Forgotten Intellectual Property Lore

ELGAR LAW AND ENTREPRENEURSHIP

Series Editors: Shubha Ghosh, *Crandall Melvin Professor of Law and Director, Technology Commercialization Law Program and Syracuse Intellectual Property Law Institute (SIPLI), Syracuse University, USA* and Robin Paul Malloy, *E.I. White Chair and Distinguished Professor of Law and Director of the Center on Property, Citizenship and Social Entrepreneurism at Syracuse University, USA*

The primary goals of this series are two-fold. The first is to develop the theoretical foundation for law and entrepreneurship. As to this goal, central research questions involve but are not limited to developing an understanding of the various meanings of entrepreneurship. Although superficially associated with the creation of a profit-making business enterprise, the concept of entrepreneurship extends to any motivation and effort to create something new. What does it mean to create? In what sense is an enterprise or project new? Is creation a process or an instantaneous, unpredictable event? What are the channels of creativity and in what venues does it occur? Is creativity in art, science, and business a coherent whole or completely different exercises? These questions serve to define the contours of entrepreneurship and its relationship to law and legal institutions.

The second goal is to translate the theoretical understanding of law and entrepreneurship into concrete policy. At one level, this goal entails identifying key legal policy levers (taxation, property rights, competition policy, financial regulation, contract law) that structure and direct entrepreneurship. At a deeper level, the second goal mandates a detailed institutional analysis of successful and unsuccessful entrepreneurship activity. This deeper goal invites an inquiry into the definitions of success and its measures. These definitions and measures, in turn, provide a benchmark for accessing and defining implementable policies.

At its core, the Law and Entrepreneurship series examines the role of law and legal institutions in promoting and sustaining entrepreneurial activity.

Titles in the series include:

Creativity, Law and Entrepreneurship
Edited by Shubha Ghosh and Robin Paul Malloy

Entrepreneurship and Innovation in Evolving Economies
The Role of Law
Edited by Megan M. Carpenter

Comic Art, Creativity and the Law
Marc H. Greenberg

Intellectual Property, Entrepreneurship and Social Justice
From Swords to Ploughshares
Edited by Lateef Mtima

Managing the Legal Nexus Between Intellectual Property and Employees
Domestic and Global Contexts
Edited by Lynda J. Oswald and Marisa Anne Pagnattaro

Forgotten Intellectual Property Lore
Creativity, Entrepreneurship and Intellectual Property
Edited by Shubha Ghosh

Forgotten Intellectual Property Lore

Creativity, Entrepreneurship and Intellectual Property

Edited by

Shubha Ghosh

Crandall Melvin Professor of Law; Director, Technology Commercialization Law Program and Director, Syracuse Intellectual Property Law Institute, Syracuse University College of Law, USA

ELGAR LAW AND ENTREPRENEURSHIP

Edward Elgar PUBLISHING

Cheltenham, UK • Northampton, MA, USA

Published by
Edward Elgar Publishing Limited
The Lypiatts
15 Lansdown Road
Cheltenham
Glos GL50 2JA
UK

Edward Elgar Publishing, Inc.
William Pratt House
9 Dewey Court
Northampton
Massachusetts 01060
USA

A catalogue record for this book
is available from the British Library

Library of Congress Control Number: 2020944312

This book is available electronically in the **Elgar**online
Law subject collection
http://dx.doi.org/10.4337/9781788978712

MIX
Paper from
responsible sources
FSC www.fsc.org FSC® C013604

ISBN 978 1 78897 870 5 (cased)
ISBN 978 1 78897 871 2 (eBook)

Printed and bound by CPI Group (UK) Ltd, Croydon, CR0 4YY

Contents

Contributors

Kosgei Kembol Alvin is an Advocate in Nairobi and an LLM candidate at the University of Nairobi.

Arpan Banerjee is Assistant Professor at Jindal Global Law School and Scientia Doctoral Scholar at the University of New South Wales.

Dana Beldiman is Professor of Law at the University of California, Hastings College of the Law and at Bucerius Law School, Hamburg, Germany.

Catherine Bond is Associate Professor of Law at the Faculty of Law, University of New South Wales.

Rebecca Schoff Curtin is Professor of Law at Suffolk University School of Law.

Graham Dutfield is Professor of International Governance at the School of Law, University of Leeds.

Samuel F. Ernst is a Professor of Law at the Golden Gate University School of Law.

Brian L. Frye is Spears-Gilbert Associate Professor of Law at the University of Kentucky School of Law.

Shubha Ghosh is Crandall Melvin Professor of Law at Syracuse University College of Law.

Jessica C. Lai is Associate Professor of Commercial Law at Victoria University of Wellington.

Jeffrey A. Lefstin is Professor of Law at the University of California, Hastings College of the Law.

Emmanuel Kolawole Oke is a Lecturer in International Intellectual Property Law at the University of Edinburgh Law School.

Mark Perry is a Professor of Law at the University of New England (Australia).

Zvi S. Rosen is an Assistant Professor, Southern Illinois University School of Law.

Mayuree Sengupta is a Research Fellow at the Indian Institute of Management Kashipur and works as Head-Patent Cell in an Autonomous Institute under the Ministry of Health & Family Welfare, Government of India.

Kshitij Kumar Singh is Assistant Professor of Law at the Campus Law Centre, University of Delhi.

Robert Spoo is Chapman Distinguished Professor of Law at the University of Tulsa College of Law.

Uma Suthersanen holds a Chair in Global Intellectual Property Law at the Centre for Commercial Law Studies, Queen Mary University of London.

Introduction

This book continues the project started in the 2018 Special Issue of the Syracuse Law Review, "Forgotten Intellectual Property Cases."[1] The issue focused on forgotten cases. This book focuses on forgotten lore. Webster's New World Dictionary defines lore as "all the knowledge of a particular group or having to do with a particular subject, especially that of a traditional nature."[2] A second proffered definition is "the space between the eye and the upper edge of the bill of a bird or between the eye and nostril of a snake or fish."[3] The first definition is intended here, but by the end of this introduction, the second definition will have surprising relevance.

Our shift in focus from case to lore reflects a broadening of our concern from traditional legal analysis to contextual understandings, rooted in history, sociology, political science, and literary studies. Contributors to the original Syracuse Law Review volume unearthed forgotten dimensions of familiar and lesser known judicial opinions. Their work set the foundation for a deeper reassessment of what may appear to be well-worn areas of intellectual property traditions and knowledge. Scholars represented in this volume go beyond cases to explore both the context of particular cases and the ramifications of specific doctrines for the evolution of intellectual property practices. From Locke's publication agreements to wartime patents and trademarks, the following chapters span a range of intellectual property concepts and history that I hope will inspire discussion and future research.

Seven types of lore are represented in these 15 chapters:

1. The Lore of Property and Contract
2. The Lore of Intangibility
3. The Lore of Authorship
4. The Lore of Common Law
5. The Lore of Courts
6. The Lore of Intellectual Property, Human Rights and Development
7. The Lore of Intellectual Property During Wartime

---

1 Forgotten Intellectual Property Cases, 68 Syracuse L. Rev. (2018).
2 Webster's New World College Dictionary (4th edn) 848 (2010).
3 *Id.*

Engaged readers may find other intellectual property lore pops out of these pages. I invite further analysis and critique. But speaking as editor, these are the categories that appeared most salient. Missing perhaps are "The Lore of Entrepreneurship" or "The Lore of Innovation." Parts of some chapters address these pieces of lore. As always, inquiry invites only more inquiry, and the stimulating topics developed here prove that proposition.

Lore is in part background understandings that permeate the law. The United States Copyright Office acknowledges this point through its own webpage titled simply "Copyright Lore."[4] A more technical term might be the tacit knowledge undergirding intellectual property law. But lore also has elements of myth, stories that are aspirational and rest on unquestioned belief. One example of lore as myth is the invocation of maxims. In his dissent in *Golan v. Holder*,[5] Justice Breyer quotes: "To every cow its calf, to every book its copy." Professor Brian Frye's contribution to this volume unravels the background to this stodgy statement, neither holding nor legislative pronouncement, but proverbial wisdom. The power of courts and of common law reasoning also rest on a mythology of judicial decision making and rationality. Samuel Ernst's examination of common law decision making in US Supreme Court patent cases dissects this mythology. Zvi Rosen's innovative article teaches us about federal courts and trademark law. More abstractly, myth and storytelling also inform the substance of the public domain, as Mayuree Sengupta reminds us in her work on Bengali folklore.

Lest we forget, there is also the lore of reform, which ostensibly guides the work of most legal scholars, of whatever political vintage. Armed with tight legal arguments, a command of facts, and normative seriousness, reformers bring change, contributing to the progress of law. Add big data to the armaments, larger quantities of numbers measuring whatever we think we are measuring to persuade judges, legislatures, leaders. Reform mindedness pervades these chapters. Sometimes the author is explicit, as with Alvin Kosgei's analysis of traditional knowledge protection or Jeffrey Lefstin on the Supreme Court's struggle to teach us about patentable subject matter, Kshitij Kumar Singh on the biotechnology sector in India, and Emmanuel Oke on human rights and economic development. Sometimes the plea for reform is more subtle, as in Mark Perry's unearthing confusions over the original meaning of copyright or Graham Dutfeld and Uma Suthersanan's reconsideration of how copyright became intangible and the implications for the author in the marketplace. Rebecca Curtin on Locke's publication agreements, unintentionally

---

4 https://www.copyright.gov/history/lore/ (visited March 8, 2020). Thanks, as always, to Zvi Rosen for pointing this site out to me.

5 132 S. Ct. 873, 902 (2012).

but perfectly, plays off the theme of author and marketplace in showing how contract law, perhaps more than clearly delineated property rights, protects authors. And Robert Spoo's literary history of self-regulated piracy in the publication of James Joyce's poetry in the United States reveals how industry governance shapes markets for creative works. Readers will find many more examples to follow.

Skeptical readers, however, may scoff at the lack of big data; numbers are few in this volume. But equally important as measurement is observation. The authors observe moments in time, and sometimes across time, and raise questions about the resilience of legal rules. One example is the lore of intellectual property during wartime, represented by two co-authored chapters. Arpan Banerjee and Dana Beldiman teach us about trademark disputes in India arising from World War I; Catherine Bond and Jessica Lai, about wartime patents in Australasia. Wartime disruptions to markets, society, and law reshape them, and to observe how demonstrates the unpredictability of change. Observation is not just casual anecdotes. Observation supports analytic narratives that can be as important and clearer than undifferentiated numbers and their mechanical manipulations.[6]

Looking at the world, whether through direct experience or archival materials, opens the mind. Remember Charles Darwin and his finches.[7] Collective observations about the natural world hinted at patterns that coalesced into theories that could be assessed for plausibility and usefulness. On this point, the second definition of lore comes into play: "the space between the eye and the upper edge of the bill of a bird or between the eye and nostril of a snake or fish." Leaping off the page of the Oxford Online Dictionary, this surprised me. "What's the connection, if any, between the first and second definitions?" I asked myself. Darwin's finches came to mind. The first definition of lore points to culture; the second, to nature. But that dichotomy is strained. Identifying forgotten intellectual property lore involves observing many artifacts—agreements, practices, judicial opinions, inventions, writings—to reconstruct memory and point the way to where we could and should be.

As editor and contributor, I hope this volume inspires further research identifying what should not be forgotten in intellectual property lore. For those who worry about the law's future, rethinking the narratives we have can offer hope. "All sorrows can be borne if you put them into a story or tell a story about them."[8] The colleagues who contributed to this book and to the law review

---

6 Robert Bates, et al., Analytic Narratives (1999).

7 David Lack, Darwin's Finches (1947).

8 Elizabeth Young-Bruehl, Hannah Arendt: For Love of the World 19 (2004) (quoting a talk by Isak Dinesen that influenced the young Hannah Arendt).

issue offer a range of methods and a host of ideas. Their work individually and collectively offers a hopeful story, rigorous, analytical, and critical.

PART I

THE LORE OF PROPERTY AND CONTRACT

1. Locke's (own) literary property

Rebecca Schoff Curtin[1]

...[I]t costs, as I have already told you,
not a little pains and patience to be at any rate an author.
(John Locke)[2]

INTRODUCTION

In May of 1689, when John Locke negotiated a contract for the publication of his *Essay Concerning Human Understanding*, he had no way of knowing that he would become one of the most influential philosophers of the emerging modern era.[3] At the age of 56 he had published very little and even less under his own name.[4] At that moment, he was at a threshold, having just that February returned to England from exile in Holland after the downfall and death of his long-time patron, the Earl of Shaftesbury.[5] Though his return to favor under William and Mary seemed secure, the anxieties engendered by his own close brush with prosecution for treason under James II remained fresh. His correspondence from Holland had been full of pseudonyms and references veiled by initials, discretions meant to shield the privacy of his

1 I wish to thank participants of IPSC 2018 at Berkeley Center for Law and Technology, IPSC 2019 at Depaul University College of Law, and in particular Carys Craig, for helpful comments on an earlier draft. This chapter also benefitted from the generous feedback of participants in the M3 Workshop 2020 at the University of Houston Law Center, in particular Sarah Burstein, Dave Fagundes, Guy Rub, and Zahr Said.

2 Letter from John Locke to Benjamin Furly (January 19, 1688), *in* 3 The Correspondence of John Locke, 330, 331 (E.S. De Beer ed., 1978) [hereinafter Correspondence].

3 On Locke's influence, see Hans Aarsleff, *Locke's Influence*, in The Cambridge Companion to John Locke 252 (Vere Chappell ed., 1994).

4 W.M. Spelman, John Locke 25 (1997).

5 Maurice Cranston, John Locke 312 (1979). For a summary of the events that sent Locke into exile, see J.R. Milton, *Locke's Life and Times*, in The Cambridge Companion to John Locke 5, 13 (Vere Chappell ed., 1994).

opinions and associations.[6] The very idea of publishing his work in England must have required a shifting of gears. Nonetheless, within a year of his return, three of Locke's major works appeared in print, the *Essay Concerning Human Understanding*, the *Two Treatises of Government*, and *A Letter Concerning Toleration*.[7] Of those, only the *Essay* was signed. Locke was apparently so anxious to maintain the secret of his authorship of the *Two Treatises* that he destroyed all of the correspondence and documentation related to its printing.[8] The contract for the first edition of the *Essay*, however, has survived, along with a handful of other agreements regarding rights to the works he published in the final years of his life.[9] These documents provide a unique opportunity to observe how one of the great theorists of property rights and epistemology, not to mention the economic and monetary policy of his time, managed the rights to print his own works. How, if at all, was philosophical theory translated into commercial practice in Locke's case?

This chapter explores the relationship between Locke's philosophical views regarding property and his actual commercial dealings with publishers, as evidenced by the series of transactional documents that have survived in the Lovelace Collection of Locke's papers at the Bodleian Library. It builds on prior work in which I have argued that in the agreements between publishers and authors of the seventeenth and early eighteenth centuries, we can find evidence of an emerging sense of author's copyright prior to the passage of

---

6 Locke's name had appeared on a list of English conspirators that James II sought to extradite from Holland in 1685, and a warrant was put out for his arrest. Locke then spent some time in hiding at the houses of friends and associates, variously using the pseudonyms "Dr. van der Linden," "Lamy," or "Dr. Lynne." CRANSTON, *supra* note 5, 253–56. For an example of a secretive letter, see Letter from John Locke to Edward Clarke (June 22, 1688), *in* CORRESPONDENCE, *supra* note 2, at 471–72, in which Locke refers to James Tyrell as "Mr. Oakley," to Mrs. Rabsy Smithsby as "Mr. R. S." and to the Earl of Pembroke as "N. F." (perhaps for "noble friend"). For his relative security after returning to London, see CRANSTON, *supra* note 5, at 316.

7 SPELMAN, *supra* note 4, at 25.

8 CRANSTON, *supra* note 5, at 318.

9 There are seven contracts in the collection, all preserved in Bodleian Library Locke MS b.1. The contracts have previously been described and analyzed in the work of Peter Lindenbaum, see Peter Lindenbaum, *Authors and Publishers in the Late Seventeenth Century, II: Brabazon Aylmer and the Mysteries of the Trade*, 3 THE LIBRARY 32, 57 (2002), and Peter Lindenbaum, *Authors and Publishers in the Late Seventeenth Century: New Evidence on their Relations*, 17 THE LIBRARY 250, 262 (1995). The contract for the *Essay* is discussed and partially reprinted in CRANSTON, *supra* note 5, at 318. There is further information on the compensation Locke received from publishers in his account books, partially reprinted in Lord King, 2 THE LIFE OF JOHN LOCKE 50–51 (1830).

the Statute of Anne.[10] One interest of this chapter is in understanding if and how theory informed Locke's practice. But perhaps more importantly, these transactions provide a case study in how a sophisticated author of the day, who was demonstrably well informed on both the theoretical ideas and the economic realities at play in the market, managed his literary property. In these agreements, Locke and his publishers deployed a diverse set of transactional tools that give dimension to the way they conceived of the "sole right of and in the Copy." I will also argue that the agreements reflect a set of concerns that we can also see in Locke's theory. In them, there is a link between labor and compensation. Across Locke's commercial decisions, we can see a balance struck between the author's personal, reputational desire to control his work and the needs of the public good.

There are several issues complicating the endeavor of understanding the relationship between Locke's theory and practice. The first issue is how to understand what Locke's theory of literary "property" actually was. While Locke did not address the issue directly in the *Two Treatises on Government*, there have been a number of important interpretations of Locke's philosophy of property rights as applied to rights in expressive works, or in what we would today term copyrightable subject matter, by modern legal scholars, including Wendy Gordon, Justin Hughes, Alfred Yen, and others.[11] This literature is rich and complex, as is, for that matter, critical interpretation of Locke's views on the origins and justification of physical property rights. Not all scholars agree that Locke's philosophical ideas regarding physical property rights do justify a natural right to intellectual property[12] and not all scholars agree that we should even look to Locke's ideas for justification at all.[13]

In addition to the modern applications of Locke's philosophical views on physical property to intangible property, we also know a good deal about Locke's views on the actual legal status of literary property in his own time. During his life, Locke expressed his opinions on the Licensing Act of 1662, which he thought harmful in a variety of ways, and regarding the stationers'

---

[10] Rebecca Schoff Curtin, *The Transactional Origins of Authors' Copyright*, 40 Colum. J.L. & Arts 175 (2016).

[11] *See e.g.*, Wendy J. Gordon, *A Property Right in Self-Expression: Equality and Individualism in the Natural Law of Intellectual Property*, 102 Yale L. J. 1533 (1993); Justin Hughes, *The Philosophy of Intellectual Property*, 77 Georgetown Law Journal 287 (1988); Alfred C. Yen, *Restoring the Natural Law: Copyright as Labor and Possession*, 51 Ohio St. L. J. 517 (1990); but see Seana Valentine Shiffrin, *Lockean Arguments for Private Intellectual Property*, in New Essays in the Legal and Political Theory of Property 138 (Stephen R. Miunser, ed. 2001).

[12] Shiffrin, *supra* note 11, at 141.

[13] Carys Craig, *Locke, Labour, and Limiting the Author's Right: A Warning against a Lockean Approach to Copyright Law*, 28 Queen's L.J. 1 (2002).

monopoly on the printing of ancient classical works, which he thought deleterious and absurd.[14] He corresponded with friends at some length about these issues as they came before Parliament in the 1690s. He provided comments on the proposed renewal of the Licensing Act of 1662, in a document known as the *Memorandum of 1694*,[15] and, in a later manuscript, made proposals for securing authors' rights to their works in a draft bill sent to him in March of 1695, in the hand of his friend John Freke.[16] Legal scholars and book historians have found these texts to be fertile ground for unpacking Locke's understanding of literary property and how those views might relate to his larger philosophical corpus.[17]

I have used the word "property" in the context of "literary property" because Locke used the word himself in these discussions, but I do not think its use is determinative of the scope of the rights in question.[18] (Locke also used the word "priviledg" when proposing legislative language for authors' rights

---

[14] Raymond Astbury, *The Renewal of the Licensing Act in 1693 and its Lapse in 1695*, 33 The Library 296, 304–15 (1978); Ronan Deazley, On the Origin of the Right to Copy: Charting the Movement of Copyright Law in Eighteenth-Century Britain (1695–1775) 1–10 (2004); Justin Hughes, *Locke's 1694 Memorandum (And More Incomplete Copyright Historiographies)*, 27 Cardozo Arts & Ent. L.J. 555 (2010); Mark Rose, Authors and Owners: The Invention of Copyright, 32–33 (1993).

[15] Preserved as Bodleian Lib. MS Locke b.4, ff. 75–6; reprinted in 5 Correspondence, *supra* note 2, at 785–91; reprinted (with an introductory essay) in Hughes, *supra* note 14, from 1 Lord Peter King, The Life of John Locke 375 (London, Henry Colburn, 1830).

[16] Preserved as Bodleian Lib. MS Locke b.4, f. 78; reprinted in 5 Correspondence, *supra* note 2, at 795–96; proposals discussed in Hughes, *supra* note 14, at 559–60. *The Memorandum of 1694*, a summary of the draft bill, and Locke's comments on it were gathered and reprinted with the title *Liberty of the Press*, *in* Locke: Political Essays 329–39 (Mark Goldie ed., 1997).

[17] Lior Zemer, *The Making of a New Copyright Lockean*, 29 Harv. J.L. & Pub. Pol'y 891 (2006); Astbury, *supra* note 14, at 308; Deazley, *supra* note 14, at 10, 142; Hughes, *supra* note 14, at 557–63; Shiffrin, *supra* note 11, at 154–56.

[18] Use of the word "property" in the copyright context has engendered controversy in contemporary scholarship, but it was not unusual in the eighteenth century, see Justin Hughes, *Copyright and Incomplete Historiographies: Of Piracy, Propertization, and Thomas Jefferson*, 79 S. Cal. L. Rev. 993, 1008–20 (2006); on the limits of what Locke's use of the word can tell us, see Jordan Peterson, *Lockean Property and Literary Works*, 14 Legal Theory, 257, 272–73 (2008); Shiffrin, *supra* note 11, at 154–56. But see, Shubha Ghosh, *Deprivatizing Copyright*, 54 Case W. Res. L. Rev. 387, 502 (2003) (arguing that historically the deployment of a literary property construct is better understood in the context of privatization or "devolution of the sovereign's role in cultural production," 389–90); Alina Ng, *Literary Property and Copyright*, 10 NW. J. Tech. & Intell. Prop. 578 (2012) (arguing that literary property is a legal concept distinct from copyright, which "safeguards an author's creative interests and expectations against the

and the word "monopoly" when discussing the powers of members of the Stationers' Company to claim exclusive rights to print works.)[19] Even among early proponents of the existence of a common law right of authors in their literary works, questions as to its scope and duration persisted well into the eighteenth century, and beyond.[20] Given the multivalent forms of "property" understood in Locke's time, use of the word only begs the question as to the nature, extent and limitations of the rights involved.[21]

To complicate matters further, the *Memorandum of 1694* and the discussions of the book trade in Locke's correspondence were deployed at a highly political moment and were undeniably calculated to influence real deliberations ongoing in Parliament. Seana Shiffrin's caution not to "make too much of these brief, political remarks on their own" is reasonable, even as she saw parallels between Locke's political comments and his philosophical views.[22] Yet, an eminent editor of Locke's works has asserted that Locke's early political writing

> reveals a Locke whose sense of the political was more practical than might be deduced from the theoretical abstractions of the *Two Treatises*, for he frequently addressed constitutional, administrative and policy matters. "True politics," he told

---

rest of society, including printers and publishers who purchased the right to print the manuscript," 531).

[19] For use of the word "priviledg," see Locke's comments to the draft bill sent to him by John Freke, 5 Correspondence, *supra* note 2, at 796; on Locke's multiple uses of the word "monopoly," see Lewis Hyde, *Frames from the Framers: How America's Revolutionaries Imagined Intellectual Property*, 11, available at http://web.mit.edu/writing/2011/June/June_Arg_Hyde2005.pdf (arguing that Locke's "framing issue was monopoly privilege, not property rights"), but see Hughes, *supra* note 14 at 560–63 (arguing that Locke distinguishes between the "monopoly" held by the stationers in the printing of Classical authors and the "'property' belonging to authors," 562).

[20] Tomas Gómez-Arostegui, *Copyright at Common Law in 1774*, 47 Conn. L. Rev. 1, 20–21 (2014) (noting the questions posed to the judges in *Donaldson v. Becket* and the differences of opinion among them); Lionel Bently, *A Few Remarks on Copyright at Common Law in 1774*, 23, 24–25, 27–28, in *What is the Point of Copyright History?: Reflections on Copyright at Common Law in 1774*, CREATe Working Paper 2016/4 (2016), available at https://www.create.ac.uk/publications/what-is-the-point-of-copyright-history-reflections-on-copyright-at-common-law-in-1774-by-h-tomas-gomez-arostegui/ (arguing that "after *Donaldson*, what remained was a plethora of divergent views as to the position at common law before 1710, and with respect to protection of books both before and after publication," 24).

[21] Hyde, *supra* note 19 (analyzing different conceptions of property rights used as metaphor for intellectual property, including leaseholds, common stock, and allodial estates).

[22] Shiffrin, *supra* note 11, at 155.

Lady Peterborough, "I look on as a part of moral philosophy, which is nothing but the art of conducting men right in society."[23]

So it seems that Locke himself saw a link between politics and philosophy. This chapter draws parallels between Locke's contemporary political commentary on the Licensing Act and the ways in which some modern legal scholars have understood Locke's philosophy to apply to literary property, which together give some fundamental principles as to what Locke might have thought "an author's property in his copy" meant, or at least, what it should have meant. The first section of the chapter surveys some of this literature and highlights a number of aspects of Locke's theory that are relevant to or consistent with the transactional drafting tools at work in the contracts that have survived.

Assuming that we can establish a working definition of Locke's theory, the next problem is determining what the relationship between his theory and praxis was, and we have to consider the possibility that Locke's theory had no influence on his practical commercial transactions. As scholars concerned with other elements of Locke's theories have come to confront, the relationship between Locke's philosophy and his real-life commercial and political dealings can be fraught. Scholars have now long noted the tension between Locke's liberalism and his involvement with the slave trade.[24] On the one hand, in the opening of the *Two Treatises*, Locke wrote: "Slavery is so vile and miserable an estate of man, and so directly opposite to the generous temper and courage of our nation, that tis hardly to be conceived, that an Englishman … Should plead for it."[25] On the other hand, in his professional life, Locke played a role in the drafting of the Fundamental Constitutions of Carolina, which gave slaveholders "absolute power and authority" over African slaves,

---

[23] Mark Goldie, *Introduction*, in Locke: Political Essays xi, xiii (Mark Goldie, ed. 1997).

[24] Holly Brewer, *Slavery-entangled Philosophy*, Aeon, September 2018, available at https://aeon.co/essays/does-lockes-entanglement-with-slavery-undermine-his-philosophy (noting these facts but resolving the tension by attributing the genesis of the slave trade in the absolute monarchy that Locke resisted); Brad Hinshelwood, *The Carolinian Context of John Locke's Theory of Slavery*, 41 Political Theory 562 (2013) (arguing that actual circumstances of Native American slavery in the context of conflict with native peoples in the Carolina colony may have motivated Locke to argue that "just-war slavery" is legitimate, but tensions between his rejection of other forms of slavery and his investments in African slavery remain, 581–83); David Armitage, *John Locke, Carolina, and the "Two Treatises of Government,"* 32 Political Theory 602 (2004) (arguing that critiques of the "complicity of Lockean liberalism with English colonialism" were historically accurate, 620).

[25] John Locke, Two Treatises of Government 5 (Mark Goldie, ed., 1993); Brewer, *supra* note 24. Though there is also a limited justification of slavery in the state of war in the *Second Treatise* (Hinshelwood, *supra* note 24, at 563).

and he was, for a time, an investor in the Royal African Company.[26] In our own political discourse today, the word "transactional" has itself taken something of a beating lately—at best, it is frequently used to mean "concerned only with the cost/benefit analysis of the exchange at hand" but more and more I see it used with a pejorative valence to mean "free of ideology" or, worse, by definition "unprincipled."[27] It must be acknowledged that the founding documents of liberalism are shadowed by the transactional realities in which they were written. That is to say, why should we expect to find Locke's ideals in his transactions, when we know that, for instance, we cannot find Thomas Jefferson's theory of equality and inalienable rights for all men in his own actual pursuit of happiness?[28] So, there are limits to how much theoretical freight the real transactions can carry. Nonetheless, the documents are compelling, because you cannot do things with ideas that you do not have, and the documents are historical records of what authors and publishers did to bring literary property to the market and thus to readers. The second part of the chapter will read the surviving transactional documents closely and reflect on the relevance of Locke's political and philosophical views to the commercial practices they reveal.

The final issue is whether enough historical evidence of Locke's publishing deals has survived to give us a fulsome picture of his commercial practices. There are only seven documents in the Bodleian Library's collection, and it is not clear that you could even call all of them contracts. Some of them clearly do not cover the complete publication agreement, though I think they all suggest powerful and interesting things about the assumptions of the parties with respect to literary property. Above all, the documents are a strong antidote to the temptation to imagine that Locke's writing reflects on the market for literary works without ever having been affected by it. That temptation set in as early as Lord Camden's stirring speech before the House of Lords in

---

[26] Hinshelwood, *supra* note 24, at 563.

[27] *See e.g.*, Andra Gillespie, *Trump and the Limits of Transactional Politics*, CNN: Opinion, January 18, 2018, https://www.cnn.com/2018/01/18/opinions/trump-transactional-politics-problem-gillespie-opinion/index.html; Caterina Bulgarella, *The Art of Deal Making: Why Ethical Leadership Trumps Transactional Leadership*, Forbes, Jan. 31, 2019, https://www.forbes.com/sites/caterinabulgarella/2019/01/31/the-art-of-deal-making-why-ethical-leadership-trumps-transactional-leadership/#3c34dc1f2a88; Cleve W. Stevens, *We Can Survive President Trump's Soulless Transactional Leadership*, Seattle Times, August 14, 2017, https://www.seattletimes.com/opinion/we-can-survive-president-trumps-soulless-transactional-leadership/.

[28] Henry Wiencek, Master of the Mountain: Thomas Jefferson and his Slaves (2012).

Donaldson v. Becket in 1774. Camden railed against the idea of a perpetual copyright at common law, declaiming that

> glory is the reward of science, and those who deserve it, scorn all meaner views. ... It was not for gain, that Bacon, Newton, Milton, Locke, instructed and delighted the world; it would be unworthy such men to traffic with a dirty bookseller for so much a sheet of a letter press.[29]

But Locke did traffic with booksellers, and "for so much a sheet" at that, though not merely for economic gain. This chapter concludes that Locke's commercial practices in the publishing market were consistent with a number of his theoretical principles, and the transactional documents that have survived show how valuable the contractual tools Locke employed were to his emergence as one of the greatest authors of his age.

1. IN THEORY: LABOR, THE COMMONS, AND THE STATIONERS' COMPANY

Locke's own entry point in the debate regarding renewal of the Licensing Act was not as an author, but as a reader. His first recorded comments on the issue come in a letter to his close friend Edward Clarke, a member of parliament, in which he focuses on the harm the Act inflicts on scholars and book buyers. The renewal of the Licensing Act involved renewal of the pre-publication censorship system that it regulated, but it also facilitated the ability of the Stationers' Company to leverage and regulate amongst themselves the exclusive right to print particular works via two separate mechanisms, patents or printing privileges granted to stationers by the Crown and rights claimed through entrance of a work in the Stationers' Register by the first company member to publish a work. When Locke wrote to Clarke in January of 1693, Locke was disappointed that Parliament had just voted to extend the Licensing Act for an additional year and his chief complaint concerned the Act's enablement of exclusive rights to print and sell Classical authors via the former mechanism:

> I wish you would have some care of Book buyers as well as all of Booke sellers ... who have got a Patent for all or most of the Ancient Latin Authors (by what right or pretence I know not) claime the text to be their and soe will not suffer fairer and

29 The Parliamentary register; or, History of the proceedings and debates of the House of Commons [and of the House of Lords] 1000 (London, Printed for J. Almon, 1775–804).

> more correct Editions than any thing they print here or with new Comments to be imported ...[30]

Thus Locke's chief concern was the Act's impact on the public's access to the best possible editions of Latin authors. He goes on to argue that the result is that "these most usefull books are excessively dear to schollers and a monopoly is put into the hands of the company of ignorant and lazy stationers."[31] The letter contains two examples from Locke's personal experience, anecdotal evidence from his still relatively new connections amongst booksellers, and then finishes the discussion with this proposal:

> And particularly I think that clause where printing and importation of any books to which any have a right by Patent is prohibited should be at least thus far restraind, that it should be lawfull for any one to print or import any Latin booke whose author lived above a thousand year since. ... [F]or it is a great oppression upon schollers and what right can any one pretend to have to the writeings of one who lived a thousand years agoe, He that prints them best deserves best and should have the sale of them. ...[32]

Locke objects to the harmful effects of a monopoly power in printing these authors' works as a "great oppression upon schollers." Locke seems to object as well on the basis that the stationers have done nothing to deserve the right, partly because they are "ignorant" and "lazy," but also because their connection to the authors who created the works is so attenuated, and "what right can any one pretend to have to the writeings of one who lived a thousand years agoe." Locke explicitly argues that those who work to create the best editions should have the market. He also asked that Clarke speak with two booksellers, including Awnsham Churchill, who was Locke's publisher by that time, because "I believe [he] will be able to shew you other great inconvencys of that act."[33]

There are a number of themes in this opening salvo that are picked up in modern applications of Locke's philosophy to copyright. In the plea to have care of book buyers as well as sellers is a value articulated in Wendy Gordon's observation that "[n]atural rights theory ... is necessarily concerned with the rights of the public as well as with the rights of those whose labors create intellectual products."[34] From the Lockean rule that all people have a right to

---

30 Letter from John Locke to Edward Clarke (January 2, 1693 n.s.), in 4 Correspondence, *supra* note 2, 614–15.

31 *Id.* at 615.

32 *Id.*

33 *Id.*

34 Gordon, *supra* note 11, at 1535.

take from the common for sustenance, Professor Gordon derives the idea that "people must have access not only to the physical common of which Locke explicitly writes, but also to a common of intangibles. Our common encompasses not only our physical country but our culture as well."[35] This sense of a public entitlement to common heritage seems consistent with Locke's account of the harm done, the "great oppression," when scholars cannot obtain accurate editions of the Latin classics, which were the bedrock foundation of learning in his day. In reading Locke's political comments alongside his philosophy, Lior Zemer has argued insightfully that "a comprehensive Lockean approach to copyright would provide significant recognition for the public role in the making of authorship and art."[36] This observation is borne out by the first points Locke makes in this letter, with the focus on book buyers in the market and on an international, intergenerational group of scholars whose work depends on access both to old texts and new commentaries.

Locke's questioning of the "lazy" stationers' right and his assertion that "he that prints them best deserves best" seems a reflection of Locke's labor theory of property, which is commonly emphasized in modern Lockean justifications of copyright.[37] As encapsulated by Alfred Yen, the application of labor theory to modern copyright initially plays out in this way:

> Locke's views on property stemmed from his assumption that persons owned their bodies. They therefore owned the labor of their bodies and, by extension, the product of their labor. This argument seems peculiarly applicable to authorship. An author owns her body, and therefore her mind. When her mind labors, it seems that the resulting work is not just the product of the author's labor, it is practically an extension of the author herself.[38]

As Professor Yen notes, the bare extension of this argument to authors' rights is vulnerable to the criticism that it opens the door to an unlimited scope of such rights. Yet, Yen and others have derived limitations on authors' rights from Lockean principles of natural law.[39] As we will see, it has also been observed that Locke himself eventually proposed a limited author's right post-publication, but for now it is interesting to note that Locke's letter implies a lack of justification for the printer's exclusive rights to print Classical authors for two reasons. First, the printers have not diligently worked to bring out

---

35 *Id.* at 1556.
36 Zemer, *supra* note 17, at 892.
37 Gordon, *supra* note 11, at 1540.
38 Yen, *supra* note 11, at 546–47.
39 *Id.* at 548–57 (exploring how the concept of possession and the moral consequences of labor provide natural limits to copyright); see also *infra* notes 49–65 and accompanying text.

accurate editions (they have not applied their own labor), and thus lack a justification for their right to exclude others from doing so. Second, the printers are too far removed from the labor of the author to be considered successors to the author's interest (for "what right can any one pretend to have to the writeings of one who lived a thousand years agoe"?), an issue that returned in Locke's later grappling with drafting appropriate legislation. Professor Hughes notes that there are two possible interpretations of Locke's labor theory of property, one which rewards labor with property rights on "instrumental grounds that we must provide rewards to get labor," and another which rewards labor on normative grounds that "labor should be rewarded."[40] Interestingly, in the case of the letters patent given to the stationers, Locke seems to object on both grounds—the exclusive rights conferred to the stationers have failed to incentivize the desired work in diligent editing and the stationers can have no moral claim deriving from the work of the authors.

When the Licensing Act approached expiration again in late 1694, Locke prepared a manuscript of notes analyzing and critiquing the Licensing Act.[41] The structure of the text is that Locke copies out a summary of a section of the Act and then follows with commentary on it. As with the initial letter to Clarke, Locke's primary focus is the stationers' monopoly in printing Classical authors. The longest comment is on Section 6, the paragraph prohibiting the printing or importing of books "which any ... persons by force ... of any letters patents have the right priviledg authority or allowance solely to print."[42] As Justin Hughes has noted, this context of responding to Section 6 of the Licensing Act is important to understanding the import of Locke's commentary.[43] This time, Locke augments his criticism with a proposal:

> Upon occasion of this instance of the Clasick authors I demand whether if an other act for printing should be made it be not reasonable the noebody should have any peculiar right in any book which has been in print fifty years, but anyone as well as an other might have the liberty to print it for by such titles as these which lie dormant and hinder others many good books come quite to be lost.[44]

---

40 Hughes, *supra* note 11, at 296.

41 There is disagreement regarding exactly when Locke prepared the manuscript, a copy of which survives in his own hand as Bodleian Lib. MS Locke b. ff. 75–6, and was endorsed by Locke "Printing 94." Astbury concludes that the most likely timeline is for Locke to have sent a copy to Edward Clarke in November or December of 1694. Astbury, *supra* note 14, at 305, n.47.

42 Locke, *Appendix, Documents relating to the termination of the Licensing Act*, 1695, 5 Correspondence, *supra* note 2, at 786.

43 Hughes, *supra* note 14, at 562.

44 Locke, *supra* note 42, at 787.

Up until this point the argument was focused on the stationers' monopoly in printing the Classical authors, but it must surely have occurred to Locke that the issues attending a perpetual right to stationers via letters patent would also be relevant to the perpetual exclusivity claimed via entry in the Stationers' Register.[45] The proposal of a 50-year limitation, as articulated above, would have applied to all printed texts, posing the problem of how the proposal would affect the commercial transactions of living authors.

By the time of the writing of the *Memorandum*, Locke was familiar with the typical transaction between living authors and their publishers, in which authors sold their "copies" to booksellers, where the sale of the copy both transferred physical possession of the manuscript to the publisher and authorized publication. If it posed a problem for Locke to imagine what impact such a limitation in the duration of booksellers' exclusivity would have on the value of the "copies" sold by authors, he sidestepped it quickly in favor of emphasizing again the inequity in the printing privileges for Latin works:

> But be that determined as it will in regard of those Authors who now write and sell their copys to booksellers. This certein is very absurd at first sight that any person or company should now have a title to the printing of the works of Tullie Caesars or Livys who lived soe many ages since. … nor can there be any reason in nature why I might not print them as well as the Company of Stationers if I thought fit.[46]

The quick turn away from living authors in part just illustrates that the *Memorandum* was a polemic. Locke acknowledged that his readers would be worrying about how living authors got paid, and indeed the issue became an important one in the debates that led to the Statute of Anne, but for now Locke wants those readers to focus on the easy case, the one against perpetual rights in long-dead authors.

Nonetheless, Locke returned to the problem of transactions with living authors in the closing sentences of the *Memorandum*, arguing that: "And for those who purchase copies from Authors that now live and write it may be reasonable to limit their property to a certein number of years after the death of the Author or the first printing of the book as suppose 50 or 70 years."[47] As has been noted, this prescient proposal anticipates (or perhaps influenced?)

---

[45] Locke did write a comment on Section 3 of the Licensing Act, which required entry of works on the Register, but his complaint was that it opened up the opportunity for fraud, because the manuscript, once disclosed to the Company in order to be entered, might be falsely claimed by some stationer other than the one who brought it in for entry. Locke claimed that his own publisher, Awnsham Churchill, could provide an example. *Id.* at 786.

[46] *Id.* at 787–88.

[47] *Id.* at 791.

the modern duration of copyright, currently set in the United States at 70 years after the death of the author, with the crucial difference that here "their property" referred to the property of stationers, who had bought "copies" from authors, leaving ambiguous the nature of the "copies" authors were selling.[48] The word "copy" was used by stationers in their entries in the Stationers' Register to mean something like "the right to print," but in Locke's time it was not clear whether an author's "copy" could be enforced as a matter of common law after the first publication.[49] In any event, only stationers were given a legal mechanism for enforcing exclusive rights to print under the Act Locke was criticizing. Locke suggested a solution to that problem later, when his friends John Freke and Edward Clarke sought his guidance on a draft bill to replace the Licensing Act, and, as we will see, Locke addressed the issue with transactional tools in some of his agreements with booksellers.

The *Memorandum of 1694* raises important issues for the application of Locke's theory to the commercial world of bookselling that he knew. First, Locke was clearly open to limitations on rights in literary property. This is consistent with multiple modern applications of Lockean thought to copyright. For instance, Lior Zemer sees a connection between the *Memorandum*, copyright and Locke's no-spoliation proviso, which he describes as "an absolute condition set on appropriation," which "ensures that 'Nothing' was made by God to spoil or be destroyed."[50] Professor Zemer acknowledges that spoliation in "intellectual goods" is different from that in physical goods, but nonetheless intellectual goods are "perishable" and there is a loss of value, even to the original author, when a work is not shared with others: "For example, the owner deprives himself of the true value of the creation in light of the potential that someone will generate a derivative idea and then the owner would develop his initial creation even further."[51] This loss of creative exchange, albeit long after the original author is dead, was perhaps what Locke had in mind when he complained that the result of the stationers' perpetual monopoly in Classical authors was that "many good books come quite to be lost." As Professor Zemer

---

[48] Hughes, *supra* note 14, at 559; see also Zemer, *supra* note 17, at 905.

[49] For parsing of the use of the word "copy" in Stationers' Register entries, see Curtin, *supra* note 10, at 183–84, 188. The status of an author's common-law copyright was eventually taken up in late-eighteenth-century cases, though there has been some disagreement among modern scholars regarding the interpretation of these cases. See H. Tomas Gomez-Arostegui, *Copyright at Common Law in 1774*, 47 Conn. L. Rev 1 (2014) (arguing that a majority of jurists in the two landmark cases of *Millar* and *Donaldson* "favored an antecedent common-law copyright in authors," 6).

[50] Zemer, *supra* note 17, at 921.

[51] *Id.* at 925.

writes, "Locke is aware that in situations of perpetual right in works of authorship, spoilage of social value is inevitable."[52]

Another Lockean principle that has been used to justify limitations on modern copyright is the "enough and as good" proviso: "For this labour being the unquestionable property of the labourer, no man but he can have a right to what that is once joined to, at least where there is enough, and as good left in common for others."[53] Wendy Gordon summarizes its effect in the following way: "If the proviso is satisfied, others are no worse off if they are excluded from the resource the laborer has marked off as her own."[54] The proviso is central to Professor Gordon's thesis "that creators should have property in their original works, only provided that such grant of property does no harm to other persons' equal abilities to create or draw upon the preexisting cultural matrix and scientific heritage."[55] From the proviso, Professor Gordon derives the prohibition against owning abstract ideas and a limitation on the duration of copyright, with a compelling account that access to and a right to use a common heritage is crucial to human creativity: "Just as land is necessary for farmers to bring forth fruit (in Locke's imagery), a common of previously-created intangibles is necessary for creators to bring forth new works of the imagination."[56] In particular, Professor Gordon argues that "too broad a set of intellectual property rights gives one set of persons potential control over how that 'created' reality can be interpreted."[57] This account resonates deeply with Locke's indignation in the *Memorandum* that "by this Act Scholers are subjected to the power of these dull wretches [the stationers] who doe not soe much as understand Latin whether they shall have any true or good copys of the best ancient Latin authers."[58]

Thus, Locke's proposal of limiting the duration of rights in literary property seems consistent with both the no-spoliation and the enough and as good provisos. In addition, both Professor Gordon and Professor Hughes have seen in Locke's philosophy a requirement that such rights be limited in order to ensure equitable access to the commons from one generation to the next.[59] Perhaps this is why Locke considered as one possibility a term of the life of the author plus 50 or 70 years, as a rough estimate of granting exclusive control lasting

---

52 *Id.*

53 JOHN LOCKE, TWO TREATISES ON GOVERNMENT, 128 (Book II, Ch. 5, §27) (Mark Goldie, ed., Everyman 1993) (1690).

54 Gordon, *supra* note 11, at 1563.

55 *Id.*

56 *Id.* at 1556.

57 *Id.*

58 Locke, *supra* note 42, at 787.

59 Gordon, *supra* note 11, at 1557; Hughes, *supra* note 11, at 323–25.

no longer than the lifespan of one generation after the author's time, or perhaps one generation's lifespan (50 years), plus the minority of the next generation (an extra 20 years).[60] It is similar to the term under which property owners are allowed to impose unvested contingent interests under the modern formulation of the Rule Against Perpetuities (RAP).[61] At the time when Locke wrote the *Memorandum*, the common law foundations of the RAP had recently been laid in the Duke of Norfolk's Case, in 1681.[62] The alternative he proposed, a term of 50 or 70 years running from first publication, ensures that a published work would remain outside the public domain for no longer than roughly one generation's lifespan.

Finally, Locke's repeated allusion to authors selling their copies in the *Memorandum* is a reminder that commerce played a role in his philosophy of property. Professor Gordon notes that "Locke assumes contracts can be made in the state of nature."[63] She observes that "the entitlements in intellectual products can nevertheless be transferred: the creator can impose on herself by contract a duty to cease using what she has made, and transfer all her rights and powers over the use of the intangible to someone else."[64] She characterizes the "power to transfer" as one of the "three crucial entitlements in Locke."[65] For Professor Hughes, "Locke relies upon the money economy to facilitate" the addition of new physical value to the commons, through "gifts or com-

---

60 While the average life expectancy at birth was low in Locke's time, the figure sometimes seen (35 years) is heavily affected by infant mortality, while "those who survived the early years had a respectable chance of living at least into their late forties." It might be more indicative of Locke's perception of an author's lifespan to note the following statistic: "The average age of death of the nine 17th century archbishops of Canterbury was 73 and the average age of appointment 60." Anne Stott, *Old Age*, EARLY MODERN EUROPE (2011), http://early-moderneurope.blogspot.com/2011/11/old-age.html.

61 John Chipman Gray encapsulated the rule as follows: "No interest is good unless it must vest, if at all, not later than twenty-one years after some life in being at the creation of the interest." JESSE DUKEMINIER ET AL., PROPERTY 285 (7th ed., 2010). Dukeminier notes that "the effect was to permit a donor '[to] provide for all those in his family whom he personally knew and the first generation after them upon attaining majority.'" *Id.*

62 George L. Haskins, *Extending the Grasp of the Dead Hand: Reflections on the Origins of the Rule Against Perpetuities*, 126 U. PA. L. REV. 19 (1977). Haskins's account of the ruling in the Duke of Norfolk's case, as a compromise allowing some dead hand control while still preserving freedom to transfer land within a reasonable period of time, seems germane to the balancing of interests between the booksellers' need to profit and the public's need for freer access to ancient texts.

63 Gordon, *supra* note 11, at 1551.

64 *Id.*

65 *Id.*

merce."[66] So, it seems fitting that Locke would have been mindful of the commercial pathways that authors used to publish their works when considering the effects of exclusive rights to print them.

Locke turned to face squarely the issue of authors' rights in their works within a few months of composing the *Memorandum*. In March of 1695, Locke's friends, John Freke and Edward Clarke sent Locke a draft bill for his consideration. Clarke, who was a member of parliament, had presented the bill in the House of Commons earlier that month.[67] Locke's notes suggesting alterations of the bill have survived. Locke is now focused solely on "secur[ing] the Authors property in his copy, or his to whom he has transferd it."[68] As discussed above, under the contemporary legal regime, there was no legal default rule allowing anyone other than a member of the Stationers' Company (or a holder of a printing privilege from the Crown) to enforce an exclusive right to print a work after the first publication, but authors commonly succeeded in controlling (and receiving compensation for) the right to print in the first instance.[69] This was the "property" authors held in their copy, and could transfer to stationers, but Locke sought to find a way to "secure" those rights to authors (or their assigns) beyond the first publication under a new regime not controlled by the Stationers' Register. Property had become the touchstone issue in debates regarding the replacement of the Licensing Act because, in John Freke's words, "property is a very popular word, which Licencer is not."[70] The leap Locke made in his proposals was that authors could be conceived as holding a right to print for a term of years generally, not merely a right of first publication, and in this respect he anticipated the terms of the Statute of Anne.[71] He offered two alternative proposals to extend an author's legal right to control printing beyond the first edition. Interestingly, both proposals explicitly allow that the rights will be transferable, recognizing the role of commerce in the dissemination of works. The first proposed provision was to be appended to an existing clause in the draft that prohibited printers from

---

66 Hughes, *supra* note 11, at 317. However, by contrast, he argues, "intellectual property systems release the added value of a new idea without requiring the property owner's active and intentional introduction of the idea into commerce." *Id.*

67 Astbury, *supra* note 14, at 312.

68 Locke, *supra* note 42, at 795.

69 This was undoubtedly in part because authors had initial control over physical access to the manuscript, but there is evidence that an author's intangible right to control the first printing was customarily respected and there are examples of the Court of Assistants enforcing such a right where complaints arose. See Lyman Ray Patterson, Copyright in Historical Perspective 68–70 (1968).

70 Letter from John Freke and Edward Clarke to John Locke (14 March 1695), 5 Correspondence, *supra* note 2, at 291; Astbury, *supra* note 14, at 312.

71 Astbury, *supra* note 14, at 313.

printing the name of any person as author or publisher of any book without authority in writing for doing so, on penalty of paying a set sum to the person falsely named as author or publisher.[72] Once a "book, pamphlet, portraicture or paper" has been printed the first time with the name of the author or publisher on it, then it could not be printed again *with or without* the name of the author "without Authority given in writeing by the Author *or somebody intituled by him*" for a term of years after its first publication. In this proposal, the ability for an author to control reprints of the work is triggered when the work is published with identification of someone (the author or the publisher) who would be accountable for its contents.[73]

The second, alternative, proposal was a provision to be inserted under an existing paragraph in the draft regarding the deposit of books in three designated libraries. Locke added,

> And for the better encouragement thereof be it farther enacted that upon delivery of three copys for the use of the said three librarys. A receit under the hand of the Kings Library Keeper and under the hand of the Vice Chancelor of each university … who are hereby required to give such receits, for the said books, shall vest a priviledg in the Author of the said book his executors administrators and assignes of solely reprinting and publishing the said book for [____] years from the first edition thereof.[74]

In the second proposal, the exclusive right to reprint a book for a term of years following the first edition is conditioned on compliance with a deposit requirement. The language is explicitly instrumental—the clause is included for the "better encouragement" of depositing books at the King's library and those of the Universities.

---

[72] The draft copy of the bill sent to Locke was missing the words "author or" before "publisher" in the first part of the clause, but included authors in the clause laying out the remedy. Therefore it seems likely that the omission of authors from the first clause was a transcription error. The copy of the draft bill that was sent to Locke in Freke's hand is transcribed in *Appendix: Documents relating to the termination of the Licensing Act*, in 5 CORRESPONDENCE, *supra* note 2, at 791–95. Locke recopied the provision and wrote a note in the margin next to the passage: "NB the words as Author are left out in my copy but I suppose are in the bill." Locke, *supra* note 42, at 795 note b.

[73] The draft bill provided that "whosoever shall order his name to be printed to any matter or thing shall be answerable to the Law as if he were the Author of the same nevertheless the Author to be also answerable …" *Appendix*, in 5 CORRESPONDENCE, *supra* note 2, at 793.

[74] Locke, *supra* note 42, at 795. The remedy given for violation of the privilege is the "power to seize all copys of the said book reprinted by any other person which by virtue of this act shall be forfeited to the said author his executors administrators and Assignes." *Id.* at 796.

With these proposals, we come full circle in considering the interaction between Locke's political interventions and his philosophical theory. His strong advocacy for author's rights is consistent with the labor theory of property discussed above. Locke's insight is most powerfully formulated in Professor Gordon's phrase: "all persons have a liberty right to dispose of their efforts."[75] This liberty right, however, is paired with the liberty right of all persons to use the common and is limited by the no-spoliation proviso and the enough and as good proviso, such that its scope is not absolute and not perpetual.[76] Professor Gordon's interpretation of these Lockean principles as protective of expressive speech interests is true to the origins of Locke's proposals to limit literary property in the context of rejecting the Licensing Act, in which the registration process used by stationers to police printing rights was yoked with pre-publication censorship. Note that Locke's proposals limit the rights to a term of years and also express them merely as rights to control reprint of the original work. This resonates with Professor Gordon's observation that a derivative work right "would have to be quite narrow" to be justified under Lockean theory, "giving an initial creator control over only those new works by others that significantly interfere with her own plans for the work."[77] In the conditioning of the second proposal on the donation of books to libraries, Locke displayed the commitment to public benefit and access to knowledge that has been recognized in his theory, for instance, by Professor Zemer: "Locke combines arguments for freedom of expression and social exchange, economic equality, common equity, and recognition of authors' rights."[78]

There was significant connection between Locke's political and philosophical views. Modern scholars have applied Locke's general theory of property to copyright doctrine in ways that are consistent with Locke's writings in the literary property debates of his own day. In the next section of the chapter, I will analyze the relationship between these principles in theory and Locke's commercial practices. Given the principles discussed above, we might expect, for instance, to see compensation tied to labor. We should expect to find a balance struck between the author's desire to control the fruits of his efforts and a commitment to the public benefit. But above all, we should expect to find ingenuity in the deployment of diverse transactional tools as we see Locke learn about the publishing industry in the midst of his own evolution as an author from patronage to proprietorship.

---

[75] Gordon, *supra* note 11, at 1542.

[76] *Id.* at 1542, 1550–51, 1562–65. See also, Zemer, *supra* note 17, at 934–35 (arguing that perpetuity would violate the provisos of the *Second Treatise*).

[77] Gordon, *id.* at 1608.

[78] Zemer, *supra* note 17, at 900.

2. IN PRACTICE: LOCKE'S PUBLICATION AGREEMENTS

Locke had been writing for decades before he made any concerted effort to become a published author. As the epigraph to this chapter suggests, Locke discovered that writing and publishing were two different things and navigating the process by which a manuscript was printed and sold to the public was challenging.[79] This section works through the surviving agreements between Locke and his publishers in roughly chronological order. Discussing the contracts in the order that they were executed shows the development in the range of tools Locke and his publishers used to craft their deals. Locke learned over time, from the first contract in 1689, shortly after he returned to England, to the last surviving one in 1699, just a few years before his death. The contracts span the same time period during which he attempted to influence members of Parliament on the issue of literary property, as discussed above. That experience no doubt resonated in Locke's decisions regarding his own literary property. Professor Lindenbaum has noted that "Locke's contracts of the mid-1690s reflect precisely his stand that authors should have some power in controlling the publication of reprints of their works."[80] This is certainly true, and there is more to say about how Locke and his advisors engineered that control. However, it is also true that Locke's commercial dealings reflect other principles of scope and limitation in literary property.

2.a Controlling the Text: *An Essay Concerning Human Understanding*

In May of 1689, John Locke and bookseller Thomas Bassett contracted to publish the first complete edition of *An Essay Concerning Human Understanding*. The contract has been described as "complicated," "trade-oriented" and

---

[79] The context of the letter to Benjamin Furly was that Locke had gone to Amsterdam to be able to work closely with a printer who was reprinting an abridgement of the *Essay Concerning Human Understanding*, which Locke had originally prepared as a contribution to the serial journal, the *Bibliotheque Universelle*. Locke's plans for the reprint were to privately circulate it himself among his patronage circle in England. CRANSTON, *supra* note 5, at 290–91. He further lamented to his friend, who was working with a medieval manuscript, "I envye your imployment in that musty manuscript, which you will easily allow to be a great deale better than to wait here the leisure of drunken workmen [the printers], who have soe great a reverence for the holydays, that they could not till today quit the Cabarets … and betake themselves to their profane callings." Letter from John Locke to Benjamin Furly, *supra* note 2, at 330–31.

[80] Lindenbaum (1995), *supra* note 9, at 262.

"technical."[81] It is notable for its focus on two issues, a complex formula for calculating Locke's compensation and covenants covering the process by which Locke and Bassett will work together to bring the book through the press. Thomas Bassett was nearing the end of his career. The prominent publisher Jacob Tonson had once been his apprentice and the catalogue of law books for which he was best known had been printed in the 1670s.[82] Notably, the contract was witnessed by Edward Clarke and John Freke. These were the friends, a member of parliament and a lawyer, respectively, with whom Locke corresponded regarding literary property at the expiration of the Licensing Act. It was John Freke who copied out the draft bill for Locke and Edward Clarke who presented it in Parliament. That they both had a front seat at the dawn of Locke's adventures in London publishing is remarkable. Given that Locke was relatively new to publishing, he may not have negotiated much, and yet we can see some resonance with the issues Locke considered philosophically and politically.

The first issue is an author's right to control his work. The contract frames the deal as a limited authorization to publish the work in a specified time and manner:

> Whereas the said John Locke hath composed and written a Boooke or Treatise in English Entituled an Essay concerning Humane Understanding the said John Locke doth grant & Agree to & with the said Thomas Basett that he the said Thomas Basett shall have the same to Print & Publish on ye Times & in the Manner & forme following. That is to say the same shall be Printed on as good Paper & in a volume of the size and Character of the History of the Councill of Trent Printed in English in the yeare 1676. The Printing thereof shall be begun immediately & continued after the rate of at least fower sheets a weeke until the whole booke be Printed.[83]

The agreement regarding the rate of printing may reflect Locke's dissatisfaction with his experience with the printers of an abridgement of the *Essay* in Amsterdam, in which delays forced him to stay in the city longer than he had wished.[84] By choosing an exemplar for the format of the printing, Locke received some *ex ante* assurance as to the quality of the finished volume. Locke apparently cared about the caliber of the paper and the presentation of the text, an indication that the agreement is not merely about economic compensation, but also channels the author's reputational concerns. The parties

---

81 Lindenbaum (2002), *supra* note 9, at 57.

82 Henry Plomer, *Bassett (Thomas*), in A Dictionary of the Booksellers and Printers who were at work in England, Scotland, and Ireland from 1641 to 1667 16 (1910).

83 Locke MS b.1, f.109.

84 Cranston, *supra* note 5, at 290–91.

anticipated that there might be disputes during the process and appointed John Freke "umpire ... by whose judgment & Award In the Case they will be concluded."[85] That the arbitration of disputes would be adjudged by Locke's friend is a sign that the negotiations were favorable to the author, or at least, that Bassett was willing to assuage any lingering anxieties on Locke's part.

Compensation for Locke was tied to how much text he produced. The longer the book, the higher the compensation, at a rate of "ten shillings a sheet for every sheet the said booke shall contein counting for a sheet the same as is conteined in a sheet of Milton's History of England in octavo." Because the *Essay* was printed in folio (four pages to a sheet), a much larger format than octavo (16 pages to a sheet), this pay scale required a separate accounting, using the number of ems of text in a sheet of the Milton octavo as the unit quantifying what a "sheet" would be for Locke's payment, rather than the number of sheets in the actual edition.[86] This was advantageous to Locke not only because payment was proportionate to his labor, but also because the pay scale by its nature required Bassett to make every em count, literally. The care with which Locke wanted to make his debut in the London book market is reflected in the technicality of the terms. The ten-shillings-a-sheet came out to 58 sheets, according to a postscript in Thomas Bassett's hand, and Locke was paid 29 pounds.[87] This was a relatively modest amount of money for Locke, who had been appointed Commissioner of Excise Appeals that year at an annual salary of two hundred pounds per year and whose estate upon his death in 1704 was valued at more than twelve thousand pounds.[88] The benefit to Locke I think was in the precision, more than in the payment, though certainly the recognition of the value that he was transferring to Bassett was meaningful. Bassett's investment was, if nothing else, further incentive to sell the books in order to recoup his payment to Locke.

In addition, the contract specified that Locke (or his assigns) would receive 25 copies in sheets. These were the cheapest copies, unbound and uncut, suggesting that Locke preferred to receive a higher quantity of copies over

---

85 Locke MS b.1, f.109v.

86 Lindenbaum (2002), *supra* note 9, 57.

87 Locke MS b.1, f.109v. Lindenbaum walks through the conversion of sheets in the Milton octavo to the number of sheets in the Locke folio and verifies that the calculations in the postscript are correct. Lindenbaum (2002), *supra* note 9, 57. This seems to have been close to the going rate, Locke had heard via a friend about London booksellers like the Churchills, with whom he ultimately published a great deal, 'that for good books of which they may venture to print 1,000 or 1,120 copies they give sometimes £20, sometimes £30.' CRANSTON, *supra* note 5, at 298.

88 J. R. Milton, *Locke, John (1632–1704)*, in OXFORD DICTIONARY OF NATIONAL BIOGRAPHY (2008), https://doi.org/10/1093/ref:odnb/16885; Milton, *supra* note 5, at 21.

more expensive bound editions, to maximize his ability to circulate the text to chosen recipients. It seems likely that this was a priority for Locke, as Locke was also given the option to buy up to 25 more such copies "at the sale of one half penny a sheet as he the said John Locke shall desire within twelve monthes after the Publishing of the same … all such money paid for any of the said five and twenty Books the said Thomas Bassett shal repay to the said John Locke when ever he shall Reprint the said Treatise."[89] The phrase "whenever he shall Reprint the said Treatise" implies that Bassett had the power to reprint without further consent from Locke, but that point remained somewhat ambiguous until subsequent agreements regarding new editions.

Finally, the contract specified a strict timeline for production of the first impression: "And the said John Locke doth promise to ye said Thomas Bassett to deliver to him on demand from time to time so much of ye said Booke or Treatise as shall make five sheets to be Printed as above said upon the said Thomas Bassetts delivery of a Copy in Print to the said John Locke of what he then last received from him."[90] The process nonetheless took considerable time, with Locke making edits right up until the printing was complete in December of that year, so the close working relationship between author and press throughout the process paid off for Locke, who had staked and won his reputation on the essay.[91] In June of 1693, Bassett reached out to Locke to let him know "that the Impression of your Books are so neare sold that I am ready to Reprint it but thought it necessary to acquaint you first with it because you shewed me some alterations and Additions that you had made, and if you have finished what you intended, I desire you would be pleased to send it by the first opportunity."[92] Apparently, Bassett did not expect to have to ask for permission to reprint the work, but was interested in acquiring an update. As it happened, Locke did not merely send the new material for inclusion, but rather signed a new deal with Bassett, in which Locke was again paid ten shillings, this time for "each sheet of the bigness of the sheets of the former edition that shall be added to this second edition, whether in text or table."[93] He was also compensated with 20 copies in sheets and a fairly bound copy of Spencer's *de Legibus Ritualibus*. A postscript signed by Thomas Bassett adds that if Locke

---

89 Locke MS b.1, f.109.

90 *Id.* We know that Locke sent copies of the *Essay* to several friends. CRANSTON, *supra* note 5, at 327.

91 Milton, *supra* note 5, at 17.

92 Letter from Thomas Bassett to John Locke (Feb. 28, 1693), in 4 CORRESPONDENCE, *supra* note 2, at 645–46.

93 Locke MS b.1, f.168.

needs more copies of the edition, "I will let him have them cheaper than I allow them to booksellers."[94]

For all of Locke's interest in controlling the details of the *Essay*'s publication under this deal, it is perhaps worth noting a deal that Locke did not do during this period. In May of 1689, his *Epistola de Tolerantia* was published in Latin anonymously in the Netherlands, under the mystifiying initials "P.A.P.O.I.L.A."[95] Locke had left the manuscript behind when he returned to England and a friend "saw it through the press."[96] It was a controversial work that Locke never publicly acknowledged while he was alive.[97] He did, however, tolerate an English translation to be prepared and published in London by William Popple in October 1689. Locke was aware of the translation, having sent a copy of the original to Popple.[98] He casually commented to a friend in June that year, "I learn that some Englishman is now engaged in translating one of the tracts."[99] However, Locke never attempted to interfere with or profit from the translation. Perhaps this was because he did not want to admit his authorship of the original, but it is also probable that Locke did not feel it was within his rights to do so. This is consistent with the limitation in the scope of the derivative work right anticipated by Professor Gordon's understanding of Lockean labor theory, as Locke had no plans to translate the letter himself.[100] When Locke confessed authorship of the *Epistola* in a codicil to his will, he merely commented that it was "afterwards translated into English without my privity."[101] Cranston interprets "privity" here as "knowledge" and observes that Locke was being "mendacious."[102] There being no reason to lie in his will, I think it likely that Locke meant something more like "privity" in the legal sense, meaning that he had no contractual interest in the translation.[103]

---

94 *Id.*

95 Milton, *supra* note 5, at 16. Cranston reports a claim that the initials stood for Pacis Amico, Perscutionis Osore, Johanne Lockio Anglo (A Friend of Peace, a Hater of Persecution, John Locke, Englishman). CRANSTON, *supra* note 5, at 320.

96 Milton, *supra* note 5, at 16.

97 CRANSTON, *supra* note 5, at 320–21.

98 Milton, *supra* note 5, at 17–18.

99 CRANSTON, *supra* note 5, at 320.

100 See *supra* note 75 and accompanying text.

101 Locke, *Locke's Will*, in 8 CORRESPONDENCE, *supra* note 2, 419–27 at 426.

102 CRANSTON, *supra* note 5, at 321.

103 The *Oxford English Dictionary* cites uses of the word meaning "a relation between two parties that is recognized by law as a consequence of their mutual participation or interest in a transaction, covenant, tenure, lease, service, etc." going back to 1523. The earliest cited use of the phrase "privity of contract" is in 1650.

2.b Retaining "Copy": Considerations and *A General History of the Air*

If the contract for the *Essay* is notable for its involvement with the technical details of the publication process, then the next two documents that have survived are remarkable for their focus on the aftermath of publication. In them, Locke asserts control of the right to reprint the texts with a very simple provision. The most prevalent form of documentation for author-publisher agreements that has survived from this era is a simple receipt acknowledging payment, usually signed only by the author, often purporting to transfer title in the copy to the publisher in return for a single lump sum.[104] In 1692, however, Locke had his booksellers sign two agreements that exactly reverse this formula. Instead, they are declarations that the "coppy" remains with Locke. The first regarded an economic treatise and reads:

> Wee doe hereby declare that the sole right of and in ye Coppy or booke called *Some Considerations of the Consequences of the Lowering of Interest & Raising the value of money* is & remayns in Mr. John Locke witness our hands 2d March 1691/2.[105]

It is witnessed by Edward Clarke and signed on behalf of Awnsham and John Churchill, who had by then become Locke's regular publishers.[106] The most extraordinary part of it is that it was signed after the Churchills had already printed *Some Considerations*. The treatise had been hastily published in December, 1691, in order to intervene publicly in the debates regarding a controversial interest bill then before Parliament.[107] This short agreement would function as a kind of covenant not to interfere with Locke's rights in the book. Clearly, Locke was concerned to maintain complete control of the treatise. Similarly, later that same year, Locke had the Churchills sign the following agreement as they were in the midst of printing *A General History of the Air*:

> Wee doe hereby declare that the Sole Right of and in the Coppy or book called *A General History of the Ayr* begun by the Honorable Robert Boyle Esq. is &

[104] Lionel Bently and Jane C. Ginsburg, *The Sole Right ... Shall Return to the Authors: Anglo-American Authors' Reversion Rights from the Statute of Anne to Contemporary U.S. Copyright*, 25 BERKELEY TECH. L. J. 1475, 1496. For an image of a typical example, see Curtin, *supra* note 10, at 231.

[105] Locke MS b.1, f.161.

[106] Awnsham Churchill had published the *Two Treatises of Government* and the *Letter Concerning Toleration*. CRANSTON, *supra* note 5, at 326–27.

[107] Patrick Hyde Kelly, *General Introduction*, in 1 LOCKE ON MONEY 19 (1991).

> remains in Mr. John Locke after the Impression wee are now printing. Wittness our hands 25 July 1692.[108]

Here we see the strongest assertion of authors' rights in Locke's publishing agreements, a complete reservation of rights.

The words "sole right of and in the Coppy or book" in these declarations must refer to a general right to print, not merely a right of first publication, in the first note because it was executed after publication and in the second note because of its explicit terms. Had the words referred only to a right of first publication, there would have been nothing to "remain" in Locke. In the case of *A General History of the Air*, the Churchills did enter the copy in the Stationers' Register on their own behalf on July 16, 1692.[109] Thus, the Churchills were in a position to block any attempts by another bookseller to have the work printed. However, having subsequently signed the document above, they presumably had bound themselves contractually not to print the work themselves, at least, not without consent from Locke. Thus, with the cooperation of the Churchill brothers, Locke used the strength of the Stationers' Register against itself, to wrest control of reprints from the booksellers.[110]

It is irresistible to ask why Locke pressed for such control over these particular works. The stakes were more likely reputational and personal than monetary. In the case of *Some Considerations*, the work was published anonymously and Locke insisted on keeping his authorship a secret, even in the face of encouragement from Edward Clarke to reveal himself.[111] The issues of monetary policy that the work covered were politically sensitive and Locke may have wanted to control the timing of any additional interventions a new edition might make. As for *A General History of the Air*, the reputational interest was chiefly not Locke's own. The work was pulled together from the papers of Robert Boyle, Locke's recently deceased mentor and friend, from his days on a studentship at Oxford.[112] In the final months of Boyle's life, Locke helped him to organize the work and then brought it to press as one of Boyle's executors.[113] Locke had a very high opinion of Boyle. In the *Epistle to the Reader* in the *Essay Concerning Human Understanding*, Locke commented,

---

[108] Locke MS b.1, f. 164.

[109] Edward Arber, 3 A Transcript of the Registers of the Worshipful Company of Stationers, 1640–1708 A.D. 421 (London, 1914).

[110] Though the rights retained by Locke in these arrangements were theoretically perpetual at the time, the Statute of Anne not having been passed, Locke's will does not make mention of them. Locke, *supra* note 101, at 426

[111] Cranston, *supra* note 5, at 350–51.

[112] *Id.* at 75–77.

[113] *Id.* at 353.

"everyone must not hope to be a Boyle."[114] Yet, when Boyle passed, Locke was concerned about the disarray of the papers. Boyle had also entrusted him and Sir Isaac Newton with a secret alchemical recipe for multiplying gold, which Newton regarded as utterly worthless and eventually convinced Locke to abandon as bunk.[115] So there were reasons that Locke might have felt particularly protective of his former teacher's reputation, and wished to maintain the power to choose when to further disseminate his work.

2.c Striking a New Balance: *Some Thoughts* and *The Reasonableness of Christianity*

The next two agreements, dated June of 1694 and June of 1695, were executed after Locke had entered into the debates on literary property, having written to Edward Clarke in January 1693 to begin his complaints. Both agreements are with Awnsham and John Churchill. Some of Locke's expectations remained constant. For instance, his compensation is still scaled to his labor. But there are also new tools the parties use to resolve the issues of subsequent editions and title to the copy. In the agreement covering *Some Thoughts Concerning Education*, Awnsham and John Churchill agreed to pay Locke *during his life* five pounds upon every impression, with the first impression not to exceed fourteen hundred copies.[116] In addition, Locke would be paid ten shillings per sheet for all additions to the same, plus 25 books bound in calfskin and lettered. The limitation of Locke's contractual claims for compensation to the term of his life may well be a reflection of his thoughts on the unreasonable burden on the prices of books caused by the stationers' perpetual claims. Finally, the agreement binds the Churchills, their heirs, executors, administrators and assigns that "during his life that neither we nor they will or shall dispose of the right or title to the Coppy of the said booke to any person whatever without the consent of the said John Locke."[117] So the parties conceived of the booksellers holding the right to print, but they could not transfer it without Locke's consent. This arrangement may have been suggested to Locke by the circumstances surrounding the bankruptcy of Thomas Bassett, resulting in a jarring letter in March 1694 from Bassett's successor in interest.[118] Locke trusted the Churchills with ownership of the copy, but had learned that he wanted to be

---

[114] John Locke, An Essay Concerning Human Understanding 8 (Peter Nidditch, ed., Oxford University Press 1975).

[115] Cranston, *supra* note 5, at 353, 361.

[116] Locke MS b.1, f.173.

[117] *Id.*

[118] Letter from Samuel Manship to John Locke (March 10, 1694), in 5 Correspondence, *supra* note 2, at 29.

able to choose his partners in disseminating his work. This provision was an artful solution.

The contract regarding *The Reasonableness of Christianity* is similar, except that, instead of requiring consent for transfer of the "Coppy," the agreement requires that "no edition ... be made during his Life without his knowledge and Consent."[119] This provision is likely an indication of the sensitivity of the subject matter, which was theologically controversial enough to cause accusations of heresy.[120] In particular, the work provoked a virulent string of exchanges in print with the Calvinist provocateur, John Edwards.[121] The Churchills promised to pay Locke (or his executors, administrators, and assigns) ten shillings per sheet for every impression printed during Locke's life, with the exception that if "John Locke shall dy before the second Impression of the said booke, then wee promise and covenant to pay his Executors, Administrators or assigns ten shillings per sheet in full Consideration for the said Coppy." So his estate would be entitled only to payment for the second impression. There is also a postscript promising to deliver to Locke 22 bound copies of every impression. Because the delivery is directly to Locke (and not his assigns), in this context it seems reasonable to assume that the provision also applies only to impressions printed during his life. So this contract similarly limits the contractual claims of Locke's estate, but supports his control of and compensation for the work during his life.

2.d Giving Back to the Public Good: 4th Edition of the *Essay* and Locke's Will

The last agreement in Locke's papers covered the fourth edition of the *Essay* and at last cleared up any lingering ambiguity there might have been as to whether Locke's consent was needed for new editions. The agreement was signed by Samuel Manship and Awnsham Churchill, who eventually succeeded to half-shares of Bassett's interest in the rights to the *Essay*. According to a letter Manship sent to Locke in March of 1694, "Mr. Basset has disposed of the Copy to me and one more. We shall take care to satisfye you as if he had it him selfe, he having left your agreement with us, Mr. Basset sence is removed to the fryers and his shop is shet up."[122] Though Manship claimed to have retained the plate and the effigies of Locke that Bassett had prepared, Locke can hardly have been comforted by the letter. A third edition of the

[119] Locke MS b.1, f.178.
[120] Astbury, *supra* note 14, at 313.
[121] Cranston, *supra* note 5, at 390–91.
[122] Letter from Samuel Manship to John Locke, *supra* note 118, at 29.

Essay was printed in December of 1695, almost unchanged from the second edition,[123] but for the fourth edition, the parties negotiated a new agreement. In June of 1699, Manship and Churchill each agreed to the following terms "for my half part in the said Copy." Locke, or his assign, was to be paid six books, well-bound in calfskin and gilt, "as soon as the next edition of the *Essay* shall be printed and six other such books for every impression that shal be hereafter made of the said *Essay* during the life of the said Mr. John Lock," plus ten shillings per sheet for all the additions. The reduction of the number of copies down to 12 books per impression (six from each bookseller), but bound in gilded calfskin, was perhaps an indication that Locke was beyond the stage at which his priority was to circulate his own work in higher numbers, or to benefit commercially from selling copies. Instead, he opted for more expensive presentation copies of the kind that might prove durable and have long lives in library collections. The parties did not appear to anticipate needing to contract again in the event of new impressions.

Nonetheless, we know that Locke did have plans for the copies of his works that he retained in his own library. Locke's will contains the final transaction he entered into regarding his works. In a codicil dated September 15th 1704, he granted the request of the Library Keeper of the Bodleian Library for a full set of the books authored by himself for the public library at Oxford University, "in acknowledgement of the honour done me in thinking my writings worthy to be placed among the works of the learned in that August repository."[124] He then confessed authorship of the works published during his lifetime without his name. Finally, he also donated copies of the works of his theological opponent, John Edwards, saying: "Both which treatises it is my Will should be bound up in one volume with my three letters on the same subject that therein any one who pleaseth may have the convenience to examine what my Opponent and I have seyd in this controversy."[125] Locke died just a few weeks later.

The legacy of books bequeathed to the Bodleian Library was a fitting tribute to a life dedicated to intellectual work that became truly public only in the last 15 years before his death. That he also confessed authorship of his remaining works in the same transaction was a kind of cashing out (or in) of the reputational currency he had stewarded throughout his life, giving it over to history to judge its final value. Locke's resourceful use of transactional tools to disseminate his work did faithfully reflect his political and philosophical views in a number of ways, or perhaps it was his experience as an author and

---

[123] Milton, *supra* note 5, at 20–21.
[124] Locke, *supra* note 97, at 425–26.
[125] *Id.* at 426.

reader that helped to inform his political views on the literary property debates of his day. When he “trafficked” with booksellers, it was not merely “for gain” but to safeguard the integrity of his work, to advance the cause of science, and to contribute to the intergenerational, intangible commons imagined in his philosophy.

2. The lawful piracy of James Joyce's poems

Robert Spoo

1. INTRODUCTION

What would happen if the U.S. Congress withdrew copyright protection from an entire class of works? Would authors stop producing them? Would there be a mad rush by sellers to profit from existing copies that now lacked the safeguards of an enforceable federal monopoly? Would there be a surge in sales as unrestrained competition caused prices to fall, followed by a sharp decline in supply as authors and sellers watched profit margins dwindle and vanish in the frenzy? Would sellers eventually find a way to rebuild a market by agreeing informally among themselves to check their impulse to compete for the same unprotected works? Could market failure be avoided in this market without copyrights, with the help of improvised, informal protections?

This is no exotic thought experiment, and we need not guess at the answers to many of the questions posed. Throughout most of the nineteenth century, foreign authors lacked copyright protection in the United States as a matter of congressional fiat.[1] By expressly withholding copyrights from foreign authors, lawmakers hoped to shield American book manufacturers from competition from abroad and to render foreign works—gifted in plenteous supply to domestic publishers—an affordable commodity for an increasingly literate populace.[2]

When U.S. copyright at last became available to foreign authors in 1891, protection was conditioned on burdensome requirements that often left those

[1] The text of the 1790 copyright statute expressly excluded foreign authors from protection. Act of 31 May 1790, ch. 15, § 5, 1 Stat. 124, 125. Later U.S. copyright acts perpetuated this disability. Act of 3 February 1831, ch. 16, § 8, 4 Stat. 436, 438; Act of 8 July 1870, ch. 230, § 103, 16 Stat. 198, 215.

[2] The 1850 U.S. Census reported a literacy rate of approximately 90% among white men and women. Candy Gunther Brown, *The Word in the World: Evangelical Writing, Publishing, and Reading in America, 1789–1880* (University of North Carolina Press, Chapel Hill 2004), 10.

authors no better off than they had been under pre-1891 law. The 1891 Chace International Copyright Act granted copyright protection to foreign authors only if they or their publishers managed to comply with the requirement that their books be typeset on American soil and, in effect, published in the United States simultaneously with or before their appearance abroad.[3]

For foreign-origin works in English, this manufacturing clause, as it was called, was expanded in 1909 to include, in addition to typesetting, the express requirement of printing and binding within the United States.[4] For foreign authors who were new, or had not yet won an American readership, or whose writings were controversial or spoke in an unfamiliar idiom, the manufacturing clause effectively barred acquisition of copyright in the United States. Largely forgotten today, the clause in its time was every bit as feared by authors and publishers as were copyright notice, renewal, and other formalities the omission or bungling of which could destroy or impair U.S. copyright.[5]

How maddening it must have been in 1870 to enjoy copyright protection in one's own country—Britain, say—but to lack it entirely in the United States with its enormous English-speaking population and high literacy rate. Incentives to create would still exert their pull on the English author because copyrights could be enforced at home.[6] But just across the Atlantic lay an immense tract in which a governmentally decreed commons waited to claim her work just as soon as it came off the press in London. A few copies of the book, or even unbound sheets, would be hurried across the ocean and into the hands of printers. Within a few days, bookstores in the larger American cities would be supplied with ample stock, and a great scramble would ensue to extract profits from this statute-gifted resource.[7] Born into native protection, the English author's work found itself annexed by the world's busiest, hungriest public domain.

How did American publishers monetize such a public domain when its chief resource—popular foreign titles—could be reprinted abundantly, by anyone and everyone, without permission or fear of liability? How did lawful piracy survive, let alone thrive? Or, to put it another way, where a rights vacuum

---

3 Act of 3 March 1891, ch. 565, § 4956, 26 Stat. 1106, 1107–108. These requirements mandated not only U.S. typesetting, but also, as a practical matter, first or simultaneous printing and publication on U.S. soil. *See* Commissioner of Labor, *A Report on the Effect of the International Copyright Law in the United States* (Government Printing Office, Washington, DC 1901), 5–6.

4 Act of 4 March 1909, ch. 320, § 15, 35 Stat. 1075, 1078–79.

5 Herbert A. Howell, *The Copyright Law*, 2d ed. (Bureau of National Affairs, Washington, DC 1948), 84–87.

6 Robert Spoo, *Without Copyrights: Piracy, Publishing, and the Public Domain* (Oxford University Press, New York 2013), 31–32.

7 *Id.* at 49–53.

exists, what will come to fill it? Unbridled freeriding? But "freeriding" seems an uncharitable word where no property right is being invaded. Multilateral exploitation? "Exploitation," too, seems less than the *mot juste*, given its connotation of unfair advantage. It is difficult to characterize IP's negative spaces, except to say that they are just that, spaces devoid of formal entitlements, supporting doubtful contracts, engendering no sustainable lawsuits.[8] Scholarship has uncovered such spaces in likely and unlikely domains: fashion design, stand-up comedy, chefs' recipes, roller derby, tattooing, even clown makeup—but the domain of books has received much less attention.[9]

No negative space of which I am aware is as impressive for its historical longevity and social impact as the copyright vacuum that existed for foreign works in America in the nineteenth and early twentieth centuries. Rather than forgo the opportunity of reprinting the latest transatlantic titles—works by Charles Dickens, George Eliot, Walter Scott, and many other popular authors—American publishers learned to live in the immediate moment, to extract quick profits through first-mover tactics. They planted agents in England to watch for the latest publications; engaged lightning-fast typesetters, printers, and distributors; and had the grit and resilience to face the inevitable prompt competition for the same work and to move on when rivals swallowed up the early advantages.[10] Publishers were selling intellectual perishables—books with a profitable street life of days or weeks. They had to strike while the press was hot.

---

[8] Elizabeth Rosenblatt, "Intellectual Property's Negative Space: Beyond the Utilitarian," 40 Fla. St. U.L. Rev. 441–86 (2013).

[9] *See* Kal Raustiala and Christopher Sprigman, "The Piracy Paradox: Innovation and Intellectual Property in Fashion Design," 92 Va. L. Rev. 1687–777 (2006); Dotan Oliar and Christopher Sprigman, "There's No Free Laugh (Anymore): The Emergence of Intellectual Property Norms and the Transformation of Stand-Up Comedy," 94 Va. L. Rev. 1787–867 (2008); Christopher J. Buccafusco, "On the Legal Consequences of Sauces: Should Thomas Keller's Recipes Be Per Se Copyrightable?", 24 Cardozo Arts & Entm't L.J. 1121–56 (2007); David Fagundes, "Talk Derby to Me: Intellectual Property Norms Governing Roller Derby Pseudonyms," 90 Tex. L. Rev. 1093–152 (2011); Aaron Perzanowski, "Tattoos and IP Norms," 98 Minn. L. Rev. 511–91 (2013); David Fagundes and Aaron Perzanowski, "Clown Eggs," 94 Notre Dame L. Rev. 1313–79 (2019). *See also generally* Kate Darling and Aaron Perzanowski, eds., *Creativity without Law: Challenging the Assumptions of Intellectual Property* (NYU Press, New York 2017).

[10] Charles A. Madison, *Book Publishing in America* (McGraw-Hill, New York 1966), 10.

2. LAWFUL PIRACY AND TRADE COURTESY

Even for nimble and tough businessmen, the hectic trade stimulated by the copyright vacuum for foreign works could be wearing and nerve-wracking. If one house could reprint a novel, so could another, and publishers often undersold one another in a publishing environment one historian likens to a "Hobbes-like State of nature."[11] Critics called the practice "piracy" and assumed that Americans were getting rich off the unremunerated labor of British writers. Both charges were inaccurate. These reprinters were not pirates, legally speaking, and most were not getting rich. In fact, reprinting was far from universally profitable, in part because this celebrated free market was actually too free. Realizing that self-regulated coordination would be more profitable than unregulated competition, American publishers began to work together to find a way to stabilize the public domain. The result, emerging in the 1830s and 1840s, went by various names: the "usage of the trade," "etiquette," "good faith," or even the "laws of honor." Usually, however, it was called "courtesy of the trade," "trade courtesy," or just "courtesy."[12]

Whatever name it went by, it was a process by which publishers recognized informal publishing rights in literary texts that had no legal status as property. It was premised on an intuitive prior-rights logic: the first firm to declare its intention to publish a foreign book had a monopoly stake in that book and sometimes also in subsequent books by the same author.[13] In time, the custom was expanded, especially as the field of American publishing grew. For example, Publisher A would publicly claim the latest novel by George Eliot; Publisher B would recognize this claim so long as its own association with Charles Dickens was respected; and Publisher C would, ideally, acknowledge the claims of both A and B if its entitlement to the sole reprinting of Walter Scott went unchallenged. Turn-of-the-century publisher Henry Holt

---

11 James J. Barnes, "Edward Lytton Bulwer and the Publishing Firm of Harper & Brothers," 38 Am. Lit. 35, 36 (1966).

12 For contemporaneous names for courtesy, see J. Henry Harper, *The House of Harper: A Century of Publishing in Franklin Square* (Harper & Brothers, New York 1912), 358 ("law of courtesy"); Publishers' Wkly., No. 479, 19 March 1881, at 316, 316 ("trade usage"); Publishers' Wkly., No. 480, 26 March 1881, at 322, 322 ("the courtesy of the trade"). Trade courtesy was sometimes called the "Harper Rule," from the role that the publisher Harper & Brothers played in establishing courtesy rules. Adrian Johns, *Piracy: The Intellectual Property Wars from Gutenberg to Gates* (University of Chicago Press, Chicago 2009), 300–301.

13 Spoo, *supra* note 6, at 37–38.

boasted that courtesy was "a brief realization of the ideals of philosophical anarchism—self-regulation without law."[14]

By means of such coordination, publishers, within and between the major publishing centers of Philadelphia, New York City, and Boston, avoided a public-goods problem and market failure for this profitable foreign resource.[15] Steadily, the system of courtesy grew in extent and complexity. Publishers evolved rules for announcing and perfecting their improvised rights. They created procedures for securing options on a foreign author's subsequent writings and for associating authors with their firms on an exclusive basis.[16] These practices became so well recognized that publishers were able to pay honoraria or royalties to foreign authors; many authors received payments, large or small, solicited or unsolicited, from courtesy-abiding houses. Often the payments were modest (£10 or £15), but some American publishers paid British authors considerable sums, even though they were not required to do so by law. Scott received £75 for advance sheets of each of the Waverley novels, and £300 for his *Life of Napoleon Bonaparte*.[17] Harper & Brothers paid Charles Dickens £360 for magazine rights to *Bleak House*, £250 for *Little Dorrit*, £1000 each for *A Tale of Two Cities* and *Our Mutual Friend*, £1250 for *Great Expectations*, and £2000 for the never-finished *Mystery of Edwin Drood*.[18] One publisher in 1876 estimated that courtesy payments for advance sheets of foreign works averaged between £25 and £100; and payments were sometimes made to a deceased author's estate.[19]

To enforce the rules of courtesy, participating houses crafted penalties for publishers who trespassed on other firms' recognized claims. These sanctions escalated in severity, beginning with a private protest lodged with the trespasser, rising, if necessary, to public shaming in trade journals or newspapers, then to predatory pricing to match or undersell the trespasser, and climaxing, when all else failed, in retaliatory reprinting of one of the trespasser's own books.[20] Courts were no help; they did not recognize these strange courtesy

---

14 Henry Holt, "Competition," 102 Atlantic Monthly, October 1908, at 516, 522–23.

15 Spoo, *supra* note 6, at 30–32.

16 *Id.* at 37–42.

17 Donald Sheehan, *This Was Publishing: A Chronicle of the Book Trade in the Gilded Age* (Indiana University Press, Bloomington 1952), 62.

18 Madison, *supra* note 10, at 26.

19 *Minutes of the Evidence Taken Before the Royal Commission on Copyright Together with an Appendix* (Eyre & Spottiswoode, London 1878), 63, 91.

20 For overviews of trade courtesy, see Michael J. Everton, *The Grand Chorus of Complaint: Authors and the Business Ethics of American Publishing* (Oxford University Press, New York 2011), 44–47, 125–27; Harper, *supra* note 12, at 110–11; Johns, *supra* note 12, at 295–302; Sheehan, *supra* note 17, at 61–62; Siva

claims as property or business assets.[21] The more severe courtesy sanctions were rarely necessary. Often a publisher would surrender a lucrative British title, not out of fear of reprisal but because he had not secured his opportunity under the courtesy principles, and doing so would be, quite simply, discourteous.[22]

Thus, publishers responded in one of two ways to the American commons of foreign works: by engaging in lawful piracies or by observing informal courtesies. Here were two distinct professional ethics. One claimed shelter under the letter of U.S. copyright law; the other recognized a spirit of fairness in publishing, a moral imperative referred to by one Philadelphia publisher in the 1830s as the "rules that govern gentlemen."[23] Both ethics involved risks and expended resources. Courtesy required communal trust and proper behavior, coordination and cooperation. It was a fragile bulwark against the temptations of lawful piracy of foreign works. Though there is evidence of proto-courtesy agreements as early as the 1820s,[24] and the rules of engagement were likely articulated in the mid-1830s during a series of clashes between two powerful houses, courtesy's heyday was between the 1850s and 1870s.[25]

By the late 1870s, changes in the publishing world shifted the ground on which courtesy once stood. The growth of book manufacturing; the glut of cheap fiction; the arrival of new publishers lacking allegiance to the older houses; interference from Canadian publishers to whom the ethic did not apply; and the rise of literary agents who encouraged competition rather than comity among publishers, thus fraying the paternal treatment of authors which courtesy had boasted—all these forces eroded the stability of the system.[26] Above all, changes in the legal landscape disrupted the efficacy of courtesy. By the 1890s, with calls for trust-busting on the rise, competitors outside the

---

Vaidhyanathan, *Copyrights and Copywrongs: The Rise of Intellectual Property and How It Threatens Creativity* (NYU Press, New York 2001), 52–55; Jeffrey D. Groves, "Courtesy of the Trade," in *The Industrial Book, 1840–1880*, ed. Scott E. Casper et al., vol. 3 of *A History of the Book in America*, ed. David D. Hall (University of North Carolina Press, Chapel Hill 2007), 139–48; Holt, "The Recoil of Piracy," 5 Forum, March 1888, at 27, 27–32.

[21] *See* Sheldon v. Houghton, 21 F. Cas. 1239, 1241–42 (C.C.S.D.N.Y. 1865) ("[Courtesy can] hardly be called property at all—certainly not in any sense known to the law").

[22] For a discussion of the moral, religious, and customary underpinnings of nineteenth-century American publishing, see generally Everton, *supra* note 20.

[23] Letter from Carey, Lea, and Blanchard to Harrison Gray, 27 April 1835, Lea & Febiger Records, ms. 227B, Letterbook, Carey, Lea, and Blanchard, 17 June 1834 to 2 September 1835, 336–37, Historical Society of Pennsylvania, PA.

[24] Groves, *supra* note 20, at 141.

[25] Johns, *supra* note 12, at 295–302; Spoo, *supra* note 6, at 32–36.

[26] Spoo, *supra* note 6, at 53–64.

courtesy fraternity were accusing its adherents of engaging in anticompetitive practices and erecting barriers to entry.[27] And Congress's passage of the 1891 Chace Act gave foreign authors and publishers a legal alternative to extralegal courtesies, if they could satisfy the statutory manufacturing requirements. Not all authors could.[28]

In this changed world, it might seem that trade courtesy had no place. Yet it did not vanish completely. True, it became less extrovert, no longer the trumpeted boast of prestige houses as formerly; but it survived as an internalized ethic practiced by certain publishers, a recognized obligation to deal fairly with competing firms and foreign authors, a method for preventing and settling disputes and playing the game in a sporting way. But such unsystematic courtesy was ever vulnerable to the impromptu deviations or the calculated amnesia of rival houses or to the brash indifference of newcomers to the trade.[29] Courtesy in a world not bound by courtesy gave rise to sporadic noble gestures, occasional grumbling about bad conduct, and nostalgic praise of better behavior in better times. Courtesy had become less a shared practice than a private observance.[30]

This chapter explores a brief collision of these two very different, largely forgotten practices—lawful piracy and informal courtesy—in the twilight of courtesy's moment, the early twentieth century. The history of the Irish author James Joyce's first book of poems, *Chamber Music*, published in England in 1907, highlights the continuing problem of U.S. copyright for many non-U.S. authors in the first half of the twentieth century. The lack of U.S. copyright protection for *Chamber Music* invited two responses from American publishers: an unapologetic act of lawful piracy by the Cornhill Company of Boston, and a firm display of honesty and integrity by B.W. Huebsch of New York. Huebsch considered himself Joyce's authorized publisher in America. In his dealings with Joyce and Cornhill, he deployed the old traditions of trade courtesy, both in his promise to pay Joyce a fair royalty on sales of the uncopyrighted poems and in his indignant protests against Cornhill. Huebsch's and Cornhill's very different responses to the American public domain offer a glimpse of the publishing world of 1918 as it contended with a U.S. copyright law that had yet to divest itself of the protectionism and isolationism that had characterized it for more than a century.

---

27 *Id.* at 53–58 (discussing the anticompetitive nature of trade courtesy).

28 *Id.* at 59–64.

29 Raymond Howard Shove, *Cheap Book Production in the United States, 1870 to 1891* (University of Illinois Library, Urbana 1937), 37–38, 130.

30 *Id.*

3. THE CORNHILL COMPANY'S LAWFUL PIRACY

James Joyce was probably the most famously pirated English-language author of the twentieth century. The story of Samuel Roth's unauthorized serialization of Joyce's *Ulysses* in his New York magazine *Two Worlds Monthly* has received much scholarly attention over the years and has been examined in detail in two recent monographs.[31] First published as a book in Paris in 1922, *Ulysses* was widely assailed as indecent and obscene in America. Joyce was unable to have the controversial book manufactured in the United States within the statutory window mandated by the 1909 U.S. Copyright Act (an authorized edition would not be published in America until 1934), and so *Ulysses* lost its chance for U.S. copyright protection within months of its appearance in France. It had fallen victim to the manufacturing clause.[32]

Joyce responded to Roth's lawful piracy of *Ulysses* by organizing and publishing an international protest, signed by more than 150 writers and intellectuals, and by bringing a lawsuit against Roth in a New York State court for appropriating his name for commercial purposes (not for copyright infringement). Joyce's lawyers succeeded in obtaining a consensual injunction against Roth, but not before the New York publisher had printed a substantial portion of *Ulysses* in his magazine. Roth also issued unauthorized fragments of what would later become Joyce's last work, *Finnegans Wake* (1939), after Joyce was unable to reprint those portions—originally published abroad—in the United States in compliance with the manufacturing clause.[33]

The lawful piracy of Joyce's book of poems titled *Chamber Music*—his first significant publication—has received almost no attention from scholars and little more than a passing reference in biographies and bibliographies of Joyce.[34] *Chamber Music* was a slim volume of 36 poems gathered from lyrics Joyce had written in his youth. They are delicate and fastidious in style, spare and musical, moody and lovelorn, and reminiscent of Elizabethan songs touched with fin-de-siècle aestheticism. The London publisher Elkin Mathews issued the book in May 1907 in an edition of around 500 copies. The volume received some critical praise—notably in a review by the British poet and critic Arthur Symons—but it did not sell well, and Joyce received no royalties from

---

[31] Jay A. Gertzman, *Samuel Roth, Infamous Modernist* (University Press of Florida, Gainesville 2013), 63–100; Spoo, *supra* note 6, at 153–232.

[32] Robert Spoo, "Copyright Protectionism and Its Discontents: The Case of James Joyce's *Ulysses* in America," 108 Yale L.J. 633–67 (1998).

[33] Spoo, *supra* note 6, at 165–72.

[34] *See, e.g.*, Herbert Gorman, *James Joyce* (Rinehart & Company, New York 1948), 262–63; John J. Slocum and Herbert Cahoon, *A Bibliography of James Joyce* (1953; rpt. Greenwood Press, Westport, CT 1971), 10.

Mathews, who did not release a second edition until 1918, after Joyce had begun to make his name as a fiction writer in the United States and abroad.[35]

Chamber Music was protected from the outset in Britain, where the Copyright Act 1842 granted copyright for the author's life plus seven years after death, or 42 years from first publication, whichever was longer.[36] Although the 1842 Act provided that copies of a published work were to be delivered to certain British libraries, there were no formalities that had to be observed for acquiring copyright.[37] Americans and other non-British authors could secure British copyright by publishing their works in a British dominion simultaneously with publication elsewhere.[38] When Britain adopted a new, comprehensive Copyright Act in 1911, the British copyright in *Chamber Music* was increased to the author's life plus 50 years after death.[39]

The United States was a different story. The 1891 Chace Act granted an initial copyright term of 28 years from first publication only if a work was "printed from type set within the limits of the United States, or from plates made therefrom," and if two copies of such work were deposited in the Copyright Office on or before the date of first publication anywhere else. Collectively known as the manufacturing clause, these provisions made first or simultaneous manufacture and publication in America a condition of U.S. copyright for any book published abroad.[40] A 1905 amendment granted foreign authors a small reprieve: They could enjoy a one-year "ad interim" U.S. copyright if a copy of the foreign publication was deposited in the Library of Congress within 30 days after publication abroad.[41] But the ad-interim copyright would become a full U.S. copyright only if the book was manufactured and published in the United States promptly after ad-interim protection was secured.[42] The 1909 Act continued the ad-interim opportunity with its narrow

---

35 Slocum and Cahoon, *id.*, at 5–10.

36 5 and 6 Vict. c. 45, § III.

37 *Id.* §§ VI–VIII.

38 7 and 8 Vict. c. 12, § 19; E.J. MacGillivray, *A Treatise upon the Law of Copyright* (John Murray, London 1902), 193; Stephen P. Ladas, *The International Protection of Literary and Artistic Property* (Macmillan, New York 1938), 899.

39 1 and 2 Geo. 5 c. 46, §§ 3, 24.

40 Act of 3 March 1891, ch. 565, §4956, 26 Stat. 1106, 1108; Spoo, *supra* note 6, at 60.

41 Act of 3 March 1905, ch. 1432, 33 Stat. 1000; Dorothy M. Schrader, "Ad Interim Copyright and the Manufacturing Clause: Another View of the *Candy* Case," 16 Vill. L. Rev. 215, 222 n.21, 234 (1970).

42 Schrader, *id.*, at 234.

window for compliance.[43] Such rigorous conditions were impossible for many foreign authors to satisfy.

Neither Joyce nor his London publisher complied with the 1891 Act's manufacturing requirements or the 1905 ad-interim provision. Joyce, a virtual unknown at the time, had neither the connections nor the prestige to secure simultaneous manufacture and publication in Britain and America. As a result, *Chamber Music* quietly entered the American public domain just as soon as it was published in London in May 1907. For nearly a decade, the work lay in the American public domain, uncelebrated, part of the heterogeneous mass of unclaimed writings.

By 1917, Joyce was making his mark in the United States. With two books of fiction—*Dubliners* (1914) and *A Portrait of the Artist as a Young Man* (1916)—receiving critical praise, and the serialization of *Ulysses* in a New York literary magazine soon to commence, Joyce's name had at last become marketable.[44] Sometime around October 1917, a small Boston publisher calling itself the Cornhill Company announced in the *Boston Evening Transcript* that it would be publishing *Chamber Music* at one dollar per copy. Joyce's patron and attorney, John Quinn, viewed it as "a clear case of piracy."[45] But it would be case of lawful piracy; Joyce would have no remedy in the courts.

Cornhill was a newcomer to publishing. Its offices were at 69 Cornhill in one of the oldest sections of Boston, an area long familiar for its narrow, winding alleyways, quaint, cluttered bookshops, and hives of printers, publishers, and book designers. By 1902, the publisher Alfred Bartlett had installed himself at 69 Cornhill and made his small office "a rendezvous for young enthusiasts in arts and letters."[46] Between 1900 and 1905, and again in 1914, Bartlett published *The Cornhill Booklet*, a thin letterpress pamphlet offered to middle-class purchasers as "a means of self-improvement, a way to cultural education [through] sanctioned and respected works," and an example of "the private press movement [with its] beautiful typography and original decoration."[47] The covers of *The Cornhill Booklet* were a "strange fin de siècle compound of dainty halftone, ruggedly medieval, and more or less

---

43 Act of 4 March 1909, ch. 320, § 21, 35 Stat. 1075, 1080. Under the 1909 Act as originally adopted, applicants had 30 days from publication abroad to secure ad interim protection, which lasted for 30 days from the date of deposit.

44 Jeanne Redman, "New Ireland," Los Angeles Sun. Times, pt. III, 29 July 1917, at 23, 23.

45 Letter from John Quinn to B.W. Huebsch, 26 October 1917, B.W. Huebsch Papers, Library of Congress, ID No. MSS50013 [hereinafter Huebsch Papers].

46 Carl Purington Rollins, quoted in Ellen Mazur Thomson, "*The Cornhill Booklet*, 1900–1914," Printing Hist., No. 9, at 31, 32 (January 2011).

47 Thomson, *id.*, at 31.

decadent 'art for art's sake.'"[48] The *Booklet* contained selections of stories, poems, letters, choice quotations, and inspirational mottoes, some of it drawn, without permission, from recent British authors such as Oscar Wilde, Robert Louis Stevenson, Rudyard Kipling, and W.S. Gilbert.[49] Bartlett operated in the tradition of lawful American piracy that had flourished in previous decades; his was an amiable, genteel buccaneering, blending a relaxed antiquarianism with leisurely collectability, not unlike the activity of Thomas B. Mosher, the dedicated pirate-publisher of Portland, Maine.[50]

In 1918, Bartlett still had an office at 69 Cornhill, the same address from which the Cornhill Company operated. There was evidently some connection between Bartlett and Cornhill, since Cornhill listed some of Bartlett's titles in its catalogues.[51] Bartlett had been ill for several years, and it is possible that Cornhill moved into his office and helped him to sell off his stock.[52] There is no evidence that Bartlett was actively involved in Cornhill's publishing operations, however, and the suggestion of some scholars that Bartlett himself was responsible for the unauthorized reprinting of *Chamber Music* is unfounded.[53]

The owner and manager of Cornhill was a man named Walter Reid (or W.E. Reid); and the noted African-American poet and anthologist William Stanley Braithwaite acted as a talent-finder and editor. Braithwaite was not, as one scholar has suggested, an owner of Cornhill.[54] He had neither the capital nor the time for significant involvement with the firm. He was, however, a figure of continuity between Bartlett's activities and those of the Cornhill Company. Braithwaite had contributed brief pieces on current American poetry to Bartlett's short-lived revival of *The Cornhill Booklet* in 1914, which had also been published from 69 Cornhill.[55] But the look and sensibility of the Cornhill

---

48 *Id.* at 42.

49 For example, 3 The Cornhill Booklet 8–10 (Autumn 1902) contained W.S. Gilbert's "A Nightmare," from the libretto of Gilbert & Sullivan's light opera, *Iolanthe* (1882).

50 *See* Spoo, *supra* note 6, at 13–19.

51 "Trade List and Catalog of the Cornhill Company," in *The Publishers' Trade List Annual 1918* (R.R. Bowker Co., New York 1918), 15.

52 Thomson, *supra* note 46, at 37.

53 Slocum and Cahoon, *supra* note 34, at 10; Jean C. Evans, "Cornhill 1900–1915: Where Our Story Begins," in *The SP Century: Boston's Society of Printers through One Hundred Years of Change*, ed. Scott-Martin Kosofsky (Society of Printers, Boston 2006), 27.

54 Amy Lee, "Cornhill," in *The Encyclopedia of the Harlem Renaissance*, vol. 1, eds., Cary D. Wintz and Paul Finkelman (Routledge, New York 2004), 252–53.

55 *E.g.*, W.S.B., "Preaching the Gospel of Beauty," 4 *The Cornhill Booklet* 48–49 (November 1914).

Company's books were entirely different from Bartlett's quaintly designed *Cornhill Booklet.*

Braithwaite was largely responsible for the Cornhill Company's most significant contribution to literary history: its publication of African-American writers such as James Weldon Johnson, Angelina Weld Grimké, Joseph S. Cotter, Maud Cuney-Hare, and Georgia Douglas Johnson, some of whom were to become significant voices of the Harlem Renaissance.[56] In this respect, Cornhill was among the "new insurgents in the late teens and early twenties"—including Alfred Knopf, Harcourt & Brace, Boni & Liveright, and B.W. Huebsch—that actively published African-American writers, in contrast to long-established publishers whose lists were more conservative and unadventurous.[57]

Several of the new publishers who printed black authors also specialized in experimental modernist writing. The fact that these publishers "all identified with the American cultural nationalist, cultural pluralist 'movement' is crucial to understanding their relationship to the Harlem Renaissance," according to one scholar.[58] Although in its most prolific years Cornhill published a number of African-American authors, it differed from these other progressive new publishers in largely shunning modernist poetry and in showcasing traditional verse characterized by diluted romanticism, religious and spiritual sentiment, the sorrows of disappointed love, and the rewards of chaste living.

Braithwaite was an ideal poet-finder for a publisher like Cornhill, and he played an important role in shaping the firm's poetry list. An African-American with conservative tastes in verse and strong ties to Boston's genteel literary circles, he viewed poetry as a universalizing influence that could achieve the assimilationist goal of transcending racial and class divides. "Beauty and Art," he once wrote, "were the leveler of all distinctions, [a] transfiguring power … in the common unity of all men, sharing and participating in the same interests and the same privileges."[59] He distrusted modernism's radical experiments in form, believing that poetry's supreme attributes were intuition, vision, and, above all, "spiritual substance," as he declared in the introduction to one of his

---

[56] Lee, *supra* note 54, at 252–53.

[57] George Hutchinson, *The Harlem Renaissance in Black and White* (Harvard University Press, Cambridge, MA 1995), 342–44.

[58] *Id.* at 350.

[59] William Stanley Braithwaite, "The House under Arcturus: An Autobiography," pt. V, 3 Phylon 183, 186 (Second Quarter 1942).

many anthologies of magazine verse.[60] In the craft of poetry, he wrote in 1917, "[n]ot the form, but the substance is the main thing."[61]

The Cornhill Company operated largely as a vanity press, and Braithwaite was skillful at attracting novice authors desperate to be published and willing to pay the costs of producing their slim volumes. Cornhill issued, for example, Caroline Giltinan's *The Divine Image: A Book of Lyrics* (1917), with its somber religious themes and traditional rhymed forms, and Katharine Adams's *Light and Mist* (1918), with its breathless celebration of Irish moors, silver pools, and peasant girls.[62] Not all of Cornhill's self-subventing authors were of this sort, however. The important Harlem Renaissance figure James Weldon Johnson published his early volume, *Fifty Years and Other Poems* (1917), with Cornhill, paying three installments of $100 to see it to press and personally canvassing subscriptions for a special signed edition.[63]

Piracy might seem an odd practice for a vanity press to employ, yet Cornhill's operations were not always irreproachable. Walter Reid's management style eventually plunged the company into financial and legal trouble. Authors complained about slow production, unreturned manuscripts, and unpaid royalties; suppliers and advertisers wearied of sending invoices and receiving only promises in response.[64] Lawful piracy is, in a sense, the counterpart of vanity publishing. In both models, the publisher spares itself some or all of the expense of publishing—in the former instance paying no permission fees or royalties, in the latter, shifting the costs of typesetting, printing, and binding to the author. Lawful piracy relies on a generous public domain; vanity publishing, on a cooperative author. Yet Cornhill was no serial pirate. Joyce's *Chamber Music* is the only clear case of piracy that I have found in the firm's booklists.

Braithwaite undoubtedly played a role in adding *Chamber Music* to Cornhill's list. Joyce's poems resembled, superficially, the simple verse forms and accessible love themes of other Cornhill offerings, and the company

---

[60] *Anthology of Magazine Verse for 1914 and Year Book of American Poetry*, ed. William Stanley Braithwaite (William Stanley Braithwaite, Cambridge, MA 1914), xii, xvi. For a discussion of Braithwaite's tastes in poetry, see Hutchinson, *supra* note 57, at 352–55.

[61] *Anthology of Magazine Verse for 1917 and Yearbook of American Poetry*, ed. William Stanley Braithwaite (Small, Maynard & Company, Boston 1917), ix.

[62] Caroline Giltinan, *The Divine Image: A Book of Lyrics* (Cornhill Company, Boston 1917); Katharine Adams, *Light and Mist* (Cornhill Company, Boston 1918).

[63] Letter from Johnson to Braithwaite, 20 August 1917, William Stanley Braithwaite Papers, 1897–1930, MS Am 1444(571), Houghton Library, Harvard University [hereinafter Braithwaite Papers, Harvard]; James Weldon Johnson, *Fifty Years and Other Poems* (Cornhill Company, Boston 1917).

[64] *See infra* Part 5.

plainly hoped, with Joyce's and Adams's books, to exploit Irish atmosphere and melancholy for a readership that included Irish-Americans in New England. Moreover, Braithwaite had long admired Joyce's poems; they had precisely the recognizable lyric form and "spiritual substance" that he idealized. In 1910, he had sought and received Joyce's permission to publish a poem from *Chamber Music* ("Gentle lady, do not sing") in a verse anthology he was planning, but no such anthology seems to have been published.[65]

In 1919, less than a year after Cornhill issued its piracy of Joyce's volume, Braithwaite published *The Book of Modern British Verse* with two different poems from *Chamber Music* ("Bid adieu to girlish days" and "Love came to us"), but made no mention in his otherwise extensive acknowledgments of any permission received from Joyce.[66] It is almost as if, with the *Chamber Music* piracy in circulation, Braithwaite was drawing on a confirmed public domain for Joyce's poems. Courtesy had always been a fragile barrier against piracy. For any given title, it could be impaired or destroyed overnight by the aggressions of reprint houses. In the 1890s, the young firm of Grosset & Dunlap justified reprinting Rudyard Kipling's uncopyrighted works without permission on the ground that his books had lost the aura of courtesy protection "by having been reprinted indiscriminately by about everyone else in the business."[67]

4. B.W. HUEBSCH: TRADE COURTESY IN ACTION

The Cornhill edition of *Chamber Music*, announced in the fall of 1917, was published in May or June 1918. The book was bound in green cloth with the title and author's name gilt-stamped on the cover and spine, and it sold for one dollar.[68] The title page bore Cornhill's small oval device showing a bespectacled man in a hat and coat, a rolled newspaper in his pocket, a cane hooked over his arm, examining a book taken from a pile in a bookstore. The copyright page was blank, and there was no indication of a printer, unlike other Cornhill books of this period. Cornhill's 1918 catalogue, which advertised *Chamber Music* along with roughly fifty other titles, described the volume, not without cheek, as "the first American edition of the poems by the author of 'The Portrait of

---

[65] Letter from Joyce to Braithwaite, 23 September 1910, James Weldon Johnson MSS 72, Box 1, Folder 37, William Stanley Braithwaite Papers, Series I, Correspondence, Beinecke Library, Yale University [hereinafter Braithwaite Papers, Yale].

[66] *The Book of Modern British Verse*, ed. William Stanley Braithwaite (Small, Maynard & Company, Boston 1919), 60–61.

[67] George T. Dunlap, "The Fleeting Years," in *Publishers on Publishing*, ed. Gerald Gross (Grosset & Dunlap, New York 1961), 271–72.

[68] Slocum and Cahoon, *supra* note 34, at 10.

an Artist as a Young Man' [*sic*] and 'Dubliners.'"[69] Cornhill was exploiting the popularity that Joyce had at last been earning from his prose fiction. The catalogue went on to characterize his poems as being "of a substance which reveal[s] a subtle imagination and a glowing vision."[70] The word "substance," Braithwaite's favorite, betrays his hand in the drafting of this promotional language. Notices of *Chamber Music* appeared in the press in June 1918 along with other Cornhill titles, such as Katharine Adams's *Light and Mist*.[71]

The New York publisher B.W. Huebsch had considered himself Joyce's exclusive American publisher since 1916 when he issued both *Dubliners* and *A Portrait of the Artist as a Young Man*. In May 1918, he also brought out Joyce's play, *Exiles*.[72] Because Huebsch was able to produce *Exiles* and *A Portrait* in compliance with the 1909 U.S. Copyright Act, those works may have qualified for copyright protection in the United States. But the small window of opportunity for complying with the manufacturing clause had already closed for *Dubliners*, which had been published in England in 1914, and for *Chamber Music*, first issued in London in 1907.[73] No U.S. copyright existed or could exist for those two works. Even so, as early as 1915, Huebsch was negotiating with Joyce and Joyce's attorney Quinn to issue *Chamber Music* in New York. Everyone involved in the negotiation, including Joyce's English publisher, behaved as if the little volume of poems was fully protected in the United States, even though they all knew it was not. Huebsch's part in this courteous performance was motivated by his desire to be the authorized American publisher of all of Joyce's works, copyrighted or not.[74]

Here was trade courtesy in action. Faced with the checkerboard effects that U.S. copyright law had inflicted on Joyce—some of his works protected, others not—Huebsch applied a principle of bundling. If an author's output contained both protected and unprotected works, a courtesy publisher would sometimes agree to treat all of them as protected and worthy of compensation. Through bundling, the whole of an author's output became more valuable than any of its uncopyrighted parts.[75] This is exactly what Huebsch did to position himself as the approved American publisher of all of Joyce's works. In contrast to the Cornhill Company, which seized a discrete opportunity to exploit the poetry of a rising author, Huebsch invested in his own future as Joyce's preferred American publisher by bundling all of his writings into a contractual

---

69 "Trade List and Catalog of the Cornhill Company," *supra* note 51, at 6.
70 *Id.*
71 *E.g.*, Wash. Herald, 2 June 1918, at 6, 6.
72 Slocum and Cahoon, *supra* note 34, at 22–23.
73 Spoo, *supra* note 6, at 109–12.
74 *Id.*
75 *Id.* at 112.

relationship that treated him courteously as a fully protected author. Huebsch and Cornhill thus represented divergent practices in American publishers' response to copyright law: Huebsch used his reputation for honesty to secure a relationship of trust with Joyce and to inspire other firms to respect that relationship. Cornhill took its chance as a lawful pirate to build its list and capitalize, however briefly, on the prestige that Joyce's name might bring.

Huebsch practiced norms of courtesy even before he worked with Joyce. He was keenly aware of what he referred to, in 1917, as "the honor that obtains among publishers."[76] One contemporary called Huebsch "the best of the younger publishers in this country—by 'best' I mean most imaginative honourable and resourceful."[77] In 1913, he published H.G. Wells's lecture, *The Discovery of the Future*—a work previously issued in England and plainly in the American public domain—and drew up a contract to pay Wells a royalty. During their negotiations, Wells cryptically warned Huebsch that he "could not protect [Huebsch] in the copyright." Huebsch later learned that Wells allowed another American publisher to reprint the lecture, and when he wrote to express his indignation, Wells replied, "You will remember that I told you I couldn't protect you in the copyright." "I didn't suspect that when he told me this," Huebsch later reflected, "he meant that he wouldn't protect me against himself." "[I]t isn't common," he went on, "for a man to give book rights without giving exclusive book rights. I think it was a mistake on Wells' part."[78] A stark difference existed between Wells's sharp-elbowed attitude and Huebsch's observance of courtesy. Huebsch had been willing to pay royalties on a public-domain text in exchange for an exclusive courtesy right to publish the text in America. Instead of reciprocating this good faith, Wells flouted it.[79]

On learning of Cornhill's plans to publish *Chamber Music*, Huebsch resorted to the tradition of courtesy sanctions. His first step, in late October 1917, was to lodge a polite private protest by "mak[ing] inquiries" with Cornhill.[80] He directed these inquiries to Braithwaite, with whom he was acquainted. Braithwaite replied, with studied innocence, that Cornhill was "setting up the Joyce book as I learned talking with them on the phone the

---

[76] Letter from Huebsch to Quinn, 12 May 1917, quoted in Ann Catherine McCullough, "A History of B.W. Huebsch, Publisher," Ph.D. diss., University of Wisconsin-Madison, 1979, at 120, 197 n.54.

[77] E. Byrne Hackett quoted in *id.*

[78] "The Reminiscences of Ben W. Huebsch," Oral History Research Office, No. 581, I-A PRCQ, Columbia University, 1965, at 384–85.

[79] For a discussion of how Charles Dickens similarly angered American publishers in the 1860s by ignoring courtesy norms in order to maximize returns, see Robert Spoo, "Courtesy Paratexts: Informal Publishing Norms and the Copyright Vacuum in Nineteenth-Century America," 69 Stan. L. Rev. 637, 666–72 (2017).

[80] Carbon copy of letter from Huebsch to Quinn, 29 Oct. 1917, Huebsch Papers.

other day … I told them you were thinking of a book of poems by Joyce and they replied they would communicate with you."[81] But Cornhill communicated nothing, so Huebsch wrote the firm directly a week later, stating that he was "Joyce's authorized publisher in this country and that arrangements have been concluded with him for the issue of 'Chamber Music' together with more recent poems that are protected by copyright."[82] The plan to add new material to the volume as a way of bolstering copyright protection was a familiar one for American publishers who dealt in otherwise unprotected works of foreign authors.[83] (Joyce later refused, characteristically, to augment or alter the original text of *Chamber Music*.)[84] In his 9 November letter to Cornhill, Huebsch went on to invoke courtesy principles explicitly: "Now that the circumstances have been laid before you I am confident that you will not violate the moral right of the author to his property and that you will withdraw the volume that you have announced."[85] In the midst of these exchanges, Huebsch asked the lawyer Quinn not to get involved: this was a matter between publishers, not a litigable one for lawyers.[86] Courtesy and lawyers did not mix.

In the end, Cornhill was not intimidated by the accusation of having violated Joyce's courtesy rights or by Huebsch's threat to add copyrighted poems to his edition. Thus, both of Huebsch's strategies—the pure courtesy appeal and the legal threat of a revised copyright volume—availed nothing. Huebsch went ahead and published his edition of *Chamber Music* in late September 1918, calling it the "Authorized Edition" and pricing it the same as the Cornhill volume at one dollar.[87] In a swipe at Cornhill's piracy, a Publisher's Note in the front matter cautioned, "This is the only American edition of *Chamber Music* that is authorized by Mr. Joyce."[88] This Note, too, was an

---

[81] Quoted in carbon copy of letter from Huebsch to Quinn, 7 November 1917, Huebsch Papers.

[82] Quoted in carbon copy of letter from Huebsch to Quinn, 9 November 1917, Huebsch Papers.

[83] Spoo, *supra* note 6, at 94–97.

[84] Joyce's partner, Nora, wrote Quinn in October 1917 to report Joyce's firm decision that *Chamber Music* was "to be printed in America without additions." Quoted in McCullough, *supra* note 76, at 141–42, 203 n.135.

[85] Quoted in carbon copy of letter from Huebsch to Quinn, 9 November 1917, Huebsch Papers. By "moral right of the author," Huebsch meant courtesy right, not rights of authorial attribution and aesthetic integrity that some legal systems recognize for creative personalities.

[86] Huebsch wrote Quinn: "I thought it more likely that they would consider the plea of a fellow publisher than a letter from you because they might resent the implied intimidation of a lawyer's letter. In this case the book being without legal protection honey may prove more efficacious than vinegar." *Id.*

[87] Slocum and Cahoon, *supra* note 34, at 10–11.

[88] James Joyce, *Chamber Music* (B.W. Huebsch, New York 1918), n.p.

inheritance from nineteenth-century courtesy practices; American publishers often inserted paratextual statements or letters of authorization in courtesy printings.[89] Strangely, Huebsch's volume bore the notice, "Copyright, 1918, by B.W. Huebsch," and Huebsch obtained a copyright registration for the edition,[90] though it is unclear what he could have claimed as protectible matter; the text was the same as the unprotected English and Cornhill editions. The only noticeable difference was Huebsch's menorah colophon on the title page instead of Cornhill's browsing man or the harpsichord design that bordered the title page of the English edition.[91] It is hard to imagine that Huebsch or Cornhill made much profit out of their competing volumes, especially with yet another competitor on the scene: A second authorized English edition, issued in January 1918, had also entered the American market.[92]

Huebsch's courtesy sanctions did not end with the several private protests he made to Cornhill. Nettled by a review of the Cornhill edition that appeared in *The Nation* in October 1918[93]—Cornhill's *Chamber Music* had appeared several months before Huebsch's edition—Huebsch informed *The Nation* that "the only authorized American edition of the book is published by [Huebsch], and that the Cornhill Company had taken advantage of the fact that the author's rights were not protected under the copyright law, to hurry out an edition over Mr. Huebsch's head, in spite of previous notification that Mr. Huebsch had arranged with Mr. Joyce to publish the book."[94] Huebsch's whistle-blowing was an example of the sanction that norms scholars call truthful negative gossip,[95] and it had the desired effect of spurring *The Nation* to action. After Huebsch provided documents to back up his claim, *The Nation* reported that

> [these documents] appear to make good his statements about the arrangement with Mr. Joyce and also his notification to the Cornhill Company. They also show what might be gently called an evasive disposition on the part of the latter concern. Mr. Huebsch's letters, covering a period of four months, elicited only very tardy and vague replies from the Cornhill Company. The entire impression one gets from the Cornhill Company's share in the correspondence is that of a fixed intention to shirk the whole issue.[96]

---

[89] Spoo, *supra* note 79, at 672–94.

[90] Catalogue of Copyright Entries, pt. 1, gp. 1, Books, vol. 15, n.s. (Government Printing Office, Washington, DC 1919), 781.

[91] Slocum and Cahoon, *supra* note 34, at 5–9.

[92] *Id.* at 9–10.

[93] O.W. Firkins, "Assorted Poets," 107 The Nation 488, 488–89 (26 October 1918).

[94] "Unfair Enterprise" (editorial), 108 The Nation 7, 7 (4 January 1919).

[95] *E.g.*, Robert C. Ellickson, "Law and Economics Discovers Social Norms," 27 J. Legal Stud. 537, 540 (1998).

[96] "Unfair Enterprise," *supra* note 94, at 7.

Huebsch had now administered the courtesy sanction of public shaming, but the penalty phase was not quite over. In November, *The Nation* itself wrote to Cornhill to request "any information or statement that it might think appropriate" to explain the *Chamber Music* question, but received no reply. The magazine wrote to Cornhill again in December; again, there was no response. Cornhill's silence seemed self-incriminating.[97] Exasperated by these evasions, *The Nation* ran an editorial in January 1919 "to call attention to the unsatisfactory terms of the copyright law as touching the rights of foreign authors in their literary property."[98] This critique of the statutory source of Cornhill's piracy was reminiscent of earlier attacks on the protectionist, discriminatory U.S. copyright law. During the nineteenth century, charges of piracy often carried a double and shifting valence. Critics assailed specific American publishers for their unauthorized reprints, yet they also attacked Congress for failing to protect foreign authors. Protests sometimes blurred the target, making it unclear whether the inertia of politicians or the moral failing of businessmen was more to blame.[99] *The Nation* discharged its censure with similar double-barreled outrage: "The Cornhill Company is quite within its legal rights, apparently, whatever may be thought of its notions of civility or of the morals of the trade."[100]

The Nation's editorial concluded with a strange, utopian wish for the abolition of monopoly copyright and the creation, in its place, of "some social arrangement, purged somehow of the mischievous nature of a subsidy, whereby writers could live and make their literary work a free and common property."[101] If government or private patronage was to be ruled out as "mischievous," it is uncertain how authors would survive in a world of legally unprotected creativity. Perhaps *The Nation* had in mind something like an inexpensive compulsory license according to which authors could receive reasonable remuneration and readers could acquire books cheaply, but the dream of a comprehensive recasting of copyright law as a royalty system had already come and gone.[102] Or perhaps the "social arrangement" the editorialist had in mind was a full return of the courtesy tradition unimpeded by antitrust laws. In any case, until some new creative economy could come to pass, publishers

---

97 *Id.*
98 *Id.*
99 Spoo, *supra* note 6, at 22–23.
100 "Unfair Enterprise," *supra* note 94, at 7.
101 *Id.*
102 A comprehensive effort to replace copyright with a royalty system was made by minority members of the British Royal Commission on Copyright in the 1870s. Paul K. Saint-Amour, *The Copywrights: Intellectual Property and the Literary Imagination* (Cornell University Press, Ithaca, NY 2003), 53–89.

might at least be expected to behave more like Huebsch than like the cagy Cornhill, which the editorial referred to cuttingly as "a thrifty concern."[103]

"Notions of civility," "the morals of the trade:" *The Nation*'s words of 1919 might have been written in 1850 or 1880; these were phrases straight out of the courtesy lexicon. True to the script written by copyright's manufacturing clause, the Cornhill Company acted the part of the lawful pirate, and Huebsch played the courtesy publisher. Huebsch claimed his rights—and those of Joyce—under the courtesy banner, and, when Cornhill defied him, he administered punishment in the calibrated manner approved by courtesy's code, beginning with urbane private protest, escalating to negative gossip and public shaming, and finally competing directly by selling Joyce's poems for a dollar. The only punishment spared the Boston pirate was retaliation in kind: Huebsch did not reprint any of Cornhill's books. That would have been a sanction too far, and Huebsch was not that sort of businessman. He had too much reverence for the morals of the trade to start a publishing war that would invite a return of the lawlessness that courtesy had been framed to replace. If Congress would not bridge the copyright gap for foreign authors, courteous publishers would have to supply an impromptu span.

5. CONCLUSION

James Joyce died in 1941 without ever experiencing an American law that completely favored foreign authors. It was not until the mid-1950s that these disabling conditions began to change after the United States joined the Universal Copyright Convention (UCC) and enacted legislation that exempted other UCC countries from the requirements of the manufacturing clause.[104] Weakened to the point of irrelevance, the clause was finally repealed, to no one's notice, in 1986.[105] Then, in 1989, after a century of playing the lone wolf, the United States joined the international Berne Convention for the Protection of Literary and Artistic Works.[106] Under Berne, the United States was required to abolish statutory formalities, such as mandatory copyright notices, as conditions of legal protection for Berne members. With America's adherence to

---

103 "Unfair Enterprise," *supra* note 94, at 7.

104 Act of 31 August 1954, Pub. L. No. 83-743, 83d Cong., 2d Sess., 61 Stat. 655.

105 Repeal of the manufacturing clause, originally set for 1 July 1982, as provided by the 1976 Act, see Act of 19 October 1976, Pub. L. No. 94-553, § 601(a), 90 Stat. 2541, 2588, was postponed to 1 July 1986, by congressional amendment. Act of 13 July 1982, Pub. L. No. 97-215, 96 Stat. 178, 178 (current version at 17 U.S.C. § 601(a)).

106 Berne Convention Implementation Act of 1988, Pub. L. No. 100-568, § 7, 102 Stat. 2853, 2857 (codified at 17 U.S.C. § 401(a)).

Berne, foreign authors could at last look for equal, national treatment under U.S. copyright law.[107]

As added reparation, in 1994 the United States joined both the World Trade Organization (WTO) and the Agreement on Trade-Related Aspects of Intellectual Property (TRIPS)[108]—commitments that led Congress to grant further concessions to foreign authors in the form of the Uruguay Round Agreements Act (URAA), which restored copyright protection to foreign works that had prematurely entered the American public domain for, among other causes, "noncompliance with … any manufacturing requirements."[109] In restoring protection to foreign works that had lost copyright because they had not been printed and bound on U.S. soil, Congress was making amends for America's controversial history of copyright protectionism. The American public domain was forced to give back some of its spoil, better late than never. *Chamber Music* had been published too early, however, to benefit from URAA restoration.

B.W. Huebsch and the Cornhill Company had their respective rewards according to their natures, if we can believe that character is destiny in the publishing world. Cornhill enjoyed a short-lived success, capped by its publication of a handful of writers who later made important contributions to the Harlem Renaissance. By early 1918, however, the firm was receiving complaints from authors who had heard nothing for months after sending sizable checks for the birthing of their books. "Where oh where is my poor pathetic little book?" Katharine Adams wailed after months of "ghostly silence" from Cornhill's Walter Reid.[110] When her volume of insipid verse finally appeared in late April 1918, totaling 49 pages, it was bound in predictably green boards, but her name, stamped in gold lettering above a curling shamrock, was misspelled on the cover; fearing exactly this, she had earlier told Braithwaite that her father, the American consul at Dublin, "would be greatly distressed if the book came out with the name not right."[111]

Cornhill's problems multiplied. By February 1920, Braithwaite was urging James Weldon Johnson to sue Cornhill for unpaid royalties and to seek

---

[107] Act of 31 October 1988, Pub. L. No. 100-568, 100th Cong., 2d Sess., 102 Stat. 2854.

[108] Marrakesh Agreement Establishing the World Trade Organization, 15 April 1994, 1867 U.N.T.S. 154.

[109] Uruguay Round Agreements Act, Pub. L. No. 103-465, 108 Stat. 4809, 4976–81 (1994) (codified at 17 U.S.C. § 104A); 17 U.S.C. § 104A(h)(6)(C)(i).

[110] Letter from Adams to Braithwaite, 11 February 1918, Braithwaite Papers, Harvard.

[111] Letter from Adams to Braithwaite, 26 October 1917, Braithwaite Papers, Harvard.

a judicial attachment of the company's account. "You are only one of many authors," Braithwaite wrote, "who are claiming and have been for some time for an accounting, but Reid has disregarded them."[112] In April of the same year, an associate editor at the newspaper *Negro World* directed a letter on behalf of the poet Lucian B. Watkins to protest Cornhill's having kept his manuscript for nearly a year without publishing it or returning it to him.[113] In 1921, Cornhill offered to settle one poet's legal claims for 35 cents on the dollar.[114] Cornhill was shortly to be acquired by a new owner, Brookes Moore, who dismissed Reid as manager, downsized the firm's output, and used the company to issue a small selection of books that included his own minor poems and translations.[115] Cornhill continued on for some years in relative obscurity before closing its doors.

Huebsch remained James Joyce's acknowledged publisher in America and continued to operate his firm until he merged it with the Viking Press in 1925, adding Joyce's titles to Viking's list and becoming an editor and vice president there.[116] For various reasons, he was unable to acquire Joyce's *Ulysses* for Viking when publication of that controversial work in America, free of obscenity prosecutions, became possible in the early 1930s. Instead, Bennett Cerf of Random House became the authorized American publisher of *Ulysses*—but not before Huebsch had blessed Cerf's project with a touching gesture of courtesy. In late 1931, after failing to get the uncopyrighted book for Viking, Huebsch tendered Cerf a formal note of surrender: "You graciously stood aside for us, and naturally we cannot object if you should now determine to try to get the book."[117] Cerf later recalled the moment: "There are some publishers who respect the rights of others. Viking and Random House would never dream of doing anything to hurt each other."[118] This was classic trade

---

112 Letter from Brathwaite to Johnson, 15 February 1920, James Weldon Johnson MSS 49, Box 3, Folder 55, James Weldon Johnson & Grace Nail Johnson Papers, Series I, Correspondence, Beinecke Library, Yale University.

113 Letter from Hubert H. Harrison to the Cornhill Company, 20 April 1920, Hubert H. Harrison Papers, Butler Library, Columbia University.

114 Letter from Ethel W. Hallett to Braithwaite, 21 January 1921, William Stanley Braithwaite Papers, 1882–1970, Accession #8990-b, University of Virginia Library, Charlottesville, VA.

115 Lee, *supra* note 54, at 252; Hutchinson, *supra* note 57, at 358–59.

116 Al Silverman, *The Time of Their Lives: The Golden Age of Great American Book Publishers, Their Editors and Their Authors* (St. Martin's Press, New York 2008), 148.

117 Letter from Huebsch to Cerf, 17 December 1931, in Michael Moscato and Leslie LeBlanc, eds., *The United States of America v. One Book Entitled* Ulysses *by James Joyce: Documents and Commentary* (University Publications of America, Frederick, MD 1984), 100.

118 Bennett Cerf, *At Random: The Reminiscences of Bennett Cerf* (1977; rpt. Random House, New York 2002), 95–96.

courtesy, performed with a courtliness that recalled the previous century—one publisher bowing out of the scene so that another could publish a work that, as far as U.S. copyright law was concerned, was free for anyone to reprint.[119]

Joyce came to trust Huebsch so completely that when he made a contract with Viking for the publication of his final masterpiece, *Finnegans Wake*, he inserted a clause stating that "[i]f at any time during the continuance of this agreement Mr. B.W. Huebsch should sever his connection with the said Viking Press and either set up publishing on his own account or acquire interest in another firm of publishers than the Viking Press, then the said Author shall have the option of transferring the benefits of this contract to such new firm."[120] Huebsch's place with Viking was secure, and the clause was never invoked. Joyce, in many ways ruthless and unyielding when it came to publishing decisions, felt a personal attachment and debt of gratitude to Huebsch. He had found security and a measure of success with his publishing house.

What American protectionism and its instrument, the manufacturing clause, often denied to foreign authors—shelter from depredations—the norms of courtesy could supply, at least sometimes. Joyce's gesture of fidelity towards Huebsch was, in its way, pure courtesy, just the way publishers had dreamed it could be in the turbulent 1880s—a current of personal warmth and fair dealing flowing between publisher and author, a refuge from hard bargains and sharp practices on the darkling plain of American publishing. Joyce showed that author and publisher could be true to one another in the evening of courtesy, in the midst of the tempting commons.

---

119 For a complete account of Cerf's use of the courtesy tradition, see Spoo, *supra* note 6, at 233–62.

120 Quoted in *Letters of James Joyce*, vol. 1, ed. Stuart Gilbert (Viking Press, New York 1966), 38.

PART II

THE LORE OF INTANGIBILITY

3. Pope versus Curll (1741) revisited: being a fair and true account of the views of certain well-respected authors on publishing, pyracy and propertie in the eighteenth century

Graham Dutfield and Uma Suthersanen

1. INTRODUCTION

Pope versus Curll is frequently presented as a seminal case in copyright law and intellectual property more generally; one that marked—perhaps shaped even—the evolutionary trajectory of copyright leading to today's configuration of the right. Mostly, this is because of the way the case bifurcated property in the physical embodiment of the work placed on the market from that in its intangible expression. As we will show, once background and context come into play, the case can be seen also as heralding a new stage towards the professionalization of the author who becomes a key property holder in the capitalist system and an independent market actor. But it tells us much else besides, as we will see.

In what sense was it ground-breaking? We agree with those that suggest that the 1710 Statute of Anne was not merely a codification of the book industry's regulation but embodied more metaphysical considerations as characterized in *Millar v. Taylor*.[1] However, it does not appear that the legislators had truly thought through any of the radical legal implications that would unavoidably arise. At some point, presumably, it would be for the courts to tease these out. Accordingly, before the landmark decisions of the—arguably nowadays

[1] *Millar v. Taylor* 4 Burr. 2303 ("I have avoided a large field which exercised the ingenuity of the bar. Metaphysical reasoning is too subtile; and arguments from the supposed modes of acquiring the property of acorns, or a vacant piece of ground in an imaginary state of nature, are too remote. Besides, the comparison does not hold between things which have a physical existence, and incorporeal rights", at 2335).

Figure 3.1 Detail from William Hogarth's "The Distrest Poet" (1737)

Note: It is assumed that the figure depicts Pope thrashing Curll, though there are some who assert that Pope is the victim lying on the ground as the physically weaker man. The work is in the public domain. This image was screen captured from William Hogarth, 1697–1764, British, Lewis Theobald: Detail of the Poet, Etching on wove paper, Yale Center for British Art, Yale Art Gallery Collection, available at https://collections.britishart.yale.edu/vufind/Record/3624069.

better-known—*Millar v. Taylor* and *Donaldson v. Beckett* on perpetual copyright, courts struggled to lay down a statutory pathway for copyright law. The statutory language provided little or nebulous guidance as to the application of the traditional concepts of tangible or corporeal property in land and goods to the incorporeal. We claim that while one should be cautious in presenting any case as if it turns the world upside down, Pope versus Curll did more than just separate the tangible from the intangible.

By contrast, the judgment in *Pope v. Curll* uniquely and clearly evinced a necessary recognition of the distinction between the *corpus mechanicum* and the *corpus mysticum*, the latter being the repository of literary property retained by the author. Inadvertently or otherwise, this opened up copyright to other doctrines and principles now considered inherent to copyright law. This is perhaps not so well appreciated by most scholars.

As our tale shows, this was an era of layered hierarchies, chaotic trade norms and endless author-centric discourses during which the fundamental principles of modern copyright were, as we can now see, being worked out. What often escapes attention concerning this apparently 'simple' dichotomy is that the ground was being laid for the emergence of several crucial intellectual property doctrines including exhaustion (or first sale), privacy, and—some time before the French—moral rights. We explore the milieu in which Pope's complex authorial personality was forged, a milieu which metamorphoses with the advent of the Statute of Anne 1710 away from the old-fashioned social author gaining his reputation through manuscripts and patronage, to the entrepreneurial and financially astute noble genius having legally enforceable rights.

In unravelling several personalities of the era, we come across the antagonistic relationship between Alexander Pope and Edmund Curll—a relationship which usually casts Pope as the celebrated albeit not universally popular English poet and gentleman, personifying an author-centric legal regime, who battles the renegade publisher Curll who "pyrates" manuscripts, poems, and even private letters. Reviewing the circumstances leading to their final court battle forces us to reflect on the new marketplace for literature, one in which the author becomes increasingly centred within legal discourses on the new "copyright" law. Whether the one causes the other, or the novelty in the marketplace and in the law merely coincide, that eighteenth-century London is when and where copyright comes of age is hardly anomalous.

2. THE BOOK TRADE

It is true that the 1735 Engravers' Act had extended copyright beyond literary works.[2] Nonetheless, the decline in the political and legal dominance of the book traders was quite slow to give way. It took time for the liberal culture of possessive individualism, the notion of a property right deriving from "invention and labour" and finally the newly emerged "creative author" to predominate. Nonetheless, *Pope v. Curll* can be seen as an important step forward.

A critical re-analysis of the case allows us to investigate the antagonistic relationship between two eighteenth-century mavericks, which, in turn, reflects

---

2 An Act for the encouragement of the arts of designing, engraving, and etching historical and other prints, by vesting the properties thereof in the inventors and engravers, during the time therein mentioned, 1735, 8 Geo.II, c.13 (Hogarth's Act).

a new type of marketplace with growing stakeholder conflicts between authors and publishers that persists to this day. Edmund Curll has undoubtedly been cast as the villain of the publishing world. He was one of the last figures in the book trade to be pilloried, being wrongly held responsible for the invention of the obscene publications law, and serving as the "negative icon" to Alexander Pope's carefully nurtured authorial persona.

This era also saw deep changes in authorship and trading styles. In many ways it was a world that we can recognize today. There was a shift from the carefully prepared and handwritten manuscript work to the printed work; this coincided with the decline in the accepted practice of collaborative and social authorship in such manuscript works, subvented by patronage. There was an expansion in the discourse of copyright and authorship, with authors claiming their "unique individual style and genius as the basis of literary property".[3] In more modern terms, Pope is seen as the noble author who became an innovator in defining and using copyright to protect his dignity, whilst Curll employs an equally innovative publishing style akin to today's publicity and social media machinations.

Even with the shift to the print medium, patronage remained (until the late eighteenth century) an important leverage to gain "bestseller" status for young authors. And the emergence of the Kit-Cat Club as a powerful political and cultural institution encapsulates such relationships and shifts (see below). The club adopted and promoted Whig objectives by offering patronage as well as literary norms to young authors, embracing the view of "writing as primarily communication with an audience—a social gesture among friends, or to a larger audience whom one flattered by addressing as though they were one's friends".[4]

Woodmansee notes that the eighteenth century (and especially between 1773 and 1794) saw the author becoming individualized, thus breaking free of the patronage system in the German-speaking world.[5] Others however have pointed out that Woodmansee's view, valuable as it is in demonstrating the relationship between romantic ideology and copyright law in Germany and the United States, does not reconcile with British legal or literary history.[6]

---

3 Scott Hess, *Authoring the Self: Self-Representation, Authorship and the Print Market in British Poetry from Pope through Wordsworth*, Routledge, 2005, at 4.

4 Ophelia Field, *The Kit-Cat Club*, Harper Perennial, 2008, at 383.

5 Martha Woodmansee, "The Genius and the Copyright: Economic and Legal Conditions of the Emergence of the Author" (1984) 17 Eighteenth-Century Studies 425–48.

6 Field, *supra* note 4, at 230; James McLaverty, *Pope, Print and Meaning*, Oxford University Press, 2001, at 51.

The English era comprising printing privileges, guild monopolies, licensing regulations, and booksellers' disputes has been accepted as the leading basis for the origin of copyright norms, culminating in what is now seen, justifiably, as the first modern copyright law: the Statute of Anne 1710, formally titled "An Act for the Encouragement of Learning, by Vesting Copies of Printed Books in the Authors or Purchasers of Such Copies, During the Times therein mentioned."[7] While there was an implicit acceptance of some sort of property rights in the copies of books, it has been said that a conceptual recognition of innate authors' rights is absent in the period preceding the enactment of the Act. What about after it? Feather resolutely states that an author's right "to be treated as the creator and owner of literary property is not defined in any English statute before the Copyright Act of 1814."[8] Consequently, the drivers of such a transformation needed to be societal or jurisprudential, rather than statutory law per se, which of course in this area of law as in others can struggle to keep up. This era also saw changes in the status of the author, the business models adopted by booksellers, and the understanding of copyright doctrines. It is true that prior to the Statute of Anne 1710, the book trade was governed by royal printing privileges derived from the Crown and State, the private legal regime of the Stationers' Company (which excluded non-stationers and non-Londoners from printing), and the licensing regime. The stationers' guild controlled the book trade based on two fundamental principles: (i) a mutual trust and respect of company members' claims; and (ii) a registration scheme for the manuscript or "copy". In order to extend its private monopoly to the entire book trade in the country, the company sought and obtained a royal charter in 1557. The newly incorporated Stationers' Company was empowered to legally limit all printing to its members and to pursue non-company members engaging in unlicensed copying. By the end of the seventeenth century, a further statutory layer was introduced, namely the Licensing Acts, which was to sustain the Company's grip on the book trade until the lapse of the Licensing Act of 1695.[9] At most the Statute of Anne heralded change in the governance of the book market. But it did not make it happen.

---

7 Statute of Anne, 1710, 8 Anne c.19.

8 John Feather, "From Rights in Copies to Copyright: The Recognition of Authors' Rights in English Law and Practice in the Sixteenth and Seventeenth Centuries", in *The Construction of Authorship: Textual Appropriation in Law and Literature*, eds M. Woodmansee and P. Jaszi, Duke University Press, 1994, at 191.

9 Joseph Loewenstein, *The Author's Due: Printing and the Prehistory of Copyright*, University of Chicago Press, 2002, chapter 4; Mark Rose, *Authors and Owners: The Invention of Copyright*, Harvard University Press, 1993, at 12–16; Joseph Lowenstein, *Ben Jonson and Possessive Authorship*, Cambridge University Press, 2002, at 3–9, 29–32. For a detailed history of the charter, and the Star Chamber decrees, Interregnum Ordinances and Licensing Acts which followed, see generally Lyman

The book trade itself was dominated by several types of sellers from the "mercuries" and hawkers who sold ballads, to the bookstall sellers by St Paul's Churchyard, to those who operated on a wholesale basis. Within this taxonomy was a further socio-economic sliding scale, with those seller/publishers who owned the copyrights (as understood *ex ante* 1710 Act) being placed at the top.[10] One such person was the notable publisher Jacob Tonson who worked with and obtained publishing rights for the works of important living writers such as Alexander Pope, John Milton and John Dryden, as well as having purchased the rights to over 100 "copies" of Shakespeare's works.[11] Tonson's further fame lay in the founding of the Kit-Cat Club in the 1690s, whose humble beginnings lay in the world of bookselling. Through a rather "eccentric publishing rights deal",[12] Tonson would obtain first options on new works from promising young authors, and would subsidize such publications of "true copies" of authorial works. In return, authors would be fed pies at Mr. Christopher (Kit) Catling's Cat and Fiddle Inn.[13] The club has unsurprisingly been called "the first expense-account publisher's dinner on record".[14] At any event, due to Tonson's substantial investment in "copy"-rights, he and his fellow Kit-Cat members were to lobby earnestly for the 1710 Act in order to curtail the growth of piracy.

And so we come to the other end of the publishing spectrum where the mechanical book makers and sellers, the "hack writers", and the Grub Street "pyrates" stood. When booksellers and publishers complained of piratical acts, it was not to secure rights or income on behalf of authors (who remained elusive figures rhetorically) but to curtail Grub Street publishers, such as Edmund Curll and Henry Hills, from printing "pirated editions" of works which were circulating in manuscript form, either through lawful purchases of the physical copies of manuscripts or by other surreptitious means.

Ray Patterson, *Copyright in Historical Perspective*, Vanderbilt University Press, 1968; Ronan Deazley, *On the Origin of the Right to Copy: Charting the Movement of Copyright Law in Eighteenth Century Britain (1695–1775)*, Hart Publishing, 2004.

[10] Paul Baines and Pat Rogers, *Edmund Curll, Bookseller*, Oxford University Press, 2007, at 13.

[11] Jeffrey M. Gaba, "Copyrighting Shakespeare: Jacob Tonson, Eighteenth Century English Copyright, and the Birth of Shakespeare Scholarship" (2011) 19 J. Intell. Prop. L. 21.

[12] Field, *supra* note 4, at 33.

[13] The Kit-Cat Club would become a powerful cultural and political institution boasting Whig-Establishment members such as John Locke, John Vanbrugh, Robert Walpole and the Dukes of Somerset, Devonshire, Richmond, Manchester and Dorset. Field, *supra* note 4, at 232–36.

[14] Field, *supra* note 4, at 33

Confusingly, the term piracy did not have a legal context prior to the 1710 Act and instead was a reference to the era's publishing and authorial norms in controlling the manuscript. Another way of viewing piracy is in the context of the licensing regime that had governed the book trade since the incorporation of the Stationers' Company in 1557. In exchange for a monopoly over the printing of books, the company took on the task of authorizing their production and marketing. By doing so, members of the company treated such publication rights as a type of property, with the "copy" of a book entered in the register, with reference to the publisher, creating a right in perpetuity. The company viewed this arrangement as being in the natural order of commercial life, going so far as to tag such authors who demanded benefits from their labours as being "too mercenary that write books for money" thereby making "their labours fruitless".[15]

Feather points out that by the end of the sixteenth century, company members treated such copies as business assets to be used as debt securities, and transferred "by purchase, inheritance and gift, [and] subdivision into shares".[16] Thus, piracy in the book trade was understood as being concerned with transgressions of the quasi-property rights of a Stationers' Company member; ironically, such "pirate" booksellers could also be members of the company (such as the legendary book pirate Henry Hills who became the Master of the company).[17]

With the rise of the print culture and as dissemination of works became broader, authorial dissonance grew about their lack of control over the quality of the printed work and as to their moral reputations.[18] Not only were printed materials produced without the express consent of authors but works were often falsely attributed, even where such poems or plays were written collaboratively by various hands through circulation within private social circles.[19]

---

[15] James Hepburn, *The Author's Empty Purse and The Rise of the Literary Agent*, Oxford University Press, 1968, at 9, referring to the early battle between the Stationers' Company and George Withers, a seventeenth-century author.

[16] Feather, *supra* note 8, at 197–98.

[17] Jody Greene, *The Trouble with Ownership: Literary Property and Authorial Liability in England, 1660–1730*, University of Pennsylvania Press, 2005, at 46–47; Adrian Johns, *Piracy: The Intellectual Property Wars from Gutenberg to Gates*, University of Chicago Press, 2009, at 43–44; Feather, *supra* note 8, at 205; Field, *supra* note 4, at 12–13.

[18] For the suggestion that this was the rationale for Pope's litigious attitude, see McLaverty, *supra* note 6, at 54.

[19] Field, *supra* note 4, at 230; for a humorous and salutary account of Samuel Richardson's claims of "originality" and "sole authorship" in light of the Irish piracies of his works, see Kathryn Temple, *Scandal Nation: Law and Authorship in Britain, 1750–1832*, Cornell University Press, 2003, at 62–69.

The argument for quelling such adulterated versions of classics had already become an authorial litany. John Locke, for example, argued against the extension of the Licensing Acts, which, in his opinion, prevented the publication of "fairer and more correct Editions".[20] In contrast is the view that authors had no need for publishing or property rights, as they derived their remuneration in the form of sinecures or gratifications. Indeed, as a group, authors wielded little power, as shown in Milton's denouncement of the licensing system which forces an author to "appear in print like a puny with his guardian, and his censor's hand on the back of his title to be his bail and surety that he is no idiot or seducer". This was condemned as "a dishonour and derogation to the author, to the book, to the privilege and dignity of learning".[21] Yet, one can enquire as to whether authors were as weak, absent and disorganized as is sometimes suggested.

Moreover, the piratical acts of Grub Street publishers including Curll would eventually begin to benefit both publishers and authors. For a publisher, unauthorized editions prompted authors to rush to print the correct versions.[22] For a gentleman author who shirked from commercial printing (as opposed to allowing the manuscript text to circulate in Establishment circles), the norm was to have his or her work created as a corrupt text through print, and then to have it rescued with a second authorized printed version that replicated the original text.[23]

---

[20] Simon Stern, "Creating a Public Domain in Eighteenth-Century England", *Oxford Handbooks Online*, 2015, at 6. Locke's position on the renewal of the Licensing Act 1662 which had conferred a monopoly on the booksellers was clear, having written a memorandum that the act should not be allowed to remain in effect. Nevertheless, there is dispute as to whether Locke, by decrying piracy and the monopoly, was also advocating authorial rights, or advocating that the author alone should be responsible for the work, and should also be responsible for transgressions of law under libel or sedition laws. See Greene, supra note 17, at 129–31.

[21] J. Milton, *Areopagitica: A Speech For The Liberty Of Unlicensed Printing To The Parliament Of England*, 1644, available on Project Gutenberg at http://www.gutenberg.org/files/608/608-h/608-h.htm (last accessed February 2019). For a fluent critique, see M. Rose, "The Public Sphere and the Emergence of Copyright: Areopagitica, the Stationers' Company, and the Statute of Anne", in *Privilege and Property: Essays on the History of Copyright*, eds R. Deazley, M. Kretschmer and L. Bently, OpenBook Publishers, 2010, at 67–88.

[22] Field, *supra* note 4, at 230.

[23] Margaret J.M. Ezell, *Social Authorship and the Advent of Print*, John Hopkins University Press, 1999, at 59.

3. AUTHORIAL REPUTATION AND PROPERTY

Piracy and the related notions of property were also used to designate the publisher's or printer's reputation, which reflected directly on the "social reputation" of the author. Indeed until the advent of the 1710 Act and *Pope v. Curll*, the only means for authors themselves to anchor their personalities to their works and protect the benefits thereof was to "own" authorship of pirated copies of manuscripts, especially "in the face of rapacious booksellers and mercenary pirates".[24] Thus, from this perspective, when authors complained of piracy, they were not complaining that there were no copyright laws to protect their own interests but rather complaining about "the denial of the opportunity for the author to be informed in the process of production" of the manuscript. This denial of the right to participate in the production of the printed text resulted in "a text that was no longer created by the author but instead by the bookseller".[25]

A more passionate argument as to why authors were entitled to property was made by the author Daniel Defoe. He was excoriating as to piracy, likening it to theft, arson and kidnapping.[26] From his perspective, the law as it stood only sought to recognize authorial ownership for the purposes of criminal sanctions. As Rose argues,

> The parliamentary decree of 1641/2 is, so far as I know, the only state affirmation of any kind of authorial right in England earlier than the Statute of Anne and is essentially a criminal edict. It is probably not an inaccurate generalization, to say that before the statute, an English author effectively had no place in court except as a criminal defendant charged with libel, blasphemy, or sedition.[27]

The nascence of the discussion on ownership in textual material in *Pope v. Curll* is found, perhaps, in Defoe's earlier experiences as expounded in his essays. So great was Defoe's need to claim his exclusive right to control the printing and publishing of his work that in 1703 he voluntarily admitted to the authorities his authorship of an alleged seditious work (*The Shortest Way*), which consequently led to his prosecution. For Defoe, herein lay a discriminatory paradox, namely the law as it stood recognized an author only to punish him, in stark contrast to the piratical activities which flourished without

---

24 Greene, *supra* note 17, at 111.

25 Ezell, *supra* note 23, at 58–59.

26 Daniel Defoe, *A Review of the State of the British Nation*, No. 105 (December 6, 1709); no. 129 (February 2, 1710).

27 Mark Rose, "The Author in Court: Pope v Curll (1741)" (1991–92) 10 Cardozo Arts & Ent. L.J. 475, at 479.

punishment and, perhaps more importantly, without any commensurate benefit to the author. The paradox would be solved if the law accepted the author as a key stakeholder. Hence his response to a pirated collection of his works was to produce his own (more expensive) volume of collected works in 1702/3, including not only a copy of his actionable *The Shortest Way* essay but also his first public statement on authorial property rights. He continued to advocate on authors' rights and their entitled benefits in his later essays, pressing for the recognition of the author as being the centre of the discourses on property in books and the existing antiquated licensing system, arguing repeatedly that if they could be punished for a libellous or seditious book, they must reap benefits:

> For if an Author has not the right of a Book, after he has made it, and the benefit be not his own, and the Law will not protect him in that Benefit, 'twould be very hard the Law should pretend to punish him for it.[28]

It was within this multi-varied stakeholder environment that the 1710 Statute of Anne was promulgated, which unmistakably shifted the balance of power to control the literary scene from the patron, the State and the bookseller/publisher to the author and the reading public. The law was premised on the notion that it was to prevent unauthorized "printing reprinting and publishing" of books and other writings, as well as "for the encouragement of learned men to compose and write useful books". The Act secured for the author the "sole right and liberty of printing" a book, and recognized "property" in books to be secured to "the proprietor or Proprietors thereof". Booksellers gained a 21-year right if they had held earlier stationer's copyright on old texts, whilst being granted a 14-year copyright term on living authors, after which the remaining 14-year term would revert to authors. Authorial dependence on aristocratic patrons was weakened as the literary author began to emerge as a respected lone genius who could rely, albeit slowly, on the Act as a means of income.[29]

Despite the temporal limits to the right of printing, booksellers continued to deal with manuscripts and printed copies on the basis of a perpetual copyright under common law by requiring authors to sell the copy as a condition of publication, thus evading the renewal period. This practice continued until the House of Lords decision in *Donaldson v. Beckett* (1774).[30] The individual

---

28 Daniel Defoe, *An Essay on the Regulation of the Press*, 1704, as cited in Rose, *supra* note 27, at 215.

29 Field, *supra* note 4, at 230; Hepburn, *supra* note 15, at 6 (referring to the "inevitable refinements in legal doctrine" as being one factor in the improvement of authors' conditions, as well as the rises in population, literacy, wealth and leisure).

30 *Donaldson v. Becket* (1774) Hansard, 1st ser., 17 (1774): 953–1003.

speeches indicate that most of the peers were concerned with the monopolies held by booksellers. Note for instance, Lord Camden's tirade:

> All our Learning will be locked up in the Hands of the Tonsons and the Lintots of the age, who will set what price upon it their avarice chuses to demand, till the public becomes as much their slaves, as their own hackney compilers are.[31]

Although ostensibly defending the rights of authors against the booksellers, especially such authors who wrote not for gain or monies but for fame and posterity (the "genius" versus the "hack" dichotomy), the House of Lords decision curtailed the powers of authors to the statutory term and ushered in a more competitive bookselling market. In a roundabout manner, the 1774 decision forced booksellers to publish more literature from living authors as previously popular and long-established works entered the public domain. A noteworthy fact is that booksellers featured as both plaintiffs and defendants in most eighteenth-century disputes. Both Stern and Deazley note that out of the 70 English copyright cases in this period, only ten featured authors or their heirs as plaintiffs. And four cases had the same plaintiff: Alexander Pope.[32]

4. MR. POPE AND MR. CURLL

Two biographers of Curll describe the first half of eighteenth-century British culture as being typified:

> by the dramatic clash between Pope, the uncrowned laureate of his age, representative of high classical culture and urbane values, and Curll, a self-made bookseller with a reputation for piracy, deviousness, and obscenity.[33]

By the 1730s, Pope was a well-established and independent author, who was *au fait* with flitting between two contrasting worlds of readership, between being 'a court-poet' and a professional writer aiming at a large market, and between manuscript writings and collaborations within private spheres and commercial print publications which made money.[34] Ezell argues against the popular view of Pope as being a product of the print medium using copyright as a control

---

[31] Patterson, *supra* note 9, at 178; R. Deazley (2008), Commentaries on: "Commentary on Donaldson v. Becket (1774)", in *Primary Sources on Copyright (1450–1900)*, eds L. Bently and M. Kretschmer, www.copyrighthistory.org.

[32] Deazley, *Origins*, *supra* note 9, at vii–ix; Simon Stern, "From Author's Right to Property Right" (2012) 62 U. Toronto L.J. 29.

[33] Baines and Rogers, *supra* note 10, at 1.

[34] At 29 years old, Pope had self-published *The Works of Mr. Alexander Pope* in 1717, McLaverty, *supra* note 6, at 14, 53–56.

tool, and for a more nuanced perspective of Pope as being very committed to the earlier world of manuscript culture. In her opinion, Pope would have benefitted from the exchange and circulation of his manuscripts—"the creation of inter-active, dynamic texts involving his friends, overrode the need to control absolutely access to his works...".[35]

What were the key constituents of the manuscript world? Pope, in parallel with other eminent authors, indulged in such gentlemanly writing whereby poems and fragments would circulate in manuscript form within small social groups. Several versions of a verse would circulate simultaneously as "the dynamics of social, manuscript texts" meant that they were open to alteration and adaptation by the readers and re-circulated to new readers. This inevitably led, at times, to confused attribution due to multiple authorship and contributions.[36] With several versions of such works circulating, booksellers would advertise for "excellent Copies by Pope, etc. etc.", especially after Pope's market value had increased with the publication of his bestseller *Iliad* translation. Thereafter, authors including Pope would intervene and request/demand a second corrected publication. In Ezell's opinion, Pope's involvement and commitment in the manuscript era may have even furthered Pope's career in the parallel world of print. Thus we see that despite the dangers of commercial publication, Pope himself engaged in the commercial print world actively to the point of "drafting the advertisements, remodelling the dedication, supervising the printing, designing the illustrations, publishing his sources, and writing his own criticism".[37]

Hence we see literary historians struggle with Pope's rather schizophrenic personality as evidenced within his letters and dealings. Pope's assertion that he was a gentleman writing for gentlemen (as opposed to a commercial hack) is the usual basis for explaining his surreptitious publications of letters and his reputation for deviousness in dealing with the agents of print culture.[38] Some have attempted to restore his image as a manuscript author who enjoyed social literature rather than as a modern publishing author with purely commercial objectives.[39] Others point to how he took full advantage of the printing technology and the new copyright rules. As an astute businessman, Pope managed to obtain considerable sums (ranging from £15 to £26 per manuscript) for selling his copyright on individual pieces in the period 1711–1727. His bestseller *Epistle to Dr. Arbuthnot* was licensed to the bookseller Gilliver for £50 for merely one year's rights of copy, after which the copyright would revert to

35 Ezell, *supra* note 23, at 83.
36 *Ibid*, at 78–81.
37 McLaverty, *supra* note 6, at 14.
38 Ezell, *supra* note 23, at 63.
39 *Ibid*, at 65.

Pope. And he managed to negotiate a sum ranging between £5000 and £6000 for the subscription edition of his translation of the *Iliad* in 1714.[40] As one scholar asserts:

> Pope drew aggressively on the new copyright regime as he improvised a literary career, and he was virtually alone among eighteenth-century writers in his ability to exploit the statutory provisions at the booksellers' expense.[41]

Turning to the other end of the trade spectrum, Curll's fame is embedded in his antagonistic relationship with Pope. Such animosity has been documented back to 1714 but then it escalated from 1716 onwards when Curll had published a collection entitled *Court Poems*. These letters had been vaguely attributed to the collective authorship of Pope, John Gay and Lady Mary Montagu. Whether Curll had indeed been responsible for publishing the letters or had earned profits from it, is as yet uncertain.[42] Possibly in defence of Lady Montagu, or possibly for other reasons, it is a fact that Pope entreated, and failed, to curb the publication and subsequently singled Curll out for punishment in the form of an emetic he personally delivered whose effects he joyfully recounted:[43]

> And while his guts the keen emetics urge,
> Smiles on the vomit, and enjoys the purge.[44]

The two men would be textually linked for eternity with the publication of Pope's mock heroic *The Dunciad*. Written as a satire on, *inter alia*, booksellers and Grub Street writers, Curll was to feature prominently in this work, which replayed the story of Pope's crude revenge and introduces Curll into a "pissing contest" and other scatological activities; Curll retaliated in print, parodying

---

40 Ezell, *supra* note 23, at 75. Taking 1710 as the basis for period conversion from the eighteenth century to 2017, £15 = £1573.92; £26 = £2728.14; £50 = £5246.41; £6000 = £629,569.80. Based on the U.K. National Archives currency converter, http://www.nationalarchives.gov.uk/currency-converter/.

41 Stern, *supra* note 20, at 5.

42 Baines and Rogers, *supra* note 10, chapter 2 generally. On the tempestuous relationship between Pope and Lady Montagu and the authorship of these "eclogues", see Robert Halsband, "Pope, Lady Mary, and the Court Poems (1716)" (March 1953) 68(1) PMLA 237–250.

43 Ralph Strauss, *The Unspeakable Curll: Being Some Account of the Life of Edmund Curll, Bookseller*, Chapman and Hall, 1927, at 52; Baines and Rogers, *supra* note 10, at 82–85.

44 Alexander Pope, "A Full and True Account of a Horrid and Barbarous Revenge by Poison, on the Body of Mr. Edmund Curll, Bookseller: with a faithful Copy of his Last Will and Testament." (1716), as reprinted in *Alexander Pope: The Major Works*, Oxford University Press, 2006, at 124.

Pope, *inter alia*, in the *Popiad*. This was followed by Pope's counter-attack, and the battle continued.[45] Describing Curll's inclusion in the *Dunciad* as "a place in the lexicon of literary scandal … suspended between comedy and tragedy, a situation Pope did much to engineer",[46] Curll's biographers claim that Pope was fully aware of how he had free ridden on Curll's business practices, of how he had been complicit in Curll's "unauthorized" publications of his works, and of how his own fame had been extended favourably and widely by Curll's repetitive print editions.[47]

It is difficult at times to draw clear fault lines between the behaviours of these two men. What one can surmise from the literature is that Pope is considered a "literary success", with one account going as far as to claim that he was "possibly the first eminent writer earning his living by his pen who was freely able to do so", allowing publishers to bid against one another for his works.[48] On the other hand, Curll can also be considered notable for being a precursor of celebrity and entertainment news.[49] Curll's Grub Street business model was to publicize authors and their works. By continuously advertising his editions and by planting apocryphal tales and scandals relating to their authorship in the press, Curll "made authorship into news, and literature a locus of scandal, a temple of infamy, a whispering gallery of rumour".

For intellectual property aficionados, it is during this *tempus belli* that one senses the genesis of disputes metamorphosing from the tangible to the intangible manifestations emanating from their personalities including even their images. During this period, Curll shifted his shop premises, renamed it "Pope's-Head" and began using Pope's countenance on printed works, thus transforming the author's visage and head into his business trade mark, and property (Figure 3.2). This mercantile era already recognized that the images

45 Joanna Maciulewicz, *Representations of Book Culture in Eighteenth-Century English Imaginative Writing*, Palgrave Macmillan, 2018, at 99–101; Baines and Rogers, *supra* note 10, at 194.

46 Baines and Rogers, *supra* note 10, at 187.

47 Curll and other booksellers and authors responded to the *Dunciad* in a variety of pamphlets and essays, including *The Curliad, The Popiad, The Female Dunciad* and *A Popp upon Pope*. Pope meanwhile had further published *Dunciad Variorum*, which satirized Curll again. Baines and Rogers, *supra* note 10, at 190–98.

48 Hepburn, *supra* note 15, at 6–7; also see Harry Ransom, "The Rewards of Authorship in the Eighteenth Century" (1938) 18 University of Texas Studies in English 47, at 51.

49 Some of his earlier publications included such works as: *Cases of Impotency and Virginity*; *Onanism Display'd*; *Eunuchism Display'd*; *A Treatise of the Use of Flogging in Venereal Affairs*; *and The Case of John Atherton, Bishop of Waterford in Ireland: Who Was Convicted of the Sin of Uncleanness with a Cow*, see Baines and Rogers, *supra* note 10, at 10–62, 371–77.

and heads of male authors were quasi-property and were to be employed as economic goods. The commercialization of Pope's head "might have signaled Curll's ownership of Pope, whose head would also sing for Curll's profit".[50]

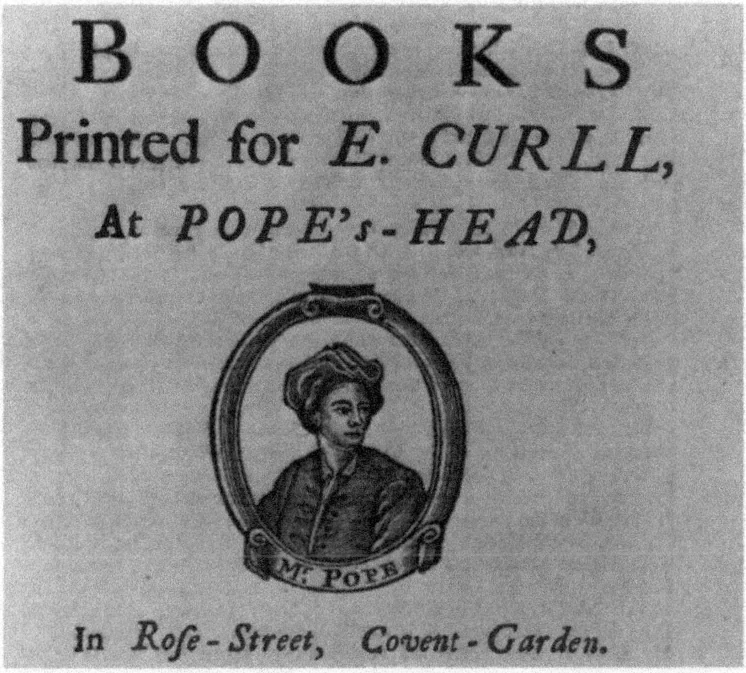

Figure 3.2 Shop sign for Edmund Curll

Source: Image captured from: Stephanson, note 50, at 186; and Baines and Rogers, note 10, at 244.

In that same period, Pope clandestinely tricked Curll into publishing his letters in 1735; this paved the way for him to openly claim (though not as a court action) an author's moral right of attribution, enabling him to reap financial gains with his own authorized version two years later.[51] Both McLaverty and

---

[50] Raymond Stephanson, *The Yard of Wit: Male Creativity and Sexuality, 1650–1750*, University of Pennsylvania Press, 2004, at 187.

[51] McLaverty, *supra* note 6, at 178, 195; Baines and Rogers, *supra* note 10, chapter 13.

Rose aver a further underlying reason for Pope's deceit against Curll in that year. The London booksellers were in the midst of a campaign to extend the term of protection under the 1710 Act and Pope is thought to have been concerned as to the absence of authors' rights in the bill. Thus the entanglement with Curll was to serve to highlight the author's anguish at an irresponsible bookseller who would benefit from the hoped-for change to the law.[52] The 1735 bill failed and Pope wrote that should another booksellers' bill be presented, Parliament should reject it unless authorial rights were clearly protected:

> Since in a Case so notorious as the printing a Gentleman's PRIVATE LETTERS, most Eminent, both Printers and Booksellers, conspired to assist the Pyracy both in printing and in vending the same.[53]

5. METAPHYSICAL PROPERTY

Several years later, Pope set out again to trick Curll into publishing a volume of letters, namely *Dean Swift's Literary Correspondence for Twenty-Four Years*. Having "printed secretly an edition in small octavo", Pope sent a copy to Dublin where, as intended, the book was reprinted without authorization. Yet another copy found its way into Curll's hands who claimed that the reprint was "lawfully" based on the Dublin edition for his text. In June 1741, Pope obtained a preliminary injunction claiming protection under the Statute of Anne 1710 Act in respect of letters authored and sent by him to others, and also letters addressed to him from Jonathan Swift, then Dean of St. Patrick's Cathedral, Dublin. The bill of complaint asked for a restraint on further distribution, an account of profits as well as an account of unsold copies. Nine days later Curll filed a request to lift the injunction. Besides pleading ignorance of copyright in the letters authored by Pope, the response argued several legal points: Pope had no property rights residing in letters sent to him; letters were not copyrightable subject matter under the Act; it was lawful to reprint such works in London after their first publication in Dublin; and one-third of the volume comprised materials written by other authors, the rights to which Curll had obtained through gift or purchase. Four days later, on June 17, 1741, the Lord Chancellor Hardwicke handed down his decision continuing the injunction to prevent the publication of the letters written by Pope, but not those letters which were written to him.[54]

---

52 Rose, *supra* note 27, at 481.
53 *Ibid* (Pope's capitalization).
54 *Pope v. Curl* (1741) 2 Atk. 342; Baines and Rogers, *supra* note 10, at 284–88.

5.a "Writings", Expressions and Ideas

The 1710 Act referred vaguely to the object of the authorial right as "book", "writing", "printed book" and "copy".[55] Given that writings took forms other than books, were the statutory-based entitlements to be denied to other expressive genres such as musical notations or letters or unpublished manuscripts?[56] Indeed, the 1710 Act was silent as to unpublished manuscripts or indeed private correspondence.

According to Deazley, it is arguable that Hardwicke's decision was guided by the Preamble to the Act, namely that the authors' rights were anchored to the statutory aphorism that the Act was passed "for the Encouragement of Learning" and the continued production of "useful Books": "[I]t would be extremely mischievous ... to make a distinction between a book of letters which comes out into the world, either by the permission of the writer, or the receiver of them, and any other learned work."[57] Hardwicke went further as to why private correspondences qualified as a learned work and were thus protectable subject matter under the Act:

> It is certain that no works have done more service to mankind, than those which have appeared in this shape, upon familiar subjects, and which perhaps were never intended to be published; and it is this makes them so valuable; for I must confess for my own part, that letters which are very elaborately written and originally intended for the press, are generally the most insignificant, and very little worthy any person's reading.[58]

As Ezell's treatise affirms, judges were now being asked to prescribe the Act of 1710 as imbibing the manuscript as authored by the individual natural author. Deazly similarly opines that Hardwicke was pressed to extend the Act,

---

[55] "The Act was lobbied for and secured on behalf of the book trade ... if the statute said nothing as to an author's rights over his unpublished work, this was simply because it was a question that held no real interest for the bookseller", Deazley, "Commentary", *supra* note 31; see also Benjamin Kaplan, *An Unhurried View of Copyright*, Columbia University Press, 1967, at 9.

[56] *Bach v. Longman* (1777) 2 Cowper 623 (published music protectable as "writing" under the 1710 Act); *Duke of Queensberry v. Shebbeare* (1758) 28 ER 924 (an inconclusive decision holding that the recipient of an unpublished manuscript could not claim profit from its publication). See also Stern, *supra* note 32, at 65; Jane Ginsburg, "'Une chose publique'? The Author's Domain and the Public Domain in Early British, French and US Copyright Law", in *Copyright Law: A Handbook of Contemporary Research*, Paul Torremans (ed.), Edward Elgar, 2007, at 138–41 (for a discussion on eighteenth-century subject matter).

[57] *Pope v. Curll* (1741) 2 Atk. 342.

[58] *Ibid.*

as letter-writing in the eighteenth century served disparate functions including as instructional, educational, news and entertainment tools: "while the Statute of Anne remained silent as to an author's unpublished correspondence, to deny the letter-writer any protection might discourage the very practice of this kind of writing."[59]

5.b *Corpus Mysticum*, Imports and Exhaustion Doctrine

Having established the copyrightability of letters, Hardwicke then made what may be considered the most notable aspect of the decision, namely its distinction between the receiver's special property in the physical letter and the writer's property in the writing (or "the text" as many would put it nowadays) as vested according to the Copyright Act. Thus the injunction could be continued in relation to the letters authored by Pope as the copyright vested in him for the duration of the copy *right*. In contrast, the receiver of a letter has "only a *special property* ... possibly the property of the paper may belong to him" to which one might include the dried ink. The sender does not abandon any property claim that in doing so would leave the letters open for "any person whatsoever to publish them to the world, for at most the receiver has only a joint property with the writer".[60] As Deazley notes, "Lord Hardwicke divorced Pope's physical letter from its metaphysical content, splitting the book and the text asunder in a way that the legislators responsible for the Act had never contemplated."

This then is the first English decision articulating the author's property right in the creative expression as opposed to the physical embodiment of that expression. It is also the basis of recognizing that intangible rights can overcome the possessor's rights, and that the intellectual property right in the immaterial creation (*corpus mysticum*) can trump the real property right in the physical embodiment (*corpus mechanicum*). The right (in this case of printing and reprinting) is thus unmoored from the purchase, sale, exchange and consumption of the work. However many transactions take place, and whatever the possessor of the work does with it, the author's right including inherent moral interest persists (such as the right of attribution and integrity).

This recognition would, in due course, be refined into the U.S. first sale doctrine and the European doctrine of exhaustion as courts and legisla-

---

[59] Deazley, "Commentary", *supra* note 31.

[60] *Pope v. Curll* (1741) 2 Atk. 342 (italics added). Also see Stern discussing the slight dispute that has arisen as to whether Hardwicke refers to "special property" or to "qualified interest", depending on whether one relies on the Atkyns's reports or on Campbell's account in the *Lives of the Lord Chancellors*—Stern, *supra* note 32, at 62–63, and note 115.

tures struggled to draw a demarcation line between the rights of purchase/possession vis-à-vis the rights of the intellectual property owner.[61] In fact, we can see a further genesis of the wider exhaustion debate when we study Hardwicke's pronunciation on Curll's ingenious argument that Irish books were a "Lawful-Prize" in London. Hardwicke remarked that to agree would

> have very pernicious consequences, for then a bookseller who has got a printed copy of a book, has nothing else to do but send it over to *Ireland* to be printed, and then by pretending to reprint it only in *England*, will by this means intirely evade the act of parliament.[62]

This is rather ironical as our readers will have already guessed that part of the rationale of publishing a Dublin edition was to enable Pope to argue for a "corrected version" of the correspondence out of concern for the public, rather than vanity.[63] There is little else written on this particular strand of argument: Deazley does not comment on it, while Rose states that Hardwicke's decision on this question is "comparatively straightforward and requires little comment".[64] And so it may well be—the 1710 Act did not extend to Ireland at that time, the Irish booksellers were lawfully entitled to reprint copies of books and export them to England, but the statute also incorporated the right to prevent *importing* of books if done without the consent of the proprietor.

However, from another perspective, what Curll was arguing for was—in effect—international exhaustion (*avant la lettre*), namely if a work is released anywhere in the world with the consent of the proprietor (and Curll would have known this popular Popian tactic), then should not any person be entitled to import such editions into the copyright-protected territory?[65] The problem

---

[61] For a legislative example of the exhaustion doctrine in relation to the distribution right, see ss.16(1)(b), 18 U.K. Copyright, Designs and Patents Act 1988, and ss.106(3), 109(a), U.S Copyright Act 1976. For a general discussion on the U.S. first sale doctrine, see Michael J. Madison, "Creativity and Craft", in *Creativity, Law and Entrepreneurship*, eds Shubha Ghosh and Robin Paul Malloy, Edward Elgar, 2011, at 30–33; and Shubha Ghosh, "The Persistent Policy Pull of Exhaustion", in *Exhausting Intellectual Property Rights: A Comparative Law and Policy Analysis*, eds S. Ghosh and I. Calboli, Cambridge University Press, 2018.

The vital principle of incorporeal versus tangible property continues to be of great import within EU copyright law and the exhaustion doctrine and is well discussed in Case C-419/13, *Art and Allposters International BV v. Stichting Pictoright*, Advocate General's Opinion, ECLI:EU:C:2014:2214.

[62] *Pope v. Curll* (1741) 2 Atk. 342 (original italics).

[63] Rose, *supra* note 27 at 482.

[64] *Ibid*, at 486.

[65] But this would have meant condoning what was viewed as the "Irish piracy" problem; though probably welcomed by the Irish printers who had begun claiming that

of course is whether at the time of the case one could openly declare Pope's surreptitious behavior as consent to reprinting. Moreover, perhaps 1741 was not the right time to introduce the doctrine of international exhaustion.

5.c Right of Publication, Divulgation or Privacy?

Hardwicke's decision also implied an author had the authority to decide whether to bring a work of authorship to market or not. Thus, it has been argued that the case clearly constructs a right of first publication of a work, irrespective of the ownership of the physical manuscript. This was arguably very different from the previously accepted right of publication which arose upon ownership of the physical "copy" of the manuscript and the registration of the title in the Stationers' Company register, this proto-copyright lasting in perpetuity. Both principles were applied in subsequent decisions, including *Duke of Queensberry v. Shebbeare* and *Millar v. Taylor*.[66] The right to authorize the first publication of one's work can be viewed as an economic right similar to the right to issue copies under current UK copyright law and the right of first publication under today's U.S. copyright law.[67] However, perhaps this authorial right, as recognized first in *Pope v. Curll*, and then subsequently in *Millar v. Taylor*, can be more appropriately classified as a moral right of disclosure. Thus, under French copyright law, the *droit de divulgation* vests a perpetual right in the author to determine when and where to publish a work.[68] If we view the discussion in *Pope v. Curll* as setting out not only authorial rights, but those which have personality and reputational-based roots, it is a logical jump to view Lord Mansfield's pronouncement in *Millar v. Taylor* as stemming from the same bases. Stern notes that Mansfield, who would pronounce several copyright rulings in his term, treated copyright not only as a property right but also showed "a pronounced interest in the repu-

---

English copyright law was ending the Irish print business—see Johns, *supra* note 17, at 147–59.

[66] *Duke of Queensberry v. Shebbeare* (1758) 28 ER 924; *Millar v. Taylor* (1769), 4 Burr 2303.

[67] Ss.16(1)(b), 18 U.K. Copyright, Designs and Patents Act 1988; ss.106(3) U.S. Copyright Act 1976, and *Harper & Row Publishers, Inc. v Nation Enterprises*, 471 U.S. 539, 564 (1985) ("The right of first publication encompasses not only the choice whether to publish at all, but also the choices of when, where, and in what form first to publish a work").

[68] Art. 121-2, French Intellectual Property Code 1992; *Whistler v. Eden case*, Cass. civ., 14 March 1900: DP 1900, I, 497, rapp. Rau/Desjardins/Planiol (the French Court of Cassation holding that the author's right to dispose of the work overrides the terms of a commissioned contract); Whistler recounts the story in Whistler, James McNeill, *Eden versus Whistler: The Baronet and the Butterfly* (1899).

tational aspect of the question".[69] Thus *Pope v. Curll* should also be claimed as a direct legal precedent for moral rights which Mansfield for the first time clearly set out in *Millar v. Taylor* when explaining why an author's rights to a copy arose from natural principles:

> [B]ecause it is *just*, that an Author should reap the pecuniary Profits of his own Ingenuity and Labour. It is *just*, that Another should not use his Name, without his consent. It is *fit*, that He should judge when to publish, or whether he will ever publish. It is *fit* he should not only choose the Time, but the Manner of Publication; how Many; what Volume; what Print. It is *fit*, that he should choose to Whose care he will Trust the Accuracy and Correctness of the Impression; in whose Honesty he will confide it, not to foist in Additions … I allow them sufficient to shew it is agreeable to the Principles of Right and Wrong, the Fitness of Things, Convenience, and Policy, and therefore to the Common Law to protect before Publication … The 8th of Queen *Ann* is no Answer. We are considering the *Common* Law, upon Principles *before* and *independent* of that Act.[70]

The nascence of moral rights can be clearly sighted in the above paragraph—the right of attribution (name), the right of divulgation (first publication), and the right of integrity (manner, accuracy and correctness). The argument that perhaps both Hardwick and Mansfield were conceiving the initial principles within copyright law on personality/reputation/moral rights bases in *Pope v. Curll* and *Millar v. Taylor* is also supported by our earlier discussion on authors' own discourses, namely that the right to *control* the time and means of publication was as important to them as the right to receive benefits. The moral rights view of these judgments further enables us to see the line of reasoning which derives the right of privacy from the right of first publication (and of course, under a civil law moral rights paradigm, the right to privacy is subsumed under the right of divulgation).[71] Indeed, in *Lytton v. Devey,* Vice-Chancellor Bacon easily relied on a pre-*Pope* decision to set out a basic notion of the principle in privacy:

> … in my opinion, the law upon the subject is plain, and has existed since long before *Pope v. Curl* was decided, namely, that the property in letters remains in the person to whom they are sent … but the sender of the letters has still that kind of interest, if not property, in the letters, which gives him a right to restrain any use being made of the communications which he has made in the letters … It would be strange indeed,

---

69 Stern, *supra* note 32, at 130.

70 *Millar v. Taylor* (1769), 4 Burr 2303, 115–16 (original italics).

71 Graham Dutfield and Uma Suthersanen, *Global Intellectual Property Law*, Edward Elgar, 2020, at 128–35 (for an overview of moral rights internationally and nationally).

> if, because a man writes to another a confidential communication, that other has a right to publish it to the world.[72]

6. REPERCUSSIONS OF *POPE V. CURLL*

In recognizing the distinction between the *corpus mechanicum* and the *corpus mysticum*, the case opened the door to doctrines and principles old and new that could hardly have been conceived without the retention of an intangible right whose existence was not to be denied by the exchange, use or consumption of the work in question. As we have seen, these range from exhaustion of rights to moral rights and privacy.

The split between the property right in the physical and the intangible is arguably responsible also for the birth of the idea versus expression principle within copyright law today. Thus, as Deazley recounts, the idea of property in the composition was taken up by William Blackstone in *Tonson v. Collins* who stated that the subject matter of copyright was the "doctrinal composition" (or literary composition) rather than the paper and print (the latter being "vehicles to convey" such compositions). Moreover, in Blackstone's opinion, the doctrinal composition comprised of ideas and the style and language of the author in communicating such ideas:

> [F]or he who obtaineth my copy may appropriate my stock of ideas, and by opposing my sentiments, may give birth to a new doctrine; or he may coincide with my notions, and by employing different illustrations, may place my doctrine in another point of view: and in either case he aquireth an exclusive title to his copy, without invading my property: for though he may be said to build on my foundation, yet he rears a different superstructure.

As Deazley states, this is tantamount to the doctrine that once a book is conveyed to the public, all ideas contained within the book were open to the public to use; however "[w]hat remained with the author after publication was his individual expression, the particular sentiments he employed in conveying his doctrine to the reader". This is perhaps another significant doctrinal consequence of the legal climate in which *Pope v Curll* was very much embedded, albeit one that took time to become apparent.

A statute does not necessarily reveal a doctrine but merely lays down the parameters of ensuing debate both societal and jurisprudential. Such debate is likely to lead to doctrines and principles unforeseen by the legislators as they argued vehemently over the text of this or that article of the legislative instrument being drawn up. This was certainly the case with the 1710 Statute

---

[72] [1881–85] All ER Rep 1135, at 1136.

of Anne, and revisiting the era surrounding *Pope v. Curll* goes some way to reveal the shifts within the doctrinal bases of copyright law, and the rise of the author.

4. *Neilson v. Harford*: shape and form in patent law

Jeffrey A. Lefstin[1]

Neilson v. Harford at first blush seems a strange choice for a volume on forgotten intellectual property lore. Since it was decided by the Court of Exchequer in 1841, *Neilson* and related cases have featured in some forty patent opinions from American courts. At the United States Supreme Court, *Neilson* played a decisive role in the nineteenth-century cases that laid the foundations of American patent law, such as *O'Reilly v. Morse* and *Tilghman v. Proctor*. More recently, *Neilson* was key in two of the cases that established the Court's modern framework for patent-eligible subject matter, *Parker v. Flook* and *Mayo v. Prometheus*. In *Flook*, Justice Stevens drew from *Neilson* the idea that an algorithm or other fundamental principles should be treated as "as though it were a familiar part of the prior art,"[2] leaving eligibility to depend on whether the rest of the claim set forth an "inventive application" of the principle.[3] And in *Mayo*, Justice Breyer turned to *Neilson* to revive *Flook*'s requirement for an inventive application,[4] explaining that the Court of Exchequer had sustained Neilson's patent because he had applied the underlying discovery in an inventive and unconventional way.[5] Beyond the case law, *Neilson* was a major focus of the great patent treatises of the nineteenth century,[6] and is still examined by commentators today.[7]

---

1 I thank Shubha Ghosh for very useful comments on the manuscript, and for his efforts in assembling and editing this volume.

2 *Parker v. Flook*, 437 U.S. 584, 592 (1978).

3 See *id.* at 594.

4 *Flook*'s approach was abandoned by the Court just three years later in *Diamond v. Diehr*, although *Diehr* pretended otherwise. See Jeffrey A. Lefstin, *Inventive Application: A History*, 67 Fla. L. Rev. 565, 570–76 (2015) (reviewing the development of the Supreme Court's modern patent-eligibility jurisprudence).

5 See *Mayo Collaborative Servs. v. Prometheus Labs., Inc.*, 566 U.S. 66, 83–84 (2012).

6 See Lefstin, *supra* note 4, at 605–08.

7 See, e.g., Alan L. Durham, *Two Models of Unpatentable Subject Matter*, 31 Santa Clara High Tech. L.J. 251, 266–67 (2015); Michael Risch, *America's First Patents*, 64 Fla. L. Rev. 1279, 1300–01 (2012); Joshua D. Sarnoff, *Patent-Eligible*

Yet there is more than one way of forgetting. Constructing the past requires us both to remember what we wish to retain, and to forget what we wish to discard. Even as a case is born, not all of the incidents that gave rise to the case find their way into the courtroom. More are lost when an appellate court constructs a different version of the case from what it hears on appeal. And once a case enters the stream of precedent, succeeding courts may read it only through the medium of opinions that have quoted it before. Each generation of interpreters impresses its own meaning upon the case, until we know it only as a reflection of a reflection of the original.

Neilson v. Harford is such a case. An examination of *Neilson* reveals a very different story than the one told in *Flook* and *Mayo*, which derives from quotations in earlier cases themselves quoting from an abbreviated report of the original. *Neilson* did not stand for the proposition that discoveries should be treated as part of the prior art, nor that inventive application was necessary to transform scientific discoveries into patentable inventions; the patent in *Neilson* was sustained only because the application of Neilson's discovery was conventional and obvious. *Neilson* was instead about the relationship of invention to shape and form: Was a patentee's invention bounded by the instrumentalities disclosed in the specification, or could it extend beyond them? If so, how far? The Court of Exchequer would ultimately conclude that Neilson's patent was not confined to his apparatus, provided that one of ordinary skill in the art could embody Neilson's principle in forms other than those he had disclosed. For courts in both England and the United States, *Neilson* would become the touchstone to determine when an invention might transcend shape and form.

1. THE FOUNTAINHEAD OF "INVENTIVE APPLICATION"

Although *Neilson v. Harford* was a central fixture in nineteenth-century American patent law, the case had slumbered for most of the twentieth century, last cited by the Supreme Court in 1898.[8] Its revival came in 1978 with *Parker v. Flook*, the Supreme Court's second major case on patent eligibility under the 1952 Act. While the Court's earlier decision in *Gottschalk v. Benson* had suggested preemption or tangibility as tests the for patent eligibility of claims involving fundamental principles such as mathematical algorithms,

---

Inventions after Bilski: History and Theory, 63 Hastings L.J. 53, 67–69 (2011); Norman Siebrasse, *The Rule Against Abstract Claims: History and Principles*, 26 Can. Intell. Prop. Rev. 205, 210 (2011).

[8] *Boyden Power-Brake Co. v. Westinghouse*, 170 U.S. 537, 577–80 (1898).

Flook instead adopted the notion that an algorithm, even if novel, should be disregarded in the patent eligibility analysis: "treated as though it were a familiar part of the prior art."[9] Once the algorithm was discarded, patent eligibility would then depend on whether the claim included a further "inventive concept" representing an inventive application of the underlying principle.[10]

Flook purportedly drew this approach from the Court's 1852 decision in *O'Reilly v. Morse*. But *Flook* did not engage with *Morse*'s facts or analysis. To support the premise that algorithms should be treated as part of the prior art, *Flook* pointed to *Morse*'s reliance on *Neilson v. Harford.* In particular, *Flook* referred to the following passage from *Neilson* that had been quoted by the Court in *Morse*, as well as glossed in some of the other foundational nineteenth-century patent cases, such as *Tilghman v. Proctor*, *Risdon Iron & Locomotive Works v. Medart*, and *Boyden Power-Brake Co. v. Westinghouse*:

> It is very difficult to distinguish [Neilson's claim] from the specification of a patent for a principle, and this at first created in the minds of some of the court much difficulty; but after full consideration, we think that the plaintiff does not merely claim a principle, but a machine embodying a principle, and a very valuable one. *We think the case must be considered as if the principle being well known, the plaintiff had first invented a mode of applying it* by a mechanical apparatus to furnaces; and his invention then consists in this—by interposing a receptacle for heated air between the blowing apparatus and the furnace. In this receptacle he directs the air to be heated by the application of heat externally to the receptacle, and thus he accomplishes the object of applying the blast, which was before of cold air, in a heated state to the furnace.[11]

Flook then concluded: "We think this case must also be considered as if the principle or mathematical formula were well known."[12] Thus the key premise of *Flook*—that the discovery of a fundamental principle cannot itself contribute to the patentability of a claim—was grounded in the supposition that *Neilson* had assumed fundamental principles to be "well known" in assessing patent eligibility.

Flook's approach was rejected by the Court three years later in *Diamond v. Diehr*, where the Court reverted to the traditional position that practical applications of fundamental principles were patent-eligible without regard to the "inventiveness" of the means of application. But in 2012 the Court turned back

---

9 *Flook*, 437 U.S. at 592.

10 *Id.* at 594.

11 *Neilson v. Harford*, as reported in Thomas Webster, Reports and Notes of Cases on Letters Patent for Inventions 371 (1844) [hereinafter Web. P. C.] (emphasis added). *Flook* only quoted this passage up to and including the italicized language.

12 *Flook*, 437 U.S. at 592.

to *Flook* in *Mayo v. Prometheus*, this time in the context of "laws of nature." While not repeating *Flook*'s conceit of assuming fundamental principles to be part of the prior art, *Mayo* revived *Flook*'s requirement for a further "inventive application" before a newly discovered law of nature could become patent eligible. To support the notion that conventional means of application could not transform a discovery into a patent-eligible invention, *Mayo* turned again to *Neilson v. Harford.* Pointing to the passage from *Neilson* quoted in *Morse*, *Mayo* asserted that Neilson's patent had rested not on the mere discovery of a principle, but had also included an unconventional means of application.[13] The Exchequer had sustained Neilson's patent, according to *Mayo*, because it "did more than simply instruct users to use the principle that hot air promotes ignition better than cold air, since it explained how the principle could be implemented in an inventive way."[14]

Mayo's requirement for an inventive means of application for new discoveries, as interpreted by the lower courts, led to the withdrawal of patent-eligibility for inventions as diverse as medical diagnostics[15] and automobile driveshafts.[16] One of the most significant changes to United States patent law since the 1952 Act thus rested in large part on a particular story the Supreme Court has told about *Neilson*—a story in which the Exchequer reached a landmark decision that patents could not be based on discoveries alone, and sustained the hot-blast patent only because Neilson had invented a new and unconventional way to apply the discovery that hot air was preferable to cold. And by extension, that became the story told about *O'Reilly v. Morse* as well, since the Courts' modern engagement with *Morse* has been essentially limited to *Morse*'s treatment of *Neilson.* Through that story the Court can confidently proclaim, as it did it in *Bilski v. Kappos*, that its limitations on patent eligibility are simply "a matter of statutory stare decisis going back 150 years."[17]

But behind that facade, the true story of *Neilson* and the other hot-blast cases has been forgotten. Turning back to the original case, and not merely its reflection in later opinions, reveals a very different story than the one the Supreme Court has told. In that story we find neither the disregard of discoveries nor a requirement for inventive means of application. The hot-blast cases—and the

---

[13] See *Mayo*, 566 U.S. at 84.

[14] *Id.* at 83.

[15] See *Athena Diagnostics, Inc. v. Mayo Collaborative Servs., LLC*, 915 F.3d 743 (Fed. Cir. 2019) (denying eligibility of a diagnostic method employing conventional assay techniques).

[16] See *Am. Axle & Mfg., Inc. v. Neapco Holdings LLC*, 939 F.3d 1355 (Fed. Cir. 2019) (holding that the method for designing an automobile driveshaft represented a conventional application of Hooke's law).

[17] *Bilski v. Kappos*, 561 U.S. 593, 602 (2010).

nineteenth-century American cases that relied upon them—were quite clear that discovery could be the foundation of patentability, and that routine and conventional means of application sufficed to transform a discovery into an invention. The judges in *Neilson* were grappling with a question more subtle and more interesting: to what extent was an invention bound by shape and form? Did the invention reside in the particular instrumentalities constructed by the patentee, or could it transcend those physical forms? *Neilson*'s answers to those questions would have a profound influence on American patent law, for like today's Supreme Court, jurists of the nineteenth century sought to justify their decisions by reference to a case whose correctness, according to Henry Merwin's 1883 treatise, "has never been doubted or denied."[18]

2. JAMES BEAUMONT NEILSON AND THE DEVELOPMENT OF THE HOT BLAST

Neilson v. Harford originated with Scottish inventor James Beaumont Neilson's development of the hot-blast iron smelting process, which industrial historian Alan Birch described as "the most important single innovation in the industry in the age of iron."[19] Iron smelting relies on hot carbon monoxide to reduce iron oxides into elemental iron. In the blast furnace—so called because air is supplied at higher than atmospheric pressure—the necessary carbon monoxide is produced by the reaction of oxygen from air with a carbon fuel such as coke or coal. Prior to the development of the hot blast, conventional wisdom held that the air introduced into the blast furnace should be kept as cold as possible.[20] Neilson proposed instead that the blast should be heated before it was introduced into the furnace.

The hot blast would revolutionize the production of iron. Once perfected, it reduced by two-thirds the fuel required for smelting.[21] Perhaps more significantly, it also permitted the use of raw coal rather than coke for fuel, making the exploitation of lower-quality iron ores economically feasible.[22] The great expansion of iron production in Wales and Pennsylvania was founded on the

---

[18] Henry Childs Merwin, The Patentability of Inventions 539 (1883).

[19] Alan Birch, The Economic History of the British Iron and Steel Industry 1784–1879, at 181 (1968).

[20] This prejudice stemmed from the observation that blast furnaces were more productive in winter than in summer. Paul Belford, *Hot Blast Iron Smelting in the Early 19th Century: A Re-appraisal*, 46 Historical Metallurgy 32, 33 (2012). Belford notes that other workers in the field, such as Thomas Botfield, may have been experimenting with hot blast prior to Neilson. See *id.* at 37–42.

[21] Birch, *supra* note 19, at 183.

[22] See *id.* at 173.

hot blast as well, because the process permitted, for the first time, the economical use of local anthracite deposits for fuel.[23]

But none of those advantages was apparent upon Neilson's invention. Nor did Neilson's invention arise from a deep understanding of the chemistry or physics of iron smelting. At the time of his invention, Neilson was employed as the manager of a gas works, where he had developed a process for removing ammonia from coal gas.[24] His original interest in blast furnaces came about when a local ironmaster asked him to investigate whether air purification might improve the output of the blast furnace, likely on the supposition that the lower productivity observed in summer resulted from contaminants in the air.[25] According to Neilson's own account, the idea of preheating the blast came about from the observation that a furnace located far from the blowing engine operated less efficiently than furnaces located near the source of the blast. Supposing that the greater volume of air when heated might deliver more oxygen to the blast furnace, he attempted the simple experiment of heating an iron vessel placed between a smith's forge and the air bellows that fed it:

> To the nozzle of a pair of common smith's bellows, I attached a cast iron vessel heated from beneath, in the manner of a retort for generating gas, and to this vessel, the blow pipe by which the forge or furnace was blown, was also attached. The air from the bellows having thus to pass through the heated vessel above mentioned, was consequently heated to a high temperature before it entered the forge fire, and the result produced, in increasing the intensity of the heat in the furnace, was far beyond my expectation, and so evident as to make apparent to me the fallacy of the generally received opinion, that the coldness of the air of the atmosphere in the winter months, was the cause of the best iron being then produced.
>
> In overthrowing the old theory, I had however established new principles and facts in the process of iron-making, and by the advice and assistance of Charles M'Intosh, Esq., of Crossbasket, I applied for and obtained a patent, as the reward of my discovery and improvements.[26]

In Neilson's account, published as litigation on his patent began, this small-scale experiment immediately demonstrated the superiority of hot blast for iron smelting, and prompted the immediate filing of his patent. Glossed over are such details that his experiment involved only a smith's forge, that

---

23 Thomas Turner, The Metallurgy of Iron 23 (1908); R.D. Corrins, *The Great Hot-Blast Affair*, 7 Industrial Archaeology 233, 233–34 (1970).

24 David P. Miller, *Of Patents, Principles, and the Construction of Heroic Invention: The Case of Neilson's Hot Blast in Iron Production*, 160 Proc. Am. Phil. Soc'y 361, 365 (2016).

25 *Id.* at 367.

26 James B. Neilson, *On the Hot Air Blast*, 1 Transactions Inst. Civ. Engineers 81, 82 (1836).

any practical utility of the hot blast for iron smelting lay in the future, and that his rationale for attempting preheating—the supposed increase in oxygen delivered—had nothing at all to do with the actual reasons why preheating the blast improved the efficiency of iron smelting.[27]

Neilson's first experiments with a blast furnace proper took place at the Clyde Iron Works in early 1829.[28] The air entering the blast furnace was heated in a simple wrought-iron box placed over a fire grate. This heating vessel was placed between the blowing apparatus and the blast furnace (Figure 4.1).[29]

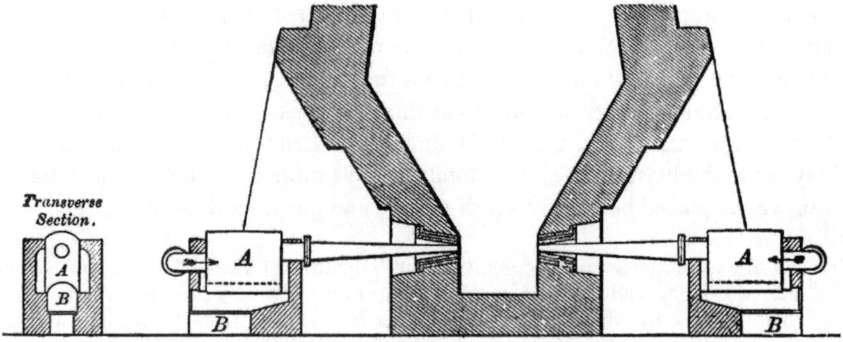

Fig. 5.—Neilson's original hot blast apparatus, 1829.

Figure 4.1 *Neilson's original hot blast apparatus, 1829*

This simple apparatus only raised the temperature of the blast to about 200°F, and the wrought-iron heating vessel easily succumbed to the heat and oxidation from the fire.[30] Later in 1829, Neilson replaced the wrought-iron box with a cast-iron retort, and succeeded in raising the temperature of the blast to about 280°F (Figure 4.2). A subsequent design implemented in 1830 extended the heating surface with a large bore pipe (Figures 4.3 and 4.4)[31] and achieved a blast temperature of about 600°.

While achieving satisfactory heating of the blast, the continuous pipe easily ruptured in use, because the entire length of the pipe expanded and contracted

---

27 The improved efficiency of the hot blast resulted from several effects of increased combustion temperature, none of which related to an increase in oxygen availability. See Turner, *supra* note 23, at 133–34.

28 See Miller, *supra* note 24, at 370.

29 This illustration appears in Turner, *supra* note 23, at 22.

30 See Henry Marten, *On the Construction of Hot Blast Ovens for Iron Furnaces*, Proc. Inst. Mechanical Engineers 62, 63–64 (1859).

31 *Id.* at 62.

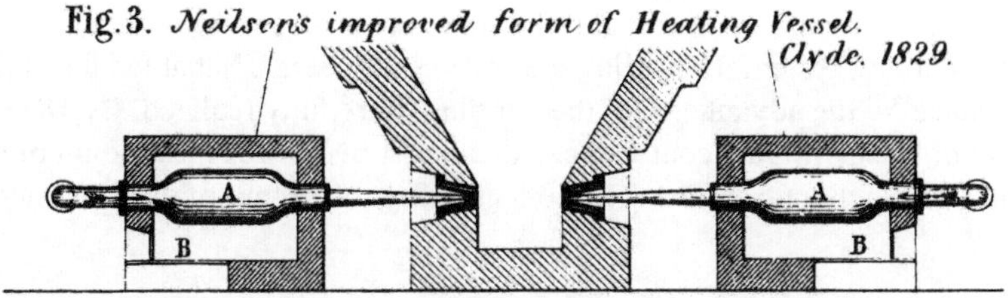

Figure 4.2 Neilson's improved form of heating vessel, Clyde 1829

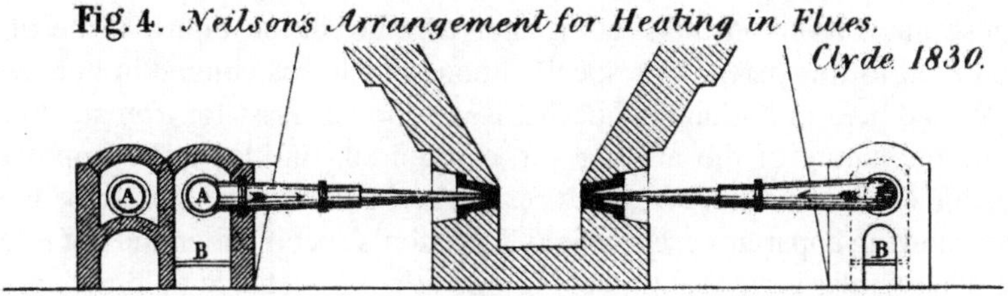

Figure 4.3 Neilson's arrangement for heating in flues, Clyde 1830

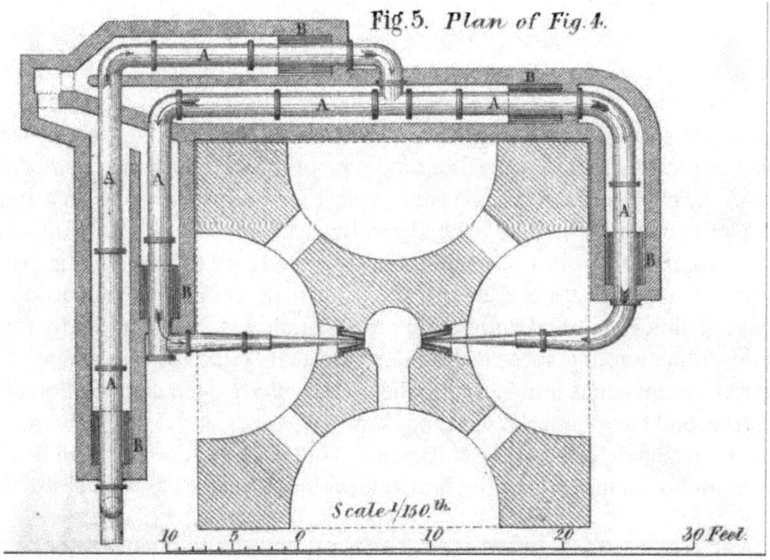

Figure 4.4 Plan of Fig. 4 [Figure 4.3]

when heated and cooled. Designs employed at Clyde by 1832 used a series of arched tubes over the heating grate, which proved far more durable while achieving the same degree of heating.[32] When coupled with two further innovations—the use of raw coal rather than coke as fuel for the furnace, and a water-cooling system for cooling the nozzles (or "twires") that fed the air into the furnace[33]—the advantages of the hot blast were fully realized. By 1833 the use of hot blast with raw coal reduced by almost two-thirds the amount of coal required to smelt a ton of iron, while increasing the output of each furnace by 67%.[34]

3. NEILSON'S PATENT

But those innovations in the heating apparatus lay in the future at the time Neilson filed for his patent. His specification, which was entered in February of 1829, said next to nothing about the use of the hot blast for iron smelting, let alone the nature of the heating vessel required. Entitled "The improved application of air to produce heat in fires, forges, and furnaces, where bellows or other blowing apparatus are required," Neilson's specification did not reference any particular industrial process or operation. It included no drawings or diagrams. It simply stated that air produced from a bellows or other blowing apparatus "must be artificially heated to a considerable temperature. It is better that the temperature be kept to a red heat or nearly so, but so high a temperature is not absolutely necessary to produce a beneficial effect." As far as the process or apparatus for heating the air, Neilson merely directed that an air current "is to be passed from the bellows or blowing apparatus into an air vessel or receptacle made sufficiently strong to endure the blast, and through or from that vessel or receptacle by means of a tube pipe or aperture into the fire, forge or furnace." The specification suggested typical vessel volumes for "an ordinary smith's fire or forge" and for "a cupola of the usual size for cast iron founders." In the case of larger blast furnaces—the only reference to iron smelting in the patent—the specification recommended that "air vessels of proportionably increased dimensions and numbers are to be employed." Most critically for the ensuing litigation, the specification declared that "[t]he form or shape of the vessel or receptacle is immaterial to the effect," as were the composition of the air vessel and the manner of applying heat.[35]

To understand Neilson's specification—indeed to understand the *Neilson* case at all—we must remember how undeveloped patent law was at the time.

---

32 See Miller, *supra* note 24, at 372–74.

33 See Belford, *supra* note 20, at 33. The water-cooled twire was already known, but prior to the development of the hot blast iron smelting usually employed coke (a coal derivative) rather than raw coal, and anthracite coals could not be ignited.

34 See *id.* at 33.

35 The specification is set out at 1 Web. P. C. 273–74.

English patent law of the late eighteenth and early nineteenth centuries was particularly plagued by uncertainty about the role of the patent specification.[36] Early patents had not required a written specification, and the patentee might satisfy the quid pro quo of the patent system by instructing apprentices in the "mystery" of the invention.[37] By the time of *Neilson*, it was settled that patentees were required to provide a specification enabling one of ordinary skill in the art to practice the invention. However, the specification was not examined for substance by the Crown before the grant.[38]

Drafting the specification was thus a perilous task for the patentee.[39] Patents did not include separate claims as we know them today; the description in the specification defined the scope of the patent. The specification therefore had to describe the invention with sufficient detail and particularity to enable practice of the invention, yet also in sufficiently general terms to provide useful scope. At the same time, patentees had to be wary of disclosing what was old and known, lest that description defeat the novelty of the patent.[40] Thus Neilson's attorneys would later argue in *Neilson v. Harford* that if Neilson had described a particular vessel for heating air, or otherwise given specific directions for heating, his patent would have been void for claiming what was already known.[41] Moreover, if the specification described unnecessary material or

---

[36] See Harold Irvin Dutton, The Patent System and Inventive Activity during the Industrial Revolution, 1750–1852, 72–76 (1984).

[37] See Helen Gubby, Developing a Legal Paradigm for Patents 155–56 (2012).

[38] See *id.* at 196.

[39] Godson's 1840 treatise lists the various ways a faulty specification might invalidate a patent:

> 1. The terms are *ambiguous*. 2. Necessary *descriptions are omitted*. 3. Parts claimed are *not original*. 4. Things are put in to *mislead*. 5. The *drawings* are incorrect. 6. *One of different ways*, or different ingredients named, fails. 7. *One of several effects specified* is not produced. 8. The things described are *not the best known* to the patentee.

Richard Godson, A Practical Treatise on the Law of Patents for Inventions and of Copyright 119–20 (2d ed. 1840) (original emphases).

[40] As Godson explained:

> It is a *fundamental rule*, on which all others for making and judging of a specification depend, that the secret must be disclosed, and the invention described in such a manner, that men of *common understanding*, with a *moderate knowledge* of the art, may be enabled to make the subject of the patent.
>
> The description must be *confined* to the manufacture, that the novelty may be known. Extraneous matter, however learned, must not be introduced to darken it.

Id. at 118 (original emphases).

[41] See G.B. Snell, Trial before Mr. Baron Parke and a Special Jury in the Case of Neilson and Others v. Harford, for Infringement of a Patent 220–21 (1841) (plaintiff's motion for a rule on the adequacy of the specification). This account of the case, taken from Snell's shorthand notes and printed in Edinburgh by Thomas

parts that had not in fact been used by the patentee, the patent might be voided on the grounds that the specification was misleading—even if the remainder correctly and completely described the invention and distinguished it from the prior art.[42]

In drafting the specification, Neilson and his partners benefitted from the advice of James Watt Jr. and others in his circle, who from the litigation on Watt Sr.'s patent knew well the problem of drafting a specification with either too much or too little detail.[43] The generality of Neilson's specification therefore did not just reflect the relatively unsophisticated heating apparatus he had employed at the time he filed. That generality was also a careful legal choice, attempting to balance the competing functions of the specification and the pitfalls posed by the state of patent law at the time.

4. THE HOT-BLAST CASES

Apart from some preliminary cases, litigation on Neilson's patent was slow to develop. Neilson and his partners offered a license to the patent at the relatively low rate of 1s per ton of iron produced, a rate they hoped would not be so high as to encourage resistance to the patent.[44] By the end of the 1830s, nearly every ironworks in Scotland, as well as a large number in England and Wales, employed the hot blast and had taken out a license to the Neilson patent.[45] However, in 1839, Scottish ironmakers led by the William Baird works organized a coalition of firms to resist and challenge the Neilson patents.[46] Ironmakers of the coalition agreed to coordinate litigation strategy and appor-

---

Constable, is the most complete account of the trial, post-trial motions, and the argument before the full Court of Exchequer on the plaintiff's rule. A nearly identical text was published in Edinburgh by Alex, Lawrie & Co. as REPORT OF THE CASE, NEILSON, ETC. V. HARFORD, ETC. TRIED IN THE COURT OF EXCHEQUER, BEFORE MR. BARON PARKE AND A SPECIAL JURY (1841). I have referred to the Snell version in this chapter.

[42] Godson, *supra* note 39, at 132–33.

[43] In addition to James Watt Jr, Neilson had the aid of his business partners with patent experience, and prominent politician (and future Lord High Chancellor) Henry Brougham. See Miller, *supra* note 24, at 369–70.

[44] See Corrins, *supra* note 23, at 245.

[45] See *id.* Scottish ironworks found the hot-blast process particularly valuable, because coal suitable for coking was scarce in Scotland, and the efficiency of the hot blast was key to the economical exploitation of local blackband iron ore deposits. See *id.* at 240.

[46] The Bairds were newcomers to the Scottish iron industry, and some of Nelson's early experiments had taken place at their works. See *id.* at 239. The Bairds had at first resisted taking a license, but had acquiesced after some preliminary court battles. See *id.* at 240–44.

tion the costs of the defense by volume of production.[47] English ironmasters also determined to resist the Neilson patent. The English firms were in regular communication with the Baird coalition, and adopted similar tactics and legal arguments as the Scottish group.[48]

Neilson v. Harford, brought against a Welsh ironworks, was only one of some twenty actions asserting Neilson's patents against defendants in England and Scotland.[49] Litigation against members of the Baird coalition in Scotland had begun first, but *Neilson* was the first to trial and the first to rule on the validity of Neilson's patent.[50] The case was tried in the Court of Exchequer, Baron James Parke presiding, from May 4 to May 6, 1841. Both sides had retained eminent counsel. Arguing for Neilson was former Solicitor-General and future Attorney-General Sir William Follett, who was regarded as one of the greatest advocates of his generation.[51] Appearing for the defendants was the Attorney-General, Sir John Campbell, as well as Sir Frederick Pollock, past and future Attorney-General and future Lord Chief Baron of the Exchequer.[52]

The defendants' pleas raised the usual array of defenses: non-infringement; that Neilson was not the first and true inventor; prior use; that the specification failed to truly and accurately describe the invention; and that the invention lacked utility.[53] However, the trial itself was devoted almost exclusively to the question of whether Neilson's specification adequately described his invention. Most of Neilson's witnesses (the defendants called none) would devote their testimony to establishing that, despite the lack of detailed instruction in the patent, the specification would be "perfectly plain and perfectly intelligible"[54] to workmen of ordinary skill in the field.

Parke's summation after trial left open only the question of the specification for the jury. On all the other defenses he directed a verdict for Neilson.[55] On

---

47 *Id.* at 245–46.

48 See *id.* at 248.

49 See *id.* at 245.

50 The Bairds adopted a strategy of delay and of pressing litigation through junior members of their coalition, hoping to wear down Neilson and his partners. See *id.* at 246–49. In hindsight, that strategy may have been a serious blunder: while the Exchequer's ruling in *Neilson v. Harford* was not binding on the Scottish courts, the Exchequer's decision to sustain Neilson's patent would prove persuasive in the Scottish cases.

51 See Miller, *supra* note 24, at 380 and 416 n.45. Neilson was also represented by Fitzroy Kelly, who would later become Solicitor-General and Attorney-General, as well as Lord Chief Baron of the Exchequer.

52 See *id.*

53 See Snell, *supra* note 41, at 176–77 (Parke's summation to the jury).

54 *Id.* at 17.

55 See *id.* at 178–79.

the specification, the jury found for Neilson as well. Responding to a series of special questions, the jury determined that while the shape and form of the heating vessel was material to the extent of benefit of the hot blast, the process would yield some benefit regardless of the shape and form.[56] The jury further answered that the specification alone would enable a person of ordinary skill to practice the invention with beneficial effect, and that a person of ordinary skill would not be misled by the specification's statement that the form and size of the heating vessel was immaterial to the effect. Parke nonetheless directed a verdict for the defendants, on the grounds that the assertion that shape and form were immaterial was a misdirection in the specification, and that such a misdirection in the patent itself could not be cured by the knowledge of those in the field.[57]

After the trial, Follett promptly moved before the full Court of Exchequer to enter judgment for Neilson, or, in the alternative, for a new trial. Having granted Follett a rule to show cause, the full Exchequer (consisting of Parke, Chief Baron Abinger, and Barons Alderson and Rolfe) heard arguments in the case over two days in June. The famous opinion of the case is the judgment of the full Exchequer, which was delivered for the court by Parke himself on 26 June. "[A]fter much consideration, and not without some doubt and hesitation," the Exchequer construed the specification to mean that once a particular degree of heating was achieved, the shape and size of the heating vessel was indeed immaterial to the effect on the smelting process. Given the jury's finding that an ordinarily skilled workman could construct a heating vessel sufficient to achieve some degree of beneficial effect, the court directed judgment for Neilson. [58]

4.a "The shape and form are of the very essence"

To understand why the materiality of form was so central to the *Neilson v. Harford* litigation, we must consider not only the parties' legal arguments at trial, but also the larger context of how the hot blast developed. As we have seen, Neilson drafted his specification at a point when he was just beginning to experiment with different arrangements for preheating the blast, and the specification described the heating vessel in the most general terms. The drafting of Neilson's specification set the stage for the parties' central dispute in *Neilson*

---

[56] See *id.* at 234–35 (Parke's summary of the jury verdicts for the full court).

[57] See *id.* at 235 ("[A]ccording to the grammatical construction of it, there was an averment that the form and shape was immaterial to the extent of the effect; that it was a misdirection; that there being a misdirection in the instrument itself, it could not be corrected by parole evidence ….").

[58] See *id.* at 375–76.

v. Harford: whether the invention of the hot blast was independent of form, specifically the form of the heating apparatus. For dependence on form was the fulcrum on which both infringement and the validity of Neilson's patent would be decided.

As a matter of infringement, Neilson's case could not succeed unless his patent extended beyond the apparatus he had implemented at Clyde in 1828 or 1829. In the years since, the forms of heating ovens employed by English, Welsh, and Scottish ironworks had multiplied profusely, as the illustrations from an 1859 report[59] show (see Figure 4.5a and Figure 4.5b).

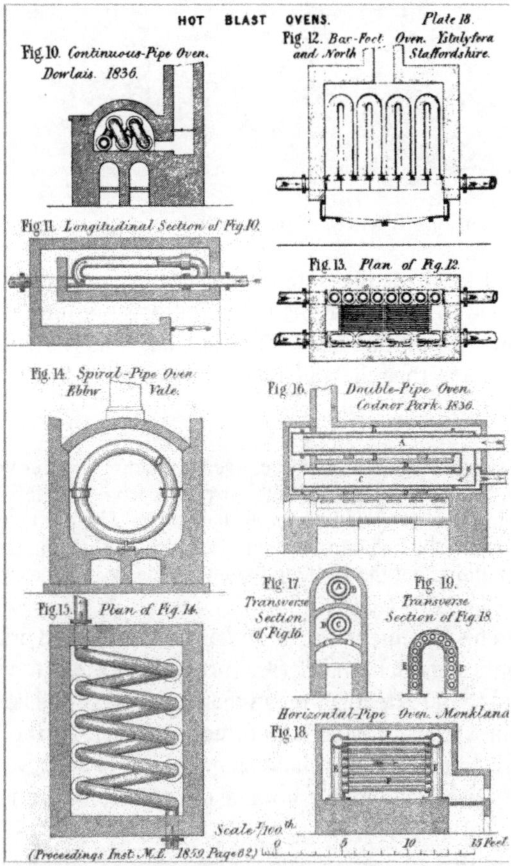

Figure 4.5a *Hot blast ovens, Figs 10–19*

---

59 Marten, *supra* note 30, at 62.

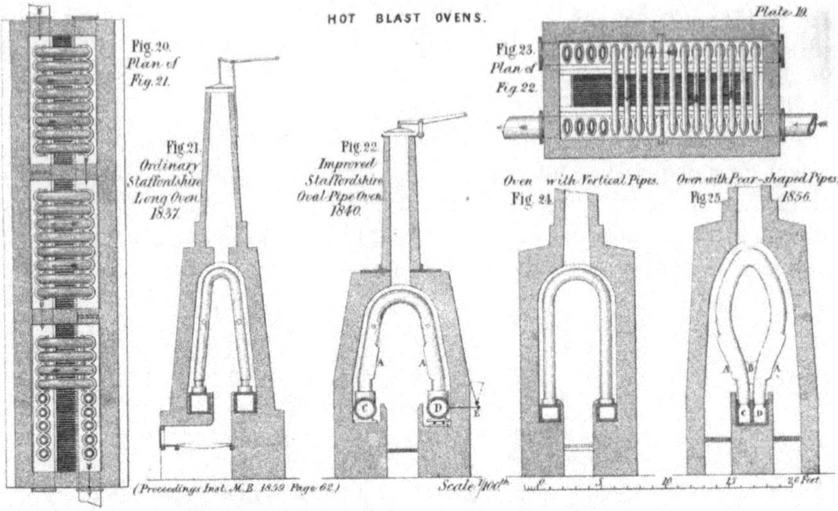

Figure 4.5b Hot blast ovens, Figs 20–25

If Neilson hoped to cover the defendants' heating apparatus[60]—let alone all the others—he had to argue that his invention was not limited to the forms of heating ovens he himself had used. Thus at trial, Follett's opening contention on infringement was that the patent encompassed a heating vessel of any conceivable form:

> Whilst Mr. Neilson's patent is in force, every vessel, no matter what its shape—no matter what its size, through which the air passes from the blowing power, for the purpose of being heated to go into the furnace, would be protected and covered by this patent, because the patent is for that discovery of applying the heated air to the furnace, and pointing out the mode in which that heated air may be applied.[61]

Form was key to his argument on validity as well. At trial, Parke had construed the specification's statement that "[t]he form or shape of the vessel or receptacle is immaterial to the effect" to mean that the form of the heating vessel was immaterial to the extent of beneficial effect produced by the invention. Once the jury determined that the form and shape of the heating vessel affected the degree of benefit produced by the hot blast, that became a misstatement in the

---

[60] At trial the defendants' apparatus was depicted by a model. Based on the descriptions at trial, the Harford heating apparatus probably resembled the arched tubular ovens shown in Marten's figures 20 and 23. See, e.g., Snell, *supra* note 41, at 141, 227–28 (the Attorney-General's descriptions of the defendants' apparatus).

[61] *Id.* at 10.

specification.[62] For the specification's statement to be true—and thus the specification to be good—Follett would have to convince the full Exchequer that Neilson's invention was not bound by form. In his motion for a rule, Follett conceded that the form and shape of the heating vessel was material to the heating of the air.[63] The question was whether the heating of the air in a vessel, or the *effect* of heating the air in the vessel, was the subject of Neilson's patent:

> But this patent was never taken out for heating the air, nor has it any reference to the form or shape of the vessel for heating air. It is that when you have heated the air, and heated it for the purpose of raising a stream proper to convey it into the furnace, then the form and shape of the vessel is immaterial, as far as regards the working of the blast furnace.[64]

In other words, because Neilson's patent was independent of the form of the heating apparatus, the form of the heating apparatus was not material to *the invention*. That was the theme to which he would return again and again in the extended argument of the case, and the argument that would ultimately convince the Exchequer that Neilson's patent was valid.

For their part, the defendants in *Neilson* sought to establish that form was the essence of Neilson's invention. When the defendants' principal attorney, Attorney-General John Campbell, opened his case to the jury, he centered his argument on the requirement of form. In the Attorney-General's framing, the defendants had done nothing but "mak[e] use of the apparatus that now lies before you"—a particular series of cross-connected pipes—and the question for the jury was "whether there is anything in point of law to prevent these respectable gentlemen from manufacturing iron according to that apparatus."[65] Form was key because only with tubular forms of the heating oven could the hot blast yield any practical benefit—and those forms had not even been developed when Neilson entered his specification.[66] The defendants therefore could not have infringed.[67] And if it were the case, as the defendants contended, that "the shape and the form are of the very essence"[68] of carrying out the hot blast,

---

62 See *id.* at 374.

63 See *id.* at 218 ("It [the form and shape of the vessel] is not immaterial to the heat of the air ….").

64 *Id.*

65 *Id.* at 141.

66 See *id.* at 143–44 (Campbell's address to jury). See also *id.* at 228 (defendants' motion for a rule) ("My Lords, it is only by means of the tubular form of some sort, that it can be beneficially exercised, and the effect depends entirely upon the form of the vessel.").

67 See *id.* at 158 (defendants' argument to the jury).

68 *Id.* at 268 (defendants' argument before the full Exchequer).

then the specification's assertion that the form and shape of the heating vessel was immaterial to the effect could not possibly be true—and the patent was void as a matter of law.

4.b "The principle being well known"

If the central question in *Neilson* was whether the hot-blast patent was independent of the form of the heating apparatus, then how could the case, in *Flook*'s telling, have required treating the discovery of a fundamental principle as part of the prior art? Or how could it depend, as *Mayo* claimed, on whether an inventor implements his or her discovery by inventive means? If neither of those stories is true, what did Parke mean when he stated that "the case must be considered, as if the principle being well known"? And why was the patentability of "principles" even at issue in the case?

The Supreme Court's treatment of *Neilson* in *Flook* and *Mayo* is limited to the Court's earlier quotation of the case in *O'Reilly v. Morse*. Probably few modern commentators have even consulted the widely available report of the case, which appeared in Thomas Webster's 1844 compilation.[69] But even that report is highly condensed.[70] Full reports of the arguments taken from shorthand at trial were published in 1841, but were not widely circulated and have not been readily available.[71] Crucially, the complete reports of the case include the arguments before the court that gave rise to the oft-quoted passage in Parke's opinion. That material, largely excised from Webster's version, at last makes clear the real meaning of that famous passage.

The objection that Neilson's patent claimed a "principle" was not pressed by the defendants at trial, and does not even seem to have been raised with the defendants' pleas.[72] It first surfaced at the close of the defendants' motion for a new trial, when Baron Alderson asked whether the defendants took the objec-

---

[69] Thomas Webster, Reports and Notes of Cases on Letters Patent for Inventions 273 (1844).

[70] While Webster's report includes both the trial and appellate arguments and runs to nearly 80 pages, Snell's version is 376 pages long.

[71] No more than a half-dozen copies of the Constable and Lawrie editions combined appear in OCLC's catalog of nearly 18,000 libraries.

[72] The objections pled by the defendants were read at trial, and did not include the objection that Neilson claimed a principle. See Snell, *supra* note 41, at 173–74. When the issue was raised by the Exchequer in the course of the defendant's motion for a new trial, one of the defendants' attorneys stated that it was an objection raised by the court's permission a few days before trial. See *id.* at 232. Webster's account, however, inserts the text "that the said patent is void, as being for a principle" at the beginning of the defendants' objections. *Neilson*, 1 Web. P. C. at 296.

tion that the patent claimed only a principle.[73] The Attorney-General's showed little interest in following that lead.[74] Nevertheless, Alderson persisted: "If the form of the vessel is immaterial then it is difficult to distinguish this from a patent for a principle."[75]

Alderson, and the other judges of the court, saw the implication of Follett's position that the invention was independent of form. To sustain the validity of the patent, Follett needed to argue that Neilson's invention was independent of form. Yet if Neilson had not claimed the heating apparatus, nor any particular mode of heating the air, then had he claimed anything more than the abstract principle that hot air was better than cold? Alderson would raise that point again and again in the subsequent argument on the patentee's rule. When Parke's final judgment for the court referred to the difficulty "created in the minds of some of the court" in distinguishing Neilson's patent from a principle, he clearly meant Alderson. To be more than a mere principle, the specification would have to disclose a practical mode for applying it—and there was serious doubt in Alderson's mind whether Neilson had sufficiently disclosed *any* mode of carrying out his invention. As Alderson stated in the course of the defendants' argument:

> The difficulty which presses on my mind here is, that this party has taken out a patent in substance like Watt's for a principle—that is, the application of hot air to furnaces; but he has not practically described any mode of carrying it into effect. If he had, perhaps he might have covered all other modes as being a variation.[76]

Remarkably, the attorney arguing for the defendants at that point—Sir Frederick Pollock—responded by contradicting Alderson, rather than agreeing that Neilson could not patent a principle:

> With respect to what has fallen from your Lordship about taking out a patent for a principle, it is theoretically true, but practically it is not true. Practically you can have a patent for a principle that is, if you embody your principle in any clear, defi-

---

[73] See Snell, *supra* note 41, at 232.

[74] In response to Alderson's question, the Attorney General replied only "There are other things open to me on the argument of the rule," and attempted to turn the objection into one about the title of the patent, which did not reference the hot blast. See *id.* at 232.

[75] *Id.* at 232. Baron Rolfe made the same point: "If the form and shape of the vessel is immaterial, and the mode of heating is immaterial, it only comes to this, that this person has discovered something which may be a most useful discovery, but it is the discovery of the principle that hot air is better than cold." *Id.* at 233.

[76] *Id.* at 268.

> nite, and distinct form, no other person shall be allowed to take that principle and embody it in some other form merely copied from yours.[77]

Why would the *defendants'* attorney have argued that a patent could effectively preempt all application of a fundamental principle? The likely answer is that Pollock had been counsel for a patentee in a prior case before the Exchequer, *Minter v. Wells*, where his principal contention had been that the patent in suit extended to any similar application of the underlying principle, regardless of shape or form.[78] Both Pollock and Campbell had appeared for Minter in a subsequent case.[79] Whether their prior representation explains their reluctance to raise the question of principle in *Neilson* must remain speculation—but *Minter* was soon to play a critical role in the case.

It was Alderson who would later introduce the notion of treating the principle of the invention as "well-known." In the argument before the full Exchequer, one of Follett's main arguments was that a challenge to the adequacy of the specification was foreclosed by the jury's finding that one of ordinary skill in the art could practice the invention with beneficial effect.[80] His principal support for that argument was *Boulton v. Bull*, a case on Watt's patent for the steam engine. Watt's patent, like Neilson's, had also been subject to the charge that it pointed out no particular mode of carrying his discovery into effect. That similarity prompted Alderson to remark that he had always been puzzled why Watt's patent was not held to be an unpatentable abstract principle:

> It is very difficult to see on what ground, though the Court certainly held it to be so—it is very difficult to distinguish why Watt's patent was not for a principle. I have always been puzzled with that. … It is very difficult to see what is a patent for a principle and what is a patent for a principle embodied in a machine, because the patent can only be for the principle embodied in a machine.[81]

---

77 *Id.* Pollock went on to argue that once the principle was put into shape, "no person can be allowed to come and steal the spirit of the invention, and put it into some other shape different from yours, provided the Jury think that that other shape is an imitation of your shape." *Id.* Perhaps realizing that this was not a position favorable to his client, he quickly returned to the argument that shape and form were the essence of Neilson's invention.

78 *Minter v. Wells*, 1 Carpmael's Reports 622 (1834).

79 Both Pollock and Attorney-General Campbell represented Minter in a subsequent case before the King's Bench, in which they would again argue that the patent claimed the application of a principle rather than a principle itself. *Minter v. Mower*, 1 Carpmael's Reports 650, 651 (1837).

80 See Snell, *supra* note 41, at 302. The Exchequer would ultimately reject that argument.

81 *Id.* at 306.

He continued by suggesting a test to determine whether a patent claimed a principle or not: imagine that the principle was already known, and ask whether the inventor could have a patent for a machine carrying the principle into effect:

> I have always thought that the real test was this, that in order to discover whether it is a good or bad patent, you should consider that what you cannot take out a patent for, must be considered as invented *pro bono publico*, that is to say, the principle must be considered as having had an anterior existence before the patent. Now, supposing in Watt's case, it had been known that to condense in a separate vessel was a mode of saving fuel, then Watt certainly could have taken out a patent for carrying into effect that principle by a particular machine, but then his patent would have been for a machine, and if I invented a better machine for carrying out the principle, I do not infringe his patent, unless my machine is a colourable imitation. ... Now here, supposing it had been known that hot air applied to a furnace, was a great improvement on cold air, and that this person had taken out his patent, and this patent was a patent for the application of a well known thing, the hot air to furnaces—then he takes out a patent for applying it by means of an intermediate reservoir between the blast furnace and the bellows, then surely any body else may apply the same principle, provided he does not do it by a reservoir intermediately between the blast furnace and the bellows, and the question for a Jury is, whether or not a long spiral pipe is a reservoir—if it be not a reservoir, or a colourable imitation of a reservoir, it is no infringement.[82]

The full text makes clear that Alderson's notion of considering the principle of the invention to be well known—"having an anterior existence before the patent"—was never a rule that discoveries must be discarded when assessing the patentability of an invention. In an era when patents lacked separate claims, his notion was a hypothetical device for clarifying exactly what the patentee had claimed. Had the patentee claimed a *machine*, as required by the patent statute? Or had he merely claimed a principle in the abstract? If he had properly claimed a machine, then the question of infringement would not be whether the defendant had employed the same principle, but whether his apparatus was equivalent—"a colourable imitation"—to the patentee's apparatus.

Alderson's device laid bare Follett's dilemma. The case had been tried on Baron Parke's assumption that the patent covered any heating vessel interposed between the blowing apparatus and the blast furnace.[83] To concede Alderson's point could open the case for a new trial, since the jury had not been asked to decide whether the defendant's apparatus was equivalent to Neilson's. Follett's case for infringement, and his rule supporting the validity of the specification, rested on the argument that Neilson's invention was independent of

---

[82] *Id.* at 306–07.

[83] See *id.* at 307.

form. But then the patent might be void as a patent for an abstract principle. That dilemma was clearest when Follett returned to his argument that the specification was accurate in asserting that shape and form of the heating vessel was immaterial to the invention. Alderson objected:

> *Mr. Baron Alderson.* That will reduce it to this. This is the very point upon which the infringement takes place, the shape of the vessel; it is the very point in the cause. Therefore, if you are to take it in this sense, he is in effect claiming every thing; he is claiming a principle, and there is no particular machine, a machine of any shape, or any size, or any form.
> *Sir W. Follett.* That is the question upon the infringement, but I should answer it with great deference thus. I say we do claim every vessel and every shape of vessel, closed vessel, in which air can be heated between the blowing apparatus and the furnace.
> *Mr. Baron Alderson.* Then I think that is a principle. If you claim every shape—if you claim a specific shape, and go to the Jury, and say that which the other people have adopted is a colourable imitation, then I can understand it. If you claim every shape you claim a principle. There is a difference between a principle to be carried into effect in any way you will and claiming the principle itself. You must detail some specific mode of doing it. Then the rest is a question for the Jury.

Alderson did not disagree that a patentee could effectively claim all practical applications of a principle.[84] Rather, he distinguished between claiming "the principle itself"—that is, the principle in the abstract—and claiming "a principle to be carried in effect in any way you will." But if Neilson had not limited his claim to any particular shape or form of heating vessel, then had he not claimed an abstract principle rather than a machine?

Follett would thread that needle with a case the Exchequer had decided seven years earlier. After a series of questions from the bench asking whether various hypothetical heating arrangements would also infringe Neilson's patent—to which Follett had to answer in the affirmative—Follett responded by raising *Minter v. Wells*,[85] a case that seven years earlier had been tried by Alderson and considered by the full court, including Parke, on the defendant's motion for a rule.

Minter's patent had claimed a reclining chair embodying the principle of self-adjusting leverage. Because Minter had declared that his patent was not confined to "the precise shape or forms" depicted in the specification, but rather

---

84 Alderson seems to have been distinguishing between claiming a specific shape and then establishing equivalence of the accused subject matter before a jury, and claiming all shapes as a matter of law. He regarded the former as a claim to a specific mode of application, versus the latter as a claim to an abstract principle.

85 See Snell, *supra* note 41, at 310. *Minter* is reported in 1 Carpmael's Patent Cases 622 (1834).

"the application of a self-adjusting leverage to the back and seat of a chair," the defendants sought to invalidate the patent on the ground that Minter had merely claimed a well-known principle of mechanics.[86] The Exchequer had rejected that argument. Though the court agreed that Minter's patent was not confined to any particular form, the court held that Minter had claimed not the principle of the self-adjusting leverage, but the *application* of that principle to the construction of a chair. The patent was therefore drawn to a machine: "the chair constructed on this principle in whatever shape or form it may be."[87]

If Minter could claim the application of a well-known principle to all chairs, regardless of shape or form, then Neilson could claim the application of a new principle to the blast furnace, regardless of the shape or form of the heating apparatus. Using Alderson's device, Follett argued that if the principle of the hot blast had been well known, then one could have taken out a patent for applying the principle by heating the air between the blowing apparatus and the furnace. That would be a patent not for a principle, but for the mode of carrying the principle into effect.[88] The same was true in Neilson's case, where the principle was newly discovered rather than well-known. As Follett responded to Alderson's objection that claiming every shape or form of the heating apparatus was tantamount to claiming a principle:

> Is it, or is it not, the subject matter of a patent that a person has discovered a valuable principle, namely, that heated air passing into a blast furnace is better than cold air, and that he points out a mode by which that principle can be carried into effect. And, my Lords, what is that mode? The mode is, that you shall heat the air in its passage from the blowing apparatus to the furnace,—that you shall pass it into a closed vessel under which a fire is to be placed between the blowing apparatus and the furnace, and that in that vessel so placed between the blowing apparatus and the furnace the air is to be heated, and, I say, with great deference to your Lordships, that until this Court decides otherwise I shall venture respectfully to submit that there could not be a doubt that that was a good patent, that it was a good subject matter of a patent, and that the party had a right to complain of an infringement against any persons who should heat the air in its passage between the blowing apparatus and the furnace by means of any vessel, whatever be its shape, provided that vessel was a closed vessel, placed between the blowing apparatus and the furnace, subject to the heat there, and the air heated in its passage. That is precisely the same principle which is laid down in these other cases, and what I venture to submit to your Lordships is the

---

[86] See *id* at 641–42.

[87] *Id.* at 646 (Lyndhurst, C.B.) That scope may have extended the patent too far; in a subsequent suit against different defendants, the King's Bench determined that a prior art chair had also embodied a self-adjusting leverage. *Minter v. Mower* (1837) 112 Eng. Rep. 282, 282 (K.B.). Minter was thereby nonsuited. *Id.* at 286.

[88] Snell, *supra* note 41, at 310.

> subject matter of this patent; and I say the form and shape of the vessel are entirely immaterial.[89]

I have quoted this argument in full for two reasons. First, Follett's framing of the invention as the heating of air in a vessel between the blowing apparatus and the furnace seems to have at last convinced the Exchequer that Neilson had not claimed an abstract principle. Alderson would raise no more objections about principle, and Lord Abinger concurred in Follett's characterization of Neilson's patent. For Abinger, that brought the case within the holding of *Boulton v. Bull*, where Watt's patent had been sustained even though he had not described the shape or size of the condensing vessel.[90] Neilson's patent would therefore be valid, provided that the specification did not mislead by stating that the effect did not depend on the shape or form of the heating vessel.

And that would be the Exchequer's ultimate disposition of the case. Despite Alderson's initial doubts, Parke's judgment for the court determined that Neilson had claimed a machine: "after full consideration, we think that the plaintiff does not merely claim a principle, but a machine embodying a principle, and a very valuable one."[91] Employing Alderson's device of supposing the principle to be already known, the patent would be regarded not as a claim to the abstract principle that hot air was better than cold, but as a claim to the application of the preheating principle, by means of a heating vessel placed between the blowing apparatus and the furnace.

What of the specification's assertion that the form and shape of the heating vessel was immaterial to the effect? Although Parke himself "still entertain[ed] great doubt," the rest of the court would agree that the specification should be construed to assert that some beneficial effect would result from preheating the air, regardless of the shape of the heating vessel.[92] That being the case, the Exchequer was bound by the finding of the jury, which had determined that a workman of ordinary skill could practice the hot blast with beneficial effect, based only on the directions of the specification. The specification was therefore valid, and the verdict was entered in Neilson's favor.[93]

4.c "It was no discovery of Mr. Neilson, every body knew it"

The other point of interest in Follett's argument is his framing of the general question of patentability—a framing with significance well beyond the

---

[89] *Id.* at 329–30.
[90] See *id.* at 330.
[91] *Id.* at 374.
[92] See *id.* at 375.
[93] See *id.* at 375–76.

argument in *Neilson v. Harford* itself. Follett asked whether it sufficed for a patentee to discover a valuable principle, and point out a mode by which that principle can be carried into effect. The distinction between the principle, which is *discovered*, and the mode of application, which is *pointed out*, differentiates the act of invention into one act requiring an inventive act—the discovery of the principle—and one seemingly less creative—the pointing out of the mode of application. If that distinction between the discovery and the means of application were only found in the patentee's argument in *Neilson* then it would hardly be worth mentioning. But Follet's argument seems to be one the earliest expressions of that distinction, which would later become embedded in English law.[94]

For example, in *Neilson v. Househill*, a later suit against one of the Scottish members of the Baird coalition, Lord Moncreiff would explain that though Neilson's patent embraced all modes of heating and all forms of the heating vessel, it would still be valid if "it is clear that there is a principle *discovered*, and a mechanical process for carrying that principle into operation *pointed out*."[95] And that view would become a staple of English law. In *Otto v. Linford*, which became one of the canonical cases on patentable subject matter in English law, Master of the Rolls Jessel explained that a new principle was patentable so long as the patentee could *show* a mode of carrying into effect.[96] He relied on *Neilson* for the proposition that applying a discovery by means of old and known machinery sufficed for patentability:

> One of the strongest illustrations that I know of is the patent for the hot blast in the iron manufacture, where there was nothing new at all except the idea that the application of hot air instead of cold air to the mixture of iron ore and fuel would produce the most remarkable results in the shape of economy in the manufacture of iron. … In the case of the hot blast the man did not pretend to invent anything; he said a machine of any shape in which you can heat air is sufficient.[97]

---

[94] That distinction was adopted in American patent law as well, largely under the influence of the hot-blast cases. Nineteenth-century courts and commentators in the United States endorsed the position that routine and conventional means of application sufficed to transform discoveries into patentable inventions. See Lefstin, *supra* note 4, at 601–08.

[95] *Neilson v. Househill Coal & Iron Co.* (1841) 14 Scottish Jurist 626, 651 (Moncreiff, L.J.) (emphases added).

[96] See *Otto v. Linford* [1882] 46 LT (N.S.) 35, 39 (Jessel, M.R.). See also *id.* at 45 (Holker, L.J.) ("The idea, no doubt, would not be patentable, but if the discoverer of this idea points out in his specification the means by which all this may be accomplished … that is the subject-matter of letters patent").

[97] *Id.* at 39–40.

That view of *Neilson* is very hard to square with the story of *Neilson* told in *Mayo,* in which the Exchequer sustains Neilson's patent only because he invented a new and unconventional means for applying his discovery.

But in truth *Mayo*'s interpretation of *Neilson* was never sustainable, even from Webster's condensed report of the case. Recall that the defendants' main argument against Neilson's patent was not that Neilson had claimed a principle, but that he had not adequately disclosed any means for heating air.[98] To rebut this challenge, Follett emphasized that the development and application of the hot blast had required no invention whatsoever, once Neilson had made the principle known. At trial Follett had drawn out testimony from multiple witnesses that the heating apparatus and the water twire were known and conventional at the time of Neilson's invention. His opening argument to the full Exchequer emphasized that point:

> The mode of heating air was perfectly well known; it was no discovery of Mr. Neilson, every body knew it. Air had been heated, and there had been different shaped vessels employed for heating the air, for heating the air economically, and for heating it to a higher or lesser degree of temperature, all that was perfectly well known.[99]

It was a point Follett would repeat throughout his argument.[100] It was also the Exchequer's premise, at least for Alderson. When the Attorney-General argued that Neilson's specification failed to teach anyone how to apply the principle of the hot blast to a practical iron smelter, Alderson dismissed the challenge on the grounds that all the instrumentalities necessary to practice the hot blast were "perfectly well known" at the time of Neilson's invention:

> The blowing apparatus was perfectly well known before,—the heating of air was perfectly well known before,—the twire was perfectly well known before, as applicable to blast-furnaces: then, what he really discovered is, that it would be better for you to apply air heated up to red heat, or nearly so, instead of cold air, as you have hitherto done. That is the principle; that is the real discovery. But, in order to take out a patent, you must have an imbodyment of the principle; and his imbodyment of the principle is, the heating of air in a separate vessel intermediately between the blowing apparatus and the point where it enters the furnace.[101]

---

[98] See, e.g., Snell, *supra* note 41, at 149–52 (defendants' argument attacking specification for lack of disclosure concerning the heating apparatus).

[99] *Id.* at 270.

[100] See *id.* at 271, 276, 315, 327, 331; see also *id.* at 218 (plaintiff's motion for rule nisi).

[101] *Id.* at 253 (interposition of Baron Alderson). See also *id.* at 357 (Alderson, B.) (noting that evidence "that these things were perfectly well known in the application of

The great irony, then, of the Supreme Court's reliance on *Neilson* in *Flook* and *Mayo* is that Neilson's patent was not sustained because Neilson had applied the principle of the hot blast in an inventive or unconventional way. His patent was sustained precisely because the application of his discovery was well-known, routine, and conventional in the field.

Exactly the same point—that discovery alone sufficed to support a patent, provided the patentee had pointed out the means of application—was voiced by the Scottish courts in subsequent trials of Neilson's patent against other members of the Baird coalition.[102] It was the discovery that mattered, not the patentee's means of application. For example, in *Househill Coal & Iron Co. v. Neilson*, the first major case on Neilson's patent in Scotland, the court instructed the jury that

> The main merit, the most important part of the invention, may consist in the conception of the original idea—in the discovery of the principle in science, or of the law of nature, stated in the patent, and little or no pains may have been taken in working out the best manner and mode of the application of the principle to the purpose set forth in the patent.[103]

Thus, contrary to *Flook* and *Mayo*'s assertions, the hot-blast cases did not stand for the proposition that scientific discoveries or other fundamental principles should be disregarded in the patentability inquiry, and that only inventive applications of fundamental principles are patent-eligible. They stood for the proposition that routine, conventional, and obvious applications of fundamental principles were patent-eligible—a position endorsed by American courts and commentators at least through the middle of the twentieth century.[104]

4.d The End of the Hot-Blast Affair

Neilson v. Harford and *Househill v. Neilson* did not end the hot-blast litigation. The Bairds finally took the field on their own account against Neilson in 1843. The trial at the Court of Session lasted for a record ten days, took testimony from over a hundred witnesses, and was litigated by many of the leading attorneys of the time.[105] Unlike *Neilson v Harford*, the question of whether Neilson had claimed a principle was raised directly, as Lord Justice-General Boyle

---

hot air" might affect a court's interpretation of the specification, but that such evidence must be grounded in the jury's findings).

[102] See Lefstin, *supra* note 4, at 588–91 (discussing subsequent hot-blast cases).

[103] *Househill Coal & Iron Co v. Neilson*, 1 Web. P. C. 673, 683 (1843).

[104] See Lefstin, *supra* note 4, at 593–623 (reviewing American law).

[105] See Corrins, *supra* note 23, at 250.

directed the jury that the patent was not for a mere abstract principle.[106] The defendants having excepted to that instruction, that question was also before the First Division of the Court of Session on appeal, when the defendants brought their bill of exceptions, following a jury verdict in Neilson's favor.[107] Yet the judges of the court regarded the legal question as conclusively settled by *Neilson* and *Househill*: the patent might be founded on the discovery of a principle, but if the inventor had disclosed a practical mode of applying the principle, the patent was good.[108]

The Court of Session's decision effectively ended resistance to Neilson's patents. Upon rejection of their bill of exceptions, the Bairds settled with Neilson for £100,000 plus his costs.[109] Neilson went on to be celebrated as one of the great inventors of the Industrial Revolution.[110]

Conversely, for subsequent English commentators, Neilson's patent became the cardinal example of the rule that for patents based on a new discovery, the

---

[106] Boyle's instruction was as follows:

> 2. That the patent is not void, as being merely for an abstract philosophical principle which the law does not acknowledge, because it combines a principle with the special purpose and important result of having atmospheric air heated in a vessel or receptacle between the blowing apparatus and fires, forges and furnaces, into which it is introduced, as an improved application of air to produce heat.

Neilson v. Baird (1843) 15 Scottish Jurist 618, 618. Boyle also directed that the patent claimed no particular mode of heating air or form of heating vessel. *See id.* (third instruction).

[107] See *id.* at 619.

[108] See *id.* at 622 (Fullerton, L.) ("Then as to the abstract principle, the question is settled both by [the Court of Exchequer] and by the Lord Chancellor. The patent was not for a general property, but for a mechanical contrivance, viz., for heating the receptacle between the blast and the furnace."); *id.* at 619–20 (Mackenzie, L.) (providing that a valid patent must, in addition to discovery, contain the invention of a practical mode of application); *id.* at 626 (Boyle, L.P.).

[109] The Bairds had given notice of their intent to appeal to the House of Lords, but settled before any appeal was heard. See Corrins, *supra* note 23 at 256–57. The settlement prompted further disputes among the members of the anti-Neilson coalition as to whether those damages, or just the legal expenses alone, should be borne pro rata by the members. See *id.* at 257–58.

[110] See Miller, *supra* note 24, at 366–67.

law did not require that the means of application be inventive.[111] That continues to be the position of English law today.[112]

5. *NEILSON* IN AMERICAN LAW: TRANSCENDING FORM

In the United States, the hot-blast cases became some of the most important authorities on patent law in the mid to late nineteenth century. All of the major treatises devoted extensive sections to the hot-blast cases: discussions of the patentability of principles, the scope of patents based on discoveries, the requirements for a specification, and the role of courts in construing patent specifications all began with the hot-blast cases as their starting point.[113] Here I will focus only on the aspect of *Neilson* that I have emphasized in the narration of the case: the independence of Neilson's invention from shape and form. *Neilson*'s principle that invention might transcend form was key to three of the Supreme Court's nineteenth-century cases that built the foundations of American patent law: *Winans v. Denmead,* frequently viewed as the origin of the doctrine of equivalents; *Tilghman v. Proctor*, which confirmed the patentability of processes separate from the apparatus used to carry them out; and *O'Reilly v. Morse*, which established the commensurability between claim scope and an enabling disclosure.

5.a Patent Scope and the Doctrine of Equivalents

Though American courts cited *Neilson* as early as 1844,[114] the Supreme Court's first significant engagement with the hot-blast cases came in 1852, with *Le Roy v. Tatham.*[115] *Le Roy* later became the fountainhead of subject matter exclusion in American patent law, via its oft-quoted (and largely tauto-

---

[111] See Jessel's comments in *Otto v. Linford, supra* note 96. See also, e.g., David Fulton, THE LAW AND PRACTICE RELATING TO PATENTS, TRADE MARKS AND DESIGNS 49–50 (1905):

> It was not and cannot be pretended that [Neilson's] air-heating means involved any invention at all. … [W]herever it is a question of claiming anything which seems to be of the nature of a principle, the rule is to claim it in conjunction with and as effected by the means for carrying the principle into effect, however simple and self-evident such means may be.

[112] See Lefstin, *supra* note 4, at 593 (discussing recent English cases).

[113] See *id.* at 605–609 (discussing nineteenth-century treatises).

[114] See, e.g., *Washburn v. Gould*, 29 F. Cas. 312, 325 (C.C.D. Mass. 1844) (No. 17,214).

[115] 55 U.S. (14 How.) 156 (1853).

logical) pronouncement on the unpatentability of principles in the abstract.[116] But the real question in *Le Roy* was about the dependence of the invention on form. The patent in the case was directed to the manufacture of wrought pipe by extrusion through a die, as compared to casting in a mold. That invention was said to have been based on the patentee's discovery that solid lead will re-anneal under heat and pressure. But the machinery used for the extrusion was old.[117] The novelty of the patent therefore turned on whether the patentees' invention subsisted in the particular machinery they disclosed, or in the application of their discovery to the manufacture of pipe.

The Court determined that the inventors had claimed their apparatus, not the more general application of their discovery.[118] But more significantly for the course of the law, the Court explained that a patent need not be bound to a particular form. Based on the authority of *Househill*, the Court allowed that "a new property discovered in matter" could be patented if practically applied. The only question was whether the patentee had adequately taught one of ordinary skill in the art "the process through which the new property is developed and applied."[119] Since Neilson had not claimed any particular machinery, the lesson of the hot-blast cases was that a patent might extend to the effect or result of a process, "without a claim to the invention of the machinery," so long as the patentee had supplied an enabling specification.[120]

The seed planted by *Le Roy* germinated quickly. The next year, the Court decided *Winans v. Denmead*,[121] which is often regarded as the foundation of the doctrine of equivalents in the United States.[122] The issue in the case

---

[116] "A principle, in the abstract, is a fundamental truth; an original cause; a motive; these cannot be patented, as no one can claim in either of them an exclusive right." *Id.* at 175.

[117] Similar machinery had been in prior use for the extrusion of clay pipes, and even macaroni. The trial judge had instructed the jury that the patentee's invention lay not in his machinery, but in first applying a newly discovered principle to the manufacture of wrought pipe, which made the invention novel. See *id* at 174.

[118] See *id.* at 177. The question of whether the patentees might have more broadly claimed the application of their discovery to the manufacture of pipes therefore "was not in the case." *Id.* Nonetheless, when the case was retried (in equity) and reached the Supreme Court again, the Court sustained the patent on the grounds that the patentee claimed the old machinery only in connection with the process of forming metal pipes under heat and pressure. *Le Roy v. Tatham*, 63 U.S. (22 How.) 132, 138–40 (1860).

[119] *Le Roy*, 55 U.S. (14 How.) at 175.

[120] *Id.* at 176 (stating that in such cases "a precise specification is required; and the test of infringement is, whether the defendants have used substantially the same process to produce the same result").

[121] 56 U.S. (15 How.) 330 (1853).

[122] See, e.g., Michael J. Meurer and Craig Allen Nard, *Invention, Refinement and Patent Claim Scope: A New Perspective on the Doctrine of Equivalents*, 93 Geo. L.J.

was again form: whether Winans's patent for a railroad hopper car was limited to the conical form disclosed in the specification. In part, the Court's decision rested on the argument that if mere changes in form did not give rise to patentable invention, then neither should they nullify infringement.[123] But the more significant argument was the Court's presumption that patents were not bounded by form: "the patentee, having described his invention, and shown its principles, and claimed it in that form which most perfectly embodies it, is, in contemplation of law, deemed to claim every form in which his invention may be copied, unless he manifests an intention to disclaim some of those forms."[124] *Winans* sets forth an essentialist concept of invention: while form might be paramount for some inventions where form and substance were inseparable, in cases where form and substance where separable "it is the duty of courts and juries to look through the form for the substance of the invention ...."[125] In support of this position, the Court cited a number of precedents for the proposition that "specifications are to be construed liberally."[126] But of those, only two addressed the real foundation of the Court's decision—that the invention might subsist in the patentee's "mode of operation," rather than the form in which that mode was embodied.[127] Those were *Le Roy v. Tatham* "and opinion of Parke, Baron, there quoted," and *Neilson* itself.[128]

5.b Processes and their Instrumentalities

The second area where the hot-blast cases would have a major influence on American jurisprudence was in the patentability of processes. In England, where the Statute of Monopolies constituted the only statutory basis of patent law until 1852, the restriction of the Statute to "new manufactures" meant that methods and processes lacked clear authority for patentability.[129] Nonetheless, by the latter half of the eighteenth century, and especially after the cases on James Watt's patent for the separate condenser, patents on processes were

1947, 1963–66 (2005). Cf. Joshua D. Sarnoff, *The Historic and Modern Doctrines of Equivalents and Claiming the Future, Part I (1790–1870)*, 87 J. PAT. & TRADEMARK OFF. SOC'Y 371, 393–98 (2005) (arguing that *Winans* was a case of liberal claim construction, and not a case of extending the patentee's rights beyond the construed claim).

[123] See *Winans*, 56 U.S. (15 How.) at 341.

[124] *Id.* at 343.

[125] *Id.*

[126] *Id.* at 341.

[127] See *id.* at 343–44

[128] *Id.* at 342.

[129] Sean Bottomley, THE BRITISH PATENT SYSTEM DURING THE INDUSTRIAL REVOLUTION 1700–1852, at 148–50 (2014).

routinely obtained by inventors and approved by the courts.[130] In the United States the use of "art" in the Act of 1793 provided a statutory foundation for patenting processes; early commentator Willard Phillips viewed the Act's categories of "art, machine, manufacture, or composition of matter" as an elaboration of the practical construction that English courts had given to the Statute of Monopolies.[131]

Early American cases such as *Corning v. Burden* readily acknowledged the patentability of processes, in the sense of chemical operations that resulted in a product or manufacture.[132] However, especially in the period when patents lacked claims to define the scope of the invention, the relationship between a process and the machinery that might be used to implement the process was one of the more contested grounds of mid- to late-nineteenth-century patent law.[133] One aspect of that debate was the extent to which a process could transcend the instrumentalities that the patentee had described for implementing it.[134] *Corning* had endorsed the theoretical patentability of a process independently of any machine or combination of mechanical devices used to carry it out.[135] Yet in *Mitchell v. Tilghman*, the Court had bound the patentee's process—a method for decomposing fats into fatty acids—tightly to the physical means he had disclosed to carry it out. The Court acknowledged, relying on *Househill*, that "the discovery of some principle of science or property of matter" could be patented "without including in the claim any new arrangement of machinery to accomplish the object," so long as the specification disclosed the means for applying the principle to practical effect.[136] Yet the Court deter-

---

[130] See *id.* at 150–53.

[131] Willard Phillips, The Law of Patents for Inventions 74 (1837).

[132] *Corning v. Burden*, 56 U.S. 252, 267–68 (1853).

[133] For an overview, *see* William B. Whitney, *Patentable Processes*, 19 Harv. L. Rev. 30 (1905–1906).

[134] The other major question arose when a patentee described a process as too closely bound to a particular apparatus. In such a case the claim might be invalid under the doctrine that one could not claim the "function of a machine." See *Corning*, 56 U.S. at 268–69; see generally Whitney, *supra* note 133. Here too, *Neilson* served the Court as an important marker of the boundary between patentable and unpatentable processes. See *Risdon Iron & Locomotive Works v. Medart*, 158 U.S. 68, 72–74 (1895) (discussing *Neilson* and *Househill*). The question was whether the mechanism was "subsidiary to the chemical action"; if so, to deny the patentee a process claim would deny him "the benefit of his real discovery, which might be applied in a dozen different ways." *Id.* at 72. Questions about the unpatentability of the "function of a machine" continued until the Court of Customs and Patent Appeals proclaimed the doctrine abolished in *In re Tarczy-Hornoch*, 397 F.2d 856 (C.C.P.A. 1968).

[135] *Corning*, 56 U.S. at 267–68. But the Court determined that Burden had disclosed and claimed a new machine, rather than a process. See *id.* at 268–69.

[136] *Mitchell v. Tilghman*, 86 U.S. 287, 392 (1873) (citing *Househill v. Neilson*).

mined that there was nothing in the patent to support the conclusion that the patentee was "the original and first inventor or discoverer of the scientific truth that such fatty and oily substances may be decomposed by high heat or water heated to a high temperature."[137] Tilghman's claim was therefore limited to the method and apparatus he had described in the specification. For the Court, "the characteristic conditions of the complainant's invention" included not only the steps and reaction conditions described in the patent, but the precise details of the machinery disclosed to carry it out.[138]

Seven years later, the Court reversed itself. In *Tilghman v. Proctor*, the Court unanimously concluded that Tilghman's patent was for the general process of manufacturing fatty acids by decomposing fats with water at high temperature and pressure, not for any specific mechanism for carrying that process out.[139] Justice Bradley's main support for this conclusion, and for the broader principle that a process claim could extend to all the modes and forms of apparatus by which the process might be applied, was *Neilson*. He noted that Tilghman's patent faced the same criticisms that had been leveled at Neilson's: that the particular apparatus disclosed in the specification was not well suited for large-scale industrial use.[140] More importantly, Bradley proposed that the Exchequer had sustained Neilson's patent as a patent for a process. In his view, Baron Parke's opinion "drew the true distinction between a mere principle, as the subject of a patent, and process by which a principle is applied to effect

---

[137] *Id.* at 392–93. The Court's inference that Tilghman would have been entitled to a broader patent if he had discovered the underlying "scientific truth" obviously challenges *Mayo*'s stance that patents should not be allowed to preempt all applications of the patentee's discovery.

[138] See *id.* at 416. These included the piston used to emulsify the fat, the strength and rating of the heating vessel, the pump used to introduce the emulsion into the heating vessel, the gauges for monitoring temperature, and the means for cooling the mixture as it exited the heating vessel.

[139] *Tilghman v. Proctor*, 102 U.S. 707, 710 (1880). The unanimous opinion in *Tilghman* was written by Justice Bradley, who had dissented in *Mitchell*. The majority opinion in *Mitchell* was written by Justice Clifford. Between *Mitchell* and *Tilghman* Bradley had written *Cochrane v. Deener*, 94 U.S. 780 (1876), which, like *Tilghman*, held that a claim to a process extended beyond the particular instrumentalities that the patentee had disclosed for carrying it out. *Id.* at 786–88. Clifford dissented in *Cochrane*, arguing that the change in instrumentalities employed by the defendant removed his process from the patent's ambit. By the time *Tilghman* was decided, Clifford was still on the Court, but was in severe mental decline and did not actively participate in any cases during the Court's October 1880 term. See David J. Garrow, *Mental Decrepitude on the U.S. Supreme Court: The Historical Case for a 28th Amendment*, 67 U. Chi. L. Rev. 995, 1006–1007 (2000).

[140] See *Tilghman*, 102 U.S. at 723.

a useful result."[141] The key was that a process might be claimed independently of form. Though Neilson could not have claimed the abstract principle that hot air was better than cold, having disclosed a process for applying that principle (heating the air in a vessel between the blowing apparatus and the furnace), "he was entitled to a patent for that process, although he did not distinctly point out all the forms of apparatus by which the process might be applied."[142] For Justice Bradley, the view that Neilson's patent was regarded as a process had been confirmed when *Househill* was appealed to the House of Lords. Lord Campbell, concurring with the Exchequer's construction in *Neilson*, had opined that Neilson's patent "must be taken to extend to all machines, of whatever construction, whereby the air is heated intermediately between the blowing apparatus and the blast furnace."[143] The lesson drawn from the hot-blast cases was therefore that an invention need not be limited to the particular mode or form of apparatus disclosed by the patentee, so long as the patentee had sufficiently described a mode or apparatus for carrying the process into effect.[144] *Tilghman* thus represented the final emancipation of process claims from their instrumentalities, and here too *Neilson* supplied the principle that invention might be independent of form.

5.c Enablement and *O'Reilly v. Morse*

The third major case where the Supreme Court was influenced by *Neilson*'s separation between invention and form was *O'Reilly v. Morse*,[145] the famous case involving Morse's patent on the telegraph. *O'Reilly* is remembered today for the Court's rejection of Morse's eighth claim, which attempted to embrace every use of electromagnetism for writing at a distance, without being limited to the apparatus disclosed in Morse's specification.[146]

Despite the Court's express statements that extending Morse's patent that far would violate the statutory requirement for an enabling disclosure,[147] some commentators have advanced the notion that *Morse* was a case decided

141 *Id.* at 724.

142 *Id.* at 724–25.

143 *Id.* at 725 (quoting *Househill v. Neilson*, 1 Webster's Patent Cases 673, 715 (1843)).

144 See *id.* at 728–29.

145 56 U.S. (15 How.) 62 (1854).

146 See *id.* at 86. The validity of the eighth claim was ultimately relevant only to the question of costs, since other claims in the patent were adjudged valid and infringed. *Id.* at 121, 123–24.

147 See *id.* at 118–19 (quoting the disclosure statute and stating that Morse's patent could only cover the invention or discovery for which he had described the manner and process of making and using it); *id.* at 120–21 (again quoting the disclosure statute

on patent-eligible subject matter grounds—the unpatentability of a law of nature—rather than a case decided on enablement.[148] That characterization of *Morse* was instrumental in the Supreme Court's construction of the *Mayo* framework for patent-eligibility, since the Supreme Court relied on it both for the assertion that restricting patentability of scientific discoveries was a long-established principle of its own jurisprudence,[149] as well as the policy justification that the enablement and written description requirements of 35 U.S.C. § 112 cannot adequately prevent patents from preempting the basic tools of scientific and technological advance.[150] And it was *Morse*—and *Morse*'s treatment of *Neilson* in particular—that provided the foundation for *Flook*'s supposition that the law historically had treated scientific discoveries and other fundamental principles as part of the prior art.[151]

But at the time *Morse* was decided, it had long been trite to state that laws of nature or other fundamental principles were not patentable in the abstract.[152] And Morse did not claim to have discovered electromagnetism, or any other

---

and holding that a disclaimer was required because Morse "claims what he has not described in the manner required by law").

[148] See, e.g., *Alice Corp. Pty. v. CLS Bank Int'l*, 573 U.S. 208, 216 (2014) (citing *Morse* for proposition that the Supreme Court has been interpreting 35 U.S.C. § 101 and its predecessors in light of an exception for fundamental principles for 150 years); *Mayo Collaborative Servs. v. Prometheus Labs., Inc.*, 566 U.S. 66, 71 (2012) (same); *Athena Diagnostics, Inc. v. Mayo Collaborative Servs.*, LLC, 927 F.3d 1333, 1341 (Fed. Cir. 2019) (Dyk, J., concurring in denial of rehearing en banc) (stating that *Morse* was "the foundation of the Court's jurisprudence on patent eligibility); Mark A. Lemley et al., *Life After Bilski*, 63 Stan. L. Rev. 1315, 1332–33 (2011) (arguing that *Morse* requires ineligibility of overly abstract claims); Sarnoff, *supra* note 7, at 67–68.

[149] See *Mayo*, 566 U.S. at 70–71; *Lab. Corp. of Am. Holdings v. Metabolite Labs., Inc.*, 548 U.S. 124, 126 (2006) (Breyer, J., dissenting from dismissal of cert. as improvidently granted); *Parker v. Flook*, 437 U.S. 584, 592 (1978).

[150] To dismiss the argument that § 112 could adequately constrain claim scope, *Mayo* cited commentary asserting, inter alia, that the concerns raised in *Morse* could not be addressed under § 112 because Morse had "taught the only way known *at the time* to use magnetism to print characters at a difference [sic, distance], so arguably he had satisfied the enablement standard as we understand it today." See *Mayo*, 566 U.S. at 90–91; Lemley et al., *supra* note 148, at 1332–33. That view is in tension with a long history of cases holding that, under § 112 or its predecessor statutes, an inventor is not entitled to claim all ways of carrying out an invention merely because he has taught the only way known at the time. See, e.g., *In re Hyatt*, 708 F.2d 712, 714–15 (Fed. Cir. 1983) (citing *Morse*); *Holland Furniture Co. v. Perkins Glue Co.*, 277 U.S. 245, 256–57 (1928) (citing *Morse*); *Béné v. Jeantet*, 129 U.S. 683, 686 (1889).

[151] See *Parker v. Flook*, 437 U.S. 584, 592 (1978) (citing *Morse*).

[152] See, e.g., *Whitney v. Emmett*, 29 F. Cas. 1074, 1078 (C.C.E.D. Pa. 1831) (Baldwin, J., charging the jury) ("Nor is a discovery of some new principle, theory, elementary truth, or an improvement upon it, abstracted from its application, a new invention").

scientific truth. The question in *Morse* was whether, having disclosed one practical application of electromagnetism to permit communication at a distance, Morse was entitled to claim more broadly than the mode and apparatus he disclosed. The hot-blast cases were Morse's principal support for his claim in his argument before the Court. [153] For if Neilson's patent could encompass the use of the hot blast independent of the particular machinery he invented, then why could Morse's patent not encompass any use of electromagnetism for writing at a distance, independent of the telegraph he had disclosed?

The Supreme Court was quite clear that Neilson's patent was not bound by the shape or form of his apparatus: "Neilson claimed no particular mode of constructing the receptacle, or of heating it. … The interposition of a heated receptacle, in any form, was the novelty he invented."[154] But the Court recognized a key distinction between Neilson's patent and Morse's. The critical fact was that Neilson's disclosure had *enabled* the practice of the hot blast beyond the simple apparatus he had disclosed. As the Court explained, in *Neilson* the jury had determined that one of ordinary skill in the art could construct a heating apparatus to practice the invention with beneficial effect "in all cases of forges, cupolas, and furnaces, where the blast is used."[155] Neilson, according to the Court, had disclosed enough to enable the universal application of his discovery, no matter what form of heating or blowing apparatus was employed.[156] That was not the case for Morse, whose invention depended upon "complicated and delicate machinery, adjusted and arranged upon philosophical principles, and prepared by the highest mechanical skill."[157] Unlike Neilson's heating vessel, Morse's telegraphic apparatus was not independent of form:

> For Neilson discovered, that by interposing a heated receptacle between the blower and the furnace, and conducting the current of air through it, the heat in the furnace was increased. And this effect was always produced, whatever might be the form of the receptacle, or the mechanical contrivances for heating it, or for passing the current of air through it, and into the furnace.
> But Professor Morse has not discovered, that the electric or galvanic current will always print at a distance, no matter what may be the form of the machinery or mechanical contrivances through which it passes. You may use electro-magnetism

153 See *Morse*, 56 U.S. at 114 (stating that the hot-blast cases were "those most relied on, and pressed upon the court, in behalf of the patentee").
154 *Id.* at 115–16.
155 *Id.* at 115.
156 See *id.* at 116 ("For whatever form was adopted for the receptacle, or whatever mechanical arrangements were made for heating it, the effect would be produced in a greater or less degree …").
157 *Id.* at 117.

> as a motive power, and yet not produce the described effect, that is, print at a distance intelligible marks or signs.[158]

The Court's contrast between Neilson's discovery and Morse's discovery permits us to understand the true nature of *Morse*. Morse's claim was not rejected because the Court treated electromagnetism as part of the prior art, or because Morse's eighth claim lacked an inventive application of electromagnetism. It was rejected because Morse's disclosure did not enable the practice of his invention apart from form.[159] The Court's later glosses on *Morse* in *Tilghman* and *The Telephone Cases* would rely on that distinction between those inventions that were bound to form, and those that were not. Thus in *Tilghman*, the Court extended Tilghman's claim beyond his apparatus because, in contrast to *Morse*, his specification disclosed a general mode for carrying out a process independent of a particular apparatus.[160] And in *The Telephone Cases*, the Court explained that, unlike Morse, Bell had not claimed the use of electricity apart from the process disclosed in his patent.[161] Bell's patent would therefore be sustained, even though it might practically preempt the use of electricity for the transmission of speech.[162]

To understand *Neilson*, then, is to understand *Morse*. American law, like English law, had long recognized the unpatentability of scientific discoveries and other principles in the abstract; *Morse* added nothing new to that maxim. The Court in *Morse* was certainly concerned about patents preempting future innovation, but the Court did not treat fundamental principles as well-known, nor did it demand that patentees apply their discoveries by new or inventive means. Rather, it simply embraced the statutory requirement for disclosure as the guard against patents unduly impeding technological progress. An inventor like Neilson, whose disclosure enabled the practice of his invention beyond his

---

[158] *Id.* at 116–17.

[159] The Court expressly grounded its decision on Morse's failure to satisfy the disclosure provisions of the 1836 Act, which, like current 35 U.S.C. § 112, required the inventor to provide a written description sufficient to enable one of ordinary skill in the art to make and use the claimed invention. See *id.* at 118–20.

[160] See *Tilghman*, 102 U.S. at 725–29 (emphasizing that Morse had not described or claimed a process for employing electromagnetism beyond his apparatus).

[161] See *Dolbear v. Am. Bell Tel. Co.*, 126 U.S. 1, 534 (1888) ("The effect of that decision [*Morse*] was, therefore, that the use of magnetism as a motive power, without regard to the particular process with which it was connected in the patent, could not be claimed, but that its use in that connection could").

[162] See *id.* at 535 (explaining Bell's ability to practically preempt the use of electricity "will, if true, show more clearly the great importance of his discovery, but it will not invalidate his patent").

instrumentalities, was entitled to claim broadly; an inventor like Morse, whose invention could not transcend form, was not.

6. CONCLUSION

If there was a received scripture for American patent law, it came from across the Atlantic. Many of the basic contours of American patent law took shape in the mid to late nineteenth century. In that formative period, American jurists still looked to England for the truths of patent law—and particularly to *Neilson* to delineate when an invention might transcend shape and form. American courts relied on *Neilson* and the other hot-blast cases to resolve the boundary between abstract principles and patentable inventions, the infringement of after-arising technologies, and the patentability of processes apart from their instrumentalities.

But it seems that patent law never settles its basic truths. After decades of relative obscurity, the Supreme Court has turned again to *Neilson* to draw the boundary between discovery and invention. But the story of *Neilson* has become quite different in the Court's telling. Where *Neilson* once stood for the patentability of practical applications of discoveries, now it has become the case that denies it. Where *Neilson* once stood against a requirement for inventive application, now it has become the case that demands it.

Neilson has thus become a palimpsest of patent law. Each new generation of interpreters, seeking an authority whose "correctness has never been doubted or denied," has rewritten *Neilson*'s meaning to serve its own ends. *Neilson* laid down the principle that invention was independent of form, so long as the inventor's principle could be discerned in the embodiment. It is perhaps ironic that the case has become the vessel for so many different principles of patent law embodied in the same unchanging text.

PART III

THE LORE OF AUTHORSHIP

5. The stolen poem of Saint Moling

Brian L. Frye[1]

I do not know the tongue my fathers spoke,
I cannot sing the songs my fathers sang.
I cannot read the books my fathers wrote;
Treasure on treasure in my hungry hands:
I cannot read a word.[2]

1. INTRODUCTION

It's a truism of copyright scholarship that the modern concept of the author didn't exist until the modern era.[3] The medieval and Renaissance author was a vehicle for the text, but the modern author is the creator of the text. And in the eighteenth century, the Romantic Movement transformed authorship into self-expression. This individualization of authorship enabled the creation of copyright. While the printing press made commercial publishing possible, the modern concept of the author created "literary property."

But is the truism entirely true? The concept of the author has certainly changed over time, and taken different forms in different places at different times. But is the modern concept of the author truly unique to the modern era, or does it merely reflect a particular literary economy? In other words, did our

1 Thanks to University of Kentucky College of Law librarians Beau Steenken, Franklin Runge, Carol Skricki, and Michel Yang for their indispensable assistance on this project. Special thanks to Patrick Kabat and Morgan Davies for introducing me to the story of St. Moling.

2 Pádraig Ó Broin, *Disinherited.* See Professor O'Looney, On the Book of Leinster and its Contents, 1 Proceedings of the Royal Irish Academy. Polite Literature and Antiquities 367–378 (1879); http://www.maryjones.us/ctexts/leinster.html (full text of Book of Leinster).

3 See, e.g., Martha Woodmansee, The Genius and the Copyright: Economic and Legal Conditions of the Emergence of the "Author", 17 Eighteenth-Century Studies 425 (1984) and Peter Jaszi, Toward a Theory of Copyright: The Metamorphoses of "Authorship", 1991 Duke L.J. 455 (1991). But see, e.g., Simon Stern, Copyright, Originality, and the Public Domain in Eighteenth-Century England, in *Originality and Intellectual Property in the French and English Enlightenment* 69–101 (Reginald McGinnis ed., 2009).

concept of the author create our literary economy, or did our literary economy shape our concept of the author? Surely, the answer is a bit of both. But a medieval Irish legend at least suggests that the modern concept of the author is only a particular expression of an economic phenomenon.

2. LITERARY OWNERSHIP IN IRISH LEGEND

Copyright scholars with an antiquarian bent often puckishly refer to the Irish legend of the Battle of the Book as the "first copyright litigation." Supposedly, sometime in the sixth century, Saint Columcille borrowed a book from Saint Finnian, and copied it without permission. When Finnian caught Columcille, he demanded the copy, but Columcille refused. They agreed to let Diarmait mac Cerbaill, the King of Tara, resolve their dispute. He ruled, "To every cow its calf, to every book its copy," and awarded the copy to Finnian. Often forgotten is that Columcille rejected the king's ruling, and raised an army to reclaim the copy by force.

Of course, everyone knows that the story of the Battle of the Book has no basis in historical fact. But it remains a popular anecdote on the origins of literary ownership, introduced by Augustine Birrell in 1899, popularized by Thomas Cahill in 1995, and even recognized by the Supreme Court in 2012.[4] Why ruin a good story? After all, "When the legend becomes fact, print the legend."[5]

In fact, the story of the Battle of the Book had nothing to do with copyright or literary ownership. On the contrary, it was created in 1532 by Manus O'Donnell, Lord of Tyrconnell, in order to legitimize *An Cathatch* or "The Battler," a *cumdach* or "book shrine" belonging to the O'Donnell clan that supposedly enclosed Columcille's copied book and guaranteed the O'Donnells victory in battle.[6]

---

4 Augustine Birrell, *Seven Lectures on the Law and History of Copyright in Books* (1899); Thomas Cahill, *How The Irish Saved Civilization: The Untold Story of Ireland's Heroic Role from the Fall of Rome to the Rise of Medieval Europe* (1995); *Golan v. Holder*, 132 S. Ct. 873, 902 (2012) (Breyer, J., dissenting) (observing that the "natural rights" theory of copyright "mythically stems from a legendary 6th-century statement of King Diarmed 'to every cow her calf, and accordingly to every book its copy'").

5 *The Man Who Shot Liberty Valance* (1962).

6 See Brian L. Frye, *Saint Columcille and the Mythical Origins of Copyright* (forthcoming). An Cathatch was given to the Royal Irish Academy in 1842. The book found inside the *cumdach* is the oldest known Irish manuscript, a psalter written in the sixth century. The book is in the Royal Irish Academy, RIA MS 12 R 33, and the *cumdach* is in the National Museum of Ireland. NMI R2835.

Ironically, the manuscript in which the story appeared, O'Donnell's *Life of Columcille*, includes an intriguing claim of literary ownership. In the preface to the *Life*, O'Donnell states that he personally compiled it from many sources and dictated it to his scribes.[7] Assertions of authorship were still quite unusual in the early sixteenth century, especially in relation to hagiographic texts.[8]

O'Donnell didn't claim literary ownership for the purpose of copyright, a concept that didn't exist in Ireland or England at the time.[9] Rather, he wanted attribution in order to associate himself with the text and the saint it celebrated. For centuries, the O'Donnell and O'Neill clans had fought for dominance of the Northern Uí Néill kingdoms. O'Donnell wrote his *Life of Columcille*, at considerable personal effort and expense, in order to bolster his political legitimacy. And he was at least temporarily successful, as the leader of the Geraldine League in its short-lived challenge to English rule in Ireland. In other words, O'Donnell didn't want to own a work of authorship, he wanted to control a country.

But a different Irish legend suggests that another concept of literary ownership existed in medieval Ireland, which did resemble copyright. Supposedly, in the seventh century, the King of Leinster asked Saint Moling to end the *bórama*, a crippling tax the kings of Tara had imposed on Leinster for many

---

7 Manus O'Donnell, *Life of Columcille* 7 (1532) (O'Kelleher and Schoepperle eds. 1918).

> And be it known to the readers of this *Life* that it was Manus O'Donnell son of Aed son of Aed Ruadh son of Niall Garbh son of Toirdelbach of the Wine that bade put into Gaelic the part of this *Life* that was in Latin, and bade make easy the part thereof that was hard Gaelic, to the end it might be clear and easy of understanding to all.
>
> And he collected and assembled the part thereof that was scattered throughout the ancient books of Erin, and he set it forth with his own lips. And passing great labor had he therewith. And much time did he give thereto, conning how he might put each part thereof in its own fitting place as it is writ here below.
>
> And having conceived the affection and the love of a brother for his high saint and kinsman by lineage and his dear patron that he was bounden to in steadfast devotion.
>
> In the castle of Port Na Tri Namat in sooth this *Life* was put together in the year that twelve and a score and fifteen hundred years were fulfilled from the birth of our Lord.

The original manuscript is in the Bodleian Library, Oxford University. Rawlinson B. 514.

8 See Brian Lacey, *Saint Columba: His Life and Legacy* 204 (2013).

9 William Caxton brought the first printing press to England in 1476. While Henry VIII granted the first English printing patent to Richard Pynson in 1510, the concept of "rights in copies" was created by the Stationers' Company after it was chartered by Mary I in 1557. Humphrey Powell introduced printing to Ireland in 1551, but the concept of copyright didn't follow until long afterwards.

centuries. In exchange for remission of the tax, Moling wrote a poem for the King of Tara and taught it to his bard, who would recite it for the King. But when Moling and his retinue left for Tara, the bard stole ahead and recited the poem for the King of Tara as his own.

When Moling arrived at Tara and recited his poem, the King accused him of plagiarizing the bard. Moling responded by ordering the bard to recite the poem again. The bard could speak only gibberish, proving that Moling was the true author, so the King apologized to Moling and suspended the tax.

The story of Moling's stolen poem also has no basis in historical fact. It was probably created in the eleventh century, as part of an explanation of why the Uí Néill were not entitled to tax Leinster. But it reflects embedded assumptions about authorship, attribution, and literary ownership.

The story made sense only because medieval Irish poets observed an anti-plagiarism rule, as part of the broader set of rules governing the "poetic economy." In medieval Ireland, poets were effectively a professional class. They enjoyed special legal rights and observed special professional rules. Among other things, poets could demand compensation for their poems, but only if their poems satisfied the professional rules of composition. One of those rules prohibited plagiarism, meaning that a plagiarized poem was worthless. As a consequence, poetry was always attributed and could not be changed, while prose was often anonymous and could be changed.

Of course, these rules were often observed in the breach. But they were rules nonetheless, and they effectively governed the medieval Irish literary economy. They show that medieval Irish poets developed an idea of authorship and concept of literary ownership adapted to the literary economy in which they practiced. And they suggest that different medieval societies may have different ideas of authorship and concepts of literary ownership that we do not yet fully understand.

3. SAINT MOLING AND THE *BÓRAMA* LEGEND

Saint Moling supposedly lived from 614 to 697.[10] He founded a monastery at St. Mullins, County Carlow and became the second Bishop of Ferns. Because of the poems attributed to him, he is also considered one of the great prophets of Ireland.[11] He also became the patron saint of the Kings of Leinster.

---

10 Alternative spellings of Moling's name include Mo Ling, Mo-Ling, Molling, Mullin, and Mullins. He was also known as Moling Luachra or "Moling of the Rushes."

11 See John Healy, *Insula Sanctorum et Doctorum Or, Ireland's Ancient Schools and Scholars* 429 (1912).

> St. Moling is said to have been a great scholar, and a great writer. More ancient Irish poems, several of which are still extant, have been ascribed to St. Moling

Information about Moling is preserved in many different manuscript sources, but the most important texts are *The Birth and Life of Saint Moling*, which is a hagiography, and the *Bórama*, which is the story of a cattle tax the Kings of Tara imposed on Leinster.[12] Both texts explain how Moling convinced the King of Tara to end the cattle tax, but provide different accounts. Among other things, only the *Bórama* tells the story of Moling's stolen poem.

3.a *The Birth and Life of Saint Moling*

The Birth and Life of Saint Moling is preserved in two manuscripts, and provides the most comprehensive account of Moling's life.[13] The oldest is a vellum manuscript written in 1437–40, which is part of the *Liber Flavus Fergussiorum* ("Yellow Book of the Ó Fearghuis").[14] The other is a paper manuscript written by Michael O'Clery in 1628–29.[15] O'Clery copied his manuscript from the *Leabhar Tighe Molling* ("Book of Timulling"), which is now lost.[16] In 1907, Whitley Stokes published an English translation, which was based on both manuscripts.

Moling was born in 614, in the Luachair ("rushland") near Castleisland, County Kerry. His father was Fáelán the Fair, a prosperous landowner, and his mother was Emnait, the beautiful sister of Fáelán's wife, who Fáelán seduced and impregnated. Afraid and ashamed, Emnait secretly fled, and headed home to the Cenél Siatnai in Bréifne, hiding by day, and walking at night.

One night, as Emnait was walking through the Luachair, there was a blizzard, and she gave birth to a son. Angels came and melted the snow around

---

> than to any other of our Irish saints, with the exception, perhaps, of Columcille. Some of these have reference to that Borromean Tribute of which we have already spoken; others purporting to be prophetical, give a list of the kings of Erin, their battles, victories, and death. In consequence of these and several other prophetical poems, St. Moling has been set down as one of the four great prophets of Erin. The others are St. Patrick, St. Columcille, and St. Berchan of Clonsast.

See also Whitley Stokes, *The Birth and Life of St. Mo Ling* 57 n.3 (1907) ("He was one of the four prophets of Ireland.").

12 The Codex Kilkenniensis (Armachanus) includes a fifteenth-century Life of St. Moling written in Latin. It is in Archbishop Marsh's Library, Dublin. MS Z 3.1.5.

13 Whitley Stokes, *The Birth and Life of St. Mo Ling* (1907).

14 The *Liber Flavus Fergussiorum* is in the collection of the Royal Irish Academy. RIA MS 23 O 48 a–b.

15 The O'Clery manuscript is in the collection of the Royal Library of Belgium. Brussels, Bibliothèque Royale de Belgique. MS 4190–4200.

16 Whitley Stokes relied on both of these manuscripts, as well as other manuscript fragments, in preparing his version of the legend. See Whitley Stokes, *The Birth and Life of St. Mo Ling* (1907).

the child, but Emnait was ashamed of him. In the morning, Emnait tried to kill her son, but God sent a dove to protect him. Saint Brénainn saw the angels, and sent his priest Collanach to investigate. Collanach baptized the child and named him Tairchell, based on the *tairchellad* ("surrounding") the dove used to protect him. Then, Collanach brought Emnait and Tairchell back to Saint Brénainn's church, *Uam Brénainn* ("Brenann's Cave"), and fostered Tairchell, who became his best student.

Eventually, Tairchell left to travel the Luachair and collect alms for the church. One day, Tairchell encountered the Evil Spectre and his retinue. They were about to fight, by staff and spear, when Tairchell asked the Spectre "to let me have my three steps of pilgrimage towards the King of heaven and earth, and my three steps of folly also, so that death may be the further from me." The Spectre agreed, "for you will never get away from us, since we ourselves are as swift as wild deer, and our hound is as swift as the wind." But in three leaps, Tairchell crossed the Luachair and returned to the church. When Tairchell told Collanach what had happened, he responded, "You are the prophesied one, whom the angel Victor foretold: You will be called Moling of Luachair from the leaps that you have leapt."[17] Apparently, an angel had visited Saint Brénainn 30 years earlier and predicted Moling.

Collanach sent Moling to study with Saint Máedóc of Ferns at Clúain Cáin Maedóc ("Pleasant Meadow"), who recognized Moling's holiness. Then Moling traveled to Cashel, where the King of Munster, Fingen Mac Aed, promised to give him land for a church. But an angel appeared to Moling, and told him to build his church by the River Barrow. Fingen agreed, and Moling traveled to Sliab Mairgi ("Slieve-Margy" or "Mount Sorrow"), from which he saw a host of angels over the Point of Ross Bruicc ("Badger's Wood").[18] When Moling found a hearth built by Saint Brénainn, he chose Ross Bruicc for his church, Teach Moling ("House of Moling") (see Figure 5.1).

Even after building his church, Moling continued to wander and cause unusual miracles. In one especially peculiar episode, he offered aid to a leper, who became the Christ child:

> Thereafter as Moling was wending his way he saw before him a hideous misshapen leper. "Whence comest thou, O cleric?" says the leper. "I come out of the wood," replies the cleric. "For God's sake, take me with thee to the church." "I am willing," says Moling: "come on then," says he. "In what manner?" asked the leper. "As

---

17 "Lingis" means "leap" and "moling" means "quick leaper."

18 Eugene O'Curry, *Lectures on the manuscript materials of ancient Irish history, delivered at the Catholic University of Ireland during the sessions of 1855 and 1856* 302–303 (1861), https://archive.org/details/lecturesonmanus00ocur/page/302/mode/2up.

Figure 5.1 *Ruins of Saint Moling's monastery, St. Mullins, County Carlow*

Source: Moling's Monastery at St. Mulins, County Carlow: public domain postcard on file with the author.

thou camest hither," says Moling. "I cannot travel," says the leper, "till I get myself carried comfortably." "Come on my back then," said Moling. "I will not go," says the leper, "lest there be some of thy raiment between me and thee, for the raiment will leave none of my skin upon me." "I will do what thou desirest," says Moling, so he doffs his clothes and lifts the leper on his back. "Blow my nose," says the leper. Moling gives his hand to him to blow it. "Nay!" says the leper, "for thy fingers will strip my skin off: put thy mouth round it." The cleric puts his mouth round the nose and sucks it to him, and spits that mucus into his left hand.

When he looked a look past him he knew not whether the leper had gone into heaven or into earth. "This is right," says Moling, "if my Lord came to deceive me. I will neither sleep nor eat until my Lord comes to me clearly and evidently." He then remained in that place till midnight. Then the angel came to him and said: "In what form wouldst thou prefer thy Lord to come and hold speech with thee?" "In the guise of a boy of seven years," says Moling, "so that I may make transports of fondness around Him." He noticed nothing at the end of a time afterwards till Christ sat on his lap in the shape of a boy of seven years, and he was fondling Him till the hour of rising on the morrow. "If thou deemest that enough," says the angel, "get thee to thy monastery."[19]

[19] Whitley Stokes, *The Birth and Life of St. Mo Ling* (1907).

Eventually, Moling became the religious leader of the Laigin. When the Laigin and the Uí Néill decided to create boundaries between their lands, the Laigin asked Moling to represent them. Moling stated that the boundary would be wherever the gathering occurred, and immediately set out traveling. The Uí Néill tried to ambush Moling, but he evaded them. Moling crossed the Righe ("Rye Water") and waited for the Uí Néill at Suide Moling ("Moling's Seat"), which became the border, greatly expanding the size of Leinster.

Later, Fínnachta Fledach mac Dúnchada of the Uí Néill became the High King of Tara. For many generations, the Uí Néill had forced the Laigin to pay a *bórama* or cattle tax. But according to prophecy, a priest would end the *bórama*. Moling visited the kings of the Uí Néill and asked them to suspend the tax. Initially, they refused, but Fínnachta eventually agreed to suspend the tax until "Luan," or "Monday."

Soon afterward, Moling visited Fínnachta at Tara. When Fínnachta's son fell ill and died, Moling resurrected him. Then Moling asserted that Fínnachta had agreed to suspend the *bórama* until "Monday of Doomsday." Fínnachta agreed, and Moling recited a praise poem in his honor.

Saint Adamnán, the religious leader of the Uí Néill, was infuriated by the end of the *bórama*, and sent soldiers to catch and kill Moling. But the saints hid Moling in a dark mist, and the soldiers could not find him. When Moling could hide no longer, the saints confused the soldiers, so they killed each other.

Moling eventually died in 696, and was buried at his monastery in St. Mullins.

3.b The *Bórama* Legend

An bhoramha Laighean ("The Leinster cattle-tribute"), typically referred to as the *Bórama* or *Bóruma*, is the foundational legend of Leinster. The full text of the *Bórama* is preserved in two manuscript collections, the *Lebor Laignech* or "Book of Leinster" (Figure 5.2) and the *Leabhar Mór Mhic Fhir Bhisigh Leacain* or "Great Book of Lecan." Part 2 of the *Bórama, Cath Belaig Dúin Bolg* or "Battle of Dunbolg" is also preserved in the *Leabhar Buidhe Lecain* or "Yellow Book of Lecan" and in a vellum manuscript. Whitley Stokes and Standish Hayes O'Grady both published translations of the *Bórama* in 1892.[20]

The Book of Leinster is one of the most important sources of medieval Irish literature. The manuscripts in the Book of Leinster, including its version of the *Bórama*, were probably written between 1151 and 1201 by Áed Ua Crimthainn

---

[20] Whitley Stokes, The Boroma, 12 Revue Celtique 32 (1892). Standish Hayes O'Grady, *2 Silva Gadelica: A Collection of Tales in Irish with Extracts Illustrating Persons and Places* 401 (1892).

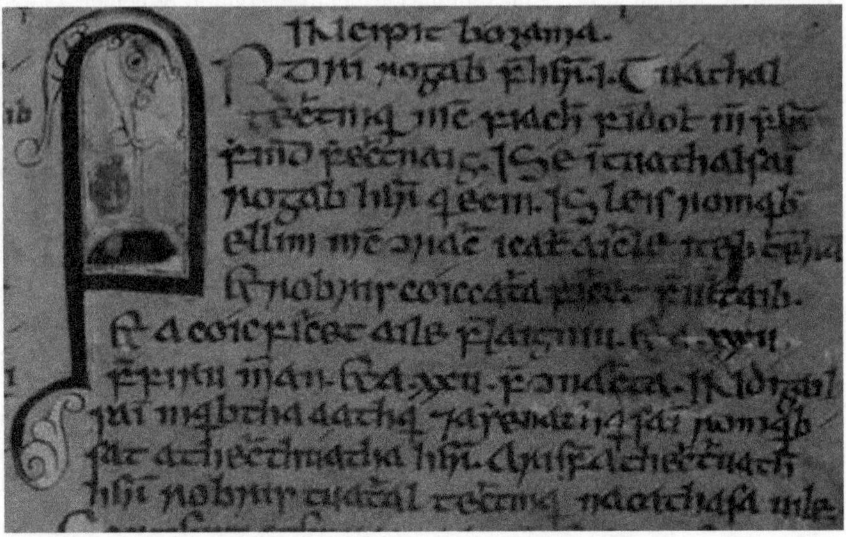

Figure 5.2 The beginning of the Bórama

Source: The Book of Leinster, Trinity College Dublin, MS 1339, folio 294.

and his students, primarily at the monastery of Tír dá Glas or Terryglass in County Tipperary. The book may have been commissioned by Diarmait Mac Murchada.[21]

The Great Book of Lecan is essentially a copy of the Book of Leinster. It was written in 1417–18 by Gilla Ísu Mac Fir Bisich and his students Adam Ó Cuirnín and Murchad Riabach Ó Cuindlis in Lecan, near Enniscrone in County Sligo. It was commissioned by Ruaidri Uí Dubda, King of the Uí Fiachrach, and delivered to Tadg Riabach, his brother and successor.[22]

The Yellow Book of Lecan is a collection of 17 manuscripts that Edward Lhuyd bound together in about 1700. The version of the Battle of Dunbolg included in the book was probably written between 1398 and 1417 by Gilla Ísa Mac Donnchaid Mhóir Mhic Fhir Bhisigh and his students, and was probably copied from the Book of Leinster. The Yellow Book of Lecan also includes the *Cath Almaine* or "Battle of Allen," which is generally considered the

21 The Book of Leinster is housed at Trinity College Dublin. H 2.18, 1339.
22 The Great Book of Lecan is held at the Royal Irish Academy. MS 23 P 2.

"sequel" to the *Bórama*, because it explains how the Uí Néill tried to reinstate the *bórama*.[23]

The *bórama* ("cattle-tribute") was a legendary tax the Uí Néill imposed on the Laigin.[24] The *Bórama* tells the story of the *bórama* in three parts. Part 1 explains why Túathal Techtmar imposed the *bórama* on the Laigin. Part 2 describes Laigin resistance to the Uí Néill and the *bórama*. And part 3 recounts how Moling ended the *bórama*.

3.b.I Part 1: the origin of the *Bórama*

The *Bórama* legend begins at the end of the first century, when Túathal Techtmar returned from exile, conquered all the tribes of Ireland, and became the High King of Tara. Túathal had two daughters. The elder was Fithir and the younger was Dáirine. Eochu, the King of Leinster, married Fithir. But when they returned to Leinster, people said he should have married Dáirine. So Eochu returned to Tara, told Túathal that Fithir had died, and asked to marry Dáirine. Túathal agreed. But when Eochu returned to Leinster with Dáirine and the sisters saw each other, Fithir died of shame and Dáirine died of grief.

When Túathal learned of Eochu's treachery and the death of his daughters, he was furious, and led the armies of Tara, Ulster, and Connacht into battle against Leinster. Eochu was killed and Túathal prevailed. Eventually, Leinster agreed to pay an *éraic*, to compensate Túathal for the death of his daughters.[25] The *éraic* consisted of:

- 15,000 cows
- 15,000 pigs
- 15,000 mantles
- 15,000 silver chains
- 15,000 wethers
- A brass cauldron large enough to hold 12 pigs and 12 calves

---

[23] The Yellow Book of Lecan is held at Trinity College Dublin. MS TCD H 2.16. The Battle of Dunbolg is also preserved in a fifteenth-century vellum manuscript held at the Royal Irish Academy. MS D iv 2 (992), ff. 86ra–87vb.

[24] *Bórama* is a compound of the words *bó* ("cattle") and *rím* ("counting"). *Dictionary of the Irish Language* 79 (E.G. Quin ed. Dublin, 2007). Whitley Stokes, The Boroma, 13 Revue Celtique 32 (1892). https://babel.hathitrust.org/cgi/pt?id=mdp.39015039641348&view=1up&seq=9.

[25] An *éraic* was a payment to compensate for a crime, analogous to the Welsh *galanas* and the Anglo-Saxon *weregild*. See *Ancient Laws and Institutes of Ireland* (Senchus Mor) xlix (1865).

- 30 white, red-eared cows and their calves, with bronze ties, tethers, and milk pails.[26]

The *éraic* became known as the *bórama*, because it consisted primarily of cows.[27] Túathal eventually died in the battle of Moin-an-chatha in Dál nAraidi, but his successors continued to levy the *bórama*, albeit with mixed success, as the Laigin often refused to pay until they were defeated in battle.

3.b.II Part 2: the Battle of Dunbolg

Áed mac Ainmerech of the Cenél Conaill became the High King of Tara in 568, and collected the *bórama* twice, with no objection from the Laigin. Then, in 593, Áed's son Cummascach asked to make a *sáerchuairt* or "free circuit of youth," in which he would visit every Irish kingdom and sleep with the wife of every king. His father agreed, and he set out, with four battalions of soldiers.

Brandub mac Echach, the King of Leinster, objected to the free circuit. When Cummascach approached Leinster, Brandub instructed the Laigin to house his soldiers individually and kill them. Cummascach himself visited Brandub's home at *Bealach Conglais* ("Baltinglass"), accompanied by one battalion of soldiers.

Cummascach occupied Brandub's home. But Brandub disguised himself as a slave, and his wife tricked Cummascach into letting her escape. Then Brandub provided Cummascach and his soldiers with a great feast, locked the doors of his home, and burned it to the ground. Cummascach barely escaped with his life, only to be beheaded by a Laigin soldier.

Brandub sent word to Áed that he had killed Cummascach and all of his soldiers. Áed responded by raising a great army and marching it to Leinster, to avenge Cummascach and levy the *bórama*. When they arrived, Brandub asked for a truce to gather his army, but Áed refused and made camp at Cell Bélat, so Brandub set an ambush. In the meantime, the Ulaid broke from the Uí Néill and secretly allied with the Laigin, and Brandub defeated the Uí Néill champion in single combat.

As the battle approached, Áed asked for Saint Columcille's cowl, which would protect him, but his servant had forgotten to bring it. Under cover of night, Brandub sent wagons of food to the Uí Néill, concealing his soldiers

---

[26] A *bratt* or "mantle" was a form of unshaped outerwear, resembling a cloak. A *molt* or "wether" was a castrated sheep or goat. In ancient Ireland, white cattle with red ears were highly prized and associated with the supernatural. Jessica Hemming, "Bos Primigenius" in Britain: Or, Why Do Fairy Cows Have Red Ears?, 113 Folklore 71 (2002).

[27] Cows were the primary form of wealth in medieval Ireland. See generally, A.T. Lucas, *Cattle in Ancient Ireland* (1989).

underneath. When the Uí Néill let the wagons into their camp, the Laigin soldiers burst out and slaughtered them. Áed fled the slaughter, but the Laigin caught and beheaded him, and presented his head to Brandub.

And yet, despite Leinster's great victory, the High Kings of Tara continued to levy the *bórama*.

3.b.III Part 3: Saint Moling and the end of the *Bórama*

Fínnachta Fledach mac Dúnchada became the High King of Tara in 675, and levied the *bórama* twice, with no objection from the Laigin. But when he levied it a third time, in 693, the Laigin refused to pay, so Fínnachta raised a great army and marched it to Leinster.

Bran mac Conaill, the King of Leinster, likewise raised an army. But he also summoned Saint Moling, because a prophecy held that a saint would end the *bórama* by repeatedly asking the High King of Tara to end it. Moling agreed to ask Fínnachta to end the *bórama*, and composed a praise-poem, which he invited the poet Tollchenn ("Hole-head") of Cluain Ena to recite for Fínnachta.

En route to Fínnachta, Moling and Tollchenn spent the night with Cobthach mac Colman of the Uí Faelain, who provided a feast in their honor. But Cobthach's poets ridiculed Tollchenn for following a priest. Tollchenn invited them to follow him instead, and they all snuck off to Fínnachta's house, where Tollchenn recited Moling's poem and claimed it as his own.

The next morning, Moling saw that Tollchenn and the poets had left and said, "The man of poetry has run away with my eulogy, and will sell it as his own to the king of Erin." But he still set off for Fínnachta's house. Along the way, Fínnachta's son Donngilla and his friends threw dirt, rocks, and other junk at Moling, but he ignored them and pressed on. And when Moling arrived at Fínnachta's house, most of the nobles ignored him.

In the meantime, Donngilla and his friends were hunting a stag, and Dongilla was killed by a stray spear, because he had dishonored Moling. Fínnachta asked Moling to resurrect Donngilla, and promised him a reward:

> "Bring the boy to life, O cleric," says Fínnachta, "and thou shalt have a reward therefor."
> "For my poem," says Molling, "and for bringing thy son to life, and for giving heaven to thyself, I ask nought save a truce as to the Boroma till *Luán*."
> "That shalt thou have," says the king.[28]

---

[28] Whitley Stokes, The Boroma, 12 Revue Celtique 32 (1892).

So, Moling recited his praise-poem, *Fínnachta a Huíb Néill* or "Fínnachta of the Ui Néill":

Fínnachta of the Ui Néill,
Rose like the sun.
He is the ship above the wave,
He is the wave over the shore.

He is the battle on the land
Because of which kings do not dare to attack;
He is the king of Tara who [tíath],[29]
He is the king to whom comes their benefit.

He is a tide of violence against fury,
He is the wave inside and outside;
He is the king of Tara in the north,
He is the harsh iron before the battle.

He is the heart of Cerna of Conn,
The royal tree of Tara, force against force.
He is the Fínnachta who isn't weak,
He is the tree of the lustrous vineyard.

It is heard by the old ones here,
It is better praising than every honor,
Who knows noble Fínnachta,
Not as long as the wealth remains.

The wealth goes into possession of everyone,
of the race of Adam for a short time.
A danger on each one, under the high heaven,
goes past each in the small world.

Coirpre and Cormac and Art,
Conn who reached the royal beds.
Although they took Tara strongly,
according to me, Fínnachta is better.[30]

When Moling finished reciting the poem, Fínnachta accused him of plagiarising Tollchenn, who had previously recited the same poem: "Worse and worse we deem thy design," said the king, "now that thou tellest a lie: inasmuch as the poem that Tollchenn the bard made, thou sellest for thine own."[31] But Moling

29 Apparently, "tíath" is an untranslatable word.

30 Whitley Stokes, The Boroma, 12 Revue Celtique 32 (1892).

31 Standish Hayes O'Grady, The Boromean Tribute in *Silva Gadelica* (1892) at 301, 421, https://play.google.com/store/books/details?id=gM84AQAAMAAJ&rdid=book-gM84AQAAMAAJ&rdot=1.

responded, "If he it be that made it, let him stand up and sing his duan."[32] And when Tollchenn tried to recite the poem again, he could speak only gibberish, proving that he had lied:

Dríbor drábor
cerca is cábail.
lachain odra.
lodra lomna áraig.

Clocha Eóre
datha déne.
benna Cuailnge
buaidre céille.

Ciall ar esbaid
grian ard uismid.
gaeth na sidi
Liffi lusmair.

Mo Lling lúamnech
lúam na fírbreth.
feidm tend tréorach
ic deilb fírbreth.

Misse romom
co muir mideng.
ticfa thorom
grogoll triball.

Messe imbárach
co muir mílach.
D'Ess Rúaid rámach
iar n-úaim trílech. D.[33]

---

[32] *Id.*

[33] There is no complete English translation of this poem, and a complete translation may be impossible. Typically, the first two words are translated as "dribble drabble," and the rest of the poem is omitted. Stokes described the poem as, "Mere nonsense, and intended as such." Whitley Stokes, The Boroma, 12 Revue Celtique 32, 107 n.3 (1892). Many of the words in the poem appear to be meaningless gibberish. But at least some of the words are meaningful and can be translated. Eyjolfsdottir translated the stanza, "Mo Lling lúamnech / Lúam na fírbreth / Feidm tend tréorach / Ic deilb fírbreth" as "Fluttering Moling / steersman of just judgement / strong energetic undertaking / by the figure of the just judgement." And she translated the stanza, "Messe imbárach / co muir mílach. / d'Ess Rúaid rámach / iar n-úaim trílech" as "I, tomorrow / towards the abounding sea. / To rowing Assaroe / after composing a poem (trilling)." Elin Ingibjorg Eyjolfsdottir, *The Bórama: The Poetry and the Hagiography in the Book of Leinster* 85–86 (2012) (unpublished dissertation).

After reciting this nonsense poem, Tollchenn was mortified by shame and ran all the way to Tirconnell, where he drowned himself in Assaroe Falls (see Figures 5.3 and 5.4).[34]

Figure 5.3 *Assaroe Falls (1908)*

Source: Assaroe Falls (1908): public domain postcard on file with the author. Image also available at https://en.wikipedia.org/wiki/Assaroe_Falls.

Fínnachta apologized to Moling for accusing him of plagiarism, asked him to resurrect Donngilla, and promised him everything he wanted. So Moling resurrected Donngilla, Fínnachta suspended the *bórama*, and Moling left for home.

Saint Adomnán was furious when he learned that Fínnachta had suspended the *bórama*. He went to Fínnachta's home and demanded a meeting, but Fínnachta was playing a game (probably draughts or checkers) and ignored him. Adomnán threatened Fínnachta with a series of increasingly severe curses, until Fínnachta finally put the game away and met with Adomnán, who explained Moling's deceit. Moling asked Fínnachta to suspend the *bórama* until *Luán* or "Monday," but he meant the Monday of Doomsday. Unless

[34] Assaroe Falls or Cathaleen's Falls was a waterfall on the River Erne near Ballyshannon, County Donegal. The construction of the Erne catchment and hydroelectric power plants in 1946–52 caused the destruction of the falls.

Fínnachta revoked his promise by the end of the day, the *bórama* would be suspended forever.

The Uí Néill gathered an army and set out after Moling. When Moling saw them coming, he raised an alarm and fled to the west. The Uí Néill followed, but God sent a mist to hide Moling and they could not find him. And so the *bórama* ended.

When Fínnachta was killed in battle in 693 at Grellach Dollaid (possibly Girley in County Meath), Moling said a prayer in his memory: "Tis sad for Findachta to day to lie in a gory bed, may he be with the men of heaven for forgiving the Boroma."[35] Moling himself died in 697 and was buried at his church.

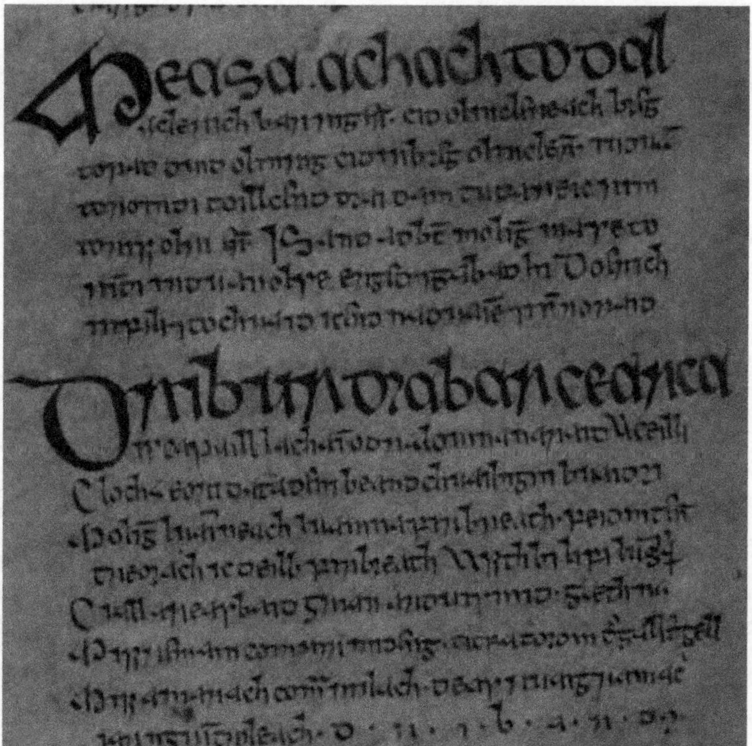

Figure 5.4 *Fínnachta of the Ui Néill and Dríbor drábor*

Source: The Book of Lecan, Royal Irish Academy, MS 23 P 2, Folio 309.

[35] Whitley Stokes, The Boroma, 12 Revue Celtique 32, 117 (1892).

4. *THE BIRTH AND LIFE OF SAINT MOLING* AND THE *BÓRAMA* AS HISTORY

The Birth and Life of Saint Moling and the *Bórama* have little or no basis in historical fact.[36] Both stories were composed many centuries after the events they purport to describe. Of course, at least some of the people featured in both stories probably actually existed, including Moling and Fínnachta. But there is no reason to believe that most of the events described in either story actually occurred. Moling probably founded the monastery at St. Mullins. And the Uí Néill were generally more powerful than the Laigin and probably imposed taxes whenever possible. But all of the other details in both stories are surely fictional.

The *Birth and Life of Saint Moling* and the *Bórama* were probably composed in bits and pieces by many different people between about 800 and 1150, when the Book of Leinster was written.[37] Both texts were probably propaganda created by Leinster in order to counter Uí Néill propaganda, which was far more voluminous.[38] Among other things, they were probably intended to show that the saints of Leinster were more clever and powerful than the saints of the Uí Néill.[39]

In any case, the story of Moling's stolen poem clearly has no basis in historical fact. On the contrary, it was created for the *Bórama*, presumably as a political allegory. While the precise meaning of the story is unclear, there are many plausible readings. The story establishes Moling as a notable poet, implicitly

---

[36] Liam Ó Buachalla, The Leinster Tribute Feud, 66 Journal of the Cork Historical and Archaeological Society 13 (1961) ("While this story in general outline is genuine historical fact, there is much which must be regarded as fanciful embellishment").

[37] Cornelius Gerard Buttimer, *The "Borama": Literature, History and Political Propaganda in Early Medieval Leinster* 328–30 (1983) (unpublished dissertation). See also Elin Ingibjorg Eyjolfsdottir, *The Bórama: The Poetry and the Hagiography in the Book of Leinster* 37 (2012) (unpublished dissertation) ("The Bórama shows various signs of having been compiled from multiple texts"). Some scholars have suggested that the *Bórama* was initially composed in the tenth century by Flann mac Máelmáedóc and was developed by other authors throughout the eleventh century. See Buttimer (citing E. Bhreathnach, Killeshin: An Irish Monastery Surveyed, 27 CMCS 33, 39 (1994)) and C. Doherty, *The Transmission of the Cult of St. Máedhóg, in Ireland and Europe in the Early Middle Ages: texts and transmission* 268, 271 (P. Ní Chatháin and M. Richter eds. 2002).

[38] Cornelius Gerard Buttimer, *The "Borama": Literature, History and Political Propaganda in Early Medieval Leinster* (1983) (unpublished dissertation).

[39] Morgan T. Davies, Kings and Clerics in Some Leinster Sagas, 47 Ériu 45, 65 (1996).

equal to Columcille, the patron saint of the Uí Néill.[40] It establishes Moling's power, which enabled him to expose Tollchenn's lie, and it emphasizes Moling's cunning. After all, Moling's praise-poem was only a ploy to trick Fínnachta into suspending the *bórama*. While *luán* did mean "doomsday," it wasn't the common meaning of the word.[41]

However, even though the story of Moling's stolen poem has no basis in historical fact and was probably always understood as a political allegory, it can still help us understand the poetic economy of medieval Ireland at the time the *Bórama* was composed. The people who composed the story knew that their audience would interpret it in relation to contemporary norms, including the norms of the poetic economy. And the poetic economy of twefth-century Ireland prohibited plagiarism.

5. THE POETIC ECONOMY OF MEDIEVAL IRELAND

In medieval Ireland, only a privileged class of people called *nemed* could travel from one political territory to another. The *nemed* included kings, lords, priests, and poets. In other words, poets were members of a professional class with a special status and social role.[42]

The poetic profession was organized by rank. Poets could increase their rank by demonstrating their poetic skills, specifically their ability to compose poems in certain forms and meters. As a poet's rank increased, he became entitled to a larger retinue and more compensation.

Specifically, poets were entitled to claim compensation in exchange for composing praise-poems for their patrons. The higher a poet's rank, the more valuable a poem he could compose and the more compensation he could demand. However, poets were entitled to compensation only if they composed a perfect poem. If a poem was flawed, the patron could withhold payment.

---

40 Morgan T. Davies, Moling and the Bórama, in *Ollam: Studies in Gaelic and Related Traditions in Honor of Tomás Ó Cathasaigh* 65 (2016) ("Now, Moling is by no means unique among Irish saints in being a poet; one thinks above all of Colum Cille in that regard").

41 *Id.*

42 Deborah Hayden, Poetic Law and the Medieval Irish Linguist: Contextualizing the Vices and Virtues of Verse Composition in Auraicept na nÉces, 54 Language & History 1, 4 (2011).

Accordingly, poets produced a body of "poetico-legal" texts describing the different ranks, explaining how a poet could increase in rank, and identifying the ways in which a poem could be flawed:

> In legal terms, poems were the merchandise at stake in a binding contract established between poet and patron, where the poet was entitled to a specified amount of compensation in return for his literary "goods"; the articulation of stylistic rules for literary compositions thus served the obvious purpose of establishing the terms by which the merchandise might be deemed faulty or otherwise. The likelihood was, of course, that other trained poets would be the first to recognize technical flaws in a rival artist's compositions, thus motivating the need for poets to maintain the quality of their wares in what was no doubt a competitive entertainment market.[43]

In the poetic economy of medieval Ireland, the counterpart to praise was satire, which poets used to shame those who behaved improperly. If a perfect praise-poem was an honor that required appropriate compensation, a perfect and justified satirical poem was a kind of magical assault that could even inflict physical harm. Poets used satire and the threat of satire to enforce the law. But unjustified satire was itself illegal and exposed the offending poet to punishment.[44]

One of the tools that poets used in order to enforce the law was the *trefocal*, a form of poetry that combined both praise and satire. *Trefocal* means "three words" or "three statements," reflecting the requirements of the form. Medieval Irish poets conceptualized praise as *find* or "white" and satire as *dub* or "black." A *Trefocal* was *brecc* or "speckled," containing both praise and satire.[45]

Essentially, a *trefocal* was a warning. A poet composed a *trefocal* in order to identify a wrong, provide an opportunity to right the wrong, and threaten satire if the wrong persisted. Like any other poem, only a perfect *trefocal* was effective. But an effective *trefocal* justified satire if ignored.

5.a The *Auraicept na nÉces* and the Prohibition of Plagiarism

One of the poetical-legal texts that explained the poetic economy of medieval Ireland was the *Auraicept na nÉces* or "Scholar's Primer," which was

43 *Id.*, 6.

44 *Id.*, 7–8.

45 See Robin Chapman Stacey, *Dark Speech: The Performance of Law in Early Ireland* (2007). See also Liam Breatnach, The *Trefocal Tract*: An Early Middle Text on Poetics, in Gordon Ó Riain (ed.), *Dá Dtrian Feasa Fiafraighidh. Essays on the Irish Grammatical and Metrical Tradition* 1–65 (Dublin 2017) and Padraig A. Breatnach, Poetics and the Bardic Imagination, 27 Celtica 95 (2013).

essentially a textbook for aspiring poets (Figure 5.5).[46] The *Auraicept* was an exceptionally important text that is preserved in many manuscript sources.[47] The core text was probably composed between 700 and 900.[48] Over the course of many centuries, many different scholars added a great deal of commentary, which differs considerably from version to version. The content and structure of the *Auraicept* resembles a Latin grammatical manual, consisting of basic linguistic principles explained by historical and literary allusions.[49]

The commentary to the version of the *Auraicept* preserved in the Book of Ballymote describes the potential faults of a *trefocal* and how they can be corrected. Among other things, it states:

> *Trefocal in so amal rocumsat na baird na patreni .i. trefocul ... Cen comman. Cen comsiudh.*
> This is *trefocal* as the bards and the *patreni* have devised it, i.e., *trefocal* ... Without plagiarism. Without sameness. ...
> *Dia nditen-sidhe cethri cenela fichet .i. co[r]raib ann: ... a oen.*
> To guard against these [flaws] are 24 kinds, *i.e. corraib* [points?] there: ... its singleness.[50]

The Book of Ballymote was written in 1390 or 1391, near the town of Ballymote, County Sligo, and contains one of the most complete versions of the *Auraicept*. It establishes that plagiarism and banality were seen as flaws

---

46 *Auraicept na nÉces: The Scholars' Primer* (George Calder trans. and ed. 1917).

47 A Middle Irish poem composed in about 1050–1150 includes the *Auraicept* in a list of the most important Irish texts. Peter J. Smith, Aimirgein Glúngel tuir tend: A Middle-Irish Poem on the Authors and Laws of Ireland, 8 Peritia 120 (1994). The oldest known version of the *Auraicept* is in the Book of Leinster and was written in about 1160.

48 *The Early Irish Linguist: An Edition of the Canonical Part of the Auraicept na n-Éces, with Introduction, Commentary and Indices* 36 (Anders Ahlqvist trans. and ed. 1982). At least apocryphally, the *Auraicept* was composed by the great scholar Longarad, about whom little else is known. According to legend, Columcille once visited Longarad and asked to borrow some of his books. When Longarad refused, Columcille said, "It is my will, if God suffer it, ... that thy books be of no avail to any other after thy death forever." Longarad relented, but Columcille could not lift the curse, and when Longarad died, his books suddenly became incomprehensible. Manus O'Donnell, *Life of Columcille* 217–19 (1532) (O'Kelleher and Schoepperle eds. 1918).

49 Deborah Hayden, Poetic Law and the Medieval Irish Linguist: Contextualizing the Vices and Virtues of Verse Composition in Auraicept na nÉces, 54 Language & History 1, 3 (2011).

50 *Id.*, 14–16. *Comman* or *commann* means "friendship," but can be taken in a negative sense to mean "false friendship." Accordingly, *cen comman* literally means "without false friendship," and is typically understood to mean "plagiarism." eDIL s.v. commann or dil.ie/11506. *Comsiudh* or *coimsiugad* is typically understood to mean "sameness" or "matching." eDIL s.v. coimsiugad or dil.ie/10295.

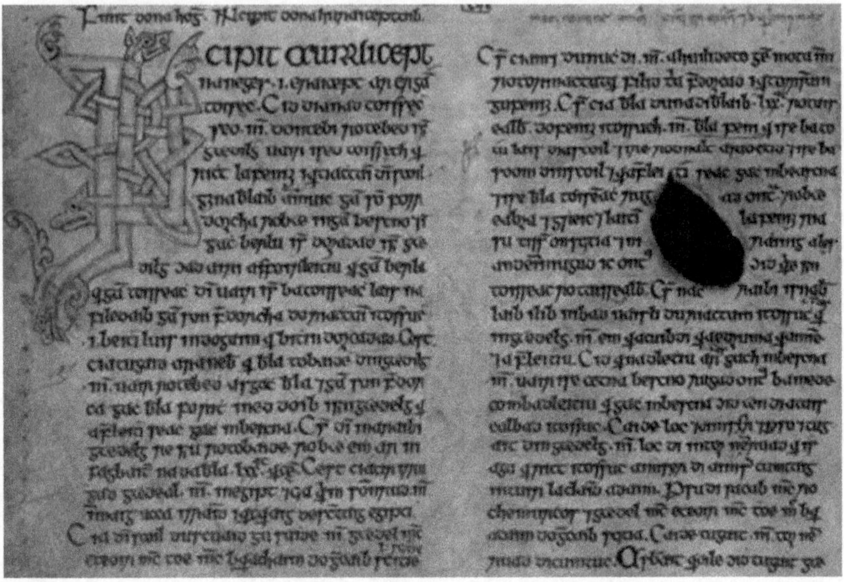

Figure 5.5 *The beginning of the Auraicept na nÉces*

Source: The Book of Ballymote, Royal Irish Academy, 23 P 12, folio 170v.

that made a poem worthless, and that they could be remedied only by uniqueness. Presumably, any amount of plagiarism constituted a fault in a poem, so plagiarism of an entire poem would have been quite an egregious offense.

5.b Moling's Stolen Poem and the Concept of Literary Ownership

Maine famously observed that "substantive law has at first the look of being gradually secreted in the interstices of procedure."[51] In much the same way, our knowledge of medieval Ireland is secreted in the interstices of the stories it told about itself. Accordingly, the *Bórama* "will be found to throw side-lights on Irish manners, customs and superstitions," especially "the incident of the piratical poet and the saint."[52] While the story of Moling's stolen poem is not literally true, it reflects the norms of the society in which it was composed. And that is the sum of the truth available to us.

---

[51] Henry James Sumner Maine, *Dissertations on Early Law and Custom* (1883).
[52] Whitley Stokes, The Boroma, 12 Revue Celtique 32, 33 (1892).

The story of Moling's stolen poem reflects the norms governing poets in twelfth-century Ireland. Among other things, it illustrates their understanding that the rules governing poets prohibited and punished both plagiarism and banality. The *Auraicept* explicitly identifies plagiarism and banality as flaws that make a poem worthless. And the story of Moling's stolen poem relied on the prohibition of plagiarism to elevate Moling at the expense of his meretricious bard.

Of course, it makes perfect sense that twelfth-century Irish poets would have regulated poetry. The poetical economy depended on their ability to compose unique poems and compel their patrons to pay for those poems. The poetic economy was explicitly transactional. The poet was expected to produce praise-poems and the patron was expected to pay for them.[53]

Poetico-legal texts like the *Auraicept* provided the rules regulating the profession, determining who could produce poems, what they could charge, and how to evaluate their quality. Indeed, they even established "fixed prices for the traditional, presyllabic meters."[54] This poetic economy persisted for several centuries, during which noble patrons were obligated to purchase poems composed in their honor.[55]

In other words, the norms governing twelfth-century Irish poets were effectively a form of professional regulation. On one level, they were a form of

---

[53] Padraig A. Breatnach, *The Chief's Poet, Proceedings of the Royal Irish Academy* 37 (1983) ("But of course the exchange of dan, 'poem', in return for duas, 'reward', is a recurring theme in Irish verse from the earliest period. In a recent article dealing with the subject Calvert Watkins has shown that in fact the very term dan takes its origin from the basic notion of such an exchange. 'Poet and patron', he writes, 'exist on a reciprocal gift-giving basis; the poet's gift is his poem. It is thus that we must understand the specialization of the word dan 'gift; talent, poetic faculty; craft, profession' as one of the words for 'poem'. It is derived not through the sense of 'poetic talent', but directly from the primary inherited meaning 'gift', 'something bestowed'. The reason why dan for duas (or ealatha, 'art', in exchange for ionnmhas, 'wealth') continues to be a pivotal aspect of an ollamh's accommodation with his chief, is best considered against the background of medieval lordship generally, and the system of tributes and services upon which it was based").

[54] Katharine Simms, Literacy and the Irish Bards, in *Literacy in Medieval Celtic Societies* 238 (Huw Pryce ed. 1998).

[55] *Id.* ("The traditional bardic eulogy was semi-public. On the one hand it was commissioned and paid for by an individual patron, whose Christian name and surname, perhaps also that of his wife and his direct ancestors, were woven into the rhyme scheme from verse to verse, making it only of value as a possession to that individual and his (or her) descendants").

quality control, ensuring that consumers could rely on quality poems. After all, no one was better able and more eager to enforce those norms than other poets:

> It has long been established that medieval Irish grammatical and metrical doctrine sheds valuable light on our understanding of the social status of poets as powerful or influential figures who could, at least theoretically, acquire high status and considerable wealth by means of their compositions. Such status was dependent, however, on the legal stipulation that poets were expected to give value for money when trading their artistic wares, leading to an emphasis in many law-tracts and other literary sources on the necessity that their poems be devoid of technical faults. At the same time, it might be argued that the explicit articulation of stylistic rules also served the converse purpose of protecting artists themselves from the potential pitfalls of a legal code so reliant on the aesthetic judgement of the individual.[56]

But the same professional norms also punished unfair competition. Specifically, the norms prohibiting plagiarism and banality ensured that poets didn't cut corners by copying, rather than composing novel poems. In other words, poets created a professional norm against plagiarism and banality to preserve their reputation and investment of labor. They certainly didn't have a concept of copyright. Indeed, they encouraged copying with attribution. But they had a concept of literary ownership, tied to the economic value of the works they produced.

6. CONCLUSION

Conventional wisdom holds that the concept of literary ownership is a modern idea, tied to the modern concept of authorship. But the story of Moling's stolen poem and the professional norms governing twelfth-century Irish poets suggest that the concepts of authorship and literary ownership long predate the modern era. Perhaps the concepts of authorship and literary ownership have always been driven by economic concerns.

---

[56] Deborah Hayden, Poetic Law and the Medieval Irish Linguist: Contextualizing the Vices and Virtues of Verse Composition in *Auraicept na nÉces*, 54 Language & History 1, 30 (2011).

6. A critical review of the quest for global protection of traditional knowledge: politico-economic concerns

Kosgei Kembol Alvin

1. BACKGROUND

There is an ongoing quest to craft a global instrument for the protection of traditional knowledge, genetic resources and cultural expressions. The need for such a regime was sparked by, among other things, the rapid rate of loss of traditional lifestyles. It is estimated that between 50 and 90 percent of such knowledge and lifestyles will be lost in the next hundred years.[1] Furthermore, indigenous peoples live where most reserves of global genetic resources are found.[2] Traditional knowledge (TK) is the sum total of innovations and practices that are used by indigenous communities around the world which have been passed from generation to generation. These have developed from the continuous interaction between the indigenous people and the ecosystems

[1] See, UNCTAD, "Elements of National Sui Generis Systems for the Preservation, Protection and Promotion of Traditional Knowledge, Innovations and Practices and Options for an International Framework," UNCTAD-Commonwealth Secretariat Workshop on Geneva, 4–6 February 2004, available at https://unctad.org/en/Docs/ditcted200518_en.pdf; or IIED, Kechua-Aymara Association for Nature and Sustainable Development (ANDES, Peru), Fundacion Dobbo Yala (Panama), University of Panama, Ecoserve (India), Centre for Indigenous Farming Systems (India), Herbal and Folklore Research Centre (India), Centre for Chinese Agricultural Policy (CCAP, China), Southern Environmental and Agricultural Policy Research Institute (ICIPE, Kenya), Kenya Forestry Research Institute; "Sui Generis Systems for the Protection of Traditional Knowledge," Paper Presented to the Information for the Secretariat of the Convention on Biological Diversity 31 October 2005, available at https://pubs.iied.org/pdfs/G02378.pdf

[2] CBD Secretariat, "Traditional Knowledge and the Convention on Biological Diversity," 10 June 2011, available at https://www.cbd.int/traditional/intro.shtml.

they live in. Traditional knowledge, therefore, encompasses all the technologies and methodologies that have been adopted to, *inter alia*, treat diseases, improve crop and livestock yield, make manual work easier, create cosmetics, enhance fertility.

On the other hand, traditional cultural expressions (TCEs) comprise different forms of indigenous art such as dance, folklore, symbols, handicraft and performances.[3] Genetic resources (GRs) refer to material that is inherent to any form of life – flora or fauna – with actual or potential value.[4] They are not intellectual property.[5] Most of the traditional knowledge of indigenous communities relates to the identification of certain resources naturally occurring in the ecosystem as being of value. The transfer of such knowledge for use by communities other than the indigenous communities is, in effect, akin to the western conception of transfer of technology.[6]

Before the Convention on Biological Diversity (CBD), the global human rights debate was, generally, centred around philosophy of human rights based on the individual and their liberty. As a matter of fact, the Universal Declaration on Human Rights, whose 30 Articles have arguably attained the status of customary international law, was based on the urgent need to fortify and protect the rights of the individual person. It was not until the CBD was developed that a communitarian approach to rights and entitlements emerged – albeit indirectly.[7] Before then, the property systems were largely based on the understanding that only an individual could own property in anything.[8] It is arguable, therefore, that the first legal document that elevated indigenous

---

3 The distinction between the two is the distinction that has existed since the Paris Convention for the Protection of Industrial Property and the Berne Convention for the Protection of Literary and Artistic Works of 1883 and 1886. The former being intended for the protection of innovation meant for industrial application, the latter focusing on the protection of artistic creativity.

4 Charles R. McManis, "Intellectual Property, Genetic Resources and Traditional Knowledge Protection: Thinking Globally, Acting Locally," *Cardozo J. Int'l & Comp. L.* 11 (2003): 547.

5 WIPO, Traditional Knowledge and Intellectual Property – Background Brief, available at https://www.wipo.int/pressroom/en/briefs/tk_ip.html.

6 This conception in Research and Development is catered for by the draft International Code of Conduct on the Transfer of Technology, 1985.

7 Peter-Tobias Stoll and Anja von Hahn, "Part II. Indigenous Peoples, Indigenous Knowledge and Indigenous Resources in International Law' in Silke von Lewinski (ed), *Indigenous Heritage and Intellectual Property, Genetic Resources, Traditional Knowledge and Folklore* (2004) 5, 5. It is argued that the fortunes of indigenous peoples started changing in the latter half of the twentieth century as the wave of decolonization swept across the global south.

8 See C. Leila, C. Sage and M. Woolcock, *Customary Law and Policy Reform: Engaging with the Plurality of Justice Systems* (July 2005), available at http://

rights to the international plane was the CDB, which expressly mentions the rights of indigenous peoples. The recognition of the need to have a regime that specifically caters for the protection of cultural intellectual property is, therefore, a key milestone in the philosophical shift and understanding of indigenes, their socio-economic life and in the human rights debate.[9]

Under the auspices of the United Nations, the World Intellectual Property Organization (WIPO) Inter-Governmental Committee (IGC) on Traditional Knowledge, Genetic Resources and Traditional Cultural Expressions has been tasked with the development of a *sui generis* regime(s) for the protection of TK, GRs and TCEs. Before the IGC was commissioned in 2000, there had been isolated attempts to utilize the existing intellectual property regimes to protect TK, GRs and TCEs.[10] However, it became clear that the existing systems were limited and the journey towards the protection of traditional knowledge began in earnest. Some scholars commented that the situation was conceptually misguided and more importantly, incoherent.[11] By 2010, the IGC had moved from reports to text-based negotiations which would see the relevant parties and interested groups review and make recommendations on the basis of draft documents.[12]

2. CONCEPTUAL FRAMEWORK: LAYING THE BASIS FOR RESPONSIVE APPROACHES

Generally, the debate on the protection of TK and related rights is based on the need to compensate indigenous communities, fortify the recognition and protection of the rights of these indigenes and the need to recognize commons as

---

siteresources.worldbank.org/INTWDR2006/Resources/477383118673432908/Customary_Law_and_Policy_Reform.pdf.

[9] In 2007 the United Nations Declaration on the Rights of Indigenous Peoples became the watershed moment for indigenous peoples in that the UN adopted a document that specifically dealt with the rights of indigenes as a group.

[10] For example, in 1967, the Berne Convention for the Protection of Literary and Artistic Works was revised to protect artistic works on the basis of originality and authorship that could be identified. See also the 1982 UNESCO Model Provisions for TCEs and the WIPO Performances and Phonograms Treaty of 1996.

[11] See generally, Graham Dutfield, “TK Unlimited: The Emerging but Incoherent International Law of Traditional Knowledge Protection,” *The Journal of World Intellectual Property* 20(5–6) (2017), available at https://www.researchgate.net/publication/320620001_TK_unlimited_The_emerging_but_incoherent_international_law_of_traditional_knowledge_protection.

[12] WIPO General Assembly 2009 – Decision on Agenda Item 28. The decision was made during the Thirty-Eighth (19th Ordinary) Session, September 22 to October 1, 2009.

being a distinct regime that requires formalization and not creation.[13] The latter conception is the origin of the north-south debate that carries the decolonization question further from political consciousness to the area of economic freedom.[14] This chapter recognizes that the recognition and validation of commons is a more potent agenda since it moves the debate from mere sentimentality to actual reform. As a matter of fact, it can be argued that the former two conceptual underpinnings gain their legitimacy from their connection to the recognition of the already existing and now recognized indigenous rights. This existence is merely validated by the formal law but exists in the indigenous systems which encompass both the innovations and the beliefs or philosophy.

Borrowing from the above, this chapter understands indigenous systems of ownership of all forms of property (and other areas of human interaction) as complete.[15] Therefore, there is no need for external validation and "formalization." Under this understanding, the indigenes – the majority of whom are in the global south – have a right, by the very fact of their personhood to be respected without the need for the subtle influence of the concept of "the other."[16] According to Achille Mbembe – one of the leading political theorists in the decolonization debate – Africa, and by extension the developing world, is viewed as the other from whence nothing proper can emanate. This non-empirical assumption led to the misguided application of Harding's theory to African land tenure systems.[17] The right to own land and make a living is inextricably linked to human dignity and therefore the question of entitlement to property in ecological resources is also a human rights issue. Further, TCEs

---

[13] David Castle and E. Richard Gold, "Traditional Knowledge and Benefit Sharing: From Compensation to Transaction" in P.W.B. Phillips and C.B. Onwuekwe (eds), *Accessing and Sharing the Benefits of the Genomics Revolution* (Springer, 2007) 65–79.

[14] Shubha Ghosh, "Reflections on the Traditional Knowledge Debate," *Cardozo J. Int'l & Comp. L.* 11 (2003): 497.

[15] H.W.O. Okoth-Ogendo, "The Tragic African Commons: A Century of Expropriation, Suppression and Subversion," Occasional Paper No. 24, Cape Town: Programme for Land and Agrarian Studies, University of the Western Cape (2002) (on file with author).

[16] See Achille Mbembe, *On the Postcolony* (University of California Press, 2001).

[17] G. Harding, "The Tragedy of the Commons," *Science* 162 (1968): 1243–1248. Harding and other theorists believe that property can only be owned by individuals. See also C. Nyamu-Musembi, "Breathing Life into Dead Theories about Property Rights: de Soto and Land Relations in Rural Africa," Working Paper No 272 (Nairobi, Institute of Development Studies, 2006), available at http://www.ids.ac.uk/publication/breathing-life-into-dead-theories-about-property-rights-de-soto-and-land-relations-in-rural-africa (on file with author). Cf. Hernando de Soto, *The Mystery of Capital: Why Capitalism Triumphs in the West and Fails Everywhere Else* (Basic Books, 2000).

and TK are part of the cultural identity of the indigenous groups.[18] In most of the post-colonial states in the global south, there is currently a push for the recognition of the indigenous laws as part of the decolonization debate.[19] This is partly fuelled by political consciousness. However, and more importantly, there is an awareness around the globe that communitarian property systems might be the answer to sustainable development. This latter understanding and much more forms the empirical basis of this chapter.

Secondly, this chapter appreciates that different systems of law can co-exist without necessarily being counterproductive. It is unnecessary for the norms that have been resilient in governing relationships among indigenous peoples to be abolished.[20] It has, hitherto, been argued that the market economy abhors joint and/or communal ownership of property.[21] This led to the abolishment of traditional property systems upon colonization. Pluralism is not extra-legality for the regimes that are outside formal law.[22] Nyamu-Musembi argues that it is a fallacious appreciation of the customary regimes of property ownership which holds that only the formalization of property rights in land that would lead to the empowerment of the poor. Among other reasons, it was argued that for efficiency in the markets, individual title to the property would be easy to settle since the decision to utilize, transfer or deal with property in any other way would be made by one person. However, despite many years of suppression and pluralism, these regimes remained resilient.[23] Currently, there is no conclusive empirical research that justifies such a bold hypothesis. Further and

---

[18] See, World Intellectual Property Organization, Publication No. 2: The WIPO Intergovernmental Committee on Intellectual Property and Genetic Resources, Traditional Knowledge and Folklore (Geneva, WIPO, 2015), available at https://www.wipo.int/edocs/pubdocs/en/wipo_pub_tk_2.pdf.

[19] See Russel Barsh, "The World's indigenous Peoples," a paper submitted to Calvert Group by First Nations Development Institute/First Peoples Worldwide, available at www.sfu.ca/~palys/Barsh-TheWorldsIndigenousPeoples.pdf.

[20] Leila Chirayath, Caroline Sage and Michael Woolcock, *Customary Law and Policy Reform: Engaging with the Plurality of Justice Systems* (July 2005), available at http://documents1.worldbank.org/curated/en/675681468178176738/pdf/336550Customary1Law01WDR060bkgd0paper1.pdf.

[21] Garrett Hardin, "The Tragedy of the Commons," *Science* 162 (1968): 1243–1248.

[22] Celestine Nyamu Musembi, "De Soto and Land Relations in Rural Africa: Breathing Life into Dead Theories about Property Rights," *Third World Quarterly* 28(8) (2007): 1457–1478. See also, Tesh Dagne, "Protecting Traditional Knowledge in International Intellectual Property Law: Imperatives for Protection and Choice of Modalities," *The John Marshall Review of Intellectual Property Law* 14(1) (2014): 2, at 47, where a pluralistic approach is proposed.

[23] See generally, A. Migai, *Rescuing Indigenous Tenure from the Ghetto of Neglect: Inalienability and the Protection of Customary Land Rights in Kenya* (Nairobi Acts Press, 2001).

more importantly, this chapter is premised on understanding these systems as having the potential to solve the problem of the finiteness of resources.[24] In any event, the global economy is moving towards the efficiency of the sharing economy in items such as cars, holiday homes, office space and fashion.[25] It is under the indigenous property systems that TK and TCEs have flourished and continue to benefit the communities. It would, therefore, be ill-advised to square the circle.

The final conceptual basis of this chapter is that of the global political economy. The treaty-making process is a political process where diverse interests are blended in a crucible.[26] This chapter appreciates the political process that precedes treaty-making. Krisch argues that international law is shaped and influenced by hegemony.[27] Further, he argues that where international law does not favour hegemony, dominant superpowers resort to withdrawal and politics. Krisch further argues that often the power struggle between the hegemon and the international law follows a well-defined pattern that leads to the application of municipal law.[28] On the face of it, the negotiations have already taken twenty years as at the time of writing this chapter. The economic and political interests that are involved have a deep influence on whether or not a treaty is concluded, its contents and consequently its utility. Therefore, this chapter is based on a practical appreciation of the fact that removing some

---

[24] It has been argued that common ownership systems can be helpful in sustainable development. See D. Bromley and M. Cernea, "The Management of Common Property Natural Resources: Some Conceptual and Operational Fallacies," Washington DC World Bank 1989 (Discussion Paper no 57). The authors observe as follows: "Resource degradation in developing countries while incorrectly attributed intrinsically to 'common property systems' actually originates in the dissolution of local level institutional arrangements whose purpose was to give rise to resource use patterns that were sustainable."

[25] This is only when the concept is used under the peer-to-peer model. See MaryAnne M. Gobble, "Regulating Innovation in the New Economy," *Research Technology Management* 58(2) (2015): 62–67. When understood under the business-to-consumer model, it ceases to refer to an economy of its own but a marketing strategy where access is preferred to ownership by consumers.

[26] Anghie is blunt in calling international treaty making a tool governing the relationship between the European and the non-European world. He argues that international law was meant to justify the agenda of civilizing the colonial world but has been overcome by the emergence of independent states both in the Oriental world and the global south. See generally, Antony Anghie, *Imperialism, Sovereignty and the Making of International Law* (Cambridge University Press, 2007).

[27] Nico Krisch, "International Law in Times of Hegemony: Unequal Power and the Shaping of the International Legal Order," *European Journal of International Law* 16(3) (2005): 369–408.

[28] *Ibid.* See also C.H. Alexandrowicz, *The European-African Confrontation: A Study in Treaty-Making* (Sijthoff, 1973).

of the knowledge that is currently deemed to be part of the public domain and requiring multinationals to pay a premium for it will be resisted. Further, if access to research areas such as the Brazilian Amazon or the Arabuko Sokoke National Park in Kenya and the utilization of the extensive mines of genetic resources will multiply the costs of players in the cosmetics, fashion and pharma trades, there is every possibility that the developed world will be slow to accept any radical changes.

3. A CRITICAL REVIEW OF THE DOMINANT JUSTIFICATIONS FOR A *SUI GENERIS* REGIME

Principally, it has been argued that the existing regimes do not comprehensively provide for both defensive and offensive protection of TK and TCEs, and rightfully so.[29] This is because, aside from the attempts by both municipal and international law to provide for – in passing – TK and TCEs, the standards of protection and the objectives are not uniform. This is true. However, the Convention on Biological Diversity and the attendant Nagoya Protocol on Access and Benefit Sharing already offer much-needed recognition and mechanisms for access and use of traditional knowledge. Furthermore, individual countries are already in the process of crafting laws that would provide for the protection of TK and TCEs in a very robust manner.

Secondly, it has been argued that the nature of TK requires special recognition.[30] This is true. As a matter of fact, TK in the wide sense covers a broad spectrum of knowledge resulting from the interaction of communities with the environment. In the narrow sense, it covers actual innovation and technical know-how. It, therefore, appears to be the case that a specialized regime that only caters to traditional knowledge would be proper. However, conceptually, traditional knowledge under customary and indigenous law has a clear legal regime that provides for recognition, ownership, transfer among the indigenous rights and utilization.[31] What is therefore new, arguably, is the interaction

---

29 Marisella Ouma, "Traditional Knowledge: The Challenges Facing International Lawmakers," *WIPO Magazine* February 2017, available at https://www.wipo.int/wipo_magazine/en/2017/01/article_0003.html; based on the keynote address to the WIPO Seminar on Intellectual Property and Traditional Knowledge in Geneva, Switzerland, in November 2016, available at https://www.wipo.int/edocs/mdocs/tk/en/wipo_iptk_ge_2_16/wipo_iptk_ge_2_16_presentation_11ouma.pdf.

30 Fulvio Mazzocchi, "Western Science and Traditional Knowledge," *EMBO Reports* 7(5) (2006): 463–466, text available at https://www.ncbi.nlm.nih.gov/pmc/articles/PMC1479546/.

31 Krystyna Swiderska, "Protecting Traditional Knowledge: A Framework based on Customary Laws and Bio-Cultural Heritage," IIED, London, UK, 2006.

between the owners – being indigenous communities and their members – and the outside world.

Thirdly, it is argued that traditional knowledge is being protected for purposes of preventing biopiracy and overexploitation and to engender sustainable development. Without a doubt, these are noble grounds. However, it is not certainly the only result that a *sui generis* regime will stop bio-piracy. Basically, biopiracy is the extraction and utilization of genetic resources without compensation of the communities from which the genetic resources are extracted.[32] What arises from this is the injustice that is visited on the community when external groups profit through the extraction of these genetic resources and the attendant knowledge, thus reaping the benefits without caring for the progress and rights of the indigenes who are often living in poverty. Often, patents are granted to such individuals – both natural and artificial – despite having originated from processes already being utilized by indigenous communities.[33] In this typology, the normative solution would be the recognition of the moral rights of the indigenes and fair compensation for the said knowledge.

Fourthly, it is expected that contracting parties will have an easier time enforcing a uniform transnational regime. This is especially true with respect to intellectual property where the use and exploitation are often cross-border.[34] However, this might not be a good idea for the following reasons. Foremost, the subject matter is wide and evolves from one corner of the globe to the other. Furthermore, indigenous mechanisms of use and *inter vivos* transfer may not be the same. Secondly, it is not necessarily the case that it is the *sui generis* regime that will make enforcement easier, as discussed in the preceding paragraph. For instance, in the area of climate change, the enforcement of the United Nations Framework Convention on Climate Change has been a hot potato.[35] However, in spite of the challenges, the Convention has given all the contracting parties a basis on which to hold each other accountable. Perhaps

---

32 Chris Hamilton, "Biodiversity, Biopiracy and Benefits: What Allegations of Biopiracy Tell Us About Intellectual Property," *Developing World Bioethics* 6(3) (2006): 158–173.

33 *Supra*, Dutfield, note 11.

34 Susy Frankel, "The Cross-Border Protection of Intellectual Property and its Relevance for the Protection of Traditional Knowledge, Traditional Cultural Expressions and Genetic Resources," Presentation to the WIPO Seminar, Geneva, 23 June 2015, available at https://www.wipo.int/edocs/mdocs/tk/en/wipo_iptk_ge_2_15/wipo_iptk_ge_2_15_presentation_susy_frankel.pdf.

35 Yong-Xiang Zhang et al., "The Withdrawal of the US from the Paris Agreement and its Impact on Global Climate Change Governance," *Advances in Climate Change Research* 8(4) (2017): 213–219, available at https://www.sciencedirect.com/science/article/pii/S1674927817300849.

to ease the jitters a soft law instrument might be appropriate.[36] This may work in the case of many of the innovations that are part of the public domain being converted to protected knowledge.

Finally, it has been argued that a *sui generis* regime for protecting TK, GRs and TCEs will help achieve environmental justice.[37] This objective borrows, partly, from the understanding that colonial regimes benefitted from and overexploited ecological resources in the colonies. This exploitation continues on the basis of free trade today and sometimes the indigenes are left to bear the brunt of pollution and dereliction.[38] As the concept developed in the United States, there emerged the appreciation that indigenous Americans suffered the brunt of environmental degradation without participating in the economic life that resulted in the degradation.[39] This is indeed true. However, a balance is crucial in order to avoid legislating impossibilities. Further, we need to learn from the past and not get stuck. Moreover, ecological justice goes beyond the global north/global south divide. It is also concerned with harmonious co-existence. More importantly, a practical approach will further avoid unnecessary resistance which will attract opposition from the developed world. Further, the developing world must realize that one of the objectives of the Earth Summit was the recognition of the fact that the resources of the globe are for the benefit of all the inhabitants of the earth. Furthermore, the global economy is interdependent.

4. SITUATIONAL ANALYSIS: CURRENT RELEVANT REGIMES

This part of the chapter reviews the existing national and global regimes that touch on TK and related rights. This will help to juxtapose the possible outlook of the intended *sui generis* regime with the current one. Currently, global regimes relevant for the protection of indigenous knowledge systems include the Convention on Biological Diversity (CBD) and the attendant Nagoya Protocol, the Universal Declaration on the Rights of Indigenous Peoples,

---

36 *Supra*, Ouma, note 29.

37 Philippe Cullet, Jonas Ebbesson and Phoebe Okowa, "Environmental Justice in the Use, Knowledge and Exploitation of Genetic Resources" in Jonas Ebesson and Phoebe Okowa (eds), *Environmental Law and Justice in Context* (Cambridge University Press, 2009) 371–389, available at http://www.ielrc.org/content/a0906.pdf.

38 Antoni Pigrau, "The Texaco-Chevron Case in Ecuador: Law and Justice in the Age of Globalization," *Revista catalana de dret ambiental* 5(1) (2014).

39 Kevin Michael Deluca, "A Wilderness Environmentalism Manifesto: Contesting the Infinite Self-Absorption of Humans" in Ronald Sandler and Phaedra C. Pezzullo (eds), *Environmental Justice and Environmentalism: The Social Justice Challenge to the Environmental Movement* (MIT Press, 2007) 27–44.

2007, the WTO Trade-Related Aspects of Intellectual Property (TRIPS), the WIPO Performances and Phonograms Treaty, the Berne Convention on Protection of Literary and Artistic Works and the WIPO and UNESCO Model Law on Protection of Expressions of Folklore against Illicit Exploitation and Other Prejudicial Actions. This list is not definitive but highlights what in the opinion of the author are the most relevant regimes. As far as national efforts are concerned, the chapter highlights the policy advances that have been made in Kenya as an example of the approach that ought to be considered by national regimes.

4.a Global Efforts

4.a.I WTO Trade-Related Aspects of Intellectual Property (TRIPS)

The TRIPS Agreement provides the basic minimum standards for the protection of intellectual property.[40] Further, it provides for the incorporation of intellectual property into global trade. It provides a uniform regime on the global plane. It also provides enforcement mechanisms for members under Part III. Under the provisions for enforcement, it is required that member states ought to provide equitable procedures that encompass the power of judicial authorities to call for evidence and orders for injunctions and damages.[41]

Relevant to the debate on the protection of TK and related rights is Article 27(3), which identifies subject matter that is excluded from patenting. Methods of treating both humans and animals are excluded from patenting. Article 27(3)(b) further excludes from patentability biological and non-biological processes.[42] The proviso here is the leeway for the protection of plant varieties by member states using the patent or a *sui generis* regime. Technically, therefore, this Agreement does not contemplate the protection of traditional knowledge and genetic resources.[43] It only recognizes the mandate of member states to protect plant varieties. To the extent that plant varieties cannot be patented, indigenous technologies are protected from individuals who claim to be the inventors but are merely copiers.[44] However, TRIPS does not directly address

---

[40] These are Patents, Copyright, Industrial Designs, Trademarks, Trade Secrets (Article 39) and Geographical Indications.

[41] See Articles 42, 43, 44 and 45 of the TRIPS Agreement.

[42] Compare with *Diamond v. Chakrabarty*, 447 U.S. 303 (1980).

[43] Olufunmilayo B. Arewa, "TRIPS and Traditional Knowledge: Local Communities, Local Knowledge, and Global Intellectual Property Frameworks," *Marq. Intell. Prop. L. Rev.* 10 (2006): 155. Examples such as the utilization of lycopene in *tamate* (Ecuador), the *ayahuasca* vine of the Amazon forest and the quinine of the Chicona Bark, whose potency was revealed to a Jesuit by Peruvian indigenes.

[44] See Elizabeth Longacre, "Advancing Science While Protecting Developing Countries from Exploitation of Their Resources and Knowledge," *Fordham Intell Prop. Media & Ent. L.J.* 13(3) (2003): 963, 970.

TK, TCEs or GRs. This loophole explains the ongoing attempts to review Article 27(3).[45]

4.a.II Convention on Biological Diversity (CBD)

Article 1 of the CBD provides that the objectives of the Convention include the conservation of biological diversity, sustainable use and equitable access to biological diversity, access to genetic resources by appropriate transfer of technology and respect for all rights over such resources. Basically, the Convention seeks to protect biological diversity and any rights that may exist over that biological diversity. The key right relevant to this chapter is that of indigenes, which is recognized by Article 8(j). This is the right of indigenous communities to innovations arising from their continuous interaction with their environments. The said article requires approval from the said right holders and the equitable sharing of resources.

On the other hand, Article 15 provides that contracting parties shall, through national legislation, make provisions outlining the process of and conditions precedent to the access to genetic resources. Further, with respect to indigenous rights, Article 17(2) provides that contracting parties shall facilitate the exchange of information including indigenous and traditional knowledge. Further, with respect to the transfer of technology and scientific innovation, the article recognizes traditional and indigenous knowledge as part of scientific innovation and hence relevant to co-operation.

As a means of implementing the Convention, the Nagoya Protocol on Genetic Resources and the Fair and Equitable Sharing of Benefits Arising from their Utilization to the Convention on Biological Diversity (Nagoya Protocol) is meant to implement Article 8(j). The Protocol provides for the obligations of contracting parties with respect to allowing access by third parties to genetic resources that are the subject of the CBD. The states are required to ensure certainty, transparency and rules of prior informed consent, as well as promoting research in sustainable development, and providing fair rules of dispute resolution. It is the obligation of contracting parties to ensure that the utilization and commercialization of genetic resources result in equitable sharing of the benefits that accrue after ultimate commercial exploitation.[46]

---

[45] Council for Trade-Related Aspects of Intellectual Property Rights, Review of the Provisions of Article 27.3(B) Summary of Issues Raised and Points Made IP/C/W/369/Rev. (06-1042) (World Trade Organization, March 2006), available at https://www.wto.org/english/tratop_e/trips_e/ipcw369r1.pdf.

[46] Article 1 as read with Article 5 of the Nagoya Protocol; Article 3 states that the Protocol also applies to access to genetic resources provided for under Article 15 of the CBD.

Critically, under Article 6(2), the Protocol provides that the contracting party shall, through appropriate measures, ensure that the prior and informed consent of the indigenes is sought and that indigenous communities are involved in the process of access. However, in terms of entitlement, Article 6, in keeping with the generally accepted rule of sovereignty, recognizes the state as the final owner of naturally occurring resources – in this case, genetic resources. The Protocol also identifies the important relationship between traditional knowledge and genetic resources, it being the case that knowledge of the worth of certain genetic resources is often utilized without reference to the indigenous communities and with no benefits accruing to them.[47]

Further, it is the obligation of states to establish mechanisms, through legislation, for promoting compliance. Importantly, the Protocol requires members to develop model contractual clauses on access to genetic resources and TK. In all, the role of the government as the powerful middle man and go-between is clearly fortified.

4.a.III WIPO Performances and Phonograms Treaty, 1996

Despite not mentioning traditional cultural expressions, this WIPO-administered Treaty provides for the protection of the rights of performers and those who develop phonograms. Under the convention, phonograms are defined as the incorporation of sounds from performance into audiovisual works. The sounds may be as a result of a performance wherein only sounds are captured and are later transferred to visual works. A performer, on the other hand, is an actor, musician, dancer or singer who performs and uses sounds to convey artistic expressions to audiences. Article 5 provides that the moral right of being identified as the source of a performance or a phonogram shall subsist even after the transfer of economic rights. The only exception is where the said recognition would be inimical to the reputation of the owner of moral rights. This protection is challenged in this era of the internet where the revenues of performers have been eroded.[48]

---

[47] Article 7 of the Nagoya Protocol as read with Article 12 requires state parties to take into consideration customary laws and procedures applicable to knowledge relating to traditional knowledge. Article 12(2) requires state parties to ensure effective participation of the indigenous communities in the establishment of mechanisms of access, obligations of users and measures made available via the Access and Benefit-Sharing Clearing-House.

[48] Branislav Hazucha, "Copyright and New Technologies: Technology Providers as 'New' Old Actors in Copyright Law and Policy," *Intellectual Property Law and Policy Journal* (2014): 45–81, available at https://www.juris.hokudai.ac.jp/riilp/wp-content/uploads/sites/6/2014/03/IP01-03_Hazucha.pdf.

Article 7 provides for the exclusive right of reproduction, while, on the other hand, Article 8 preserves the right of distribution. Traditional cultural expressions are transmitted from one generation to the other. Therefore, where members of a particular community perform songs and dances, they will still be protected against the use of such performances for commercial gain by third parties. Article 9(1) grants the performer(s) the exclusive right of authorizing commercial performance to the public by third parties. This is to be circumscribed by national law.[49] Article 15 provides for the right to be compensated for making such performances available to the public by any third party. These provisions are capable of protecting the rights of communities to inter-generational TCEs.

4.a.IV The United Nations Declaration on the Rights of Indigenous Peoples, 2007 (UNDRIP)

Probably one of the most comprehensive documents on the rights of the indigenes, this soft law instrument is evidence of the desire of the international community to move away from years of discrimination against the millions of indigenous communities across the globe. The political undertones of and discomfort with the document were seen when New Zealand, Canada, Australia and the United States of America voted against it.[50] Although not meant to create new rights, the declaration recognizes the rights of cultures, customs, identity, language and more importantly the right to cultural and ceremonial expression.[51] The latter is important for the purposes of the current research because this is where matters touching on TCEs or folklore arise.

Other than the general objective in the preceding paragraph, the declaration is meant to form a basis for requiring the commitment of state parties to allow indigenous communities to develop their own institutional arrangements and traditions.[52] This objective can be viewed as a shift from the hitherto prevalent view of such traditional systems as backward and undeserving of recognition, and so vulnerable to annihilation. It must be noted that cultural intellectual property derives its legitimacy from customs and customary law and further that the same customs delineate the procedures of transfer *inter vivos*.[53]

---

[49] Under Part III, these very rights shall apply to the producers of phonograms.

[50] Provisions such as Articles 3 and 4 providing for self-determination could have informed the stances taken by these countries which are distinctly controlled by British settler populations but still have large populations of indigenous communities.

[51] This is provided for under Articles 11, 12 and 13 of the UNDRIP.

[52] Article 5; further, Article 21(1) recognizes the right of indigenous peoples to pursue their indigenous economic activities.

[53] Andre Lalonde, "African Indigenous Knowledge and its Relevance to Environment and Development Activities, " The Common Property Conference,

Arguably, since the property is deemed to be for the benefit of the community, transfer to neighbouring communities was made on the basis of barter.[54] It can be argued by extension that modern-day transfers to other third parties or commercial exploitation were not contemplated but the principle of equitable sharing of benefits must apply.[55]

Article 24 recognizes the right of these people – on top of access to state-provided health care – to their own systems of medication. They are meant to have access to these medicinal resources and plants and to have them conserved under Article 25. Furthermore, the Declaration provides that the indigenous groups have the right to strengthen their spiritual relationship with their habitats, to use and develop lands that they have traditionally occupied and receive due recognition of their traditions and laws. It is provided that, where possible, such rights must be given back to the indigenes and if restitution is not possible, just and fair compensation must be granted.[56]

Article 31 recognizes the rights of these indigenous groups to their traditional knowledge. Traditional knowledge is defined as the sciences of the indigenes and their technologies in relation to genetic resources, seeds, medicines and artistic expressions.[57] Groups of indigenous people are granted the right to control, develop and protect their entitlements over cultural TK heritage and traditional knowledge.

September 26–29, 1991, Winnipeg, Manitoba (held by the International Association for the Study of Common Property (IASCP)), available at https://dlc.dlib.indiana.edu/dlc/bitstream/handle/10535/904/African_Indigenous_Knowledge_and_its_Relevance_to_Environment_and_Development_Activities.pdf?sequence=1.

[54] James Fenske, "Ecology, Trade, and States in Pre-Colonial Africa," *Journal of the European Economic Association* 12(3) (2014): 612–640.

[55] However, Article 35 provides that the indigenous groups have the right to determine the rights and responsibilities of individuals and groups within the indigenous community. Basically therefore, it is the customs as passed from generation to generation that will determine issues of ownership and transfer. Okoth-Ogendo, *supra* note 15, discusses the role of customary law in this respect but in the context of land.

[56] See Articles 25–28.

[57] Article 31 provides verbatim as follows: "Indigenous peoples have the right to maintain, control, protect and develop their cultural heritage, traditional knowledge and traditional cultural expressions, as well as the manifestations of their sciences, technologies and cultures, including human and genetic resources, seeds, medicines, knowledge of the properties of fauna and flora, oral traditions, literatures, designs, sports and traditional games and visual and performing arts. They also have the right to maintain, control, protect and develop their intellectual property over such cultural heritage, traditional knowledge, and traditional cultural expressions."

4.a.V Model Law on Protection of Expressions of Folklore against Illicit Exploitation and Other Prejudicial Actions (WIPO and UNESCO)

As opposed to the WIPO Performances and Phonograms Treaty, this Model Law specifically focuses on the protection of folklore. Folklore is defined as including artistic productions consisting of distinct traditional content.[58] If reduced to tangible form in, *inter alia*, paintings, sculptures, pottery, textiles and weaving, these are also offered protection under the Model Law. Under Section 3, it is proposed that reproduction, publication and distribution or public recitation is subject to authorization by either the relevant Authority established under Section 9 or the community concerned.

Other regimes that are relevant to TK protection include the International Convention for the Protection of New Varieties of Plants (UPOV). This offers protection to plant breeders who meet the criteria set out under Chapter III of the Convention.[59] However, there have been concerns that this regime favours the commercialized competition that engineers crops with a view to increasing yield at the expense of traditional systems of seed saving. On the other hand, we also have the International Treaty on Plant Genetic Resources for Food and Agriculture under the Auspices of the Food and Agriculture Organization. It aims to achieve food security through the conservation and exchange of the world's genetic resources for agriculture.[60] In establishing a multilateral system of access and benefit sharing, based on co-operation and exchange of information, the Convention also requires the developed world to provide technical assistance to the developing world. Important for the purpose of this chapter is the recognition of the role played by indigenous groups in conservation under Article 9. The principle of equitable sharing of benefits as provided for under the CBD and the Nagoya Protocol is also provided for under Article 13.

4.b National Efforts

4.b.I The Kenyan case

Kenya is one of the first countries to develop a *sui generis* regime that protects TK and TCEs. The Protection of Traditional Knowledge and Cultural Expressions Act, 2016 gives effect to Articles 11, 40 and 69(1)(c) of the Constitution. Article 11 recognizes culture as the foundation of the nation. It

---

58 See Sections 1 and 2 of the Model Law.

59 Articles 5–9.

60 Article 3 clearly indicates that the purpose of the Convention is the utilization of plant genetic resources obtained both *in situ* and *ex situ* agriculture.

tasks the state with the mandate of promoting indigenous artistic expressions and traditional scientific innovation. On the other hand, Article 40 provides for the right to property including intellectual property.

With respect to the environment and natural resources, Article 69(1)(c) sets out the obligation to "protect and enhance intellectual property in, and indigenous knowledge of, biodiversity and the genetic resources of the communities". Therefore, the Kenyan Act of 2016 has a solid backing in the constitutional imperatives that are based on the recognition and respect for indigenous systems of innovation and artistic expression.[61] It must be noted that before the law was enacted, a policy was developed in 2009, which, at paragraph 4.5.3, recognized the need for a *sui generis* regime.[62] It was at the same time that Kenya developed a national land policy and recognized Community Land Ownership as a system of tenure.[63]

Section 4 of the Act grants the County Governments – being closer to the people than the national government – the mandate to collect and develop databases of traditional knowledge and cultural expressions. On the other hand, the national government is tasked with developing a repository at the Kenya Copyright Board. It is also the mandate of the national government to facilitate access to TK and TCEs and to protect them from misuse. The assumption is that the national government is in contact with external entities that may require access and has the capacity to interact and negotiate on behalf of the indigenous groups. Upon development of a database, the counties shall register the interests including competing interests from communities outside the county or the country.[64]

The Act grants the community exclusive rights over TK and TCEs.[65] Any exploitation of such TK and TCEs shall be subject to authorization and the community shall have the right to bring legal action against any persons violating this right. Section 11 requires recognition in the case of the use of TCEs.

---

[61] See Ben Sihanya, "Traditional Knowledge, Traditional Cultural Expressions and Intellectual Property Management in Kenya," *Law Society of Kenya Journal* 12(2) (2016): 32–33.

[62] See generally, The National Policy on Traditional Knowledge, Genetic Resources and Traditional Cultural Expressions, 2009, available at https://www.wipo.int/edocs/lexdocs/laws/en/ke/ke022en.pdf. Among the guiding principles of the Policy are respect for indigenous systems, prior informed consent, confidentiality and access.

[63] See Sessional Paper No. 3 of 2009, available at http://extwprlegs1.fao.org/docs/pdf/ken163862.pdf. Customary land ownership which is administered generally under customary law – codified or otherwise – was non-existent before the national land policy.

[64] Section 7.

[65] Part II deals with the conceptualization and protection of traditional knowledge, whereas Part III deals with traditional cultural expressions.

Under Section 12, the Cabinet Secretary may grant a compulsory licence subject to Article 40(3) of the Constitution which requires fair and prompt compensation. Section 18(2) requires prior informed consent in the case that TK or TCEs are exploited by third parties. In the case of derivative works, an authorized user agreement has to be prepared setting out the terms under which the community owning the original rights has allowed the production of derivative works.[66] However, the intellectual property right will be granted to the person who has derived new works from the original TCEs.

According to Section 22, the owners under customary law have the right to license or assign rights to third parties under a licensing agreement.[67] In this case, they are required to notify the Cabinet Secretary of all the authorization agreements entered into. The role of the Cabinet Secretary under this arrangement is merely to provide advice.[68] Further, in the event such rights are accessed, Section 24 requires that the principle of equitable sharing of benefits is respected. This extends beyond monetary compensation into community projects. However, the community may give this right to any of the two levels of government after consultations. Critically, Section 26 excludes access to genetic knowledge from access to genetic material.[69]

The owner of TK or TCEs is mandated under Section 32 to consider an application for use and may accept or reject it.[70] The terms of the User Agreement must contain matters such as benefit-sharing, dispute resolution, nature of use, disclosure requirements, term, access by owners themselves, controls on publication, moral rights and confidentiality.

---

66 Section 20 of the TK Act; under Section 21, the holders of the knowledge under customary law shall have the moral rights vested in them. Among other things, this includes the right not to have their knowledge distorted or prejudicially altered.

67 Section 25(1)(a).

68 Section 22(5); unless the community under Section 25(1)(b) grants the county government the mandate to exploit the TK and TCEs on their behalf. However, benefits ought to go directly to the community save for the administrative costs and fees in dispute resolution (Section 30 where there is a dispute on who the rights holders are) and publication as under Section 28.

69 This is the Environmental Management and Coordination (Conservation of Biological Diversity and Resources, Access to Genetic Resources and Benefit Sharing) Regulations, 2006 under the Environmental Management and Co-Ordination Act.

70 Under Section 32(2), the Cabinet Secretary must always be notified of the decision of the owners on an application to use.

5. THE PROMISE OF A NATIONAL *SUI GENERIS* REGIME

On the basis of the preceding sections of this chapter, it has emerged that alongside the progress towards the development of a global instrument, national laws can be developed by member states of the international community. As a matter of fact, some of the obligations in existing instruments such as the CBD, TRIPS and UPOV require national legislation. This is going to be a much easier route for the IGC owing to the challenges that arise and continue to be faced in crafting a global treaty. Furthermore, this would be much easier if the global instrument carries the nature of a model law or a declaration. In this case, the minimum standards shall be set by the instrument. In any event, global instruments on intellectual property such as TRIPS just provide for the minimum standards. Thereafter, the global regime relies on jurisdictional enforcement. The benefits of this approach are ventilated as follows.

Firstly, all factors constant, a national regime is likely to be responsive and alive to the needs of the indigenous communities. This is because as opposed to the crafting of a regime under the auspices of international agencies, the municipal government is closer to its people and actually understands the nature of indigenous rights to TK and TCEs. This is especially so where upon independence the government was taken over by the original occupants of the land. However, in areas such as Australia, the United States of America and Canada, the case might be different.

Secondly, the utilization of national law-making processes is a better avenue to get around the challenge of global politics in treaty-making.[71] In this case, it will be much easier for the law to form a representation of the local interests. The international interests can effectively be pushed to the periphery. At the same time, there are already established principles of international law that local laws cannot circumvent.[72] These include the principle of access based on the understanding that natural resources are a shared heritage. Therefore, national governments will be precluded from acting contrary to existing glob-

---

[71] This is not to say that global politics cannot interfere in local law-making processes; see Robert S. Ratner and Andrew Woolford, "Mesomobilization and Fragile Coalitions: Aboriginal Politics and Treaty-Making in British Columbia," *Research in Social Movements, Conflicts and Change* 28 (2008): 113–136.

[72] In the Alabama claims of the United States of America against Great Britain (RIAA) 1871, Volume XXIX, pp. 125–134 (available at https://legal.un.org/riaa/cases/vol_XXIX/125-134.pdf) it was held, *inter alia*, that municipal law cannot be used as an excuse to violate international law. Discussed by Edwin Borchard, "The Relation Between International Law and Municipal Law," *Virginia Law Review* (1940): 137–148, 141.

ally agreed standards. Furthermore, allowing national regimes to legislate for TK, genetic resources and TCEs can be seen as promoting principle 2 of the CBD which requires decentralization of management to the lowest level.[73] As has already been seen from the process that led to the UNDRIP, politics can easily overshadow well-meaning efforts.[74] This can be solved by using soft law instruments such as the Declaration itself or model laws to ensure that as far as possible, all member states of the global community are involved in the process. In the event developed countries opt-out, the resulting regime will have little or no effect. As the principles become globalized and accepted, then they can attain the status of international law through custom.

Thirdly, municipal law can be directly enforced as compared to international treaties. It has been argued that Kenya is a monist regime owing to Articles 2(5) and 2(6) of the 2010 Constitution.[75] However, generally, international law still needs to be domesticated into municipal law before it can be enforced. Unless the international instrument directly demands enforcement of certain principles or requires the establishment of certain administrative mechanisms, the process of domestication must be undertaken. Therefore, in the event that member states of the UN participating in the debate under the auspices of the IGC were to enact municipal laws like Kenya, enforcement will be easier and instant. Furthermore, the disputes that will arise in the case of illegal exploitation of TCEs may not necessarily touch on the relationship between states or state actors. It is likely that they will touch on the communities as owners of TK and TCEs and multinationals.[76] In this case, the best way to regulate is using national laws but relying on accepted principles of international law. It will be easier to enforce such interactions at that level by denying access to cultural IP or through arbitration with the help of national governments.

Fourthly, the appreciation of the juristic nature of customary indigenous systems is better handled by the national governments which are in contact with the indigenes. As discussed earlier, key among the reasons for the suppression of communal patterns of ownership of property is the international

[73] See, Principles, Convention on Biological Diversity, 2 July 2007, available at https://www.cbd.int/ecosystem/principles.shtml.

[74] See generally, Louis Henkin, "US Ratification of Human Rights Conventions: The Ghost of Senator Bricker," *American Journal of International Law* 89(2) (1995): 341–350. See also Jeff Corntassel, "Toward Sustainable Self-Determination: Rethinking the Contemporary Indigenous-Rights Discourse," *Alternatives* 33(1) (2008): 105–132.

[75] Tom Kabau and John Ambani, "The 2010 Constitution and the Application of International Law in Kenya: A Case of Migration to Monism or Regression to Dualism?," *Africa Nazarene University Law Journal* 1(1) (2013): 36–55.

[76] Chenguo Zhang, "How Is the Owner of 'Traditional Knowledge Right'? A Perspective of International Law and the Case of China," *Journal of Legal, Ethical and Regulatory Issues* 21(2) (2018): 1–14.

fallacy that indigenous regimes are backward and inimical to progress.[77] Since the national governments are closest to the indigenes, theoretically they are better placed to appreciate the nature of such rights. That they are in contact with these communities gives them access to study and identify appropriate solutions. Furthermore, they are the closest competent administrative arrangement that can assist in vouching for these interests. The economic life of the indigenous communities will directly affect the development of the countries at large.[78] This gives national governments more impetus to craft proper laws and will engender a stronger sense of ownership of the process, which is crucial.

Finally, municipal law can inform the general principles of an international framework. As the national and international efforts develop simultaneously, the experiences of the national laws can be used to develop a responsive and working international regime. In this case, the regime can take the form of a model law. Working examples include the UNCITRAL Model Law on International Commercial Arbitration, the UNCITRAL Model Law on Electronic Transactions and the OECD Model Tax Convention on Income and on Capital. It will be easier to come up with international standards which can carry the nature of custom if they develop from tried and tested experiences based on already agreed principles under existing regimes. On the critical twin issues of access and benefit-sharing, there are already international standards in the nature of the UNDRIP and the Nagoya Protocol. Further, the emerging international instruments such as the Model Law on Protection of Expressions of Folklore against Illicit Exploitation and Other Prejudicial Actions (WIPO and UNESCO) and the WIPO Performers and Phonograms Treaty can be used as foundational instruments to guide the process of crafting an international regime. Furthermore, national regimes can directly engage the communities and consider their interests. The national regimes can fortify already existing instruments to ease the work of the IGC.

6. CONCLUSION

Based on the evidence of existing regimes, the urgent need to realize the protection of indigenous peoples' rights to TK and TCEs and the need for a responsive regime, this chapter concludes that national legislation supple-

---

[77] Nyamu-Musembi, *supra* note 17 and Okoth-Ogendo, *supra* note 15.

[78] Melisande Middleton, "Using Traditional Knowledge in Economic Development: The Impact of Raised Field Irrigation on Agricultural Production in Puno, Peru," World Bank Group, No. 99, January 2007, available at https://openknowledge.worldbank.org/bitstream/handle/10986/10719/391330PE0iknt9901PUBLIC1.pdf?sequence=1&isAllowed=y.

mented by a model law would be an appropriate solution. This will, generally, receive support from the international community. Possible resistance owing to the economic implications of the erosion of matters currently constituting the public domain will be diminished. On the other hand, this will take the pressure off the IGC and move their efforts towards a close. Further, this will, at the same time, help to validate the UNDRIP. Furthermore, if the national governments take the right steps, indigenous communities will receive much-needed unconditional validation of their systems of property ownership and control.

Borrowing from the Kenyan legislation, the proposed international law instrument can then set standards relating to applicable principles, ownership of rights, access, the role of national governments, the content of licensing agreements, compulsory licensing, dispute resolution, and institutionalization of the community, among other things. The regime can also, *inter alia*, establish its own administrative framework for the purposes of research and development, monitoring legislation and offering legislative support, considering the interests of the indigenes as being distinct from those of the national governments.

Despite the above, challenges abound. The national governments may stifle the voice of the indigenous communities. It is also not clear whether all the governments of the developing world have the capacity and experience to craft responsive and comprehensive legislation. However, considering the case of Kenya, this is possible. There is also the challenge of the apparent conflict between the entitlement by the government to natural resources and the entitlement of the communities to their indigenous knowledge. This must be resolved in favour of the community with respect to the knowledge, whereas the naturally occurring resources – in terms of title – can be the property of the state. In all, the exploitation of such genetic resources must still benefit the local communities living in the ecosystems where the GR is mined.

7. Folklore vis-à-vis intellectual property in Bengal since the seventeenth century: a study

Mayuree Sengupta[1]

1. INTRODUCTION

"Folklore is one of these three: a body of knowledge, a mode of thought, or a kind of art. These categories are not completely exclusive of each other."[2] When folklore juxtaposes with intellectual property,[3] the knowledge resource that results is unparalleled in stature and aids in understanding the wisdom of Bengal, a land steeped in ancient history, cultural legacy, political patronage, colonial hegemony and a weary independence at the cost of being partitioned. An undivided Bengal as depicted in Figures 7.1 and 7.2 was partitioned in 1947 into the state of West Bengal in India and East Pakistan, which later gained freedom to form a new country, Bangladesh. It would be prudent to consider that political uncertainty after close to two hundred years of colonial subjugation led to a lull in the appraisal of local lore and the assemblage of credible intellectual property.

Based on this premise, this chapter embarks on an in-depth study pertaining to three case studies concerning folklore and intellectual property of Kohitoor, Muslin and Rosogolla from Bengal, setting off on a journey from the pre-British Nawabs' regime to the current democratic jurisdiction.

---

[1] I wish to gratefully acknowledge the immense contribution of Professor Ghosh as the Editor in tirelessly bringing together the diverse chapters of the book.

[2] Ben-Amos, D. (1971). "Toward a definition of folklore in context", *The Journal of American Folklore* 84(331), 3–15 at p. 5.

[3] Intellectual property (IP) refers to creations of the mind: inventions, literary and artistic works, and symbols, names, images and designs used in commerce.

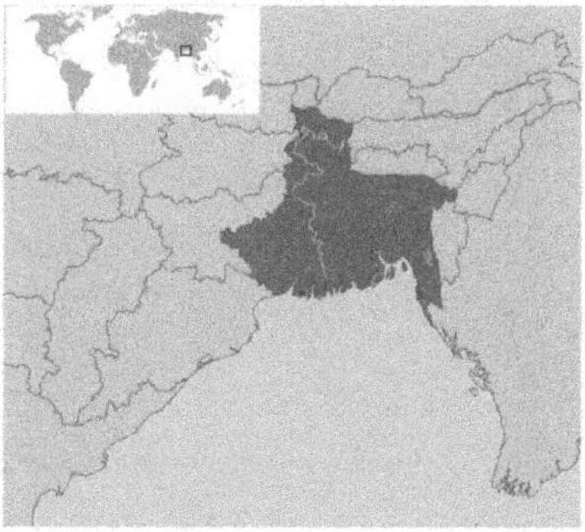

Figure 7.1 *Undivided Bengal*

Source: Retrieved from https://en.wikipedia.org/wiki/Bengal (last visited on 10 August 2019).

2. THE LORE OF MANGO

The mango[4] is considered one of the choicest fruits in the world.[5] India is the leading producer[6] of mangos (*Magnifera indica*), or the "king of fruits" as it is popularly termed. Among all Indian states, West Bengal (as shown in Figure 7.3) is a notable producer[7] of different varieties of mango. "No other fruit has such a conspicuous register in written works, verses, mythical tradition, chronicles, painting and statuesque [*sic*] as that of mango".[8] Local folklore[9] on mango in indigenous Bengali language exalts the richness of the seasonal

---

4 The word found salience in an Italian text written by Ludovico di Varthema in 1510 and was also mentioned by Hendrik Van Rheedein his book *Hortus Malabaricus*, a compendium of the plants of economic and medical value in the Malabar (Northern Kerala), published in 1678.

5 Mirta, S. and Baldwin, E. (1997). "Mango". Excerpt summary retrieved from https://www.ars.usda.gov/research/publications/publication/?seqNo115=88473 (last visited on 10 August 2019).

6 Retrieved from http://agriexchange.apeda.gov.in/Market%20Profile/one/MANGO.aspx (last visited on 10 August 2019).

7 Retrieved from http://mangifera.res.in/indianstatus.php (last visited on 10 August 2019).

8 Chakraborti, K. and Bandyopadhyay, M. (2015). "Mango-Lore of Bengal", *International Journal of Environmental & Agriculture Research* 2(1), at p. 12.

9 Translated, it eulogises the mango through rhymes:

Rhyme 1: Mango starts developing from flower in the month of *Magh* (January–February), in *Falgun* (February–March) it develops, in *Boisakh* (April–May) the seed is formed and in *Joistha* (May–June) one gets to savour the ripe fruit in full glory, leaving only the seed intact.

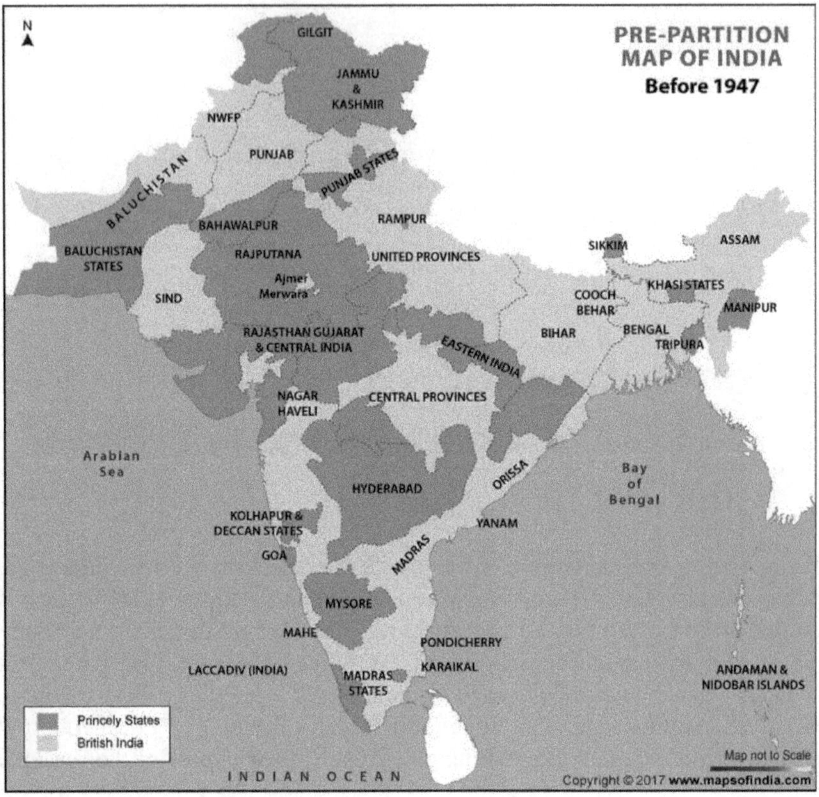

Figure 7.2 *Undivided India in the pre-1947 era*

Source: Image reproduced with permission from https://www.mapsofindia.com/maps/india/prepartitionmap.htm.

fruit and enumerates the varieties in rhyme songs sung during the harvest and local festivals.

So ingrained are the characteristics of each mango variety with the climate and soil of Bengal, that no fewer than three varieties of mango, namely

---

Rhyme 2: Mango is the best of fruits, Shyam (Hindu God Krishna) best among humans, white cloth among clothes, Radha (God Krishna's associate/beloved) amongst women and water from River Ganges (considered holy river by Hindus) is the best.

Figure 7.3 *Present-day West Bengal*

Source: Image reproduced with permission from https://www.mapsofindia.com/maps/westbengal/westbengal-district.htm.

Malda[10] Laxman Bhog,[11] Malda Khirsapati (Himsagar)[12] and Malda Fazli,[13] have been recognised as geographical indicators[14] by the Government of

---

[10] Malda is an agrarian district in West Bengal, famed for abundant and varied Mango production. Excerpt retrieved from http://malda.gov.in/economy_about.htm (last visited on 10 August 2019).

[11] GI Application No. 111, retrieved from http://www.ipindia.nic.in/registered-gls.htm (last visited on 10 August 2019).

[12] GI Application No. 112, retrieved from http://www.ipindia.nic.in/registered-gls.htm (last visited on 10 August 2019).

[13] GI Application No. 113, retrieved from http://www.ipindia.nic.in/registered-gls.htm (last visited on 10 August 2019).

[14] Article 22.1 of the Trade Related Intellectual Property Rights Agreement defines geographical indications as "indications which identify a good as originating in the territory of a Member [of the World Trade Organization], or a region or locality in that territory, where a given quality, reputation or other characteristic of the good is essentially attributable to its geographical origin".

India.[15] Interestingly, the neighbouring country Bangladesh (erstwhile Eastern Bengal until 1947 and east-Pakistan until 1971) also registered the Khirsapat (Himsagar) mango of Chapainawabganj as a GI in 2019;[16] a glaring example of how the intellectual property of Bengal still converges, blurring man-made jurisdictional borders. In West Bengal, mangoes are primarily cultivated in the districts of Malda, Murshidabad, Nadia and 24 Parganas (North) which have a rich collection of varieties.[17] The districts of Murshidabad and Malda are especially celebrated for distinct mango varieties. However, these are at significant risk of genetic erosion of the mango germplasm,[18] as the traditional varieties are low yielding and increasingly being replaced by new high yielding hybrids. More than 200 varieties of mango were recorded during the time when these districts were under royal rule.[19] This number has sharply declined in recent times.

Though efforts have been made for the recognition of Malda mangoes, Murshidabad, another border district, had been relegated to anonymity until the recent past, when in 2018 the West Bengal state government applied for GI recognition for Murshidabad's famed and rare Kohitoor (also Koheetur) mango variety. Of the 12 noteworthy royal mango varieties,[20, 21] Kohitoor has scant availability, and hence it is rare. Kohitoor is also noted as a significant variety in neighbouring Bangladesh.[22]

Folklore has it that the last independent Nawab (King) of Bengal, Siraj ud-Daulah (reign: 1756–57), was a connoisseur of mangoes. Such was his avid love for the famed fruit that he acquired saplings of the best mangoes from all over the country for his garden in Murshidabad. Nawab Siraj ud-Daulah even

---

[15] Retrieved from http://www.ipindia.nic.in/registered-gls.htm (last visited on 10 August 2019).

[16] Retrieved from http://www.itfnet.org/v1/2019/02/bangladesh-khirsapat-mango-wins-gi-tag/ (last visited on 10 August 2019).

[17] Kundu, S., Sanyal, N. and Datta, P. (2009). "Studies on potentiality of some mango varieties in West Bengal", *Journal of Crop and Weed* 5(2), 68–71.

[18] Germplasm is living tissue from which new plants can be grown. It comprises the information for a species' genetic makeup, a valuable natural resource of plant diversity.

[19] De, M., Das, J., Saha, M., Pal, A. and Dey, S.R. (2014). "Documentation and characterization of the indigenous Mango (Mangiferaindica L.) varieties of Malda and Murshidabad districts of West Bengal", *J. Environ. & Sociobiol.* 11(2), 187–198.

[20] Anaras, Bhabani, Bira, Borosinduria, Chandankhosa, Daudi, Dhobani, Dilpasand, Gulabkhas, Kohitoor, Michridana, Rumali.

[21] Developed under Nawabi patronage in mango orchards from Lalbag to Palashi, present-day Murshidabad district.

[22] Ara, R., Motalab, M., Uddin, M. N., Fakhruddin, A.N.M. and Saha, B.K. (2014). "Nutritional evaluation of different mango varieties available in Bangladesh", *International Food Research Journal* 21(6).

went to the extent of employing highly skilled mango breeders who carried out research and undertook cross-breeding between various mangoes to create new varieties. Historical accounts also state that there was a research centre in the Nawabi administration for conceiving new varieties of mangoes. For enhancing flavour, fragrance, and taste many novel methods were adopted. The mango seeds were soaked in fruit juice, rose water and herbal extract to change the traits of the mango.[23]

Many of these processes were lost with the fall of the Nawab administration. Ironically, the decisive Battle of Plassey (1757), which led to the ousting and death of the last independent Nawab of Bengal, Siraj ud-Daulah and the advent of British imperialism and the rule of the East India Company, was fought in the shaded groves of the mango orchards in Plassey (locally termed Palashi).

The Kohitoor, an exclusive variety, is believed to have been created by a royal mango breeder called Hakim Ada (also Aga) Mohammadi, by cross-breeding between a mango called Kalopahar and another variety at the bidding of the last independent Nawab of Bengal Siraj ud-Daulah. The variety was reportedly only consumed by royals and was out of bounds for subjects. It is also stated that only deseeded mangoes were served to royal guests and courtiers so that the famed variety did not fall into common hands. The fruits were hand plucked individually, or by *thoosi.*[24] It was believed that after harvesting, the mangoes were moved carefully to cane baskets lined with soft cotton. The delicate Kohitoor would supposedly lose its taste if it fell on hard ground. After every 12 hours, the mango had to be turned on its side for uniform ripening. It was also required that the Kohitoor be sliced by a sharp bamboo wedge and not a traditional metal knife. Nawabs would supposedly use golden toothpicks to savour the fruit. During the Nawabi era, the Kohitoor was doused in honey to augment shelf life and aid in preservation.

Even after Company rule was established in Bengal province and Siraj ud-Daulah's treacherous general Mir Jafar ascended the throne as a dependent ruler, the prestige of the Kohitoor remained untarnished. Mir Jafar's eldest son, Miran, was fond of this variety and employed skilled persons to manage this delicate affair. Faiyaz Ali Khan, the sixth generation descendant of Nawab Mir Jafar, set up a mango orchard at Jafraganj and planted the Kohitur variety there.

However, with the passage of time and Bengal being subjected to ruthless colonial rule, neither the delicate variety nor the knowledge and finesse sur-

---

23 Chopra, P. (2019). "Things you can do with Murshidabad mangoes", iLEAD Foundation.

24 Ibid 23. A *thoosi* is a thin bamboo pole, with an open mouthed net bag at the top end, into which fruits fall when drawn in with a slight jerk.

rounding it could be preserved fully. Until the 1970s, the Nawabi orchard of the Maharaja of Cossimbazar had 50 Kohitoor plants. Soon after, most of these orchards were sold for urbanisation and saplings were lost or re-planted elsewhere, leading to a dilution of the breed and loss of purity of the germplasm. Growers assert that the mango production is neither plentiful nor annual. However, the Kohitoor is sold at around fifteen hundred Rupees per piece, a sum which would comfortably fetch a few kilograms of other varieties. In the present-day scenario, 25 to 30 numbered trees are left in Murshidabad despite the state government initiating efforts to preserve the variety and have the GI registered. Elite by birth, made still more exclusive by traits, rarity, and now by price, the heritage, folklore and rich germplasm of the Kohitoor is way too precious to fade into anonymity.

3. THE ALLURE OF MUSLIN

The world-famous Dacca (also Dhaka[25]) muslin,[26] described as "a web of woven winds" is believed to have been spun from a superior variety of cotton[27] called "Forma Bengalenese".[28] Dacca sent its muslins and embroidered fabrics to Western Asia, Syria, Babylon, Persia, China, Java, Pegu (Myanmar), Malacca, Greece, Rome, Egypt, Provence, Italy, Languido and Spain.[29] They

---

[25] The present-day capital of Bangladesh; an important city located on the eastern part of the erstwhile undivided Bengal.

[26] Muslin is a loosely-woven plain cotton fabric and brand name of a pre-colonial Bengal textile, especially of Dacca origins. The true origin of this fabric was in Bangladesh and certain parts of West Bengal in Eastern India.

[27] Analysing the cotton plant from which the Dacca spinners took their cotton, an expert noted down these four points, "(1) The branches are more erect and the lobes of the leaves more pointed. (2) The whole of the plant is tinged with a reddish colour, even the petioles and nerves of the leaves are less transparent. (3) The tendrils which support the Bowers are longer and the exterior margin of the petals is tinged with red. (4) The staple of the cotton is longer, much finer and softer compared to other Bengal cottons." Reproduced from Puntambekar, S.V. and Varadachari, N.S. (1926). *Hand spinning and hand weaving: An essay*. All India Spinners Association, Ahmedabad, at p. 31.

[28] The finest sort of muslin was made of *phuti* cotton, which was grown in certain localities on the banks of the Brahmaputra and her branches. The other kinds of cotton called *bairait* and *desee* were inferior and were produced in different parts of Dhaka and neighbouring areas; they were used for manufacturing slightly inferior and course clothes. Information sourced from Shah, J.J. (1985). "A comparative analysis of two major cotton textile centres of India-Bombay and Ahmedabad", *Treballs de la Societat Catalana de Geografia*, 87–106.

[29] Banerjei, N.N. (1900). "The cotton fabrics of Bengal", *The Journal of Indian Art, 1886–1916* 8(61–69), 221–258 and Puntambekar, S.V. and Varadachari, N.S. (1926). *Hand spinning and hand weaving: An essay*. All India Spinners Association, Ahmedabad.

were some of the finest offerings from Bengal and India to the world.[30] The art of spinning and weaving involved in the production of the finer muslin fabrics required a very high degree of skill and a great deal of labour and patience.[31] Narratives state that the expert weavers of Dacca used no fewer than 126 distinct processes for muslin.[32] Specific procedures for warping, sizing, dressing and bleaching the muslin were studied by contemporary European researchers. A piece of muslin had 500 counts of thread and took 10–180 days to manufacture, depending upon the quality and finesse.

The Dacca muslin trade was almost entirely carried on by Hindu weavers and spinners who flourished under the enduring and benevolent patronage of the Dacca Nawabs and the Emperors at Delhi.[33] The East India Company had not concentrated on Bengal for sourcing textiles until the second half of the seventeenth century; their main station of trade until then was the Coromandel coast, which was prone to civil wars and thus marred Company interests.[34] British rule, established by the East India Company, marked the death knell for the local royalty, and most of Muslim aristocrats were dispossessed of their wealth. Consequently, there was a decline in the consumption of domestic muslin. The population of Dhaka declined from about 300,000 in the eighteenth century to 50,000 in the mid-nineteenth.[35] This could be attributed both to the onset of British colonial rule and the removal of the Nawab's court from Dacca to Murshidabad earlier in 1702.[36] After the Battle of Plassey, "Bengal

---

30 Dugvekar, T.G. (1957). "Management of nationalised industry", *The Indian Journal of Political Science* 18(3/4), 268–276, at p. 268.

31 Pal, N.M. (1930). *Industrial development of India*. The Book Co, Calcutta, at p. 16.

32 The starch they used comprised of parched rice. The starch used for "shabnam" was always mixed with a small quantity of lamp-black. The weavers plied their looms under shelter and worked most during the rainy season (the months of *Ashadh, Shravan* and *Bhadra)* which was the most favourable for their operations. The probable reason attributed to this was that the moisture prevented the thread from snapping. The mode of packing and shipping fine muslins was to enclose them in hollow bamboo tubes sufficiently large to contain yards of cloth. Often a muslin fabric was judged for its quality based on its ability to pass through a finger ring.

33 Puntambekar, S.V. and Varadachari, N.S. (1926). *Hand spinning and hand weaving: An essay*. All India Spinners Association, Ahmedabad. However, a conflicting view states that most of the finer textiles like Dacca muslin and Kashmir shawls were woven by Muslim master weavers (Qureshi, I.H. (1977). *The Muslim community of the Indo-Pakistan subcontinent, 610–1947: A brief historical analysis*. Ma'aref).

34 Glamann, K. (1981). "Piece-goods", in *Dutch-Asiatic Trade 1620–1740*. Springer, Dordrecht (pp. 132–151).

35 Maddison, A. (1970). "The historical origins of Indian poverty", *PSL Quarterly Review* 23(92).

36 Murshid quli Khan, the Diwan of Bengal (holding allegiance to the Mughal Sultanate of Delhi under Emperor Aurangzeb) removed the seat of administration

plunder" from the Nawab's treasury was so colossal that it fuelled Britain's Industrial Revolution from 1760 and affected the world's lifestyle forever.[37] It eventually led to the collapse of the traditional industrial structure of the country, including textiles. Bengal was compelled to act as an absorber or emerging market for British mill manufactured textiles; it was a planned strategy of British colonial policy to drive indigenous textiles to extinction.

> The people of Bengal had been used to tyranny, but had never lived under an oppression so far-reaching in its effects, extending to every village market and every manufacturer's loom. They ... had never suffered from a system which touched their trades, their occupations, their lives so closely. The springs of their industry were stopped; the sources of their wealth dried up.[38]

The ruthless economic suppression was also condemned worldwide:

> England has broken down the entire frame-work of Indian Society, without any symptom of reconstitution yet appearing. This loss of his old world, with no gain of a new one, imparts a particular kind of melancholy to the present misery of the Hindu and separates Hindustan ruled by Britain from all its ancient tradition and from the whole of its past history.[39]

The East India Company was anxious to maintain its trade in Indian muslins, which depended on a restricted supply.[40] It increased its investments and Indian (Bengal) muslin reached England.[41] Alarmed by the popularity of

---

from Dhaka to Murshidabad in 1702. He became Nawab of Bengal in 1716. A document at the archives in Hazar Duari Palace of the Nawabs of Murshidabad, shows that Nawab Murshid Quli Khan (reign: 1716–1727) bought one khanda of the 1,000-count muslin from a weaver for Rs 400. The Nasiri Dynasty of Murshid Quli Khan ended in 1740 and was replaced by the Afshar Dynasty founded by Alivardi Khan. Nawab Siraj ud-Daulah was the maternal grandson of Alivardi Khan. An interesting story states that Nawab Alivardi Khan once banished a Hindu weaver from the capital due to the weaver's having left a piece of muslin on grass which was devoured by a cow.

[37] Sengupta, S. (2010). "Bengal's plunder gifted the British Industrial Revolution", *The Financial Express*.

[38] Dutt, R.C. (1902). *The Economic History of British India: A Record of Agriculture Land Settlements, Trade and Manufacturing Industries, Finance and Administration*. Kegan Paul, London, at p. 27.

[39] Marx, K. and Engels, F. (n.d.). *The First Indian War of Independence 1857–9*. Moscow; and Marx, K. and Engels, F. (n.d.). *On Colonialism*. Moscow.

[40] Chapman, S.D. (1987). "The cotton industry in the industrial revolution", in *The Industrial Revolution. A Compendium*. Palgrave, London (pp. 1–64).

[41] Thomas, P.J. (1924). "The beginnings of calico-printing in England", *The English Historical Review* 39(154), 206–216.

Indian (Bengal) muslin abroad,[42] local English manufactures started an active lobbying against the import of Indian textiles. Muslins were thus made to pay a 10% (conversely 17.5%) duty[43] on importation and £31 6s 8d on home consumption.[44] In fact, "in 1824 the exports of British muslins to India hardly amounted to 6 million yards, while in 1837 it surpassed 64 million yards".[45]

The quest for commercial opportunities, backed up by lust for political ascendancy of the British, led to a continuous assault on the rich cultural and commercial heritage of the muslin trade.[46] A "Regulation for Weavers" passed by the Governor General in Council, on 23 July 1787 exploited Indian cotton weavers with regard to price, purchase, sale and with non-economic compulsion or extraterritorial jurisdiction.[47]

The British atrocities on the colonised population and unethical trading practices that can be deemed anticompetitive at best and destructive at worst led to the decline and ultimate death of the muslin trade in the mid-nineteenth century. Weavers during early 1800s used to manufacture on own accord and sell to merchants profitably. However, towards the 1850s, due to dearth of patronage, capital and other ancillary causes, they undertook weaving only on an advance payment and made-to-order basis. By the 1840s–1850s the systematic destruction of the art and trade was so thorough that the art of muslin weaving went into oblivion. The scarcity of long stapled cotton was another decisive reason. Even towards the later part of the nineteenth century, researchers deemed that the art of the manufacture of superfine muslin fabrics was dead.[48]

It was only after India gained independence in 1947 that attempts were made to revive the lost art of muslin. Muslin was experimentally revived in West Bengal with the aid of a few Khadi institutions. Presently Kalna in Burdwan

---

42 In the great 1851 Exhibition of London, Dacca muslin occupied a prominent place and attracted a large number of visitors, while the British Press spoke very highly of the marvellous muslin fabrics of Dacca.

43 Other accounts peg the import duty at 75–80%.

44 Tripathi, A. (1949, January). "Some reflections on the East India Company's Charter of 1813", in *Proceedings of the Indian History Congress*. Indian History Congress (Vol. 12, pp. 227–239).

45 Marx, K. in June 10, 1853 edition of *New York Daily Tribune*.

46 In 1787, the then Collector of Dacca, Mr Day had estimated the Dacca muslin trade to be worth between Rs. 30 lakh to Rs. 1 crore.

47 Nishimura, T. (1964). "The Indian cotton industry in the age of the industrial revolution", *Bulletin of University of Osaka Prefecture. Ser. D, Sciences of economy, commerce and law* (8), 13–26.

48 Banerjei, N.N. (1900). "The cotton fabrics of Bengal", *The Journal of Indian Art, 1886–1916* 8(61–69), 221–258 and Pal, N.M. (1930). *Industrial Development of India*. The Book Co, Calcutta.

district, Nabadweep in Nadia district and Chok Islampur in Murshidabad district are the frontrunners in producing high count muslin.[49] In West Bengal there are primarily seven districts which can be identified as major pockets of muslin fabric: Murshidabad, Birbhum, Nadia, Burdwan, Malda, Hooghly and Paschim Medinipur. The West Bengal Khadi and Village Industries Board[50] (WBKVIB) has applied for registration of "Bengal Muslin" as GI (Application no. 676) on 18 November 2019 and it is currently awaiting examination.

The *jamdani* or the loom-figured muslin was the most exquisite production of the Dacca[51] loom. In Bangladesh the notable areas for muslin were Dhaka, Sonargaon, Dhamrai, Teetbady, Junglebary and Bajitpur. Bangladesh granted GI registration for Jamdani to the applicant Bangladesh Small and Cottage Industries Corporation (BSCIC) in 2016, the first product registered for that country.

4. THE CHRONICLE OF ROSOGOLLA

The sweet temptation, or rosogolla,[52] has been the subject of a sticky affair, much like the sugary syrup it is soaked in. West Bengal and Odisha, two states of independent India had staked a claim over rosogolla at the GI Registry. According to local lore, the chhena-based[53] sweets for which Kolkata[54] is renowned acquired their current form as late as the mid-nineteenth century. This could be partially attributed to shifting attitudes of Hinduism and a general

[49] Notable institutions producing high count muslin are: 1. Nabadweep Kutir Shilpa Pratishtan, Nabadweep. 2. Chandrakant Lalit Mohan Resham Shilpa Samiti, Murshidabad. 3. Bharat Khadi Sevak Sangh, Murshidabad. 4. Muslin Katai Mandal, Murshidabad.

[50] The board is supposedly in the final stages of conducting extensive research work collating the age-old gazette notifications, different publications and literature to establish the rich history of muslin in Bengal. It is also making a detailed record of the steps taken in recent times for the rejuvenation of muslin.

[51] In the Narayanganj area of Dacca specific localities such as Noapara, Dakkhin Ruposhi, Ruposhi Kajipara, Gandabpur, Shiddhirgonj, Mugrakul, Khidirpur, Imkoli, Tarabo, Khalpara, Dighborar, Khadun, Pabankul, Sultanbagh and some areas of Sonargaon upazila are famous for *jamdani*.

[52] Rasogolla is one of the ultimate delicacies of Bengal which is made from ball-shaped dumplings of chhana (an Indian cottage cheese) and is cooked in a light and somewhat transparent syrup made of sugar. Note on spelling: it is also called "roso-golla" (being a native term it is prone to different spellings in English).

[53] When hot milk is curdled, chhena (cottage cheese) is formed. Note on spelling: in Bengal it is called chhana. While in northern parts of India it is pronounced chhena. Both variants can be found in this chapter.

[54] Present-day capital of West Bengal, erstwhile capital of British India until 1911.

evolution of society.[55] It should be noted that in earlier times, only kheer was considered pure and could be offered to the Gods.[56] Kabi Kankan Mukunda Chakraborty mentioned the term "chhana" and its product in the form of "chhana naru" in his noted *Chandimangal*.[57] In *Chaitanyacharitamrita*,[58] authored by Krishnadas Kabiraj in the sixteenth century, the name of a different sweet product made of chhana is mentioned, though not explicitly "rosogolla".

Nobin Chandra Das was one of the many moiras (sweetmeat sellers) who trace their roots to nineteenth-century Kolkata. In 1868[59] Nobin Moira, after substantial experimentation,[60] was successful in creating the modern-day rasogolla.[61] It soon became popular with Bengal's elite[62] and a worthy competitor to traditional sandesh. According to divergent sources of information, Braja Moira, who was an ancestor of Dinu Moira, an inhabitant of Sitanath Ghosh Street of Beniatola, Kolkata, had started a shop near Calcutta High Court and discovered how to prepare rasogolla.[63] Rasogolla's origin has also been attributed to Haradhan Moira from Fulia town in Nadia district.[64] Rasogolla was appreciated as a treasure of Bengal by Rakhaldas Adhikari in his poem.[65]

---

55 Krondl, M. (2011). *Sweet invention: A history of dessert*. Chicago Review Press.

56 Chhana, which is produced by cutting milk with citric acid was considered impure. It was considered unworthy of the Gods, hence prohibited at temples.

57 *Chandimangal* is a noted medieval literary Bengali work dating back to the sixteenth century. Its edited version (Chakrabarti, M., *Chandimangal*, edited by Sukumar Se. Calcutta, Sahitya Akademi, 1986, 63) is referred to here.

58 A hagiography on the life of the mystic and saint Chaitanya Mahaprabhu, Hindu mystic of the Vaishnava sect.

59 Information retrieved from a Promotional Information Booklet of K.C. Das Private Limited.

60 He made small balls of casein (cottage cheese) and boiled them in hot sugar syrup. It resulted in a succulent, spongy sweet with a unique, distinctive taste.

61 Different historical accounts state conversely. According to the eminent writer Panchanan Bandyopadhyay, rasogolla was invented in the Nadia district of Bengal. He wrote that rasogolla was no more than around sixty years old. The birthplace of Krittibas, Fuliya is the place where rasogolla originated. A confectioner of that village named Haradhan used to prepare sweets for the Paul Chowdhury family of the Ranaghat area. One day his daughter was crying and to console her Haradhan the confectioner threw the balls of chhana into the sugar syrup kept on the oven. An innovative new sweet was thus created which the landlord of the Paul Chowdhury family named rasogolla.

62 Raibahadur (an English title given to influential and loyal Indians) Bhagwandas Bagla was one of the first customers of rosogolla. Maharani (Queen) Swarnamoyee Devi, the dowager of the House of Cossimbazar was also a connoisseur.

63 Bhowmik, H. (2015). "Rasogolla Banglar Jagatmat no Abiskar", *Gangchil*.

64 Retrieved from https://www.anandabazar.com/national/rasgulla-of-odisha-also-gets-geographical-indication-1.1024801 (last visited on 10 August 2019).

65 Adhikari, R. (1896). Rasikata, 30.

Mrs. J Halder, in her eminent book *Bengal Sweets*[66] had depicted the recipe of rasogolla and sponge rasogolla along with its ingredients in detail. The word rosogolla found mention as "desoj" (indigenous word) in *Bangla Biswakosa*, the first encyclopedia in Bengal, published by Nagendranath Basu in 1911.

Nabin Moira's descendants, modern-day sweet baron K.C. Das's in-house R&D laboratory in Bangalore, has been recognised by the Government of India's Department of Science and Technology (DST).[67]

Armed with a barrage of folklore, rich heritage and the legacy of the advent and evolution of rasogolla, West Bengal State Food Processing and Horticulture Development Corporation Limited filed a GI application[68] for the same on 18 September 2015 and was granted registration on 14 July 2017 (Figure 7.4). The detailed specification[69] designated "Banglar Rasogolla" as a syrupy dessert made up of pure chhana dumplings dipped in light sugar syrup.

BANGLAR RASOGOLLA

Figure 7.4 *GI logo of Banglar Rasogolla*

Source: Retrieved from Geographical Indications Journal No. 99 from http://www.ipindia.nic.in/journal-gi.htm (last visited on 10 August 2019).

[66] *Bengal Sweets* by Mrs J Halder, second edition, 1926, pp. 98–101.

[67] Information retrieved from http://www.dst.gov.in/sites/default/files/Directory%20of%20R%20%26%20D.pdf (last visited on 10 August 2019).

[68] Application No. 533 in respect of Food Stuff falling in Class 30, titled Banglar Rasogolla.

[69] Chhana is the sole ingredient of "Banglar Rasogolla" which is obtained from the curdling of pure milk. Starch is not used while preparing the chhana dumplings. The dumplings are spherical in shape to give them a ball-like structure. The size of rasogolla varies from 3.7 to 6.2 cm approx. The colour of the sweet is usually white/off white. The spongy character of "Banglar Rasogolla" has made the product unique from the

The registered GI was intended to be used by a substantial number of rasogolla manufacturers and sellers. According to the declaration of Paschim Banga Mistanna Byabsayee Samity (loosely translated West Bengal Sweetmeat Seller's Association) there are more than 1 million confectioners in West Bengal, excluding the district Darjeeling, making and selling rasogolla.

Religion and sweets (rosogolla) intertwined in a heady cocktail even under the apparent religion-neutral rule of the British. However, nowhere was the impact more pronounced than in the case of rosogolla when the neighbouring state Odisha took up in arms against West Bengal's registration of the GI and staked a claim based on the *bhog* (offering) made to Mahaprabhu Jagannath[70] (a Hindu deity) of Puri (the capital of Odisha). A reference to "Rasagola" is found in the late fifteenth-century, *Odia Ramayana*[71] written by Balaram Das.

A petition was even filed contesting West Bengal's precedence. Odisha also adduced numerous literary evidences in explicit support of its claim.[72] Eventually, the Odisha Small Industries Corporation Limited (OSIC Ltd., a Government of Odisha undertaking) and Utkal Mistanna Byabasayee Samiti

---

rest. In terms of texture, "Banglar Rasogolla" are soft, smooth and have better cohesiveness. The chewiness is much less, within a range of 400–850 gm. The average moisture content of the sweet is 50%. The sugar syrup is light in consistency and somewhat transparent in nature, and the concentration of sugar syrup is usually maintained within a range of 30–40%. The pH of the sugar syrup is usually within the range of 5.5–6.2. No extraneous colouring matter is added. The Brix range of the sugar syrup is between 30 and 40.

70 As part of the last ritual of Rath Yatra, known as "Niladri Bije" (Lord Jagannath's return to his abode after nine days), it is offered to goddess Lakshmi on behalf of Lord Jagannath.

71 In its "Ajodhya Kanda", one comes across elaborate descriptions of chhena and chhena-based products including rasagola. According to the description, after Lord Rama left for the forest, Bharata and Satrughna went to bring him back and on their way accepted the hospitality of sage Bharadwaj. The sage served them and their respective followers various types of food and delicacies which included dudha chhena (cottage cheese prepared from milk) and the products from chhena, namely chhenapuri, chhenaladu, rasagola and rasabali.

72 The reference to rasagola was first found in the late fifteenth century, *Odia Ramayana* written by Balaram Das. Fakir Mohan Senapati, in his writing *Utkal Bhramanam* published in "*Utkal Deepika*" on 27 August 1892 mentioned plentiful use of rasagola in Odisha during those days. On 14 December 1893, a poem titled, "Bali Jatra" was published in the weekly "Indradhanu" written by poet Damodar Pattanayak. The poem was an eye-witness account of Cuttack's famous, historic fair, Bali Jatra (Journey to Bali Island of Indonesia) and mentioned that sweets shops were looking attractive in the presence of rasagola and other sweets. This shows that rasagola was a much-relished sweet as far back as 1893 in Bali Jatra, the grand fair of Odisha. Important evidence relating to the popularity of rasagola is available in a travelogue named Waltier Darshan written by Fakir Mohan Senapati, which was published in the *Utkal Sahitya*, a monthly Odia literary magazine in 1904.

jointly applied for a GI[73] on the 23 of February 2018 and were granted registration on 29 of July 2019 (Figure 7.5). OSIC named all the 30 districts in Odisha as areas that will fall within the GI purview.

4.a Odisha Rasagola

Figure 7.5 *GI logo of Odisha Rasagola*

Source: Retrieved from Geographical Indications Journal No. 116 at http://www.ipindia.nic.in/journal-gi.htm (last visited on 10 August 2019).

The detailed specification[74] designated "Odisha Rasagola" as a soft, juicy and non-chewy sweet prepared using the principle of caramelization of sugar applying specific methods.

---

73 Application No. 612 in respect of Food Stuff falling in Class 30, titled Odisha Rasagola.

74 "Odisha Rasagola" is a sweet from the state of Odisha made up of chhena cooked in sugar syrup, which is very soft to the touch, juicy and non-chewy in consistency and can be swallowed without using much teeth pressure. The colour development of "Odisha Rasagola" is very specific, where without the addition of external colour, rasagolas of various intensity of colour are prepared using the principle of caramelisation of sugar with specific methods of preparation. Generally, "Odisha Rasagola" are white in colour with a round shape, but off-white rasagolas in various shades are plentifully prepared by cooking the rasagola at 110^{0}C for about 40 minutes, in which caramelisation of sugar takes place, giving the off-white colour.

For "Odisha Rasagola" chhena is prepared from the natural milk of a local breed of cow without the removal of cream. The presence of fat makes it softer compared to the chhena of other parts, where the cream is removed from the milk before chhena preparation leading to coarse-textured chhena. "Odisha Rasagola" is prepared by following a unique chhena-processing technique called "chhena chakata", in which chhena is kneaded a number of times for about 15 minutes on a wooden base to cause the disinte-

The contest over the sweetmeat between two neighbouring states is not merely about recognition for their respective fares but under the intellectual property regime it also translates into potentially sound business for the confectioners of the two states and revenues for the state governments. Rosogolla is proof of how folklore, culture and traditions form the evidentiary foundation on which intellectual property matters are contested and wrested from a rival. While both states have obtained their respective registrations after the contentious issue began in 2015, it is pertinent to point out that Bengal won the registration for "Banglar Rasogolla" while Odisha obtained it for "Odisha Rasagola". As per colloquial indigenous dialect and taste perception, the above-mentioned two sweets are vividly distinct.

Also, rosogolla has not been limited to the confines of its geographical indication only, but a patent has also been filed over its preparation.[75]

5. CONCLUSION

The study of knowledge embedded in a synergism of folklore and a modern intellectual property regime, as depicted in the above three cases, indicate that these are not in conflict with each other. Often, it is extraneous factors such as regime change (governing authority), lack of preservation of indigenous lore, the non-profitability of produce or product owing to prohibitive prices, or the absence of patronage for a skill set are the reasons which lead to setbacks in augmenting and sustaining valuable and intangible assets such as intellectual property. Bengal, both in its erstwhile unified state and within its currently divided geopolitical boundaries, is one such inimitable case in point. The heartening instances of revival of Kohitoor, Muslin and Rosogolla are worthwhile reminders that knowledge, both lore and intangible, need nurturing to thrive and prove economically advantageous to the local populace.

---

gration of its particles from the tissue. In this process the strength of chhena's particles is reduced and it becomes softer. The addition of "suji" and "maida" acts as a binding agent for the development of soft, round-shaped, non-spherical rasagola.

[75] Application No. 553/KOL/2002 (IN212143B) titled "A process for preparing nutrient fortified ayurvedic sweets like sandesh and rosogolla containing at least one herb" was filed at the Indian Patent Office by a group of individual inventors in 2002. Their governmental affiliation, if any, has not been revealed.

PART IV

THE LORE OF COMMON LAW

8. Radical patent law reform in a common law enabling system: a metahistory

Samuel F. Ernst[1]

INTRODUCTION

A volume such as this one about lost intellectual property lore is necessarily about history. Postmodern historians tell us that history is not a science whereby we discover facts about what happened in the past.[2] Absent a time machine, recreating the past is impossible. Rather, historians select and interpret 'facts,' which are themselves 'always refracted through the mind of the recorder,' such that '[h]istory means interpretation.'[3] Accordingly, histories are constructed narratives that use literary tools and tropes to shape the present by making an argument about the past.[4] So, too, are judicial decisions. In a common law system such as U.S. patent law,[5] the law develops through appellate opinions that construct the current law by selectively interpreting prior judicial opinions that are themselves rhetorical constructs built according to the same methods. Appellate opinions must selectively construct and construe what happened in the trial courts. And the trial courts engage in 'fact-finding,' which is itself an historical construct based on testimony and documentary evidence, which are themselves human constructs of something that may or may not have actually

[1] Thanks to Dr. Johann Neem, historian and friend, and to Dr. Eldon G. Ernst, historian and father.

[2] See, e.g., Edward Hallett Carr, *What is History?* (Vintage Books 1961) 3–29.

[3] Id. at 24, 26.

[4] Hayden White, *Metahistory: The Historical Imagination in 19th-Century Europe* (Fortieth Anniversary Ed., Johns Hopkins University Press 2014) 1–41.

[5] Or, to be precise, a common law enabling system, because Congress does enact broadly sketched patent law statutes that the courts purport to interpret. However, as discussed below, the statutes are largely codifications of past judicial decisions and leave so many gaps for the courts to fill in that the U.S. has, in practical effect, a common law system for patent law. See Section 1, *infra*.

happened. Using the medium of these cycles of historical construct, the appellate courts and occasionally the Supreme Court paint the current patent law.

Hence American[6] patent law is made out of history, which is actually only lore. This is surprising given Americans' constant focus on the present, with little knowledge or sense of the vast history leading up to the latest Tweet or soundbite.[7] Major patent litigation reform typically occurs in the United States when the Supreme Court resuscitates history to correct the lower courts; specifically, the Court revives its judicial precedent on patent law from prior historical periods that witnessed abuses of the patent system. This does not necessarily mean that we should view the development of U.S. patent law cynically. Along with the postmodern recognition that judicial decisions are constructs comes the metamodern[8] recognition that such constructs can nonetheless serve an essential social function; in this example, to reform the patent law to promote innovation. However, this requires active litigation campaigns to influence judge-made law, because judicial decisions are constructs that can also be used to facilitate or wreak injustice.[9]

Although the U.S. Congress has periodically throughout our history passed major patent legislation, such as the Patent Act of 1952, these are what are known as 'common law enabling statutes.' Congress generally spoke in broad

---

[6] Here I use the narcissistic term 'American' to refer solely to the United States merely as convenient shorthand, neither wishing nor qualified to pass judgment on the other 34 American nations.

[7] Benjamin M. Schmidt, 'The History BA Since the Great Recession' *Perspectives on History: The News Magazine of the American Historical Association* (26 November 2018) https://www.historians.org/publications-and-directories/perspectives-on-history/december-2018/the-history-ba-since-the-great-recession-the-2018-aha-majors-report, accessed 8 July 2019; Alan C. Brownfeld, 'The Danger Ignorance of History Poses to the Future of a Free society' *American Council of Trustees and Alumni* (22 April 2018) https://www.goacta.org/news/the-danger-ignorance-of-history-poses-to-the-future-of-a-free-society, accessed 8 July 2019; Max Boot, 'Opinion: Americans' Ignorance of History is a National Scandal' *Washington Post* (Washington, D.C. 20 February 2019).

[8] 'Metamodernism' refers generally to an optimistic view of the postmodern insight that such things as history, religion, and even science are human filtered constructs; these constructs can be powerful tools for social good. See generally John Higgs, *Metamodern: Making Sense of the Twenty-First Century* (Weidenfeld and Nicolson 2019).

[9] See, e.g., *Scott v. Sandford*, 60 U.S. 393 (1857), *superseded by* U.S. Const., Am. XIV, § 2 (1868) ('The Dred Scott decision,' holding, *inter alia*, that Scott was not a citizen because of his race and could not, therefore, bring suit in federal court); *Korematsu v. United States*, 323 U.S. 214 (1944) (holding that an executive order excluding American citizens of Japanese descent from their homes to hold them indefinitely in internment camps without any evidence of wrongdoing was valid under the Constitution), *abrogation recognized by Trump v. Hawaii*, 138 S. Ct. 2392, 2423 (2018).

strokes, codifying past judicial decisions on patent law by the Supreme Court and intermediate appellate courts (the circuit courts) and allowing those courts to fill in the interstices of the statutes going forward with further precedential decisions. This is perhaps distinguished from a civil law system, wherein the legislative codes are more detailed and the role of the courts is, at least in theory, merely to interpret the codes.[10]

But the Supreme Court does not work continuously at the task of shaping patent law. Historically, the Supreme Court has engaged in periods of relative disengagement from patent law for decades at a time until there arose a perceived or real crisis in society with respect to the abuse of patent rights to harm the economy, a competitive marketplace, and/or powerful business interests.[11]

The most recent example of this phenomenon occurred in the wake of the creation of a specialized appellate court, the Court of Appeals for the Federal Circuit (hereafter 'the Federal Circuit'), which was created to unify patent law, but instead disrupted and distorted the law in favor of those asserting patent rights. To curb this imbalance, the Supreme Court has affected major reforms in patent law in the last two decades on a wide range of issues, from patent validity standards, to the availability of injunctions, to defenses to patent infringement, and a host of other issues.[12]

The Supreme Court's method in undertaking this task was to revive its forgotten precedential decisions from decades or centuries past; cases that were often issued prior to the passage of the Patent Act of 1952. This method gives the perception that the Court is neutrally applying its precedent, and not making new law or policy, but this is deceptive because the Court selects which of its precedents to augment and which to disregard or diminish.[13]

This raises the issue of what motivates judges in making their disguised policy choices. Scholars have proposed a wide range of hypotheses to answer this question, including formalism, economic rationality, unconscious psychological or sociological influences, political biases, pragmatism, and other theories. None of these theories provides an all-encompassing explanation. They are partial explanations that overlap in some respects and contradict one another in other respects, containing half-truths and half-fictions. In fact, judges are human beings and therefore motivated by incalculable complexities and contradictions.[14]

---

10 See Section 1, *infra*. Detailed citations to sources are provided in the sections below and not in this introductory outline.

11 See Section 2, *infra*.

12 See Section 3, *infra*.

13 See Section 3, *infra*.

14 See Section 4, *infra*.

Be that as it may, in the context of patent law, this process has resulted in useful patent reform far more efficiently and decisively than anything Congress could achieve. But is it democratic to allow unelected judges to perform this task? Would a code-based civil law system give more power to the people? Or, in actual practice, is a code-based system really so very different? Finally, given the domination of Congress in the U.S. by lobbying interests and powerful corporations, and the unequal apportioning of voting influence by our antiquated Constitution, are we faced with a choice between two essentially undemocratic institutions to affect legal reforms?[15]

1. PATENT STATUTES TO CODIFY AND ENABLE THE COMMON LAW

In 1789 the U.S. Constitution went into full effect and granted to the federal congress the power to grant copyrights and patents. Specifically, Congress would have the power '[t]o promote the Progress of Science and useful Arts, by securing for limited Times to Authors and Inventors the exclusive Right to their respective Writings and Discoveries.'[16] Congress seized this power to pass major patent legislation from time to time, including in 1790, 1793, 1836, 1870, 1952, and most recently the 'America Invents Act' of 2011.[17] With the passage of all these patent codes, how then can we call American patent law a common law system? The answer lies in the understanding of what constitutes a 'code.' In civil law systems a code is 'a forward-looking new lawbook, written as one coherent whole and intended to create a new legal order rather than to present a summary and an inventory of the old.'[18] But in a common law system, statutes often codify the existing judge-made common law (with some occasional corrections), and create new law only insofar as they are written in broad strokes, allowing for interpretation and indeed law-making by the judiciary.[19] In simple and general terms, appellate judges in a common law system can make law in the interstices of statutes and through broad interpre-

---

15 See Section 4, *infra*.

16 U.S. Const. art. I, § 8, cl. 8.

17 Patent Act of 1790, 1 Stat. 109; Patent Act of 1793, 1 Stat. 318; Patent Act of 1836, 5 Stat. 117; Patent and Copyright Act of 1870, 16 Stat. 198; Patent Act of 1952 (codified as amended at 35 U.S.C. §§ 1 et seq.); Leahy-Smith America Invents Act, Pub. L. No. 112-29, 125 Stat. 284 (2011) (codified in scattered sections of 35 U.S.C.).

18 R.C. van Caenegem, *European Law in the Past and the Future* (Cambridge University Press 2002) 40.

19 Id. at 40–41.

tation, even in areas where the legislature has enacted statutes; civil law judges theoretically only interpret and apply the code.[20]

So it is with U.S. patent law. Even the first patent statute was a common law enabling statute, codifying in part the judge-made law that came before it and enabling further common law development in the future. The Patent Act of 1790 was enacted against 'a patent custom extant in both the infant United States and in Great Britain.'[21] Hence, the Act was influenced by the British Statute of Monopolies, which itself was largely a codification of existing British common law on patents.[22] The British Statute was written in broad strokes, such that 'English patent practice also was governed by certain common law judicial decisions.'[23] And the first U.S. Congress sought to incorporate some aspects of this British common law into the new U.S. law.[24] The patent law practices of various states within the Union were even more influential,[25] and so the first Patent Act was in significant part a codification of existing British and state common law. The Act itself 'was fairly short and comparatively simple,' leaving it to the Department of State to examine and issue patents and even fix their terms, and to the courts to develop the details of the patent law in the context of litigation.[26]

Hence, the courts developed the common law of patents under this statute and the subsequent patent acts. Over the centuries, the courts invented out of whole cloth or through interpretation of the broad statutes the standards for

---

20 Martin Vranken, *Fundamentals of European Civil Law* (The Federation Press 1997) 65. This characterization is simple, general, and theoretical because there are numerous variations between civil law systems. See, e.g., Stuart J.H. Graham and Nicolas Van Zeebroeck, 'Comparing Patent Litigation Across Europe: A First Look' [2014] 17 Stan. Tech. L. Rev. 655. Moreover, Alan Watson argues, '[t]he claim that the main distinction between civil law systems and common law systems is that the former are codified and the latter are not is full of defects.' Alan Watson, *The Meaning of Civil Law* (Harvard University Press 1981) 3. But even Watson admits, '[i]n common law systems, in contrast, legal emphasis is on what the courts do rather than on systematic exposition.' Id. at 29.

21 Edward C. Walterscheid, 'Charting a Novel Course: The Creation of the Patent Act of 1790' [1997] 25 AIPLA Q. J. 445, 449.

22 Id. at 450.

23 Id. at 451.

24 Id.

25 Id. at 451.

26 P.J. Federico, 'Operation of the Patent Act of 1790' [1990] 72 J. Pat. & Trademark Off. Soc'y 373, 373–374, 381 (reprinted from 18 J. Pat. & Trademark Off. Soc'y 237 [April 1936]).

patent infringement,[27] for equivalent infringement,[28] for novelty,[29] for priority of invention,[30] for patent eligible subject matter,[31] for sufficient enablement and description in the patent specification,[32] for claim interpretation and claim definiteness,[33] for infringement remedies,[34] and for a host of other legal and equitable issues.

Even when Congress enacted the massive Patent Act of 1952, it largely codified the existing judge-made law (with a few futile attempts at correction discussed below) and enabled the development of further common law.[35] As Craig Allen Nard observes:

> [T]he patent code, much like the Sherman Act, is a common law enabling statute, leaving ample room for courts to fill in the interstices or to create doctrine emanating solely from Article III's province. Indeed the common law has been the dominant legal force in the development of U.S. patent law for over two hundred years.[36]

The Supreme Court openly recognizes this, repeatedly making such statements as, '[i]n the context of infringement, we have already held that pre-1952 precedent survived the passage of the 1952 Act';[37] and 'the 1952 Patent Act was primarily intended to codify existing law.'[38] And the Act requires the development of future common law by employing very broad standards that must as a practical matter be developed into rules.

For example, the statutory standard for infringement states merely that 'whoever without authority makes, uses, offers to sell, or sells any patented

---

27 See, e.g., *Winans v. Denmead*, 56 U.S. 330 (1853).

28 See, e.g., *Graver Tank & Mfg. Co. v. Linde Air Prods. Co.*, 339 U.S. 605 (1950).

29 See, e.g., *Gaylor v. Wilder*, 51 U.S. 477 (1850).

30 See, e.g., *City of Elizabeth v. American Nicholson Pavement Co.*, 97 U.S. 126 (1878).

31 See, e.g., *O'Reilly v. Morse*, 56 U.S. 62 (1853).

32 See, e.g., *Consolidated Electric Light Co. v. McKeesport Light Co.*, 159 U.S. 465 (1895).

33 See, e.g., *McClain v. Ortmayer*, 141 U.S. 419 (1891).

34 See, e.g., *Continental Paper Bag Co. v. Eastern Paper Bag Co.*, 210 U.S. 405, 424 (1908).

35 See Samuel F. Ernst, 'A Patent Reformist Supreme Court and its Unearthed Precedent' [2018] 29 Fordham Intell. Prop. Media & Ent. L.J. 1, 35.

36 Craig Allen Nard, 'Legal Forms and the Common Law of Patents' [2010] 90 B.U. L. Rev. 51, 53. 'Article III' refers to Article III of the U.S. Constitution, which established the Judiciary, and the Sherman Act refers to the Sherman Antitrust Act of 1890, currently codified as amended at 15 U.S.C. §§ 1–38.

37 *Warner-Jenkinson v. Hilton Davis Chem. Co.*, 520 U.S. 17, 26 (1997); see also *Aro Mfg. Co. v. Convertible Top Replacement Co.*, 377 U.S. 476, 505 n. 20 (1964).

38 *SCA Hygiene Prods. Aktiebolag v. First Quality Baby Prods.*, 137 S. Ct. 954, 968 (2017) (Breyer, J., dissenting).

invention … during the term of the patent therefor, infringes the patent.'[39] It has been left to the courts through centuries of precedent to specify that infringement is determined by (1) interpreting the language of the claims under complicated claim construction rules;[40] (2) comparing the claim limitations to the elements of the accused product or process;[41] (3) requiring that all claim limitations be present in the accused product or process;[42] (4) unless any different structure performs substantially the same function in substantially the same way to achieve the same result under a 'doctrine of equivalents' that is nowhere mentioned in the statute;[43] (5) but not if there is some defense to equivalent infringement, such as 'prosecution history estoppel.'[44]

With respect to damages, the Patent Act merely states, 'Upon finding for the claimant the court shall award damages adequate to compensate for the infringement, but in no event less than a reasonable royalty for the use made of the invention by the infringer, together with interest and costs as fixed by the court.'[45] Needless to say, it has required a vast library of judicial law often informed by the economic analysis of legions of experts to determine what constitutes 'damages adequate to compensate' and 'a reasonable royalty' in any given case. One leading treatise on patent damages law is 1,382 pages long, has a list price of $1,145, and is updated annually to keep pace with the ever evolving judicial law on damages.[46]

Hence, Judge Howard T. Markey was incorrect in his famous article, 'Why Not the Statute?', when he wrote, '[T]he patent laws are entirely statutory. There is no common law of patents.'[47] This statement is at best true only as some needling technicality. A stickler may insist on the use of the term 'statutory interpretation' rather than 'judge-made law' or 'common law.' Judicial decisions theoretically serve only to fill gaps in the patent statutes. But the patent statutes are composed almost entirely of gaps. Indeed, the statutory gaps are so vast and the judicial rules so comprehensive and detailed that it obliterates Melvin Eisenberg's distinction between statutory interpretation and

---

39 35 U.S.C. § 271(a).

40 See *Phillips v. AWH Corp.*, 415 F.3d 1303, 1312–1319 (Fed. Cir. 2005) (en banc).

41 *Lemelson v. United States*, 752 F.2d 1538, 1551 (Fed.Cir.1985).

42 Id.

43 *Graver Tank & Mfg. Co. v. Linde Air Prod. Co.*, 339 U.S. 605, 608 (1950).

44 *Festo Corp. v. Shoketsu Kinzoku Kogyo Kabushiki Co.*, 535 U.S. 722, 727 (2002).

45 35 U.S.C. § 284, ¶ 1.

46 See John M. Skenyon et al., *Patent Damages Law and Practice* (Clark Boardman Callaghan 2019).

47 Howard T. Markey, 'Why Not the Statute?' [1983] 65 J. Pat. Off. Soc'y 331, 331.

common law.[48] With such sparse guidance from the Patent Act, we would be at sea without the vast common law of patents.

One of the very few exceptions where the Patent Act of 1952 did not purport to codify existing judge-made law was with respect to rules for determining whether a patent is invalid for 'obviousness.' Prior to the Act the courts had developed from the broad language of the Constitution rules surrounding a requirement of 'invention' for something to be patentable. In a foundational case from 1850, *Hotchkiss v. Greenwood*, the Supreme Court held that novelty alone did not suffice for a claimed invention to be patentable; there had to exist an inventive leap beyond any minor improvement to the prior art that an ordinary mechanic could make.[49] The Court thereby invalidated a patent on the basis that the claim at issue did 'not rise to the dignity of an invention or discovery, but is a mere substitution of one material in place of another, for making the same common article.'[50] This 'invention' standard evolved and developed through judge-made law until the passage of the Patent Act of 1952. One of the authors of the Act, Judge Giles Rich, abhorred the 'invention' standard because he found it unpredictable and ill defined. Judge Rich wrote:

> You really have to be on the Supreme Court to find a 'standard' there because the only way it can work is this: if you [i.e., the Supreme Court] think the lower court was wrong in sustaining the patent, you proclaim that it applied too low a standard and reverse its decision, saying '*That* was not an *invention*.'[51]

In particular, Judge Rich pointed to the Supreme Court's *Hotchkiss* decision as the corrupt origin of what he viewed as the lawless 'invention' requirement.[52] Judge Rich wanted a more rigid, predictable rule.

Accordingly, the Patent Act of 1952 set forth a broadly sketched requirement that has been given the clumsy moniker, the 'non-obviousness' requirement. The statute provides:

> A patent may not be obtained though the invention is not identically disclosed or described as set forth in section 102 of this title, if the differences between the subject matter sought to be patented and the prior art are such that the subject matter as a whole would have been obvious at the time the invention was made to a person

---

[48] Melvin Aron Eisenberg, *The Nature of Common Law* (Harvard University Press 1988) vii.

[49] *Hotchkiss v. Greenwood*, 52 U.S. 248, 262 (1850).

[50] Id.

[51] Giles S. Rich, 'The Vague Concept of "Invention" as Replaced by Sec. 103 of the 1952 Patent Act' [1964] 46 J. Pat. Off. Soc'y 855, 861 (emphases in original).

[52] Id. at 859–860.

having ordinary skill in the art to which said subject matter pertains. Patentability shall not be negated by the manner in which the invention was made.[53]

But this too provided only a general standard, rather than a detailed rule, because '[t]he drafters of the 1952 Act, however, were circumspect in their attempt to strike a balance between reining in judicial discretion and inviting judicial intervention.'[54]

Hence, the Supreme Court began the task of giving actual substance to the new non-obviousness requirement in the 1966 case, *Graham v. John Deere Co. of Kansas City*, by articulating a five-step process for determining obviousness.[55] The Supreme Court directed lower courts to (1) determine the scope and content of the prior art; (2) determine the level of ordinary skill in the art; (3) ascertain the differences between the prior art and the claimed invention; (4) determine against this background the technical obviousness or non-obviousness of the invention; and (5) consider non-technical secondary considerations bearing on obviousness such as 'commercial success, long felt but unsolved needs, failure of others, etc.'[56] One might argue that the Court was acting somewhat as a civil law court in this instance, rather than in its typical common law mode, because the Court's test does require, among other things, analyzing the differences between the prior art and the claimed subject matter as the statute commands. But the courts conducted this analysis before the passage of the Act too. In the *Hotchkiss* case itself the Court ascertained the differences between the prior art and the claimed invention.[57] And, in any event, the *Graham* Court explicitly stated that even on this issue, where many felt that Congress was supplanting the 'Invention' test with legislation, in fact the pre-1952 common law survived:

We believe that this legislative history, as well as other sources, shows that the revision was not intended by Congress to change the general level of patentable invention. We conclude that the section was intended merely as a codification of judicial precedents embracing the Hotchkiss condition, with congressional direc-

---

[53] 35 U.S.C. § 103(a) (pre-AIA). The America Invents Act slightly modified the language of this provision to accommodate the newly adopted 'first-to-file' system. See 35 U.SC. § 103.

[54] Nard, *supra* note 36 at 72–73.

[55] *Graham v. John Deere Co. of Kansas City*, 383 U.S. 1, 17–18 (1966).

[56] Id. at 18.

[57] *Hotchkiss*, *supra* note 49 at 265 ('But in the case before us, the knob is not new, nor the metallic shank and spindle, nor the dovetail form of the cavity in the knob, nor the means by which the metallic shank is securely fastened therein. All these were well known, and in common use; and the only thing new is the substitution of a knob of a different material from that heretofore used in connection with this arrangement').

> tions that inquiries into the obviousness of the subject matter sought to be patented are a prerequisite to patentability.[58]

Despite Judge Rich's Sisyphean efforts, *Hotchkiss* and its progeny survived. And like countless waves depositing sand on the shore, subsequent opinions by the Courts of Appeals further developed the obviousness inquiry. This task was necessary in particular to round out the details of the circular black box that was step four of the Supreme Court's test: 'Against this background, the obviousness or nonobviousness of the subject matter is determined.'[59]

But eventually the Court of Appeals for the Federal Circuit inserted too many rule-based strictures into the obviousness inquiry, requiring, for example, that '[t]he party seeking patent invalidity based on obviousness must also show some motivation or suggestion to combine the prior art teachings' (commonly called the 'teaching, suggestion, motivation' or 'TSM' test).[60] Accordingly, in 2007, the Supreme Court rejected the Federal Circuit's obviousness rules as 'unduly rigid' and erroneous because '[t]hroughout this Court's engagement with the question of obviousness, our cases have set forth an expansive and flexible approach inconsistent with the way the Court of Appeals applied the TSM test here.'[61] The Court then relied on its precedent from before the passage of the 1952 Patent Act, including *Hotchkiss*, because 'the principles laid down in *Graham* reaffirmed the "functional approach" of *Hotchkiss*.'[62]

In short, the answer to Judge Markey's rhetorical question, *Why Not the Statute?*, is: you can read the statute as much as you like, but the real patent law in the U.S. is judge-made law.[63]

---

58 *Graham*, *supra* note 55 at 17.

59 Id. at 17.

60 *Al-Site Corp. v. VSI Int'l, Inc.*, 174 F.3d 1308, 1323–1324 (Fed. Cir. 1999).

61 *KSR Int'l Co. v. Teleflex, Inc.*, 550 U.S. 398, 415 (2007).

62 Id. at 415. And the cycle continues, as certain panels of the Federal Circuit have recently begun to reinsert the 'teaching, suggestion, motivation' requirement into the obviousness inquiry. See, e.g., *Metalcraft of Mayville, Inc. v. The Toro Co.*, 848 F.3d 1358, 1367 (Fed. Cir. 2017) (upholding the validity of a patent where the challenger failed to demonstrate a motivation to combine because 'while we understand that "[t]he obviousness analysis cannot be confined by a formalistic conception of the words teaching, suggestion, and motivation," we also recognize that we cannot allow hindsight bias to be the thread that stitches together prior art patches into something that is the claimed invention') (citing *KSR*, *supra* note 61 at 419).

63 Of course, there are a handful of exceptions where the statutes are highly detailed and technical, such as the requirements for petitioning the Patent and Trademark Office ('the PTO') to review the validity of an issued patent, the new *inter partes* review procedure. See 35 U.S.C. §§ 311 to 319. But even these statutes require judicial interpretation and law-making in the interstices. See, e.g., *Fresenius USA, Inc. v. Baxter Intern., Inc.*, 721 F.3d 1330 (Fed. Cir. 2013) (holding that the cancellation of patent claims by

2. HISTORICAL PATTERNS OF SUPREME COURT JUDICIAL REFORM

The Supreme Court's ability to make law through this common law process empowers it to affect reforms to the patent law much more quickly and much more radically than Congress can achieve. Congress is fettered by powerful lobbying interests that are at war with one another (such as the pro-patent pharmaceutical industry versus the often anti-patent Silicon Valley high-tech industry), resulting in the need for watered-down compromises, vague, general standards, or no legislation at all. Radical and speedy reforms are also foiled by the necessity of obtaining a majority in the House of Representatives, a filibuster-proof majority in the Senate for legislation, and the signature of the President. In addition, Congress has limited attention to give to patent law due to its infinite competing priorities, many of which are far more important than patent reform. Then there is the need to spend countless hours raising money and campaigning to win the next election.[64] Hence, while Congress occasionally makes a significant reform, such as the enactment of *inter partes* review in the 2011 America Invents Act,[65] generally Congress does not act or merely issues the common law enabling statutes discussed above.

In contrast, the Supreme Court can set its own priorities because it needs only four out of nine votes to accept a case. Supreme Court justices are appointed for life and need spend no time on re-election, raising money, or worrying about the wishes of constituents and wealthy patrons. And making new law through a majority opinion requires only five votes. From these facts we get the famous anecdote about the late Justice William Brennan:

> Brennan liked to greet his new clerks each fall by asking them what they thought was the most important thing they needed to know as they began their work in his chambers. The pair of stumped novices would watch quizzically as Brennan held up five fingers. Brennan then explained that with five votes, you could accomplish anything.[66]

---

the PTO during pending infringement litigation is binding in the litigation if it occurs at any time prior to final judgment).

[64] Ryan Grim and Sabrina Siddiqui, 'Call Time for Congress Shows How Fundraising Dominates Bleak Work Life' *Huffington Post* (8 January 2013) https://www.huffpost.com/entry/call-time-congressional-fundraising_n_2427291, accessed 29 July 2019 (reporting that an incoming orientation for freshman congressmen recommended spending five hours per day raising campaign donations and only three to four hours per day doing congressional work).

[65] See 35 U.S.C. §§ 311 to 319.

[66] Seth Stern and Stephen Wermiel, *Justice Brennan: Liberal Champion* (Houghton Mifflin Harcourt 2010) 196.

Accordingly, throughout the history of U.S. patent law, we have seen the same pattern. Decades pass where the Supreme Court is relatively inactive in its engagement with patent law. Then, in apparent response to a crisis related to the abuse of patent rights, the Court enacts radical and rapid reforms. For example, in the late 1800s there arose a phenomenon of non-practicing entities (called 'patent sharks' in those days) acquiring and asserting farm implement patents against farmers.[67] Specifically, as Colleen Chien has explained, 'patent "sharks" became infamous for using patents to demand payments from farmers for articles the farmers had purchased.'[68] Congress failed to act despite the plight of these sympathetic defendants. At the same time, 'patent sharks' also asserted patents against the most powerful corporations of the day, the railroads.[69] The result was that '[i]nstead of the sometimes awkward alliance between Silicon Valley giants and hacker activists, the nineteenth century offered railroad companies and farmers.'[70] These lobbying interests proposed a range of measures to curb patent abuse,[71] but Congress was unable to act. The legislative proposals were largely stymied by a handful of powerful Senators.[72]

Then the Supreme Court took active measures to confront this nineteenth-century patent thicket. Steven Usselman writes that 'if a small tribunal in the Senate could block railroads from securing a legislative remedy to their problems by altering the patent laws, a handful of justices on the Supreme Court might offer at least a measure of relief through their interpretation of those laws.'[73] In fact, the Supreme Court provided more than a measure of relief; it produced radical patent law reform. And the Court did not merely interpret the patent laws; it created new doctrine out of whole cloth. For example, in the 1800s the Court created the patent exhaustion doctrine, whereby the authorized first sale of a patented product exhausts all rights in that product, thus prohibiting 'patent sharks' from chasing it down the stream of commerce to collect additional royalties from farmers and other consumers.[74] The Court created the reverse doctrine of equivalents, whereby even if

---

67 Colleen V. Chien, 'Holding Up and Holding Out' [2014] 21 Mich. Telecomm. & Tech. L. Rev. 1, 10.

68 Id. at 10.

69 Steven W. Usselman, *Regulating Railroad Innovation* (Cambridge University Press 2002) 169.

70 Christopher Beauchamp, 'The First Patent Litigation Explosion' [2016] 125 Yale L.J. 848, 935.

71 Id. at 934–935 (describing proposals).

72 Usselman, *supra* note 69 at 169.

73 Id.

74 See Samuel F. Ernst, 'Patent Exhaustion for the Exhausted Defendant: Should Parties be able to Contract Around Exhaustion in Settling Patent Litigation?' [2014] 2014 J.L., Tech. & Pol'y 445, 451.

an accused product falls within the literal scope of the patent claims, it escapes infringement if it is so far changed in principle that it constitutes a substantial improvement over the patented invention.[75] The Court sowed the seeds of the modern day inequitable conduct defense, holding that the government could sue in equity to void a patent if the applicant had committed fraud on the patent office.[76]

Another such period of Supreme Court patent law reform came in the early to mid-twentieth century, the 'antitrust era.' The courts were suspicious of powerful, monopolistic trusts and this bled over into an aversion to potentially monopolistic patent rights.[77] Nard describes the Supreme Court patent reforms undertaken in this era:

> For example, the Court expanded the patent misuse doctrine, did away with the common practice of drafting claims in functional terms, and, most significantly, enhanced the so-called 'requirement for invention' by invoking the 'flash of genius' test. The Court also cast doubt on the patentability of 'combination' patents (i.e., combination of old elements) by requiring a display of synergism; that is, the combination, to be patentable, had to equal more than the sum of its parts.[78]

In sum, one can observe historical cycles of Supreme Court disengagement from patent law; followed by the growth of patent thickets and patent abuses harmful to innovation; followed by periods of intense Supreme Court involvement in patent law as it enacts common law judicial reform.

---

[75] See Samuel F. Ernst, 'The Supreme Court Case that the Federal Circuit Overruled: *Westinghouse v. Boyden Power Brake Co.*' [2018] 68 Syracuse L.R. 53, 55–69. Despite being faithfully applied by the Courts of Appeals for over eighty years after *Boyden*, the Federal Circuit has effectively overruled *Boyden sub silentio*. See id. at 69–75. See also Samuel F. Ernst, 'The Lost Precedent of the Reverse Doctrine of Equivalents' [2016] 18 Vand. J. Ent. & Tech. L. 467, 473–488 (describing the circuit court precedent applying the reverse doctrine of equivalents prior to the 1982 creation of the Federal Circuit).

[76] *United States v. Am. Bell Tel. Co.*, 128 U.S. 315, 355 (1888) ('It seems to us that if Bell was aware, at the time that he filed his specifications, asserted his claims, and procured his patents that the same matter had been previously discovered and put into operation by other persons, he was guilty of such a fraud upon the public that the monopoly which these patents grant to him ought to be revoked and annulled'); see Robert J. Goldman, 'Evolution of the Inequitable Conduct Defense in Patent Litigation' [1993] 7 Harv. J.L. & Tech. 37, 43–44.

[77] See Ernst, 'A Patent Reformist Supreme Court,' *supra* note 35 at 56.

[78] Nard, *supra* note 36 at 72 (internal citations omitted).

3. THE RISE AND FALL OF THE PATENT COURT

Then came an interesting plot twist. The pendulum against patents began to swing in the opposite direction. Patent stakeholders, such as certain businesses and the patent prosecution bar, began to believe that the Supreme Court and the regional circuit courts were diminishing patent rights to a vanishing endpoint. In the words of Judge Marion T. Bennett (one of the original judges on the Federal Circuit): 'Some of the regional circuit courts, expressing strong feelings about the dangers of monopoly and having a low regard for the expertise of the Patent Office, tended not to give any deference to the administrative examination process and invalidated many patents.'[79] Or, in the words of Justice Robert H. Jackson, 'I doubt that the remedy for such Patent Office passion for granting patents is an equally strong passion in this Court for striking them down so that the only patent that is valid is one which this Court has not been able to get its hands on.'[80]

During a cycle of economic stagnation in the 1970s that was doubtless caused by a myriad of complicated, interrelated, and unknown causes, these patent stakeholders blamed it all on weakened patent rights. Judge Bennett opined that 'technological innovation was being impeded by the lack of uniformity in application of the patent laws' and that this 'diminish[ed] the patent system further as an incentive to industrial innovation.'[81]

This equation of innovation with patented invention is highly problematic. A patent is merely an abstract articulation of an invention that may or may not prove to be a success. 'An innovation is the "debugged" and functional version of the invention.'[82] 'A tremendous amount of work and investment must occur in order to turn a patented invention into a commercial product that will directly benefit the public, including the development and testing of working prototypes, product modifications and improvements, market research and marketing, distribution, and so forth.'[83] At the very least, investment in the infrastructure, public universities, and the skilled labor necessary for this

---

[79] Marion T. Bennett, 'The United States Court of Appeals for the Federal Circuit – Origins' in *The United States Court of Appeals for the Federal Circuit: A History: 1990–2002* (2002) 11.

[80] *Jungersen v. Ostby & Barton Co.*, 335 U.S. 560, 572 (1949) (Jackson, J., dissenting).

[81] Bennett, *supra* note 79 at 10.

[82] Robert T. Merges, 'Commercial Success and Patent Standards: Economic Perspectives on Innovation' [1988] 76 Calif. L. Rev. 803, 807.

[83] Samuel F. Ernst, 'Protecting the Boundaries: Unclaimed Consideration in the Patentee's Social Contract' [2015] 18 Tulane J. Tech & Int. Prop. 1, 7 (citing Ted Sichelman, 'Commercializing Patents' [2010] 62 Stan. L. Rev. 341, 347–354).

process would do more to spur innovation than strengthening patent rights. Moreover, there are strong arguments that patents often hinder, rather than spur, innovation.[84]

Be that as it may, in 1982 Congress created the Federal Circuit for the perceived purpose of addressing, in the words of Judge Pauline Newman, 'the practical urgency of recovering the incentive that can be provided by an effective patent system.'[85] The new court got straight to work, not only in unifying patent law, but in strengthening patent rights. Among the court's pro-patent reforms were the following:

- The Federal Circuit made the issuance of permanent injunctions virtually automatic upon a finding of patent infringement, without any necessity to show irreparable harm;[86]
- The court made it more difficult to prove a patent invalid for obviousness by interposing inflexible rules such as the teaching, suggestion, motivation test discussed above;[87]
- The court watered down the patent eligible subject matter requirements to nothing, allowing for patenting of business methods, empty internet configurations, and other abstractions;[88]
- The court ruled that patent holders could evade patent exhaustion through contract, even contracts of adhesion, unless those contracts violated the antitrust laws;[89]
- The court made it difficult to prove a patent invalid for claim indefiniteness, holding that a claim is indefinite only if it is 'insolubly ambiguous' and not amenable to interpretation using all of the available tools of claim construction;[90]

---

[84] Id at 2–4 (collecting citations).

[85] Pauline Newman, 'The Court of Appeals for the Federal Circuit, After Three Decades' [2013] 23 Fordham Intell. Prop. Media & Ent. L.F. 553, 555.

[86] See, e.g., *Richardson v. Suzuki Motor Co.*, 868 F.2d 1226, 1247 (Fed. Cir. 1989) ("It is the general rule that an injunction will issue when infringement has been adjudged, absent a sound reason for denying it"), *overruled by eBay Inc. v. MercExchange, L.L.C.*, 547 U.S. 388, 391 (2006).

[87] See Section 1, *supra*.

[88] See, e.g., *State St. Bank & Tr. Co. v. Signature Fin. Grp., Inc.*, 149 F.3d 1368, 1373 (Fed. Cir. 1998), *overruled by In re Bilski*, 545 F.3d 943 (Fed. Cir. 2008).

[89] *Mallinckrodt v. Medipart*, 976 F.2d 700, 708 (Fed. Cir. 1992), *overruled by Impression Products, Inc. v. Lexmark Int'l, Inc.*, 137 S. Ct. 1523 (2017).

[90] *Exxon Research and Engineering Co. v. United States*, 265 F.3d 1371, 1375–1380 (Fed. Cir. 2001), *overruled by Nautilus, Inc. v. Biosig Instruments, Inc.*, 572 U.S. 898 (2014).

- The court gave generous construction to the patent venue statute, making it easy for patent holders to choose favorable forums for their lawsuits;[91]
- The court made it exceedingly difficult to prove a patent unenforceable for inequitable conduct, famously calling it a 'plague' on the patent system;[92]
- The court interposed on accused infringers a 'duty of care' to avoid patent infringement, meaning that a party with notice of a patent had to demonstrate affirmative acts to investigate the infringement or validity of the patent on pain of being declared a 'willful infringer' liable for treble damages;[93]
- The court decided that if an accused infringer failed to obtain an opinion from its counsel as to the validity or non-infringement of an asserted patent, or declined to produce such an opinion to the court, it resulted in a presumption of willful infringement and treble damages;[94]
- The court declared that if, on the other hand, the accused infringer did decide to produce an opinion of counsel, it resulted in the waiver of that party's attorney-client privilege,[95] resulting in an obligation to produce to the patent holder all communications and work product with its opinion counsel and, according to some district courts, with trial counsel as well;[96]
- The court all but overruled the reverse doctrine of equivalents (discussed above), creating what the Sixth Circuit Court of Appeals once maligned as 'the doctrine of literal infringement,'[97] whereby infringement is proven merely by the semantic word game of determining that some part of the accused device falls within the literal scope of the claims, without regard to whether the accused device is also a substantial improvement operating in a wholly different manner to achieve a wholly superior result.[98]

---

[91] *VE Holding Corp. v. Johnson Gas Appliance Co.*, 917 F.2d 1574, 1584 (Fed. Cir. 1990), *overruled by TC Heartland LLC v. Kraft Foods Grp. Brands LLC*, 137 S. Ct. 1514 (2017).

[92] *Burlington Indus., Inc. v. Dayco Corp.*, 849 F.2d 1418, 1422 (Fed. Cir. 1988) ('[T]he habit of charging inequitable conduct in almost every major patent case has become an absolute plague').

[93] *Underwater Devices Inc. v. Morrison-Knudsen Co.*, 717 F.2d 1380, 1389–1390 (Fed. Cir. 1983), *overruled by In re Seagate Tech., LLC*, 497 F.3d 1360 (Fed. Cir. 2007) (en banc), *overruled on separate grounds by Halo Elecs., Inc. v. Pulse Elecs., Inc.*, 136 S. Ct. 1923, 195 L. Ed. 2d 278 (2016).

[94] *Fromson v. Western Litho Plate & Supply Co.*, 853 F.2d 1568, 1572–1573 (Fed. Cir.1988), *overruled by Knorr-Bremse Systeme Fuer Nutzfahrzeuge GmbH v. Dana Corp.*, 383 F.3d 1337 (Fed. Cir. 2004) (en banc).

[95] See, e.g., *In re EchoStar Commc'ns Corp.*, 448 F.3d 1294, 1299 (Fed. Cir. 2006).

[96] See, e.g., *Informatica Corp. v. Bus. Objects Data Integration, Inc.*, 454 F. Supp. 2d 957, 965 (N.D. Cal. 2006).

[97] *Mead Digital Systems, Inc. v. A.B. Dick Co.*, 723 F.2d 455, 462 (6th Cir. 1983).

[98] See note 75, *supra*, and accompanying text.

This list of ways the Federal Circuit evolved the law to favor patent holders is necessarily inexhaustive due to the constraints of this chapter.

Then the pendulum swung back in the other direction. In the late 1990s and early 2000s stakeholders in industry, scholars, and others complained of a 'patent thicket,' a labyrinth of low-quality patents that imposed a tax on true innovation or blocked it altogether.[99] This resulted from a series of interrelated flaws in the patent law and patent system. There was a glut of overly broad patents that claimed a function to be achieved, rather than the particular means of obtaining it.[100] The law allowed for excess royalties because it failed to apportion damages properly by accounting for the phenomenon of royalty stacking, whereby a single product was covered by dozens, hundreds, or thousands of patents.[101] The Federal Circuit required the virtual automatic granting of injunctions to patent holders even if they produced no commercial product and were not irreparably harmed.[102] There also loomed the threat of International Trade Commission ('ITC') exclusion orders prohibiting the importation of allegedly infringing products into the United States, even where the patent holder instituting the ITC proceeding had no domestic industry to protect, other than the licensing of its patents.[103] These threats combined with the high cost of litigation resulted in law suits asserting low-quality, invalid, or non-infringed patents that patent holders correctly calculated defendants would settle because the risk and cost of defense outweighed the pursuit of justice.[104] All of these problems were famously exacerbated by the plague of 'patent trolls' (or to be polite, 'non-practicing entities'), who acquired patents not in order to develop and introduce new innovations, but to extract licensing

---

[99] The literature on this topic is vast. See, e.g., Amber Rose Stiles, 'Hacking Through the Thicket: A Proposed Patent Pooling Solution to the Nanotechnology "Building Block" Patent Thicket Problem' [2012] 4 Drexel L. Rev. 555, 562; Carl Shapiro, 'Navigating the Patent Thicket: Cross Licenses, Patent Pools and Standard-Setting,' in Adam B. Jaffe et al. (eds), *Innovation Policy and the Economy* (2001) vol. 1, 119–126; Stu Woolman et al., 'Evidence of Patent Thickets in Complex Biopharmaceutical Technologies' [2003] 53 IDEA 1, 3; Amit Makker, 'The Nanotechnology Patent Thicket and the Path to Commercialization' [2011] 84 S. Cal. L. Rev. 1163, 1175–1176; Christopher A. Cotropia, 'The Folly of Early Filing in Patent Law' [2009] 61 Hastings L.J. 65, 112.

[100] Mark A. Lemley and A. Douglas Melamed, 'Missing the Forest for the Trolls' [2013] 113 Colum. L. Rev. 2117, 2173.

[101] Id. at 2174.

[102] See *Richardson, supra* note 86 at 1247.

[103] See *InterDigital Communications, LLC v. ITC*, 707 F.3d 1295, 1299 (Fed. Cir. 2013) ('InterDigital has engaged in some production of products, but it is principally dedicated to research and licensing intellectual property in the cellphone industry').

[104] Samuel F. Ernst, 'Introduction to the 2015 *Chapman Law Review* Symposium' [2015] 18 Chapman L.R. 611, 612.

fees from companies that were endeavoring to innovate;[105] a problem that was particularly crippling to startup companies as they attempted to embark on the path to innovation.[106]

Against this background, the Federal Circuit began a sporadic and gradual retreat, as new members of the court, litigation campaigns, and outside pressure evolved its common law direction.[107]

And then the Supreme Court awakened. Since the passage of the Patent Act of 1952 and in particular since the 1982 founding of the Federal Circuit, the Supreme Court had decided relatively few patent law cases compared to our own century: five in the 1950s, 16 in the 1960s, ten in the 1970s, seven in the 1980s, and eight in the 1990s.[108] But at the time of writing the Supreme Court

---

[105] Robin Feldman et al., 'The AIA 500 Expanded: The Effects of Patent Monetization Entities' [2013] 17 UCLA J. L. & Tech. 1, 16. The counter-argument is that non-practicing entities are 'patent dealers' who provide liquidity and efficiency to the patent market when inventors cannot, thereby providing an incentive to invent and giving the public efficient and broad access to inventions. James F. McDonough III, 'The Myth of the Patent Troll: An Alternative View of the Function of Patent Dealers in an Idea Economy' [2006] 56 Emory L.J. 189, 201.

[106] Colleen Chien, 'Startups and Patent Trolls' [2014] 17 Stan. Tech. L.R. 461. Elsewhere Chien points out that disproportionate blame was placed on patent trolls, as only 17% of the patent suits brought from 2000 to 2008 were brought by non-practicing entities, with 4% brought by individual inventors, 18% brought by small companies against large companies, 16% brought by one small- or medium-sized company against another; and 8% brought by a large firm against a small one. Colleen V. Chien, 'Of Trolls, Davids, Goliaths, and Kings: Narratives and Evidence in the Litigation of High-Tech Patents' [2009] 87 N.C. L. Rev. 1571, 1571–1572.

[107] See, e.g., *Knorr-Bremse Systeme v. Dana Corp.*, 383 F.3d 1337 (Fed. Cir.) (en banc) (holding that no adverse inference of willful infringement was to be drawn from the failure to obtain or disclose an opinion of counsel); *In re Seagate*, 497 F.3d 1360, 1371–1376 (Fed. Cir. 2007) (en banc) (holding, *inter alia*, that there is no affirmative duty of care to avoid infringement that can only be satisfied by obtaining an opinion of counsel; and that a party who chooses to rely on an opinion of patent counsel to defend against a charge of willful infringement does not thereby waive privilege with respect to litigation counsel), *overruled on separate grounds by Halo Elecs., Inc. v. Pulse Elecs., Inc.*, 136 S. Ct. 1923, 1931–1936 (2016) (holding that the Federal Circuit's requirement that the district court find objective and subjective recklessness prior to enhancing damages for willful infringement was unduly rigid and failed to give sufficient discretion to the district court); *DyStar Textilfarben GmbH & Co. Deutschland KG v. C.H. Patrick Co.*, 464 F.3d 1356, 1367 (Fed. Cir. 2006) ('Our suggestion test is in actuality quite flexible and not only permits, but *requires*, consideration of common knowledge and common sense') (emphasis in original); *Alza Corp. v. Mylan Labs., Inc.*, 464 F.3d 1286, 1291 (Fed. Cir. 2006) ('There is flexibility in our obviousness jurisprudence because a motivation may be found *implicitly* in the prior art. We do not have a rigid test that requires an actual teaching to combine ...') (emphasis in original).

[108] See Ernst, 'A Patent Reformist Supreme Court,' *supra* note 35 at 9 (and references cited therein).

has decided 43 cases on substantive patent issues since the year 2000 and 33 in the 2010s alone.[109] The Supreme Court reviewed decisions from the Federal Circuit in all but three of these cases and it reversed that court in 73% of the cases.[110]

This surge in Supreme Court activity largely constitutes a sustained reform of the law in favor of accused infringers, counter-balancing the pro-patent holder slant of the early Federal Circuit (whether wittingly or unwittingly on the part of the Supreme Court). By this author's count, of the 43 Supreme Court cases on substantive patent law issues this decade, 25 established a rule to favor accused infringers (58%); 12 established a rule to favor patent holders (28%); and six established a rule that could favor either party in a given case (14%).[111]

These numbers do not paint the entire picture, however. The substance of the Supreme Court's rulings worked far more fundamental changes to patent law in favor of patent holders than did the handful of rulings favoring patent holders. Here again, space constraints permit only the listing of a few examples:

- In *eBay Inc. v. MercExchange*, the Supreme Court held that an injunction did not automatically issue upon a finding of infringement and that the court must weigh traditional equitable factors before imposing an injunction.[112] As a practical matter, this made it difficult for non-practicing entities to prove they were irreparably harmed by ongoing infringement and thereby entitled to an injunction.[113]

---

[109] Id. at 5–6, nn. 8–10 (citing 41 of the cases); see also *Return Mail, Inc. v. United States Postal Serv.*, 139 S. Ct. 1853 (2019); *Helsinn Healthcare S.A. v. Teva Pharm. USA, Inc.*, 139 S. Ct. 628 (2019).

[110] See Ernst, 'A Patent Reformist Supreme Court,' *supra* note 35 at 5–6, nn. 8–10; see also *Return Mail*, *supra* note 109 at 1867–1868 (affirming the Federal Circuit); *Helsinn*, *supra* note 109 at 634 (reversing the Federal Circuit).

[111] See Ernst, 'A Patent Reformist Supreme Court,' *supra* note 35 at 35–40; see also *Helsinn*, *supra* note 109 at 634 (holding that an inventor's sale of an invention to a third party counts as prior art to invalidate the patent for anticipation even if the sale was confidential); but see *Return Mail*, *supra* note 109 at 1867–1868 (favoring patent holders by holding that the U.S. government is not a 'person' who may challenge a patent through *inter partes* review in the PTO).

[112] *eBay Inc. v. MercExchange, LLC*, 547 U.S. 388, 394 (2006).

[113] Colleen V. Chien and Mark A. Lemley, 'Patent Holdup, the ITC, and the Public Interest' [2012] 98 Cornell L. Rev. 1, 2 ('In the wake of the Supreme Court's 2006 *eBay Inc. v. MercExchange, LLC* decision, district courts rarely grant injunctions in patent infringement cases to patent-assertion entities (PAEs, also known as "patent trolls")').

- In *KSR*, as discussed above, the Court rejected the Federal Circuit's rigid rules for proving a patent invalid for obviousness in favor of a more flexible standard.[114]
- In *Impression Products*, the Court revitalized the exhaustion doctrine by holding that parties could not write contracts to evade patent exhaustion whether or not those contracts violated the antitrust laws or constituted patent misuse.[115] The Court also held that the sale of a patented product overseas exhausts all patent rights in that item, even in the United States.[116] This made the United States one of the few countries in the world to adopt such an 'international exhaustion' regime,[117] and it did so through judge-made law. No longer can companies use patent law to attempt to shut down the used resale market, lock end users into particular brands and secondary products, or otherwise chase patented products down the stream of commerce extracting royalties or pursuing new law suits at each bend in the river.[118]
- In a series of cases the Court resuscitated the doctrine of patent ineligible subject matter, making it easier to prove a patent invalid for claiming abstract ideas, natural phenomena, or laws of nature.[119] This allowed accused infringers to obtain early dismissals of cases asserting low-quality patents before mounting litigation costs could force a settlement.[120]

---

114 *KSR, supra* note 61 at 415–422.

115 *Impression Products v. Lexmark Int'l, Inc.*, 137 S. Ct. 1523, 1532–1533 (2017).

116 Id. at 1535–1538.

117 See Shubha Ghosh and Irene Calboli, *Exhausting Intellectual Property Rights: A Comparative and Policy Analysis* (Cambridge University Press 2018) 88–133 (describing and comparing the patent exhaustion regimes of the United States, the European Union, Canada, Mexico, Australia, New Zealand, India, China, and member countries of ASEAN).

118 Samuel F. Ernst, 'Total Patent Exhaustion!' [2018] 59 IDEA 41.

119 See, e.g., *Alice Corp. v. CLS Bank Int'l*, 134 S. Ct. 2347, 2360 (2014); *Bilski v. Kappos*, 561 U.S. 593, 602–606 (2010); *Ass'n for Molecular Pathology v. Myriad Genetics, Inc.*, 569 U.S. 576, 580 (2013); *Mayo Collaborative Servs. v. Prometheus Labs., Inc.*, 566 U.S. 66, 70–73 (2012).

120 However, the Federal Circuit has begun to erode this practical advantage by holding that factual disputes underlying the ineligible subject matter claim preclude invalidating the patent on the pleadings or on summary judgment. See, e.g., *Berkheimer v. Hewlett-Packard Co.*, 881 F.3d 1360, 1370 (Fed. Cir. 2018) ('We do not decide today that claims 4–7 are patent eligible under § 101. We only decide that on this record summary judgment was improper, given the fact questions created by the specification's disclosure').

- In *TC Heartland* the Court reinterpreted the patent venue statute in a way that reduces forum shopping by patent holders and reduces their ability to sue in forums that are inconvenient or hostile to accused infringers.[121]
- In *Nautilus, Inc. v. Biosig Instruments* the Court made it easier to prove a patent invalid for claim indefiniteness, rejecting the Federal Circuit's rule that a claim was indefinite only if every conceivable tool of claim interpretation did not result in a definite meaning for the claim.[122]
- In *Oil States Energy v. Greene's Energy* the Court affirmed the constitutionality of post-grant *inter partes* review proceedings in the PTO, which give patent holders a less expensive forum than the federal courts to prove a patent invalid and allow for the stay of federal court proceedings pending such review.[123] This too reduces settlement pressure and allows for the relatively inexpensive disposal of lawsuits asserting low-quality patents.

Hence, we are living through a period of common law reform of U.S. patent law and can closely observe its operation.

What are the Supreme Court's methods? On what bases does it typically overrule the Federal Circuit on patent law issues? Scholars have correctly identified several overlapping and interrelated rationales the Supreme Court typically relies upon in reversing the Federal Circuit in patent law cases. The Court frequently faults the Federal Circuit for failing to grant the trial court sufficient discretion, for example in determining whether to enhance damages or grant an injunction.[124] Somewhat more frequently, the Court reverses the Federal Circuit on the basis that it has imposed a rigid rule rather than a flexible standard, for example in determining whether a patent would have been obvious or in applying the doctrine of prosecution history estoppel.[125] Yet more frequently, the Court has corrected the Federal Circuit for creating a special rule for patent law, rather than applying general legal and equitable principles.[126] But by far the most frequent rationale articulated by the Supreme Court for reversing the Federal Circuit on patent law issues is that the Federal Circuit improperly disregarded or cabined Supreme Court precedent from prior to the 1982 creation of the Federal Circuit and prior to the 1952 Patent Act.[127] This unearthing of precedent from prior to the passage of the most

---

[121] See *TC Heartland LLC v. Kraft Foods Grp. Brands LLC*, 137 S. Ct. 1514, 1517 (2017).

[122] See *Nautilus, Inc. v. Biosig Instruments, Inc.*, 134 S. Ct. 2120, 2124 (2014).

[123] See *Oil States Energy v. Greene's Energy*, 138 S. Ct. 1365, 1379 (2018).

[124] Ernst, 'A Patent Reformist Supreme Court,' *supra* note 35 at 12, 17–20 (collecting citations).

[125] Id. at 13, 20–23 (collecting citations).

[126] Id. at 13, 23–27 (collecting citations).

[127] Id. at 16, 27–36 and Fig. 3.

important, foundational patent statute in nearly 200 years indicates once again that in the United States, patent law is common law.

All four of these rationales are interrelated and sound in the nature of the two institutions, the Federal Circuit and the Supreme Court. As discussed above, the Federal Circuit is a specialized court created to unify patent law and, perhaps, though unstated, to reform it in favor of patent holders.[128] To achieve that task the new court had to cabin trial court discretion by imposing rigid rules rather than standards and often had to disregard Supreme Court precedent and traditional legal and equitable principles. The Supreme Court, on the other hand, is the highest court in the land and maintains that stature by jealously guarding its precedent. Further, the Supreme Court (unwittingly or not) nudges the law in different policy directions that affect the nation as a whole, and not just the litigants before it (whether or not we agree with those policies). Thomas G. Hansford and James F. Spriggs write:

> The justices recognize that the legal rules or precedents established in the Court's majority opinions represent their most important tool for influencing social, political, and economic outcomes. Their behavior on the bench is therefore principally motivated by the distributional consequences of their opinions, and they want these consequences to reflect their preferences.[129]

But how do the Justices achieve these policy goals in the light of day? Why do the people not rise up in revolt against this anti-democratic law-making? After all, the Supreme Court typically has a higher approval rating with the American public than the political branches, Congress and the President.[130]

The answer is that common law judges rely on a subtle and deceptive tool called 'precedent vitality.'[131] The Court issues reasoned opinions purporting to say that the decisions it makes are dictated, not by personal preference, but by the need to follow the binding precedent of previous Supreme Court decisions; in other words, *stare decisis*.[132] Alexander Hamilton wrote that judges 'should be bound down by strict rules and precedents, which serve to define and point out their duty in every particular case that comes before them.'[133] But because

---

[128] See *supra* text accompanying notes 79–85.

[129] Thomas G. Hansford and James F. Spriggs II, *The Politics of Precedent on the U.S. Supreme Court* (Princeton University Press 2006) 17–18.

[130] See, e.g. Megan Brenan, 'Supreme Court Approval Highest Since 2009' *Gallup* (18 July 2018) https://news.gallup.com/poll/237269/supreme-court-approval-highest-2009.aspx, accessed 29 July 2019.

[131] See generally, Hansford and Spriggs, *supra* note 129 at 206.

[132] See William M. Lile et al., *Brief Making and the Use of Law Books* (3rd ed. 1914) 321.

[133] The Federalist No. 78 (Alexander Hamilton).

the Supreme Court has such a vast selection of precedent to choose from, *stare decisis* is, in fact, a very loose and flexible garment, not an 'inexorable command.'[134] Even without explicitly overruling a case, the Court can distinguish it, narrow its application, or ignore it altogether. Alternatively, the Court can determine a particular outcome while appearing neutral by emphasizing particular precedent, citing it and discussing it repeatedly, and expanding its application to new situations. In the words of Judge Richard Posner, '[o]ften "following" precedent really means a policy-based choice among competing precedents or a policy-influenced interpretation of a precedent's scope.'[135]

Which precedent did the Supreme Court rely upon in affecting the radical patent reforms of this century? This author has concluded that in those portions of its opinions where the Court explains why the Federal Circuit was incorrect, it most frequently cites its cases from the late nineteenth century (the era of the 'patent sharks') and the early to mid-twentieth century (the antitrust era).[136] Hence, the Supreme Court has affected efficient, seemingly neutral patent reform in favor of accused infringers by selectively unearthing its precedent from prior historical periods when patents were viewed as harming, rather than fostering, innovation.

4. COMMON LAW JUDICIAL REFORM AND DEMOCRACY

We are confronted with this dangerous phenomenon: unelected judges who serve for life pushing the nation in different policy directions through the deceptive tool of selectively enhancing or diminishing their own precedent. It raises an urgent issue: what motivates these invisible rulers in choosing their policy directions? Are they benevolent and wise or tainted by self-deception and frailty?

Judge Posner thoroughly surveys various scholarly theories of 'how judges think.'[137] Like all such theories, each has its truths, its flaws, and they are often overlapping.

There is formalism (or what Posner calls 'legalism'), the notion that judicial decisions are objectively forged out of precedent, canons, statutes, and the Constitution by dispassionate judges who do their duty even if they disagree

---

134 *Burnet v. Coronado Oil & Gas Co.*, 285 U.S. 393, 405 (1932) (Brandeis, J., dissenting) ('Stare decisis is not, like the rule of res judicata, universal inexorable command').

135 Richard A. Posner, *How Judges Think* (Harvard University Press 2008) 45.

136 See Ernst, 'A Patent Reformist Supreme Court,' *supra* note 35 at 28, n. 102.

137 Posner, *How Judges Think*, *supra* note 135 at 9–56.

with it.[138] This theory is unpopular among scholars and political scientists of all stripes because judges are necessarily biased, imperfect humans working in a fabric of social constructs and unwitting prejudices using the imperfect tool of language. Law is not arithmetic. Nonetheless, because formalism is what most judges earnestly proclaim they are doing,[139] we must assume that they often conscientiously make an imperfect attempt.

There is the political theory (or what Posner calls 'attitudinalism'), 'which claims that judges' decisions are explained by the political preferences that they bring to their cases.'[140] While there is some data to support this position,[141] it is an incomplete explanation as well. The theory is complicated, for example, by the fact that sometimes Republican presidents appoint judges who drift to a liberal ideology and vice versa.[142] Many cases either do not involve high political stakes or 'pose a conflict between two political values, both of which are important to a judge.'[143] And, at least in the area of patent law, we see far more unanimity among the justices than we see dissents.[144]

There is the 'strategic theory,' which is a somewhat more nuanced version of the political theory. This theory posits that judges vote strategically, sometimes not voting in alignment with their alleged party, because the reaction of other judges, society, voters, and Congress will be counter-productive to the judges' long-term policy goals.[145] For example, a conservative Supreme Court might affirm the constitutional right of a woman to medical and bodily privacy in order to avoid a backlash against the anti-choice movement, but continue to enlarge the 'reasonable restrictions' states can put on abortion to the point

---

[138] Id. at 41–42 (citing Frederick Schauer, 'Formalism' [1988] 97 Yale L.J. 509).

[139] In the words of Chief Justice Roberts at his confirmation hearing, 'I have no agenda … [I]t's my job to call balls and strikes and not to pitch or bat.' CNN.com, 'Roberts: "My Job is to Call Balls and Strikes and Not to Pitch or Bat"' *CNN.com* (12 September 2005) http://www.cnn.com/2005/POLITICS/09/12/roberts.statement/, accessed 29 July 2019.

[140] Posner, *supra* note 135 at 19–25.

[141] Id. at 19–25.

[142] As examples, Justice John Paul Stevens, appointed by Republican President Gerald Ford, Justice David Souter, appointed by Republican President George H.W. Bush, and Justice Brennan, appointed by Republican President Dwight D. Eisenhower.

[143] Posner, *supra* note 135 at 27.

[144] Gregory N. Mandel, 'Institutional Fracture in Intellectual Property Law: The Supreme Court Versus Congress' [2017] 102 Minn. L. Rev. 803, 805 ('Over the period of study, the Supreme Court issued unanimous opinions in intellectual property cases at a rate almost twice that of its general docket. This difference was not uniform across intellectual property fields. The Supreme Court issued a unanimous decision in a remarkable 81% of patent and trademark cases that substantively affected the strength of intellectual property rights.').

[145] Posner, *supra* note 135 at 29–30.

where the right to choose becomes practically nugatory.[146] On some issues the Court appears to act in this way. But there are plenty of decisions, such as *Scott v. Sanford*[147] and *Bush v. Gore*,[148] in which the Court was wholly tone deaf to the immediate political backlash against its policy trajectory the rulings would have.[149] In general, this theory largely suffers from the same incompleteness as the political theory.

The sociological theory contends that such things as gender, racial, and socioeconomic identity, the small group dynamics of an appellate court, the aversion to triggering dissents, and moderation by association with others unconsciously push judges in different policy directions.[150] This is undoubtedly true to a degree, but these are not the only influencing factors; there is conscious decision-making as well.

The 'economic theory' assumes that judges are dispassionate, self-interested utility maximizers.[151] Judge Posner sees some truth in this theory in judges' 'fondness for doctrines such as harmless error, waiver, and forfeiture; the pressure some judges exert on litigants to settle cases before trial; and excessive delegation of judicial tasks to law clerks and other staff.'[152] This theory is the most incomplete of those listed, however, because all of its conclusions rest on the false premise that human beings are characterized primarily by rationality. They are not, as research in cognitive psychology demonstrates.[153] In fact, various studies demonstrate that in the legal system, 'decision-making under

---

[146] See, e.g., *Planned Parenthood of Southeastern Pennsylvania v. Casey*, 505 U.S. 833, 846 (1992) (affirming the right to choose but with 'a confirmation of the State's power to restrict abortions after fetal viability, if the law contains exceptions for pregnancies which endanger the woman's life or health').

[147] *Scott*, *supra* note 9 ('The Dred Scott decision').

[148] *Bush v. Gore*, 531 U.S. 98 (2000) (holding that Florida's recount of its votes for President violated the Equal Protection clause, thereby having the practical effect of appointing George W. Bush President by a 5–4 vote).

[149] See David W. Blight, *Frederick Douglass: Prophet of Freedom* (Simon & Schuster 2018) 277–278 ('To antislavery Northerners the idea of a Slave Power conspiracy had never seemed so evident. ... In the wake of *Dred Scott*, the operative emotion in Northern black communities and among abolitionists was either despair or revolutionary outrage'); David Cole, 'The Liberal Legacy of *Bush v. Gore*' [2006] 94 Geo. L.J. 1427 (describing the outrage against *Bush v. Gore* by the public, the press, and the scholarly and legal community and how this led to a period of moderation in the Court).

[150] Posner, *supra* note 135 at 31.

[151] Id. at 35–36.

[152] Id. at 36.

[153] See Ernst, 'Patent Exhaustion for the Exhausted Defendant,' *supra* note 74 at 469–471.

risk and uncertainty may not comport with rational theories of behavior.'[154] This has been shown with respect to litigants settling litigation,[155] the assessment of pain and suffering damages by juries,[156] the awarding of punitive damages,[157] eyewitness investigations,[158] law firm management,[159] and antitrust policy.[160] Unless we are to assume that upon swearing the oath of office, judges transform from human beings into robots, the assumption without evidence underlying the economic theory causes the entire edifice to crumble.

This is why the 'psychological theory' (along with the sociological theory) trumps the economic theory as an absolute explanation of judicial behavior.[161] The psychological theory 'focuses on strategies for coping with uncertainty' and 'highlights the importance and the sources of preconceptions in shaping responses to uncertainty [and] is supported by studies of judges.'[162] Related to the psychological theory is the 'phenomenological theory,' which emphasizes the influence of the conscious psychological experience of being a judge, rather than just the unconscious experience.[163]

But even the psychological and sociological theories are not all encompassing, because sometimes judges act as conscious pragmatists. The pragmatist theory holds that judges base decisions on the ultimate policy effects decisions will have in society, rather than on legalistic readings of cases and statute.[164] There is rich scholarship to support the notion that this is what often motivates the Supreme Court in its decision-making.[165] However unconsciously clouded

---

[154] Jeffrey J. Rachlinski, 'Gains, Losses, and the Psychology of Litigation' [1996] 70 S. Cal. L. Rev. 113, 114.

[155] Id. at 116–145.

[156] Edward J. Mccaffery et al., 'Framing the Jury: Cognitive Perspectives on Pain and Suffering Awards' [1995] 81 Va. L. Rev. 1341.

[157] Cass R. Sunstein et al., 'Assessing Punitive Damages (with Notes on Cognition and Valuation in Law)' [1998] 107 Yale L.J. 2071.

[158] Daniel L. Schacter et al., 'Policy Forum: Studying Eyewitness Investigations in the Field' [2008] 32 Law & Hum. Behav. 3.

[159] Daniel Kahneman and Gary Klein, 'Law Firm Leadership Decisions: Can You, Should You, Trust Your Gut?' [2010] 10-9 Law Off. Mgmt. & Admin. Rep. 1.

[160] Max Huffman, 'Marrying Neo-Chicago with Behavioral Antitrust' [2012] 78 Antitrust L.J. 105.

[161] Posner, *supra* note 135 at 37.

[162] Id. at 35 (citing C.K. Rowland and Robert A. Carp, *Politics and Judgment in Federal District Courts* (University Press of Kansas 1996)).

[163] Posner, *supra* note 135 at 40.

[164] Id.

[165] See, e.g., Hansford and Spriggs, *supra* note 129 at 17–18; Robert L. Boucher and Jeffrey A. Segal, 'Supreme Court Justices as Strategic Decision Makers: Aggressive Grants and Defensive Denials on the Vinson Court' [1995] 57 J. Pol. 824; Gregory A. Caldeira et al., 'Strategic Voting and Gatekeeping in the Supreme Court' [October 1999] 15 J.L. Econ. & Ord. 549; C. Herman Pritchett, *The Roosevelt Court: A Study in*

justices might be in this task by psychological and sociological influences, they are often admirably forthright in admitting that policy pragmatism is what they consciously attempt. Justice Vinson wrote: 'What the Court is interested in is the actual, practical effect of the disputed decision – its consequence for other litigants and in other situations.'[166]

If all of these theories refute and overlap with each other in different ways, each one suffering from its own flaws and incompleteness, which theory is correct? The answer is that they are all correct. As in most areas of law and life, the embrace of monism leaves one as clueless as the group of men feeling different parts of an elephant in the dark, with one believing it to be a snake, another a fan, another a tree trunk, and another a rope, according to an ancient Indian parable.[167] Pluralist approaches to legal descriptions and arguments attempt to embrace aspects of all theories and are therefore the most convincing.[168]

In other words, judges are human beings. Hence, common law judges' phenomenological experience is to read the precedent and use it to justify their decisions; except that they may disagree with it and therefore distinguish or disregard it; because they also act pragmatically to achieve a certain policy direction or political result; in this way acting strategically to achieve those results; all of which is influenced, consciously or unconsciously, by sociological and political attitudes and utilitarian self-interest.

Is it therefore undemocratic to leave law and policy-making in the hands of these unelected human beings with their complex and unknowable motivations? Was Jeremy Bentham correct when he wrote to President James Madison about the common law, 'the yoke of which in the wordless, as well as boundless, and shapeless shape of common, alias Unwritten law, remains still about your necks'?[169] Yes, to a disturbing degree. Would a code-based civil law system be more democratic? Perhaps not. Even in civil law systems,

---

Judicial Politics and Values, 1937–47 (The Macmillan Co. 1948); David W. Rhode and Harold J. Spaeth, *Supreme Court Decision Making* (W.H. Freeman 1976).

[166] Fred M. Vinson, 'Work of the U.S. Supreme Court' [1949] 12 Tex. Bar. J. 551, 552.

[167] See John D. Ireland, *Udana and the Itivuttaka: Two Classics from the Pali Canon* (Buddhist Publication Society 2007) 81–84. The parable has Hindu, Buddhist, and Jain versions with different variations on why the men are sightless: either blind, blindfolded, or in the dark.

[168] See Samuel F. Ernst, 'Pluralism Applied: A Concordant Approach to Selecting Contract Rules' [2017] 101 Marquette L.R. 87, 95–98.

[169] Andrew P. Morriss, 'Codification and Right Answers' [1999] 74 Chi.-Kent L. Rev. 355, 355 (quoting Letter from Jeremy Bentham to President James Madison (30 October 1811), in 8 Jeremy Bentham, *The Correspondence of Jeremy Bentham* 182 (Stephen Conway ed. 1988)).

'[c]ontemporary legal scholars – especially those who have had some exposure to common law – admit readily that, in reality, the courts never find law. Each time it is purported to apply a legal rule to a specific problem situation, the rule as it applies to the case at hand is formulated.'[170]

This American lawyer cannot judge the civil law. In the context of American patent law, the common law process has resulted in useful patent reform far more efficiently and decisively than anything Congress could achieve. And it is uncertain that congressional policy-making is any more democratic, given the domination of Congress in the United States by lobbying interests and powerful corporations, and the unequal apportioning of voting influence by our antiquated Constitution. In this democracy, California, with a population of close to 40 million people, gets two votes in the Senate; Wyoming, with a population of under 550,000 people, also gets two votes; and of course Washington D.C., the nation's capital, with a population of over 630,000 people, gets zero.

5. CONCLUSION

Because we cannot time travel, every history is necessarily a literary narrative that reconstructs the past, rather than recreates it.[171] Edward Hallett Carr observed that '[t]he belief in a hard core of historical facts existing objectively and independently of the interpretation of the historian is a preposterous fallacy, but one which it is very hard to eradicate.'[172] Instead, 'the facts of history never come to us "pure," since they do not and cannot exist in a pure form: they are always refracted through the mind of the recorder.'[173] As a result, history 'is a continuous process of interaction between the historian and *his* facts, an unending dialogue between the present and the past.'[174] Hayden White added to this the insight that historical narratives are literary in character, applying literary tropes and rhetorical devices: 'Histories (and philosophies of history as well) combine a certain amount of "data," theoretical concepts for "explaining" these data, and a narrative structure for their presentation as an icon of sets of events presumed to have occurred in the past.'[175] When constructing a history of judicial decisions, such as this one, the 'data' are further emplotted histories—the judicial decisions with their rhetorical reasoning, controversial conclusions, and factual backgrounds determined by

---

170 Vranken, *supra* note 20 at 65.

171 Hayden White, *Metahistory*, *supra* note 4 at 1–41.

172 Carr, *supra* note 2 at 10.

173 Id. at 24.

174 Id. at 35 (emphasis added).

175 Id. at xxix.

preponderances of evidence by imperfect factfinders. Because all histories of the common law of U.S. patents rely on similar data sets (these judicial decisions), their power lies not in how accurately they replicate the past (again, an impossibility), but in how well they select their judicial decisions and how persuasively they use them to construct a literary metanarrative. This chapter is the history of a Supreme Court reforming patent law to disentangle us from the patent thicket and encourage innovation. Others use much of the same data to write about a generalist Supreme Court that misunderstands patent law and squelches innovation.[176] Future authors on this topic will enlighten or darken the picture with more layers of metanarrative about metanarratives.

---

[176] Cf. Greg Reilly, 'How Can the Supreme Court Not "Understand" Patent Law?' [2017] 16 Chi.-Kent J. Intell. Prop. 292, 295–296 (describing but not endorsing this view).

9. The legacy of *The Seasons*: confusion and misdirection

Mark Perry[1]

> The historical context removes obstacles—long-continued acceptance of certain ideas, self-interest, and the pressing need to resolve immediate problems—which may be present when analysis occurs in a wholly contemporary context. And it yields a basis for employing the logic of experience. The historical perspective thus provides the opportunity to compare the ideas of copyright and the problems to which those ideas were directed in origin and development with the ideas of the concept and the problems of today.[2]

1. INTRODUCTION

Patterson's words describing how the history of copyright can reflect upon our current attitudes to perceptions and issues surrounding copyright are as true today as they were fifty years ago. As this author noted over twenty years ago, the concepts around the protection of expression before and after the passage of the Statute of Anne[3] were not as clear as some of the major copyright texts of the twentieth century suggested,[4] and indeed remain confused to this day. In many standard copyright texts as late as the last century,[5] the accepted

[1] Thanks are given to my research assistant, Cristina Avallone, and to the longanimity of Professor Shubha Gosh.

[2] L. Ray Patterson, *Copyright in Historical Perspective* (Charlotte, Vanderbilt University Press, 1968) 223.

[3] Copyright Act 1709 8 Ann c.21 (Gr. Brit); An Act for the Encouragement of Learning, by vesting the Copies of Printed Books in the Authors or purchasers of such Copies, during the Times therein mentioned. The Act came into force in 1710 and is sometimes cited with that latter date.

[4] M. Perry, "Acts of Parliament: Privatisation, Promulgation, Crown Copyright—is there a Need for a Royal Royalty" (1998) New Zealand Law Review 493–529. This current work has been buzzing around in my head since 1992, where the issues came up in the background to my MJur thesis.

[5] Eaton S. Drone, *A Treatise on the Law of Property in Intellectual Production in Great Britain and the United States* (New Jersey, Hackensack, Reprint, 1972), and E.P. Skone James et al., *Copinger and Skone James on Copyright* (12th and 14th Eds,

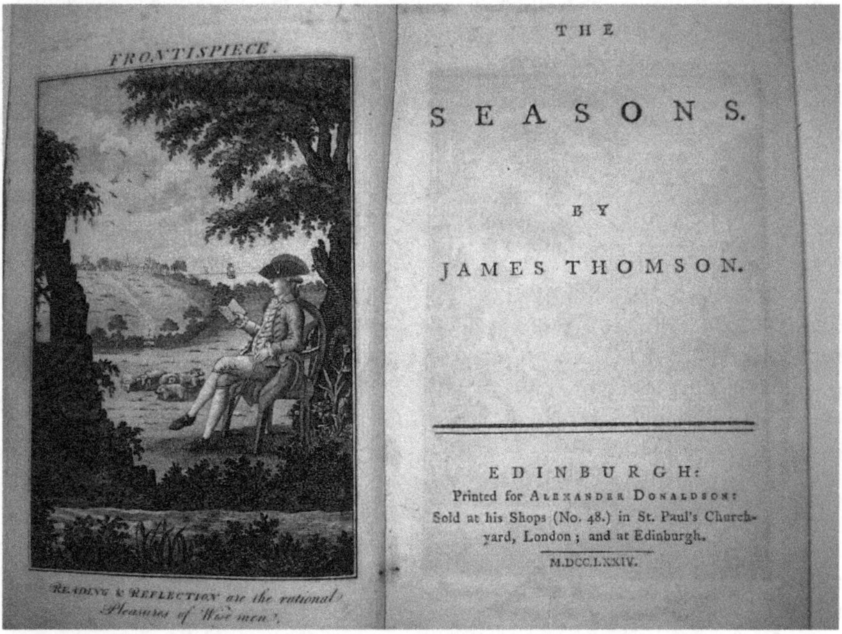

Figure 9.1 *The frontispiece of Thomson's The Seasons 1774*

Source: Image from http://www.thepublicdomain.org/2009/08/17/donaldson-v-beckett/; photo by James Boyle, all rights waived.
Note: James Thomson's *The Seasons* was first published in 1730. It was also the work in question in both *Millar v Taylor* (1769) and *Donald v Beckett* (1774), see text accompanying notes 7 and 8. Oscar Wilde, "To Read or Not to Read", *Pall Mall Gazette*, February 8, 1866, divided readings into three class, the third of which was "Books not to read at all, such as Thompson's Seasons …", a sentiment appreciated, but one that was not followed in the year of its publication.

approach was that prior to the Statute of Anne there had been a clearly a developed doctrine of copyright at common law, as held by the Court of King's Bench in *Millar v Taylor* (1769).[6] This common law right, it was stated, was only subsumed by the Statute of Anne. Such texts often conclude that the House of Lords in *Donaldson v Beckett* (1774)[7] decided that although a per-

---

London, Sweet & Maxwell, 1980) (hereafter referred to as *Copinger and Skone James* 12th or 14th Ed).

[6] *Millar v Taylor* (1769) 4 Burr. 2303, 98 ER 201.

[7] *Donaldson v Beckett* (1774), *The Parliamentary History of England* Vol XVII (1771–1774) *Proceedings in the Lords on the Question of Literary Property* (1774) 954. An incomplete report is also given in 4 Burr 2408; 98 ER 257 and in 2 Bro PC 129; 1 ER 837. See also the report of *A Gentleman of the Inner Temple*, first published in

petual copyright did exist under the common law, the right was "impeached" by the Statute of Anne 1710 for published works. Drone, author of a standard text in the USA into the 1970s, stated for example: "It is a fact which may be regarded as judicially conceded, that copyright in printed books was not created by legislation, but that it existed by the common law long before, and when the Statute of Anne was passed".[8] *Copinger*, the extensive English Copyright tome currently in its 17th edition, took the view that "this case must be taken to have decided finally that publication put an end to the common law perpetual right, and that after publication an author had to base his claim for protection upon his statutory right".[9] There has been some scholarly analysis that pointed out that this was not the case and that the common law had never recognised copyright as a protectable right.[10] Today we can reflect on how our early conceptions of copyright still have an influence in the interpretation given to current copyright laws, and the romantic and reverential view of expressions of authors, even though any claims to a common law right have long been abandoned.

This discussion looks at the history behind the confusion over the basis for copyright, ponders over the idea of recognising common law copyright as a concept, even though it either never existed or has been subsequently removed by legislation. The interpretation of *Donaldson* on the issue of common law copyright has importance as setting the basis for our thoughts over the genesis of this now broad suite of monopoly rights. Of particular focus are the perspectives provided by the Lords in *Donaldson*, and some excerpts of Lord Camden's long speech are reproduced here (a) to illustrate one very strong opinion against any claim of common law copyright; (b) to show the strength of feeling that can be raised on a copyright issue, and the passion that is often seen in some of the arguments today; and (c) for the beautiful expression. His passion, perhaps reinforced by his dislike of Lord Mansfield, resonates through the ages into our modern-day considerations of copyright.[11] Lord Camden was very much a driving force of the discussion in *Donaldson*,

---

1774 and reproduced in *The Literary Property Debate: Six Tracts 1764–1774* (Garland, 1974).

[8] Drone, *A Treatise on the Law of Property in Intellectual Production in Great Britain and the United States*, 20 (cited in note 5).

[9] *Copinger and Skone James* 14th Ed at ¶ 5.

[10] Howard B. Abrams, "The Historic Foundation of American Copyright Law: Exploding the Myth of Common-Law Copyright" (1983) 29 Wayne Law Review 1119–91, 1164 and 1128: "there is no historical justification whatsoever for the claim that copyright was recognized as a common-law right of an author".

[11] It is clear from many accounts that Lord Camden and Lord Mansfield did not like each other, nor was there harmony in their approaches to law, J. Buchan, "Lord Mansfield" *The Atlantic Monthly* (1857–1932), 88(000530), 1901, 777.

and passionately reflects the view that the claims to common law copyright were a misdirection of the prior rights claimed and granted by the Crown.

1.a Overview of the Early History

Lord Camden: The Arguments attempted to be maintained on the side of the Respondents, were founded on patents, privileges, Star-chamber decrees, and the bye laws of the Stationers' Company; all of them the effects of the grossest tyranny and usurpation; the very last places in which I should have dreamt of finding the least trace of the common law of this kingdom: and yet, by a variety of subtle reasoning and metaphysical refinements, have they endeavoured to squeeze out the spirit of the common law from premises, in which it could not possibly have existence. They began with their pretended precedents and authorities, and they endeavoured to model these in such a manner, as to extract from them something like a common law principle, upon which their argument might rest.

I shall invert the order, and first of all lay out of my way the whole bead-role of citations and precedents, which they have produced—that heterogeneous heap of rubbish, which is only calculated to confound your lordships, and mislead the argument. After the first invention of printing, the art continued free for about fifty years; I mean to lay no stress upon this; I mention it only historically, not argumentatively; for as the use of it was little known, and not very extensive, its want of importance might protect it from invasion; but as soon as its effects in politics and religion were felt, all the Crowned heads in Europe at once seized on it, and appropriated it to themselves. Certain it is, that in England, the Crown claimed both the power of licensing what should be printed, and the monopoly of printing. Two licences were granted to those who petitioned for them. An author not only was obliged to sue for a Licence to print at all, but he was also obliged to sue for a second licence that he might print his own works.

When the King had once claimed the right of printing, he secured that right by patents and by charters. Still further to secure his monopoly, he combined the printers, and formed them into a company, then called the Stationers' Company, by whose laws, none but members could print any book at all. They assumed powers of seizure, confiscation and Imprisonment, and the decrees of the Star-Chamber confirmed their proceedings. These transactions, I presume, have no relation to the common law; and when they were established, where could an author, independent of the company, print his works, or try his right to it? Who could make head against this arbitrary prerogative, which stifled and suppressed the common law of the land? Every man who printed a book, no matter how he obtained it, entered his name in their books, and became a member of their company: then he was complete owner of the book. Owner was the term applied to every holder of copies; and the word "author" does not occur once in all their entries.[12]

---

[12] From the speech of Lord Camden delivered in *Donaldson v Beckett* (1774) as reported in *The Parliamentary History of England from the Earliest Period to the Year 1803*, Vol XV11 (1771–1774), printed by TC Hansard (Johnson Reprint Corp) (cited in note 7). The version so reported corresponds almost word for word to the report by a Gentleman of the Inner Temple in *The Cases of the Appellants and Respondents in the cause of Literary Property before the House of Lords: wherein The Decree of*

Most commentators do not dispute the major factors in the history of copyright's development up to the Statute of Anne, as recounted by Lord Camden,[13] and indeed for some they reflect many of the sentiments expressed by him. Prior to the introduction of moveable type enabling the mass production of printed materials,[14] the protection of reproduction rights was not an issue of great import, being a hugely labour intensive task, although there was an association known as "Writers of Court Hand and Text Letters" in the fourteenth century. The pre-press age relied on handwritten works, and, given the time and effort required for mass duplication, copying was of little consequence.[15]

In the very early days of the printing press in England, introduced by Caxton and others, the production and distribution of materials was actively encouraged.[16] The period of nearly fifty years shortly following the introduction of the moveable type printing press to England by Caxton in 1476 was the only

---

Lord Chancellor Apsley was reversed, 26 February 1774. This was first published in 1774, and is reproduced in *The Literary Property Debate: Six Tracts 1764–1774.* Lord Camden's speech of an hour and a half was also reported in *The Scots Magazine*: Volume 36, published by Sands, Brymer, Murray and Cochran on 31 December 1774 "May 1774 Lord Camden on Literary Property" 233.

[13] Cf. John Feather, "From Rights in Copies to Copyright: The Recognition of Authors' Rights in English Law and Practice in the Sixteenth and Seventeenth Centuries" (1991) 10 Cardozo Arts and Entertainment Law Journal 455 (hereafter referred to as Feather), who takes the view that the foundation for authors' rights is to be found in the pre-revolution patents and trade practices, and suggests that legal commentators have largely ignored the practical protection of literary works that was prevalent well before statutory protection. Also note that Patterson's *Copyright in Historical Perspective* (cited in note 2), 145–147 considers that the Statute of Anne was a significant codification of rights previously limited to Members of the Company of Stationers and giving that right to "all persons".

[14] Burrow in 4 Burr 2418, records the debate between those putting the first English printing press in Oxford around 1468 and those championing Caxton soon after 1471, commenting that "it is very unsafe to trust to common history; and necessary to recur to original testimonies, if we would know the state of facts with exactness". Most commentators now agree that the printing press was introduced into England by Caxton in 1476, and there is a plaque at Westminster Abbey mounted in 1954 to this effect saying "1476 Near this place William Caxton set up the first printing press in England. This stone was placed here to commemorate the great assistance rendered to the Abbey Appeal Fund by the English speaking press throughout the world" at https://www.westminster-abbey.org/abbey-commemorations/commemorations/william-caxton.

[15] Prior to the introduction of the moveable type printing press, the main concern was with the promulgation of heretical materials. However, the case of St. Columba, recounted below, shows that some people were precious about their handwritten collections and did not countenance any copying.

[16] At the beginning of the realm of Richard III, The Importation of Books by Aliens Act 1483 (1 Ric 3 c9) was introduced with the aim of encouraging the printing of books and to foster their importation and sale, even by non-English merchants.

period of no regulation of printers and printed materials. However, within fifty years or so from the introduction of the press to England, Henry VIII assumed total control by establishing a system of licensing.[17] This provided the Crown with a handsome source of revenue for the royal coffers and an effective means of censorship.[18] The nearly two and a half centuries of total Crown control, whether by Crown prerogative, the enforcement of the Licensing Acts, or management of "copy" by the Stationers' Company, left the Crown with great power over the distribution of written knowledge. This was an era where the Crown was exercising censorship policies on any materials it considered detrimental to its position in England, which was aided by maintaining the monopoly of the Company of Stationers. The focus was clearly on the control of printing and distribution, with no thought of the intellectual efforts of the authors. The establishment, by charter, of the Stationers' Company in 1557 ensured that the Crown and the printers had formalised a total control over this new medium. Professor Abrams summarises the climate of that age:[19]

> Only members of the Company of Stationers could legally print books and only books authorized by the Crown could be published. The Company was authorized to seize and destroy any unauthorized books and presses, thus silencing political and religious opposition to the Crown while eliminating economic competition to themselves. This powerful economic incentive harnessed the self interest of the publishers to the yoke of royal censorship.

The decrees and ordinances of the Star Chamber continued to restrict printing severely.[20] Despite the abolition of the Chamber in 1640, Parliament was quick to bring in a series of acts to ensure that the power of the Company was maintained, a practice continued during the Restoration. For example, the Licensing

---

17 Printers and Binders Act 1533 (25 Hen 8, c15) (Gr. Brit.).

18 For a historical background to the control of printing practices (from the perspective of those writing on copyright), see *Copinger and Skone James on Copyright* 14th Ed ¶¶ 21–45 (cited in note 5); Benjamin Kaplan, *An Unhurried View of Copyright* (New York, Columbia University Press, 1967); Harold Fox, *The Canadian Law of Copyright and Industrial Designs* (Toronto, Carswell & Co, 1967) ch 2.

19 Abrams, "The Historic Foundation of American Copyright Law: Exploding the Myth of Common Law Copyright" (cited in note 10), at 1119, 1135–36.

20 *Copinger and Skone James on Copyright* 14th Ed, at ¶22 (cited in note 5): "In 1637, the Star Chamber again decreed that 'no person is to print or import (if printed abroad) any book or copy in which the Company of Stationer, or any person, hath or shall, by any letters patent, order or entrance in their register book, or otherwise, have the right, privilege, authority, or allowance, solely to print'."

Act 1662 prohibited the printing of any book unless it was registered with the Company and also forbade: [21]

> [A]ny heretical, seditious, schismatical, or offensive books or pamphlets, wherein any doctrine or opinion shall be asserted or maintained which is contrary to the Christian faith, or the doctrine or discipline of the Church of England, or which shall, or may, tend to be the scandal of religion or the church, or the government or governors of the church, state, or common wealth, or of any corporation or particular person or persons whatever.

The last in the series of such Licensing Acts expired in 1694, prompting publishers and booksellers to petition for a new statute. However, the resulting legislation was of a new kind, being the first statute to recognise that the property right in "books and writings" was first vested in the author, rather than being concerned solely with the proprietary rights of the printers and seller.[22] The preamble to the Statute of Anne 1710 states that it is:[23]

> An Act for the Encouragement of Learning by vesting the Copies of printed Books in the Authors or Purchasers of such Copies during the Times therein mentioned.

This Act is the fountainhead of subsequent copyright legislation in common law countries. It provided authors with a sole right of printing unpublished works for only 14 years, with an extension of 14 more years if the author was still living. It also provided for registration with the Company of Stationers. Between 1710 and the English Copyright Act of 1911 there was little change in the protection afforded to authors, although the Copyright Act of 1842 extended the term of protection to 42 years, or the life of the author plus seven years, whichever was longer. A variety of *sui generis* statutes were also introduced to extend the subject matter protected by the legislation, including early protection of engravings,[24] sculptures,[25] dramatic works[26] and fine art.[27]

2. PRINTING, PUBLISHING, AND "COPY" RIGHTS

> *Supreme Court of United States Justice M'Lean*: Perhaps no topic in England has excited more discussion among literary and talented men, than that of the literary

---

21 Licensing Act 1662, 13&14 Car 2 c33 (Gr. Brit).

22 Scotland and England were unified by the Union Acts 1706 and 1707, which was important for the Scottish printers.

23 Copyright Act 1709 8 Anne c.21 (cited in note 3).

24 Engraving Copyright Act 1734 (Gr. Brit).

25 Sculpture Copyright Act 1814 (Gr. Brit).

26 Dramatic Copyright Act 1833 (Gr. Brit).

27 Fine Arts Copyright Act 1862 (Gr. Brit).

property of authors. So engrossing was the subject, for a long time, as to leave few neutrals, among those who were distinguished for there [sic] learning and ability.[28]

Lord Camden: In short, the more your lordships examine the matter, the more you will find that these rights are founded upon the charter of the Stationers' Company and the royal prerogative; but what has this to do with the common law right? for never, my lords, forget the import of that term. Remember always that the common law right now claimed at your bar is the right of a private man to print his works for ever, independent of the Crown, the company, and all mankind. In the year 1681 we find a bye law for the protection of their own company and their copy-rights, which then consisted of all the literature of the kingdom; for they had contrived to get all the copies into their own hands. In a few years afterwards, the revolution was established, then vanished prerogative, then all the bye laws of the Stationers' Company were at an end; every restraint fell from off the press, and the old common law of England walked at large. During the succeeding fourteen or sixteen years, no action was brought, no injunction obtained, although no illegal force prevented it; a strong proof, that at that time there was no idea of a common law claim. So little did they then dream of establishing a perpetuity in their copies, that the holders of them finding no prerogative security, no privilege, no licensing act, no Star Chamber decree to protect their claim, in the year 1708 came up to parliament in the form of petitioners, with tears in their eyes, hopeless and forlorn; they brought with them their wives and children to excite compassion, and induce parliament to grant them a statutory security. They obtained the Act. And again and again fought for a further legislative security.

Thus, my Lords, stands the pretence on the score of usage, of which your lordships have heard so much on one side of the question. I come now to consider upon what foundation stand the prerogative copies; and these were in fact cases between co-patentees (for I must consider the Stationers' Company itself as a patentee of the Crown), and no authorship right occurs here. The right in the Crown is supposed to come either from purchase or contract; and our law argues from principles, cases, and analogy; but not a word of this in the judgment of the court; but the arguments of counsel are adduced to prove the point. The argument of counsel is a sorry kind of evidence indeed, in most cases it would be very dangerous to rely on it, but here it is such stuff as I am ashamed to mention. You have them at length in Carter. First, it is put on the topic of prerogative, next of ownership. 1. Henry the Sixth brought over the printers and their presses, ergo, say the counsel, he has an absolute right to the whole art, and all that it can produce. 2. Printing belongs to nobody's, and what is nobody's is of course the King's. 3. The King pays his judges, ergo, he purchases that right for a valuable consideration. 4. He paid for the translation of the Bible, therefore, forsooth, he bought a right to sell bibles. Away with such trifling! Mr. Yorke put it on its true footing. Ought not the Promulgation of your venerable codes of religion and of law to be entrusted to the executive power, that they may bear the highest mark of authenticity, and neither be impaired, or altered, or mutilated? These printed Acts are Records themselves, are Evidence in a court of law, without recurring to the original parliamentary roll. Will you, then, give this honourable

[28] *Wheaton and Donaldson v Peters and Grigg* 33 U.S. (8 Pet.) 591 (1834). This case is also of note for it being the first consideration by the Supreme Court of the United States on a copyright issue, and also as mistakenly looking to the judges' votes in *Donaldson* rather than the decision of the Lords.

> right to your sovereign as such? or will you degrade him into a bookseller? indeed, had he no other title to this distinction, that could hardly be maintained.[29]

Looking at the period from the end of the sixteenth century to the late eighteenth century, any discussion of the development of the copyright doctrine also requires taking account of the relationship to the Crown prerogative. The Crown prerogative to print certain works was delimited at that time and is still occasionally invoked in modern times, but usually without reference to the circumstances that originally gave rise to the Crown's right. There are only very few cases from this era, and they are commonly cited to support the contention that the Crown has rights over publishing particular works, such as bibles and statutes. However, much of the confusion over the boundaries of copyright and Crown prerogative stems from the terms "prerogative" and "copyright" being used interchangeably in a mixture of contexts in the early cases and writings. This can be seen as one of the areas leading to the confusion around the existence of a common law copyright, i.e. a form of copyright which was a misnomer applied to the seemingly unrestrained prerogative claims by the Crown became associated with claims to a common law right.

Thus in the seventeenth century, and into the eighteenth, the words "copy-right" or "copyright" did not carry with them the connotations of current thinking (that is, protecting the intellectual efforts of authors' original expressions by giving them a limited monopoly in the reproduction rights over the product of their labours). Prior to the Statute of Anne,[30] there were three rights that regulated the publication of any work: the Stationer's rights over the "copy"; the printer's right to print the work; and the patents issued under the Crown prerogative. Once authors had released their hold (and typically this would be literally) on their manuscripts,[31] there was little they could do to control replication of the materials. During the Middle Ages the "ownership" of an original manuscript related to possession of the physical work, much like the physical ownership of the medium that remains today,[32] and whose quill, ink and parchment were used, rather than deriving from the creativity of an author.[33] This right was one of ownership of the physical manuscript

---

[29] Lord Camden in *Donaldson v Beckett* (1774) (cited in note 7).

[30] Copyright Act 1709 8 Ann c.21. Due to the calendar changes later in the century this Act may be seen cited as the Copyright Act 1709, but the "normalised" date of 1710 is most frequently used.

[31] In the seventeenth century this would be virtually exclusively into the hands of one of the members of the Company of Stationers.

[32] See *Re Dickens* [1935] Ch 267.

[33] See generally, Elizabeth Armstrong, *Before Copyright: The French Book Privilege System 1498–1526* (Cambridge, UK, Cambridge University Press, 1990)

itself, rather than any ownership of the thought or the words in the text. That an author of a work had any rights of ownership, other than over pen, ink and parchment, was an alien concept in law. The introduction of the printing press in Europe brought forth not only a new era in the dissemination of literature, poetry and information, but also protectionism.[34]

The Royal Charter of incorporation of the Company of Stationers in 1557 was the single most important event in publishing in sixteenth-century England. This was probably at the instigation of the government of the day and certainly for the purpose of giving the Crown greater control over the content of published materials.[35] The Charter gave the Company a complete monopoly over publishing in England.[36] The Company developed its own internal management system for dealing with texts that came under its control. Disputes between members were settled primarily in the Company's own Court of Assistants.[37] All texts were by the seventeenth century referred to as "copy", sometimes meaning the content, which today we would consider the work of original expression, and at other times the physical work. The right to the copy was purely a matter of regulating works within the Company and its members. As those who held the right to copy were the publishers, that is the Stationers, the reproduction right of necessity was an integral part of the

---

and Mark Rose, *Authors and Owners: The Invention of Copyright* (Cambridge, MA, Harvard University Press, 1993).

[34] The arguments that arose at that time have an interesting analogy with those being promoted today, principally by the United States. Faced by new technologies allowing for easy global distribution at a very low cost, there have been calls for further extending the realm of copyright. In Geneva, on December 20, 1996, the World Intellectual Property Organization (WIPO) Diplomatic Conference on Certain Copyright and Neighboring Rights Questions adopted two new treaties, including the WIPO Copyright Treaty. This Treaty contains provisions that treat copyright protection of computer programs, original databases and rental rights in a similar way to the Agreement on Trade-related Aspects of Intellectual Property Rights Agreement (TRIPS), which most jurisdictions have now implemented. A third proposal in Geneva, seeking highly restrictive regulation of data use, was promoted principally by the United States, but was not adopted.

[35] See Patterson, *Copyright in Historical Perspective* (cited in note 2).

[36] The Charter provided: "No person within this our realm of England or the dominions of the same shall practise or exercise by himself, or by his ministers, his servants or by any other person the art or mistery of printing any book or thing for sale or traffic within this our realm of England or the dominions of the same, unless the same person at the time of his foresaid printing is or shall be one of the community of the foresaid mistery or art of Stationery of the foresaid City, or has therefore license of us or the heirs or successors of us the foresaid Queen by the letters patent of us or the heirs or successors of us the foresaid Queen." Quoted in Patterson, *Copyright in Historical Perspective* at 32 (cited in note 2).

[37] *Id* at 32–36.

Stationers' right to the copy. The primary purpose of this Stationers' right to the copy, also know later as "stationer's copy-right", was to enable administration within the Company. This, it must be stressed, was for the regulation of publishing amongst the members to the exclusion of anyone else. The main restriction to publishing a work was not any right in the work, but rather to the status of membership of the Company. There was a complete change in under a century, from the medieval simple licence to print a work, into ownership by the Stationers of an exclusive right to publish and otherwise deal with a work. This was used to control how the copy would be distributed amongst members, whether by sale or upon the death of the holder. On the use of the word copy by Lord Mansfield, it is recounted that he had explained that he used the word "copy" "in the technical sense in which it had been used for ages to signify the incorporeal right to the sale, printing, and publishing of somewhat intellectual, communicated by letters".[38]

By the end of the sixteenth century the licence to print a work had evolved as a separate entity to that of the "copy-right". The printer's right was the right of a particular printer (the craftsman and exerciser of the *mystery* of setting type) to produce the printed versions of a work. "The printer's right was to the printer what the copyright was to the publisher, in that they both provided economic protection."[39] This was a valuable right and was often preserved within assignments of the copyright. The power to exercise control over a particular work effectively shifted from the printer to the stationer.

Related to this printer's right was the Crown's privilege, exercised in much the same way as the grant of a patent. Typically the Crown would give a grant to print a particular work or class of works. In Europe at large, usually these grants were for an exclusive right to print within a particular geographical area, such as the grants given to Johann de Spira in 1469 from the government of Venice. However, in the same year Aldus Manutius received a 20-year grant for all his works printed in Greek, and later, in 1502, an exclusive privilege for his type design from the Venetian Government and the Pope. In 1479, three printers were granted the exclusive right to print the Wurzburg breviary, and such episcopal privileges were not uncommon during the remainder of the fifteenth century in most of Europe.[40] The earliest English book privilege was

---

[38] John Lord Campbell, "The Lives of the Chief Justices of England" 3rd Ed, Vol III (London, John Murray, 1874) 301.

[39] *Id* at 51 (footnotes omitted).

[40] See Rose, *Authors and Owners: The Invention of Copyright*, at 9, and Armstrong, *Before Copyright: The French Book Privilege System 1498–1526*, at 2 (both cited in note 33).

granted to the University of Oxford for a commentary on Aristotle's *Ethics*.[41] The first privilege to be granted by the English Crown was that of the printed oration of the proposed marriage of Princess Mary and the Dauphin of France, in 1518.[42] At that time it would have been unthinkable, and possibly fatal, to challenge the right of the Crown to grant such a patent.[43] The printing press in England had been in use just thirty years, and printing was treated as a new art akin to other inventions of the day. Almost all early English grants of privilege were given to printers to print a particular work, but by the middle of the sixteenth century grants were being given to printers to produce certain classes of books, such as bibles, almanacs and law-books. Elizabeth I made extensive use of letters patent to govern the application of industrial devices and printing, primarily for raising money and conferring benefits on favourites. The distinguishing feature of the Elizabethan patents is that they usually included monopoly clauses. The general abuse of Crown prerogative stimulated the enactment of the Statute of Monopolies,[44] which placed some restrictions on the Crown's use of these grants. However, the statute explicitly exempted letters patent concerned with printing, and the Crown continued to make such grants under the prerogative.[45]

Typically, an author in the seventeenth century who wished to have a work printed would sell the manuscript to a publisher, probably a member of the

---

[41] Oxford 1518, 4° Bodl. Arch.A.E.76 (STC 6458). This book dated May 1518 carries the privilege on the last page, cited in Armstrong, *Before Copyright: The French Book Privilege System 1498–1526*, at 10 (cited in note 33). "*Cum privilegio. Vetitum est per edictum sub sigillo cancellariatus ne quis in septennio hoc insigne opus imprimat vel aliorum ductu impensis venditet in universitate Oxonie: aut infra precinctum eiusdem: sub pena amissionis omnium librorum et quinque librarum sterlingarum pro singulis sic venditis ubiubi impressi fuerint preter penam pretaxatam in decreto.*" [With privilege. It is forbidden through an edict under the seal of the Chancellor that anyone, within seven years of this seal, print the work or under the leadership of others sell the work for payment in the university of Oxford or with in the precinct of the same under the penalty of the surrender of all books and 5 pounds sterling for each individual book thus sold, wherever they have been printed, in accordance with the penalty appointed in the decree.] (Translated T. Taylor, The University of New England, 2019).

[42] See Armstrong, *Before Copyright: The French Book Privilege System 1498–1526*, at 10 (cited in note 33).

[43] Even 250 years later, that the book was just an industrial device subject to patent was still given consideration, as in *Donaldson v Becket* (1774) XVII Parliamentary History of England, 953, 974, Baron Eyre: "considered a book precisely upon the same footing with any other mechanical invention".

[44] 21 Jac I c3.

[45] Patterson, *Copyright in Historical Perspective*, at 86 (cited in note 2): "The reason for [the printing patent] exception is not clear."

Company of Stationers, and would have little to do with the work thereafter.[46] Depending on the prospects of the work, the publisher would perhaps offer a fixed sum to the author, or some free copies, or discounted copies. The Company did recognise a "right" of authors to receive some compensation for their works, but this was in the nature of recompensing them for the original property, not for the reproduction of the work. A different order of expectations on the part of the author existed then from today's presumption of an author's copyright.[47] The question of "books" was primarily within the realm of printers and stationers, not authors. The granting of patents and the payments individual authors received for their scripts has been interpreted as evidence of an early form of copyright, and indeed that is a valid interpretation so far as it goes.[48] Although publishers may have recognised the rights of authors to a reward for their labour and the need for the protection of the works once the publisher had control of them, this was part of the complex symbiotic relationship between the Company and the writer. The protection was desired to ensure that the economic interests of the Stationer were not threatened. The laws of the day did not give credence to authors' rights as such in the content of their work. Unless an author had a Royal patent, or a publisher had registered the work, there was little that could be done at law to prevent unauthorised publication. Indeed, it was often the threat of unauthorised publication that prompted authors to arrange for their publication, primarily for erudite reasons than thought of any economic return.

The concept of a common law copyright was espoused by Mansfield in the Court of King's Bench in *Millar v Taylor*[49] (1769) and the commonly reported decision of the Judges in the House of Lords *Donaldson v Beckett*[50] (1774), the latter's misreporting suggesting that although a perpetual copyright did exist

---

[46] *Id* 64–77, suggesting that the relationship between authors and publishers was more cooperative than competitive.

[47] D. Defoe, *Tatler* 101, 1 December 1709, for example, was still arguing: "All Mechanic Artizans are allowed to reap the Fruit of their Invention and Ingenuity without Invasion; but he that has separated himself from the rest of Mankind, and studied the Wonders of the Creation, the Government of his Passions, and the Revolutions of the World, and has an Ambition to communicate the Effect of half his Life spent in such noble Enquiries, has no Property in what he is willing to produce, but is exposed to Robbery and Want, with this melancholy and just Reflection. That he is the only Man who is not protected by his Country, and the same Time that he best deservers it."

[48] See Feather, "From Rights in Copies to Copyright: The Recognition of Authors' Rights in English Law and Practice in the Sixteenth and Seventeenth Centuries" (cited in note 13), which also takes the view that the foundation for authors' rights is to be found in the pre-revolution patents and trade practices.

[49] *Millar v Taylor* (1769) 4 Burr. 2303, 98 ER 201.

[50] *Donaldson v Beckett* (1774) (cited in note 7).

under the common law the right was (merely) "impeached" by the Statute of Anne 1710 for published works. However, it was the prerogative powers of the Crown that were extremely unpopular in the eighteenth century, reaching a *crescendo* in the late 1760s.[51] Lord Mansfield's approach to claims to print that were based on patents issued under the Crown prerogative to print was to suggest the claims were founded in a common law property right of the Crown. This culminated in his judgment in *Millar v Taylor*.[52] Although it may seem strange that *Millar*, despite being overruled, is cited more often than the House of Lords decision in *Donaldson*, there are several possible reasons. The reporting of *Millar* was more complete, and it was the first King's Bench case where Lord Mansfield was challenged by a dissenting judgment.[53] The case also had notoriety at the time, due in part to Lord Mansfield's status. In *Millar* Lord Mansfield again stressed that the Crown had no control over the act of printing in general, and referred to *Basket* in his judgment:[54]

> [I]t is, and has all along been admitted … that by the common law, the King's copy continues after publication; and that the unanimous judgment of this court in the case of Basket and The University of Cambridge is right.

He continued: [55]

> We had no idea of any prerogative in the Crown over the press; or of any power to restrain it by exclusive privileges, or of any power to control the subject-matter on which a man might write, or the manner in which he might treat it. We rested upon property from the King's right of original publication.

---

[51] E Heward, *Lord Mansfield* (Chichester, UK, Barry Rose Ltd, 1979) 75 (hereafter referred to as Heward).

[52] *Millar v Taylor* (1769) 4 Burr. 2303, 98 ER 201.

[53] Cecile Fifoot, *Lord Mansfield* (Oxford, Clarendon Press, 1936) 47, notes that the dissenting Justice Yates "nursed a grievance until reticence became intolerable. In 1770 he expressed his desire to 'retire into the Court of Common Pleas' and was succeeded by Sir William Blackstone. Blackstone himself shrank under the immediate eye of his patron and was glad to seek the same shade before the end of the year". It was the plaintiff in *Millar* who was claiming a common law copyright in Thomson's *Seasons* and it was Blackstone who acted for the plaintiff.

[54] *Millar v Taylor* (1769) 4 Burr. 2303, 98 ER 201 at 2401.

[55] *Id* at 2404.

His Lordship went on to solidify the proposition that the Crown prerogative was simply a proprietary right of the Crown recognised at common law in much the same way as authors' rights:[56]

> The King has no power or control over the subject-matter: his power rests in property. His whole right rests upon the foundation of property in the copy by the common law. What other ground can there be for the King's having a property in the Latin Grammar, (which is one of his most ancient copies,) than that it was originally composed at his expense? Whatever the common law says of property in the King's case, from analogy to the case of authors, must hold conclusively, in my apprehension, with regard to authors.

The argument here is based on reasoning that the right relied on in the judgment given in *Basket*[57] was a "copyright" of the Crown at common law, and one that had not been pre-empted by the Statute of Anne. This reasoning is highly suspect. It was this notion of the Crown prerogative merely being a property of copyright that was dismissed emphatically by Lord Chief Justice De Grey a few years later in *Donaldson*:[58]

> The case of Basket and the University of Cambridge ... appeared upon the pleadings to be a question arising between two parties who claimed under concurrent and inconsistent grants of the Crown. My late honourable and learned friend (Mr. Yorke) who argued that case, endeavoured to shew that his client's right might arise from the power of the Crown, and to illustrate his argument said, it might perhaps be 'property founded on prerogative'—a language, however allowable for counsel, not very admissible by, or intelligible to a judge, but the certificate [of the court] in the above case does not say a word of property, and indeed if such a claim as that had been founded on property, every one would have as good a right to publish abridgments of the statutes, as of any other book.

Lord Camden also devoted part of his speech in *Donaldson* to criticising judges who assume the role of lawmakers: "their business is to tell the suitor how the law stands, not how it ought to be"—a gibe undoubtedly aimed at Lord Mansfield.[59]

---

56 *Id* at 2405.

57 *Basket v The University of Cambridge* 1 Black W 106; 96 ER 59 (KB 1758).

58 *Id* at 989.

59 Lords Camden and Mansfield had very different approaches to the function of judging, see Heward, *Lord Mansfield* (cited in note 51) at 131. The criticism of judge-made law was likely aimed at Lord Mansfield and his role in *Millar*, and Mansfield was well known for moving out of precedent in order to achieve what he thought was justice.

With regard to *Donaldson v Beckett*[60] (1774) Drone's treatise on the law of intellectual property emphatically takes the traditional position:[61]

> It is a fact which may be regarded as judicially conceded, that copyright in printed books was not created by legislation, but that it existed by the common law long before, and when the Statute of Anne was passed. This doctrine was declared by the King's Bench in Millar v Taylor; and it has never been judicially overruled. It was expressly approved by a majority of the judges in Donaldson v Beckett; and was in effect affirmed in that case by the House of Lords, whose judgment was not, that copyright had been created by the Statute of Anne, but that the common-law right had been superseded by the statutory.

Copinger and Skone James on Copyright takes the view that "this case must be taken to have decided finally that publication put an end to the common law perpetual right, and that after publication an author had to base his claim for protection upon his statutory right".[62] This position, that the outcome of *Donaldson* was simply that publication brought an end to a copyright at common law, is reiterated with little clarification: "[in] the case of *Donaldson v Beckett*, the House of Lords finally decided that the effect of the statute was to extinguish the common law copyright in published works, though leaving the common law copyright in unpublished works unaffected".[63] Professor Ricketson takes a similar approach,[64] but does note that he is discussing the opinions of the judges called to advise the House of Lords in *Donaldson* rather than the ultimate decision of the full House.

A detailed analysis of *Donaldson* by Professor Abrams reveals that the Lords voted against the existence of common law copyright by 22 to 11.[65] Ironically, the confusion is mainly attributable to the ban on reporting House of Lords proceedings at that time, ostensibly because of a fear of possible errors in the reporting process. At that time it was contempt of the House,

---

60 *Donaldson v Beckett* (1774) (cited in note 7).

61 Drone, *A Treatise on the Law of Property in Intellectual Production in Great Britain and the United States* (cited in note 5) at 20 (footnotes omitted). Although Drone does note that it was the advisory opinions of the judges reported, he does not discuss the decision of the full House of Lords, only those of the judges. Drone's treatise was first published in 1879.

62 *Copinger and Skone James on Copyright* 12th Ed, ¶ 2-03 (cited in note 5).

63 *Copinger and Skone James* 12th Ed, ¶ 20-16 (cited in note 5), citing the limited Burrows report on *Donaldson* (1774) 4 Burr 2407.

64 Staniphort Ricketson, *The Law of Intellectual Property* (North Ryde, New South Wales, Law Book Company, 1991) 70.

65 Abrams, "The Historic Foundation of American Copyright Law: Exploding the Myth of Common Law Copyright" (cited in note 10) 1157–1158. See also Richard Tompson, "Scottish Judges and the Birth of British Copyright" (1992) The Juridical Review 18.

punishable by imprisonment, to report the speeches of the Lords.[66] It was thus prudent for reporters to confine their work to the advisory opinions of the judges. Burrow's report, almost invariably the only one cited, thus omits the speeches in House of Lords deliberations in *Donaldson* and simply reports some advisory opinions of the judges solicited to assist. Some of the Lords' speeches are reported in the *Parliamentary History of England*. These are indicative of the total rejection by the full house of the notion of common law copyright.[67] However, the judicial statements commonly have been interpreted to be the controlling opinions in this case, whilst the actual decision and opinions expressed in the House of Lords have been overlooked. Although the advisory opinions of the judges were frequently followed, it was the Lords that had the final say in matters before them. A clear and well documented illustration of this is found in *Bishop of London v Ffytche*[68] (1783), another case where the opinion of the judges was not followed and the ruling of the lower court reversed upon the urging of the Episcopalian members of the House.[69] In *Jefferys v Boosey*[70] (1854) common law copyright again came before the

---

66 The reporter Shower suffered the wrath of the House of Lords at the end of the seventeenth century when his reports on its deliberations were ruled a breach of privilege. Regular reporting of the House did not reappear until the reports of Josiah Brown at the end of the eighteenth century. See Robert Stevens, *Law and Politics: The House of Lords as a Judicial Body, 1800–1976* (Chapel Hill, University of North Carolina Press, 1978) 12; William Holdsworth, *A History of English Law* (London, Methuen, 3rd Ed, 1945) 572; and Abrams, "The Historic Foundation of American Copyright Law: Exploding the Myth of Common-Law Copyright" (cited in note 10), at 1159. The House of Lords judgments to 2009 are now within the scope of Parliamentary Copyright under s 165 of the United Kingdom Copyright, Designs and Patents Act 1988. There is a Parliamentary Copyright notice posted at the site of the reports, https://publications.parliament.uk/pa/ld/ldjudgmt.htm, and for the Supreme Court judgments (https://www.supremecourt.uk) there is a Crown Copyright notice, under s 163 of the United Kingdom Copyright, Designs and Patents Act 1988.

67 Abrams, "The Historic Foundation of American Copyright Law: Exploding the Myth of Common Law Copyright" (cited in note 10), at 1164.

68 *Bishop of London v Ffytche* (1783) 2 Bro. Parl. Cas. 211.

69 See Stevens, *Law and Politics: The House of Lords as a Judicial Body, 1800–1976* (cited in note 66), at 11–12.

70 *Jeffereys v Boosey* (1854) 4 HLC 814. Also William Cornish, *Intellectual Property: Patents, Copyright, Trade Marks and Allied Rights* (London, Sweet & Maxwell, 3rd Ed, 1996), at ¶ 9-03 comments that the House of Lords consulted the judges, but rejected their majority opinion and unanimously agreed with Lord Chief Baron Pollock, who put the case against a common law right strongly at 4 HLC 814, 937: "Weighing all the arguments on both sides, and looking to the authorities up to the present time, the conclusion I have arrived at is, that copyright is altogether an artificial right, not naturally and necessarily arising out of the social rules that ought to prevail among mankind assembled in communities, but is a creature of the municipal law of

House of Lords, and again it was rejected. The Scottish Court of Session in *Hinton v Donaldson* (1773) decided that once a manuscript was published it was only protected by the Statute of Anne.[71] Despite the pronouncements of the Lords in *Donaldson*, as opposed to the widely promulgated opinions of the judges, several cases have applied the concept of a common law copyright in unpublished works,[72] although a direct claim of copyright at common law was never made by the Crown.

The Lords' decision was also overlooked in *Wheaton and Donaldson v Peters and Grigg*,[73] where only the advice of the judges was considered. This was the first United States Supreme Court case on copyright which focused on the judgment of Lord Mansfield in *Millar* and the votes of the judges in *Donaldson*, rather than the House's binding decision. This confusion across the Atlantic persevered for longer than may have been expected in the new world, even though the *Wheaton* court recognised that "From the above authorities, and others which might be referred to if time permitted, the law appears to be well settled in England, that, since the Statute of 8 Anne, the literary property of an author in his works can only be asserted under the statute."[74] The presumption of the common law was nonetheless assumed in the United States, "At common law, the author of an unpublished manuscript had a property in his production, which continued in him until publication by his consent."[75]

---

each country, to be enjoyed for such time and under such regulations as the law of each state may direct, and has no existence by the Common law of England".

[71] *Hinton v Donaldson* (1773, 5 Brn 508). A discussion of this case can be found in R Deazley (2008) "Commentary on Hinton v. Donaldson (1773)", in *Primary Sources on Copyright (1450–1900)*, (eds) L. Bently and M. Kretschmer.

[72] A full discussion of these cases can be found in *Re Dickens* [1935] Ch 267, although this case is better known for its clear distinction between the physical document, subject to personal property rights, and the rights in the expression of the author—i.e. the ability to separate rights of ownership over the paper and those copyrights in the work.

[73] *Wheaton and Donaldson v Peters and Grigg* 33 U.S. (8 Pet.) 591 (1834).

[74] See Ralph S. Brown, Jr., "Publication and Preemption in Copyright Law: Elegiac Reflections on Goldstein v. California", Faculty Scholarship Series 2720 (1975), for a discussion on the development of legislation in the United States and its uneasy relationship with a perceived common law right. See also Ralph S. Brown, Jr., "Unification: A Cheerful Requiem for Common Law Copyright", Faculty Scholarship Series 2719 (1977). Shortly after the new US copyright provisions in 1976 it seemed that the use of common law copyright could be finally buried, even in the USA, though the myth prevailed.

[75] Henry Wade Rogers, *Literary Property* (1881). Faculty Scholarship Series. 4047, https://digitalcommons.law.yale.edu/fss_papers/4047.

3. WHY DOES IT MATTER TODAY?

> *Lord Camden*: At length, my lords, having removed every stumbling-block that opposed our progress to the pure source of common law; having cleared the way of all those spurious, pretended authorities, which will not bear the test of a moment's serious examination, the question begins to assume its natural shape: Here, then, I feel myself upon my own ground, and I challenge any man to produce any adjudication, a precedent, a case, or any thing like legal authority on which this claim can be grounded. Does there a scintilla, a glimpse of common law appear under any of those different heads I have mentioned, and which have been so often repeated to us? For my own part, I find nothing in the whole that savours of law, except the term itself, Literary Property. They have borrowed one single word from the common law, and have raked into every store-house of literary lumber to find out how to apply it to the subject, and to deduce some principles to which it may refer, and be governed by.
>
> And now what are they? What are the foundations of this claim in the English common law? Why, in the first place, say the respondents, every man has a right to his ideas. Most certainly every man who thinks, has a right to his thoughts, while they continue his; but here the question again returns; when does he part with them? When do they become *publici juris*? While they are in his brain no one indeed can purloin them; but what if he speaks, and lets them fly out in private or public discourse? Will he claim the breath, the air, the words in which his thoughts are clothed? Where does this fanciful property begin, or end, or continue? Oh, say they, the ideas are marked in black and white, on paper or parchment—now, then, we get at something; and an action, I allow, will lie for ink and paper: but what says the common law about the incorporeal ideas, and where does it prescribe a remedy for the recovery of them, independent of the materials to which they are affixed? I see nothing about the matter in all my books; nor were I to admit ideas to be ever so distinguishable and definable, should I therefore infer they must be matters of private property, and objects of the common law?[76]

The question remains as to the legacy that common law copyright has left with us today. It could be argued that this subtle idea pervading historical analysis, i.e. one of their having always been protection for authors, has provided succour to those proponents of deontological moral positions for supporting stronger copyright, even though this is not the fact. The notion of ownership of something you create is attractive, like the plant you grow from seed, but what if the seed is taken from someone else (most ideas are stimulated by the ideas of others), the soil is someone else's, and the water is stolen. This acceptance of protection having always been there then means that legislation (from the Statute of Anne onwards) is simply a codification of a common law right, albeit extended into modern realms, even though it was really founded on an interpretation of Crown Privileges and Patents.

---

[76] *Donaldson v Beckett* (1774) at 954 (cited in note 7).

The benefits of having legal protection of ideas is naïve: it diminishes the role that all the external influences and inputs have played in order for that idea to ferment. The existence of a creation from nothing is unlikely, but it is this conception of literary genius, and today also for music, film, photography, sculpture, and even digital locks, that is readily adopted by many. Indeed, some reflect on the story of Columba and Finnian as a confirmation for the natural right over your own text. It is related that Columba secretly copied the text of a new version of the Holy Book which belonged to Finnian in sixteenth-century Ireland. Finnian was not happy with this activity when he found out,[77] but they agreed to take the issue to the High-King of Ireland, Diamit.[78] Columba claimed

> But I hold, that Finnian's book has not decreased in value because of the transcript I made from it; also that it is not right to extinguish the divine things it contained, or to prevent me or anybody else from *copying it, or reading it, or circulating it throughout the provinces*. I further maintain that if I benefited by its transcription, which I desired to be for the general good, provided no injury accrued to Finnian or his book thereby, it was quite permissible for me to copy it![79]

However, Diamit is recorded as giving judgment: "To every cow her calf, to every book its transcript. Therefore the copy you have made [Columba] belongs to Finnian". Columba was not happy about this, and this was one of the reasons for the battle of Culdreimhne, which he won.[80] The story, apocryphal or not, gives succour to those claiming a long history in protection of works, and the natural relationship between a work and the need for its derivatives to be protected, despite the book not being authored by Finnian and the loss of the battle by the King.

There are many great scholarly works surrounding and following the Great Literary Debate, the creation of copyright under statute, legal analysis, historical analysis, philosophical analysis, Supreme Court cases and reams of

---

[77] Which seems odd. First, it would be good to have the word of God, in the new format, spread widely. Second, presumably it was not his original writing, but rather a new copy of the Holy Book that he picked up on his travels to Rome. Indeed, Lucy Menzies, *Saint Columba of Iona: A Study of his Life, his Times and his Influence* (JM Dent and Sons Ltd, 1920) at 35 suggests the book was possibly a copy of Jerome's translation of the Psalter, along with some other works.

[78] This is recounted from the description given by Menzies, *id.*

[79] *Id* at 25.

[80] The battle was won by Columba, but at a cost of 3,000 lives. However, Columba defended this outcome "I am not responsible, it was the unjust judgment passed on me by Diarmit that caused the battle", *id* at 32.

legislation.[81] However, the essence of the myth highlighted by Lord Camden persists in the consciousness of civil society, that is, that there is something so special in an idea that you should have extensive protection for its fixation.[82] Of course, this is reinforced by the bombardments of advertisements of those spruiking the value of literature, music, art, and even radio waves (though rarely owned by the creator), pressing the ideology of "theft" by copyright owners, such as those represented in the puffery of FAST, MPAA and other trade and publisher organisations. [83] Although we are now in an age that is undergoing a revolution in the ability to disseminate works, after thirty years of a disruptive technology that is no less important than the introduction of the printing press, in which the fair use of copyrighted works and the realm of the public domain is becoming more restrictive.[84] Some of the principles of the doctrine of copyright, such as providing public access to knowledge by offering only a limited monopoly for authors, are being eroded within a framework

---

[81] Some works cannot be omitted from any study of this realm, such as Rose, *Authors and Owners: The Invention of Copyright* (cited in note 33); Abrams, "The Historic Foundation of American Copyright Law: Exploding the Myth of Common Law Copyright" (cited in note 10); Patterson, Copyright in Historical Perspective (cited in note 2); Abraham Drassinower, *What's Wrong with Copying?* (Cambridge, MA, Harvard University Press, 2015).

[82] However, the existence of common law copyright in the eighteenth century is still reflected in a number of intellectual property texts of today, such as some recognition of a common law right in Andrew Stewart et al., *Intellectual Property in Australia* (6th Ed, LexisNexis, 2018).

[83] UK Federation Against Software Theft (http://www.fast.org) and the Motion Picture Association of America (http://www.mpaa.org) are examples of such organisations. The message usually exceeds simply one of "don't infringe copyright", but rather demonises the "thief" and their destruction of the represented industry. Cf. Nicolas P. Suzor, Brian F. Fitzgerald and Mark Perry, "Free Software as a Democratic Principle", in Mark Perry and Brian F. Fitzgerald (eds), *Knowledge Policy for the Twenty-First Century: A Legal Perspective* (Toronto, ON, Irwin Law, 2011) 17–28.

[84] For a discussion of the threat to the public domain by implementation of the Agreement on Trade-related Aspects of Intellectual Property Rights (TRIPS) in the United States, see Peter Jaszi, "Goodbye to All That—A Reluctant (and Perhaps Premature) Adieu to a Constitutionally-Grounded Discourse of Public Interest in Copyright Law", 29 Vanderbilt Journal of Transnational Law 595 (1996); James Boyle, "The Second Enclosure Movement and the Construction of the Public Domain", in B. Atkinson (ed), *Copyright Law Volume III: Copyright in the 21st Century* (Abingdon, Routledge, 2017). See also Shubha Ghosh, *Deprivatizing Copyright*, 54 Case W. Res. L. Rev. 387 (2003).

that stresses an economic analysis of copyright. However, this approach is not fully developed, as one commentator suggests:[85]

> Essentially the history of economic thinking about copyright suggests that the analysis has progressed only to the point of presenting a serious alternative to the natural rights rationale: an alternative rationale based normatively on the criterion of economic welfare and on an explicit balancing of the costs of the copyright system against the economic objective of improving the operation of the unregulated ... market.

At the end of the twentieth century, we saw the beginnings of a new philosophy of protection in works of the intellect. Copyright legislation is now highly complex and codified, with the acceptance of digital-specific international conventions. The provisions for a limited monopoly have been extended in both term and extent.[86] This millennium has seen radical changes in the application of copyright doctrines worldwide, and challenges to the efficacy of the doctrine by digital media. Mass reproduction of works on a printing press is not now the concern for copyright holders, and even at the time of the Statute of Anne the act of copying a work was a very expensive and possibly not very profitable venture.[87] The widespread use of the photocopier in the 1980s, digital media since the 1990s, and global networks today, have given every user of literary and other works the potential to infringe copyright on an unprecedented scale.

It is apt to conclude along with Lord Camden, taking his words as a prescience of the need for protecting open access and the dangers of the corporatisation of knowledge, something that we face today with the consolidation of corporate interests over publishing of all kinds, the extensions of the terms of protection to the extreme, exceeding anything that would have been contemplated in the consideration of a common law right. Even today, though publishers serve an important role in the distribution of works of literature, music, film and art, their position is not as complementary to the advancement of knowledge as they suggest. Copyright is often used as a tool to protect the

---

[85] G Hadfield, "The Economics of Copyright: An Historical Perspective" (1991) 38 Copyright Law Symposium 1.

[86] The United Kingdom Copyright Act 1911 ran to 37 sections, compared to the New Zealand Copyright Act 1994 which has 236 sections and four schedules, and the latest version of the Australian Copyright Act 1968, which has been amended into hundreds of sections over the last 50 years and needs replacing—it now runs to 657 pages, the last 42 being lists of its amendment history. Further extensions to the realm of copyright are constantly under consideration.

[87] Richard Posner, *Law and Literature* (Cambridge, MA, Harvard University Press, 1998). However, this did not prevent a great deal of copying, and thus the many cases in the eighteenth century.

publishers, the same outcome as the printers of old desired, namely to shore up their profits rather than the often claimed reason of supporting the creators of works. Although some change can be seen, driven by the courts in cases such as *CCH v Law Society of Upper Canada*,[88] where a counter-balance to the natural law basis of copyright is given by way of exceptions, limitations and even user rights,[89] it is perhaps time for our conception of the basis for protecting expression to be reformed. The imminent growth in the production of materials that fall into copyright's subject matter, generated by software, automatons, expert systems, and artificial intelligence, is already presenting challenges to the idea of authoring being an expression of an individual. However, in many cases today it could be argued that 14 years, let alone life plus 75, is indeed too long for some of the perishable trash circulated.

> *Lord Camden*: Why did we enter into society at all, but to enlighten one another's minds, and improve our faculties, for the common welfare of the species? Those great men, those favoured mortals, those sublime spirits, who share that ray of divinity which we call genius, are intrusted by Providence with the delegated power of imparting to their fellow-creatures that instruction which heaven meant for universal benefit; they must not be niggards to the world, or hoard up for themselves the common stock. We know what was the punishment of him who hid his talent, and Providence has taken care that there shall not be wanting the noble motives and incentives for men of genius to communicate to the world those truths and discoveries which are nothing if uncommunicated. Knowledge has no value or use for the solitary owner: To be enjoyed it must be communicated. "Scire tuum nibil est, nisi te scire, hoc sciat alter."[90] Glory is the reward of science, and those who deserve it, scorn all meaner views; I speak not of the scribblers for bread, who teaze the press with their wretched productions; fourteen years is too long a privilege for their perishable trash. It was not for gain, that Bacon, Newton, Milton, Locke, instructed and delighted the world; it would be unworthy such men to traffic with a dirty bookseller for so much a sheet of letter-press. When the bookseller offered Milton five pounds for his Paradise Lost, he did not reject it, and commit his poem to the flames, nor did he accept the miserable pittance as the reward of his labour; he knew that the real price of his work was immortality, and that posterity would pay it. Some authors are as careless about profit as others are rapacious of it, and what a situation would the

---

[88] *CCH Canadian Ltd. v Law Society of Upper Canada* [2004] 1 SCR 339.

[89] Carys Craig, "Globalizing User Rights-Talk: On Copyright Limits and Rhetorical Risks" (2017) 33(1) American University International Law Review 1.

[90] This quote is attributable to Aulus Persius Flaccus, a Roman poet "it is nothing for you to know a thing unless another knows that you know it", Jon Stone, *The Routledge Dictionary of Latin Quotations* (2004) 121, which connects well to a counterpoint of the need to share knowledge in order to advance it, reflected in Sir Isaac Newton's sentiment in a letter to Robert Hooke dated 5 February 1676: "If I have seen further it is by standing on the sholders [sic] of giants". However, the idea of relying on earlier work to make advances had been expressed some centuries prior to Newton, and was no doubt known to Lord Camden.

public be in with regard to literature, if there were no means of compelling a second impression of useful work to be put forth, or wait till a wife or children are to be provided for by the sale of an edition. All our learning would be locked up in the hands of the Tonsons and the Lintons of the age, who would set what price upon it their avarice chuses to demand, till the public became as much their slaves, as their own hackney compliers are.

PART V

THE LORE OF COURTS

10. "If music did not pay": the state court roots of Justice Holmes' intellectual property jurisprudence

Shubha Ghosh

1. WHY HOLMES?

While Justice Holmes' intellectual property opinions are established canon, long forgotten are his intellectual property related opinions authored while on the Massachusetts Supreme Court. Such neglect is perhaps justified as intellectual property law is a matter of federal, not state law. Except in some narrow areas, what relevance do Holmes' state court opinions have? However, his state court opinions should not be forgotten. His experiences with intellectual property in state courts foreshadow the fundamental approach guiding the more well-known Supreme Court canon.

Judging from the few discussions of his state court decisions, Holmes' tenure on the Massachusetts Supreme Court was not marked by memorable cases or serious developments in the law. He himself described his time on the state bench as consisting of "a thousand cases, many of them on trifling or transitory matters."[1] Professor Mark Tushnet's systematic study of Holmes' decisions on the Massachusetts Supreme Court reveals rather routine, collegial decision-making as the judge engaged with his colleagues on the bench to achieve cohesive judgments.[2] As Professor Gordon summarizes:

> Few of these cases, it turned out, provided much scope for Holmes' talents as a general theorist and historian of the common law, and even when they did, Holmes proved a cautious judge, usually inclined to decide on narrow grounds rather than on broad ideas of policy.[3]

---

[1] See Robert W. Gordon, "Introduction" in Robert W. Gordon, ed., *The Legacy of Oliver Wendell Holmes*, Jr. 2 (1992) (citing a Holmes' bar speech from 1900).

[2] Mark Tushnet, "The Logic of Experience: Oliver Wendell Holmes on the Supreme Judicial Court" 63 Va. L. Rev. 975 (1977).

[3] See Gordon, supra note 1.

A study of the intellectual property cases authored by Judge Holmes does not contradict this general assessment. There are no grand flourishes of language, no memorable phrases, no attempts to speak in grand aphorisms, as we observe in his United States Supreme Court opinions. As Professor Tushnet argues, Holmes' time on the state bench seems to have tempered the grand ambitions he articulated in his book *The Common Law*, published one year before he assumed the position on the Massachusetts bench.[4] The vision of the judge in shaping the law set forth in that book contrasts with the staid, quotidian workmanship we see in his state court opinions. Even the broad language in his federal opinions masks a more technical ambition to resolve cases and author opinions that might serve to guide future litigants in their citation of the law.

But without making too broad a point, Holmes' state court intellectual property opinions did shape his later more well-known federal intellectual property decisions. To follow on from Professor Tushnet's point: Holmes' tenure as a state court judge provided the experience that molded the logic of his more memorable intellectual property opinions. Perhaps the most surprising conclusion of this chapter is that Holmes' opinions in the largely federal area of intellectual property law were shaped by his time as a judge on the Massachusetts Supreme Court from 1882 to 1902. In fact, a complete picture of Holmes' intellectual property jurisprudence requires careful study of his two decades on the state court.

This conclusion is surprising because intellectual property is largely federal law, with trade secret law based solely in state law during the period from 1882 to 1932, the span of Holmes' tenure in the state and federal judiciary. While on the Massachusetts Supreme Court, Judge Holmes authored 22 opinions that touched on intellectual property. None of these opinions dealt with trade secrets, which one might expect to arise within the state court system. Instead, as summarized in Table 10.1, these 22 cases consisted of 13 patent-related cases and nine trademark cases. Since federal courts share jurisdiction over trademark cases with state courts, trademark cases before the state Supreme Court should not be surprising. However, the large number of patent cases before a state court is surprising since federal courts have exclusive jurisdiction over patent law.

This conundrum is readily explained by examining the specific patent and trademark issues that came before the Massachusetts Supreme Court. At issue in each of these 22 cases were state law issues of contract, commercial law, or trust and estate law. Even before Holmes joined the federal judiciary, his exposure to intellectual property while on the state bench shaped his understanding of patents and trademarks within the framework of commercial law. It

---

4 Tushnet, supra note 2.

Table 10.1 Decisions authored by Holmes on Massachusetts Supreme Court

Name	Year	Subject matter	Description
Squires v Mason Mfg Co	1902	Patent	Libel based on patent infringement
Martin v Meles	1901	Patent	Contribution arrangement in patent dispute
Flagg Mfg Co v Holway	1901	Patent	No unfair competition in absence of patents
Prouty v Union Hardware Co	1900	Patent	Contract dispute arising from patent license
Garst v Harris	1900	Patent	Minimum resale price maintenance enforced
Lawrence v Hull	1897	Patent	Trade name issue. Expresses disagreement with *Proctor v Tilighman* over recovery of both profits and damages
Currier v Hallowell	1893	Patent	Contract dispute arising from sale of patented invention
Standard Button Fastening v Harney	1892	Patent	Royalty dispute from patent license
Bi-Spool Sewing Machine v Acme Mfg Co	1891	Patent	Contract for transfer of patents
Reeve v Dennett	1887	Patent	Fraudulent representation as to patent in stock fraud case
Pratt v Tuttle	1884	Patent	Contract for transfer of patents
Smith v Moore	1883	Patent	Patent held in trust
Burt v Tucker	1901	Trademark	Knickerbocker as applied to shoes/ boots. Prior use defense
Commonwealth v Rozen	1900	Trademark	Registration requirements and criminal conviction for counterfeit cigars
American Waltham Watch Co v US Watch Co	1899	Trademark	First in time principle. Place name has secondary meaning beyond geography
Tracy v Banker	1898	Trademark	Name used by trade union
New England Awl & Needle Co v Marlboro Awl & Needle	1897	Trademark	Use of guarantee on label analogized to trademark
Russia Cement v LePage Co	1897	Trademark	Bond in TM injunction
H.A. Williams Mfg Co v Noera	1893	Trademark	Not generic term. Use of phrase public property
American Order of Scottish Clans v Merrill	1890	Trademark	Trade name and trademark

Name	Year	Subject matter	Description
Chadwick v Covell	1890	Trademark	Transfer of TM in inheritance as gift and assignment in gross
National Machine & Tool v Standard Shoe Machine	1902	Patent	Contract dispute arising from patent license

is no surprise that in writing his 50 majority opinions in the field of intellectual property while on the United States Supreme Court (see Table 10.2), Holmes developed a jurisprudence of intellectual property law that emphasized the treatment of patent, copyright, trademark, and trade secrets as commercial assets. Such a jurisprudence mirrors his modernist understanding of economic regulation, property as a construct of the state, and free speech as supporting the "marketplace of ideas." Intellectual property was not so much the hallmark of artistic creativity or technological invention but a legal construct operating within the world of commerce. Such a conception has implications, I argue in this chapter, not only for our understanding of Holmes but also of his influence on contemporary debates in intellectual property law and policy.

Before fleshing out my thesis, I should address the question of why Holmes. There are other prominent Supreme Court justices whose views on intellectual property resonate in modern debates over intellectual property. Justice Douglas, with his suspicions of patent law, comes to mind, as do the first Justice Harlan, who wrote a stirring and somewhat overlooked dissent to a famous Justice Holmes' copyright opinion,[5] and Justice Brandeis, who wrote an important dissent in the *INS v AP* case[6] extolling the importance of Congressional legislation creating intellectual property rights. Of course, articles or books could be written on any or all of these historically towering figures. But Holmes is an iconic figure, arising at a point in American history where the ascendancy of free markets was giving away to the cohesion of national governmental power. Perhaps more than any of the other judges mentioned, Justice Holmes' vision of the law framed the relationship between government and individual citizens, whether acting in the economic or in the political sphere, in a way that shaped doctrinal debates. Perhaps, Justice Holmes' iconic status was of his own making. But given the wide scholarly attention paid to Holmes, his less than shameless self-promotion has paid off.

At the very least, Justice Holmes' oft quoted aphorisms demonstrate his prominence, at least for the rhetoric of judging. Citations of Justice Holmes in recent intellectual property cases are one such indication. In a 1995 case involving patent claim construction, Judge Mayer of the United States Court

5 See *Bleistein*, infra note 41.
6 248 U.S. 215 (1918).

Table 10.2 Holmes' IP decisions at the United States Supreme Court

Name	Year	Subject Matter	Description
United States v Freights of the Mount Shasta	1927	Copyright	Copyright not *res* as analogy in admiralty case
Fox Film Corporation v Knowles	1923	Copyright	Renewal right and executor
Manners v Morosco	1920	Copyright	Right to make moving pictures from dramatic work not in grant
Herbert v Shanley Co	1916	Copyright	Performance right of music in restaurant. "If music did not pay" ASCAP
Louis Dejonge v Breuker & Kessler	1914	Copyright	Copyright-patent distinction with respect to design in a case about notice for copyright in panel drawing
Smith v Hitchcock	1912	Copyright	Mailing privileges for circulars. Books for copyright purposes but not for postal regs
Kalem v Harper Brothers	1911	Copyright	Movies as derivatives. Jobbers/distributors and inducement
United Dictionary v G&C Merriam Co	1908	Copyright	Notice requirement not applicable to sales overseas. Importation issue not addressed.
Bleistein v Donaldson Lithographic	1903	Copyright	Personality. Commercial ads and copyright
Lektaphone Corp v Rola Co	1930	Patent	Variation from claim means no infringement
Minerals Separation North American v Magma Copper	1930	Patent	Prior art anticipation
Becker v Contoure Labs	1929	Patent	Estoppel based on assignment
Milburn v Davis Bournoville Co	1926	Patent	Patent application as prior art
Electric Boat Co v United States	1924	Patent	Interpretation of assignment signed with US government
Hayer v Duplicator Mfg Co	1923	Patent	Repair
Adamson v Gilliland	1917	Patent	First to invent with cite to *Barbed Wire* case about oral testimony
American Well Works Co v Layne Bowler	1916	Patent	Jurisdiction case in a libel action involving patent infringement
Healy v Sea Gulf Specialty Co	1915	Patent	Jurisdiction in patent license dispute: patent or contract?
United States v Winslow	1913	Patent	Antitrust case. Patents and business success

Name	Year	Subject Matter	Description
Cook v Beecher	1910	Patent	Lack of diversity in suit against corporation for damages in patent infringement action
Brill v Washington Ry & Electric Co	1910	Patent	Doctrine of equivalents
Rumford Chemical Works v Hygienic Chemical Co	1910	Patent	Review of direct infringement judgment
Steward v American Lava Co	1909	Patent	Invalidity of a patent
Eclipse Bicycle Co v Farrow	1905	Patent	Contract for sale of invention
United States v Harvey Steel Co	1905	Patent	Contract for use of patented invention
Renziehausen v Lucas	1930	Trademark	Treatment of TM under IRC for depreciation of goodwill
US Printing &Litho v. Griggs, Cooper & Co.	1929	Trademark	No remedy under trademark act for use of mark wholly within a state or if mark has not been used in a state
Larson Co. v Wrigler Co	1928	Trademark	Taxes not included in determining infringer's profits
Beech-Nut Packing Co. v Lorillard Co.	1927	Trademark	Laches case. Language about goodwill, qualified property. Dilution issues. TM owner and female customers
Yu Cong Eng v Trinidad	1926	Trademark	TM case cited in opinion on commerce clause
Prestonettes v Coty	1924	Trademark	Repackaging of TM owner's products. Goodwill and consumer deception. Comparison with copyright
Bourjois v Katzel	1923	Trademark	Gray market goods infringing, analogy to patent and imports. Misleading use of TM
Stark Bros. Nurseries v Stark	1921	Trademark	TM damages available from date of notice of registered mark
Coca-Cola v Koke of America	1920	Trademark	Coca-Cola did not have unclean hands. No injunction against "dope"
Schlitz Brewing v Houston Ice & Brewing	1919	Trademark	Trade dress of bottle. Mistake not likely.
Strauss v Notaseme Hosiery Co	1916	Trademark	Mark not registered so no TM claim. Unfair competition based on deception. No taking of goodwill
Waterman v Modern Pen Co.	1914	Trademark	Limitations on use of surname
Ubeda v Zialcita	1913	Trademark	Analysis of treaty and Philippine law with respect to Spanish TM

Name	Year	Subject Matter	Description
Jacobs v Beecham	1911	Trademark	Formula uncovered for patent medicine. Not generic.
Saxlehmer v Wagne	1910	Trademark	"Artificial Hunyadi" natural water from region in Hungary. Only a geographic expression.
Herring-Hall-Marvin Safe Co. v Hall's Safe Co	1908	Trademark	Rights in surname
Burt v Smith	1906	Trademark	Malicious prosecution pursuant to TM infringement case
United States v JuToy	1905	Trademark	TM case cited as precedent in habeas corpus case
Chattanooga Foundry & Pipe Works v Atlanta	1906	Trademark	Antitrust case. Distinction between industry to property versus industry to business
FTC v American Tobacco	1924	Trade secret	FTC mandamus against company. Holmes points to protection of trade secrets
duPont v Masland	1917	Trade secret	Disclosure in litigation. Confidential relationship and property
Chicago Board v Christie Grain	1905	Trade secret	Price of grains analogized to trade secret
American Colortype v Continental Colortype	1903	Trade secret	Jurisdiction case does not get to revelation of TS issue
State of Missouri v State of Illinois	1906	Patent	Reference to patent in border dispute. Setting of time is matter for legislature
Ingenohl v Walter E. Olsen & Co.	1927	Trademark	Philippines case extraterritorial app of TM in Hong Kong
Donnell v Herring-Hall-Marvin Safe Co.	1908	Trademark	Companion to *Hall's Safe*. Discussion on corporation as fiction

of Appeals for the Federal Circuit cited Holmes for the proposition that "[a] word is not a crystal, transparent and unchanged: it is the skin of a living thought."[7] Not only does Holmes serve as handy reminder of the malleability of words, he also urges us to recognize the thin line between law and policy. For example, in 2009, Judge Newman, also sitting on the Federal Circuit, turned to *The Common Law* for a defense against a charge by a colleague that she was engaging in policy making:

> Every important principle which is developed by litigation is in fact and at bottom the result of more or less definitely understood views of public policy; most generally, to be sure, under our practice and traditions, the unconscious result of instinc-

[7] *Markman v Westview Instruments, Inc.*, 52 F.3d 967 (Fed. Cir. 1995).

> tive preferences and inarticulate convictions, but nonetheless traceable to views of public policy in the last analysis.[8]

Justice Stevens, in one of his final Supreme Court opinions, also saw fit to quote Holmes' aphorism: "A page of history is worth a volume of logic."[9] Appearing in Justice Stevens' concurrence in the patent case, *Bilski v Kappos*, it is yet another indication of Holmes' noted appearance in intellectual property cases. Perhaps such a reference reflects only his ability to turn a phrase. But behind these citations lies some intellectual influence, which I demonstrate and explore in this chapter.

Appeals to Justice Holmes are made in judicial opinions outside the United States. Indian courts have cited Holmes in their intellectual property opinions. The Madras High Court in an appeal by Yahoo!, Inc.[10] of a patent rejection punctuated its affirmance with Holmes' famed quote, "It is sometimes more important to emphasize the obvious than to elucidate the obscure."[11] While such language appears to be mainly rhetorical flourish, another court made more substantive reference to Justice Holmes and his assertions about copyright law:

> In copyright property has reached a more abstract expression. The right to exclude is not directed to an object in possession or owned, but is in vacuo, so to speak. It restrains the spontaneity of men where but for it there would be nothing of any kind to hinder their doing as they saw fit.[12]

Foreshadowing Justice Holmes' concerns in his free speech opinions, this quotation demonstrates how Holmes serves as a touchstone for courts to strengthen the logic of their opinions and provide a strong sense of legitimacy and gravitas.

The exploration of Holmes' intellectual property jurisprudence in this chapter proceeds as follows. Section 2, the following part, provides a discussion of the Justice's intellectual opinions written during his tenure on the

---

[8] *In re Ferguson*, 558 F.3d 1359 (Fed. Cir. 2009).

[9] *Bilski v Kappos*, 562 US 593 (2010).

[10] *Yahoo! Inc. v Intellectual Property Appellate Board*, in the High Court of Judicature at Madras (July 29, 2010).

[11] This quotation appears to be part of the Holmes folklore, perhaps something he actually spoke. For other references to this statement, see, e.g., Thomas L. Jefffers, *Norman Podhoretz: A Biography* 113 (2010). See also the discussion at Yatendra Singh, "Who was Justice Oliver Wendell Holmes, One of the Most Famous Judges of the Anglophone World?" The Leaflet (October 23, 2018), available at https://theleaflet.in/who-was-justice-oliver-wendell-holmes-one-of-the-most-famous-judges-of-the-anglophone-world/ (last viewed July 4, 2020).

[12] *White-Smith Music Co. v Apollo Co.*, 209 U.S. 1 (1908).

Table 10.3 *Universe of cases*

	Massachusetts Supreme Court (1882–1902)	U.S. Supreme Court (1903–1932)	Total
Trade Secret	0	4	4
Copyright	0	9	9
Trademark	9	21	30
Patent	13	17	30
Total	22	51	73

Massachusetts Supreme Court. Section 3 connects the ideas and themes from the Massachusetts Supreme Court cases to Justice Holmes' jurisprudence, both within and outside intellectual property, developed in the United States Supreme Court. Section 4 presents implications for contemporary intellectual property law and policy.

2. HOLMES AND IP AT THE MASSACHUSETTS SUPREME COURT

Judge Holmes interrupted a teaching career at Harvard Law School to accept a position on the Massachusetts Supreme Court in 1882. He served as a judge, and then chief judge, on the court until 1902, when he was appointed by President Theodore Roosevelt to the United States Supreme Court. While his tenure on the United States Supreme Court has been closely studied, less attention has been paid to his two decades on the highest court in Massachusetts. A review of his intellectual property decisions during his time as a state court judge reveals a burgeoning understanding of patents and trademarks, the relationship between commercial law and intellectual property, and issues of markets, regulation, and speech that take a more sophisticated and seasoned form in his United States Supreme Court jurisprudence.

To trace the origins of Holmes' intellectual property jurisprudence, I analyzed majority opinions he authored both as a state court judge and a Supreme Court Justice from 1882 to 1932. The intellectual property cases are divided into four categories: trade secret, copyright, trademarks, and patents. Counts of the respective opinions are summarized in Table 10.3.

The absence of copyright opinions authored by Holmes on the Massachusetts Supreme Court is not surprising given the exclusive federal jurisdiction over copyright law. A bit more surprising is the lack of opinions in the area of trade secret. In fact, only one trade secret case, *Peabody v Norfolk*, came before the

Massachusetts Supreme Court in 1868.[13] In *Peabody*, the court declined to enforce a trade secret under a contractual duty of confidentiality because it was found to be an unreasonable restraint of trade. The lack of cases after that date perhaps reflects a reluctance of Massachusetts courts to enforce trade secrets or of the parties to use the court system to enforce rights in secret or confidential information.

Since trademark law falls under both federal and state jurisdiction, it is not surprising to see a number of trademark opinions authored by Holmes during his time on the Massachusetts bench. In fact, prior to the enactment of the Lanham Act in 1947, federal jurisdiction over trademark claims was quite narrow, limited to marks actually used in interstate commerce. But the majority of Holmes' trademark opinions, combining his 50 years as a state and federal judge, were written while on the United States Supreme Court. This division contrasts with the split between state and federal court for Holmes' patent law opinions. During his 50 years as a judge, Justice Holmes authored as many patent opinions as trademark ones. But nearly half were authored while Holmes was on the Massachusetts Supreme Court. This division is truly surprising given the exclusive federal jurisdiction over patent law. The answer to this puzzling result is the central motivation for this chapter.

How did cases involving patents arise at the state court level? The answer is straightforward. The 13 patent opinions authored by Holmes during his 20 years as a state court judge addressed issues of commercial law. As discussed in more detail below, six of these 13 cases raised contract questions arising from disputes over patent licenses. One involved an inheritance issue over a patent. Others raised traditional state law questions of defamation, unfair competition, and fraud in the sale of a patent. In short, Justice Holmes' initial foray into federal intellectual property law was at the intersection of commercial law and patent. My contention is that these initial cases shaped Justice Holmes' intellectual property jurisprudence more broadly, especially provocative and influential questions of economic regulation and speech.

I develop this point by a close reading of Holmes' state law opinions in trademark and patent laws in the next two sections respectively. These cases illustrate themes, policies, and tropes that foreshadow many of the issues that permeate Justice Holmes' Supreme Court opinions. These latter issues are the subject of Section 3 of this chapter.

---

13 98 Mass. 452 (Mass. Sup. Ct. 1868).

2.a Trademarks, Holmes, and the Massachusetts Supreme Court

Contemporary trademark law illustrates the place of signs and symbols in a market economy. Judge Holmes' early trademark decisions are a harbinger, and perhaps even the source, of this modern understanding of names in a transaction-based economy. Brands, whether in the form of names, colors, logos, or other indicators of source, have no inherent meaning except as associated with particular products and services originating from certain sources, whether as manufacturer or distributor. Two implications derive from the convention of naming in markets. What matters for naming conventions is the identification of source, whether a natural person or a legal fiction, like a corporation, a partnership, or a union. The concept of source levels differences between natural and artificial persons. In market transactions, brands are what matter, whatever the reference. Related to this severance between naming and personhood is the arbitrariness of value. There is no inherent value that market transactions seek to realize. Instead, value arises from the transacting itself. Convention and artifice define market transactions, and fraud and deception serve to undermine these conventions by creating confusion in the act of naming.

Holmes' trademark decisions from his tenure on the Massachusetts Supreme Court demonstrate these changes in the market economy. There is no claim that Holmes introduced these changes. More likely, his decision making in trademark cases was symptomatic of broader shifts in commercial culture. Whether cause or effect, his opinions are signs of a reconfiguration of meaning and value in a transaction-driven society.

A well-known and oft-cited decision is Holmes' analysis of geographic place names in the Waltham Watch case.[14] In this 1899 decision, Holmes addressed the claim by a watchmaker that it had the right to use Waltham on its manufactured watches because they in fact were made in the town of Waltham, Massachusetts. This claim was made against a plaintiff watchmaker that it owned rights in the name "Waltham" as indicating the source of its own watches, whether made in Waltham or not. According to the plaintiff, the use of Waltham on competing watches, even if in fact made in the town, would create confusion among consumers and divert trade to the competitor. Judge Holmes affirmed a finding for the plaintiff, rejecting any specific geographic meaning in the name. Once the plaintiff had shown an association among consumers between the word Waltham and the plaintiff's watches, a concept referred to as secondary meaning, the word "Waltham" was not limited to its

---

[14] 53 N.E. 141 (Mass. Sup. Ct. 1899).

marker as a place name. Instead, the plaintiff had the right to prevent a competitor from diverting traffic by unauthorized use of the name.

Often taught and referenced, the Waltham decision came two years after another Holmes' decision in which he recognized the arbitrariness of names and the creation of meaning, and hence value, through commercial transactions. In his 1897 decision in *New England Awl*, Judge Holmes addressed trademark rights in colors.[15] Starting from the unquestionable premise that no company could have a monopoly in a color, Holmes affirmed rights that could attach to colors when used in conjunction with other aspects of packaging a product. The distributor of brown colored awls, the judge concluded, could enjoin a competitor that sold awls of a similar color whose "meaning" was "calculated to cause confusion." Colors, like place names, take on different meanings when used as a tool for merchandizing and promoting commercial transactions. This meaning was arbitrary, could not be the basis for a monopoly, and could serve to avoid confusion in the marketplace.

Words, colors, and other symbols were hollow vessels that are bestowed with meaning through interactions between buyers and sellers. This deracination of signs and symbols from any notion of inherent meaning or value echoes in a series of Judge Holmes' decisions about public property and abandoned marks. Discontinuing the use of a mark announces to the public that the mark is free for others to use and imbue with a new meaning. But such discontinued use, or abandonment, must be certain and the user can retain rights to resume use after a short period. The legal rights are attendant to the practice in the marketplace, as Judge Holmes found in his 1901 Burt decision.[16] There, the plaintiff sought to enjoin the use of the Knickerbocker mark by a shoe manufacturer that had ceased to use the mark for a few years. Judge Holmes affirmed the right of the first user of the Knickerbocker mark not only to resume use, but also to use the mark on a different type of shoe. Rebranding, or redefinition of the meaning associated with a mark, is permissible and understood as accepted practice, according to Holmes, as mark owners and brand creators seek to establish connections in the marketplace.

Implicit in the treatment of signs and symbols as hollow vessels is the possibility of their loss of association and meaning altogether. As Judge Holmes described, words can "become public property, and [acquire] a generic meaning, descriptive of a general kind, quality, and class of goods."[17] When this happens is a matter of social convention and understanding. Usage, as with geographic terms, trumps any notion of constant, unchanging meaning. As

---

15 46 N.E. 386 (Mass. Sup. Ct. 1897).
16 59 N.E. 1111 (Mass. Sup. Ct. 1901).
17 *H.A. Williams Mfg. Co. v Noera*, 32 N.E. 1037 (Mass. Sup. Ct. 1893).

public property, former marks lose any specialized meaning or association and become terms available to everyone for expression of meaning. Presumably, this generic use resides not only in the marketplace to refer to classes of goods, but also in other domains for the purposes of communication even when no commercial transaction is intended. There is no reason to think that the realm of public property is one that is unchanging. Meaning as convention would apply equally to the marketplace and to other domains. But once symbols are public property, trademark law has no force to limit or regulate their usage.

As the meaning of words becomes a matter of convention, so does the identity of their owner. A series of Holmes' state court opinions illustrate an expansive meaning of the word "person" as the party that can own a trademark. "If the words of the statute are to be taken with grammatical nicety upon a question evidently not before the minds of the legislature," wrote Judge Holmes in 1900, "we may say that the firm is a 'person,' within the meaning of that word, or we may extend the word 'association' to include associations without as well as with officers."[18] Several decades before the U.S. Supreme Court's pronouncement in *Santa Clara* that a corporation was a person for the purposes of the Fourteenth Amendment,[19] Holmes was broadening the usage of the word person to include business associations of all types, at least for the purposes of trademark registration. Such protection was also extended to entities like trade unions and fraternal organizations, such as the American Order of Scottish Clans.[20] While recognizing that ownership of names extended to business entities, Holmes admonished that businesses "choose the name at their peril, and that, if they take one so like that of an existing corporation as to be misleading, and thereby to injure its business, they may be enjoined."[21]

Names are choices that have consequences, whether attached to things, natural persons, or artificial ones. They lack intrinsic meaning or value. Legal rights are similarly constructing, a point made by Holmes in his 1890 opinion in *Chadwick v Covell*.[22] At issue were rights in a trademark devised by will from the widow of Dr. Spencer, whose name was associated with a brand of secret medicine used to treat pain. In determining whether trademark rights could be transferred by gift, Holmes pondered how rights in words arose through use by a particular manufacturer of the trademarked product. Rights in words did not attach independently of use to label and advertise the product to the consuming public. More to the point, the advertising value was not the source of the legal right. As Judge Holmes put it, "the fact that a right would

---

[18] *Commonwealth v Rozen*, 57 N.E. 223 (Mass. Sup. Ct. 1900).
[19] *Santa Clara County v Southern Pac. R. Co.*, 118 U.S. 394 (1886).
[20] *American Order of Sottish Clans v Merrill*, 24 N.E. 918 (Mass. Sup. Ct. 1890).
[21] Id.
[22] 23 N.E. 1068 (Mass. Sup. Ct. 1890).

have a money value, if it existed, is not a conclusive reason for recognizing the right."[23] Instead, rights reflect a purpose to enact certain policies and their desirable consequences. Holmes reinforces this point with reference to myth:

> When the common law developed the doctrine of trade-marks and trade-names, it was not creating a property in advertisements more absolute than it would have allowed the author of Paradise Lost, but the meaning was to prevent one man from palming off his goods as another's, from getting another's business or injuring his reputation by unfair means, and, perhaps, from defrauding the public.[24]

The invocation of the common law is mythic because it comes without a citation to some iconic, precedent-making decision. Instead, the policy, echoed through the ages, rationalizes the convention of legal rights in words as trademarks. Language, meaning, and law interact in a seemingly arbitrary manner but coalesce into a social understanding that makes sense. Judge Holmes concludes in the case that a gift of trademark does not transfer any rights unless the transfer also passes on the goodwill, such as the underlying secret process for making the medicine or some specially designed manufacture. The doctrine is recognized now as a rule against "naked licensing" or trademarks in gross.

It perhaps should not be surprising that imaginative, fanciful creatures like trademarks should be assessed in terms of convention and the arbitrariness of meaning. Such analysis is no mere post-modern dalliance, but a recognition by a hard-nosed modernist in the most rational and modern of times that creative works have their own points of reference. What should be surprising is if notions of conventions also were found to apply to the objective, scientifically dissectible notion of inventions, the subject matter of patent law. Judge Holmes authored a number of patent opinions while on the Massachusetts Supreme Court, and these opinions are the subject of the next subsection. What they show is that Judge Holmes' understanding of legal rights and property, even in the context of patents, represented the role of convention and arbitrariness of value as hallmarks of a market-based commercial culture.

2.b Patents, Holmes, and the Massachusetts Supreme Court

Over the past 30 years, patent law has grown in importance as a field of federal law jurisprudence. The establishment of the United States Court of Appeals for the Federal Circuit in 1980 as a specialized appellate court with expertise in patent law marked the emerging importance of patents as a means to identify intellectual property rights over new technologies and inventions. More

---

23 Id.
24 Id.

recently, the Federal Circuit has been a forum for legal debates over the scope and breadth of patent rights, the enforcement of these rights through litigation, and the mechanisms for monetizing and commercializing patents as a business asset. Each of these issues were foreshadowed in the over a dozen opinions authored by Judge Holmes for the Massachusetts Supreme Court.

From 1883 to 1902, Judge Holmes authored 13 state court opinions that engaged with a substantive issue related to patents. Seven of these opinions addressed an underlying contract dispute, raising questions such as payment of royalties, contractual restrictions on patent licenses through practices like minimum resale price maintenance, and transfers of patent interests. Under contemporary federal jurisdiction, most if not all of these cases would have been raised in a federal court that has exclusive jurisdiction even over mixed questions of patent and contract law. As a purely strategic matter, disputants would prefer a federal court as the venue for these mixed patent and contract disputes even if state court jurisdiction would be appropriate. However, the very different rules of federal jurisdiction in the late nineteenth century provide a window into how Holmes as a state court judge learned to adjudicate matters of federal intellectual property law.

In the mixed patent-contract disputes, Judge Holmes not surprisingly resolved the disputes as pure questions of contract law. Royalty disputes were addressed through the plain meaning of the contract.[25] Transfer of patent rights, which are of special importance for reasons discussed below, were settled according to the agreement of the parties as set forth in the contractual language. While the opinions do not raise particularly striking innovations in contract law, they do illustrate a range of commercial contexts in which patents played a part. Business entities purchased patents from the United States and from England, established practices for their dissemination through licensing, and set price and non-price terms for the transfer of inventions. Fields represented included mostly pharmaceutical or medical inventions, such as secret elixirs (referred to as patented medicines) and pain relievers, but also included inventions involving zithers, looming, manufacturing, switching mechanisms for railroads, and hydraulics.

One well known opinion from this time is Judge Holmes' decision on resale price maintenance in *Garst v Harris*,[26] in which Holmes ruled that minimum resale price maintenance was per se legal as a business practice contrary to claims of anti-competitive conduct under the common law. When the same issue came before the United States Supreme Court in *Dr. Miles* in 1911, the Court ruled the practice of setting the minimum price at which a product

---

25 *Prouty v Union Hardware Co.*, 57 N.E. 352 (Mass. Sup. Ct. 1900).

26 58 N.E. 174 (Mass. Sup. Ct. 1900).

could be sold per se illegal under the Sherman Antitrust Act.[27] Justice Holmes authored a vigorous dissent, citing his earlier Massachusetts opinion. But even when the Supreme Court addressed the issue again in 2008, in its *Leegin* decision, the Roberts Court overruled *Dr. Miles* only to the extent of making the practice subject to the rule of reason under federal antitrust laws.[28] Holmes' ruling of per se legality remains an elusive judgment for some contemporary commentators.

While more than half of his state court opinions dealt with the patent-contract intersection, the remainder touched on other matters of state and federal law in patent related disputes. One opinion, discussed in the previous subsection on trademark law, referred to the now-outdated rule that trademarks on products subject to expired patent are unenforceable.[29] Another case, *Lawrence v Hull*, considered in dicta the application of this old rule to the enforcement of rights in a trade name.[30] In his *Lawrence* opinion, Judge Holmes addressed, also in dicta, the question of whether profits earned by a patent infringer could be recovered by the patent owner, ruling that lost profits were not recoverable in the dispute over unauthorized use of a trade name. Foreshadowing an issue in the dispute between Lexmark and Static Controls over unfair competition and trade libel, Judge Holmes ruled that statements about ownership of an invention were libelous to the actual patent owner.[31] Finally, in a 1901 decision, Judge Holmes referred to patent infringement as a species of unfair competition, refusing to find a claim for unfair competition in the copying of a zither that was unpatented.[32] In 1964, the United States Supreme Court would rule that an unfair competition claim brought to prevent copying of an unpatented design was preempted by patent law.[33] Judge Holmes reached a similar result through judicious application of state law, rather than engaging with the complexities of federal jurisdiction and constitutional law.

What these varied opinions demonstrate is the role of patents in state law commercial disputes during the 20 years Holmes served as a state court judge. Two pairs of cases further exemplify the commercialization of patents and echo current debates over patent reform. At issue in the *Reeve*[34] and *Smith*[35] cases were claims of fraud over the transfer of patents in corporate acquisitions

---

[27] 220 U.S. 373 (1911).
[28] *Leegin Creative Leather Products, Inc. v PSKS, Inc.*, 551 U.S. 877 (2007).
[29] See *Burt*, supra note 16.
[30] 47 N.E. 1001 (Mass. Sup. Ct. 1897).
[31] *Lexmark Intern. Inc. v Static Control Components Inc.*, 572 U.S. 118 (2014).
[32] *Flagg Mfg. Co. v Holway*, 59 N.E. 667 (Mass. Sup. Ct. 1901).
[33] See *Sears, Roebuck & Co. v Stiffel Co.*, 376 U.S. 255 (1964).
[34] *Reeve v Dennett*, 11 N.E. 938 (Mass. Sup. Ct. 1887).
[35] *Smith v Moore*, 134 Mass. 405 (Mass. Sup. Ct. 1883).

and the establishment of business trusts (under Massachusetts law). In both instances, Judge Holmes looked to state law fraud principles to resolve the disputes. Holmes found for the complainant in *Reeve* because the underlying patent was "worthless," purporting to be a pain reliever that did not provide any benefit to patients. In the other case, *Smith v Moore*, he found for the defendant charged with fraud on the grounds that the patent owner had not transferred the patent to a trust as promised.

The second pair of cases, *Pratt v Tuttle*[36] and *Bi-Spool Sewing Machine Co. v Acme Mfg Co.*,[37] dealt with agreements to transfer rights in patents. Again, the two decisions differed as to liability. Holmes found for the patent owner in *Pratt*, but against the patent owner in *Bi-Spool*. In the latter case, the court found that the defendant had fulfilled obligations for purchase of the patent and therefore the patent owner had to transfer ownership. By contrast, in *Pratt*, the defendants had failed to meet the conditions for purchase and therefore had to compensate the patent owner. Under the terms of the agreement in *Pratt*, the purchaser of the patent was required to transfer proceeds from the sales of the patented item until the accumulated proceeds equaled the purchase price of the patents. In each case, Judge Holmes had to assess a commercial transaction for the dissemination and use of a patented invention.

Holmes' familiarity with the commercial side of patents parallels current debates over the role of non-practicing entities in the furtherance of patent policy. There are good reasons to be wary of non-practicing entities and their strategies to enforce rights through litigation, rather than practice in the marketplace. At the same time, non-practicing entities are touted as creating a market for patents which permits the monetization of patents by small inventors and businesses that lack the capital to manufacture and disseminate patented technology. Non-practicing entities allegedly serve an intermediary function as a conduit between those who invent and those who commercialize. Whether, and to what extent, this point is true for non-practicing entities is a debatable question. Holmes' state law opinions demonstrate that patents fuel commercial interests that implicate legal interventions.

While the trademark cases illustrate the role of naming and language in a market-driven culture, the patent cases show how federal intellectual property took seed in the same culture as commercial ventures fostered the dissemination of technology. As notions of fixed meaning and value were giving way to the utilitarian calculus of market transactions, so government grants of legal rights in the form of patents, dating back in the Anglo-American tradition to at least the sixteenth century, were transformed into private commodities.

---

36 136 Mass. 233 (Mass. Sup. Ct. 1884).
37 26 N.E. 991 (Mass. Sup. Ct. 1891).

The corporate and commercial arrangements involving patents evinced in the several disputes that came before Judge Holmes illustrate the monetization of federal grants of rights as parties sought to realize value. Notions of fraud, good faith, and fair dealing were brought to bear on these transactions as markets for inventions sprang from federal patent rights. Holmes witnessed and participated in these transformations as the judge resolving these commercial patent disputes. My contention, the subject of Section 3, is that this experience shaped his approach to intellectual property during his tenure as a Supreme Court justice.

3. HOLMES' JURISPRUDENCE

Over the combined 50 years that he served on the Massachusetts Supreme Court and then United States Supreme Court, Holmes developed a broad and distinct jurisprudence, marked by a mixture of bluster and insight. Scholars disagree as to the proportions in which these two elements exist in his voluminous opinions. Whatever the exact mix, there is no doubt that Holmes symbolizes a modern judicial temperament that brought to the surface legal debates that continue today. This section synthesizes three main themes in Holmes' jurisprudence and traces parallels in his intellectual property opinions from both the state and United States Supreme Courts.

There is a fractaline quality to my analysis, identifying patterns in the narrow range of intellectual property cases that appear in Holmes' broader jurisprudence. However, these patterns do not necessarily neatly repeat themselves through microscopic focus on specific areas of law. But the word fractaline is more appropriate than the word causal. I do not suggest that Holmes' experiences with patent and trademark in state cases influenced or shaped his later, more mature opinions. Such causal stories would be pure fantasy to say that least.

My point is that there are important themes in Holmes' intellectual property jurisprudence that are reflected in his state court experiences and in his broader juridical writings. These common themes resonate with current policy debates. The sole lesson may be that the more things change, the more they stay the same (translated from the French for the less cosmopolitan reader). Somewhat less mundane is a lesson about how policy battles in contemporary intellectual property fit into a more comprehensive skein of thought about the relationships among law, the marketplace, and commercial culture. Correspondingly, I focus on two principal themes in Holmes' jurisprudence: his approach to economic regulation and his metaphor of the marketplace of ideas in which speech functions, especially as it pertains to artistic expression. In this section, I look at each of these areas, first within the broader scholarly understanding and second within his state and federal intellectual property opinions.

3.a Economic Regulation

Professor G. Edward White reminds us that Holmes was not interested in the short run political consequences of an individual case. Instead, his interest was in "larger questions of economic policy, such as whether government regulation had any significant effect on the distribution of wealth or on the effectiveness of markets for goods and services."[38] "He did not believe it did," Professor White succinctly assesses Holmes' views on this question.

Professor Gordon captures Holmes' views on economics and law in light of Judge Richard Posner's own admiration of the Justice:

> What Posner overtly responds to in Holmes is primarily his utilitarian economism: the conception of law as a risk-allocation mechanism of incentives and disincentives rather than as a set of commands or moral precepts; the quasi behaviorism in Holmes's insistence that law is a set of "external" standards directed to outward behavior; and the programmatic ambition (which Holmes himself, in contrast to Posner, did nothing to fulfill) to reconstruct law on a foundation of welfare economics, a science of satisfying measurable desires.[39]

Holmes' approach to intellectual property contrasts with modern approaches to intellectual property law, grounded in various forms of utilitarian understanding. Intellectual property rights seek to facilitate economic views of the marketplace. Similarly, reforms of intellectual property rights seek to identify the correct levers through which to reach desirable ends, such as access or social justice, often framed counter to utilitarian goals, but often assuming consequentialist ends of their own. Intellectual property is a set of legal rules that govern conduct and regulate various activities. As regulation, intellectual property reform can improve distributive ends and the effectiveness of markets.

Holmes displays a different view towards intellectual property. Drawing on his experience with patents and trademarks in the Massachusetts Supreme Court, where intellectual property rights appear as objects of commerce, Justice Holmes emphasized the commercial ends of intellectual property. His copyright opinions reveal this attitude. For example, in Shanley, a case where Justice Holmes rules that a music copyright owner had a right to be compensated when the work was performed in a restaurant, the Justice reduces the musical work to an ordinary commodity.

> The defendants' performances are not eleemosynary. They are part of a total for which the public pays, and the fact that the price of the whole is attributed to a par-

---

38 G. Edward White, *Oliver Wendell Holmes, Jr.* 84 (2006).

39 Gordon, supra note 1 at 6.

> ticular item which those present are expected to order, is not important. It is true that music is not the sole object, but neither is the food, which probably could be got cheaper elsewhere. … If music did not pay, it would be given up. If it pays, it pays out of the public's pocket. Whether it pays or not the purpose of employing it is profit and that is enough.[40]

It is not too much of a leap from the commercial world of patents and trademarks that shaped Holmes' thinking on the Massachusetts court to the world of music copyright and entertainment that Holmes saw on the federal bench. It is not surprising that intellectual property would come entwined in commerce as it does today. But Justice Holmes moves beyond these factual surroundings to fashion a particular intellectual property jurisprudence, one grounded not in regulation but in business.

Holmes' first intellectual property opinion while on the United States Supreme Court heralded this commercial view of copyright. In *Bleistein*, Justice Holmes expanded the scope of copyright protection to include advertisements, expanding copyright's domain beyond the realm of artistic genius. Copyright should be expanded, he writes, and not be limited by the narrow acumen of a judge:

> At the other end, copyright would be denied to pictures which appealed to a public less educated than the judge. Yet if they command the interest of any public, they have a commercial value—it would be bold to say that they have not an aesthetic and educational value—and the taste of any public is not to be treated with contempt … That these pictures have their worth and success is sufficiently shown by the desire to reproduce them without regard to the plaintiffs' rights. We are of the opinion that there was evidence that the plaintiffs have rights entitled to the protection of the law.[41]

Justice Holmes makes a logical error here. He seems to conclude that the existence of economic value implies the need for legal protection. But arguably he eludes this general observation (about which more is said below). Instead, Holmes may be avoiding the converse proposition, that existence of commercial, as opposed to educational or aesthetic value, negates copyright. What speaks in Holmes is a pragmatic recognition of the marriage of intellectual property and commerce.[42]

---

40 *Herbert v Shanley Company*, 242 U.S. 591 (1917).

41 *Bleistein v Donaldson Lithographic Company*, 188 U.S. 239 (1903).

42 But see Barton Beebe, "Bleistein, the Problem of Aesthetic Progress, and the Making of American Copyright Law" 117 Columbia Law Review 319 (2017) (finding in the decision, germs of a theory of aesthetic progress as middle ground between judicial deference and market deference to identifying copyrightable subject matter).

Holmes' pragmatism combines a historicist evolutionary perspective on law with scientific naturalism.[43] What we see in decisions like *Shanley* and *Bleistein* are examples of Holmes' naturalistic jurisprudence. Building on his experience with patents and trademarks while on the Massachusetts Supreme Court, Holmes observes intellectual property in the environment of commerce and from there extrapolates the commercial nature of patents, trademarks, and by inference copyright. Strengthening this naturalist orientation is Holmes' own fascination with the business world. In a 1913 letter to Felix Frankfurter, offering advice on whether to join the ranks at Harvard Law School, Justice Holmes shared his views:

> Academia is but half a life—it is withdrawal from the fight in order to utter smart things that cost you nothing except the thinking them from the cloister. Business in the world is unhappy, often seems mean, and always challenges your power to idealize the brute fact—but it hardens the fibre and I think is more likely to make more of a man of one who turns it into success.[44]

Holmes' hardheadedness shines through even in a somewhat romanticized view of the business world. But the hallowed world of commerce informed his vision of intellectual property, much as it shaped his understanding of speech, as we shall see in the next section.

There is a naiveté to Holmes' naturalism. The danger is in confusing the is with the ought. To defend Holmes, he perhaps does not think in terms of ought and all that matters is a cold realism of what legal categories, like intellectual property, actually map onto. However, once this realism is embedded in judicial opinions, it takes on a normativity which affects future generations. As those living in the shadow of Holmes' jurisprudence, we cannot be sanguine about the commercial veil shrouding intellectual property. Instead, the ought requires a rethinking of the reality Holmes presents. If intellectual property is regulation, however, we cannot escape the realities either and must be wary of elusive generalities.

3.b Speech and Exchange

Given how Holmes imagines the business world, it should not be surprising that we inherit the conception of the marketplace of ideas as the mental map for understanding free speech. Holmes' advice to Frankfurter about academia also reveals a seemingly prophetic view of speech within universities. For

---

[43] See Gordon, supra note 1 at 7, discussing Thomas Grey, "Holmes and Legal Pragmatism" 41 Stanford Law Review 787 (1989).

[44] White, supra note 38 at 45.

Holmes, speech in the ivory tower is cloistered, not subject to the challenges of the marketplace, and therefore lacks the imprimatur of commercial competition. Perhaps current debates on various media outlets are taking a leaf out of Holmes' book. Like his modern avatars, Holmes ignores the forces of competition and market pressures within even academic walls.

Nonetheless, the marketplace of ideas has been a robust foundation for protecting the right to speak. Faith in the ability of market success to validate truth and the robustness of viewpoints pervades discussions of the First Amendment and intellectual property. Some point to how intellectual property supports the marketplace of ideas by creating property rights in expression. Others point to how these same property rights can limit the marketplace of ideas through suppressing certain forms of creative inquiry. For the narrow purposes of this chapter, the focus is on how Holmes' metaphor equates speech with exchange and results in a pursuit of certainty that reinforces a rigid marketplace.

Professor Peter Gibian enhances our understanding of the marketplace of ideas by situating that metaphor in an implicit conversation that Justice Holmes was having with his father, a renowned doctor and poet. As Professor Gordon aptly summarizes:

> The younger Holmes, Gibian says, rebelled strenuously against his father's questioning of everything and lightness of being. For the young Civil War veteran, the model of social life was the battlefield rather than dinner-table conversation. The Justice found his style in "blunt declarative sentences," terse conversation stoppers that put an authoritative end to discussion. Although a skeptic, he believed the end of law was certainty, even if final certainty was impossible. To his father's belief in the "free play" of ideas he opposed the free trade in ideas, a Darwinian marketplace in which only the strongest survived. Even Holmes' model of civil law, Gibian points out, is martial law; he recognizes as "rights" only what people have been willing to die for.[45]

As we discuss in more detail below, Gibian uncovers in Justice Holmes' search for certainty a paradoxical disdain for facts over "general observations," combined with a skepticism that general observations are ever possible.[46] By contrast, Doctor Holmes exhibited his own form of skepticism in the careful prescription of medicines to address a patient's symptoms. His demeanor eschewed autocracy as he favored the free play of ideas, especially among his children. But such free play led one of his children to seek in law certainty grounded in the shifting battles of the marketplace. For Dr. Holmes, free

---

[45] Gordon, supra note 1 at 14.

[46] See Peter Gibian, "Opening and Closing the Conversation" in Gordon, ed., supra note 1.

speech was about conversation; for Justice Holmes, free speech was about battle.

These two visions perhaps inform contemporary debates over free speech. Those who seek to regulate speech by tempering it envision free speech as a civil, courteous exchange, suitable for the parlor or public venues. Those who seek unregulated speech prefer the battle and the validity secured for the victor. One can contrast the two views in terms of a preference for a healthy, ruled-guided competition over a free for all. Other metaphors follow: soccer versus rugby, bridge versus poker, Greco-Roman wrestling versus the WWF.

What does this mean for intellectual property? Those who strictly follow Holmes' metaphor of the marketplace of ideas should recognize the dark side of that vision. Put another way, in adopting the marketplace of ideas as the mental rubric for free speech, one needs to think about threshold choices about what that marketplace would look like. Justice Holmes ignored those choices. Perhaps his father did as well in presuming that calm deliberation and exchange best yields proper conversation; perhaps, such conversation is composed of mere banal niceties masking conformity. Holmes the lawgiver, however, offers no guidance on these foundational questions about the marketplace. Instead, he succumbs to a naturalistic vision that leads an allegedly anti-authoritarian figure to yield to the authority of the market. Perhaps, he would argue, there is no real alternative. But perhaps skepticism itself should be brought into the marketplace.

Justice Holmes' experience on the state Supreme Court can teach us about how to approach the marketplace for ideas. First, that metaphor stems from a particular set of experiences, as Gibian suggests, experiences honed on the battlefield. By the time Holmes the soldier becomes a judge for the first time, his range of experience shifts to resolving disputes in the courtroom, among them commercial disputes over patents and trademarks. These experiences as a disinterested arbiter, rather than active paladin, shaped Holmes' thinking not only about judging but also about certain realities of the marketplace. The second lesson is how Holmes' perception of commercial reality in turn shaped his understanding of intellectual property. This understanding is one we still debate today. But our engagement in that debate cannot be overshadowed by the contingent experiences of the judge. The past cannot be allowed to cast too long a shadow on the present.

4. LAW, HISTORY, AND FAITH

Holmes is admired and condemned for his tough mindedness. Critics view his distance and objectivism as deferential to the power of the majority; admirers find in his tough mindedness a commitment to the progress of law and society. Arguably we are living in times that favor the tough minded both as necessary to check political power of an executive, elected by a minority, and to aid in the search for clear answers to complex policy questions. Holmes' tough mindedness is rooted in secularism and is echoed in some (admittedly shallow) blows at faith-based law making. Facts, grounded in big data, are the preferred guide. But, surprisingly, the tough-minded secularist was skeptical of facts. In a 1919 letter to Sir Frederick Pollock, Holmes brashly wrote:

> I hate facts. I always say the chief end of man is to form general propositions—adding that no general proposition is worth a damn. Of course, a general proposition is just a string of facts and I have little doubt that it would be good for my immortal soul to plunge into them.[47]

As with many passages authored by Holmes, one could go dizzy trying to separate irony from sincerity in distilling a guiding message. But there is almost a trivial meta-narrative here: general propositions are the goal but fuel a futile search. One may be left with facts to ponder, but facts, like general propositions, are elusive and not "worth a damn." Is there just a sullen resignation to Holmes' ruminations?

Holmes' tough mindedness leads us to a brutal confrontation with reality. Professor Kellogg teaches in his book on Holmes and judicial restraint:

> As a Massachusetts judge, Holmes routinely conceptualized close cases as invoking competing lines of precedent, involving conflicts that must be resolved through line drawing, thus applying his model of common law rulemaking as it emerged in the early 1870's.[48]

In drawing these lines, Holmes, like any judge, had to rely on "the materials of each case—claims, facts, defenses—...already packaged by counsel to suit the interests of opposing parties."[49] The requisite skepticism towards facts led to Holmes removing "arguments from case law into a wider perspective, disrobing principles and maxims, translating conflicting precedents into the continuum of conflicting activities."[50] Experience is what guides but also calls into question logic. And individual experiences, that of parties, their attorneys, and judges, translate into the experience of the legal system, society, and history.

One might be tempted to reduce the interplay of facts, judicial opinions, and law into what Professor Gibian calls a conversation. Gibian frames this conversation, as one between Holmes and his father. Framed more broadly, the

---

[47] Id. at 213 (quoting from letter to Pollock, May 26, 1919).

[48] Frederic R. Kellogg, *Oliver Wendell Holmes, Jr., Legal Theory, and Judicial Restraint* 161 (2007).

[49] Id. at 162.

[50] Id.

conversation is within the oft-heralded marketplace of ideas, a brutal exchange without any overarching direction. If there is a teleology to the market, in Holmes' mind, it would not be worth a damn. The tough-minded judge, however, might say that all we have are words, whether in the pages of judicial opinions or in ephemeral conversations.

However, we can seek to reconstruct the past and make observations, elusively general but more than specific. Experience shapes logic, as Holmes' state court experience with intellectual property shows. And the logic in turn shapes our own experience in how we engage with and reform intellectual property. Tough mindedness has its virtues, but its principal vice is in dismissing the experiences of the future in the ongoing conversation with the past.

11. In the shadow of the *Trade-Mark Cases*: the 1881 Trademark Act and the Supreme Court

Zvi S. Rosen[1]

In 1879, the US Supreme Court famously struck down the entirety of federal trademark law in the *Trade-Mark Cases*, leading Congress to leap into action and pass a new trademark statute within two years. Much less famously, though, the same thing, at least in substance, happened again 24 years later in a largely forgotten 1903 case, *Warner v. Searle & Hereth.* Instead of holding the entire law unconstitutional, though, the Supreme Court narrowly construed the 1881 Trademark Act's restriction to foreign commerce to hold that it would only allow federal courts to hear cases under the Act in a tiny sliver of trademark infringement cases—cases where the suit was actually about foreign commerce. This was unacceptable to American businesses, and Congress passed the 1905 trademark law less than two years later. This is the story of how a commercial dispute between two early pharmaceutical companies led to the first American trademark law of the twentieth century.

These cases were especially important because the challenges of interstate enforcement of trademarks were significant. To this day every state has a provision for trademark registration,[2] but they are currently subsidiary to the modern trademark law of the Lanham Act.[3] However, at the time the concern was much greater—if federal trademark registration was not effective for

[1] The author would like to thank those who provided comments and other feedback on this piece, including the participants of the fall 2019 Trademark Works in Progress Conference at the American University Washington College of Law.

[2] Summary of State Trademark Registration Provisions, available at https://www.uspto.gov/trademarks-getting-started/process-overview/state-trademark-information-links.

[3] Lee Ann Lockridge has studied these provisions and argued that they serve no real purpose in this era and should be abolished. *Abolishing State Trademark Registrations*, 29 Cardozo Arts & Ent. L.J. 597 (2011). Every state except South Carolina has had a law providing for trademark registration as of 1904 as well. Titian W. Johnson, *Trade-Mark Law: Present Statute Declared Inadequate and New One Needed*, Wash. Post, January 11, 1904 at 9.

domestic protection, you would potentially need to register in every single state separately to ensure that you could litigate to protect your mark, and the injunctive remedies available would likewise be limited.[4]

In telling the story of *Warner v. Searle*, it became apparent that I should also explore other Supreme Court cases—*Ryder v. Holt, Elgin National Watch v. Illinois Watch Case*, and *Gaines v. Knecht*. *Ryder v. Holt* was actually a direct predecessor to *Warner v. Searle* regarding construction of the 1881 Act, decided in 1888, but it did not have much impact, perhaps because it is so terse at 118 words. If *Warner v. Searle* is a footnote in the history of trademark law, *Ryder v. Holt* is a footnote to a footnote, and a full accounting of this period requires that it be brought out of the shadows. In the *Elgin National* case, on the other hand, the Supreme Court avoided deciding the question of jurisdiction under the statute but the issue was argued heavily, setting the stage for *Warner v. Searle* two years later. Finally, in *Gaines v. Knecht* the Supreme Court was faced with a direct Constitutional assault on the new 1905 Trademark Act which replaced the 1881 Act at issue in the other cases, but chose to avoid the issue.

This entire chapter is, in many ways, a history of the 1905 Trademark Act, and the legislative history of the Act is explored in detail, showing the origins and purpose of many of its sections. One benefit of this approach is that it allows us to understand provisions that have endured in the law ever since, and as a case study I have explored the origins of a rule which has been before the Supreme Court in recent years—that a trademark must be rejected if it is "immoral or scandalous." Understanding the path the law took to enactment shows a number of sources explaining why that language was used, and its purpose in the Act. In particular, this history shows that propriety and non-disparagement was always the rationale for that aspect of trademark law.

This chapter is in some ways a sequel to my article *In Search of the Trade-Mark Cases*, which explores the period from 1860 through 1882 in terms of federal legislation and litigation and extends the narrative of that paper to after 1905.[5] As with that piece, in exploring the forgotten history of

---

4 *Current Topics*, 66 ALBANY L.J. 237 (1904).

5 Zvi S. Rosen, *In Search of the Trade-Mark Cases: The Nascent Treaty Power and the Turbulent Origins of Federal Trademark Law*, 83 ST. JOHN'S L. REV. 827 (2009). This chapter also allows me a chance to remedy an oversight in that piece—I failed to address the debates on the trademark bills under consideration on April 27, 1880; 10 Cong. Rec. 2795–2808 (46th Cong., 2nd Sess., 1880). The debates there don't change any of my conclusions but do offer additional color on the various considerations regarding whether to amend the constitution to include trademarks used in interstate commerce, and the decision not to include criminal penalties in the 1881 Act that resulted. *Id.* A reader interested in going deeper on the subject should consider reading these debates—they are surprisingly jocular at times.

the jurisdictional limits of federal trademark law, we can understand current trademark law—both its cases and laws—with a context not otherwise possible.[6] What is past is not just prologue, it is law.

1. PROLOGUE: THE CHALLENGE OF THE *TRADE-MARK CASES*

Although trademarks had long existed at common law, and the first state trademark law was passed in 1845 in New York, the first federal trademark law was not passed until 1870, following a flurry of trademark treaties with other nations.[7] The law had no limitation to use in commerce with any particular place, and according to one of the main framers of the law, when interviewed a decade later, the constitutional basis of the 1870 Trademark Act never even came up in Congress.[8] However, storm clouds over the new trademark law (and its criminal provisions, added in 1876) came when a number of defendants in criminal trademark cases asserted that the law lacked a constitutional basis. A trial court in Wisconsin agreed in a published opinion in 1878,[9] and by the time the Supreme Court was hearing a number of consolidated cases on the same issue early in the following year, the constitutional point was already essentially conceded, with the government hoping to save the law on a narrow construction of the statute. That didn't work, and in the fall of 1879 the Supreme Court issued its decision, written by Justice Samuel Miller, holding in unambiguous terms that a trademark was not a "writing" or "discovery" within

---

[6] I'm of course not the only person to write on trademark law in this period—for instance John Cross has also written an account of the period surrounding the *Trade-Mark Cases* and 1881 Trademark Act. John T. Cross, *The Lingering Legacy of Trade-Mark Cases*, 2008 MICH. ST. L. REV. 367 (2008). Paul DuGuid has also written extensively on trademark law in this period, focusing on the development of branding: *French Connections: The International Propagation of Trademarks in the Nineteenth Century*, 10 ENTERPRISE & SOC'Y 1 (2009); *A Case of Prejudice? The Uncertain Development of Collective and Certification Marks*, 86 BUS. HIST. REV. 311 (2012); *Early Marks: American Trademarks before US Trademark Law*, 60 BUS. HIST. 1147 (2018). Ross D. Petty has also written extensively on the period, also focusing on the development of brand identity and its legal context: *From Label to Trademark*, 4 J. HIST. RESEARCH IN MARKETING 129 (2012).

[7] *Id.* at 834.

[8] There are at least two possible reasons for this. Firstly, the bill was the (thus far only) true omnibus revision of federal copyright law, and most of its provisions dealt with patent and copyright law, which have their own constitutional basis. Also, the provisions for federal trademark law were included mainly to execute obligations under treaties the U.S. had signed in the past two years, so they may have thought of the provisions as being based on powers on those areas.

[9] *Leidersdorf v. Flint*, 15 F.Cas. 260 (C.C.E.D.WI. 1878).

the meaning of the Constitution, and that if the law was limited to trademarks used in interstate or foreign commerce, such limitation needed to be explicit in the law.[10] With that, the only trademark law in the United States was that provided by state common law and statutes, and the nation was likely in default of its treaty obligations to what were by now many European nations.

The initial reaction was one of serious concern—a proposed amendment to the Constitution was considered and new legislation was immediately introduced, but after the initial shock wore off stakeholders and lawmakers agreed that state law was more or less adequate for domestic trademarks, and a new federal law was enacted in 1881 which limited its protection to marks used in foreign commerce.[11] To enforce this, applicants were required to file a declaration with their trademark application asserting "that such trademark is used in commerce with foreign nations or Indian tribes."[12] The damages provision of the 1881 Act also provided a sort of bifurcated system of remedies, wherein

> [a]ny person who shall reproduce, counterfeit, copy or colorably imitate any trade-mark registered under this act and affix the same to merchandise of substantially the same descriptive properties as those described in the registration, shall be liable to an action on the case for damages for the wrongful use of said trade-mark, at the suit of the owner thereof; and the party aggrieved shall also have his remedy according to the course of equity to enjoin the wrongful use of such trade-mark used in foreign commerce or commerce with Indian tribes.[13]

In other words, injunctive relief was only available against infringing use of the trademark in foreign commerce. This language was a repeat of the language of the 1870 statute, but with the limitation at the end on the remedies available it substantially narrowed the relief available in practice in cases where the mark was used internationally, but the alleged infringement was not.[14] Section 11 of the 1881 Act included an additional limitation to the jurisdiction of the federal courts further limiting the scope of trademark protection under the new law:

> [N]oting in this act shall be construed ... to give cognizance to any court of the United States in an action or suit between citizens of the same State, unless the trade-mark in controversy is used on goods intended to be transported to a foreign country, or in lawful commercial intercourse with an Indian tribe.

---

10 *Trade-Mark Cases (in re Steffens et al)*, 100 U.S. 82 (1879). The Court also provided lengthy dicta speculating that a trademark was not used in commerce because it was not the article being sold, per se.

11 1881 Act. When I refer to foreign commerce, I also include commerce with the Indian tribes.

12 1881 Act at §2.

13 *Id.* at §7.

14 The original language is the first half of §79 of the 1870 omnibus IP revision.

In other words, this statute did not give jurisdiction to the federal courts unless the trademark at issue was being used in foreign commerce. The statute also specifically stated that "nothing in this act shall prevent … any remedy … which any party … might have had if the provisions of this act had not been passed."[15]

These provisions were all presumably motivated because, in the report accompanying the bill, the House Judiciary Committee made clear that they did not think the Congressional power to regulate trademarks extended to commerce, and instead justified the new trademark law under the power to make treaties.[16] Implicit here (and indeed to the whole Act) is whether or not a sort of *de minimis* international use is sufficient, or whether the mark needed to be in regular use in foreign commerce—or indeed if the dispute itself needed to involve foreign commerce.

2. TESTING THE 1881 ACT: *RYDER V. HOLT*

The issue first reached the Supreme Court fairly quickly, in an 1888 decision that is equal parts forgotten, cryptic, and terse. The entirety of the Court's decision in *Ryder v. Holt* is as follows:

> It was stipulated in the Circuit Court that this cause should abide the event of *Holt v. Menendez*, ante, 514, just decided, and the same decree in favor of complainants was, therefore, rendered in this as in that case. But it is now assigned for error that, as defendant and complainants below were citizens of the same State, and the bill did not allege that the trade-mark in controversy was "used on goods intended to be transported to a foreign country," Act of March 3, 1881, c. 138, § 11, 21 Stat. 502, the Circuit Court had no jurisdiction, and the decree must be reversed for that reason. The objection is well taken, and the decree is accordingly.[17]

This decision tells us nothing about the case really, and is a puzzling curio when read in the modern context online. But looking at the printed reporter the connection to *Holt v. Menendez* becomes much clearer—the *Ryder* decision is appended to the *Menendez* decision, which tells the story of the case, and *Ryder*'s relation to it.[18]

---

[15] 1881 Trademark Act, §10.

[16] Registration of Trade-Marks, H.Rep. 561, 46th Cong. (1880); Zvi S. Rosen, *Treaty Power Justifications for Early Federal Trademark Laws*, 16 U. PA. J. CONST. L. HEIGHT. SCRUTINY 1 (2013).

[17] *Ryder v. Holt*, 128 U.S. 525 (1888).

[18] *Menendez v. Holt*, 128 U.S. 514 (1888). Even so, it is perhaps a bit overly terse. Another reason is that Chief Justice Waite had died earlier that year, due in part to the rigors of a docket with 500 or so cases a year, and riding circuit on top of that. When the case was docketed with the Supreme Court years earlier Waite was still Chief Justice,

The case began as an 1882 lawsuit by Holt & Co. against Jose and Joaquin Menendez, and also a separate suit against Alfred Ryder, brother of a former partner of Holt & Co., for infringing use of their trademark "La Favorita" to denote a specific brand of flour (Figure 11.1). The printed record from the case clarifies the background—Holt & Co. was based in New York, with members residing in New Jersey as well.[19] Alfred Ryder was also a resident of New York, while the Menendez brothers were citizens of Spain doing business in New York. However, in the printed depositions from the case the brother/former partner not named in the suit, Stephen O. Ryder, makes clear that he was running the business, and his brother was the owner because Stephen had lost his money in "stock operations" and it would be untenable to have the business in his own name.[20]

The evidence brought is unclear as to the origin of the term "La Favorita" used by Holt for flour,[21] but defendants especially were adamant that "La Favorita" and another term both sides used, "La Selecta," were terms of grading quality, not trademarks. Ryder had joined Holt & Co. in a junior role around 1855 and became a partner in 1861. Holt & Co. had been using "La Favorita" as of at least 1861, and such use had initially been exclusive, although as time went on others began using the mark as well in competition, which led to the suit. When Ryder left as a partner in 1869 things had originally been cordial, but the two parties were divided as to whether complaints over his use of "La Favorita" had been lodged or not—a Mr. Busby who was a partner at Holt & Co. indicated that he had made a direct complaint as of 1871, while Stephen Ryder did not recall such conversations. Clearly some conversations had been had about trademarks—Ryder desisted from using "Potomac," which was Holt & Co.'s biggest seller, while Ryder took with him

---

and the new Chief Justice Fuller likely felt a need to plow through the backlog by whatever means worked.

[19] Holt & Co. had been founded early in the nineteenth century, and despite numerous changes in its ownership structure, as of this time the main partner in the firm was a descendant of the founder. *Evolution of the New York Flour Trade*, 9 American Hay, Flour and Feed Journal 14 (May 1907). The firm folded around 1910. *R.S. Holt is Dead*, N.Y. Times, March 26, 1933 at 31.

[20] Transcript of Record, *Menendez v. Holt*, at 73. Implicitly this was to keep the business out of reach of his creditors, but a colloquy among counsel is recorded objecting to the question, and Stephen Ryder's answer to why the business was in his brother's name was never provided.

[21] One of the witnesses for the defendants, Eldridge Goddard of St. Louis, testified that they developed the term "La Favorita" for flour in 1857 or 1858, but had stopped using it by 1861. Menendez Tr. of Record at 114. Appellant's Brief at 11–12 excerpts a letter from Holt suggesting that evidence of disuse would not be unfavorable, indicating perhaps coaching on this point.

at least "Aurora," which he had originated. But with no agreement over "La Favorita," litigation commenced. In 1882 Alfred Ryder agreed to a stipulation that the Menendez case and the case against him could be argued jointly and agreed to be bound by the results.

In all of this, the Menendez brothers do not appear. They were not deposed, and indeed are barely mentioned in the depositions transcribed in the record. Holt & Co. was entirely an export business by this time,[22] and naming them may have been an attempt to sue their domestic competitors while being less likely to fall afoul of the limitations of the new federal trademark act. In their Supplemental Brief to the Supreme Court, Holt & Co. admitted that "[o]bviously the real defendant here is Ryder."[23]

Figure 11.1 *Facsimile of trademark registration by Holt & Co., from the U.S. Supreme Court Case File for Holt v. Menendez, held at the National Archives*

Source: Photographed at the U.S. National Archives by the author.

---

22 *Evolution of the New York Flour Trade*, *supra* note 19.
23 Appellee's Supplemental Brief at 11.

In 1885, the trial court rendered a verdict.[24] The Court found that Holt & Co. had a valid trademark in "La Favorita," and the fact that they did not produce the flour itself was irrelevant. However, although the Court enjoined the defendants from use of the mark, the Court found that damages were inappropriate since Ryder had been using "La Favorita" for over a decade, in a manner known to plaintiffs, and that "[i]t would be inequitable to compel him to pay for its use during the long years that the complainants slept upon their rights."[25]

The Appellant's Brief to the Supreme Court (from Ryder et al.) seems to be the first place that Alfred Ryder's citizenship, and the court's lack of jurisdiction, might be an issue.[26] It is not mentioned in the Petition for Appeal filed April 11, 1885, to commence the appeal, or seemingly anywhere else in the record. The appellant noted the 1882 stipulation that Alfred Ryder would abide by the result in the Menendez case, but argued it did not grant the trial court jurisdiction.[27] Later in their brief, appellant's counsel expanded on this point, noting that the limitation on the jurisdiction of the federal courts in the trademark statute was constitutional, and thus no stipulation could nonetheless grant the federal courts jurisdiction in this matter.[28]

Holt & Co. did not address the question of jurisdiction until the final page of their brief, of which the entirety follows:

> The agreement upon which the decree was entered in No. 76 is valid. The presumptions are that the Court below had jurisdiction. It is shown that the mark is used in foreign commerce (fol. 167). The facts bring the case distinctly within the rule laid down in Glen Cove Mfg.. Co. vs. Ludeling, 22 Fed. Rep., 823.[29]

The *Glen Cove* case about similar marks for corn-flour did not quite hold that—it held that "[u]nless the complainant's trade-mark is used on goods intended to be transported to a foreign country, by the terms of the act of congress the court can take no cognizance of the wrong in a suit between citizens of the same state."[30] These scant pleadings placed the issue squarely before the Court—is it enough for the mark to have been used in foreign commerce by the plaintiff at some point, or did the actual infringing use at issue need to be in foreign commerce?

---

24 *Holt v. Menendez*, 23 F. 869 (C.C.S.D.N.Y. 1885).
25 *Id.* at 871.
26 Appellant's Brief at 18.
27 Appellant's Brief at 19.
28 Appellant's Brief at 41.
29 Appellee's Supplemental Brief at 13.
30 22 Fed. Rep at 825. Note that if the citizens were from different states the Act would still apply.

Referring back to the decision quoted above, the Court's position is thus clear—because it was not specifically alleged that Ryder's flour was "used on goods intended to be transported to a foreign country," the federal courts were without jurisdiction. Diversity jurisdiction did not exist regarding Alfred Ryder and thus was not addressed, and the case was dismissed. Accordingly, even though Holt won the case against the Menendez brothers, in a decision still cited today,[31] the Ryder brothers were the real target of the suit, and the case against them was dismissed.[32]

The *Ryder* decision was not treated as major news later in 1888 when it was decided, but it was important for two reasons.[33] Firstly, the Court made clear that the Act only provided federal remedies for use actually in foreign commerce—it wouldn't be enough for the trademark to generally be used in foreign commerce. However, Rowland Cox (the lawyer for Holt & Co. in these lawsuits) noted in print that the case also served as a practical vindication of the constitutionality of the 1881 Act.[34] The *Trade-Mark Cases* had only been nine years prior to *Ryder*, and the Supreme Court had not yet taken a stand on the constitutionality of the 1881 Act. In adjudicating the jurisdictional limits of the trademark statute, though, "there is a recognition of the power of Congress to legislate concerning trade-marks," at least in foreign commerce.[35] Thus the *Ryder* decision was a mixed bag for proponents of federal trademark law, making clear that the jurisdictional provisions would be strictly construed,

---

[31] The *Menendez* decision is still cited a fair bit in reference to laches and trademark law. See Brad Powers, *Note, A Crisis in Equity: Laches Doctrine and the Lanham Act*, 57 Drake L. Rev 547, 555 (2009).

[32] This news came too late for Stephen, who died the day after the case was argued before the Supreme Court, and thus the month prior to the decision (Obituary in Brooklyn Eagle, November 16, 1888). In 2015 New York Magazine ran a photo of Ryder, commenting that he "led the kind of life we don't see much anymore: that of a successful businessman who was also in the military for most of his adulthood." Christopher Bonanos and Matt Giles, *See Portraits of New Yorkers Who Served in the Civil War*, New York, June 5, 2015, available at http://nymag.com/intelligencer/2015/06/meet-your-old-civil-war-neighbors.html. Afterwards Alfred Ryder ran the business that was already in his name, but he sold it before long, and the purchaser was saddled with additional trademark claims from other parties. *Brower v. Boulton*, 58 F. 888 (2d Cir. 1893) (reversing dismissal of a trademark suit against the purchaser of the business).

[33] Indeed, there were only four case citations to the decision prior to the *Warner* case 15 years later.

[34] Rowland Cox, *The Constitution of the United States and its Relation to the Subject of Trade-Marks*, 51 Albany L. J. 118 (1895).

[35] *Id.* at 121. There had been a fair bit of turnover between the *Trade-Mark Cases* in 1879 and *Ryder* in 1888, but a majority of the Justices were still there, including Samuel Freeman Miller (who had written the opinion in the *Trade-Mark Cases*), as well as Justices Swayne, Bradley, Field, and Harlan.

but also intimating that the current law was constitutional.[36] However, the limitations of the 1881 Act were quickly becoming apparent in an era of rapid growth and national proliferation of brands.

3. REMEDYING THE 1881 ACT

The reaction to the *Ryder* decision was fairly muted—it doesn't seem to have gotten much attention at all. Perhaps the sheer brevity of the decision allowed it to be essentially forgotten, and over the next two decades businesses continued to use a token amount of international trade to register their trademarks, and then consider themselves protected against domestic infringers.[37] The "pious fraud" of engaging in *de minimis* trade with Canada or another foreign country was sufficient to allow for a registration to be filed and approved.[38] However, enforcing the trademark in federal court was another question entirely—as the Supreme Court held in *Ryder* and would confirm 18 years later.

The problem was obvious, and bills to allow for federal protection for trademarks used in interstate commerce were being proposed almost as soon as the ink was dry on the 1881 Act.[39] A bill was proposed in early 1884 to do just that,[40] and it was reported favorably the following year by the House Committee on Patents,[41] but no further action was taken. In 1888 a bill re-adding criminal remedies to federal trademark law was repeatedly proposed but didn't get much traction in Congress,[42] while a substantial revision proposed in 1890 would do not only that but also protect marks used in

---

[36] The trademark laws would have another brush with the Constitution three years later, when in a case concerning copyright in labels the Court mentioned trademarks, but neither confirmed nor denied their federal protection. *Higgins v. Keuffel*, 140 U.S. 428 (1891).

[37] Ross Housewright, *Early Development of American Trademark Law* at 18 (2007) (Unpublished Master's Thesis), available at https://www.ischool.berkeley.edu/sites/default/files/Ross%20Housewright%20TM%20Paper%20-%20FINAL.pdf; *quoting* Titian W. Johnson, *Trade-Mark Law: Present Statute Declared Inadequate and New One Needed*, WASH. POST, January 11, 1904 at 9.

[38] *Pending Trade Mark Legislation*, 74 SCIENTIFIC AM. No. 10, pg. 146 (March 7, 1896).

[39] A minor amendment was passed in 1882, but it only clarified that trademarks based on personal names and other marks used in foreign commerce before the passage of the 1881 Act could be registered. An act relating to the registration of trade-marks, 22 Stat. 298 (August 5, 1882); *Modification of the Trade Mark Law*, 47 SCIENTIFIC AM. No. 15, pg. 224 (October 7, 1882).

[40] H.R. 4553, 48th Cong. (1884); 15 Cong. Rec. 862 (February 4, 1884).

[41] Registration of Trade-Marks H. Rep. 2376, 48th Cong. (January 24, 1885).

[42] S. 2190, 50th Cong. (1888); H.R. 7732, 50th Cong. (1888); Punishment for Counterfeiting Trade-Marks, Labels, Etc, H. Rep. 2707 (June 22, 1888).

interstate commerce.[43] The House report in 1890 focused on the importance of including trademarks used in interstate commerce in the federal trademark act, noting that "that which is omitted is of far greater importance than that which is included" in the 1881 Act.[44] However, the Committee on the Judiciary objected to the re-inclusion of criminal remedies in federal trademark law, and the effort stalled in that Congress.[45] The effort continued in the following Congress, with numerous bills being proposed, and the Committee on Patents reported out its own substitute bill crafting its own composite bill and reporting on it favorably.[46] The Committee "recognize[d] that there is a crying demand for legislation upon this subject" and recommended that trademarks used in interstate commerce be protected.[47] A similar bill was proposed in the Senate shortly thereafter, but nothing further happened.[48]

There were other bills during this period as well, most of which left even less of a trace.[49] Congress was clearly aware that the trademark laws were not working, and began making inquiries. In March of 1893 the Senate resolved that the Secretary of the Interior (whose department the Patent Office was within) report back on "what legislation, if any, is necessary to enforce the provisions of existing treaties or conventions with foreign countries with respect to patents and trade marks," or to ensure parity for Americans abroad.[50] However, the effort began in earnest in 1897, when Senator Orville Platt

---

43 H.R. 3812, 51st Cong. (1890).

44 Trade-Marks and Copyrights, H. Rep. 27 at 3, 51st Cong. (February 6, 1890). The bill proposed included additional remedies for both trademarks and copyrights for labels; the report recommended reintroducing the trademark provisions as a separate bill. *Id.* at 1. The story of why copyrights for product labels were being treated differently from regular copyrights and were being registered in the Patent Office is a long one which the author has explored elsewhere. Zvi S. Rosen, *Reimagining* Bleistein*: Copyright Advertisements in Historical Perspective*, 59 J. Copyright Soc'y U.S. 347 (2012).

45 Counterfeiting Trade-Marks, Labels, Etc., H. Rep. 1749, 51st Cong. (April 26, 1890).

46 Trade-Marks and Labels, H. Rep. 1860, 52nd Cong. (July 13, 1892); *reporting* H.R. 9528. The Committee on Patents also reported on an unrelated bill on trademarks, one of the fairly few such proposed measures—they recommended that a proposed bill to refund fees for rejected trademarks should not pass. Registration of Trade-Marks, H. Rep. 410, 52nd Cong. (February 18, 1892). Other proposed bills in the period dealt with proto-certification and collective marks such as union labels. Paul Duguid, *A Case of Prejudice? The Uncertain Development of Collective and Certification Marks*, 86 Bus. Hist. Rev. 311 (2012).

47 *Id.*

48 S. 3478, 52nd Cong. (July 27, 1892).

49 The Report of the Commissioners, discussed shortly *infra*, has a complete list of all such measures proposed.

50 S. Res.

proposed to the Senate Committee on Patents, which he was chair of, setting up a commission to revise patents and trademarks. The Committee reported back positively in a week, but nothing further was done that year.[51] Later that year at the Brussels Conference the French delegation presented a resolution "That the Government of the United States of America attempt in every way to provide as soon as possible Federal legislation which will replace local legislation in reference to trademarks, and will insure an easier and more efficient suppression of trademark infringements."[52] In the following Congress, Senator Platt again proposed a commission,[53] but recommended his own bill adversely in favor of a bill to set up a similar commission which had already passed the House.[54] The Senate report adopted verbatim the House Report from two weeks prior, which noted the ongoing conference at Brussels and all the changes that had happened in the past decades without changes to the federal statutes.[55] The bill passed the house, with debates mostly limited to ensuring the costs of the commission did not exceed $250.[56] Following Senator Platt's report, the Senate passed the bill establishing the commissioners in short order, and all within the month of May the bill passed both houses and became law on June 4, 1898.[57] The Commission appointed Francis Forbes, a businessman from New York who had organized the United States Trademark Association in 1878 and directed it since then, as a Commissioner, along with Judge Grosscup from the U.S. District Court for the Northern District of Illinois, and Arthur Greeley, the Assistant Commissioner of Patents.[58] In late 1899 Arthur P. Greeley gave a speech at the International Commercial Congress in Philadelphia, urging action in passing a new trademark law, on a panel moderated by Francis Forbes.[59] There was clearly already demand both inside and outside the United States for the nation to pass a new trademark law.

---

[51] S. 3698, 54th Cong. (February 15, 1897).

[52] Reprinted in the Report of the Commissioners *infra* at p. 123.

[53] S. 671, 55th Cong. (March 18, 1897).

[54] 31 Cong. Rec. 4992 (May 18, 1898).

[55] Commissioners to Revise the Statutes Relating to Patents, Etc., H. Rep. 1256, 55th Cong. (May 3, 1898); H.R. 9815.

[56] 31 Cong. Rec. 4776 (May 10, 1898).

[57] 30 Stat. 429 (1898).

[58] *Commission Appointed by the President to Begin Its Inquiries*, WASHINGTON POST, October 28, 1898 at 9; *Francis Forbes*, 6 BULLETIN OF THE U.S. TM. ASSOC. 19 (1910), available at https://books.google.com/books?id=KQw0AQAAMAAJ&pg=PA19&lpg=PA19.

[59] Official Proceeding of the International Commercial Congress, Fifteenth Day's Session, October 30, 1899, at 311.

The Report of the Commissioners finally arrived in December of 1900,[60] although a preliminary report had been delivered earlier.[61] The report goes far beyond the questions of the jurisdiction of federal courts in trademark matters, and urged that the law be amended to include trademarks used in interstate but not foreign commerce—subject to a dissenting minority report by Arthur Greeley arguing that the bill would go too far to "abrogate the common-law rights" of trademark holders.[62] In essence, the majority bill would establish a comprehensive system for centralized registration, while the much shorter minority bill set up a simpler system where registration was a recognition of rights, not their establishment.[63] The minority report is essentially a history of trademark law in the United States, and as such is an invaluable resource given that this was lived history for the commissioners.[64] Particularly important is the minority report's extensive argument that the commerce clause includes the regulation of trademarks, which seemed to have largely settled the issue.[65] Model statutes were drafted by the majority and minority, and each explained the reasoning for their drafting.[66] These were duly introduced in Congress in the 56th and 57th Congresses, but despite persistent complaints about the 1881 Act there was no urgency to the matter, and the bills languished without even a report.[67]

---

[60] Report of the Commissioners Appointed to Revise the Statutes Relating to Patents, Trade and Other Marks, and Trade and Commercial Names under Act of Congress Approved June 4, 1898, S. Doc. 20, 56th Cong., 2nd Sess. (December 4, 1900).

[61] Preliminary Report of the Commissioners Appointed to Revise the Statutes Relating to Patents, Trade and Other Marks, and Trade and Commercial Names under Act of Congress Approved June 4, 1898, S. Doc. 43, 56th Cong., 1st Sess. (December 11, 1899).

[62] Report, *supra* note 60 at 59 (majority); *id.* at 61.

[63] The history of failed attempts to implement a national registration-based system (as opposed to the federal system through U.S. history, which has been use-based) is a story itself, although beyond the scope of this chapter. California has long had a registration-based system for trademarks, even before the 1870 Trademark Act. Paul DuGuid, *California Marking & Collective Amnesia*, 47 U.Cal. Davis L. Rev. 581 (2013). In the 1930s and 1940s there were attempts to amend the Constitution to set up a national system for trademark registration not premised on use in commerce. *In Search of the Trade-Mark Cases*, *supra* note 5 at 894–901.

[64] Report, *supra* note 60 at 89 *et seq.*

[65] *Id.* at 115–125.

[66] In the report of the Commission model statutes were included by both the majority and minority, along with explanations.

[67] Arthur P. Greeley, Registration of Trademarks Under the New Trademark Act 23–24 (1905). The majority bills were S. 5027 in the 56th Congress and S. 5290 and H.R. 15027 in the 57th Congress. The minority (Greeley) bill was S. 5026 in the 56th Congress as well as S. 5289 and H.R. 15026 in the 57th Congress.

4. RETURN TO THE SUPREME COURT

Even as Congress failed to act, litigation was bubbling up which would make it impossible for Congress to continue to avoid legislation on trademark law. Issues of the constitutionality of the 1881 Act remained despite the *Ryder* decision, and even more importantly, so did questions about the usefulness of the statute as a remedy for infringement within the United States. In two Supreme Court cases in 1901 and 1903 the Court at first dodged the issue, and then finally confirmed the toothlessness of the 1881 Act.

4.a The Dodge: *Elgin v. Illinois* Watch Case

In 1901, a dispute in the watch industry nearly brought this tension to a head. The Elgin National Watch Company was, at the time, the largest watch manufacturer in the world. Located in Elgin, IL since the 1860s, they did not make the pocket cases the watch went into (what we'd think of today as part of the watch), but instead customers generally chose the case separately.[68] Elgin National spent $75,000 a year on advertising during this period, focused on promoting their brand.[69] Meanwhile, the Illinois Watch Case Company had started in Chicago in 1888, but moved to Elgin shortly thereafter and prospered, putting out over a thousand watch cases daily by the end of the decade.[70] This led to disputes with Elgin National almost immediately when Illinois Watch Case attempted to reincorporate as the "Elgin National Watch Case Company of Elgin, Illinois," which the Illinois courts blocked on the grounds that it would cause confusion.[71] This was only compounded when the Illinois Watch Case Company began producing watch cases such as "Elgin Giant" and "Elgin Pride."[72] A lawsuit alleging trademark infringement was commenced by Elgin National in the Circuit Court for the Northern District of Illinois in January of 1896, which was immediately met with a demurrer from Illinois Watch Case arguing that the Court lacked jurisdiction, because there was no evidence that Illinois Watch Case was using the Elgin name in foreign

---

[68] https://en.wikipedia.org/wiki/Elgin_National_Watch_Company.

[69] David M. Higgins, Brands, Geographical Origin, and the Global Economy 46 (2018).

[70] E.C. Alft, Elgin: An American History at V, available at http://www.elginhistory.com/eaah/.

[71] *Elgin Nat. Watch Co. v. Eppenstein*, 25 Chi. Legal News 142 (Cir. Ct. Cook Cty. December 21, 1892) (this opinion does not seem to have been reported elsewhere).

[72] Illinois Watch Case Company of Elgin and Elgin American, http://elginwatches.org/history/illinois_watch_cases.html.

commerce.[73] The demurrer was argued May 1, 1896, and overruled on July 11, 1896—presumably a decision was given orally, but it does not survive.[74]

Following discovery, in 1898 the Circuit Court granted an injunction for trademark infringement under federal law—the Court found that "[i]t is a fair inference ... that [defendant's] product is also intended to be, and is in fact, the subject of foreign or international commerce."[75] The following year the 7th Circuit Court of Appeals reversed, finding that the geographic name "Elgin" could not be a trademark.[76] In so doing the 7th Circuit noted that "[t]here has been no ruling upon the constitutionality of [the 1881 Act], and it need only be said that its validity is fairly doubtful."[77] The Court also noted that "such [foreign] commerce in the case before us has been so slight as to be practically immaterial, and that the real controversy is concerning state and interstate commerce in the manufactured article."[78] However, because their ruling was premised on a holding about the geographic nature of the mark, the 7th Circuit did not make a clear holding on the constitutional and jurisdictional aspects of the question (beyond holding they had no jurisdiction to enforce what was not a trademark), and indeed intentionally avoided the issue to the extent possible.[79] The Supreme Court agreed to hear the case, and it seemed possible that some of the longstanding questions about the effectiveness of the 1881 Act would be put to the test

The briefs for the parties to the Supreme Court go into great length on the constitutional questions raised in this case.[80] And yet, when the case reached

---

[73] *Elgin Nat. Watch Co. v. Illinois Watch Case Co.*, October Term 1901 No. 52, Case No. 17,493, Transcript of Record at 1, 13 (U.S.). Keeping the various circuit courts straight can be a bit of a challenge. Until 1891 The District and Circuit Courts were both trial courts, but with different jurisdictions. In 1891 the Circuit Courts of Appeals were created, but the old trial-level Circuit Courts also remained until 1911, meaning that often the Circuit Court would be appealed to the Circuit Court of Appeals. https://en.wikipedia.org/wiki/Judiciary_Act_of_1891.

[74] Transcript of Record at 15 (reproducing the docket entry but not containing any reasoning).

[75] *Elgin Nat. Watch Co. v. Illinois Watch-Case Co.*, 89 F. 487, 489 (C.C.N.D. Ill. 1898).

[76] *Illinois Watch-Case Co. v. Elgin Nat. Watch Co.*, 94 F. 667 (7th Cir. 1899).

[77] *Id.* at 669.

[78] *Id.* at 672.

[79] The Court noted "if we should concur with counsel to the full extent of [Elgin National's] contention, we are, as we think, without jurisdiction to grant relief; or, to say the least, that jurisdiction is of so doubtful a nature and so limited in extent, and under an act of doubtful constitutionality, that we must decline to exercise it." *Id.* at 671.

[80] Appellant's Brief has a particularly interesting discussion of the nature of trademarks as property, and thus their use in trade constituting commerce. Appellant's Brief at 17.

the Supreme Court, the Court "refrained from any discussion of that subject."[81] Counsel for both sides also advanced different arguments for whether infringement of a properly registered mark (which was being used in foreign commerce) was sufficient to bring a case under federal trademark law, or whether the infringement needed to be in foreign commerce as well.[82] Counsel for Elgin National argued to the Supreme Court that such authority was "plenary"—that a valid registration allowed Congress to forbid any infringement of that mark.[83] These arguments were followed by a lengthy deconstruction of Section 7 of the 1881 Act, arguing that damages could be granted for domestic use of a federally registered mark, as delineated from injunctive relief specifically limited to foreign commerce.[84] Finally, counsel for Elgin National argued that "[i]f Congress had intended to limit [the jurisdictional provision of the 1881 Act] solely to trade-marks so used by the *defendant*, it would assuredly have said so in plain terms."[85] Counsel for Illinois Watch Case, on the other hand, asserted that they had only made minimal sales outside the United States, and that they were entirely focused on domestic markets.[86]

The Supreme Court's opinion is mainly notable for its holding that "words that … are merely descriptive of the place where an article is manufactured or produced, cannot be monopolized as a trade mark."[87] The Court noted that when "secondary signification has been acquired," the use of the geographic name will be prohibited if it would be a "fraud on the public."[88] However, this was not conventional trademark protection but rather a question of "protection is accorded against unfair dealing, whether there be a technical trade mark or not."[89] This outright ban on geographically descriptive marks is no longer good

---

81 *Elgin Nat. Watch Co. v. Illinois Watch Case Co.*, 179 U.S. 665, 678, (1901).

82 The brief of Elgin National in particular is voluminous at 98 pages to a degree that is no longer commonly permitted. The briefs available through Gale's Records and Briefs online archive include a lengthy excerpt from the oral argument of Lysander Hill on behalf of Elgin National over two days of oral argument in December 1900. It is however unclear if this is verbatim or taken from his prepared remarks—there are no questions or interruptions recorded.

83 Appellant's Brief at 80.

84 *Id.* at 86.

85 *Id.* at 94 (discussing Section 11 of the 1881 Act, italics in original).

86 Appellee's Brief at 45–46.

87 *Elgin Nat'l Watch Co. v. Ill. Watch Case Co.*, 179 U.S. 665, 673 (1901).

88 *Id.* at 674.

89 *Id.* "Technical" trademarks are those which are inherently distinctive, as compared to "trade names" with acquired distinctiveness. Mark P. McKenna, *Trademark Use and the Problem of Source*, U. Ill. L. Rev. 773, 781 (2009), available at https://scholarship.law.nd.edu/law_faculty_scholarship/321.

law,[90] but it is the part of the opinion that has been most widely cited. This is because, having reached a conclusion it could rest on, the Supreme Court avoided any firm conclusions on the subject of jurisdiction.

The Supreme Court simply noted that since the geographical name "could not be employed as a trade mark … and that it was not properly entitled to be registered as such," the Court of Appeals was correct to find that they had no jurisdiction.[91] The Court declined to address the counterfactual of whether the Court would have had jurisdiction if the registration was valid, concluding that since it was not necessary to reach that issue, and the constitutionality of the 1881 Act was not addressed by the lower courts, the Supreme Court "refrained from any discussion of that subject."[92]

The *Elgin* decision was noticed and commented on in the usual way in the legal papers, but didn't cause any undue controversy, as it had avoided dealing directly with the question of jurisdiction under the 1881 Act. Two years later, the Supreme Court would be ready to make its views on jurisdiction under the 1881 Act known.

4.b The Confirmation: *Warner v. Searle & Hereth*

In December of 1882, William R. Warner, a resident of Philadelphia, received a federal trademark registration for "pancreopepsine" for a medical preparation with the active ingredients of pancreatin and pepsin which he sold in foreign commerce, particularly in sales to Australia (Figure 11.2).[93] William R. Warner's firm was successful, and recognized as one of the important firms in the city.[94] When he passed away in 1901 it was front-page news in the *Philadelphia Inquirer*, which remembered him as a "famous chemist, naturalist, and scholar."[95] His firm would eventually become Warner-Lambert Pharmaceuticals in 1955, before being acquired by Pfizer in 2000.[96]

In 1888, a young pharmacist named Gideon Daniel Searle founded a pharmaceutical company in Omaha Nebraska, along with his partner at the time

---

[90] Robert Brauneis, *Geographic Trademarks and the Protection of Competitor Communication*, 96 TRADEMARK REPORTER 4, 782 (July–August, 2006); GWU Law School Public Law Research Paper No. 233, available at SSRN: https://ssrn.com/abstract=951273.

[91] *Elgin*, 179 U.S. at 677.

[92] *Id.* at 678.

[93] *Warner v. Searle*, Complaint.

[94] *The Inquirer's Portrait Gallery*, PHILA. INQUIRER, Morning, October 12, 1891 at 4.

[95] *W.R. Warner Passes Away*, PHILA. INQUIRER, April 4, 1901 at 1.

[96] https://www.pfizer.com/about/history/pfizer_warner_lambert.

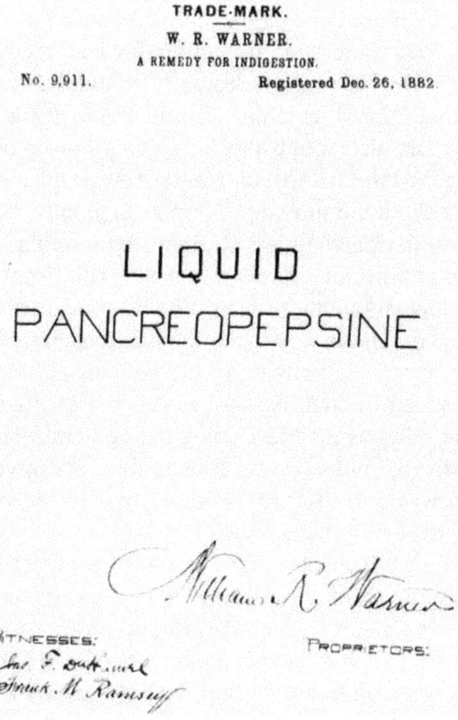
TRADE-MARK.
W. R. WARNER.
A REMEDY FOR INDIGESTION.
No. 9,911. Registered Dec. 26, 1882.

LIQUID
PANCREOPEPSINE

William R. Warner

WITNESSES: PROPRIETORS:

Figure 11.2 *Facsimile of trademark registration for Liquid Pancreopepsine*

Source: Photographed at the U.S. National Archives, Great Lakes Research Center by the author.

Franklin Ehrich, a chemist who has previously worked for Eli Lilly.[97] The company relocated to Chicago in 1890, but in that decade it was still a long way from the multibillion dollar company it would become before being acquired in 1985.[98] Searle & Ehrich specialized in selling "syrups, elixirs,

---

[97] *Searle 1888–1985* at 1, available at http://library.rumsfeld.com/doclib/sp/1822/Searle%201888-1985%20shareholder%20report.pdf. Eli Lilly refers to the man who founded the eponymous company here.

[98] *Id.*

[and] tinctures," along with other products.[99] Following a series of mergers Searle Laboratories likewise became part of Pfizer in 2003.[100]

In late 1900, the trial court ruled in an unpublished decision that the word "Pancreopepsin" was distinctive, not descriptive, and thus could be protected as a federal trademark, and enjoined Searle from using their competing mark.[101] The trial court also found that there was no unfair competition by Searle. The case reached the 7th Circuit Court of Appeals in early 1902, which affirmed the finding about unfair competition in an opinion by Judge Grosscup (one of the two Commissioners to join the majority report a few years earlier), but reversed on the validity of Warner's mark.[102] The Court found that aside from the similar trademarks, "there would be no room" to allege that Searle "were attempting in any unfair way to invade the trade built up by the merit of [Warner's] goods or by his advertising.[103] In reversing a finding that the trademark was valid, the Court noted that the name was essentially the two active ingredients together—it was just describing the contents. The "specific word … is in a sense artificial," but as it was essentially descriptive and evidence of secondary meaning was not offered, the lower court's decision was reversed, and the injunction was ordered dissolved.[104]

The Circuit Court of Appeals didn't mention jurisdiction once, but the briefs to the 7th Circuit absolutely do. The attorneys for Searle asserted that the only reason to even mention the federal trademark registration by Warner was to establish a date which it had been used since, as "[w]here foreign trade … is not involved in the controversy, the [federal trademark act] is in no way applicable, and a federal court, if it has jurisdiction at all, acquires it upon the ground of diverse citizenship alone."[105] Searle's attorneys argued that the only way the federal court had jurisdiction was due to the diverse citizenship of the parties, and then proceeded to argue the technicalities of the Illinois trademark statute, and the substance of the trademark dispute.[106] Warner did not heavily

---

[99] *Id.*

[100] https://www.pfizer.com/about/history/pfizer_pharmacia.

[101] *William R. Warner v. The Searle & Hereth Co. et al*, No. 24787 (December 14, 1900).

[102] *Searle & Hereth v. Warner*, 112 F. 674 (7th Cir. 1902). William R. Warner died between the trial and appellate ruling, and his son William R. Warner Jr. was substituted, but for purposes of clarity I'll continue to refer to Warner in a singular fashion unless it is relevant to distinguish them.

[103] *Id.*

[104] *Id.* at 676; *Scientific Names as Trademarks, Legal Notes*, 87 SCIENTIFIC AM. No. 3, pg. 43 (July 19, 1902).

[105] Appellant's Brief at 12–13, *Searle v. Warner*, No. 766 (7th Cir., October Term 1901).

[106] *Id.* at 16 *et seq.*

dispute this, instead focusing on the argument that the court had jurisdiction due to diversity of citizenship, and that the statutes granting the court diversity jurisdiction and the 1881 Trademark Act "are not inconsistent sections, but are both consistent existing laws."[107] Indeed, Warner's Brief to the 7th Circuit only alleged infringement under state law.

In the spring of 1903, counsel for Searle moved to dismiss before the Supreme Court, noting that the case was only brought on the grounds of diversity jurisdiction (that plaintiff and defendant were from different states), and that under the statute creating the Circuit Courts of Appeal passed 12 years earlier,[108] the judgment of the Circuit Courts of Appeal was final in cases where that was the only reason for federal jurisdiction.[109] In response, counsel for Warner argued that they were in fact bringing the action under federal trademark law, that the case involved the constitutionality of the 1881 Trademark Act, and that the Supreme Court had jurisdiction to hear constitutional cases from the Circuit Courts of Appeal—quite in contrast to what they had argued in their briefs to the 7th Circuit.[110] On May 4, 1903, the Supreme Court ordered consideration of the motion to dismiss "postponed until the hearing of the cause on its merits."[111]

---

[107] Appellee's Brief at 9.

[108] Judiciary Act of 1891, 26 Stat. 826 (1891) (also known as the Evarts Act). Section 6 of the Evarts Act states that "the circuit courts of appeals established by this act of appeals. shall exercise appellate jurisdiction" of the federal trial courts. However, the same section provides that "the judgments or decrees of the circuit courts of appeals shall be final in all cases in which the jurisdiction is dependent entirely upon the opposite parties to the suit or controversy, being aliens and citizens of the United States or citizens of different States." In other words, if the Seventh Circuit had jurisdiction only because of the diverse citizenship of the parties, the appeal before the Supreme Court was precluded and should be dismissed. However, if jurisdiction was based on the 1881 Trademark Act, the Supreme Court could hear the case. This rule lasted until 1925, when the "Judges' Bill" was passed expanding the scope of the Supreme Court's discretionary jurisdiction. Act of February 13, 1925, 43 Stat. 936.

[109] Brief on Motion to Dismiss the Appeal, *Warner v. Searle & Hereth*, No. 307 (U.S. October Term 1902).

[110] Brief on Behalf of Appellant Opposing Motion to Dismiss, *Warner v. Searle & Hereth*, No. 307 (U.S. October Term 1902). Counsel for Warner noted that the emphasis on state-law trademarks was especially necessary in "the Seventh Circuit, for in that regard the Court of Appeals seems to pay no regard to registered trade-marks, and has on more than one occasion expressed doubts as to the constitutionality" of the 1881 Trademark Act. *Id.* at 5. The case referred to, of course, is the Seventh Circuit's opinion in *Elgin National Watch*.

[111] Order of Chief Justice Melville Fuller, May 4, 1903, *Warner v. Searle & Hereth*, No. 307 (U.S. October Term 1902) (original in U.S. National Archives, copy on file with author).

In the briefs for Searle, they took pains to point out that the only foreign sales there was evidence of by Warner were two to Australia in 1882, and there was no evidence of any sales in foreign commerce by Searle.[112] Warner, for its part, asserted this was "entirely immaterial," the Court had jurisdiction to hear the case by virtue of its registration, and proving additional use of the mark in foreign commerce "simply would have increased the bulk of the record without accomplishing any useful object."[113] Warner likewise argued at length that foreign use by the alleged infringer is not a necessary prerequisite to federal jurisdiction.[114] When the Supreme Court reached its opinion it recited the relevant facts and statutory sections, and then immediately responded in the negative to Warner, holding that "obviously … [the 1881 Trademark Act] can only be infringed when used in that commerce, without right, by another than its owner."[115] And just like that, Warner's case under federal trademark law was over. The Court explained that jurisdiction under § 7 of the 1881 Trademark Act must be premised on infringement in foreign commerce, since the "intent and object of the act forbid a construction that would bring local commerce within its scope."[116] The Court thus held that in order to bring a successful suit for infringement under the 1881 Trademark Act, the plaintiff needed to allege (1) that their use of the trademark remained active in foreign commerce, and (2) that the infringement was on articles intended for export to a foreign nation.[117] For this proposition the Court noted that "[w]e so held, in effect, in *Ryder v. Holt*, and we see no reason to depart from that ruling."[118] Finally, the Supreme Court noted that even if the prerequisites of the 1881 Trademark Act were otherwise met, injunctions under § 7 of the 1881 Trademark Act were limited to foreign commerce anyway.[119]

---

112 Appellee's Brief at 25, *Warner v. Searle & Hereth*, No. 307 (U.S. October Term 1902).

113 Appellant's Brief at 6–7, *Warner v. Searle & Hereth*, No. 307 (U.S. October Term 1902).

114 *Id.* at 8.

115 *Warner v. Searle & Hereth Co.*, 191 U.S. 195, 204 (1903).

116 *Id.* at 205 The Supreme Court addressed the motion to dismiss here, holding that the action argued a federal question of infringement of the 1881 Trademark Act, and the Supreme Court thus had authority to hear the appeal since the premise of the case was more than diversity jurisdiction, even though it would turn out that the claim to jurisdiction as a federal question was found invalid by the Court's ruling that there was no trademark infringement. *Id.* at 205–206.

117 *Id.* at 206.

118 *Id.* (internal citations omitted). Counsel for Warner's lengthy brief does not even mention *Ryder*, suggesting the case was being forgotten already.

119 *Id.* The Court declined to address the constitutionality of the 1881 Trademark Act, noting that lower courts had not addressed the issue either. *Id.*

The Court did not address Warner's state-law trademark claims, because those were premised solely on diversity of citizenship, and, as mentioned, the 1891 Act creating the Circuit Courts of Appeal specifically stated that their rulings in cases where diversity was the only ground for jurisdiction were final. Accordingly, the ruling of the 7th Circuit was affirmed and/or final, depending on the claim, and Searle had triumphed. In the process though, the 1881 Trademark Act had been worn down to a nub—it now only applied in cases where the plaintiff was actively using the mark in foreign commerce and the actual infringement had occurred in foreign commerce—and an injunction would only enjoin infringement in foreign commerce.

The judgment was swift—following the *Warner* decision a federal trademark registration was "worthless, except in cases where it is used in foreign commerce."[120] Registering in each individual state could cost around $300, not even considering the "annoying" complications of complying with each state's rules for registration.[121] Business organizations across the country quickly began to lobby for a new trademark law that was effective within interstate commerce, not just internationally.[122] Whereas in 1879 business organizations had seen state remedies for trademark infringements as being sufficient, by 1903 interstate use of trademarks was the chief concern—the problem of intrastate-only infringement of marks was "believed … so small as to be practically … negligible."[123] America had changed, and it was time for federal trademark law to change as well.

5. A PARTIAL FIX—THE 1905 TRADEMARK ACT

Since 1881 "American business [had] chafed under the totally inadequate provisions of the 1881 Act."[124] Now Congress's hand had been forced by the Supreme Court, and work began in earnest on a new statute. Model bills for such a new law already existed in the form of the proposed bills from the Commission a few years earlier, and the American Bar Association's Committee on Patents stepped in to help mediate between majority and minority reports "which were so diverse that Congress was unable to decide between them."[125] Finding that the majority bill, with its "European theory of property

---

120 *Current Topics*, *supra* note 4.

121 *Trade-Mark Troubles*, Wash. Post, June 21, 1904 at 14.

122 *Current Topics*, *supra* note 4.

123 *Id.* at 9–20.

124 *History of United States Trademark Legislation*, 1 McCarthy on Trademarks and Unfair Competition § 5:3 (5th ed.).

125 Report of the Twenty-Sixth Annual Meeting of the American Bar Association 87–88 (1903).

in trade-marks by virtue of registration" was less "in harmony with the law of the United States" than the minority bill, they chose to focus on the minority bill as a solution.[126] Working with the minority report's author, Arthur Greeley, the ABA Committee on Patents drafted a new bill to present to Congress,[127] and adopted it at their 1903 Annual Meeting on August 26–28, 1903.[128] Critically, the bill allowed for federal remedies both when the defendant was engaged in interstate trademark infringement, and where the plaintiff's mark was being used in interstate commerce and "the acts of the defendant are such as to interfere with that commerce."[129]

The 58th Congress had started unusually, with a First Session that was only 15 days long, which ended only a few days after the Supreme Court decided *Warner v. Searle*.[130] However, as the Second Session began in earnest following the holidays, bills to remedy the problem caused by the *Warner* decision poured in. The majority and minority bills were once again introduced,[131] as was the ABA bill.[132] Numerous other bills were also proposed, typically being variants on the minority/ABA bill.[133] However, this array of bills in the

---

[126] *Id.* at 88.

[127] *Id.* The bill was not especially controversial, although there was a proposed amendment to move trademarks to a new office with its own commissioner under the Commerce Department (the Patent Office was still in the Interior Department at the time), leading W.J. Knight of Iowa to comment that the "Patent Office is already notoriously overcrowded" and that a separate trademark office would be a "relief." *Id.* at 91. The amendment was not adopted as the matter was thought best left to Congress. *Id.* at 93. Greeley meanwhile had already left the Patent Office earlier in 1900. *A.P. Greeley Leaves Patent Office*, N.Y. TIMES, March 20, 1900 at 5.

[128] Report, *supra* note 125 at 93. The report identifies the changes made to the minority bill, the main one being the inclusion of criminal remedies for trademark infringement. Report of the Committee on Patent, Trade-Mark, and Copyright Law, *Id.* at 475. The committee was Edmund Wetmore, R.S. Taylor, William C. Strawbridge, Arthur Steuart, and Lysander Hill, the last of which had been lead counsel for Elgin National Watch before the Supreme Court.

[129] Report, *supra* note 125 at 477.

[130] 50th to 59th Congresses (1887–1907), at https://history.house.gov/Institution/Session-Dates/50-59/. The First session had begun November 9, 1903 and concluded December 5, 1903, while *Warner v. Searle* was decided on November 30, 1903.

[131] S. 3219 and S. 3220, 58th Cong.

[132] H.R. 11672 and S. 3799, 58th Cong.

[133] H.R. 13297, H.R. 14945, and H.R. 15367 were all introduced by Rep. Southwick in the House, and S. 4433 and S. 5398 were the same bills as the first two, introduced by Sen. Clapp. H.R. 15223 was introduced by Rep. Currier in this session as well. The Southwick bill was designed to have the Commissioner of Patents evaluate the validity of the trademark, with an appeal to the federal court in Washington, DC, while the Currier bill provided for open registration, leaving adjudication of their validity to the Courts. Titian W. Johnson, *New Trade-Mark Law*, WASH. POST, January 6, 1907 at 15.

second session needed time to be debated, and the matter was left for the third session.[134]

With this array of bills proposed, the House Committee on Patents took it upon itself to draft a new bill which combined the attributes of a number of the bills proposed.[135] Representative Robert Bonynge became the driving force behind the bill, and reported a new substitute bill back in the third session (aka the "lame duck session"), hoping to pass a law before the end of the Congress a few months later, which would have necessitated starting essentially from scratch. In the report accompanying the bill, six objectives were identified for the new law: (1) to provide for protection of trademarks used in interstate commerce; (2) to provide uniformity in the registration of trademarks; (3) to further penalize trademark infringement; (4) to reduce the registration fee for trademarks; (5) to regulate conflicting trademark claims; and (6) to conform to international treaty obligations.[136] The bill purposely avoided making changes and attempted to use the language of the 1881 Act as much as possible.[137] As this was ongoing petitions from many major trademark interests were sent to Congress, presumably in a coordinated campaign, to urge the passage of a law which would provide protection for trademarks used in interstate commerce.[138]

The bill reached the Senate, and on January 24, 1905, the Senate issued a report recommending that the bill pass with only a few minor changes.[139] Two weeks later, a conference report was issued, where the House accepted most of the Senate's changes.[140] A few days thereafter the House agreed to the conference report,[141] and from there things progressed quickly. Nine days later, on February 20, 1905, America had a new trademark law.[142]

The new bill did not include criminal remedies, the main element removed from the ABA's proposed bill. Competing bills were introduced in the fol-

---

134 *Current Topics*, *supra* note 4.

135 H.R. 16560, 58th Cong. (December 14, 1904). Rep. Bonynge also introduced a similar bill himself a week earlier as H.R. 15803, representing his work over the recess, which became H.R. 16560 following hearings. Greeley, *supra* note 67 at 25.

136 H. Rep. 3147 at 7–8, 58th Cong., 3rd Sess. (1904).

137 *Id.* at 8.

138 These petitions are currently held in the files of the Senate Committee on Patents for the 58th Congress at the U.S. National Archives, in box/folder 56A-F26. I've scanned the contents of that folder and shared it on the Internet Archive: https://archive.org/details/1905trademarkpetitions.

139 Registration of Trade-Marks Used in Commerce with Foreign Nations, Etc, S. Rep. 3278, 58th Cong., 3rd Sess. (1905).

140 Registration of Trade-Marks, H. Rep. 4418, 58th Cong., 3rd Sess. (1905).

141 39 Cong. Rec. 2412 (February 11, 1905).

142 An Act to authorize the registration of trade-marks used in commerce with foreign nations or among the several States or with Indian tribes, and to protect the same, 33 Stat. 724 (February 20, 1905).

lowing Congress to provide criminal remedies to the law, with the United States Trademark Association proposing a bill which simply added criminal remedies to the new law, while the ABA proposed a bill which would also extend the law to commerce within a single state affecting interstate commerce.[143] At a hearing before the House Committee this divide was noted by the chair, giving a general sense of disinclination to pursue this issue.[144] Indeed, a member of the Committee on Patents made clear that there was a "disinclination of Congress to make any more statutory crimes," and that the new law had just been passed and it would be "better to have that pretty well tried out" before adding criminal remedies.[145] In the end, criminal remedies for trademark infringement would not find their way back to the federal statute until 1984.[146]

Shortly after the passage of the law, advertisements began to appear, falsely asserting that "a trade mark registered under the old law is almost worthless," from a firm seeking to profit by filing new registrations for businesses.[147] In response, Arthur Greeley, the main drafter of the 1905 Act, put out a pamphlet seeking to explain procedure under the new Act and to "correct this misapprehension" and thus prevent trademark owners from being taken advantage of.[148] At the same time, Greeley was frank that the "new law was not all that could be desired."[149]

6. THE LAST STAND OF THE *TRADE-MARK CASES*

The expected challenges to the constitutionality of the 1905 Trademark Law did appear, in another Supreme Court case even more forgotten than the others discussed *supra*. The owner of the registered trademark "Old Crow" for whiskey (Figure 11.3) opposed the registration of "'Raven Valley Whisky,"

---

[143] *Amendment of the Trade-Mark Law H.R. 10,091*, 2 BULL. U.S. TRADE-MARK ASSOC. 157 (April 1906).

[144] Argument Before the Committee on Patents of the House of Representatives on H.R. 13942, To Provide Criminal Remedies for the Willful Forgery and Utterance of Registered Trade-Marks, May 9, 1906, 59th Cong.

[145] *Amendment of the Trade-Mark Law*, *supra* note 143.

[146] Trademark Counterfeiting Act of 1984, Pub. L. No. 98-473, Tit. II, § 1502(a), 98 Stat. 2178 (1984).

[147] *Advertisement, Munn & Co.*, 42 SCIENTIFIC AM. No. 9, pg. 192 (March 4, 1905).

[148] *Preface*, ARTHUR P. GREELEY, REGISTRATION OF TRADEMARKS UNDER THE NEW TRADEMARK ACT (1905).

[149] *Id.* Although Greeley would remain a practicing lawyer for many more years, this would largely mark the close of his engagement with trademark policy and legislation. *A.P. Greeley*, PROSPEROUS WASHINGTON EDITION, WASH. POST, June 12, 1912 at L70; *Chisholm-Ryder Co. v. Buck*, 65 F.2d 735, 735 (4th Cir. 1933) (listed as counsel).

accompanied by a pictorial representation of three ravens in the bare limbs of a tree."[150] Before the Court of Appeals of the District of Columbia (now the DC Circuit Court of Appeals), counsel for W.A. Gaines & Co. did not simply argue that the two marks were excessively similar, he argued that the entire trademark registration system was unconstitutional.[151]

This argument was rejected, but the case proceeded to the U.S. Supreme Court, where counsel for Gaines requested copies of the briefs filed before the Court in the *Trade-Mark Cases* almost thirty years earlier.[152] In its brief, Gaines made clear that the "sole question involved in this case is the constitutionality of the" 1905 Trademark Act.[153]

In its brief Gaines reviewed the history of trademark laws in the United States and noted that there had not been a direct challenge to the 1881 Act.[154] Noting that the registration being prosecuted relied solely on interstate commerce, counsel for Gaines looked back to the language of Justice Miller's decision in the *Trade-Mark Cases* to the effect that a trademark was "not an article of commerce."[155] With no more decisions to cite on this exact point, counsel for Gaines instead argued some of the other major commerce clause decisions of the gilded age, focusing on the limitations of the commerce clause to argue that the "power of the state is exclusive over trade-marks."[156] Counsel for Gaines concluded with a simple argument—"if the reasoning of [the *Trade-Mark Cases*] was legally sound … the Act cannot be sustained."[157] In response,

[150] *Gaines v. Knecht*, 27 App. D.C. 530, 534 (D.C. Cir. 1906).

[151] *Id.* at 530. It is unclear why Gaines, who had a registered trademark under every previous trademark law, wanted to find the federal trademark law unconstitutional. Brian F. Haara, Bourbon Justice. How Whiskey Law Shaped America 43–59 (2018). It is plausible that a string of losses before the courts had convinced Gaines that he'd be better off relying on state law. *Id.* In 1918 Gaines lost control of the "Old Crow" mark before the U.S. Supreme Court, but the pain of that loss was mitigated by the mark becoming irrelevant with the passage of prohibition a year later. *Rock Spring Distilling Co. v. Gaines & Co.*, 246 U.S. 312 (1918); U.S. Const., Amend. 19 (1919).

[152] Letter from James Love Hopkins, Counsel for W.A. Gaines & Company, to James D. Maher, Assistant Clerk of the U.S. Supreme Court, April 12, 1907, in the file for *Gaines v. Knecht* Casefile, Record Group 267, U.S. National Archives (copy on file with author). Hopkins was particularly interested in getting a copy of the brief of George Hoadly on behalf of some of the defendants, which laid out the argument which ultimately succeeded in that case. In response the clerk noted that he only had one copy of the briefs left, but offered to make a typewritten copy for a fee. Letter from James D. Maher to J.L. Jopkins, April 15, 1907, copy attached to *Id.*

[153] Brief of W.A. Gaines & Co., Plaintiff in Error at 6, *W.A. Gaines & Co. v. C.A. Knecht & Son*, No. 52, File No. 20647 (U.S. October Term 1908).

[154] *Id.* at 10–11.

[155] *Id.* at 12.

[156] *Id.* at 19 (capitalization of section heading removed).

[157] *Id.* at 22.

counsel for the registrant addressed not just the *Trade-Mark Cases*, but the report of Congress that came with the 1881 Act, noting how times had changed and how both the dicta in the *Trade-Mark Cases* and the Congressional Report misconstrued the relationship of trademarks to commerce.[158]

Figure 11.3 Old Crow whiskey label

Source: From the U.S. Supreme Court Record and Briefs, Library of Congress, photo by author.

And yet before the Supreme Court, the result was an anticlimax—the Court dismissed the decision *per curiam* for lack of jurisdiction. The only rationale given was a cite to *Frasch v. Moore*, decided earlier that year, holding that the 1893 Act creating the DC Court of Appeals left the Supreme Court of the United States without jurisdiction to hear further appeals of actions by the Commissioner of Patents, as "there is no final judgment in the cause, but one interlocutory in its nature, and binding only upon the Commissioner."[159] Counsel for Gaines filed a petition for rehearing, noting that *Frasch v. Moore* was a patent case, brought under the special provisions of the Patent Act, and arguing that a ruling on a trademark opposition was a final decision giving the Supreme Court jurisdiction.[160] However, the Court denied the petition for rehearing a few weeks later.[161]

[158] Brief for Knecht & Son at 13.

[159] *Frasch v. Moore*, 211 U.S. 1, 9 (1908).

[160] Petition or Rehearing at 2–3, December 26, 1909 (copy on file with author).

[161] Letter from Clerk, United States Supreme Court to James L. Hopkins, January 4, 1909, in *Gaines v. Knecht* Casefile, *supra* note 152.

A few months later, the Court felt the need to explain itself if it was going to use *Gaines v. Knecht* as a precedent to dismiss trademark appeals originating from decisions of the Commissioner of Patents, noting that *Gaines* "was a case of opposition to the registration of a trademark under [the 1905 Trademark Act], the objections being that the act was unconstitutional" and that the marks were too similar.[162] The Court explained the background of its decision further, but only in the context of its jurisdiction—there was clearly no appetite for re-engaging the Constitutional question.[163]

In practice, that would essentially be the end to questions about the constitutionality of federal trademark protection. In 1917 a petition for writ of certiorari was filed with the Supreme Court in another case, in which the Bear Lithia Springs Company sought to prevent the issuance of a trademark they felt to be infringing by interference, once again by trying to bring down the whole of federal trademark law in the process.[164] However, the Court declined to hear the case.[165] By 1943, the Seventh Circuit Court of Appeals would note that "[a]lthough the question has never been squarely decided by the Supreme Court, we believe it is clear that Congress has the power to legislate upon the substantive law of trade-marks."[166] In practice, the commerce clause justification or federal trademark law would seem increasingly unassailable following cases like *Wickard v. Filburn*, which established a much broader scope for the commerce clause than imagined by Justice Miller in 1879.[167]

7. "IMMORAL" AND "SCANDALOUS" MARKS IN CONTEXT

In exploring the unfolding of the 1905 Trademark Act, it is interesting to explore how understanding this history can shed light on terms still in the law. As an example of this, the 1905 Act introduced a formal bar to registration of "immoral or scandalous" marks, and this has generally been understood as

---

[162] *E.C. Atkins & Co. v. Moore*, 212 U.S. 285, 290 (1909).

[163] The court responded to the Motion for Rehearing effectively here, noting that "In the light of the various details of the act of February 20, 1905, and of the specific provisions of § 9, we were of opinion that proceedings under the act were governed by the same rules of practice and procedure as in the instance of patents, and the writ of error was accordingly dismissed. The same result must follow in the present case." *Id.* at 291.

[164] *Fulton Water Works Co v. Bear Lithia Springs Co*, 247 U.S. 506 (1918) (Cert. Denied).

[165] *Id.*

[166] *Philco Corp. v. Phillips Mfg. Co.*, 133 F.2d 663, 668 (7th Cir. 1943).

[167] *Christian Faith Fellowship Church v. Adidas AG*, 841 F.3d 986, 990–992 (Fed. Cir. 2016).

having been done "with little explanation."[168] This language first appears in §5 of the proposed minority bill in the Commission's 1900 Report and remains in the statute despite being largely invalidated by the Supreme Court in *Brunetti* and *Tam* respectively.[169] The draft bill proposed by the minority (aka Arthur P. Greeley) indicates that all distinctive marks may be registered save for any mark which "consists of or comprises immoral or scandalous matter" or governmental insignias and coats of arms.[170] The report does not explain exactly why this bar was included, but indicates that this section is "drawn to provide for the registration of all marks which would or could under the law, as construed by the Supreme Court, be held to be capable of being appropriates as the exclusive property of the person using them as trademarks."[171] The proposed majority bill contained no such provision in the coordinate section (Section 6) or elsewhere.[172] However, the version of the majority bill introduced in the following Congress (in 1902) added to this section a provision that "[a] mark contrary to good morals" could not be registered.[173]

In his treatise on trademark law, likely the most important American one at the time, William Henry Browne opines that "[t]o be a 'lawful trade-mark,' the emblem must avoid transgressing the rules of morality or public policy."[174] He believed that "propriety must be the standard" in selection of a trademark, and "[t]he moral, religious, or political sensibilities of any people must not be shocked by the perversion of an emblem sacred in their eyes."[175] Browne notes that "[a] reader of these lines might be a [Chinese person,] His [religion] must

---

[168] Jasmine Abdel-khalik, *To Live in In-"Fame"-Y: Reconceiving Scandalous Marks as Analogous to Famous Marks*, 25 CARDOZO ARTS & ENT. L.J. 173, 180 (2007).

[169] *Matal v. Tam*, 582 U.S. ___ (2017); *Iancu v. Brunetti*, No. 18–302, 588 U.S. ___ (2019); Report, *supra* note 60 at 127.

[170] Report, *supra* note 60.

[171] *Id.* (internal punctuation removed). The Paris Convention of 1883 "also allows governments to deny registration to trademarks that are contrary to morality or public order." Lisa P. Ramsey, *A Free Speech Right to Trademark Protection?*, 106 TRADEMARK REP. 797, 806 (2016), *citing* Paris Convention for the Protection of Industrial Property art. 6ter(1)(a), March 20, 1883. Jasmine Abdel-khalik has noted that the scandalousness bar also first appeared a few years earlier, in a proposed 1892 Law. Abdel-khalik, *supra* note 168 at 184.

[172] Report, *supra* note 60 at 65–66.

[173] 57th Cong., H.R. 15027 at §6.

[174] WILLIAM HENRY BROWNE, A TREATISE ON THE LAW OF TRADE-MARKS AND ANALOGOUS SUBJECTS, at § 602—this section appears largely identical in the 1873, 1885, and 1898 versions of the treatise.

[175] *Id.* "Propriety" is emphasized – in bold in the 1873 edition and italicized in the 1885 and 1898 editions.

not be caricatured."[176] No case is offered for this proposition, but it is presented as Patent Office policy. Browne does cite the 1871 trademark registration by Walter & Shaffer of San Francisco for "Pipifax Bitters," no. 434, which he describes as being an edge case because the specification describes "a smiling half-drunk demon or devil in a sitting posture ... in his arms and hands he carries six bottles" (Figure 11.4).[177] However, "the *bottles* turned the scale," coupled with the fact that "it had been recognized in Germany."[178] If there hadn't been the moral lesson to avoid alcohol, it implicitly would not have been registrable. By the 1890s, Courts began recognizing this rule.[179]

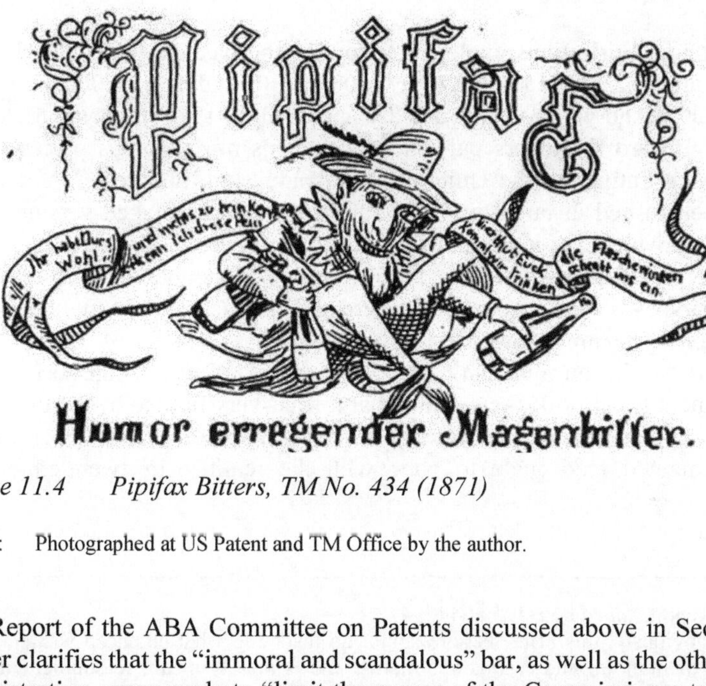

Figure 11.4 *Pipifax Bitters, TM No. 434 (1871)*

Source: Photographed at US Patent and TM Office by the author.

The Report of the ABA Committee on Patents discussed above in Section 5 further clarifies that the "immoral and scandalous" bar, as well as the other bars to registration, were made to "limit the power of the Commissioner to reject applications" by codifying traditional exceptions to trademark protection and

---

176 *Id.* The actual term Browne uses is a racial pejorative which is no longer the correct nomenclature for an Asian-American. This is somewhat dissonant with Browne's insistence on respect, and one suspects he didn't even realize the usage might be offensive, at the time or today.

177 *Id.*; Annual Report of the Commissioner of Patents for the Year 1871, Vol. 1 at 273.

178 *Id.* (emphasis in original).

179 *Cohn v. People*, 149 Ill. 486, 493, 37 N.E. 60, 62 (1894).

excluding others.[180] In other words, the bill meant to restrict the grounds for denial of an application for trademark registration by codifying certain grounds under which an application was already denied. Understanding the path the 1905 Trademark Act took to pass allows us to understand that the inclusion of this bar to registration was not an innovation of early-twentieth-century morality, but rather a codification of a longstanding rule, and a limitation on Patent Office discretion to invent other bars to registration.[181]

8. EPILOGUE—A NINETEENTH-CENTURY STATUTE IN THE TWENTIETH CENTURY

Trademark registrations exploded following the passage of the 1905 Act—from roughly 2,000 in 1904 to over 4,000 in 1905 and over 10,000 the following year.[182] And yet problems quickly appeared. In 1914 the noted trademark expert Edward S. Rogers published one of his most famous pieces—"The Expensive Futility of the United States Trade-Mark Statute."[183] A new law had been rushed in but it was still fundamentally a tweaked version of the 1881 Act, which was in turn a tweaked version of the 1870 Act. In retrospect, "the Federal Trademark Act of 1905 … reflected the view that protection of trademarks was a matter of state concern and that the right to a mark depended solely on the common law."[184]

In his treatise on trademark law, J. Thomas McCarthy is unsparing in his assessment of the 1905 Act, noting that it was "very limited by today's standards," and "even with [subsequent] amendments, the basic 1905 Trademark Act remained inadequate to cope with the realities of twentieth-century

---

180 Report, *supra* note 125 at 476–477.

181 Obviously, this brief section cannot do justice to what has been written on the subject of immoral and scandalous marks, and is merely meant to supplement it by explaining the origin of the term in the law. Ramsey, *supra* note 171 at n. 11 provides a valuable concordance on the scholarship on this subject.

182 Zvi S. Rosen, *Federal Trademark Law: From its Beginnings*, 11 LANDSLIDE NO. 4 (2019), available at https://www.americanbar.org/groups/intellectual_property_law/publications/landslide/2018-19/march-april/federal-trademark-law/; Johnson, *supra* note 133 (noting that 24,300 applications had been filed, with over 20,000 disposed of, since it went into force two years earlier).

183 12 MICH. L. REV. 660 (1914). He argued that the 1905 Trademark Act was a "slovenly piece of legislation, characterized by awkward phraseology, bad grammar, and involved sentences. Its draftsmen had a talent for obscurity amounting to genius." *Id.* at 665. Later he suggests that the term "descriptive properties" was "possibly … intended as a practical joke." *Id.* at 669.

184 *Park 'N Fly, Inc. v. Dollar Park and Fly, Inc.*, 469 U.S. 189, 658 (1985).

commerce and brand names.[185] And in terms of substance he is correct—the 1905 Act continued to not protect descriptive marks, or service marks, and the continued amendments to try to haul what was still fundamentally the 1881 Act into the twentieth century resulted "in a crazy quilt of modifications and amendments."[186] To this day, federal trademark law is shaped by these largely forgotten decisions of the United States Supreme Court, which whittled federal trademark law into near nonexistence, from which it needed to be slowly rebuilt.

---

185 *History of United States Trademark Legislation*, 1 McCarthy on Trademarks and Unfair Competition § 5:3 (5th ed.).

186 *Id.*

PART VI

THE LORE OF INTELLECTUAL PROPERTY, HUMAN RIGHTS AND DEVELOPMENT

12. Is there a constitutional right to intellectual property in South Africa? Revisiting the case of *In re Certification of the Constitution of the Republic of South Africa, 1996*

Emmanuel Kolawole Oke

INTRODUCTION

In 1996, after the South African Constitutional Assembly adopted the text for a new post-apartheid South African Constitution, it was transmitted to the South African Constitutional Court for certification, as required by the then Interim Constitution of 1993.[1] In line with the requirements of the Interim Constitution, the Constitutional Court was tasked with determining whether all the provisions in the proposed new Constitution complied with a set of constitutional principles listed in Schedule 4 of the Interim Constitution.[2] These constitutional principles included, inter alia, the principle that "everyone shall enjoy all universally accepted fundamental rights, freedoms and civil liberties, which shall be provided for and protected by entrenched and justiciable provisions in the Constitution."[3]

In the course of certifying the proposed new Constitution, the Constitutional Court invited and received representations from members of the public.[4] One

[1] See, Section 71 of the Interim Constitution of South Africa, 1993. Specifically, Section 71(2) of the Interim Constitution provides that: "The new constitutional text passed by the Constitutional Assembly, or any provision thereof, shall not be of any force and effect unless the Constitutional Court has certified that all the provisions of such text comply with the Constitutional Principles referred to in subsection (1) (a)."

[2] Schedule 4 of the Interim Constitution contained a set of 34 constitutional principles.

[3] Principle II of the constitutional principles.

[4] *In Re Certification of the Constitution of the Republic of South Africa, 1996*, Case CCT 23/96, decision of the Constitutional Court of South Africa (6 September 1996), para 4. [Hereinafter, *Certification* case.]

of the issues the Court had to deal with concerned the Bill of Rights in the proposed new Constitution. Specifically, an objection was raised by some stakeholders that the draft text of the proposed new Constitution failed to recognise a right to intellectual property.[5] Importantly, it was contended by these stakeholders that the right to intellectual property is a "universally accepted fundamental right, freedom and civil liberty."[6] The Constitutional Court however rejected this contention and it ruled that the recognition of a right to intellectual property "cannot be characterised as a trend which is universally accepted."[7] Thus, South Africa's current Constitution does not contain a right to intellectual property.

It should however be noted that, even though the right to intellectual property is not recognised in South Africa's Constitution, Section 25 of the current Constitution protects the right to property. This provision on the right to property has now become the focal point for stakeholders who want to elevate intellectual property rights into a constitutional right in South Africa. Indeed, some scholars in South Africa have construed certain judicial pronouncements from South African courts as implying that intellectual property falls within the scope of the protection of property rights guaranteed under Section 25 of the Constitution.[8] Some have even gone as far as contending that, because trademarks constitute property under the South African Constitution, any law that prevents the use of trademarks on tobacco products (such as plain packaging measures) would constitute a deprivation or expropriation of property and an infringement of Section 25 of the Constitution.[9]

This chapter is divided into three main parts. In part 1, there will be a critical re-examination of the 1996 decision of the Constitutional Court of South Africa with regard to the constitutional status of intellectual property rights in South Africa in the light of the current debates on the relationship between intellectual property and human rights in South Africa. Part 2 will question the view of those who contend that intellectual property rights fall within the scope of the constitutional protection of the right to property. In doing so, there will be a critical assessment of some of the cases where South African courts have

---

[5] *Certification* case, ibid, para 75.

[6] Ibid.

[7] Ibid.

[8] See, Mikhalien Du Bois, "Intellectual Property as a Constitutional Property Right: The South African Approach" (2012) 24 *South African Mercantile Law Journal* 177, 188; Owen Dean, "Deprivation of Trade Marks through State Interference in their Usage" (2013) 35:10 *European Intellectual Property Review* 576, 586; Andre Van der Walt and Richard Shay, "Constitutional Analysis of Intellectual Property" (2014) 17:1 *Potchefstroom Electronic Law Journal* 52, 55.

[9] Owen Dean, "Deprivation of Trade Marks through State Interference in their Usage" (n 8) 581.

dealt with the interface and tensions between intellectual property rights and human rights. In part 3, it will be contended that, even if one takes the view that intellectual property rights fall within the scope of the constitutional protection of the right to property, this should not constitute an impediment to the implementation of measures aimed at protecting the public health. Thus, it will be contended that, if measures relating to the plain packaging of tobacco products are implemented in South Africa, this would not amount to either an arbitrary deprivation or an expropriation of property rights in trademarks.

1. *IN RE CERTIFICATION OF THE CONSTITUTION OF THE REPUBLIC OF SOUTH AFRICA, 1996*

During the process of the drafting of the 1996 post-apartheid Constitution of South Africa, some stakeholders tried unsuccessfully to convince the Constitutional Assembly to include a right to intellectual property in the proposed new Constitution.[10] The Constitutional Assembly appeared to have taken the view that there was no need to include a separate provision on the right to intellectual property in the proposed new Constitution because the provision on the right to property in the proposed Constitution could be used to protect intellectual property.[11] When the proposed new Constitution was brought before the Constitutional Court for certification, these stakeholders lodged an objection against the new Constitution on the grounds that it failed to recognise a right to intellectual property.[12] Crucially, these stakeholders contended that it would be contrary to Constitutional Principle II of the Interim Constitution of 1993[13] if no right to intellectual property is included in the

[10] See, Owen Dean, "The Case for the Recognition of Intellectual Property in the Bill of Rights" (1997) 60 *Tydskrif vir Hedendaagse Romeins-Hollandse Reg* 105 (noting that, "Numerous individuals, bodies and organisations made representations to the Constitutional Assembly requesting that specific recognition and protection be granted to intellectual property in the Bill of Rights to be incorporated into the new Constitution ... Numerous other bodies, including the Association of Marketers and the South African Institute of Intellectual Property Law, also made written submissions. These petitions did not find favour with the Constitutional Assembly and the Constitution adopted by that Assembly contained no clause in the Bill of Rights dealing specifically with intellectual property").

[11] Dean, "The Case for the Recognition of Intellectual Property in the Bill of Rights" (n 10) 107, 112.

[12] *Certification* case (n 4) para 75.

[13] Constitutional Principle II contained in Schedule 4 of the 1993 Interim Constitution provides that: "Everyone shall enjoy all universally accepted fundamental rights, freedoms and civil liberties, which shall be provided for and protected by entrenched and justiciable provisions in the Constitution, which shall be drafted after

proposed Constitution.[14] Essentially, these stakeholders were arguing that the right to intellectual property is a universally recognised fundamental right.

In a rather short and pithy paragraph, the Constitutional Court dismissed the objection raised by these stakeholders and it ruled that:

> Although it is true that many international conventions recognise a right to intellectual property, it is much more rarely recognised in regional conventions protecting human rights and in the constitutions of acknowledged democracies. It is also true that some of the more recent constitutions, particularly in Eastern Europe, do contain express provisions protecting intellectual property, but this is probably due to the particular history of those countries and cannot be characterised as a trend which is universally accepted. In the circumstances, the objection cannot be sustained.[15]

While the decision of the Constitutional Court with regard to this objection is brief, it does however contain a number of crucial elements that require further critical analysis. Importantly, there are three key points that are worth noting in this regard.

Firstly, the Constitutional Court observed that "many international conventions recognise a right to intellectual property."[16] In support of this, the Court cited Article 27(2) of the Universal Declaration of Human Rights (UDHR) and Article 15(1)(c) of the International Covenant on Economic, Social and Cultural Rights (ICESCR).[17] The Court's reliance on these provisions is based on the assumption that they deal with a right to intellectual property. However, this is not necessarily a correct assumption because neither Article 27(2) of the UDHR nor Article 15(1)(c) of the ICESCR mentions the right to intellectual property. Rather, both provisions actually refer to the right of creators to benefit from the protection of their "moral and material interests."[18] It is not

---

having given due consideration to inter alia the fundamental rights contained in Chapter 3 of this Constitution."

[14] *Certification* case (n 4) para 75.

[15] Ibid, para 75 [internal citations and footnotes omitted].

[16] Ibid, para 75.

[17] Ibid, para 75, footnote 66.

[18] Article 27(2) of the UDHR provides that, "Everyone has the right to the protection of the moral and material interests resulting from any scientific, literary or artistic production of which he is the author." Article 15(1)(c) of the ICESCR is based largely on Article 27(2) of the UDHR and it provides that the states parties to the Covenant recognize the right of everyone to "benefit from the protection of the moral and material interests resulting from any scientific, literary or artistic production of which he is the author."

uncommon to find some scholars who equate the right to the protection of the moral and material interests of creators with the right to intellectual property.[19]

However, a critical examination of the history behind the drafting of Article 27(2) of the UDHR indicates that, at least for some of the countries that argued for the inclusion of this provision in the UDHR, it was aimed at protecting the labour rights of creators as "intellectual workers."[20] Thus, the provision is not intended to directly confer a right to intellectual property on creators but rather aimed at ensuring that the moral (i.e. the personal link between creators and their works) and material (or financial) interests of creators are secured.[21] States are thus free to secure these interests through any means they deem fit. This can be (and is typically) done via intellectual property laws. As Plomer points out, "Mexico's support for the inclusion of [Article 27(2)] on the protection of the rights of authors thus appeared to be primarily based on the assimilation of an individual's creations as a form of 'work' or labor to physical work or labor."[22] In the same vein, the UN Committee on Economic, Social and Cultural Rights (UN CESCR) in its General Comment No.17 on Article 15(1)(c) of the ICESCR has cautioned against equating intellectual property rights with the human right to the protection of the moral and material interests of creators.[23] Therefore, instead of interpreting Article 27(2) of the UDHR and Article 15(1)(c) of the ICESCR as conferring a right to intellectual property, it is suggested here that it is better to conceive of intellectual property rights

---

19 See for instance, Dean, "The Case for the Recognition of Intellectual Property in the Bill of Rights" (n 10) 109 (noting that Article 27(2) of the UDHR is "a clear enshrinement of the right of the individual to acquire and own IP").

20 This much can be gleaned from the speech by the Mexican delegate in support of the inclusion of a provision to protect the "material interests" of creators. According to the Mexican delegate, "The Committee had already recognized the rights of the wage earner, the family, the mother and the child; if it did not wish there to be a serious omission in the text it was drawing up it must now proclaim the rights of the individual as an intellectual worker, scientist or writer …". See, UN GAOR, "Draft International Declaration on Human Rights, Hundred and Fiftieth Meeting", 3d Sess., UN Doc. A/C.3/SR. 150 (1948) 617.

21 Lea Shaver, "The Right to Science and Culture" (2010) 1 *Wisconsin Law Review* 121, 150 (noting that, "Rather than enshrining a right to intellectual property, the 'protection' element [i.e. Article 27(2) of the UDHR] should be understood to refer only to the creator's right to obtain a decent standard of living from their work, and to preserve their moral rights of attribution and integrity").

22 Aurora Plomer, "The Human Rights Paradox: Intellectual Property Rights and Rights of Access to Science" (2013) 35 *Human Rights Quarterly* 143, 172.

23 UN CESCR, "General Comment No.17, The Right of Everyone to Benefit from the Protection of the Moral and Material Interests Resulting from any Scientific, Literary or Artistic Production of which He or She is the Author (Article 15, Paragraph 1(c), of the Covenant)", E/C.12/GC/17 (2006), para 3.

as one of the means that states can use to protect the moral and material interests of creators.[24] In other words, it is preferable to conceptualise intellectual property rights as a means to securing a human right end, i.e. protecting the moral and material interests of creators instead of conceptualising intellectual property rights as a human right in and of itself.

Secondly, the Constitutional Court noted that a right to intellectual property "is much more rarely recognised in regional conventions protecting human rights and in the constitutions of acknowledged democracies."[25] In support of its statement that a right to intellectual property is much more rarely recognised in regional conventions, the Court cited the fact that there is no provision protecting intellectual property in the American Convention on Human Rights, the Banjul Charter on Human and Peoples' Rights (i.e. African Charter), and the European Convention on Human Rights.[26] It should however be noted that, prior to the Constitutional Court's decision in this regard, the European Commission of Human Rights had held in 1990 that intellectual property rights are protected in Europe by virtue of Article 1 of Protocol 1 of the European Convention on Human Rights which deals with the right to property.[27] This approach has subsequently been affirmed by the European Court of Human Rights in a line of cases.[28] It should also be noted that Article 17(2) of the Charter of Fundamental Rights of the European Union (2000) now explicitly provides that "Intellectual property shall be protected."[29]

Thirdly, it is also important to note what the Constitutional Court did not say when it dismissed this objection. The Constitutional Court did not say that the reason for its decision in this regard was because the right to intellectual property is already contained in another provision of the proposed Constitution such as the provision dealing with the right to property (i.e. Section 25).

---

[24] See UN CESCR, General Comment No.17, ibid, para 16 (noting, among other things, that "the purpose of enabling authors to enjoy an adequate standard of living can also be achieved through one-time payments or by vesting an author, for a limited period of time, with the exclusive right to exploit his scientific, literary or artistic production").

[25] *Certification* case (n 4) para 75.

[26] Ibid, para 75, footnote 68.

[27] *Smith Kline and French Laboratories Ltd v. Netherlands*, 12633/87, Commission decision of 4 October 1990.

[28] See generally, *Melnychuk v. Ukraine*, 28743/03, ECHR 2005-IX; *Anheuser-Busch Inc. v. Portugal*, 73049/01, 11 January 2007; *Balan v. Moldova*, 19247/03, 29 January 2008.

[29] For a critical analysis of this provision, see, Christophe Geiger, "Intellectual Property shall be Protected!? Article 17(2) of the Charter of Fundamental Rights of the European Union: A Mysterious Provision with an Unclear Scope" (2009) 31:3 *European Intellectual Property Review* 113.

The Court was quite explicit that its rationale for dismissing the objection was because the recognition of a constitutional right to intellectual property "cannot be characterised as a trend which is universally accepted." Thus, the Constitutional Court did not endorse the view of the Constitutional Assembly that the right to intellectual property is already covered by the provision on the right to property. It is necessary to highlight this point because, over the years, a number of South African scholars have incorrectly read the decision of the Constitutional Court to mean that the provision on the right to property in the Constitution is broad enough to include the right to intellectual property.[30]

Ultimately, the proposed Constitution was adopted in 1996 without any specific provision on the right to intellectual property. However, the 1996 Constitution contains a number of civil and political rights such as the right to freedom of expression (Section 16) and the right to property (Section 25). The Constitution also contains economic and social rights such as the right to health (Section 27).

---

[30] See for instance Du Bois, "Intellectual Property as a Constitutional Property Right" (n 8) 178–179 (while discussing the *Certification* case, Du Bois (incorrectly and without citing any specific paragraph in the Constitutional Court's decision) notes that, "The Court concluded that the term 'property' is wide enough, when used in a generic property clause, to include rights and interests that require protection according to international human rights standards. Thus there is no need for a separate intellectual property clause, since the property clause can provide the necessary constitutional protection"). See also, Dean, "Deprivation of Trade Marks through State Interference in their Usage" (n 8) 586 (noting that, "The Constitutional Court in *In re: Certification of the Constitution of the Republic of South Africa, 1996* held that the right to hold intellectual property as a fundamental right did not require to be specifically addressed in the Constitution and implied that this was unnecessary as intellectual property was protected in terms of the property clause"). It should be noted that Dean was initially critical of the decision of the Constitutional Court in the *Certification* case and he was sceptical about relying on the property clause in the Constitution for the protection of intellectual property. In 1997, he had written that, "[i]n practical terms, Section 25 [which deals with the right to property] has no bearing whatsoever on IP as a fundamental right or in the regulation of its content or ownership". See, Dean, "The Case for the Recognition of Intellectual Property in the Bill of Rights" (n 10) 113. However, even Dean had incorrectly assumed in this 1997 article that the Constitutional Court shared the same view as the Constitutional Assembly regarding the property clause in the Bill of Rights. According to Dean, "it was the view of opinion-makers in the Constitutional Assembly that IP rights are protected by the property clause in the Bill of Rights. This view appeared to be shared by the Constitutional Court to the extent that the consideration by it of the IP rights issue was classified as an aspect of the overall debate about the property rights provision in the Bill of Rights." Ibid, 112.

2. SOUTH AFRICAN COURT DECISIONS ON THE INTERFACE BETWEEN INTELLECTUAL PROPERTY AND HUMAN RIGHTS AFTER 1996

After the adoption of the 1996 Constitution, South African courts have had the opportunity to deal with cases involving tensions between intellectual property rights and human rights. In some of these cases, the courts have also made some pronouncements on whether or not there is a constitutional right to intellectual property in South Africa. In this regard, this part of the chapter will focus on three cases that involve trademarks,[31] patents,[32] and copyright[33] respectively. The focus of the analysis below will be on what the courts said regarding the constitutional status of intellectual property rights in South Africa.

The first case that will be examined in this regard is the leading case of *Laugh It Off Promotions v. South African Breweries International*[34] (hereinafter, *Laugh It Off*) which involved a tension between trademarks and the right to freedom of expression. In this case, Laugh It Off had made parodic use of the trademarks belonging to South African Breweries and the latter sued the former for trademark dilution (relying on Section 34(1)(c) of the South African Trade Marks Act of 1993). Laugh It Off however contended that its parodic use of the trademarks should be protected by its right to freedom of expression guaranteed in Section 16 of the South African Constitution. South African Breweries won before the trial court and Laugh It Off lodged an appeal before the Supreme Court of Appeal of South Africa.

The Supreme Court of Appeal ultimately ruled in favour of South African Breweries.[35] What is however worth noting in this regard is what the Supreme Court of Appeal said about the constitutional status of intellectual property

---

[31] *Laugh It Off Promotions v. South African Breweries International*, Case No. 242/2003, decision of the Supreme Court of Appeal of South Africa (16 September 2004); *Laugh It Off Promotions v. South African Breweries International*, Case CCT 42/04, decision of the Constitutional Court of South Africa (27 May 2005).

[32] *Cipla Medpro v. Aventis Pharma* [2012] ZASCA 108, decision of the Supreme Court of Appeal (26 July 2012).

[33] *National Soccer League v. Gidani (Pty) Ltd*, Case No. 10/48519, decision of the High Court of South Africa, Gauteng Local Division, Johannesburg (28 February 2014).

[34] *Laugh It Off Promotions v. South African Breweries International*, Case No. 242/2003, decision of the Supreme Court of Appeal of South Africa (16 September 2004); *Laugh It Off Promotions v. South African Breweries International*, Case CCT 42/04, decision of the Constitutional Court of South Africa (27 May 2005).

[35] *Laugh It Off Promotions v. South African Breweries International*, Case No. 242/2003, decision of the Supreme Court of Appeal of South Africa (16 September 2004), paras 28, 41.

rights in South Africa. The Court noted that trademarks are intangible property.[36] However, it equally made it clear that "intellectual property rights have no special status" and that the South African Constitution "does not accord them special protection."[37] Thus, the Supreme Court of Appeal reaffirmed what the Constitutional Court had said about the constitutional status of intellectual property rights in the *Certification* case.

In addition, even though the Supreme Court of Appeal noted that intellectual property rights are intangible property, it did not state that they were intangible property protected by the right to property in Section 25 of the South African Constitution. In other words, intellectual property rights are property rights created by statutes, not by the Constitution. The Supreme Court of Appeal emphasised that the case required "a weighing-up of the freedom of expression and the trademark owner's rights of property."[38] However, it never said that the case required a weighing-up of the right to freedom of expression as enshrined in Section 16 of the Constitution and the right to property as enshrined in Section 25 of the Constitution. Clearly, the Supreme Court of Appeal only conceptualised the conflict as one between the constitutional right to freedom of expression and a statutory right to trademarks.

After losing at the Supreme Court of Appeal, Laugh It Off further appealed to the Constitutional Court of South Africa. The Constitutional Court eventually ruled in favour of Laugh It Off and in the process it equally made some important pronouncements on the constitutional status of intellectual property rights.[39] At the outset, it should be pointed out that the Constitutional Court equally framed the tension as one between a constitutional right (freedom of expression) and a statutory right (trademark) and not as a conflict between two constitutional rights (i.e. the right to freedom of expression and the right to property).[40] Crucially, the Constitutional Court acknowledged that the right to freedom of expression is not an absolute right in South Africa and it could be

---

36 Ibid, para 10.

37 Ibid, para 11.

38 Ibid, para 21.

39 *Laugh It Off Promotions v. South African Breweries International*, Case CCT 42/04, decision of the Constitutional Court of South Africa (27 May 2005), para 66.

40 Ibid, para 1 (the Constitutional Court noted per Moseneke J (who wrote the judgment for the Court) that "[t]his case brings to the fore the novel, and rather vexed, matter of the proper interface between the guarantee of free expression enshrined in section 16(1) of the Constitution and the protection of intellectual property rights attaching to registered trade marks as envisaged by section 34(1)(c) of the Trade Marks Act"). See also the concurring judgment of Sachs J noting that "The question to be asked is whether, looking at the facts as a whole, and analysing them in their specific context, an independent observer who is sensitive to both the free speech values of the Constitution and the property protection objectives of trademark law, would say that the

limited by the Constitution itself or a statute.[41] The Constitutional Court was however clear in noting that, in this case, the limitation of the right to freedom of expression was due to the anti-dilution provision in the Trade Marks Act[42] and not due to another right in the Constitution such as the right to property.

More importantly, the Constitutional Court agreed with the Supreme Court of Appeal that "intellectual property does not enjoy special status under the Constitution."[43] In support of this, the Constitutional Court cited its earlier decision in the *Certification* case.[44] Thus, it is instructive to note that when the Constitutional Court had the opportunity to do so, it reiterated and endorsed its earlier position with regard to the constitutional status of intellectual property, i.e. that there is no constitutional right to intellectual property.[45] Moreover, the Constitutional Court did not say that the right to property in Section 25 of the Constitution covers or applies to intellectual property rights.[46]

The next important case that is worth examining in this regard is the decision of the Supreme Court of Appeal of South Africa in the case of *Cipla Medpro v. Aventis Pharma*.[47] In this case, Aventis was seeking an interim interdict to prevent Cipla from infringing its patent relating to an anti-cancer drug. Cipla equally sought to revoke one of the key claims of this patent on the grounds, inter alia, that it lacked clarity, novelty, and inventive step.[48] Ultimately, the

---

harm done by the parody to the property interests of the trademark owner outweighs the free speech interests involved." Ibid, para 82.

41 Ibid, para 47.

42 Ibid, paras 47–48 (according to Moseneke J, "Plainly, the right to free expression in our Constitution is neither paramount over other guaranteed rights nor limitless … In appropriate circumstances authorised by the Constitution itself, a law of general application may limit freedom of expression. It is so that the anti-dilution prohibition under Section 34(1)(c) [of the Trade Marks Act] seeks, in effect, to oust certain expressive conduct in relation to registered marks with repute").

43 Ibid, para 17.

44 Ibid, para 17, footnote 11.

45 *Cf.* Du Bois, "Intellectual Property as a Constitutional Property Right" (n 8) 188 (incorrectly noting without any citation that the decision in *Laugh It Off*, at least in relation to trademarks, "may be considered authority for the statement that intellectual property rights may be recognised and protected under the constitutional property clause").

46 *Cf.* Dean, "Deprivation of Trade Marks through State Interference in their Usage" (n 8) 586 (ignoring what the Constitutional Court said to the effect that intellectual property does not enjoy special status under the Constitution and incorrectly noting that in *Laugh It Off*, "the Constitutional Court held that the right to freedom of expression … and intellectual property (more specifically trade marks) enjoyed equal status under the Constitution").

47 *Cipla Medpro v. Aventis Pharma* (n 32).

48 Ibid, para 19.

Supreme Court of Appeal ruled in favour of Aventis by upholding the validity of the patent and granting an interim interdict against Cipla.[49]

The aspect of the decision of the Supreme Court of Appeal that is most relevant to the analysis here is the Court's treatment of the framing of the dispute between the two parties as one between patent rights and the right to health. This framing had been done by Treatment Action Campaign (a South African NGO involved in issues relating to access to medicines) that had been admitted to the case as *amicus curiae*.[50] In opposing Aventis' application for an interim interdict, Treatment Action Campaign invoked Section 27 of the South African Constitution which provides for the right to health and it contended that the Patents Act must be interpreted through the prism of the Constitution and in a manner that correctly balances the rights of a patentee against the constitutional rights of others.[51] It should be noted that Treatment Action Campaign did not frame this dispute as a tension between the right to health and the right to property but as a conflict between the right to health and the Patents Act.

The Supreme Court of Appeal did not object to the manner in which the dispute was framed by Treatment Action Campaign. Citing Section 39(2) of the South African Constitution, the Court noted that it is indeed required to promote the spirit, purport and objects of the Bill of Rights when interpreting any legislation.[52] The Supreme Court of Appeal however held that this "does not open the door to changing the clear meaning of a statute" and it was not convinced that interpreting the Patents Act through the prism of the Constitution should "deny Aventis its right to enforce its patent."[53] Thus, while the Court accepted the framing of the dispute by Treatment Action Campaign, it was not persuaded that this should lead to the refusal to grant an interim interdict in this case. Importantly however, the Court did not try to correct the framing of the dispute as a tension between patent rights and the right to health. Crucially, the Court did not reframe the dispute as a tension between the right to health and the right to property.

The final important case that will be examined is the decision of the High Court in *National Soccer League v. Gidani (Pty) Ltd*[54] which relates to a copyright dispute. In this case, the plaintiff (National Soccer League) sued the

[49] Ibid, paras 25–28, 40, 62.

[50] Ibid, para 43.

[51] Ibid, para 44.

[52] Ibid, para 45. Section 39(2) of the South African Constitution provides that: "When interpreting any legislation, and when developing the common law or customary law, every court, tribunal or forum must promote the spirit, purport and objects of the Bill of Rights."

[53] *Cipla Medpro v. Aventis Pharma* (n 32) para 45.

[54] *National Soccer League v. Gidani (Pty) Ltd* (n 33).

defendant (Gidani) for infringing its copyright in its soccer fixtures which the defendant had been using in its sport stake betting business without licence or permission.[55] The defendant contended, inter alia, that its use of the fixture was protected by the right to freedom of expression. Specifically, the defendant relied on Section 16(1)(b) of the South African Constitution which deals with the freedom to receive or impart information or ideas.[56] Ultimately, the Court ruled in favour of the plaintiff and it noted that the defendant did not seek to "inform the public, but to profit from the public by inviting it to participate in its gambling game."[57]

However, in arriving at its decision, the High Court noted that the "plaintiff's property rights are also entrenched and protected in the Constitution" and it cited Section 25(1) of the Constitution to support its view in this regard.[58] The High Court did not provide any elaboration regarding this line of reasoning. It is not entirely clear how the High Court arrived at this conclusion, although one can presume that the Court must have conflated the fact that copyright is an intangible property right with the right to property in the Constitution.

It is suggested here that the High Court's statement with regard to the constitutional status of copyright was made *per incuriam* as it goes against the clear and consistent rulings of the Constitutional Court in both the *Certification* and *Laugh It Off* cases. As noted above, in both cases, the Constitutional Court affirmed that there is no constitutional right to intellectual property and that intellectual property does not enjoy a special status under the Constitution. Crucially, the High Court failed to critically engage with what the Constitutional Court has said in previous cases about the constitutional status of intellectual property rights. Moreover, it was unnecessary for the High Court to invoke the constitutional right to property in order to rule in favour of the plaintiff in this case.

3. TOBACCO, TRADEMARKS, AND THE DEBATES CONCERNING A CONSTITUTIONAL RIGHT TO INTELLECTUAL PROPERTY IN SOUTH AFRICA

Some South African scholars have contended that intellectual property rights are recognised by the South African Constitution because Section 25(4)(b) of the Constitution provides that property for the purposes of Section 25 is "not

---

55 Ibid, para 1.

56 Ibid, para 98.

57 Ibid, para 109.

58 Ibid, para 105. Section 25(1) of the South African Constitution provides that: "No one may be deprived of property except in terms of law of general application, and no law may permit arbitrary deprivation of property."

limited to land."[59] This could possibly be construed as including intellectual property rights within the framework of the constitutional right to property in Section 25 of the Constitution. It should be stressed that this particular view has not been endorsed by the Constitutional Court in any of the cases considered above. However, even if one takes the view that intellectual property rights fall within the scope of the right to property because of Section 25(4)(b), that does not mean that intellectual property rights cannot be limited by the state in order to achieve certain societal objectives. As Mikhalien Du Bois rightly points out:

> If intellectual property is recognised as constitutional property, it could be protected, but also limited by the property guarantee, just like tangible property such as land. The state is permitted to interfere with property rights in terms of the provisions in section 25(1) to (3) for deprivation and expropriation. Intellectual property rights may furthermore be limited by public interests such as the public domain and private interests such as the right to freedom of expression. In other words, the property clause cannot serve to insulate intellectual property rights completely. Like all rights, property rights may also be limited by s 36 of the Bill of Rights.[60]

Thus, even if intellectual property rights including trademarks are regarded as protected by the right to property, this should not necessarily stop the South African government from implementing plain packaging measures to curb the consumption of tobacco products in the country. In this regard, the provisions of the Constitution that can be used to challenge the implementation of plain packaging measures are Section 25(1) which deals with deprivation of property and Section 25(2) which deals with expropriation of property.[61] Section 25(1) provides that: "No one may be deprived of property except in terms of law of general application, and no law may permit arbitrary deprivation of property." Section 25(2) provides that:

> Property may be expropriated only in terms of law of general application—
> (a) for a public purpose or in the public interest; and

---

[59] See for instance, Du Bois, "Intellectual Property as a Constitutional Property Right" (n 8) 185.

[60] Ibid, 177.

[61] For instance, Dean has contended that, "South African legislation that prevents or prohibits the use of trade marks on tobacco products infringes both s.25(1) and (2) of the Constitution in that such legislation will bring about an arbitrary deprivation of property, and indeed an expropriation of such property, at least as a manifestation of constructive expropriation." See, Dean, "Deprivation of Trade Marks through State Interference in their Usage" (n 8) 581.

(b) subject to compensation, the amount of which and the time and manner of payment of which have either been agreed to by those affected or decided or approved by a court.

Addressing the question concerning whether or not Section 25 of the Constitution can be used to prevent the South African government from implementing plain packaging measures has become more pertinent because, in May 2018, the South African Department of Health published a draft bill that would introduce plain packaging in South Africa if passed into law. The bill is titled the draft Control of Tobacco Products and Electronic Delivery Systems Bill of 2018. Borrowing a leaf from countries such as Australia that have equally implemented such measures,[62] the bill mandates the South African Minister of Health to introduce regulations that provide for standardised packaging and labelling of tobacco products.[63] Specifically, the bill provides that the regulations to be introduced by the Minister of Health must at least prescribe, among other things, that: the packaging of a tobacco product must have a uniform plain colour and texture; any branding, logos or other promotional elements on, inside or attached to the packaging or on an individual tobacco product is prohibited; and, only the brand name and product name may appear on packaging in a standard colour and typeface, together with other mandatory information such as health warnings.[64] The bill also prohibits the use of false, misleading or deceptive packaging or labelling of tobacco products (including through the use of trademarks) that creates any erroneous impression about, inter alia, the composition and health effects of such tobacco products.[65]

---

[62] See, Tobacco Plain Packaging Act 2011 (Cth). This law was unsuccessfully challenged by tobacco companies at the national level (*JT International SA v. Commonwealth of Australia* [2012] HCA 43) and before an international investment tribunal (*Philip Morris Asia Limited v. The Commonwealth of Australia*, PCA Case No. 2012-12, Award on Jurisdiction and Admissibility (17 December 2015)). The law was equally unsuccessfully challenged at the WTO (WTO, *Australia—Certain Measures Concerning Trademarks, Geographical Indications and Other Plain Packaging Requirements Applicable to Tobacco Products and Packaging*, Panel Report, WT/DS435/R, WT/DS441/R, WT/DS458/R, WT/DS467/R (28 June 2018)). The implementation of the Standardised Packaging of Tobacco Products Regulations 2015 by the UK government was also unsuccessfully challenged by some tobacco companies. See, *R (British American Tobacco UK Ltd) v. Health Secretary* [2016] EWCA Civ 1182.

[63] Section 4(1) of the draft Control of Tobacco Products and Electronic Delivery Systems Bill of 2018.

[64] Section 4(2)(a), (d) and (e) of the draft Control of Tobacco Products and Electronic Delivery Systems Bill of 2018.

[65] Section 4(4) of the draft Control of Tobacco Products and Electronic Delivery Systems Bill of 2018 provides that:

It is contended here that the implementation of plain packaging measures would not amount to an expropriation of the trademark rights of tobacco companies. This is because the Constitutional Court has held in *Agri South Africa v. Minister for Minerals and Energy* that, in order to prove expropriation, "a claimant must establish that the state has acquired the substance or core content of what it was deprived of."[66] According to the Constitutional Court, there is no expropriation "where deprivation does not result in property being acquired by the state."[67] Thus, as plain packaging measures do not require the state to acquire the trademark rights of tobacco companies, implementing such measures cannot amount to an expropriation.

The most pertinent provision with regard to plain packaging measures is therefore Section 25(1) of the Constitution which deals with the deprivation of property. Essentially, this provision prohibits the deprivation of property except by a law of general application which must not be a law that permits the arbitrary deprivation of property. In *First National Bank v. Commissioner, South African Revenue Service*, the Constitutional Court defined deprivation as "any interference with the use, enjoyment or exploitation of private prop-

---

> No person shall manufacture for sale in the Republic, import or sell a tobacco product that has packaging or labeling that is false, misleading, deceptive or likely to create any erroneous, deceptive or misleading impression about its characteristics, properties, health effects, toxicity, composition, merit, safety, hazards or emissions, including any term, descriptor, trade mark, figurative, colour, number or other sign that directly or indirectly creates the impression that a particular tobacco product—
> (a) is less harmful than another tobacco product;
> (b) aims to reduce the effect of any harmful content of the product or its smoke;
> (c) has vitalising, energising, healing, rejuvenating, natural or organic properties or has other health or lifestyle benefits;
> (d) has a taste, smell or any flavouring or other additive that is prohibited by any law or that any such taste, smell, flavouring or additive is absent in a particular tobacco product; or
> (e) resembles a food or a cosmetic product.

[66] *Agri South Africa v. Minister for Minerals and Energy*, Case CCT 51/12, [2013] ZACC 9, para 58.

[67] Ibid, para 59. See also, Louis Harms, "Plain Packaging and its Impact on Trademark Law" (2013) *De Jure* 387, 397 (regarding the meaning of expropriation, Harms notes that, "[o]ur courts interpret the word as requiring not only dispossession or deprivation but also appropriation by the expropriator (on behalf of itself or another party) of the particular right"). See also, Van der Walt and Shay (n 8) 62 (noting that, "[g]iven the fact that the state would seldom acquire intellectual property interests through regulatory legislation, there seems to be very little chance of constructive expropriation in this area").

erty."[68] There is a debate amongst South African scholars regarding whether or not the implementation of plain packaging measures would amount to an expropriation of trademark rights.[69] However, even if one assumes that the implementation of plain packaging measures would amount to a deprivation, the key question is whether such measures would amount to an arbitrary deprivation of property. In *First National Bank v. Commissioner, South African Revenue Service*,[70] the Constitutional Court held that a deprivation of property is arbitrary when the law "does not provide sufficient reason for the particular deprivation in question or is procedurally unfair."[71] As Du Bois points out, the implementation of plain packaging measures would not be arbitrary because "the furtherance of public health should constitute a sufficient reason."[72]

In *First National Bank*, the Constitutional Court provided some elaboration on how "sufficient reason" can be determined, and it provided a list of factors to be considered in this regard:

> (a) It is to be determined by evaluating the relationship between means employed, namely the deprivation in question, and ends sought to be achieved, namely the purpose of the law in question. (b) A complexity of relationships has to be considered. (c) In evaluating the deprivation in question, regard must be had to the relationship between the purpose for the deprivation and the person whose property is affected. (d) In addition, regard must be had to the relationship between the purpose

---

68 *First National Bank v. Commissioner, South African Revenue Service*, Case CCT 19/01, [2002] ZACC 5, para 57. See however the subsequent case of *Mkontwana v. Nelson Mandela Metropolitan Municipality*, Case CCT 57/03, [2004] ZACC 9, para 32, where the Constitutional Court mentions *substantial* interference rather than *any* interference. According to the Constitutional Court in this latter case, "Whether there has been a deprivation depends on the extent of the interference with or limitation of use, enjoyment or exploitation. It is not necessary in this case to determine precisely what constitutes deprivation. No more need be said than that at the very least, substantial interference or limitation that goes beyond the normal restrictions on property use or enjoyment found in an open and democratic society would amount to deprivation."

69 Dean contends that "[r]estricting the use of a trade mark, let alone the complete extinguishing of an item of property, clearly falls within the scope of deprivation in this context." See, Dean, "Deprivation of Trade Marks through State Interference in their Usage" (n 8) 586. Van der Walt and Shay equally contend that, "regulatory limitations imposed on intellectual property interests would generally constitute deprivations of property for the purposes of section 25(1)." See, Van der Walt and Shay (n 8) 56. For a contrary view see, Harms (n 67) 397 (contending that "plain packaging law does not deprive the trademark owner of any trademark right but only regulates or limits the exercise of that right").

70 *First National Bank v. Commissioner, South African Revenue Service* (n 68).

71 Ibid, para 100.

72 Mikhalien Du Bois, "Trade Marks for Tobacco Products as Constitutional Property: Australian Plain Packaging Legislation" (2013) 25 *South African Mercantile Law Journal* 197, 220 at footnote 129.

> of the deprivation and the nature of the property as well as the extent of the deprivation in respect of such property. (e) Generally speaking, where the property in question is ownership of land or a corporeal moveable, a more compelling purpose will have to be established in order for the depriving law to constitute sufficient reason for the deprivation, than in the case when the property is something different, and the property right something less extensive … (f) Generally speaking, when the deprivation in question embraces all the incidents of ownership, the purpose for the deprivation will have to be more compelling than when the deprivation embraces only some incidents of ownership and those incidents only partially. (g) Depending on such interplay between variable means and ends, the nature of the property in question and the extent of its deprivation, there may be circumstances when sufficient reason is established by, in effect, no more than a mere rational relationship between means and ends; in others this might only be established by a proportionality evaluation closer to that required by section 36(1) of the Constitution. (h) Whether there is sufficient reason to warrant the deprivation is a matter to be decided on all the relevant facts of each particular case, always bearing in mind that the enquiry is concerned with "arbitrary" in relation to the deprivation of property under section 25.[73]

Importantly, the Court noted that, depending on the circumstances, sufficient reason can be established by either a "rational relationship" standard or a "proportionality evaluation" standard. It is contended here that, whichever standard is applied to the plain packaging measures in the draft Control of Tobacco Products and Electronic Delivery Systems Bill, these measures would not amount to an arbitrary deprivation.

As indicated in the preamble to the Bill, the proposed measures are aimed at deterring people from using tobacco products due to the extent of the harmful effects of the use of such products. The measures are also aimed at protecting non-smokers from exposure to tobacco product emissions and to encourage existing users of tobacco products to quit. The preamble also indicates that the proposed law is aimed at aligning the South African health system with the democratic values of the Constitution and the World Health Organization's Framework Convention on Tobacco Control (FCTC),[74] to which South Africa is a party. In this regard, it is worth noting that the South African government has a constitutional obligation to protect the right to health of its citizens by virtue of Section 27 of the South African Constitution.[75] Thus, the purpose of

---

[73] *First National Bank v. Commissioner, South African Revenue Service* (n 68) para 100.

[74] The FCTC imposes obligations on state parties with regard to the packaging and labelling of tobacco products (Article 11) and the advertising, promotion and sponsorship of tobacco products (Article 13).

[75] Section 27 of the South African Constitution provides that:
(1) Everyone has the right to have access to—(a) health care services, including reproductive health care; (b) sufficient food and water; and (c) social security,

the proposed law is to protect the health of South Africans and comply with international obligations. Moreover, with regard to the nature of the property, intellectual property rights only confer a negative right to exclude third parties and not a positive right to use. Thus, the proposed plain packaging measures do not interfere with the right of trademark owners to exclude third parties from using their marks. It is therefore suggested here that, with regard to the proposed measures, sufficient reason for the deprivation can be established by mere rational relationship between means and ends.

However, even if "a proportionality evaluation closer to that required by Section 36(1) of the Constitution"[76] is applied, this should still not lead to the conclusion that the proposed measures constitute an arbitrary deprivation of trademark rights. This view is supported by the decision of the Supreme Court of Appeal of South Africa in *British American Tobacco South Africa (Pty) Limited v. Minister of Health.*[77] This case concerned section 3(1)(a) of the Tobacco Products Control Act of 1993 as amended by the Tobacco Products Amendment Act of 2008 which prohibits the advertisement or promotion of tobacco products. The key question was whether the limitation of the right to freedom of expression of British American Tobacco South Africa (BATSA) by virtue of this law could be justified by Section 36(1) of the Constitution.[78] The Supreme Court of Appeal noted that it had to "engage in a balancing exercise on the basis of proportionality."[79] In this regard, the Court held that:

> The Minister has in my view established that the prohibition on advertising and promotion of tobacco products is reasonable and justified. There can be no question

---

including, if they are unable to support themselves and their dependants, appropriate social assistance.
(2) The state must take reasonable legislative and other measures, within its available resources, to achieve the progressive realisation of each of these rights.
(3) No one may be refused emergency medical treatment.

76 Section 36(1) of the South African Constitution provides that:
The rights in the Bill of Rights may be limited only in terms of law of general application to the extent that the limitation is reasonable and justifiable in an open and democratic society based on human dignity, equality and freedom, taking into account all relevant factors, including—
(a) the nature of the right;
(b) the importance of the purpose of the limitation;
(c) the nature and extent of the limitation;
(d) the relation between the limitation and its purpose; and
(e) less restrictive means to achieve the purpose.

77 *British American Tobacco South Africa (Pty) Limited v. Minister of Health*, Case No. 463/2011, [2012] ZASCA 107 (20 June 2012).

78 Ibid, para 14.

79 Ibid, para 16.

> that government has an obligation to protect its citizens from the ravages of tobacco use. Smoking is undoubtedly hazardous and has an adverse effect on health care. In terms of section 27(1) of the Constitution everyone has the right to have access to health care services which the State is obliged to provide and to carry the costs of, if necessary. All of these facts highlight the purpose, the importance and the effect of the limitation. The impugned prohibition is targeted at any member of the public, amongst whom are consenting adult smokers. As I have already pointed out, there are also those that are trapped in the habit of smoking and wish to rid themselves of it and those that have given up and do not wish to go back to old habits. Although I do not consider that there are less restrictive means available to enforce the impugned provisions, it is not possible to carve out an exception from the prohibition of the use of tobacco … In the circumstances a blanket ban on advertising and promotion is, to my mind, the only way to address the issue—an objective the impugned prohibition seeks to achieve.[80]

In arriving at its decision in this case, the Court also took into account the fact that South Africa is a party to the FCTC which (in its Article 13) obliges state parties to adopt measures to prohibit the advertising and promotion of tobacco products.[81] Therefore, whether the mere "rational relationship" standard is applied or the "proportionality evaluation" standard is applied, it is unlikely that a court would hold that the proposed plain packaging measures constitute an arbitrary deprivation of property.

A final issue that is worth addressing is whether or not the proposed plain packaging measures violate South Africa's obligations under the World Trade Organization's (WTO) Agreement on Trade-Related Aspects of Intellectual Property Rights (TRIPS Agreement). However, given the decision of the WTO Dispute Settlement Panel in the *Australian Plain Packaging* case,[82] where certain countries challenged similar measures introduced by Australia

---

[80] Ibid, para 26.

[81] According to the Supreme Court of Appeal, "South Africa is a signatory to the Framework Convention on Tobacco Control … South Africa ratified the Framework Convention on 19 November 2005. In relation to advertising the Framework Convention imposes clear obligations on State parties. Article 13 of the Framework Convention provides: 'Each Party shall, in accordance with its constitution or constitutional principles, undertake a comprehensive ban of all tobacco advertising, promotion and sponsorship.' I do not think that it was open to the Minister and the legislature to ignore the Framework Convention when considering what steps to take to deal with the risks posed by tobacco use … [I]n determining whether or not to impose a ban on advertising and promotion of tobacco products the Minister would have been obliged to have regard to the Framework Convention. This Court is therefore obliged, under the Constitution, to give weight to it in determining the question of justification or the limitation of the right to freedom of speech." See, *British American Tobacco South Africa (Pty) Limited v. Minister of Health*, ibid, para 23.

[82] See, WTO, *Australia—Certain Measures Concerning Trademarks, Geographical Indications and Other Plain Packaging Requirements Applicable to Tobacco Products*

and the Panel ruled in favour of Australia, it can be strongly argued that South Africa's proposed measures are TRIPS-compliant. It should be noted that Australia's plain packaging law essentially permits only the use of word marks in prescribed form on retail packaging of tobacco products and it prohibits stylized word marks, figurative marks and composite marks on retail packaging of tobacco products. Nevertheless, the WTO Panel held that the law did not violate Article 20 of the TRIPS Agreement which prohibits the imposition of unjustifiable encumbrances on the use of trademarks in the course of trade.[83]

4. CONCLUSION

In sum, this chapter has critically re-examined the decision of the Constitutional Court of South Africa in the *Certification* case. In that case, the objection against the proposed Constitution on the grounds of a failure to recognise a right to intellectual property was dismissed by the Constitutional Court on the grounds that the recognition of a right to intellectual property cannot be considered as a trend that is universally accepted. Importantly, the Constitutional Court did not endorse the view that the right to intellectual property is already protected by the right to property in the proposed Constitution. Moreover, in its subsequent decision in *Laugh It Off*, the Constitutional Court reiterated and endorsed its earlier view that intellectual property does not enjoy a special status under the South African Constitution. Nevertheless, this chapter has equally contended that, even if one assumes that intellectual

---

and Packaging, Panel Report, WT/DS435/R, WT/DS441/R, WT/DS458/R, WT/DS467/R (28 June 2018).

[83] Ibid, paras 7.2604–7.2605. According to the Panel, "While recognizing that trademarks have substantial economic value and that the special requirements are far-reaching in terms of the trademark owners' possibilities to extract economic value from the use of figurative or stylized features of trademarks, we note that the TPP [i.e. tobacco plain packaging] measures, including their trademark restrictions, are an integral part of Australia's comprehensive tobacco control policies, and designed to complement the pre-existing measures. As noted above, the fact that the special requirements, as part of the overall TPP measures and in combination with other tobacco-control measures maintained by Australia, are capable of contributing, and do in fact contribute, to Australia's objective of improving public health by reducing the use of, and exposure to, tobacco products, suggests that the reasons for which these special requirements are applied provide sufficient support for the application of the resulting encumbrances on the use of trademarks. We further note that Australia, while having been the first country to implement tobacco plain packaging, has pursued its relevant domestic public health objective in line with the emerging multilateral public health policies in the area of tobacco control as reflected in the FCTC and the work under its auspices, including the Article 11 and Article 13 FCTC Guidelines." Ibid, para 7.2604.

property is covered by the constitutional right to property, this should not impede the South African government from implementing measures aimed at achieving certain societal objectives. Thus, contrary to what some scholars have suggested, the implementation of plain packaging measures in South Africa should not amount to either an arbitrary deprivation or expropriation of property rights in trademarks.

13. The biotechnology sector in India

Kshitij Kumar Singh

1. INTRODUCTION

The biotechnology sector in India has been shaped by legislative and policy initiatives with significant institutional developments. India continues to value the potential of biotechnology to make a significant contribution in the health and agriculture sectors, and in terms of environmental sustainability and economic progress. The legislative initiatives to promote and regulate biotechnology include the IP legislations, environmental legislations, agricultural legislations and related regulations. The regulatory framework involves a number of regulatory bodies operating through a complex web of legislation. Government policies have been encouraging the biotechnology sector with remarkable initiatives encompassing tax deductions, fund raising, special schemes for start-ups, micro, small and medium enterprises (MSMEs), and academic and research institutions. These initiatives have shaped biotechnology as an organised sector with well-defined sub-sectors such as biopharmaceuticals, bio-agriculture, bio-services, bio-industry and bioinformatics. Biopharmaceuticals has remained the most dominant sub-sector of biotechnology, catering to the medicinal and health needs of the people in the face of great challenges posed by ensuring accessibility and affordability. Though the results produced by almost all the sub-sectors have been well received by the public, in the bio-agriculture sector, however, public perception largely governs the decisions as to the regulatory approval of GM food crops, and many a time it has been backed by a non-scientific opposition involving numerous farmer organisations, NGOs and other activists.

The IP landscape in India came to prominence through Patent Amendments made to comply with the TRIPS Agreement in 1999, 2002 and 2005. Though India secured its protectionist approach by utilising the flexibilities under the TRIPS agreement in drafting IP legislations, a few of the provisions of IP laws have still remained contentious, for example section 3(d) of the Patents Act 1970, which is aimed at curbing the evergreening of patents. The overlapping of two important legislations on common subject matter, viz. the Patents Act 1970 and the Protection of Plant Varieties and Farmers' Rights Act

(PPVFRA), creates enormous confusion as to their application. In recent times, India has adopted a progressive approach to biotechnology on all the fronts, for example: the Indian Patent Office has started absorbing the new realities in the biotech sector by explaining the inherent flexibilities in the patent system through guidelines; the Indian judiciary seems to recognise the distinct nature of biotechnology and its contribution in innovation; and governments (both central and state) have launched major initiatives to promote innovation through patent facilitation centres, concession schemes for start-ups and MSMEs. However, the constant focus on protecting patients and farmers against the monopoly rights of IP holders and the alleged dilution of technicalities of patents in favour of public interest has been questioned by IP proponents for the want of innovation and respect for IP laws. Moreover, because of the ambiguities in the statutory provisions, though explained through patent guidelines, a fair amount of discretion remains with the Indian Patent Office (IPO) authorities to determine the scope of protection for inventions. Against this background, this chapter attempts to revisit the legal and policy lore in the biotech sector in India and analyse the legal and policy orientations thus far established to meet the challenges in this sector. The special focus is on the policy paradigm of the biotech-IP discourse in India.

2. THE EVOLUTION AND DEVELOPMENT OF INDIA'S BIOTECHNOLOGY SECTOR

India stands among those rare countries of the developing world which realised the potential of biotechnology as a tool to boost economic growth in important sectors such as agriculture and health. The Government of India launched great policy initiatives in numerous Five Year Plans[1] long before it provided IP protection to biotechnology inventions. India came up with the first policy document to cover biotechnology development in the Sixth Five-Year Plan (1980–85) with the object of shaping it as an industry. It established an independent department, the Department of Biotechnology in 1986 well before

---

[1] Five-Year Plans were the centralised economic growth programs based on the idea of "plan[ning] public spending for equitable growth rather than leaving expenditure to the marketplace". Five-Year Plans started in 1951 with the First Five-Year Plan (1951–1956) and laid to rest after the Twelfth Five-Year Plan (2012–2017). Five-Year Plans were eventually replaced by the three-year action plan. The Niti Ayog has replaced the Planning Commission, a body responsible for giving policy direction; *The end of Five-Year Plans: All you need to know about this big policy change* The Economic Times Online (April 13, 2017) https://economictimes.indiatimes.com/news/economy/policy/the-end-of-five-year-plans-all-you-need-to-know-about-this-big-policy-change/articleshow/58162236.cms (last visited January 17, 2020)

"biotechnology" became a buzzword.[2] However, the seeds of "need-based innovation" in agriculture were sown in the Third Five-Year Plan, setting the platform for a "Green Revolution". Although this Green Revolution guided the route of agricultural biotechnology, the latter established a much wider goal of innovation. Specifically, the Sixth Five-Year Plan was focused on strengthening and developing capabilities in areas such as immunology, genetics, communicable diseases, etc., providing a pathway for biotechnology advancements.

The Indian biotechnology sector aims to find affordable solutions to pressing national needs as well as remain competitive and innovative. India's policy initiatives pertaining to biotechnology have yielded remarkable results as it registered an eight-fold growth from the Eighth Five-Year Plan to the Eleventh Five-Year Plan.[3] In addition to central government, state governments undertook great policy initiatives encompassing tax concessions and the establishment of biotech parks and incubators, ensuring significant investments in the biotechnology sector.[4] There has been a significant increase in the scientific workforce. Due to early initiative taken by the government in the biotechnology sector, a very significant bioinformatics programme termed the Biotechnology Information System (BTISnet-BioGrid India) was also introduced as early as 1986–87. This System has progressed so well that it currently boasts more than 150 bioinformatics centres located across the country.[5]

2.1 Contribution of the Green Revolution and Five-Year Plans to shaping the Biotechnology Sector in India

The "Green Revolution"[6] has been considered as a precursor of the "biotech era"[7] in India but the latter differs from the former on various counts. The

---

2 S. Natesh and M.K. Bhan, *Biotechnology Sector in India: Strengths, Limitations, Remedies and Outlook*, 97:2 Current Science 157–169 (2009), https://www.jstor.org/stable/24111912?seq=1 (last visited January 17, 2020).

3 Ibid.

4 Ibid.

5 Ibid.

6 The Green Revolution reflects a great increase in the production of food grains, especially wheat and rice with the introduction of new high yielding varieties. The Revolution started in the 20th century, registering huge success in Mexico and the Indian Subcontinent. The flipside of these varieties was that they required large amounts of chemical fertilizers and pesticides to produce high yields, raising cost issues and environmental concerns. Encyclopedia Britannica, https://www.britannica.com/event/green-revolution (last visited January 17, 2020).

7 In an interview Norman Borlaug explained how the Green Revolution started: "It started in the 1940s when I joined a new program, funded by the Rockefeller

distinction lies in areas such as the nature and complexity of policy narratives relating to agriculture, food security and poverty; the network of actors; the location of experts and sites of policy making; and the nature and extent of policy debate and dissent.[8] There has been a paradigm shift in emphasis from "national food self-sufficiency and nation building" to a "liberalised, unequal and uncertain global market economy". The focus was shifted from Cold War security concerns to liberalisation and trade issues. Although much emphasis has been given to the Green Revolution as precursor to similar advances in biotechnology in policy rhetoric in India and internationally, caution should be exercised in extrapolating too much from this.[9] In India the Green Revolution steered a path through the introduction of dwarf wheat varieties imported from Mexico which demonstrated the potential for high crop yield increases and kick-started a major technological boost to the agricultural sector. The biotechnology era, through transgenic technologies, expanded this promise to multidimensional results encompassing higher yields, reduced pest and disease incidence, and resistance to stresses of various sorts, from drought to salinity to poor soil fertility. One of the features common to both the Green Revolution and the biotechnology era was the realisation that scientific and technological revolution coupled with increased collaborative research partnerships would set the future development goals.[10]

The seeds of the Green Revolution were sown against the backdrop of India's independence and in the midst of the Cold War. With the realisation of the ideals of "Swaraj" (self-rule) coupled with "Swadeshi" (of one's own country) and a great sense of nation building, the achievement of national

---

Foundation, aimed at assisting poor farmers in Mexico to increase their wheat production." He also spoke about biotechnology: "Biotechnology will help these countries accomplish things that they could never do with conventional plant breeding. The technology is more precise and farming becomes less time consuming." AgBioWorld, *Biotechnology and the Green Revolution: An interview with Norman Borlaug*, http://www.agbioworld.org/biotech-info/topics/borlaug/bioscience.html (last visited January 17, 2020).

[8] Shaila Seshia and Ian Scoones, *Tracing Policy Connections: The Politics of Knowledge in the Green Revolution and Biotechnology Eras in India*, IDS Working Paper 188 (June, 2003), https://www.ids.ac.uk/files/Wp188.pdf (last visited January 17, 2020).

[9] Ibid.

[10] Ibid.

self-sufficiency was set as the most important goal. In this context, India's First Prime Minister observed:

> The objective for the country as a whole was the attainment as far as possible of national self-sufficiency. International trade was certainly not excluded, but we were anxious to avoid being drawn into a whirlpool of economic imperialism ...[11]

This reflects the Nehruian socialism that permits a controlled or cautious participation in international trade with a strong focus on national self-sufficiency. In line with this approach, India pursued a policy of "import-substitution industrialisation" (ISI) under Nehru and his chief economic advisor, P.C. Mahalanabois. With the due recognition of agriculture as an important sector and achieving self-sufficiency in food as a significant object, Indian planners prioritised industrialisation as the ultimate objective. During this time, in the mid-1950s, the Rockefeller Foundation supported India with scientific advisors and funds to increase cereal production and improve the Indian Agricultural Research Foundation.[12] However, it was only in the Third Five-Year Plan that agriculture gained prominence under the leadership of India's Second Prime Minister, Lal Bahadur Shastri and his Minister of Agriculture, C. Subramaniam. The Shastri-Subramaniam period was responsible for numerous institutional initiatives, for example the reorganisation of the Indian Council of Agricultural Research (ICAR) in 1965; the creation of agricultural universities and all-India agricultural research projects; and the formation of the National Seeds Corporation and Agricultural Finance Corporation.[13] This period had set the agricultural sector to give a kick-start to the Green Revolution. Emphasising self-sufficiency, Prime Minister Shastri observed:

> I consider self-sufficiency in food to be no less important than an impregnable defence system for the preservation of our freedom and independence ... In the present emergency ... every bit of land should be cultivated.[14]

Green Revolution technologies were well received by the public with increased crop yields and the achievement of self-reliance with regard to certain crops.[15]

---

[11] Jawaharlal Nehru, *The Discovery of India*, New Delhi: Jawaharlal Nehru Memorial Fund and Oxford University Press 398 (1946), cited in Seshia and Scoones, *supra* note 8.

[12] Seshia and Scoones, *supra* note 8.

[13] Ibid.

[14] Lal Bahadur Shastri, *Prime Minister Calls the Nation: Produce More Food and Preserve our Freedom*, 15:7 Indian Farming 3–4 (1965), cited in Seshia and Scoones, *supra* note 8.

[15] Seshia and Scoones, *supra* note 8.

2.2 The Influence of Liberalisation and Globalisation on India's Biotechnology Sector

Agricultural biotechnology gained prominence in 1991 through economic reforms and the globalisation of trade and production.[16] India opened its economy through the introduction of new industrial policy in the light of a changing world scenario. Two important outcomes of the Uruguay Round GATT Negotiations – the establishment of WTO and the adoption of the TRIPS Agreement – exerted a great influence on India's biotechnology policy debates.[17] One of the significant outcomes of this was the increased participation of the private sector in India's agriculture sector.[18] Private companies, both Indian and multinational, emerged as key players in the biotechnology sector, in contrast to the public research institutes and private philanthropic organisations and donors that were the predominant actors in the Green Revolution Era.[19] However, this does not mean that the public sector contribution has ended, but an increased recognition of public-private partnerships and collaborative partnerships began to replace the previous system. Irrespective of other sectors, which were still under state patronage a decade after economic reforms, biotechnology became a part of a "new economy", where the private sector was leading the alliance in collaboration with multinational players. Although the Department of Biotechnology and ICAR continued to support biotechnology research and development, this support seemed nominal as compared to the resources made available from Monsanto, DuPont or Syngenta.[20] The new policy discourse pertaining to biotechnology involves discussions as to public-private partnerships (PPP) and the compliance of trade agreements and patents, rather than major state-supported programmes and national projects.[21]

In addition to biotechnology development through economic reforms and liberalisation, other contemporary issues such as sustainable development and environmentalism started gaining momentum. An eminent Indian scientist, M.S. Swaminathan termed the biotechnology era as "the evergreen revolution"

---

[16] Ibid.

[17] Ibid.

[18] "As a result of these economic changes nationally and globally, private sector involvement in India's agricultural sector has increased." Seshia and Scoones, *supra* note 8, p. 6.

[19] Ibid.

[20] Ibid.

[21] Ibid.

and suggested GMOs as potential solutions to contemporary problems. He maintained:

> The use of GMOs has the potential to be of help in promoting an evergreen revolution rooted in the principles of ecology, economics, equity and ethics. GMOs can confer real benefits in agriculture, food quality, nutrition and health. However, consumer confidence based on an appreciation of the scientific evidence and the regulatory checks and balances will ultimately decide whether or not GMOs make a significant contribution to feeding the 8 billion people who are likely to inhabit our planet in 2020.[22]

Swaminathan envisioned "link[ing] the biovillages of Tamil Nadu and Pondicherry to the latest of transgenic technologies, making the most of the new biological sciences for the benefit of poor and marginal people in an environmentally sustainable manner".[23] In India, the future of agriculture is envisaged as large, consolidated and commercial farms competing on the world market and involving the use of high technology to contribute to economic growth. The poor marginal and small farmers without access to technology could likely be replaced by a new brand of entrepreneurs introducing new disciplines such as industrial management and financing to the rural areas.[24] These potential changes in India's agriculture sector ensure a great future for biotechnology along with new issues such as its impact on biosafety, farmers' rights, the regulation of GMOs and health. Certain economic reforms have a direct impact on biotechnology in India such as the liberalisation of the investment regime, industrial licensing, and permission as the entry point of foreign pharmaceutical, agro-chemical and seed companies.[25]

Another significant development in the biotechnology era was an increased influence of state governments on biotechnology and diffusion of policy-making to lower levels against the centrally planned economy.[26] Agriculture, being a state subject increasingly regulated and influenced by state policies though the regulatory control of biosafety issues in biotechnology, remains under the regulatory control of central government. There has been a radical transformation in the nature of areas of expertise from crop breeding to molecular biology and life sciences; from field-based to lab-based science and from public

---

22 M.S. Swaminathan, "Preface", in *National Consultation on Genetically Modified Plants: Implications for Environment, Food Security and Human Nutrition*, Chennai, January 1999, Recommendations of the participants, Chennai: M.S. Swaminathan Research Foundation (MSSRF), cited in Seshia and Scoones, *supra* note 8.

23 Seshia and Scoones, *supra* note 8.

24 Ibid.

25 Ibid.

26 Ibid, 20.

good research based on free exchange of knowledge to research governed by intellectual property concerns and commercial confidentiality clauses.[27] These transformations changed the status of the biotechnology sector in India to reflect a very promising and competitive image.

3. THE STATUS OF THE BIOTECHNOLOGY SECTOR IN INDIA

India's biotechnology sector has a very promising status, ranking among the top 12-biotech destinations in the world and third in the Asia Pacific region. It has also become the number one producer of recombinant Hepatitis B vaccine.[28] India boasts a pool of talented scientists and researchers backed by strong and world-class information technology (IT) industry. It has a very successful and vibrant pharmaceutical sector that has registered itself as a significant player on the global biotech map and is considered to be the next booming sector after IT. India's rich biological diversity, including plant, animal and human genetic diversity, enables it to take a lead in biotechnological developments.[29] A large pool of medical knowledge coupled with large patient population creates great opportunity in India for clinical research as well as significant market for biotech medicine. Given this potential, India can contribute significantly in vaccine development, regenerative medical services, biosimilars, contract manufacturing, bio agriculture and bioinformatics. The relatively low manufacturing and R&D costs attract international biotech companies to India for outsourcing.[30] Biotechnology could be a great tool for India to advance the fields of healthcare, energy security and environmental conservation. Being a strong voice of developing countries, India could take a leadership role in the global discourse on biotechnology.[31]

---

[27] Ibid.

[28] IBEF, *Biotechnology Industry in India* (last update July 2017), https://www.ibef.org/industry/biotechnology-india.aspx (last visited January 17, 2020).

[29] Ibid.

[30] Ananth Padmanabhan, R. Shashank Reddy and Shruti Sharma, *Modern Biotechnology and India's Governance Imperatives* 1–36 (Carnegie Endowment for International Peace, 2017), https://carnegieendowment.org/files/CP_311_Padmanabhan_FNL4WEB.pdf (last visited January 17, 2020).

[31] Ibid.

4. THE COMPOSITION OF THE INDIAN BIOTECHNOLOGY SECTOR

The Indian biotechnology sector is composed of five major components: bio-pharma, bio-services, bio-agriculture, bio-industry and bioinformatics.[32] The largest component of this group is the biopharmaceutical sector, with a share of 55 per cent, followed by the bio-agriculture sector with a 22 per cent market share (2018). The bio-services sector accounts for 16 per cent, as India is taking the lead in clinical trials, contract research and manufacturing activities. The remaining market is captured by the bio-industrial sector (almost 8 per cent) and a very small contribution from the bioinformatics sector, despite India's great IT base.[33]

4.1 Biopharmaceuticals

Being the largest component of the Indian biotech sector, biopharmaceuticals holds the potential for medical tourism. The Indian biopharma sector primarily consist of vaccines, diagnostics and recombinant therapeutics, which have been the major drivers of its growth. Starting with the vaccine production by the Haffkine Institute of Mumbai and the Pasteur Institute of India in the early 1990s, the sector produced globally acclaimed Indian companies, including Biocon, Serum Institute of India and Shanta Biotechnics. India helps supply vaccines to international institutions such as the World Health Organization and UNICEF.[34] Recognising the potential of Indian companies in vaccine development, Bill and Melinda Gates Foundation's Program for Appropriate Technologies for Health extended grants to Shantha Biotechnics and Bharat Biotech.[35] On the innovation front too India has shown significant progress. Indian biotech companies are joining hands with multinationals to develop vaccines. It is worth mentioning that the Indian biopharma company Regenerative Medical Services has become the fourth company in the world to receive regulatory approval from the Indian government to administer a new treatment called chodron autologous chondrocyte implantation to repair damaged cartilage in patients' knee and hip joints.[36]

After registering huge success in manufacturing generic drugs, India has shown great potential in becoming a hub of biosimilars, the generic equivalent

---

[32] Invest India, *India – A Biotech Growth Catalyst*, https://www.investindia.gov.in/sector/biotechnology (last visited January 17, 2020).

[33] Ibid.

[34] Padmanabhan *et al.*, *supra* note 30.

[35] Natesh and Bhan, *supra* note 2.

[36] Padmanabhan *et al.*, *supra* note 30.

of biological drugs.[37] Indian companies are making significant attempts to keep the prices of medicines low, for example in the case of Insugen, which remains the most affordable human insulin in the domestic market. India's premier biotech company, Biocon is in the process of developing recombinant human insulin, while Shanta Biotechnics marketed its recombinant interferon alpha (IFN-α) product.[38] Moreover, Zydus, Cadila and Dr. Reddy Laboratories have initiated research programmes to capture this emerging field, although designing and testing viable biological compounds is a challenging task given the complex structure of these compounds.[39] In diagnostics, xCyton, Span Diagnostics and J. Mitra & Co. have registered a strong presence, with xCyton, in particular, having the complete infrastructure for ELISA (Enzyme-linked Immunosorbent Assay) kit manufacture, state of the art peptide synthesis and purification systems. Having strong roots in producing ELISA kits, xCyton is switching to the development of rapid tests and polymerase chain reaction (PCR) kits. J. Mitra & Co. Pvt. Ltd is the first Indian company to manufacture the confirmatory test for HIV.[40]

4.2 Bio-Agriculture

The bio-agriculture sector is another promising sector in India that has registered significant growth yet is facing potential obstacles in the form of unscientific and political opposition, regulatory logjams and bureaucratic delays. Nevertheless, it has made significant advancements in producing non-food commercial crops including Bt cotton and other pest and insect resistant techniques including weedicides and pesticides. As of now Bt cotton is the only GM crop approved for production and commercialisation in India; however, the political climate and the government's approach seems positive for GM technologies. The NITI Ayog, a government think tank, maintains in its three-year action plan, "GM seeds have emerged as a powerful new technology that promises high productivity; improved quality; and lower use of fertilizers".[41] MetaHelix is one of the leading agri-bio companies in India, with a special focus on gene discovery for the agronomic and nutritional enhancement of food and commercial crops. A joint venture, Mahyaco-Monsanto

[37] Ibid.

[38] Natesh and Bhan, *supra* note 2.

[39] Padmanabhan *et al.*, *supra* note 30.

[40] Utkarsh Palnitkar, *Growth of Indian Biotech Companies, in the Context of the International Biotechnology Industry*, 11:2 Journal of Commercial Biotechnology 146–154 (January 2005), https://link.springer.com/content/pdf/10.1057/palgrave.jcb.3040112.pdf (last visited January 17, 2020).

[41] Padmanabhan *et al.*, *supra* note 30.

Biotech, obtained approval from the Government of India for the commercial production of Bt cotton in several states. Following this venture, many Indian seed companies started forging alliances with companies with technologies involving genetic modification for insect protection and increasing the shelf life of fruits and vegetables.[42] India has also achieved remarkable success in the production of biofuels, biofertilizers, and bio-pesticides, and exhibits great potential in marine biotechnology. For example, the Centre for Conservation and Utilisation of Blue Green Algae at the Indian Agricultural Institute has been developing algal strains as biofertilizers. It is encouraging that many private Indian biotechnology firms such as Geomarine Biotechnologies, Parry Nutraceuticals and Manglore Biotech Laboratory have also been active in formulating marine-based biotech products. It is another promising yet relatively unexplored area in India.[43]

4.3 Bio-services

The bioservices sector is comprised of contract research, manufacturing services and clinical trials. This is yet another promising area for India, given the large young population and the impending expiration of patents on many drugs with annual global sales in excess of $1 billion.[44] It is also backed by the regulatory waivers granted by the Indian Government's Drugs Technical Advisory Board (DTAB) for advanced clinical trials of certain drugs.[45] Custom research is a service model that is extremely popular among biotech start-ups in India, which enables them to earn early revenues to ensure adequate funds for infrastructure development and to pay salaries to scientists.[46] There are a significant number of contract manufacturing firms in India, namely Jubilant Life Sciences, Dishman Pharmaceuticals and Divi's Laboratories, which function as suppliers of pharmaceutical ingredients used in drug formulas. International pacts for bio-services are also apparent, for example, Syngene International, an affiliate of Biocon dealing with contract research and all set to launch a pharmaceutical research and development centre in Bengaluru for US biotech company Amgen.[47]

---

42 Palnitkar, *supra* note 40.
43 Padmanabhan *et al.*, *supra* note 30.
44 Ibid.
45 Ibid.
46 Palnitkar, *supra* note 40.
47 Padmanabhan *et al.*, *supra* note 30.

4.4 The Bio-industrial (Industrial Biotechnology) Sector

In industrial biotechnology, India has shown its aptitude in the production of enzymes for numerous purposes – food production, pharmaceuticals, textiles, and even for bioenergy – but this sector has not yet been developed to its full potential. In recent times, a great deal of emphasis has been given to this sector and private players such as Novozymes and Sea6 Energy have achieved great success. Novozymes offers a new technology to produce biodiesel, while Sea6 Energy has optimised a technology to derive biofuel from marine biomass.[48] India has also put efforts into producing ethanol from cellulose biomass, including agricultural and forestry waste and biodiesel from varied feed stocks.[49] It is noticeable that India's Department of Biotechnology has established an Energy Biosciences Centre at the University Institute of Chemical Technology, Mumbai, "to develop economically and ecologically sustainable technology for biofuel from biomass and provide a platform for evaluating bioenergy-related technologies".[50]

4.5 Bioinformatics

Despite having a strong base in IT, bioinformatics contributes very little to the biotechnology sector in India. This is due to the fact that the bioinformatics field is fragmented, with a large number of small and mid-sized players, the most notable of which are Strand Life Sciences, Ocimum Biosolutions and Molecular Connections.[51] Nevertheless, it is developing at a rapid pace and considered as a potential future segment within the biotechnology sector. Given India's large biodiversity and enormous gene pool, bioinformatics provides an immense opportunity to Indian companies for defining new drug molecules, mining novel biomarkers, and obtaining new pharmacogenomic data and high-value medical information based on phenotypic and genotypic data.[52] India's diverse gene pool may provide new information pertaining to breast and colon cancer, asthma, diabetes and a host of other diseases. Several Indian companies started harnessing this opportunity by taking numerous initiatives, for example Biocon started working in collaboration with Surromed Inc (Palo Alto, CA) to identify biomarkers for diabetes in the Indian population; Strand Genomics has registered great success through a service delivery model, relying on data management and development of customised data mining soft-

---

48 Ibid.
49 Natesh and Bhan, *supra* note 2.
50 Ibid.
51 Padmanabhan *et al.*, *supra* note 30.
52 Palnitkar, *supra* note 40.

ware for customers; the Institute of Bioinformatics (IOB), a Bangalore-based institute has successfully completed its first international project on the creation of the Human Protein Reference Database.[53] Bioinformatics is a sector which would be interesting to watch as India has a lot to offer to this sector.

5. INSTITUTIONAL DEVELOPMENT IN THE BIOTECHNOLOGY SECTOR

India also made institutional arrangements early in the development of the biotechnology sector; in 1982, the Government of India constituted an agency under the Ministry of Science and Technology, the National Biotechnology Board (NBTB), an apex coordinating body. In 1986, the NBTB was upgraded into a fully fledged separate department under the Ministry of Science and Technology, i.e. the Department of Biotechnology (DBT). The DBT was aimed to be a formidable administrative body, focused on the planning, promotion and coordination of biotechnological programmes.[54] The DBT has been instrumental in creating a scientific workforce and a large infrastructure network, as well as providing strong support to R&D in the life sciences.[55] Technology transfer in the biotech sector was accelerated with the establishment of the Biotechnology Consortium India Ltd (BCIL). This was aimed at acting as an agency for forging effective linkages between research, financial and industrial institutions and the policy framework at the government level.[56] With a view to encouraging the institutions to file patent applications on their innovations, motivating them to transfer their technologies for commercialisation and facilitating them to reward their inventors, some further instructions were issued during 2002 for institutions receiving funds for research projects from the Ministry of Science and Technology.[57] To strengthen the ties with industries and private players, the Biotechnology Industry Research Assistance Council (BIRAC) has been established. BIRAC is a not-for-profit (Section 8, Schedule B), Public Sector Enterprise, set up by the DBT as an interface agency to strengthen and empower the emerging Biotech enterprise

---

53 Ibid.

54 S.R. Rao, *Indian Biotechnology Developments in Public and Private Sectors – Status and Opportunities*, Asian Biotechnology and Development Review (November 2007), http://ris.org.in/images/RIS_images/pdf/abdr_nov1.pdf (last visited January 17, 2020).

55 Natesh and Bhan, *supra* note 2.

56 Rao, *supra* note 54.

57 Ibid.

to undertake strategic research and innovation, addressing nationally relevant product development needs.[58]

6. REGULATORY FRAMEWORK

India has well defined regulatory policies and supporting mechanisms in the form of committees; however, it has been criticised for having at present too many agencies that are involved in giving regulatory clearance. The public perception on GM foods is largely misguided. The DBT under the Ministry of Science and Technology leads as the nodal agency for policy, promotion of R&D, international cooperation and manufacturing units. The Environment (Protection) Act 1986 and Rules 1989 provide biosafety rules, procedures and guidelines "to ensure safety from the use of Genetically Modified Organisms (GMOs) and products thereof in research and application to the users as well as to the environment".[59] A Biosafety Research Programme is aimed at implementing the rules and guidelines with a three-tier mechanism consisting of Institutional Biosafety Committees (IBSCs) at the Institute/company; the Review Committee on Genetic Manipulation (RCGM) in the Department of Biotechnology; and the Genetic Engineering Approval Committee (GEAC) in the Ministry of Environment & Forests (MoE&F). These Committees are given the responsibility for "granting approval for research and development activities on recombinant DNA products, environmental release of genetically engineered (GE) crops and monitoring and evaluation of research activities involving recombinant DNA technology".[60] The IBSC is a committee necessary for the institutions intending to carry out research activities dealing with "genetic manipulation of microorganisms, plants and animals".[61] The GEAC works under the MoE&F in coordination with the DBT, with the prime responsibility of granting approval for activities involving the large-scale use of hazardous microorganisms and recombinant products in research and industrial production from an environmental angle.[62] The RCGM holds the responsibility under the DBT to act as "a body to monitor the safety related

---

[58] Biotechnology Industry Research Council (BIRAC), https://birac.nic.in/desc_new.php?id=89 (last visited January 17, 2020).

[59] Department of Biotechnology, Ministry of Science and Technology, Government of India, *Biosafety Programme*, http://dbtindia.gov.in/regulations-guidelines/regulations/biosafety-programme (last visited January 17, 2020).

[60] Ibid.

[61] Vibha Ahuja, *Regulation of Emerging Gene Technologies in India*, 12 (Suppl 8): 14 BMC Proceedings (2018), https://www.ncbi.nlm.nih.gov/pmc/articles/PMC6069684/pdf/12919_2018_Article_106.pdf (last visited January 17, 2020).

[62] Ibid.

aspects of ongoing research projects and activities dealing with genetically engineered organisms/hazardous microorganisms".[63] Its composition involves representations of scientific organisations or departments such as the Indian Council of Medical Research (ICMR), the Indian Council of Agricultural Research (ICAR) and the Council of Scientific and Industrial Research (CSIR), as well as other experts working in an individual capacity.[64] In addition to these three committees, there are another three: the RDNA Advisory Committee (RDAC), focused on giving recommendations from time to time on safety regulations in research and application of GMOs and products thereof; the State Biotechnology Coordination Committee, a state-level committee with monitoring responsibility, constituted in each state in which research and applications of GMOs are underway; and the District Level Committee (DLC), which is constituted in those districts "where monitoring of safety in installation[s] engaged in the use of GMOs/hazardous microorganisms and its applications in the environment" is required.[65]

The Indian regulatory mechanism dealing with biotechnology suffers from numerous shortcomings, namely: its multi-layered complex regulatory system; the fact that its regulatory mechanism is not holistic, with a lack of coordination among various committees; no proper definition of the role and responsibilities of the GEAC, and a great deal of uncertainty as to its autonomy as an approval authority; the regulatory committees lack of a pro-innovation approach; and an approval process which usually takes between three to five years, and sometimes even more than ten years.[66] The creation of a single window for the approval of genetically engineered organisms and a specifically dedicated body for biotech regulations has been demanded for a long time in India. In this context, India came up with a proposed regulatory body, the Biotechnology Regulatory Authority of India (BRAI), to regulate uses of biotechnology products, including genetically modified organisms (GMOs). As regards the approval of biologics or biosimilars, the Central Drugs Standard Control Organisation (CDSCO), headed by the Drug Controller General of India (DCGI) under the Ministry of Health and Family Organisation, is the responsible body. For biosimilars, the RCGM makes recommendations for clinical trials based on data from pre-clinical studies to the DCGI, who then considers these recommendations and takes an independent decision as to the approval for clinical trials followed by permission for marketing and manufacturing.[67] The Indian Pharmacopoeia Commission was established with

---

63 Ibid.
64 Ibid.
65 Ibid.
66 Padmanabhan *et al.*, *supra* note 30.
67 Ibid.

the aim of promoting the safe use of medicines, and functions as the National Coordination Centre (NCC) for the Pharmacovigilance Programme of India (PvPI).[68] However, the CDSCO lacks functional and financial autonomy, good infrastructure and adequate human resources, and the pharmacovigilance machinery in India badly needs technical and skills upgrades.[69]

The regulatory environment for bio-agriculture in India has been controversial due to an incomplete social understanding of biotechnology coupled with the politicisation of the same. The regulation of GM crops is a subject that comes under state jurisdictions in India, where states wield significant influence over the trials and commercial cultivation of GM crops.[70] Bt cotton received approval for commercial cultivation in 2002, and thus far remains the only crop to do so. States have been reluctant to even offer a regulatory pathway for testing other GM crops. Bt eggplants raised huge controversy in India and despite the recommendation of the prime regulatory body, the GEAC, for the commercialisation of Bt eggplants, the Ministry of Environment, Forest and Climate Change (MOEFCC) had to announce a moratorium in February 2010. The underlying reason for this was a dearth of long-term studies to establish human and environmental safety.[71] It is noteworthy that a few episodes of growing illegal Bt eggplants are coming up in India, defying the Government's moratorium.[72]

GM mustard has encountered the same fate in terms of the anti-GMO campaigner filed public interest litigation against it, despite the GEAC's inclination to approve the commercial cultivation of the crop.[73] A year after the government put the commercial release of genetically modified (GM) mustard on hold, the GEAC approved "field studies of GM mustard on honey bee and other pollinations at its recently held 136th meeting", in spite of fierce opposition and criticism by anti GM crop activists.[74] Being a biodiversity-rich country and a signatory of the Convention on Biological Diversity 1993 and other related treaties, India came up with the Biological

---

[68] Ahuja, *supra* note 61.

[69] Padmanabhan *et al.*, *supra* note 30.

[70] Ibid.

[71] Ibid.

[72] Colin Todhunter, *Illegal Bt Brinjal in India: A Call to Initiate Criminal Proceedings Against Regulators and Corporations*, Counterpunch (May 14, 2019), https://www.counterpunch.org/2019/05/14/illegal-bt-brinjal-in-india-a-call-to-initiate-criminal-proceedings-against-regulators-and-corporations/ (last visited January 17, 2020).

[73] Padmanabhan *et al.*, *supra* note 30.

[74] *GEAC Approves Field Studies of GM Mustard on Honey Bee*, Down To Earth (October 26, 2018) https://www.downtoearth.org.in/news/agriculture/geac-approves-field-studies-of-gm-mustard-on-honey-bee-61947 (last visited January 17, 2020).

Diversity Act 2002. However, IP proponents view India's approach to biodiversity as over-protectionist and consider it as an obstacle to innovation. This approach, however, stems from various episodes of wrongful misappropriation of bio-resources, for example patents pertaining to the healing properties of turmeric and fungicidal properties of the Neem plant in the United States and EU respectively.[75] The regulatory regime in India for biotechnology is still in an evolving phase, with significant legal and institutional reforms and a promising atmosphere for GM crops, yet it is raising enormous concerns regarding the vulnerability of various stakeholders pertaining to biotechnology due to the non-conducive regulatory climate.

7. IPR CLIMATE FOR BIOTECHNOLOGY IN INDIA: AN INQUIRY INTO POLICY AND LEGISLATIVE LORE AND EVOLVING IP JURISPRUDENCE

IP protection for biotechnology in India is primarily governed through two specific legislations, the Patents Act 1970 and the Protection of Plant Varieties and Farmers' Rights Act (PPVFRA) 2001, though other IP protections, such as copyright protection, trademark protection and protection of trade secrets, are also relevant to biotechnology with the introduction of new subject matters in the domain of biotechnology such as genetic and genomic databases, bioinformatics software, etc. In India, it has been patents which have dominated the biotechnology and IPR debate, along with the interface of the Patents Act 1970 and the PPVFRA. India has revised its IP laws using the flexibilities provided under the TRIPS Agreement to cater to its socio-economic needs as well as to ensure that its IP laws remain TRIPS compliant. However, many developed countries, particularly the USA, consider the statutory framework of IP in India non-conducive to innovation and investment.[76]

7.1 Statutory Framework of Patent Law for Biotechnology Patents

Patent proponents and biotechnology companies consider Indian patent law overprotective and the patent approach conservative. This is due to numerous statutory hurdles that a patent applicant has to face: narrow standards of patentability; a prohibitive filing fee for sequence listings; burdensome requirements (e.g. the mandatory disclosure of the source and geographical origin

---

[75] Padmanabhan *et al.*, *supra* note 30.

[76] *USTR puts India on "Priority Watch List" on "Intellectual Property" Concerns*, Economic Times (April 26, 2019), https://economictimes.indiatimes.com/news/economy/foreign-trade/ustr-puts-india-on-priority-watch-list-on-intellectual-property-concerns/articleshow/69050830.cms?from=mdr (last visited January 17, 2020).

of biological material); and the hurdle of prior approval from the National Biodiversity Authority (NBA).[77] Section 3 of the Patents Act 1970 contains a long list of patent exclusions, which usually create hurdles to patenting on life forms. Section 3(b) excludes inventions, the commercial exploitation of which is "contrary to public order or morality" or "causes serious prejudice to human, animal or plant life or health or to the environment".[78] In India, public order and morality could play a major role in excluding inventions; however, India seldom uses this criterion as the sole basis to exclude inventions from patenting.[79] Patent proponents remain susceptible regarding this provision and consider it a potential hurdle to obtaining patents on life forms. Section 3(c) of the Patents Act 1970 stipulates that the "discovery of any living thing or nonliving substances occurring in nature" does not constitute patent-eligible subject matter.[80] In the biotechnological context, the IPO Guidelines on the Examination of Biotechnology Applications for Patents, 2013 expressly state that sequences isolated directly from nature are not patentable.[81] One of the most controversial sections dealing with patent exclusions is section 3(d), which stipulates that mere discovery of a new form of a known substance is not patentable unless it enhances the known efficacy of the substance.[82] In an illustrative manner in the explanation, section 3(d) also prohibits under "new forms of known substance", new salt, ester, polymorphic, or isomeric forms of known compounds for want of enhanced efficacy.[83] The legislative intent behind section 3(d) was to prevent evergreening, a practice that denies the ingenuity of invention.[84]

---

[77] Debashish Banerjee and Pankaj Musyuni, *Biotechnological Inventions in India: Law, Practices and Challenges* Remfry and Sagar (October 23, 2015), https://www.lexology.com/library/detail.aspx?g=8405b078-b301-4672-8850-84f74ca23aa7 (last visited January 17, 2020).

[78] Section 3(b) of the Patents Act 1970.

[79] Shamnad Basheer *et al.*, *Patent Exclusions That Promote Public Health Objectives*, SCP/15/3 ANNEX IV, https://www.wipo.int/edocs/mdocs/scp/en/scp_15/scp_15_3-annex4.pdf (last visited January 18, 2020).

[80] Section 3(c) of the Patents Act 1970.

[81] Office of the Controller General of Patents, Designs and Trade Marks, *Guidelines on the Examination of Biotechnology Applications for Patents* (March 2013), http://www.ipindia.nic.in/writereaddata/Portal/IPOGuidelinesManuals/1_38_1_4-biotech-guidelines.pdf (last visited January 18, 2020).

[82] Section 3(d) of the Patents Act 1970.

[83] Jodie Liu, *Compulsory Licensing and Anti-Evergreening: Interpreting the TRIPS Flexibilities in Sections 84 and 3(d) of the Indian Patents Act*, 56:1 Harvard International Law Journal 207–227 (2015), https://harvardilj.org/wp-content/uploads/sites/15/561Liu.pdf (last visited January 18, 2020).

[84] Aditya Kant, *Section 3(d): "New" Indian Perspective*, 14 Journal of Intellectual Property Rights 385–396 (2009), https://pdfs.semanticscholar.org/d779/642cc0a5953b4a40c77219458137a7d66a01.pdf (last visited January 18, 2020).

However, although section 3(d) was not exclusively applicable to pharmaceutical inventions, the legislative debates were more focused on preventing the evergreening of patents in the pharmaceutical field as India was about to lose its practice of excluding food, drugs and chemicals from patentability.[85] The potential application of section 3(d) of the Patents Act to other fields, particularly biotechnology, largely depends on how it is interpreted by the patent authorities as much leeway is left with them to ascertain whether any modification in a substance meets the requirement of enhanced efficacy or not. Though the requirement of efficacy was explained in pharmaceutical patent cases,[86] no specific parameters were laid down to determine efficacy. Its impact on biotechnology patents could not be fully ascertained but it created a complex and overprotective image of the Indian patent system for potential patent applicants.[87] Section 3(e) excludes "a substance obtained by a mere admixture resulting only in the aggregation of the properties of the components thereof or a process for producing such substance",[88] meaning thereby that a combination of two known components may be worthy of being protected through patents if they exhibit synergism. Many suspect that similar to the ambiguities attached to the term efficacy under section 3(d), synergism in the case of biotechnology patent applications lacks a clear statutory definition, leaving much discretion to the IPO to determine the same on a case-by-case basis.[89]

Section 3(h) excludes "a method of agriculture or horticulture" from patenting.[90] A plain reading of section 3(h) suggests that it may obstruct a very wide range of biotechnology inventions in the agriculture field. The Biotechnology Guidelines limit the scope of section 3(h) by restricting its application to "conventional methods" performed on open fields.[91] However, in practice, great uncertainty persists as to what constitutes "conventional methods on open fields" and the practice of the IPO in interpreting section 3(h) has not been con-

---

[85] Liu, *supra* note 83.

[86] *Novartis A.G. v. Union of India & Others*, Civil Appeal Nos. 2706-2716 of 2013.

[87] See William J. Bennett, *Indian Pharmaceutical Patent Law and the Effects of Novartis Ag v. Union of India*, 13 Wash. U. Global Stud. L. Rev. 535–557 (2014), https://openscholarship.wustl.edu/cgi/viewcontent.cgi?article=1500&context=law_globalstudies (last visited January 18, 2020); Janice Mueller, *The Tiger Awakens: The Tumultuous Transformation of India's Patent System and the Rise of Indian Pharmaceutical Innovation*, 68 U. Pitt. L. Rev. 491, 514–515 (2007), http://d-scholarship.pitt.edu/17944/1/79-157-1-SM.pdf (last visited January 18, 2020).

[88] Section 3(e) of the Patents Act 1970.

[89] Banerjee and Musyuni, *supra* note 77.

[90] Section 3(h) of the Patents Act 1970.

[91] Biotechnology Guidelines 2013, *supra* note 81.

sistent.[92] Diagnostics is seen as a very promising sector under biotechnology, but section 3(i) of the Patents Act 1970 seems to obstruct the diagnostic patent applications. Section 3(i) excludes from patenting "any process for the medicinal, surgical, curative, prophylactic, diagnostic, therapeutic or other treatment of human beings or any process for a similar treatment of animals to render them free of disease or to increase their economic value or that of their products".[93] Although the IPO has granted patents for "in vitro diagnostic methods" performed on tissues or fluids which had been permanently removed from the body, the Biotechnology Guidelines brought *in vitro* diagnostic methods under the remit of section 3(i), so the IPO is unlikely to grant such patents in the future.[94] However, since the Guidelines are not binding, a liberal interpretation of section 3(i) by the courts would define the contours of *in vitro* diagnostic methods.[95] Section 3(j) of the Patents Act 1970,[96] though broadly modelled on Article 27.3(b) of the TRIPS Agreement,[97] has some distinctive features. It is rather broad in scope on two counts: first, Article 27.3(b) refers to "plants or animals" but section 3(j) further limits it to "plants and animals in whole or any part thereof"; second, while Article 27.3(b) is silent about "seeds", section 3(j) makes it specific that seeds are excluded from patenting.[98] The scope of the terms "microorganism", "microbiological process", "essentially biological process" and "non-biological process" are enormously contentious in India[99] and much depends on how they are interpreted.

Section 3(p) is a distinct addition to the Patents Act 1970, which excludes traditional knowledge from patentability. It precludes from patentability "an invention which in effect, is traditional knowledge or which is an aggregation or duplication of known properties of traditionally known component or com-

---

92 Sharavan S. Acharya and Prosenjit Chattopadhyay, *Scope of Section 3(h) of the Patents Act, 1970 – An Analysis* (December 2017), https://www.lakshmisri.com/insights/articles/scope-of-section-3h-of-the-patents-act-970-an-analysis (last visited January 18, 2020).

93 Section 3(i) of the Patents Act.

94 Banerjee and Musyuni, *supra* note 77.

95 Ibid.

96 Section 3(j) of the Patents Act 1970 states: "plants and animals in whole or any part thereof other than micro-organisms but including seeds, varieties and species and essentially biological processes for production or propagation of plants and animals".

97 Article 27.3(b) provides "plants and animals other than micro-organisms, and essentially biological processes for the production of plants or animals other than non-biological and microbiological processes. However, Members shall provide for the protection of plant varieties either by patents or by an effective *sui generis* system or by any combination thereof".

98 Essenese Obhan, *IP Rights for GM Seeds*, https://www.obhanandassociates.com/blog/ip-rights-for-gm-seeds/ (last visited January 18, 2020).

99 See *Nuziveedu v. Monsanto* discussion *infra*.

ponents".[100] To clear the traditional knowledge bar set by section 3(p), patent claims are examined against searches of traditional knowledge databases, including the Traditional Knowledge Digital Library.[101] In *Dhanpat Seth and Ors. v. NilKamal Plastic Crates Ltd,*[102] Himachal Pradesh (HP) High Court had examined the validity of the Patent No. 195917, a patent granted to the plaintiffs for a "device used for manually hauling agricultural produce", on the basis of its alleged similarities to a traditional handicraft called "Kilta" (an all-purpose bamboo basket used to carry any type of load, supported by a rope and tied to the forehead).[103]

The Court revoked the patent under section 64 of the Patents Act 1970 on several counts: first, on the inventive step criterion, defined under section 2(1)(ja),[104] the Court maintained that the defendants successfully proved that change in size or raw material could not contribute to a "technical advance" or "economic significance" as ordained in the section; second in the absence of any significant inventive features in the plaintiff's patented product and having resemblance with Kilta, the Court concluded that the patented product does not appear to be non-obvious to a person skilled in the art; third, referring to section 3(d),[105] the Court held that the patented invention attracts the said provision, since mere replacement of the raw material (bamboo replaced by plastic) falls under a new discovery of a known substance (i.e. traditional Kilta) and no enhancement could be recorded in the known efficacy.[106] Finally, coming to section 3(p), the Court observed that Kilta has been used in the countryside

---

[100] Section 3(p) of the Patents Act 1970.

[101] Banerjee and Musyuni, *supra* note 77.

[102] AIR 2008 HP 23, MIPR 2008 (2) 370, 2008 (36) PTC 938 NULL.

[103] Prarthana Patnaik, *The Himanchal Pradesh Court Revokes Patent Grant Invoking Section 3(p)*, Spicy IP (July 15, 2018), https://spicyip.com/2018/07/the-himachal-pradesh-high-court-revokes-patent-grant-invoking-section-3p.html (last visited January 18, 2020).

[104] Section 2(1)(ja) states: "'inventive step' means a feature of an invention that involves technical advance as compared to the existing knowledge or having economic significance or both and that makes the invention not obvious to a person skilled in the art".

[105] Section 3(d) of the Patents Act 1970: "the mere discovery of a new form of a known substance which does not result in the enhancement of the known efficacy of that substance or the mere discovery of any new property or new use for a known substance or of the mere use of a known process, machine or apparatus unless such known process results in a new product or employs at least one new reactant". Explanation: "For the purposes of this clause, salts, esters, ethers, polymorphs, metabolites, pure form, particle size, isomers, mixtures of isomers, complexes, combinations and other derivatives of known substance shall be considered to be the same substance, unless they differ significantly in properties with regard to efficacy".

[106] Patnaik, *supra* note 103.

of Himachal Pradesh since time immemorial and fits under the traditional knowledge domain; therefore, the patented product is nothing but a "mere aggregation or duplication of traditionally known components".[107] Based on the above grounds, the Court revoked the patent granted under section 64[108] of the Patents Act 1970. As a point of criticism, it could be argued whether Himachal Pradesh High Court has certain defined parameters to determine whether Kilta has been used from time immemorial or it has just worked on a vague assumption.[109] Moreover, the Court missed an opportunity to lay down certain parameters for determining traditional knowledge. Another aspect of the case was its long pendency in the court, as it was filed in 2002 and decided in 2018. Though the Guidelines were issued in 2013, an interpretation by the courts could bring clarity to this segment.[110]

7.2 Judicial Response to Biotechnology: Evolving IP Jurisprudence

The Patent Policy adopted by the Ayyangar Committee,[111] which laid the foundation of the Patents Act 1970 in India, was a thoughtful result of the prevailing situation of patents and their socio-economic implications in India, particularly in vital areas such as food, drugs and chemicals. India travelled far after this and there has been enormous progress in the industrial sector and in technological development along with surplus production in certain sectors, which has necessitated creating a pro-innovation IP climate. By being a member of the WTO and bound by the TRIPS Agreement, India needed to make enormous transformations in patent law, which it has done through the Patent Amendments of 1999, 2002 and 2005. However, the policy control of the Ayyangar Committee Report still acts as a guardian to the Indian patent pathway.[112] This could be justified on the basis that the Report reflects the

---

[107] Ibid.

[108] See section 64 of the Patents Act 1970 for the grounds of revocation.

[109] Patnaik, *supra* note 103.

[110] Ibid.

[111] In 1957, the Government of India appointed Justice N. Rajagopala to the Ayyangar Committee "to examine the question of revision of the Patent Law and advise government accordingly". The Report of the Committee became the basis for the introduction of the Patents Act 1970, replacing the Patents and Designs Act 1911. See Office of the Controller General of Patents, Designs and Trade Marks, DPIIT, Ministry of Commerce and Industry, Government of India, *History of Indian Patent System*, http://www.ipindia.nic.in/history-of-indian-patent-system.htm (last visited January 19, 2020).

[112] Shamnad Basheer, *"Policy Style" Reasoning at the Indian Patent Office*, I.P.Q. (2005) 309–323, https://www.researchgate.net/publication/228146700_%27Policy_Style%27_Reasoning_at_the_Indian_Patent_Office (last visited January 19, 2020).

underlying policy levers for granting patents in India and demonstrates the roots of legislative intent relating to the same.[113]

Nevertheless, given the transformations in the IP discourse, India's IP regime is bound to be reviewed to accommodate the new realities and ensure that the explicit legislative provisions should not be diluted in favour of the policy to find different interpretations. Accordingly, the Indian Patents Office is bound by the legislative mandate and it should abide by it. However, the old policy ordained in the Ayyangar Committee Report still acts as a guiding force for the IPO. Professor Shamnad Basheer reflected on the policy-type reasoning as to the application of patent law provisions.[114] There are a few important cases that reflect the policy lore, responsible for the patent trends in India.

7.2.1 *Dimminaco AG v. Controller of Patents* – setting the IP jurisprudence for life forms

The *Dimminaco*[115] case could be seen as a precursor for patenting on life forms, though India was under an obligation to make "microorganisms" and "micro-biological processes" patentable, which it did through the Patents Amendment Act 2002. The decision came before this Amendment and demonstrates the IPO's policy-style reasoning for rejecting patents on methods/processes the end product of which was living organisms.[116] Coming to the facts of the case, the applicant Dimminaco AG was a subsidiary of American Home Products, Inc., which applied for a process patent the end result of which was a live vaccine for infectious bursitis.[117] Dimminaco AG specifically claimed: "[a] process for the preparation of a vaccine, which is capable of protecting poultry against infectious, bursitis infection".[118] The IPO rejected the patent application on numerous grounds, the most prominent being the fact that the definition of "invention"[119] in the Patents Act did not include a living organ-

113 Ibid.
114 Ibid.
115 *Dimminaco AG v. Controller of Patents and Designs* (2002) I.P.L.R. July 255.
116 Basheer, *supra* note 112.
117 Ibid.
118 App. No.135/Cal/98 (filed on January 28, 1998).
119 The definition of "invention" under the Patents Act 1970 was ordained under section 2(1)(j): invention would mean any new and useful (i) art, process, method or manner of manufacture; (ii) machine, apparatus or other articles; (iii) substance produced by manufacture and includes any new and useful improvement of any of them and an alleged invention. This definition was replaced by the Patents Amendment Act 2002 under section 2(1)(j) of the Patents Act 1970: "'invention' means a new product or process involving an inventive step and capable of industrial application", http://ipindia.nic.in/writereaddata/Portal/IPOAct/1_31_1_patent-act-1970-11march2015.pdf (last visited January 19, 2020).

ism. As a result, any process that resulted in a "live vaccine" would not qualify as "a manner of manufacture". Kolkata High Court rejected the findings of the IPO by maintaining that, first, there is no statutory bar to the patentability of living organisms and second "[t]he dictionary meaning of the word 'manufacture' does not exclude the process of preparing a vendible commodity which contains a living substance".[120] An inference could be drawn from the previous decisions that a manufacture ought to result in an article or substance, meaning, thereby, that a process that did not result in an article or substance did not merit protection.[121] Adopting this approach, a large number of patents were denied to a number of processes, including a method of generating electricity from solar energy and a "method for the generation of power from solid carbonaceous fuels".[122]

English courts moulded this approach by inventing a new test, termed a vendible test, to accommodate those inventions which were industry breakthroughs. In *Elten & Leda Chemicals Ltd's Application*,[123] which involved an application for a method of fog dispersal, the court went to the extent of stretching the vendibility test to hold that the vendible product in this case could be the fog-free atmosphere. This clearly shows the influence of policy implications on the judgment, as the reasoning given in the case was beyond common sense.[124] However, while dealing with an application relating to the method of magneto metric survey, the Controller of Patents maintained that "unlike the United Kingdom, the definition of 'manufacture' within the Indian context would not admit of a 'vendible product' test". Though the method of magneto metric surveying was not a "manufacture", it satisfies the vendibility product test.[125] With the profound realisation that foreigners held almost 90 per cent of Indian patents and that the majority of them were not even worked in India, and given an increasing probability that foreigners would exploit the patent system to the maximum, the Ayyangar Committee recommended that certain inventions such as pharmaceutical inventions and food and other chemical inventions be granted only process patent protection.[126]

Against this background, with regard to the meaning of manufacture in the Indian context, the Committee stated, "a narrow interpretation of the term

[120] *Dimminaco, supra* note 115, at 269.

[121] Basheer, *supra* note 112.

[122] Re Texaco Development Corp, Decisions on Patents and Designs (The Patent Office Technical Society, Calcutta, 1982) (2) 11.

[123] *GEC's application* [1943] 60 R.P.C. 1.

[124] Basheer, *supra* note 112

[125] Patent No. 34986.

[126] Basheer, *supra* note 112

would serve India's interest in a more optional manner".[127] A clear influence of the Ayyangar Report could be seen on many patent decisions in India. An illustration of the same could be found in Thomas Brandt's application,[128] where a patent application claiming a process for dispersing fog was refused, relying on the restrictive interpretation of the term "manufacture", which necessitates that a process must involve an end product, as recommended by the Ayyangar Committee Report.[129] In line with the restrictive meaning given to the term "manufacture", it is obvious that living organisms as end results may be precluded from patenting. The policy ordained by the Ayyangar Committee influenced the patent authorities in rejecting patent applications for processes involving life forms as their end results. In this matter, it is worth mentioning that the Controller of Patents issues an inner circular to preclude patent applications involving living entities.[130] The *Dimminaco* judgment could be considered a progressive judgment in the sense that "in stark contrast with the policy-driven approach of the Patent Office, … the Kolkata High Court judge … reached his conclusion without any reference whatsoever to policy implications".[131] The Court maintained that the vaccine in question would clear the vendibility hurdle to qualify as a "manufacture". The Court then adopted the vendibility test, which has been persistently rejected by the IPO. However, the Court would have explained various parameters of biotechnology patents before declaring that there is no bar to patent law in general. It could have analysed the policies more effectively and come up with a clearer distinction based on sound reasoning.[132]

Going by the analogy that fewer patents result in better economy, Professor Basheer argued that patent offices are ignoring the basic precept of the legal system, i.e. the rule of law. Though Patent Amendments in 1999, 2002 and 2005 brought in explicit provision relating to biotechnology inventions, yet since the parent Act remains the same, the ghost of the Ayyangar Committee may still halt the patent practice.[133] However, there has been a growing realisation by the IPO regarding the changing demands in the realm of IP, and, therefore, patent offices in India are granting patents on biotechnology as per the revised and updated guidelines; though they are not perfect, they are making a significant contribution. The *Dimminaco* judgment reflects a pro-

---

[127] Ayyangar report, 22.
[128] [1990] I.P.L.R. 280 Patent Office.
[129] Basheer, *supra* note 112.
[130] Ibid.
[131] Ibid, 316.
[132] Ibid.
[133] Ibid.

active approach of the judiciary in recognising the potential of biotechnology patents to contribute to economic progress.

7.2.2 Pharmaceutical cases defining the patent pathway for biotechnology inventions: *Bayer v. Natco* and *Novartis AG v. Union of India*

Two important cases[134] relating to pharmaceutical patents gained enormous popularity as they were closely watched not only by giant pharmaceutical companies but also the companies seeking biotechnology patents in India. These cases reflect the patent trends after India lost the protectionist regime on drugs (exclusion on food, drugs and chemicals) and introduced patenting on living forms.[135] It is interesting to learn how India reacted in a globalised TRIPS-compliant national regime with the controversial addition of section 3(d) to the Patents Act 1970. India was guided by the policy reasoning in the pre-TRIPS era, but a conservative approach much in line with the old policy still subsists in the post-TRIPS era. The decisions in *Bayer v. Natco*[136] and *Novartis AG v. Union of India*[137] reflect India's approach as to compulsory licensing and the evergreening of patents respectively.[138] Both cases relied heavily on the legislative intent behind inserting compulsory licensing and anti-evergreening provisions in the Patents Act 1970.

7.2.2.1 Bayer Corp. v. Natco Pharma Ltd[139]

Compulsory licensing intends to prevent the ill effects of patent monopoly on public welfare and it is duly recognised in the TRIPS Agreement under Article 31. Member countries of the WTO are permitted to issue a compulsory licence for public health purposes; however, Members are restricted to granting a licence on an individual basis only and limited to the purpose for which it was authorised.[140] The Doha Declaration addressed the scope of public health and the ability of WTO Members to grant compulsory licensing to third parties

---

134 *Bayer Corporation v. Natco Pharma Ltd.*, Order No. 45/2013 (Intellectual Property Appellate Board, Chennai) & *Novartis AG v. Union of India & Others*, Civil Appeal No. 2706-2716 of 2013.

135 Section 3(j), *supra* note 96.

136 *Bayer Corporation v. Natco Pharma Ltd.*, Order No. 45/2013 (Intellectual Property Appellate Board, Chennai).

137 *Novartis AG v. Union of India & Others*, Civil Appeal No. 2706-2716 of 2013.

138 Jodie Liu, *Compulsory Licensing and Anti-Evergreening: Interpreting the TRIPS Flexibilities in Sections 84 and 3(d) of the Indian Patents Act*, 56:1 Harvard International Law Journal 207–227 (2015), https://harvardilj.org/wp-content/uploads/sites/15/561Liu.pdf (last visited January 19, 2020).

139 *Bayer*, *supra* note 136.

140 Liu, *supra* note 138.

when the Members themselves lack manufacturing capabilities. Through the Patents Amendment Act 2005 India specifies three conditions for issuing compulsory licensing under section 84:

> At any time after the expiration of three years from the date of the grant of a patent, any person interested may make an application to the Controller for grant of compulsory licence on patent on any of the following grounds, namely:
> (a) that the reasonable requirements of the public with respect to the patented invention have not been satisfied, or
> (b) that the patented invention is not available to the public at a reasonably affordable price, or
> (c) that the patented invention is not worked in the territory of India.[141]

In the present case, Bayer developed a drug, Nexavar, to treat late-stage liver cancer and obtained a patent over it in India. The patent practice of Bayer gave rise to a controversy due to ongoing patent infringements by Indian pharmaceutical companies including Natco. Bayer filed an action against Natco with the allegation that it was producing a generic version of Nexavar in violation of Bayer's Indian patent on the drug. Against this, Natco filed an application for compulsory licensing to the Controller General of Patents on the basis that all the grounds for issuing compulsory licensing mentioned in section 84(1) had been independently met.[142] On March 9, 2012, the Controller granted Natco the first ever compulsory licence in India and directed it to pay a royalty of 6 per cent of its sales. Bayer made an appeal to the Intellectual Property Appellate Board (IPAB), which on March 4, 2013 upheld the Controller's granting of the compulsory licence while increasing the royalty from 6 per cent to 7 per cent. The IPAB relied heavily on the fact that the sole concern of granting compulsory licensing is whether the public interest has been satisfied or not.

As regards the scope of the term "reasonably affordable" under section 84 of the Patents Act 1970, the IPAB categorically maintained that the pertinent inquiry could be made "with reference to the public"[143] and not "with reference to the inventor".[144] The natural meaning of the term "affordable" refers to the buyer rather than the seller of a product. Based on this reasoning, the IPAB concluded that the Controller of Patents had permissibly found that the price of 280,000 rupees per month charged by Bayer for Nexavar was alone relevant in determining that the drug was not reasonably affordable under section 84(1).[145] Responding to the other requirement under section 84(1)(a)

---

141 Section 84 of the Patents Act 1970.
142 Liu, *supra* note 138.
143 *Bayer*, *supra* note 136, para 40.
144 Ibid.
145 Liu, *supra* note 138.

on whether the compulsory licensing could be granted on the grounds that the reasonable requirement of the public had not been met, the IPAB pondered over section 84(7), which lists numerous circumstances under which "the reasonable requirements of the public shall be deemed to have been satisfied".[146] Referring to one of the circumstances, when "the patented invention is not being worked in the territory of India on a commercial scale to an adequate extent",[147] the IPAB categorically observed that "commercial scale" had to do with market price, which implied that "a prohibitively costly drug could not be commercially viable" and as a result it was of little relevance to section 84(1)(a) on whether importing might qualify as "working".[148] The Board maintained that "so long as the drug price was too high to be commercial the drug satisfied section 84(7)(d), which in turn deemed that section 84(1)(a) had been triggered".[149]

As regards the requirement under section 84(1)(c) that the compulsory licence could be granted on the ground that the drug was not worked in the territory of India, Bayer contended that in certain circumstances (as in the present case) importation is justified and suffice the need for working the patented invention, it therefore did not require local manufacturing in India.[150] Bayer further contended that given the quantity of drug required in India, setting up a manufacturing unit in India was not justified economically.[151] Responding to this contention, the IPAB rejected the argument that working did not require local manufacturing, leaving the question open as to what the term "working" actually requires. It held that the term "worked" under section 84(1)(c) must be decided on a case-by-case basis, for example in some cases it could mean local manufacturing entirely, while in others it could mean only importation.[152] Critics argue that while placing much reliance on compulsory licensing furthering public interest, the IPAB had avoided other public interest considerations explicitly mentioned in the provision. They maintain that while doing this the IPAB could have undercut the very public interest purpose that it seeks to advance and that probably it could act contrary to India's obligations under the TRIPS Agreement.[153]

As regards Bayer's Patient Assistance Program, the IPAB had provided the reasoning that the reasonable requirement condition contained under section

---

[146] Section 84(7) of the Patents Act 1970.
[147] Section 84(7)(d) of the Patents Act 1970.
[148] Liu, *supra* note 138.
[149] Ibid.
[150] Ibid.
[151] Ibid.
[152] Ibid.
[153] Ibid.

84(1) cannot be avoided by handing out the product for free to those who cannot afford it as such acts under the programme do not actually lower the market price of the drug.[154] Rather, in order to satisfy the requirements under section 84(1)(a), a pharmaceutical company may need to lower a drug's prices for all. Critics argue that the exclusive focus on price might reduce the number of options available to brand name pharmaceuticals in making the drug available. They suggest price differentiation as a viable option to avoid compulsory licensing in these circumstances, which the Controller had also hinted at but the IPAB had not applied.[155] The IPAB's interpretation of the term "working" as a condition for issuing the compulsory licence was wide and flexible, and in certain cases required local manufacturing too, which may not be compatible with the TRIPS Agreement. Article 27.1 of the TRIPS Agreement states: "patents shall be available and patent rights enjoyable without discrimination as to … whether products are imported or locally produced".[156] The IPAB, however, provided a justification that the non-discrimination principle affects only the patent itself and not the compulsory licence, which is a fallacy as under Article 27.1 the TRIPS Agreement categorically stipulates that "patent rights shall be enjoyable" and not merely that "patents shall be granted – without discrimination as to the place of a product's manufacture".[157] From the enjoyment of patent rights perspective, it is noteworthy that the party granted the compulsory licence may overtake the entirety of the patent holder's market value.[158]

7.2.2.2 Novartis AG v. Union of India

The *Novartis* case deals with section 3(d) of the Patents Act 1970, which seeks to prevent evergreening of patents and, at the time of its inception, had no parallel anywhere else in the world. The section prevents patenting on new forms of a known substance that does not provide an enhanced efficacy against the known one. Although section 3(d) is not restricted to pharmaceutical patents, it was designed primarily to prevent the practice of evergreening products by pharmaceutical companies.[159] While designing this provision, there was a pro-

[154] Ibid.
[155] Ibid.
[156] Ibid.
[157] Ibid.
[158] Ibid.
[159] "Evergreening is the art of extending the life of a parent patent by introducing minor physical improvements or label claims in the guise of incremental (often frivolous) innovations." Gopakumar Nair and Andreya Fernandes, *Patent Policies and Provisions Relating to Pharmaceuticals in India,* 19 Journal of Intellectual Property Rights 7–77 (2014), http://nopr.niscair.res.in/bitstream/123456789/26503/1/JIPR%2019%281%29%207-17.pdf (last visited January 20, 2020).

longed discussion in the Parliament of India in the light of the sheer vulnerability of Indian pharmaceutical companies and innovators after the loss of India's protectionist regime, which excluded product patents from food, drugs and chemicals. However, the interpretation of section 3(d) needs much caution, as it may have a serious impact on innovation. The concept of evergreening is closely connected with incremental innovation. There have been contesting debates about the patentability of the latter as there exists a thin yet significant line of demarcation between the two. Incremental innovation could be distinguished from the evergreening because it could be considered as "an important stepping stone in the development of a breakthrough drug where evergreening could not".[160] If a pharmaceutical company merely modifies the tablet colour or the inert ingredients of a drug and seeks a patent on the modification, this certainly comes under the definition of evergreening.[161] A more complex case arises when a modification increases a drug's bioavailability, a type of absorptivity defined as "the proportion of a drug that is delivered to its site of action in the body".[162] For illustration, "this is usually the amount entering the circulation and may be low when the drugs are given by mouth".[163] Increased bioavailability has the potential to produce a significant impact in terms of drug delivery and drug administration which would have beneficial implications for patients. Here, the question arises whether this type of improvement could be considered as an incremental innovation worthy of patent protection.[164] Against this backdrop, the *Novartis* judgment reflects the judicial trend in India regarding pharmaceutical patents eschewing issues in a relatively new IP regime where national regimes started feeling global influences, particularly in a new patent paradigm, which included product patenting on pharmaceuticals.

Novartis was the first case relating to pharmaceutical patents which reached the Supreme Court of India after India had made certain amendments to the Patents Act 1970 to make it TRIPS compliant. It triggered much heated debate when, on April 1, 2013, the Supreme Court of India upheld the rejection of Novartis's patent application on a life-saving anti-cancer drug Gleevec on the ground that it failed to meet the criterion fixed by section 3(d). Patient advocates welcomed the decision as a landmark one, making the medicine more

---

[160] Liu, *supra* note 138.
[161] Ibid.
[162] Oxford Reference: https://www.oxfordreference.com/view/10.1093/oi/authority.20110803095506748 (last visited January 20, 2020).
[163] Ibid.
[164] Liu, *supra* note 138.

affordable, while pharmaceutical companies, innovators and patent proponents considered it harmful for innovation and foreign investment.[165]

While deciding the case, the Supreme Court of India frequently referred to the legislative intent behind drafting section 3(d) and explained what the law is in the light of "why" and "how".[166] Three forms of imatinib mesylate which came to the forefront in relation to section 3(d) were imatinib free base, imatinib mesylate non-crystalline and imatinib mesylate beta crystalline.[167] Novartis filed a patent application on the compound imatinib in its free base form in the USA in 1993 and successfully obtained patent protection for the same. In its free base form it was not administrable to humans. Novartis improved the compound by first converting it to imatinib mesylate and second to the beta crystalline form of imatinib mesylate. It was the latter which helped produce Gleevac. Novartis filed a mailbox application in India in 1998 on "the beta crystalline imatinib mesylate, specifying in its application the use of beta crystalline imatinib mesylate in Gleevac and other aspects of the drug's solid form".[168] The Assistant Controller rejected Novartis's patents for lack of novelty and non-obviousness; however, on appeal, the IPAB reversed the decision as to the novelty and non-obviousness counts and held that Novartis's invention fulfilled both the criteria. However, it maintained that the patent failed to pass the requirement of section 3(d). Against the decision of IPAB, Novartis proceeded to the Supreme Court of India. The Supreme Court held that although the substance in question, i.e. the beta crystalline form of imatinib mesylate, was a new form of a known compound, i.e. imatinib free base, Novartis had failed to provide sufficient evidence to demonstrate that there was an enhancement in the therapeutic efficacy as compared to imatinib free base.[169] The court also maintained that the therapeutic efficacy of a medicine must be judged strictly and narrowly.[170] As regards Novartis's claim of better bioavailability and better physical characteristics, such as better storability of the compound, the Court rejected the claim by observing that these attributes do not necessarily improve the therapeutic effect.[171]

---

165 Sudip Chaudhary, *The Larger Implications of the Novartis Glivic Judgment* 48:17 Economic and Political Weekly (April 27, 2013), https://www.epw.in/journal/2013/17/commentary/larger-implications-novartis-glivec-judgment.html (last visited July 16, 2020)

166 Liu, *supra* note 138.

167 Ibid.

168 Ibid.

169 Ibid.

170 Chaudhary, *supra* note 165.

171 Ibid.

The judgment had a great positive impact on the affordability and accessibility of drugs (particularly life-saving drugs) and would be helpful in checking the practice of evergreening patents in India but the decision leaves uncertainty as to many aspects, such as what constitutes enhanced therapeutic efficacy and whether improved bioavailability would qualify under the section 3(d) criterion. These uncertainties would have an adverse impact on patent filing and investment. After the Novartis case, demonstrating enhanced therapeutic efficacy may not be that easy. Further, in an illustrative manner, under explanation, section 3(d) provides that salts, esters and other derivatives of known substance shall be considered to be the same substance, "unless they differ significantly in properties with regard to efficacy". Even if in future a new form depicts some increase in efficacy, it would be subject to the interpretation of the word "significantly".[172]

7.2.3 *Nuziveedu v. Monsanto*:[173] the overlapping of patent and plant variety legislations

After the foregoing discussion of two important cases relating to pharmaceutical patents with serious implications for the patentability of biotechnology inventions, *Nuziveedu* emerged as the first case specifically related to biotechnology patents that reached the Supreme Court of India through the complex web of different legislations and executive and judicial decisions. There are certain commonalities among all the decisions mentioned above, including *Nuziveedu*, i.e. issues of the accessibility of patented technology, controversial licensing practices and exorbitant prices charged on the end product. *Nuziveedu* also grappled with the overlapping of patent and plant variety legislations on a common plant-related subject matter (seeds). Since it was addressing the contested overlapping statutes, both IPR proponents, agri biotech companies and breeding companies on one side, and farmers and small breeders backed by farmer organisations and NGOs on the other side started following the case. The case was expected to decide the future of IP and innovation pathways for agricultural biotechnology in India, and, therefore, a detailed discussion of this case is pertinent.

As background, Monsanto developed a pest-resistant technology, popularly known as Bt technology, aimed at enabling farmers to achieve better yields of crops. Specifically, Bt technology involves the "introgression of certain genes of *Bacillus thuringiensis* (Bt), naturally occurring bacteria, into the genome of cotton-seeds to ensure that the resulting crops develop resistance against

172 Ibid.

173 *Nuziveedu Seeds Ltd. and Ors. v. Monsanto Technology LLC and Ors.*, MANU/DE/1388/2018.

certain pests of the lepidopteron species".[174] Bollworm insects were ruining the cotton crops in India and in Bt cotton "the genome of the bacteria, *Bacillus thuringiensis*, codes for a protein which eliminates the bollworm insect".[175] This gene is procured through lab-made process involving substantial human intervention; "Bt trait genes are inserted into a variety in a laboratory through a biotechnology process, which after transformation is known as a 'transgenic variety'. The Bt trait from this variety is then transferred into other varieties by traditional plant breeding methods".[176] Bt technology developed by Monsanto worked well against bollworm pests and had shown the potential for effectively reducing the use of pesticides by farmers.[177] In India, Monsanto obtained patents on Bollgard-II technology and introduced its variety in the market under the trademark Bollgard-II®.[178]

Monsanto entered into business by licensing its patent to its joint venture Mahyco Monsanto Biotech (India) Ltd (MMBL), which in turn entered into sub-licences with approximately 40 Indian seed companies.[179] It is to be clearly understood here that these seed companies produced seed varieties of their own that are eligible to be protected under the Protection of Plant Varieties and Farmers' Rights Act (PPVFRA) 2001; these seeds are then introgressed with Monsanto's patented gene technology.[180] Although the introduction of Monsanto's patented technology yielded successful results, the company has been criticized for its exorbitant licensing fee and overcharging for seeds. In addition to this, in due course allegations erupted that the Bt seeds lose their ability to resist pests over time. Due to these factors, farmers were forced into

---

174 Prashant Reddy, *A Monsanto Case that Could Alter the Dynamics of Technology Transfer to India*. IP Kitten (March 4, 2016), http://ipkitten.blogspot.com/2016/03/a-monsanto-case-that-could-alter.html (last visited January 20, 2020).

175 Rajdeep and Joyeeta Banerjee, *The Future of Genetically Modified Crops in India*, Forbes, India (May 21, 2018), http://www.forbesindia.com/blog/economy-policy/the-future-of-genetically-modified-crops-in-india/ (last visited January 20, 2020).

176 Ibid.

177 Reddy, *supra* note 174.

178 Ibid.

179 Kshitij Kumar Singh, *Bayer-Monsanto Merger and India's IP Approach to Agricultural Biotechnology: Navigating through a Complex Web of Law and Policy*, 20:1&2 Asian Biotechnology and Development Review 3–25 (2018), https://www.researchgate.net/publication/329351862_Bayer-Monsanto_Merger_and_India%27s_IP_Approach_to_Agricultural_Biotechnology_Navigating_through_a_complex_web_of_law_and_policy (last visited January 20, 2020).

180 Reddy, supra note 174.

debt and many alleged this as a compelling factor in suicides among farmers. In the light of these serious concerns, states started regulating prices in 2016.[181]

Against this background, a dispute arose over the sub-licensing agreements between MMBL and Nuziveedu, executed on March 10, 2015. Monsanto procured Nuziveedu cotton transgenic variety seeds as the "Donor Seeds", and allowed them to develop genetically modified hybrid cotton planting seeds on the licensing terms. Monsanto also licensed its registered trademarks: Bollgard and Bollgard-II.[182] Nuziveedu refused to pay the process fee to Monsanto as per the licensing agreement and agreed to pay the "trait fee" only as fixed by the State Government. Against this refusal Monsanto instituted a suit against Nuziveedu in Delhi High Court for infringement of its patents as well as trademarks.[183] In response to this, Nuziveedu, contended that Monsanto's patent is liable to be rejected as it falls under one of the exceptions, section 3(j) of the Patents Act 1970. In addition to this, it filed a counterclaim in the court that "the patent granted to Monsanto is liable to be cancelled besides praying for declaration that the Agreements are valid and binding and performance of the consequent obligations".[184]

Monsanto's patent contained 27 claims including a "method for producing a transgenic plant with increased resistance to insect[s] on account of a 'nucleic acid sequence', derived from the DNA of Bt (*Bacillus thuringiensis)* bacteria and the process to insert it in plant cells".[185] More specifically, "the invention involved identification of desired gene (Cry2Ab) from the DNA of BT (*Bacillus thuringiensis*) bacteria, making (synthesizing) nucleic acid sequence by copying the Cry2Ab for insertion into a plant cell, and the method of inserting the said nucleic acid sequence into a plant cell".[186] Out of 27 claims, claims 25 to 27 were contested on the basis that they included the biotechnological invention involving an infusion of the Bt gene into the

---

181 Disher Dhillon, *Without its GM Cotton Patents, Monsanto May Stop Doing Business in India*, Business Insider India (April 12, 2018), https://www.businessinsider.in/without-its-gm-cotton-patents-monsanto-may-stop-doing-business-in-india/articleshow/63731936.cms (last visited January 20, 2020).

182 T.V. Padma, "Explainer: SC Will Not Stay High Court Order in Monsanto v. Nuziveedu Case", The Wire (May 14, 2018), https://thewire.in/the-sciences/explainer-sc-will-not-stay-high-court-order-in-monsanto-v-nuziveedu-case (last visited January 20, 2020).

183 Singh, *supra* note 179.

184 Jacob Schindler, "India's Supreme Court will hear Monsanto's Challenge to a Recent Ruling Imperiling Agri-tech Patentability", IAM (May 7, 2018), https://www.lexology.com/library/detail.aspx?g=1c6aa834-8a8e-4968-8c5c-e926651879ae (last visited July 16, 2020).

185 Ibid.

186 Rajdeep and Banerjee *supra* note 175.

cotton gene. The contested Patent No. 214436 was entitled "METHODS FOR TRANSFORMING PLANTS TO EXPRESS BACILLUS THURINGIENSIS DELTAENDOTOXINS".[187]

The Single Bench of the High Court headed by Justice Gauba did not accept Nuziveedu's argument that Monsanto's claim was not maintainable.[188] The Court held that the determination of this issue and ascertainment of the patent claim would necessarily require formal proof and expert opinion.[189] Justice Gauba, however, agreed that GM traits involve "laboratory processes and are not naturally-occurring substances". They involved human intervention and, therefore, could be protected under the Patents Act 1970.[190] As regards the patent sub-licensing agreements, the Court observed that the "pre-mature termination of the Agreements was illegal and arbitrary" and until the suit was decided "the parties would remain bound by their respective obligations".[191] Rejecting the injunctive relief against Nuziveedu, the Court directed that the licensing fee/trait value must conform to the prevailing laws (as fixed by states).[192]

Against the single judgment, the parties preferred an appeal in the Division Bench. The Division Bench, comprised of two justices, Justice Ravindra S. Bhatt and Justice Yogendra Khanna, upheld the single judges' direction to restore the obligations of the parties under the sub-licensing agreement with the payment of a license fee or trait value by the defendant according to the prevailing law.[193] As a matter of surprise, the Division Bench also rejected Monsanto's patent while suggesting Monsanto to proceed under the PPVFRA. While deciding the case as to the patentability of the subject matter, the Court believed that the parties were agreed as to the summary adjudication of the validity of patents. The Bench observed that the transgenic plants with the integrated Bt trait in the present case came under the category of "essentially

---

[187] Pratistha Sinha, *Monsanto Technology LLC and Ors v. Nuziveedu Seeds Ltd. and Ors*, IIPRD Blog-IPR Discussion (May 15, 2018), https://www.iiprd.com/monsanto-technology-llc-and-ors-vs-nuziveedu-seeds-ltd-and-ors/ (last visited January 20, 2020).

[188] Singh, *supra* note 179.

[189] Deepa Tiku, *Indian IP Jurisprudence is the Real Winner in the Monsanto Cotton Technology Case*, iam (January 15, 2019), https://www.iam-media.com/litigation/indian-ip-jurisprudence-real-winner-monsanto-case (last visited January 20, 2020).

[190] Vivian Fernandes, "The Delhi High Court Order on Patenting on GM Traits is Confidence-Shattering", Financial Express (April 12, 2018), https://www.financialexpress.com/opinion/the-delhi-high-court-order-on-patenting-on-gm-traits-is-confidence-shattering/1130018/ (last visited January 20, 2020).

[191] Schindler, *supra* note 184.

[192] Singh, *supra* note 179.

[193] Tiku, *supra* note 189.

biological process" excluded from the patentability under the Patents Act 1970 and the patent rights of Monsanto over the gene were not maintainable.[194] The Court categorically maintained that "the nucleic acid sequence which was the invention in question had no existence of its own and after introgression, the seed material had to undergo further steps of hybridisation to suit local conditions. Thus, the product was not [a] 'microorganism'".[195] Though the Court agreed to the fact that the gene constructs having artificial features can be protected under the Patents Act, yet it maintained that once they become a part of a plant or a seed, they can only be protected under the PPVFRA rather than the Patents Act.[196] The Court clarified that the two legislations, the Patents Act 1970 and the PPVFRA are mutually exclusive and not complementary.[197]

The interpretation of the Division Bench judgment could be contended on numerous counts: the Court's logic that "the moment the DNA containing the nucleotide sequence (subject patent) is hybridized to produce the transgenic seeds/plants; the seeds/plants fall within the purview of the PV Act" is inconsequential as the patentee had limited its claim to selected genetic sequence as inserted into a plant genome and not a plant.[198] On the import of an essentially biological process, it is worth mentioning that in Bt cotton, "the gene, which produces the bollworm killing toxic protein, is derived from a soil bacterium, but insertion of this natural isolate in Bt cotton-plants is a complex affair and it could not be inserted straight away into the cotton genome". It has to be modified in such a manner that is acceptable to the plant and "it has the components attached so that the production of the toxic protein is switched on and off at particular points in the life cycle of the cotton plant".[199] Therefore, "insertion of the relevant DNA sequence into the genome of a plant could not occur without human intervention, and consequently, this step is an important technical step which has a decisive impact on the desired final result".[200] Monsanto approached the Supreme Court of India challenging the Division Bench's deci-

---

194 Padma, *supra* note 182.

195 Rajdeep and Banerjee, *supra* note 175.

196 Fernandes, *supra* note 190.

197 Padma, *supra* note 182.

198 Prashant Reddy, *Delhi HC Delivers Deadly Blow to Agro-Biotech in Monsanto-Nuziveedu Ruling*, Bloomberg Quint Opinion (April 26, 2018), https://www.bloombergquint.com/opinion/2018/04/26/delhi-hc-delivers-deadly-blow-to-agro-biotech-in-monsanto-nuziveedu-ruling (last visited January 20, 2020).

199 Fernandes, *supra* note 190.

200 Malathi, Lakshmikumaran (2019) "Genetically Modified Plants: The IP and Regulatory Concerns in India". In: Liu K.C., Racherla U. (eds) *Innovation, Economic Development, and Intellectual Property in India and China*. ARCIALA Series on Intellectual Assets and Law in Asia. Springer, Singapore, https://link.springer.com/chapter/10.1007/978-981-13-8102-7_16 (last visited July 16, 2020).

sion. The Supreme Court refrained from giving any opinion on the validity of Monsanto's patent, i.e. whether the patent falls under section 3(j) of the Indian Patents Act, 1970 (the "Patents Act"), which excludes plants, animals and *essentially biological processes* for the production of plants and animals from patent protection. The Supreme Court based its judgment on the following two issues: first, whether Monsanto had consented to a summary adjudication regarding the validation of its patent; and second, whether the Division Bench was correct in invalidating the patent without a trial.[201] Responding to the first issue the Court observed:

> The plaintiffs had never consented to a summary adjudication regarding the validity of its patent. The consent referred to by the Division Bench, had been given only to decide whether the plaintiffs' patent had been infringed or not, as also the scope of the patent, so as to allow or disallow the relief of injunction. It is incomprehensible that the plaintiffs holding a valid registered patent under the Act nonetheless would have agreed to a summary consideration and validation/invalidation of the patent.[202]

On the second issue, the Court held that the Division Bench had erred by considering such complex issues of facts without the help of expert evidence through a trial. The Court observed:

> The Division Bench ought not to have examined the counter-claim itself usurping the jurisdiction of the Single Judge to decide unpatentability of the process claims 1–24 also in the summary manner done. Summary adjudication of a technically complex suit requiring expert evidence also, at the stage of injunction in the manner done, was certainly neither desirable nor permissible in the law. The suit involved complicated mixed questions of law and facts with regard to patentability and exclusion of patent which could be examined in the suit on basis of evidence.[203]

Conclusively, the Supreme Court upheld the injunctive relief provided by the single judge by maintaining that the relief merited no interference during the pendency of the suit. Further, while restoring the patent, the Court remanded the suit to the single judge for disposal in accordance with the law.[204]

---

[201] Indus Law, *Supreme Court Sets Aside Delhi High Court Judgment, Restores Monsanto's Patent* (January 2019), https://induslaw.com/app/webroot/publications/pdf/alerts-2019/Monsanto-vs-Nuziveedu-Supreme-Court-InfoAlert.pdf (last visited January 20, 2020).

[202] *Monsanto Technology LLC thru the Authorised Representative Ms. Natalia Voruz & others v. Nuziveedu Seeds Ltd. and Others*, Civil Appeal No(s). 189–190 of 2019 (arising out of SLP(C) Nos. 16479–16480 of 2018, para 9, https://indiankanoon.org/doc/116548206/ (last visited January 20, 2020).

[203] Ibid, at para 22.

[204] Indus Law, *supra* note 201.

Although the Supreme Court has not tested the validity of patents and a few other important issues yet, it sets a good precedent for how cases relating to biotechnology patents should be approached. Many issues such as (a) whether the patented DNA sequence was a plant or a part of a plant; (b) whether the nucleic acid sequence trait once inserted could be removed from the plant variety; and (c) whether the Patent is valid in light of the provisions of the Protection of Plant Variety and Farmers' Right Act 2001, were posed before the court.[205] The overlapping of the two legislations on the present subject matter has not been explained through the judgment and it would be interesting to see how the Single Bench proceeds with the trial. Nevertheless, the Court has laid great emphasis on the fact that patent matters involve mixed questions of fact and law and categorically maintained that "summary adjudication of any technically complex suit without formal proof, particularly by way of expert opinion is neither desirable nor permissible under the law".[206] Monsanto being the first case on agricultural biotechnology may exert a great influence on patent practices and licensing strategies in the sector and it could be expected that future cases would be dealt with after giving due recognition to the technical complexity of inventions relating to biotechnology.

7.2.4 The *PepsiCo* case – vulnerability of farmers under the PPVFRA

The vulnerability of farmers was exposed in the *PepsiCo* episode in India, when PepsiCo India initiated legal proceeding against four farmers in Gujrat for "illegally growing its potato variety registered under the Protection of Plant Varieties and Farmers' Rights Act (PPVFRA) 2001". The company registered two hybrid varieties, FL1867 and FL2017, in 2016 for a period of 15 years and marketed the latter under the trademark FC-5. As regards the trademarked variety FC-5, PepsiCo alleged that farmers were using it illegally. However, due to the questions raised about the registrability of this variety by the farmer organisations, PepsiCo withdrew its case. It is worth noting that just before this withdrawal PepsiCo insisted the farmers enter into a contractual settlement.[207] Despite this withdrawal, this episode caused great alarm and raises significant concerns as to the implementation of the PPVFRA. The PPVFRA was the result of almost ten years of serious debate as to how agricultural products such as plant variety could be protected through IPR protection. After careful consideration, India opted to go for a *sui-generis* system by not abiding to the UPOV Model 1991 as it denies farmers the freedom to reuse farm-saved seeds

---

205 Ibid.

206 Tiku, *supra* note 189.

207 Biswajit Dhar, Points of law in the PepsiCo-Potato case, Business Line (May 7, 2019), https://www.thehindubusinessline.com/opinion/points-of-law-in-the-pepsico-potato-case/article27060326.ece (last visited January 20, 2020).

and exchange them with their neighbours.[208] Under the PPVFRA, farmers' rights have been distinctively recognised. It provides threefold rights to farmers: (i) farmers are recognised on a par with breeders and they can register their varieties; (ii) farmers engaged in the conservation of genetic resources of land races and wild relatives of economic plants and their improvement through selection and preservation are recognised and rewarded; (iii) farmers can protect the traditional practices of saving seeds either for sowing for their next harvest or sharing them with their farm neighbours.[209]

Farmers planting a registered variety is per se not an offence since the Act allows the farmers to reuse such varieties and to also share them with their neighbours, provided two conditions are met. First, the farmers cannot sell branded seeds; second FC-5 has been registered as an extant variety, which is a variety of common knowledge in that such a variety of potato was already available in the knowledge registries. From this case, it could be inferred from the order of the judge that the PepsiCo India company may have given the wrong information in claiming that FC-5 was a new variety instead of an extant variety.[210] It was also alleged that PepsiCo employed a private agency to collect samples from farmers' field. And the last thing, which is particularly worrisome, is that though it withdrew from the case, before withdrawal it was offering farmers the possibility of settling the dispute by entering into a contractual agreement.[211]

8. PROGRESSIVE TRENDS AND POTENTIAL CHALLENGES

The Indian biotechnology sector moved ahead from self-sufficiency to a pro-innovation approach with a promise to promote the sustainable use of biotechnology products and processes. One of the significant features in the regulatory regime is the proposed National Biotechnology Regulatory Authority of India (NBRA) with a single professionally managed mechanism that would ensure a single window clearance process for biotechnology products and processes. The NBRA recommendation was transformed into a proposed Biotechnology Regulatory Authority of India (BRAI). Another significant trend is the increasing participation of the private sector and the government's emphasis on the PPP model.[212] Many homegrown companies took a lead in the services and manufacturing sectors pertaining to biotechnology.

---

208 Ibid.
209 Ibid.
210 Ibid
211 Ibid.
212 Padmanabhan et al., *supra* note 30.

To imbibe an effective incentive model for researchers and scientists in the system has been a big ask, which seems to be well received by the government as it has given approval to the Department of Scientific and Industrial Research (DSIR) proposal "to allow scientists to set up start-up companies while retaining their jobs in academic institutions".[213] Similarly, the Biotechnology Industry Research Assistance Council (BIRAC) within five years of its establishment, initiated numerous schemes, networks and platforms that assist in bridging "the existing gaps in the industry-academia Innovation research and facilitate novel, high quality affordable products development through cutting edge technologies".[214] It has also triggered various partnership programmes with national as well as global partners to collaborate and deliver "the salient features of its mandate".[215]

There are Government's flagship programmes such as "Make in India" and "Start-up India" that have placed special emphasis on the promotion of biotechnology. Realizing the growth phase of the biotechnology industry and the immense opportunities before it, "biotechnology was chosen as one of the champion sectors in [the] Make-in-India initiative".[216] In this context, the BIRAC has been entrusted with the responsibility of establishing a Biotechnology Industry Facilitation Cell. Similarly under the "Start-Up India" programme a large number of world-class incubators have been established across India; the AcE Fund and SEED funds have been launched to provide capital assistance to start-ups; and three BIRAC Regional Centres have been established.[217] The Government of India has adopted a pro-innovation approach to create IP ecosystems in the country by making the IPO smart, efficient and up-to-date, coupled with launching fee rebates and expedited patent filing and examination processes for start-ups and academia.[218] Along with this, biotechnology has registered a strong presence in India's National IPR Policy 2016.[219] The wheel of innovation through innovation can only

---

213 Natesh and Bhan, *supra* note 2.

214 Department of Biotechnology, Ministry of Science and Technology, Government of India, BIRAC, https://birac.nic.in/desc_new.php?id=89 (last visited January 20, 2020).

215 Ibid.

216 Department of Biotechnology, Ministry of Science and Technology, Government of India, *Make in India & Start-up India*, http://dbtindia.gov.in/schemes-programmes/translational-industrial-development-programmes/make-india-start-india (last visited January 20, 2020).

217 Ibid.

218 Government of India, IPO, https://ficpi.org/news/reforms-in-indian-patent-system-and-procedure/ (last visited January 20, 2020).

219 Government of India, Ministry of Commerce and Industry, DIPP, *National IPR Policy 2016*, https://dipp.gov.in/sites/default/files/National_IPR_Policy_English.pdf (last visited January 20, 2020).

be ensured by an effective enforcement mechanism for IPRs dealing with biotechnology. The enforcement mechanism is being strengthened with the creation of commercial courts for taking up the commercial issues including IPRs.[220] In an interesting development, India registered an eight-point jump in 2019 from 44th position in 2018 to 36th position on the International Intellectual Property Index.[221] India sets an exemplary record in vaccine production by supplying more than 60 per cent of the current world requirements. Attempts are also being made to innovate in terms of different methods of vaccine production, which may provide an added advantage to India. This success could be translated into other subsectors to achieve excellence.[222] The National Biotechnology Development Strategy 2015–2020 aimed at attracting substantial investment, improving and building infrastructure for research and development, building a skilled workforce and attracting global and national alliances with international institutes.[223]

Along with significant progressive trends in the biotechnology sector, India also faces significant challenges: India lacks quality human resources of the right kind, it lacks venture/angel funding, and the structure of public-private partnership is fragile and on a small scale, while many institutions still lack units or structures that may promote such interactions. The country also suffers from bureaucratic barriers and regulatory challenges given the complex regulatory approval process, and industry-led R&D is not adequate in scale or quality. Furthermore, although IP generation exists, its scaling up is a huge challenge, as is the lack of adequate ignition grants to young innovators.[224] Despite having a great IT base, the bioinformatics field has not yet made

---

[220] Pratik Chaudhari and Anay Amin, *India commercial court: Saviour of the System* WIPR (September 24, 2019), https://www.worldipreview.com/contributed-article/india-commercial-courts-saviour-of-the-system (last visited January 19, 2020).

[221] *India jumps 8 places to 36th on International IP Index*, The Economic Times (February 8, 2019), https://economictimes.indiatimes.com/news/economy/indicators/india-jumps-8-places-to-36th-on-international-ip-index/articleshow/67884700.cms (last visited January 20, 2020).

[222] Prasanta Kumar Ghosh, *Indian Vaccines Industry Addressing Human Health Challenges*, Forum for Indian Science Diplomacy Case Study (No. 4, 2019), http://fisd.in/sites/default/files/FISD%20Case%20Study_P%20K%20Ghosh.pdf (last visited January 20, 2020).

[223] Press Information Bureau, Government of India, Ministry of Science and Technology, *National Biotechnology Strategy 2015–2020* (December 30, 2015), https://pib.gov.in/newsite/printrelease.aspx?relid=134035 (last visited January 20, 2020); Department of Biotechnology, Ministry of Science and Technology, Government of India, National Biotechnology Development Strategy 2015–2020 – Promoting bioscience research, education and entrepreneurship, http://dbtindia.gov.in/sites/default/files/DBT_Book-_29-december_2015.pdf (last visited January 20, 2020).

[224] Natesh and Bhan, *supra* note 2.

a significant contribution in the Indian biotech sector, and translating the great potential of this sector into the biotechnology field poses a great challenge for India. Given India's initiatives and positive approach to biotechnology, the country has risen up to deal with these challenges in the future.

9. CONCLUSION

The biotechnology sector has evolved into one of the most prominent sectors in India, making a significant contribution to the national economy. It is considered the technology for the future, with a huge potential to bring radical transformations in society. India being a biodiversity-rich country with diverse human, animal and plant genetic resources, can do wonders in the field of genetics, genomics and bioinformatics. The biotechnology sector in India has been well shaped by policy initiatives and institutional developments with varying objectives ranging from a successful need-based self-sufficiency model through the Green Revolution to a very competitive pro-innovation model, well in tune with modern biotechnological advances. New industrial policy recognising the waves of liberalisation and globalisation have made it possible for India to forge important collaborations for biotechnology developments in both public and private spheres. This has also made possible the increasing participation of the private sector in the biotech field and the growing acceptance of public-private partnerships (PPPs). India has shown its potential in vaccine development as it supplies almost 60 per cent of the world's requirements. This benchmark needs to be set for other sub-fields such as bio-industry and bioinformatics too as the Indian biotech sector has not yet fulfilled its real potential, making a very minimal contribution to the global share of biotechnology. Although India has registered phenomenal growth in numerous sub-sectors including biopharmaceuticals, it faces enormous challenges in others. A glaring example of this is agricultural biotechnology, where regulatory logjams coupled with non-scientific opposition often halt the innovation process. An efficient legal and regulatory system creates an ecosystem that encourages innovation in technological fields. India is on a progressive track to simplify the rules and provide a dedicated regulatory authority (the proposed BRAI) along with significant governmental schemes. However, given the pace of the rapidly changing world, a steady pace of reforms may slow down the innovation wheel.

On the innovation front, India's approach to intellectual property has been alleged as conservative and overprotective, yet recent decisions reflect a progressive trend. In the evolutionary phase every country remains more cautious about its socio-economic needs, while striking a balance in resisting the monopolies created by IPRs. India has tried to use TRIPS flexibilities to the maximum to suit its socio-economic needs. This use could be justified as developing countries have their own specific conditions requiring a particular approach, for example the *PepsiCo* case reflects the sheer vulnerability of farmers in the face of the multinational companies, which needs to be redressed specifically. But while making such adjustments the sanctity of the patent law should not be diluted, and the patent doctrines should not be disregarded; the technicalities of patent law should not be pitted against the public interest. IP in today's world has become a potential economic indicator that affects foreign investments in vital fields such as pharmaceuticals and biotechnology, and, therefore, countries are required to take thoughtful and intelligent decisions after assessing its impact on long-term growth and innovation. A balance has to be struck between the patient's right to access to medicine and the patentee's rights. It is not the static expressions in the form of provisions under the law that makes the difference but how they are applied by the patent examiners and interpreted by the courts. A policy-style reasoning devoid of the changing realities in the realm of IP may not produce the desired result; application and interpretation both have to be progressive. Irrespective of the outcome, the recognition of the distinct nature of biotechnology patents by the Supreme Court of India in the *Nuziveedu* case, pertaining to the interface of patent and plant variety legislations, may set a progressive trend at the trial court level to treat this subject as a special case to be decided after obtaining expert opinions. An increased emphasis by the Government of India on creating a viable ecosystem for biotechnology sets an encouraging tone for the flourishing of the sector.

PART VII

THE LORE OF INTELLECTUAL PROPERTY DURING WARTIME

14. International trade mark enforcement under the Versailles Treaty: a case study of Sanatogen

Arpan Banerjee and Dana Beldiman[1]

INTRODUCTION

The First World War was commonly called 'The war to end all wars'.[2] And, according to a book by HG Wells which popularised the use of the term, would 'stop this sort of thing for ever' and 'open the way to disarmament and peace throughout the earth'.[3] The end of the War was marked by a series of peace treaties. The Versailles Treaty, signed in 1919, was undoubtedly the best known and defined the economic terms of the peace with Germany.[4] However,

[1] The authors thank Catherine Bond for her comments on a draft version of this chapter.

[2] The broad facts surrounding the First World War are well known. The War began in 1914, triggered by the assassination of Archduke Franz Ferdinand of the Austro-Hungarian Empire in Sarajevo, by a Serbian militant. In response, Austro-Hungary declared war on Serbia. Russia felt obligated to support Serbia and stepped in to protect it. Germany, allied with Austro-Hungary, declared war on Russia, which, in turn, was an ally of France. Germany attacked France, passing through neutral Belgium. Belgium appealed to Britain for protection and Britain entered the War. Because the War drew on each power's colonial empire, the conflict spread across the globe. Out of the network of interlocking alliances, ultimately two adversarial coalitions emerged. On the one hand, the Triple Entente, later known as the Allied Powers, grouped together France, Russia, Britain and, eventually, the US, On the other hand, the Triple Alliance, aka Central Powers, included Austria-Hungary, Germany, Italy and their allies. The War raged for four years, as more belligerent parties were drawn into it. Its outcome marked a turning point in world history. Four empires crumbled, national borders were redrawn, and new states formed out of the remains of the former empires.

[3] HG Wells, *The War That Will End War* (Frank & Cecil Palmer, London 1914) 11, 14.

[4] Treaty of Peace with Germany (Treaty of Versailles), Treaty and Protocol signed at Versailles on 28 June 1919, https://www.loc.gov/law/help/us-treaties/bevans/m-ust000002-0043.pdf.

hopes for a long-lasting peace would prove to be horribly wrong. Barely two decades after the War had ended, the world would enter into a second conflict of even greater magnitude. During its existence, the Versailles Treaty was criticised by some for being one-sided and impractical.[5] Later assessments have seen the Treaty being 'attacked both as too severe and too lenient'.[6] Arguably, however, one of the fairest provisions of the Treaty concerned industrial property rights. Upon the outbreak of the War, warring countries adopted economic measures to prevent traders from enemy countries conducting business on their soil. These measures included the forced confiscation and sale of enemy-owned assets, encompassing both physical property and industrial property rights.[7] The Versailles Treaty sought to restore the pre-War status for all affected businesses in signatory countries.

Among the notable German targets of the property expropriation laws was Sanatogen, an internationally famous health tonic. After the War, the original German makers of Sanatogen attempted to reclaim their rights to the Sanatogen word mark from a British company that had since appropriated it. This resulted in a major trade mark case in British India, where the German company had been forced to cede its monopoly to the British usurper (as well as others). At the time, British India was the largest and most important colony in the British Empire. Its territory included present-day Pakistan and Burma. Prior to the War, British India had served as a lucrative market for the German makers of Sanatogen. Thus, the stakes involved in the case were presumably quite high. This chapter looks back on this long-forgotten case, decided by the Bombay High Court. The case is unusual for interpreting trade mark law principles in accordance with provisions of the Versailles Treaty. Yet, it still reinforces certain basic, enduring principles of trade mark and unfair competition law. The chapter begins by providing some background information on Sanatogen, followed by a discussion of how the brand was appropriated during the First World War. It then discusses the international trade mark law system during the First World War, followed by an explanation of the relevant provisions of the Versailles Treaty. This is followed by a discussion of the Bombay High Court case.

---

5 For example, John Maynard Keynes termed it 'not practically right or possible'. John Maynard Keynes, *The Economic Consequences of the Peace* (Harcourt, Brace and Howe, New York 1919) 36.

6 David Stevenson, 'France at the Paris Peace Conference', in Robert Boyce (ed), *French Foreign and Defence Policy, 1918–1940* (Routledge, London 1998) 10, 11.

7 Leske-Loewenfeld, *Die Rechtsverfolgung im internationalen Verkehr*, Teil 2 (Carl Heymanns Verlag, Berlin 1924) 5.

1. SANATOGEN: ITS HISTORY AND WARTIME ACQUISITION

1.a Historical Origins

The Wülfing Bauer & Cie company (trading using various names over time)[8] was formed in 1898 in Berlin, by businessman Abraham von Wülfing and chemical engineer Felix Bauer. The company had manufacturing facilities in Gronau, near Hanover.[9] Among its products was the health tonic Sanatogen. In the early 1900s, Sanatogen became internationally fashionable as a panacea for many malaises. It rapidly acquired fame as one of the world's most popular brands. Sanatogen was described variously as a tonic for 'all those who feel weak and worn-out',[10] 'king of tonics',[11] 'brain tonic'[12] and 'nerve revitaliser'.[13] It came in the form of a white powder which, when heated, dissolved to become a milky liquid.[14] Chemically, it consisted of casein and sodium glycerophosphorus. The product's instructions read:

> Food tonic. A concentrated nutrient with tonic properties. It is very easily digested and absorbed and is recommended as an effective means of reinforcing the daily diet

---

[8] These include Bauer & Cie, Wülfing Bauer & Ci, Wülfing AG, AJ Wülfing and Wülfing Pharma GmbH. For convenience, the company is referred to henceforth as 'Wülfing'.

[9] 'Wülfing Pharma: Mutiger Schritt in die Selbständigkeit' (1997) 16 *Pharmazeutische Zeitung*, 14 April 1997, https://www.pharmazeutische-zeitung.de/inhalt-16-1997/wuh1-16-1997.

[10] *SANATOGEN: Zur Hebung der Nerven- und Muskelkraft*, advertisement reproduced by Reklamebox, 14 March 2010, http://www.reklamebox.com/plakate-und-schilder/blechschilder/sanatogen-zur-hebung-der-nerven-und-muskelkraft/ (authors' translation from German).

[11] *Sanatogen Crowned King of Tonics*, advertisement from 1911 reproduced by Wikipedia, https://upload.wikimedia.org/wikipedia/commons/0/07/1911_adv%27t_for_Samtogen%2C_King_of_Tonics.jpg.

[12] Max KW Huang, 'Medical Advertising and Cultural Translation: The Case of *Shenbao* in Early Twentieth-Century China', in Pei-yin Lin and Weipin Tsai (eds), *Print, Profit, and Perception: Ideas, Information and Knowledge in Chinese Societies, 1895–1949* (Brill, Leiden 2014) 114, 128–35.

[13] ibid.

[14] Above n 10. The advertisement read: 'Sanatogen is a well-known soluble protein-containing nutritional preparation made by mixing casein with 5% sodium glycerophosphorus and appears as a snow-white powder which swells considerably when mixed with a little cold water and when heated dissolves completely to become a milky liquid. It contains 8.34% water, 5.37% ash, 2.49% phosphoric acid and 82.75% nitrogen' (authors' translation from German).

of anaemic and convalescent patients, including children, and in cases of weakness and exhaustion from overwork or illness.[15]

With the dawn of the twentieth century, Sanatogen was distributed in various international markets, including continental Europe, the UK, the US, China, Australia and India.[16] It achieved phenomenal success, helped by aggressive marketing. Its marketing strategy relied on endorsements by celebrities and prominent physicians. For instance, an advertisement published in a British journal read as follows:

> WHAT Celebrities Say about SANATOGEN: Thirteen thousand doctors have written in praise of Sanatogen. Thirty thousand doctors throughout the world are known to prescribe it. Hundreds of thousands of people have been restored from conditions of grave illness to complete health by its use.[17]

The advertisement went on to list praises for Sanatogen from a large number of eminent personalities, including various prelates, a Member of Parliament, and personal physicians to the King of England, the Emperor of Austria and the Tsar of Russia. A similar advertisement was published in the *Sydney Morning Herald*, with Sanatogen being described as 'The Royal Tonic'.[18] In one advertisement, published in a British newspaper, Sanatogen was advertised as the 'greatest invention of modern medical science' and 'the most rapid cure for Rickets in children'.[19] Meanwhile, a flattering piece, published in the *Times of India* proclaimed Sanatogen to be 'the most powerful revitalising and restorative agent known to the world' and both a prevention and cure against malaria, with advantages even over quinine.[20] However, the outbreak of the First World War was to interfere with Sanatogen's success.

---

[15] Sanatogen label, reproduced by the Smithsonian National Museum of American History, https://americanhistory.si.edu/collections/search/object/nmah_714696.

[16] Huang, above n 12.

[17] 'What Celebrities Say About Sanatogen' [advertisement] (1911) 66 *Educational Times and Journal of the College of Preceptors* 77, https://archive.org/details/educationaltimes64educ/page/77.

[18] *Sanatogen* (advertisement), *Sydney Morning Herald*, 6 February 1913, 4, https://trove.nla.gov.au/newspaper/article/15395894.

[19] Alan Gall, 'Sanatogen Nerve Tonic and its Role in the History of the Laboratory Supply Industry' (Autumn 2015) *The Journal: The Official Journal of the Institute of Science and Technology* 73 (quoting from an advertisement in the *Sheffield Daily Telegraph*, 21 April 1904), https://istonline.org.uk/cms/wp-content/uploads/2018/08/ist-journal-2015-autumn.pdf.

[20] 'The Scourge of Malaria', *The Times of India*, 15 April 1910, 11.

1.b Wartime Acquisition

In 1906, Wülfing AG of Germany established in London a wholly-owned subsidiary, named A Wülfing & Co.[21] During the War, the use of products of German origin was considered undesirable. It thus became imperative to produce Sanatogen but dissociate it from its German origins. Wülfing's London subsidiary, conscious of prevailing anti-German sentiments and wary of a takeover, issued a statement claiming that it had always employed only British workers, and that 'Mr Wülfing ... is over 60 years of age and is incapable of fighting with the German forces'.[22] Eventually, the British government de-recognised German patents and trade marks during the War, with Sanatogen becoming a casualty. A string of copycat products were manufactured, including Sanaphos (from the British Milk Products Company), Sanagen (from the Casein Limited Company) and Regesan (by Boots).[23] Such products were frequently publicised using nationalistic language. For example, the British Milk Products Company claimed that the 'extravagant price of Sanatogen' had 'enriched its German owner',[24] while Boots issued a call to 'haul down the German flag'.[25] In the *British Medical Journal*, the British Milk Products Company advertised Sanaphos as an 'all-British article' that had 'surpassed and superseded' Sanatogen.[26] Even the British Home Secretary declared Sanaphos to be 'in every way a superior product' to Sanatogen.[27] Meanwhile, at Wülfing's London subsidiary, employees attempted to take advantage of nationalist sentiments, oust its German manager, and launch their own copycat product.[28]

Ultimately, with Sanatogen having been declared by the British Home Secretary as 'a national necessity',[29] the Board of Trade, pursuant to its powers

---

21 'Genatosan', *Grace's Guide to British Industrial History*, 1 January 2017, https://www.gracesguide.co.uk/Genatosan.

22 Gall, above n 19, 74.

23 Laura Robson-Mainwaring, *Branding, Packaging and Trade Marks in the Medical Marketplace c.1870–c.1920*, PhD Thesis, University of Leicester, 351 (2019), https://lra.le.ac.uk/handle/2381/45069.

24 Gall, above n 19, 74.

25 ibid 352.

26 'Front Matter' (24 June 1916) 1 *The British Medical Journal* 16.

27 'In Parliament: Home Secretary's Statement Re "Sanatogen"', *The Times of India*, 24 February 1915, 11 (quoting Reginald McKenna).

28 Gall, above n 19, 74.

29 'Why a British Syndicate Bought Sanatogen', *The Primitive Methodist Leader*, 7 December 1916, 791, https://www.escholar.manchester.ac.uk/api/datastream?publicationPid=uk-ac-man-scw:15m1854&datastreamId=FULL-TEXT.PDF; 'Why Lord Rhondda Bought Sanatogen', *The Cambrian News and Welsh Farmers Gazette*, 1 December 1916, 5, https://cymru1914.org/en/view/newspaper/3778839/4.

under the Trading with the Enemy Act, was able to place Wülfing's London subsidiary for sale by public tender. It was acquired by a British syndicate, which took over the factory, machinery, staff and stock of ingredients.[30] The management put in place by the syndicate proceeded to de-Germanise the enterprise and declared that the management and staff were all British, making Sanatogen 'absolutely British'.[31] However, there remained the question of the brand name. Officially, Wülfing's new British owners had acquired its business and goodwill, inclusive of trade marks.[32] Yet, the names 'Wülfing' and 'Sanatogen' were still associated by consumers with Germany. This led to a curious situation where the scientific properties of Sanatogen (ordinarily protectable by patent laws) were valued, but perhaps not its brand name and house name (ordinarily protectable by trade mark laws). If anything, these names may even have repelled some British consumers. Thus, the new owners renamed Wülfing to 'Genatosan', an anagram of Sanatogen, and took care in promotions and product packaging to use the Sanatogen logo in conjunction with terms like 'British' and 'Manufactured in England', and even the Union Jack.[33] Nevertheless, valuable mass goodwill was probably still attached to Sanatogen, as a German badge of origin, in countries with no discernible anti-German sentiment. In India, prior to the forced sale of Wülfing's London subsidiary, the *Times of India* even called for British companies profiting from Wülfing's industrial property rights to share profits with it after the War. In an indication of possible dissonance between Indian and British public opinion, an annoyed Englishman attacked the newspaper for 'taking up the cudgels on behalf of Sanatogen' and wrote to its editor:

> [I]t is *per se* a German concern and therefore highly undeserving of any support. ... It is common knowledge that the German people have made the quarrel of their militarist leaders their own and they are in the mass haters of England and all that is English.[34]

---

30 Gall, above n 19, 74.

31 ibid.

32 See Letter from the Assistant Comptroller, UK Patent Office, to Albert Oppenheimer, 17 December 1920, in Board of Trade, Industrial Property Department, File No. 22660.

33 For examples, see https://i.etsystatic.com/16257361/r/il/28550c/1421060715/il_570xN.1421060715_13jc.jpg (photograph of a tin, courtesy of Etsy.com) and https://iiif.wellcomecollection.org/image/L0023921.jpg/full/full/0/default.jpg (a poster, courtesy of the Wellcome Collection museum in London).

34 JD Jenkins, 'The Case of Sanatogen: To the Editor of the *Times of India*', *Times of India*, 23 December 1914, 8.

In India, copycat products like Sanaphos reportedly came to be used by doctors and patients.[35] Yet, as will be later discussed, the Sanatogen brand name and original German product continued to be held in high regard. After the War, the Versailles Treaty provided for the reinstatement of the pre-War status of industrial property rights. During the War, Wülfing had obviously been unable to control the use of the Sanatogen mark in India. Thus, Wülfing Pharma GmbH, which had continued to produce Sanatogen in Germany, sought to reclaim exclusive rights to the mark in India. Against this background, Bombay High Court decided the case of *AJ Von Wülfing v DH Jivandas*, on 19 December 1924.

2. INDUSTRIAL PROPERTY RIGHTS DURING THE FIRST WORLD WAR

2.a International Law

Until the onset of the First World War, the enforcement of industrial property rights among nations was regulated by the Paris Convention of 1883, as revised by the Washington Act of 1911. Its signatories at the time included Britain, the US, Germany, Austria and France. The Convention provided for national treatment, both with respect to the grant of an application and protection against infringement, and further introduced a system of granting international priority to trade marks registered in member countries. A separate system, the Madrid System for the International Registration of Marks, enabled international registrations valid across designated contracting states. Fourteen countries had adhered to the Madrid System by the outbreak of the War, including Austria, Germany and France. Britain, however, was not a member of the Madrid System, nor were any of its territories.

The outbreak of the War placed such treaty obligations in a state of uncertainty. Different theories were put forward on whether the Paris Convention and the Madrid Treaty stood abrogated or remained in full force.[36] The Paris Convention's International Bureau in Berne, which acted as a central information agency regarding industrial property and conducted communications with warring states, took the position that the Convention remained in effect during the War. It requested all parties to the Convention to respect and apply it as much as possible during the War. No country refused outright

35 'In Parliament', above n 27

36 See Stuart Hull MacIntyre, *Legal Effect of World War II on Treaties of the United States* (Martinus Nijhoff, Hague 2012) 234–6; Stephen Ladas, *Patents, Trademarks and Related Rights: National and International Protection* vol 1 (Harvard University Press, Cambridge, MA 1975) ch 49.

to cooperate directly with the Paris Convention's International Bureau.[37] Accordingly, international registrations of patents and trade marks under the Paris Convention continued to be accepted as valid by member states, even when registered by enemy nationals.[38] Furthermore, member states like the US continued to contribute to the maintenance of the Bureau throughout the War,[39] and publication of the Bureau's journal carried on without interruption.[40] However, some countries refused to recognise enemy industrial property and considered international conventions suspended in this respect. Notably, the British government was advised by its law officers that industrial property conventions were suspended between Britain and enemy powers during the War.[41]

2.b National Laws

Trade mark law has historically functioned on the basis of the principle of territoriality. Signatories to the Paris Convention were free to enact their own substantive legal standards, subject to the standards specified by the Convention (which were quite general, if not vague). The Madrid System, being primarily procedural in nature, had little impact on the substantive provisions of national law. At the onset of the War, trade mark law in Britain was governed by the Trade Marks Act of 1905. The law provided for the registration of marks[42] and defined a mark as 'a device, brand, heading, label, name, signature, word, letter, numeral or any combination thereof.'[43]

During the War, most Allied countries enacted laws against German economic interests in their territories. On 5 August 1914, Britain passed the Trading with the Enemy Proclamation, which declared transactions with 'subjects of, or resident or carrying on business in, a state for the time being at war with His Majesty' as unlawful.[44] Soon after, on 18 September 1914, the Trading with the Enemy Act was enacted. The law required enemy aliens to register their property in Britain and prohibited them from engaging in banking, selling or acquiring assets in the country or transferring money abroad. It created special custodians of alien property in Britain and empowered the courts 'to vest in the

---

37 MacIntyre, ibid.

38 ibid.

39 ibid.

40 ibid.

41 ibid.

42 Trade Marks Act 1905 s 1.

43 ibid s 3.

44 Daniela L. Caglioti, 'Property Rights and Economic Nationalism', *International Encyclopaedia of the First World War*, 8 October 2014, https://encyclopedia.1914-1918-online.net/article/property_rights_and_economic_nationalism.

custodian any property, real or personal, belonging to or held or managed for or on behalf of any enemy'.[45] The Board of Trade was empowered to appoint administrators which enjoyed extensive powers over enemy aliens' businesses and firms.[46] The Patents, Designs and Trade Marks (Temporary Rules) Act 1914 covered industrial property, effectively suspending German patents and trade marks and permitting compulsory licensing.[47]

However, there existed a perception that German companies could still operate in Britain, subject merely to restrictions on profits.[48] The government, responding to public pressure, adopted even more drastic measures against companies with German connections. The Trading with the Enemy (Amendment) Act of 1916 authorised the Board of Trade to wind up or confiscate British companies with German affiliations, thus conclusively putting 'an end to trade activities of persons of enemy nationality'.[49] By the end of the War, almost 600 companies were wound up.[50] Other Allied countries also enacted economic measures against German businesses. For example, in the US, a Trading with the Enemy Act was enacted in 1917, under which the US President appointed an Alien Property Custodian to take control of alien property that might hinder the war effort.[51] The law also extended to industrial property rights. US authorities made available several German-owned patents for licence to any bona fide US individual or corporation, in the public interest. A licensing fee of 5 per cent of the gross income via the licences was to be paid to the Alien Property Custodian. [52]

Through such laws, several valuable German trade marks were affected. For example, the German pharmaceutical company Merck had roots as far back as 1668, when Jacob Merck set up the Engel Pharmacy in Darmstadt. In 1891, the then owner of the company established Merck & Co in the US, as its distribution subsidiary. Merck & Co was confiscated by US authorities during the

---

[45] ibid.

[46] ibid.

[47] Leske-Loewenfeld, above n 7, 6. See also Catherine Bond, '"This is Not a Bill to Legalize Looting": Wartime Regulation of Enemy-Owned Intellectual Property in Australia' (2015) 2 *Intellectual Property Quarterly* 79.

[48] John McDermott, 'Trading With the Enemy: British Business and the Law During the First World War' (1997) 32 *Canadian Journal of History* 201, 219.

[49] Caglioti, above n 44.

[50] McDermott, above n 48.

[51] Daniel Gross, *The U.S. Confiscated Half a Billion Dollars in Private Property During WWI*, Smithsonian (2014), https://www.smithsonianmag.com/history/us-confiscated-half-billion-dollars-private-property-during-wwi-180952144/#XzqsWu3UjqCERLkl.99>; Leske-Loewenfeld, above n 7, Teil 1, 58–60. See also Bond, above n 47 (discussing the suspension of German patents in Australia).

[52] Leske-Loewenfeld, ibid.

War. After the War, both US and the German companies continued using the Merck trade mark. The rights between the entities were not clearly defined at any point, a situation which has been the source of litigation even in relatively recent years.[53] Similarly, 'Pebeco' was the flagship brand of the German cosmetics firm Beiersdorf (better known as the producers of Nivea). Prior to the War, Pebeco was a leading brand for toothpastes. The mark was expropriated in the US during the War. Following this, problems of quality control developed, with the non-uniform use of the mark.[54] To cite another example, the US subsidiary of the German chemical company Bayer was auctioned off in New York. Bayer lost its US patent for aspirin, one of the most valuable drugs ever produced. Eventually, it also lost its trade mark.[55] Some companies partly shielded themselves through proactive measures. For instance, the US subsidiary of Robert Bosch GmbH created a new mark in order to avoid confusion: an anchor inside a circle, which remains associated with the company to the present day.[56] Nevertheless, there is no doubt that German industrial property was a major casualty of enemy property wartime laws, the damage often being irreparable.

2.c The Versailles Treaty

With the return of peace, Britain, the US, and other countries, were eager to resume economic relations. The Versailles Treaty aimed to restore industrial property rights to parties. Article 306 of the Treaty accordingly stated that:

> rights of industrial, literary and artistic property, as … defined by the International Conventions of Paris and Berne … shall be re-established or restored, as from the coming into force of the present Treaty … in favour of the persons entitled to the benefit of them at the moment when the state of war commenced or their legal representatives.

The provision was applicable to the 'territories of the High Contracting Parties', thus including regions such as British India. Article 309 provided immunity to acts in Allied countries infringing the industrial, literary and artistic property rights of entities based in Central countries (and vice versa) in the period between the date of the declaration of the War and the date of the coming into the force of the Versailles Treaty.

---

[53] Thiemo Heeg, MERCK:Keimzelle Engel-Apotheke, FAZ, 18.03.2006; Handelsblatt, US-Konzern holt zum nächsten Schlag aus, 15.01.2016.

[54] Beiersdorf Chronicle 04 (on file with the authors).

[55] Gross, above n 51.

[56] Bosch Corporation, *History – Global Steps 1906–1925*, https://www.bosch.com/stories/1906-1925-globalization-and-new-beginning/.

Notwithstanding these provisions, the resolution of post-War property disputes proved to be difficult. Intellectual property, being non-rivalrous in nature, had especially been prone to losses, being subject to simultaneous use by multiple parties. After the War, many brands were bereft of their original owners or disappeared altogether.[57]

2.d Indian Law

In British India, the Governor General was authorised to apply British enemy property laws and suspend industrial property rights.[58] However, the legal regulation of trade marks in India was dissimilar to that in Britain. Although India was a territory of the British Empire, it adopted a trade marks statute allowing trade mark registration and protection much later than Britain, via the Trade Marks Act of 1940.[59] Demands for legislation on the registration of trade marks in India were made as early as 1877, by the Bombay Mill Owners' Association, and supported by the Bombay Chamber of Commerce.[60] The demand culminated in the drafting of an Indian Trade Marks Bill in 1880. However, the law could not be passed owing to various disagreements, which also resulted in India not joining the Paris Convention.[61]

At the time of the First World War, a degree of protection was available to trade mark owners via the Indian Merchandise Marks Act of 1889.[62] This law worked synchronously with the Indian Penal Code of 1860 and referenced its provisions. It defined a trade mark as a 'mark used for denoting that goods are the manufacture and merchandise of a particular person', and automatically protected any trade mark registered in Britain.[63] It prohibited, among other

---

[57] For example, the French government had liquidated and sold the formerly German-owned champagne producer Mumm & Co, Reims. In addition, French authorities prohibited the use of any of Mumm's trade marks registered in third countries, taking the position that trade mark rights outside France had been transferred as part of the liquidation. The decision has been criticised as being contrary to local French law. See Leske-Loewenfeld, above n 7, Teil 2, 130.

[58] US House of Representatives Committee on Interstate and Foreign Commerce, *Trading With the Enemy*, House Report 4704, 94 (1914) (quoting extracts from a patent and trade mark law bulletin).

[59] P Narayanan, *Law of Trade Marks and Passing Off* (6th edn, Eastern Law House, New Delhi 2004) 3.

[60] S Venkateswaran, *The Law of Trade and Merchandise Marks in India* (Madras Law Journal Office, 1937) 1–2.

[61] ibid 3.

[62] The text of the legislation is available at https://www.wipo.int/edocs/lexdocs/laws/en/in/in129en.pdf.

[63] Indian Merchandise Marks Act 1889 s 2 (referring to Indian Penal Code 1860 s 478). See also MH Starling, *Indian Criminal Law* (7th edn, WH Allen, 1897) 599–600.

things, the act of using a 'false trade mark' (i.e. the use of a mark 'in a manner reasonably calculated to cause it to be believed that the goods so marked … are the manufacture or merchandise of a person whose manufacture or merchandise they are not'), and made the act punishable with a fine and/or imprisonment.[64] However, the law was criticised as 'thoroughly useless' in practice, as it only allowed for criminal proceedings against infringers, as opposed to civil remedies like an injunction or damages.[65] Furthermore, it seemed to privilege foreign trade mark owners who had registered their marks in Britain (and could automatically assert their rights) over Indian traders who could not do so in their own country.[66] Referring to government notifications, an early edition of *Kerly's* had observed that although India lacked a registration system, trade marks 'can be, and sometimes are' registered under the Indian Registration Act of 1877, which had been enacted to protect traditional forms of property rights.[67] However, an Indian treatise clarified that this practice was 'not of any material assistance' to trade mark owners. What was registrable was not a trade mark but merely a declaration of ownership in a mark, equivalent to 'no more than the recorded opinion of the registrant' and not granting rights analogous to those under statutory trade mark law in Britain.[68]

Notwithstanding the absence of adequate statutory protection, trade marks, as a component of goodwill, could be protected in India under the common law tort of passing off. In the 1990s, in a widely-cited modern description of the tort, Nourse LJ summarised the 'classical trinity' of requirements in a passing off action as follows: '(1) a reputation (or goodwill) acquired by the plaintiff in his goods, name, mark, etc., (2) a misrepresentation by the defendant leading to confusion (or deception), causing (3) damage to the plaintiff'.[69] Although not articulated with the same succinctness, the rudiments of the action had been visible in English cases a century before, i.e. even prior to the First World War.[70] This period also witnessed one of the first reported passing off cases in India, before the Madras High Court. The case, involving two clothiers, saw the court hold that a defendant had deliberately used an image that bore 'a general resemblance' to the plaintiff's mark 'without being exactly the same

---

[64] Indian Merchandise Marks Act 1889 s 3 (referring to Indian Penal Code 1860 ss 480, 482).

[65] Venkateswaran, above n 60, 16–17.

[66] ibid 17.

[67] FG Underhay, *The Law of Merchandise Marks by DM Kerly* (3rd edn, Sweet & Maxwell, London 1909) 176.

[68] Venkateswaran, above n 60, 11–15.

[69] *Consorzio del Prosciutto di Parma v Marks & Spencer* [1991] RPC 351, 368 (CA).

[70] See Christopher Wadlow, *The Law of Passing Off: Unfair Competition by Misrepresentation* (4th edn, Sweet & Maxwell 2011) 35.

... with a view to have their goods to pass under the name' of the plaintiff.[71] In another Indian passing off case, also predating the First World War and involving image marks, Benson J acknowledged that '[t]here is no system of registering trade marks in India'.[72] Yet, the judge cited English cases and observed that if a 'person has by user acquired a reputation which couples his name with the mark or combination of marks or symbols .... the user acquires a property in the mark or combination which the law will protect just as much as if it were a registered trade mark'.[73]

Thus, the legal situation in India for German trade mark owners during the War would ostensibly have been as follows: (1) the suspension of trade mark registrations in Britain would preclude criminal action by German businesses with British trade mark registrations under the Indian Merchandise Marks Act of 1889, and (2) a civil suit for trade mark infringement under Indian law was not possible because India did not have a system of trade mark registration (and, even if it did, the applicability of British enemy property laws in India would very likely have precluded such an action). In theory, the tort of passing off did exist, but in practice it would probably have been difficult, if not impossible, for a trader from an enemy country to bring such an action in another enemy country. After the War, there was no registration system available to trade mark owners until the Trade Marks Act of 1940. An action for passing off, however, could conceivably be brought, as had happened in *AJ Von Wülfing v DH Jivandas*.

Before moving on to the case, it is interesting to consider a wider historical issue. Indian political leaders were broadly supportive of Britain during the War, and Indian soldiers formed one of the largest contingents in the War (suffering thousands of casualties).[74] Yet, it has also been argued that there existed 'a far greater ambivalence than is usually acknowledged' among Indians, unhappy over being dragged into a foreign conflict by a colonial power.[75] In fact, during the Second World War, there would prove to be large-scale resentment in India over joining the War effort. The revered nationalist leader Subhash Chandra Bose would meet with Adolf Hitler to lobby for Indian independence from the British, and form an anti-British military force with help from Axis Japan.[76] Thus, it would perhaps not be a stretch to assume that the

---

71 *Taylor v Chetti* (1883) 6 ILR Mad 108, para 6 (Madras High Court).

72 *Nooroodeen v Sowden* (1905) 15 MLJ 45, para 12 (Madras High Court).

73 ibid.

74 See generally, Budheswar Pati, *India and the First World War* (Atlantic, 1996).

75 Santanu Das, *India, Empire, and First World War Culture: Writings, Images, and Songs* (CUP, Cambridge 2018) 106–15.

76 See generally, Sugata Bose, *His Majesty's Opponent* (Harvard University Press, Cambridge, MA 2011).

anti-German sentiment that had existed in Britain during the First World War, which made traders dilute the German connotations of the Sanatogen mark, did not echo in India to the same extent (if at all). And, therefore, that considerable consumer goodwill and loyalty may have been associated with the mark in India, as a German badge of origin.

3. THE SANATOGEN DISPUTE IN INDIA

The case of *AJ Von Wülfing v DH Jivandas* arose after the War had ended. It was decided by the Bombay High Court on 19 December 1924. The sole judge hearing the case was Vikaji Fardunji Taraporewala. A member of India's industrious Parsi community, Taraporewala had qualified as a barrister in England, admitted to Lincoln's Inn. After an apparently nondescript start to his career, he rapidly rose in prominence and impressed peers in two notable cases.[77] He was appointed in 1924 at as an Additional Judge (acting judge) of the Bombay High Court. However, he resigned in 1926 (apparently insulted that a lawyer junior to him had been promoted as a permanent judge before him) and resumed legal practice.[78] A search of online case databases suggests that *Wülfing v Jivandas* was possibly the only intellectual property rights case that Taraporewala had presided over in his short-lived judicial career. Nevertheless, Taraporewala was obviously held in high regard by his peers. He eventually rose to become the acting Advocate General of Bombay, and has been described as being among a small group of lawyers that 'consolidated the reputation of the Indian Bar in Bombay'.[79] Thus, it can be assumed that the author of *Wülfing v Jivandas* was among the more esteemed minds within the Indian legal community at the time.

Following the War and the conclusion of the Versailles Treaty, Wülfing (as a German entity) had sued Genatosan in the Calcutta High Court, claiming the exclusive right to use the word 'Sanatogen'. The case was settled and resulted in Genatosan withdrawing from the Indian market.[80] However, apparently, some traders in Bombay continued to import and sell Genatosan's product, which resulted in a fresh civil suit being filed at the Bombay High Court by Wülfing. During the case, it was admitted that 'a very small quantity of Sanatogen other than the Sanatogen of the plaintiffs in the Indian market' was

---

[77] See Mitra Sharafi, *Law and Identity in Colonial South Asia: Parsi Legal Culture, 1772–1947* (CUP, Cambridge 2014); PB Vaccha, *Famous Judges, Lawyers and Cases of Bombay* (NM Tripathi, 1962) 156–8.

[78] Vaccha, ibid; Chimanlal Harilal Setalvad, *Recollections and Reflections: An Autobiography* (Padma Publications, 1946) 68–9.

[79] Vaccha ibid 157.

[80] *AJ Von Wülfing v DH Jivandas* (1926) 28 Bom LR 243, para 19.

being sold.[81] Hence, the probable intention of the suit was to firmly secure Wülfing's rights across India and warn others not to use the Sanatogen mark. Along with rights to the Sanatogen mark, Wülfing also claimed rights over the word 'Formamint', used in relation to another of its successful products.

The facts surrounding *Wülfing v Jivandas* were as follows: Wülfing claimed that it had sold Sanatogen in India 'for several years prior to 1914'.[82] It claimed that Sanatogen (along with Formamint) had 'acquired a very high reputation throughout India and the sales thereof were large and profitable'.[83] Thus, 'the names of Sanatogen and Formamint had come to mean chemical compounds of the plaintiff's [Wülfing's] manufacture'.[84] Wülfing claimed that, following the outbreak of War, Sanatogen continued to be imported in India through Wülfing's London subsidiary. Following the sale of the subsidiary to Genatosan Limited, the latter continued to trade in India, using the Sanatogen mark (presumably continuing until the post-War settlement with Wülfing, following the Calcutta High Court case). After the War, Wülfing resumed importing Sanatogen into India from Germany. By this time, the patent rights in Sanatogen had expired. Nevertheless, Wülfing claimed that the 'original exclusive right to the use of' the Sanatogen mark had been restored to it under the Versailles Treaty.[85] In other words, Wülfing's claim was effectively this: other traders were free to manufacture products using the chemical composition of Sanatogen (as its patent had expired), but not to use the Sanatogen mark. Accordingly, Wülfing sued an Indian firm for importing and selling Genatosan's Sanatogen variant in India. It cited certain consignments allegedly imported in India (in 1923) and sold 'at a much lower rate' than Wülfing's product.[86] Wülfing claimed that, in addition to the use of the Sanatogen mark, Genatosan's packages were deceptively similar in the 'general make up, marking and appearance' to those used by Wülfing.[87] Wülfing claimed that the defendant firm was acting 'to deceive the public and lead them to believe that in purchasing the inferior compounds offered for sale they were buying the genuine articles of' Wülfing.[88] It thus sought an injunction against the defendant to restrain it 'from passing off or attempting to pass off' its goods as that of Wülfing's.[89] A similar claim was also made with respect to Formamint.

---

81 ibid.
82 ibid para 1.
83 ibid.
84 ibid.
85 ibid.
86 ibid.
87 ibid.
88 ibid.
89 ibid.

Thus, Wülfing had submitted a textbook passing off claim, on the basis of protectable reputation attached to both its word mark and trade dress. As the court noted, there was 'no Registration Act giving a right of property in trade marks by registration' in India, and 'the only right of action a trader or manufacturer' had lay in passing off.[90] This, however, raised an elementary question: could the Versailles Treaty be invoked to protect unregistered marks through a passing off action?

In reply to Wülfing's claims, the defendant firm denied that the Sanatogen mark was synonymous with Wülfing. It asserted that the name had become 'public property both in England and India' after being suspended from the Trade Marks Register in Britain during the War, and that the Versailles Treaty did not restore to Wülfing the exclusive right to use the name[91] (indeed, this also appeared to be the position of the Board of Trade in Britain).[92] The defendant added that Sanatogen referred to the constituent compound of the product. As the patent in the product had expired, the name was public property. The defendant further argued that 'the common law right to a trade mark is not a right to industrial property in the same sense as a right in a registered trade mark'.[93] With reference to the argument concerning packing, the defendants claimed that it was 'common to the trade'.[94] Hence, before delving into the question of passing off, there were two elementary questions surrounding the admissibility of Wülfing's claim: whether the reputation and goodwill associated with the *unregistered* Sanatogen mark was protected under the Versailles Treaty, and whether the word 'Sanatogen' had become *publici juris*.

On the Versailles Treaty issue, the court noted that Article 306 of the Treaty referred to the Paris Convention's definition of industrial property. The judge thus reproduced various provisions of the Paris Convention, important among which were Articles 1, 2, 6 and 10.[95] To elaborate, Article 1 (which was not too dissimilar to what it states today) read: 'The words "industrial property" are to be taken in their broadest sense; they extend to all productions of the agricultural industries (wines, corn, fruits, cattle, etc) and of the mining industries (minerals, mineral waters, etc).' Article 2 (like it continues to do today) rec-

---

[90] ibid para 8.

[91] ibid para 2. Indeed, this also appeared to be the position of the Board of Trade in Britain.

[92] The Board of Trade claimed, in correspondence concerning Sanatogen and Formamint, that the marks were 'open to be used by any person manufacturing the articles of which they are the name'. See Letter from Cecil Litchfield, Board of Trade, to Evan R Davies, 11 November 1919, in Board of Trade, Industrial Property Department, File No. 22660.

[93] *AJ Von Wülfing v DH Jivandas* (1926) 28 Bom LR 243, para 4.

[94] ibid para 2.

[95] ibid paras 38–42.

ognised the principle of national treatment. Article 6 stated: 'Every trade mark duly registered in the country of origin shall be admitted for registration and protected in the form originally registered in the other countries of the Union.' Article 10 (whose present-day successor is the similarly-worded Article 10*bis*) read: 'All the contracting countries undertake to assure to those who enjoy the benefits of the Union effective protection against unfair trade competition.' Examining these provisions, the court observed that the signatories to the Paris Convention '[p]robably … did not contemplate or provide for rights in trade marks which are not acquired by registration'.[96] However, the court added that if it interpreted the Convention strictly, it 'would be frustrating the very object with which the Convention was made', and hamper foreign traders 'in a country like India'.[97] The court thus held that under the Paris Convention (and, therefore, under the Versailles Treaty), the 'right to a trade mark is not affected by the method by which it is acquired'.[98] Hence, 'a common law right to a trade mark' was protectable.[99] The judge remarked: 'I would not be giving full effect to the clauses of the Peace Treaty if I construed the definition of "industrial property" in the narrow sense in which I am asked to do by the defendants in this case.'[100] The court further referred to an observation in *Kerly's* (based around the English case of *Millington v Fox*[101]) that 'a definite property-right in the use of a trade mark was set up' in England in the nineteenth century, prior to the advent of trade mark registration laws.[102]

On the *publici juris* issue, the court rejected the defendant firm's attempt to link the trade mark rights in Sanatogen with the expiry of the patent. The court noted that Sanatogen was not descriptive of the product. Rather, it was a 'fancy word' at the time it had been registered as a trade mark, and the fact that other traders had appropriated it during the War did not make it *publici juris*.[103] Furthermore, the court observed that even if Sanatogen was descriptive of the product and had become *publici juris* on the expiry of the patent, 'the argument could not apply in India as the said compounds were not patented in India'.[104] In other words, 'rights of industrial property in India are governed by the laws of India and are in no way affected by the laws of England or by the

---

96 ibid para 43.
97 ibid.
98 ibid.
99 ibid.
100 ibid para 44.
101 3 Myl. and Cr. 338.
102 *AJ Von Wülfing v DH Jivandas* (1926) 28 Bom LR 243, para 5.
103 ibid para 44.
104 ibid para 4.

action of parties in England'.[105] Hence, '[i]n respect of rights in trade marks and trade names any rights acquired by the parties in England have no effect on the rights of the parties in India'.[106] Thus, even while interpreting complex international law agreements, the court reiterated two elementary principles: the territoriality of intellectual property rights and the rudimentary purpose of unfair competition law in protecting the hard-earned reputation attached to a mark, whether registered or not.

On the question of passing off, the defendant's case appeared wobbly on the issue of goodwill (i.e. the first of the classical trinity of requirements in a passing off action). Various wholesale medicine dealers, produced as witnesses by Wülfing, claimed that 'there were three kinds of Sanatogen in the market: English, American and German'.[107] Of these, 'German Sanatogen' was regarded as the best, and the others 'merely a substitute and a bad substitute'.[108] The dealers also claimed that when 'they could get the German stuff again, they would not buy or import and sell to the customers any Sanatogen other than the Sanatogen of the plaintiffs' manufacture'.[109] Even a partner representing the defendant firm conceded Sanatogen's strong association with Wülfing prior to the War.[110] The court concluded that the evidence of witnesses proved that 'prior to the outbreak of War in 1914 the plaintiffs had acquired a reputation in respect of these compounds under the name of Sanatogen and Formamint, and the said names were identified in the minds of the public with the manufacture of the plaintiffs'.[111]

On the issue of misrepresentation (i.e. the second of the classical trinity of requirements), the court also ruled in favour of Wülfing. Relying again on the statements of traders appearing as witnesses, the court held: 'This evidence means, and can only mean this, that … the compound which is sold under the name Sanatogen is not Sanatogen unless it is manufactured by the original German manufacturers'.[112] The court noted that no actual consumer had appeared before it as a witness to establish confusion, but it assumed the existence of a likelihood of consumer confusion based on the evidence of a veteran English trader ('a dealer on a very large scale in chemicals' and with 'long experience of Indian markets').[113] Among the claims made by the trader

---

105 ibid.
106 ibid.
107 ibid para 12.
108 ibid.
109 ibid.
110 ibid para 4.
111 ibid para 8.
112 ibid para 13.
113 ibid.

was that 'customers complained of the inferiority of Sanatogen other than the German Sanatogen', and that 'the stock of original Sanatogen which remained in Bombay at the commencement of the War fetched a very high price'.[114] The court thus remarked of the average Indian consumer: '[W]hen he buys the compound Sanatogen, he buys the genuine article only if it is the manufacture of the plaintiffs, and if he is given anything which is not the manufacture of the plaintiffs under that name, he is not really given the article which he has asked for'.[115]

On this point, an important issue revolved around the fact that Genatosan had, as discussed earlier, consciously distanced itself from its German roots. As in England, it was marketed in India with taglines like 'absolutely British' and 'free from enemy capital or influence'.[116] However, it was accepted by the defendant that consumers of Sanatogen in India included those who did not understand English (and, therefore, could not read the label).[117] Furthermore, the court observed that the label also stated that Wülfing's assets in England had been taken over by Genatosan, and that the latter was now producing 'the genuine original Sanatogen'.[118] This, the court felt, showed that Genatosan 'tried to sell their goods in the Indian market on the faith of the representation that they were the assignees of the business and goodwill of' Wülfing, since 'the name Sanatogen is still identified in the mind of the public with the manufacture of the plaintiffs'.[119] Hence, 'the general public and those who do not know English could not have known … that Sanatogen was a common name of a compound which was manufactured by various manufacturers', and they 'bought it under the impression that they were buying the genuine articles as originally manufactured by' Wülfing.[120] The court made a similar finding with respect to Formamint.

In an acknowledgement that a *publici juris* claim could be relevant in a finding of consumer confusion, the court referred to opinions in two English cases. In one, Lord Ashbourne had stated that the question of a mark being *publici juris* in 'each case must depend upon its own facts' and could depend

---

114 ibid.
115 ibid.
116 ibid para 15.
117 ibid para 13.
118 ibid para 15.
119 ibid para 16.
120 ibid paras 16–17.

on a range of factors.[121] In the other, Mellish LJ's observations were more striking:

> [W]hat is the test by which a decision is to be arrived at whether a word which was originally a trade mark has become *publici juris*? I think the test must be, whether the use of it by other persons is still calculated to deceive the public, whether it may still have the effect of inducing the public to buy goods not made by the original owner of the trade mark as if they were his goods.[122]

Applying Mellish LJ's remarks in the context of Sanatogen, the court observed: 'Even if the word "Sanatogen" had ceased to be distinctive, there is no doubt in my mind that the way the defendants have tried to sell the goods is indicative of their intention to pass off their goods as the goods of the plaintiffs'.[123]

The court lastly visited the issue of the alleged similarities in packaging. It noted that Wülfing 'did not press the point' as its arguments mainly revolved around the word mark, but still observed that the 'get-up' of the defendant's product was 'very similar' to that used by Wülfing and 'likely to deceive the public', and hence 'they must change the get-up of the goods'.[124]

In contrast with modern-day passing off cases, the court did not go into an elaborate discussion on the issue of the likelihood of damages (i.e. the third of the classical trinity of requirements). Presumably, the court assumed that this factor would go in favour of Wülfing, given that the court had found strong evidence of confusion.

4. CONCLUSION

The ruling in *Wülfing v Jivandas* is notable, among other things, for the fact that the court elegantly bridged the conceptual gap between the civil law and common law view of trade mark law. As mentioned earlier, Justice Taraporewala noted that the Paris Convention probably did not contemplate unregistered trade marks.[125] That conclusion is supported by the fact that France, a civil law country, was the initial promoter of the Convention.[126] At the time of the First World War, the Washington Act of the Paris Convention was dominated by civil law countries, whose laws in general view registra-

---

[121] ibid paras 25–7 (discussing *National Starch Manufacturing Company v Munn's Patent Maizena* [1894] AC 275).

[122] ibid paras 23–4 (discussing *Ford v Foster* (1872) LR 7 Ch. App. 611).

[123] ibid para 31.

[124] ibid paras 30, 46.

[125] *AJ Von Wülfing v DH Jivandas* (1926) 28 Bom LR 243, para 28.

[126] See Heinz Dawid, 'Past and Present Developments in the International Law of Trademarks' (1975) 2 *Brooklyn Journal of International Law* 70.

tion as a prerequisite for the existence of a trade mark.[127] It was only later that the US and Britain joined the treaty and infused common law doctrine in subsequent amendments.[128] Thus, the court was caught between (at the time) a limited civil law conception of trade mark law and the insufficiently developed legislation in India, but with the latter still being a common law jurisdiction. This difficulty was overcome by a sweepingly broad interpretation of the intent of the Paris Convention, likely far beyond what its drafters had contemplated. In this manner, the court was able to craft a solution that navigated the inadequacies of international and Indian law, and would appear equitable in the eyes of modern jurists under the doctrines of common law trade mark and unfair competition.

By modern-day standards, *Wülfing v Jivandas* seems quaint. A search of Indian case law databases suggests that the case was cited again only twice by Indian High Courts, both mentions being perfunctory and both cases predating the 1940s, when India had no trade mark registration law.[129] Furthermore, few intellectual property lawyers in the present day would be bothered by provisions of the Versailles Treaty. Nevertheless, the decision can still be instructive for modern lawyers. At the end of the day, the court liberally interpreted and incorporated international trade mark law with a view to maintaining fair play in commerce and protecting the hard-earned reputation of a foreign trader. This remains a relevant consideration even in the twenty-first century. For example, in *ITC v Punchgini*,[130] the Indian conglomerate ITC failed to protect its famous (but unregistered) 'Bukhara' trade mark against a blatant copyist in Manhattan. A US court acknowledged the existence of a 'famous foreign marks doctrine' (protecting 'a trade mark or service mark … within a nation if it is well known in that nation even though the mark is not actually used or registered in that nation'), but nevertheless held that 'Congress has not incorporated the substantive protections of the famous marks doctrine set forth in [the] Paris Convention … into the relevant federal law, and this court cannot recognise the doctrine simply as a matter of sound policy'. Here, it could well be argued that the court in *Wülfing v Jivandas* was more farsighted. Another aspect where *Wülfing v Jivandas* could still be relevant is in its consideration of purely domestic factors in assessing whether the Sanatogen mark had

---

[127] Paris Convention, Washington Act 1911, French original, "Toute marque … de commerce regulierement enregistree" (any trade mark duly registered).

[128] Dawid, above n 126.

[129] *Thomas Bear v Prayag Narai* AIR 1935 All 7, para 6 (Allahabad High Court); *S Meera Sahib v Hajee M Abdul Azeez Sahib* (1938) 2 MLJ 651, para 14 (Madras High Court).

[130] 482 F.3d 135 (2007).

become *publici juris*. Hypothetically, in litigation involving genericide, the case could serve as a helpful precedent.

As a parting observation, a search of the UK Trade Marks Register reveals various 'live' and 'dead' registrations for Sanatogen in the UK and EU, the former comprising several registrations by the pharmaceutical giant Bayer (for, among other things, 'medicated wine',[131] 'tonic wine',[132] 'Pharmaceutical, veterinary and sanitary preparations; dietetic substances adapted for medical use',[133] and 'Professional consultancy services relating to diet and nutrition'[134]). Internet searches show that the Sanatogen mark is used in Britain today by at least three traders for dissimilar products, namely Bayer (in connection with multivitamins), a company called Power Health Products (in connection with protein powder, the fine print in its packaging suggesting a licence from Bayer), and a company called Accolade Wines (in connection with regular wine containing 'Sanatogen formula to give a unique mellow flavour', although its packaging does not suggest any licensing arrangement with Bayer). Notwithstanding Bayer's huge reputation, it is questionable whether the word 'Sanatogen' retains even a fraction of the recall it once had among consumers. While much of this can possibly be attributed to the forced loss of ownership and quality control of the mark because of the War, it is also true that 'nerve tonics' and 'brain tonics' are far less popular today than they were a century ago. While this is most likely due to advances in modern medicine and the development of more sophisticated cures, some of the claims made in advertisements of Sanatogen appear dubious. In fact, a Member of the British Parliament once accused Wülfing of 'shamming' while marketing Sanatogen, and remarked: 'If you ever saw any particularly blatant advertisement by a British company you might be sure there was something German about it.'[135] Thus, had Sanatogen been advertised today as a miracle cure for assorted diseases, it may well have fallen foul of misleading advertising and consumer protection laws and forced to resort to more objective claims, eroding its value.

---

[131] UK Trade Mark Registration No UK00000777633, Class 5.
[132] UK Trade Mark Registration No UK00000690564, Class 33.
[133] EU Trade Mark Registration No EU000328617, Class 5.
[134] UK Trade Mark Registration No UK00001383758, Class 42.
[135] House of Commons, 1 June 1921, col 155 (Gershom Stewart).

15. 'A process of experimentation': intellectual property, war and defence in Australasia

Catherine Bond and Jessica C Lai[1]

1. INTRODUCTION

In the century since the end of the First World War, the relationship between intellectual property (IP), war and defence has been largely forgotten in modern legal IP scholarship.[2] While some scholarship emerged around the time and immediate aftermath of the two world wars, any reflection on the wartime regulation and management of IP became overshadowed as the legal community grappled with the new challenges posed by rapid technological

---

[1] The quotation in the title of this chapter comes from 'New Zealand War Histories: Civilian Narrative. Patents Office', War History Branch, Department of Internal Affairs, Wellington, New Zealand (written sometime after WWII), National Archives of New Zealand (NANZ) File No. R12677394, 2.

[2] Although overlooked by the legal community, scholars in other disciplines had discussed IP and war, in historical, social and economic contexts. See, for example, Tom H O'Dell, *Inventions and Official Secrecy: A History of Secret Patents in the United Kingdom* (Clarendon Press, 1994); Kathryn Steen, 'Patents, Patriotism, and "Skilled in the Art" *USA v. The Chemical Foundation, Inc.*, 1923–1926' (2001) 92 Isis 91; Diarmuid Jeffreys, *Aspirin: The Remarkable Story of a Wonder Drug* (Bloomsbury, 2005) ch. 6; Graham Gooday, 'Combative Patenting: Military Entrepreneurship in First World War Telecommunications' (2013) 44 Stud. Hist. Philos. of Sci. Part A 247; Christine MacLeod, '"A Delicate Business": Wartime Airplane Designs and Their Post-war Evaluation, 1919–1924' (2013) 44 Stud. Hist. Philos. of Sci. Part A 269; Petra Moser and Alessandra Voena, 'Compulsory Licensing: Evidence from the Trading with the Enemy Act' (2012) 102 Am. Econ. Rev. 396; Kathryn Steen, *The American Synthetic Organic Chemicals Industry: War and Politics, 1910–1930* (University of North Carolina Press, 2015); David Zimmerman, '"A More Creditable Way": The Discovery of Active Sonar, the Langewin-Chilowsky Patent Dispute and the Royal Commission on Awards into Inventors' (2018) 25 War in Hist. 48.

growth.[3] However, the period around the global commemoration of the centenary of the First World War witnessed an increased interest in this intersection, as scholars began to explore both this legal relationship, and the economic, industrial, social and political elements thereof.[4]

As with daily life, few aspects of IP were left untouched by law during the First and Second World Wars. National governments sought to maintain existing rights and abide by international obligations during unprecedented global conflict with no foreseeable end date, requiring legal responses to deal with the minutiae of IP, including payments of fees and extensions of time. But many governments also saw IP as part of the war effort, seeking to utilise IP-protected creations as both a weapon against the enemy and to enhance local industries. Registers of IP rights contained valuable information on existing technologies – and, with war underway, local inventors soon turned their minds to new methods that would provide an edge against the enemy, subsequently seeking IP protection for these inventions. Public dissemination of such inventions could in turn be disastrous for the local war effort.

In Great Britain, the Patents, Designs and Trade Marks (Temporary Rules) Act 1914 (Imp.),[5] dated 7 August 1914, was included as part of the first wave of wartime legislation passed in that jurisdiction. It appeared alongside other statutes essential for wartime including the Aliens Restriction Act 1914 (Imp.)[6] (5 August 1914) and the Defence of the Realm Act 1914 (Imp.) (8 August 1914).[7] This IP statute extended the existing powers of the Board of Trade under the Patents and Designs Act 1907 (Imp.) and the Trade Marks Act 1905 (Imp.) 'to make rules and to do such things as they think expedient for avoiding or suspending in whole or in part any patent or licence grant to ...

---

[3] See, for example, William Macomber, 'The War and Our Patent Laws' (1915) 25 Yale LJ 396; S Mittler, 'Enemy Owned Patents and Patent Applications' (1945) 27 J Pat. & Trademark Off. Soc'y 856; Howland H Sargeant and Henrietta L Creamer, 'Enemy Patents' (1945) 11 Law Contemp. Probs 92.

[4] See, for example, Christopher Wadlow, 'The Great Pharmaceutical Patent Robbery, and the Curious Case of the Chemical Foundation' (2010) 3 IPQ 256; S Tina Piper, 'How War Creates Commons: General McNaughton and the National Research Council, 1914–1939' in Brett M Frischmann, Michael J Madison and Katherine J Strandburg (eds), *Governing Knowledge Commons* (OUP, 2014); Catherine Bond, '"This is not a Bill to legalize looting": Wartime Regulation of Enemy-Owned Intellectual Property in Australia' [2015] 2 IPQ 79; Catherine Bond, '"Through the dreadful circumstances of fate, a broken man": Anton Reznicek, War and Australian Law, 1911–1930' (2017) 17 Legal Hist. 46; Catherine Bond, 'Aspirin Pill' in Claudy Op den Kamp and Dan Hunter (eds), *A History of IP in 50 Objects* (CUP, 2019) 209.

[5] 4 and 5 Geo. 5, ch. 27.

[6] Ibid. ch. 12.

[7] Ibid. ch. 29.

a subject of any State at war with His Majesty'.[8] This statute was transmitted to countries around the British Empire, with an expectation that these dominions would introduce identical or similar legislation, and follow the British example when it came to smaller matters such as maintenance of rights, fees and term extensions for payment and protection.

This included the two jurisdictions that are the subject of this chapter, Australia and New Zealand, which, during the First World War, joined to become ANZAC – the Australian and New Zealand Army Corps.[9] In its original form, this chapter intended to explore the forgotten role of IP in war and defence across the twentieth century through to today, but it quickly became apparent that the experiences of these countries in the First World War alone provided a rich example of a forgotten legal history. While legislation in both countries prior to the First World War contained provisions around government use of IP rights, the legal experiences of these two countries illustrate the depth and breadth of regulation that faced legislators during this unprecedented period of conflict. Compared with Britain and the United States, Australia and New Zealand had – and continue to have – smaller IP systems, but nevertheless both had to grapple with major issues around the maintenance and protection of IP in the First World War.

Further, how IP was treated in each of the jurisdictions in the First World War also highlights a number of broader themes around the wartime legal experiences of these countries, in addition to IP more generally. In both countries there was a consistent failure on the part of Members of Parliament and government bodies in terms of understanding either the basics or intricacies of IP rights, with issues relating to patents, designs and trade marks considered interchangeably – a pattern that arguably continues today. The influence of local politics was also a factor in both countries, with the influence of William Morris Hughes, first Attorney-General (1914–1915) and then Attorney-General *and* Prime Minister of Australia (1915–1921), as evident in the regulation of IP as it was in all areas of law during the First World War.[10] One theme of Hughes's tenure as Attorney-General and PM was consistent overregulation; a factor that is evident in the wartime regulation of IP in Australia as opposed to New Zealand.

This chapter proceeds as follows. Part 2 considers how aspects of defence were integrated into IP statutes in Australia and New Zealand, long before the

---

8 Patents, Designs and Trade Marks (Temporary Rules) Act 1914 (Imp.) s. 1(1).

9 See generally Catherine Bond, *Anzac: The Landing, The Legend, The Law* (Australian Scholarly Publishing, 2016).

10 LF Fitzhardinge, 'Hughes, William Morris (Billy) (1862–1952)' (1983) 9 Australian Dictionary of Biography, http://adb.anu.edu.au/biography/hughes-william-morris-billy-6761, accessed 21 August 2019.

contemplation of the First World War, and the initial measures taken when war was declared in early August 1914. Part 3, 'Maintaining rights in war', examines an example of how the Australian and New Zealand governments dealt with the minutiae of maintaining IP rights, while enacting regimes similar to that introduced in Britain, discussed above, around the use of enemy-owned patents.[11] Part 4 then considers how legislatively-mandated secrecy was utilised in relation to inventions deemed potentially useful to the war effort, but also the concurrent difficulties in managing this type of system. Part 5 concludes with some general reflections.

2. THE PRE-WAR POSITION

2.a Australia

On 1 January 1901 the Commonwealth of Australia was established with the adoption of a new Constitution that, among other aspects, granted power to the Federal Parliament to make laws with respect to 'copyrights, patents of inventions and designs, and trade marks'.[12] While a number of colonies had enacted locally-based patent regimes prior to Federation, the regulation of IP now became a federal matter, though those state-based patents would remain in force until expiration.[13] Within the first five years of Federation the Parliament had passed a number of IP-related laws, including the Copyright Act 1905 (Cth), the Trade Marks Act 1905 (Cth) and the Patents Act 1903 (Cth).

The Patents Act 1903 as enacted included provisions for Crown use.[14] It allowed any public service department (either itself, an agent, contractor or

---

11 This part does not consider the range of measures for extension of times for payment of fees on account of the war, but both the Patents, Designs and Trade-marks Amendment Act 1914 (NZ) and the Patents, Trade Marks, and Designs Act 1914 (No. 2) (Cth) dealt with this issue.

12 Australian Constitution, s. 51(xviii).

13 According to Malcolm Easthope, about 8,563 state-granted patents were valid in 1909. See Malcolm Easthope, *Australian Colonial Patents 1847–1904* (Patent, Trade Marks and Designs Offices, 1992) vii, cited in Bond, '"This is not a Bill to legalize looting"' (n. 4) 83.

14 The applicable provisions in Australia and New Zealand were based on s. 27(2) of the Patents, Designs, and Trade Marks Act 1883 (Imp.) 46 and 47 Vic. c. 57, re-introduced in the UK as per s. 29 of the Patents and Designs Act 1907 (Imp.) 7 Edw. 7, ch. 29. At the end of the First World War, in Britain, a Royal Commission was undertaken to determine the appropriate fees to be paid in circumstances where s. 29 applied, in addition to inventions by those in military-related positions and circumstances where inventors had not sought patent protection but the government had used the relevant creation in the war effort. See, for example, *Royal Commission on Awards to Inventors: First Report*, 1921, cmd 1112.

any other authorised person) to use an invention from the point of application, 'for the public service'. The terms of such use were to be agreed upon with the patentee, or via arbitration.[15] Section 93 also allowed the Governor-General of the Commonwealth, or the Governor of a State, to acquire any patent. For the former, resolution of both Houses of Parliament was required.[16] For the latter, the Parliament of the State had to legislate authorisation of the acquisition.[17] The consideration was to be agreed upon with the patentee, or settled by arbitration. If a State had acquired a patent that the Commonwealth then required, the Act granted the Commonwealth the power to acquire the patent from the State.[18]

The 1903 Act also provided that the inventor of any invention could assign a patent to the Commonwealth.[19] The Minister for Defence could direct that any invention assigned to the Commonwealth and the manner in which it was worked should be kept secret.[20] This led to the patent documents being sealed and only divulged with the written permission of the Minister for Defence.[21] These patents could not be revoked.[22] On 31 December 1915, the Patent Regulations 1912 were amended to clarify that secrecy demanded that:[23]

- the Commissioner could not communicate the application or any related documents to any staff member other than an examiner or deputy examiner;
- no copy of the specification or any other document or drawing was to be published or open for public inspection;
- the application and acceptance of the specification should not be advertised, nor open to opposition;
- the secret patents should be on a secret register;
- no fees should be payable for secret patents, which automatically received the full 14-year patent period.

The Minister could direct that the invention no longer needed to be secret.[24] The Minister could also re-assign the patent to the inventor, upon which the patent would no longer be kept secret and would be moved from the secret reg-

15 Patents Act 1903 (Cth), s. 92(2).
16 Ibid. s. 93(1).
17 Ibid. s. 94(1).
18 Ibid. s. 93(5).
19 Ibid. s. 95.
20 Ibid. s. 96.
21 Ibid. s. 97.
22 Ibid. s. 98.
23 Statutory Rules 1915 No. 267, adding regs 33A–33D to the Patent Regulations 1912.
24 Patents Act 1903 (Cth), s. 100.

ister to the normal register, and fees would become payable as would normal rules of renewal.[25]

Any communication made to the Department of Defence about an invention could not prejudice the grant of a patent or validity of the patent for the invention.[26] This encouraged inventors to contact the Minister if they had an invention that might be relevant to the defence of the Commonwealth. These amendments will be significant in the discussions on secrecy, considered in Part 4 below.

At the outbreak of war, after a decade of registration under the federal system, 15,811 Commonwealth patents had been sealed in Australia.[27] Although a comparatively small country, Australia took its responsibilities in relation to both war and IP seriously, and on 12 November 1914 the Patents, Trade Marks, and Designs Bill 1914 (Cth) was read for a second time in the House of Representatives. The Attorney-General, William Hughes provided more context for the Bill than had been given when the preceding legislation had been introduced in Britain, noting that:

> We are at war with Germany and with Austria, but we do not propose to violate any principle of international law, or to sanction the expropriation of private property. ... I do not put this provision forward on the low ground that we should do unto others what we hope they may do onto us; I put it on the higher ground that a civilized community has no right to take away private property, which inheres as much in a patent as in any other form of property.[28]

That balance would continue to be tested throughout the war. But it also became apparent during the passage of the Bill that even the Attorney-General had difficulty differentiating between trade marks, designs, patents and associated rights. The examples he discussed in Parliament vis-à-vis patent law – German products Lysol and Aspirin – were both well-known brands and the type of products that Australia ultimately needed to manufacture during the war – but neither was actually protected by a valid local patent, only registered trade mark law.[29]

The Patents, Trade Marks, and Designs Bill 1914 became the Patents, Trade Marks, and Designs Act 1914 (Cth) on 19 November 1914. Its substantive provisions will be considered in more detail in Part 3 below.

---

25 Statutory Rules 1915 no. 267, adding regs 33A–33D to the Patent Regulations 1912.

26 Patents Act 1903 (Cth), s. 99.

27 Bond, '"This is not a Bill to legalize looting"' (n. 4) 83.

28 (1914) 46 Parliamentary Debates, 604.

29 Ibid. 604–605.

2.b New Zealand

The Patents Act 1860 (NZ) was the first of a series of patent-related statutes introduced for the registration of inventions in that jurisdiction.[30] In the first two decades of its operation, only 400 patents were granted in New Zealand. This figure grew exponentially over the next few decades, with 3,097 granted in the period 1880 to 1889. However, the introduction of the amalgamated statute, the Patents, Designs, and Trade-marks Act 1889 (NZ), covering all aspects of registrable IP, saw a surge of registered patents, with 7,945 granted in the last decade of the nineteenth century.[31]

Most significantly for the present purposes, the 1889 statute introduced a provision relating to Crown use of patents; pursuant to section 36(2), any Government Department (either itself, an agent, contractor or any other authorised person) could use an invention from the point of application, 'for the services of the Crown'. The terms of such use were to be agreed upon between the Department and the patentee, either before or after the use, with the approval of the Minister of Finance.[32]

That statute had been replaced by the Patents, Designs, and Trade-marks Act 1911 (NZ) by the time war broke out in August 1914, with the Crown retaining the ability to use any patent, in certain circumstances.[33] As alluded to throughout this chapter, whether the Crown had the wherewithal to take advantage of registered patents, is another matter. In a 1909 exchange between the Office of the Council of Defence and the Ministry of Justice, these two Departments were unsure of what to do when inventors wrote to them with what they perceived to be inventions useful for the military.[34]

Both the 1860 and 1911 statutes provided a 14-year period of protection for registered patents;[35] as a result, it is possible to calculate that at the time of the outbreak of the First World War there were approximately 12,661 registered

---

30 See also Patents Act 1870 (NZ); Patents Act 1883 (NZ); Patents Act 1883 Amendment Act 1885 (NZ).

31 The New Zealand historical patent statistics provided here were supplied by the Intellectual Property Office of New Zealand (IPONZ) and are on file with the authors.

32 Patents, Designs, and Trade-marks Act 1889 (NZ), s. 36(2).

33 Patents, Designs, and Trade-marks Act 1911 (NZ), s. 31.

34 'Justice Department, Wellington – 20 May 1909 – Patents Bill likely to be introduced – draws attention to certain claims regarding Defence Inventions', NANZ File No. R24755128.

35 Patents, Designs, and Trade-marks Act 1889 (NZ), s. 19(1); Patents, Designs, and Trade-marks Act 1889 (NZ), s. 22(1).

patents in New Zealand.[36] That number will become more significant when the number of 'enemy patents' in force in that country are considered below.

Although New Zealand had an established, well-functioning IP regime, the outbreak of war presented wholly new issues for the Patent Office. These issues were beyond its experience and largely met through a 'process of experimentation'.[37]

From 4 August 1914, all action on enemy patent applications was suspended;[38] on 2 November 1914 the Patents, Designs and Trade-marks Amendment Act 1914 (NZ) came into force, reproducing for the most part the provisions included in the British and Australian statutes. Its provisions will be considered in greater detail in the next part.

3. MAINTAINING RIGHTS IN WAR

The outbreak of war required consideration of both the smaller details and bigger picture aspects of IP regimes. At the most basic level, governments had to determine how to deal with existing rights now owned by those considered enemies of their country. The war would one day end and governments would need to be accountable for how IP, like other forms of 'enemy'-owned property, was managed during that period. At the same time, many jurisdictions had legislation in place around 'trading with the enemy', which limited what individuals and businesses could do in a practical sense. As a result, a range of legislation, proclamations and orders were required, from dealing with the most simple aspects of IP regimes (such as maintaining the payment of fees),[39] to avoiding or suspending 'enemy'-owned patents.

---

36 Based on annual patent registration information for the period 1900 to 1914, on file with and supplied to the authors by IPONZ.

37 'New Zealand War Histories: Civilian Narrative. Patents Office', War History Branch, Department of Internal Affairs, Wellington, New Zealand (written sometime after the Second World War), NANZ File No. R12677394, 2 [hereinafter 'New Zealand War Histories'].

38 Ibid.

39 See also (n. 11).

3.a Paying Fees in Enemy Countries and on Behalf of Enemies

On 23 September 1914, pursuant to a Royal Proclamation, the British Board of Trade granted a licence to all residents or persons carrying on business in His Majesty's dominions:

- to pay fees relating to obtaining the grant or renewal of patents, designs or trade marks in an 'enemy country'; and
- pay fees on behalf of an 'enemy' for an application or renewal of a British patent, design or trade mark.[40]

On 8 October 1914, the right to grant such a licence was extended to Governors of British Colonies. The New Zealand Governor granted an analogous licence to all persons resident, carrying on business, or being in New Zealand, on 17 March 1915.[41]

Like New Zealand, in Australia, on 28 November 1914, the Deputy Governor-General in Council granted to all persons resident, carrying on business or being on the Commonwealth of Australia licence to pay fees to obtain or renew a patent, design or trade mark in an enemy country, and to pay such a fee on behalf of an enemy in the Commonwealth.[42] On 13 April 1917, the Foreign Trade Department of the Foreign Office extended this licence to persons (including body corporates) resident, carrying on business or being in the United Kingdom.[43]

3.b Avoiding or Suspending Enemy Intellectual Property: New Zealand

Restrictions introduced pursuant to the Trading with the Enemy Act 1914 (NZ) made it difficult for individuals and businesses deemed 'enemies' – mainly those from Germany and Austria – to trade in New Zealand during the war.[44] Nevertheless, while they might not have been able to work their New Zealand patents during this time, it was open to them to sue for infringements after the war.[45] This appeared to be of some public concern.[46]

---

40 (1914) 3(24) New Zealand Patent Office Journal (NZPOJ) 662.
41 (1915) 4(8) NZPOJ 171, 171–2.
42 (1914) 20(45) Australian Official Journal of Patents (AOJP) 1998.
43 (1917) 26(24) AOJP 591. See also 'Licence' (1918) 28(15) AOJP 354; and 'Licence' (1919) 30(32) AOJP 844.
44 Trading with the Enemy Act 1914 (NZ), s. 3.
45 (1916) 175 Parliamentary Debates, 171–2.
46 'Enemy Patents (1914–18)', NANZ File No. R18323817, containing letters between the editor of the Littleton Times and the Registrar of Patents regarding this matter (dated 12, 13 and 18 August 1915).

As noted above, on 2 November 1914, New Zealand amended the Patents, Designs, and Trade-marks Act 1911, in line with the equivalent British legislation. This two-page amendment conferred on the Governor (now referred to as the Governor-General) the power, by Order in Council, to 'make regulations and do all things necessary' to avoid or suspend, in whole or in part, any patent or licence, 'the person entitled to the benefit of which is the subject of any State at war with His Majesty the King'.[47] The Governor could also do anything necessary to avoid or suspend a registered design or trade mark of such a subject,[48] and any application made under the principal statute.[49]

If a patent or registered design (but not trade mark) was avoided or suspended, the Governor could grant a licence for that patent to others (not subjects of an enemy of the State), 'on such terms and conditions, and either for the whole term of the patent or registration or for such less period as the Governor in Council thinks fit'.[50] Royalties were collected by the Government as an additional source of revenue, rather than being paid to a custodian of enemy property on behalf of the patentees.[51] This was in direct contrast to the position in Australia, discussed below. No provision was made for non-licensee use of avoided or suspended patents.

The 'subject' included:

- any person resident and carrying on business in an enemy State;
- any business managed or controlled by such a subject; or
- any business carried on wholly or mainly for the benefit or on behalf of such a subject.[52]

On 14 December 1914, the Patents (Temporary) Regulations 1914 (NZ) were enacted. These stated that the Governor in Council, 'before granting any such application, may require to be satisfied' that

- 'the person applying [for the suspension or avoidance] intends to manufacture, or cause to be manufactured, the patented article, or to carry on, or cause to be carried on, the patented process';[53] or

---

47 Patents, Designs, and Trade-marks Amendment Act 1914 (NZ), s. 2(1)(a).
48 Ibid. s. 2(1)(b).
49 Ibid. s. 2(1)(c).
50 Ibid. s. 2(1)(d).
51 'New Zealand War Histories' (n. 37) 2.
52 Patents, Designs, and Trade-marks Amendment Act 1914 (NZ), s. 2(2).
53 Patents (Temporary) Regulations 1914 (NZ), reg. 1(b), first published in (1914) 3(24) NZPOJ 659.

- 'it is in the general interests of the country or of a section of the community or of a trade that that article should be manufactured or such process carried on as aforesaid.'[54]

On 18 September 1914, about six weeks into the war, the Department of Internal Affairs sent out a list of unexpired letters patent granted in New Zealand to residents of Germany and Austria-Hungary for consideration by a number of government departments.[55] There were 72 patents listed,[56] indicating how few enemy-owned patents there were in New Zealand compared to the 12,661 overall patents in force at the time (discussed above). The Department of Internal Affairs asked recipients to

> be good enough to obtain as soon as possible reports from experts in [their] Department on such of the inventions mentioned in the list upon which they are capable of expressing an opinion as to the value of such inventions with regard to the industry affected, the prospect of successful manufacture in New Zealand and anything else affecting the matter.[57]

The reactions were mixed, and likely less helpful than the Department of Internal Affairs had hoped.[58] The Department of Labour (16 November 1914) 'made enquiries', and there did not 'appear to be anyone in this office capable of expressing an opinion' as requested. A report from the Military Forces indicated a lack of interest in any of the patents. The Public Works department sought a report from the Chief Electrical Engineer, who looked at 15 patents and found that one or two might be of direct interest to individual manufacturers in New Zealand. The Department of Agriculture, Industries and Commerce commissioned a number of reports that were dismissive of the majority of the patents, considering a range of dairy-related patents to 'have no material value'. The Railway Department responded more positively, identifying two patents (34504, a valveless reciprocating engine or steam super-heater, and

---

54 Ibid. reg. 1(c).

55 'Enemy Patents (1914–18)' (n. 46), containing 'Circular No. 730 from Under Secretary J Hislop of the Department of Internal Affairs', 18 September 1914, the list of unexpired letters patent granted in New Zealand to residents of Germany and Austria-Hungary, and a list of all the Departments that received the list.

56 The same Archive File includes a list from the Registrar of Patents of nine patents granted to nominees and assignees of German inventors, and a list of two patents of 'Doubtful cases not included in other lists'; 'Enemy Patents (1914–18)' (n. 46).

57 Ibid., containing 'Circular No. 730 from the Department of Internal Affairs', 18 September 1914 and the list of unexpired letters patent granted in New Zealand to residents of Germany and Austria-Hungary.

58 This correspondence is held in 'Enemy Patents (1914–18)' (n. 46).

23532, a process of impregnating wood) that had potential use, but they had already identified other alternatives prior to the outbreak of war.

By 23 June 1916, just under two years into the conflict, these provisions had not been utilised at all. The question arose before Parliament as to whether all German-owned patents should simply be cancelled.[59] This was discussed in Parliament during debates on the 'Supply' (or budget), where longstanding MP Thomas Wilford suggested that they reduce the allotment to the Patent Office of £3,324 by one pound, to indicate that 'the time had arrived when every German patent in New Zealand should be forthwith cancelled'.[60] The debate then centred around the confiscation of enemy German property, the value of German patents per se, and the value of avoidance/suspension and licensing versus cancellation.

The debate highlighted that many Members of the House did not have a firm grasp of patent law. As in Australia, the example of 'Lysol' was repeatedly invoked, despite the product being protected by a registered trade mark and not a patent. Indeed, Mr Wilford did not seem to understand the distinction between cancellation and avoidance/suspension, lamenting the fact that the 1914 Act had been passed, but German patents had not been cancelled.[61] Furthermore, Prime Minister William Massey was under the impression that German patents had already been cancelled, and if that was not the case, they would be in the 'very near future' in light of the 1914 Act.[62] Mr Wilford and his ilk were of the opinion that Germans were still benefitting from New Zealand patents.

A few Members had a better understanding of patent law. James McCombs understood that 'mere cancellation and wholesale destruction of patents could serve no useful purpose'.[63] He noted that patents were an international matter and the local ramifications of such disregard for property:

> [W]hile a German patent in New Zealand might not be of much value to the German owner on account of [the] small population, New Zealand patentees might suffer considerable loss if Germany adopted reprisals after the war. The Government, therefore, should not attempt to settle post-war problems, or tie itself down so that the Dominion could not fall into line with the policy that might be decided upon by England and her Allies after the war. If they cancelled all German patents now they might subsequently have to revive them in order to secure the rights of New Zealand patentees. … It was possible that if we deprived Germans of the right to exercise rights in New Zealand, with its million of population, New-Zealanders would lose

59 (1916) 175 Parliamentary Debates, 170.
60 Ibid. 169.
61 Ibid. 170.
62 Ibid.
63 Ibid.

the right to exercise their patents over a population of a hundred millions in central Europe.[64]

The fact that no one had applied to avoid or suspend an enemy patent or licence was taken to indicate that German-owned patents had very little value.[65] Charles Statham took a more nuanced understanding, stating that some German-owned patents must be 'valuable assets' such that they should not simply be cancelled, as this would make them worthless. He was, thus, in favour of Government use of any valuable patents, or suspension in favour of persons likely to use them (what was essentially enacted in the 1914 Act).

Attorney-General Alexander Herdman was 'certain that there were no patent rights in New Zealand of any value belonging to Germans'.[66] This was confirmed by the Head of the Patent Office.[67] He took this view because a list of German patents had been sent out to various Government Departments (as noted above), '[b]ut of so little value were they considered to be that no application had been made since the regulations were passed for the voiding of the German patent rights'.[68]

Mr Wilford further argued that German-owned patents should be cancelled to symbolise New Zealand's outrage at German-committed atrocities, particularly against non-combatants. While this 'might not do much harm to the Germans', it would honour the spirit of the Paris Economic Pact (reached at the Paris Economic Conference held 14 June 1916) to economically isolate enemy States.[69] Mr Wilford lost his case.[70]

No application for the avoidance or suspension of an enemy-owned patent was ever filed in New Zealand during the First World War.[71]

3.c Avoiding or Suspending Enemy Intellectual Property: Australia

On 19 November 1914, the Commonwealth passed the Patents, Trade Marks and Designs Act 1914, which was to be read together with the Patents

---

64 Ibid.
65 Ibid. 171.
66 Ibid. 169.
67 Ibid. 187.
68 Ibid. 172.
69 Ibid. 175.
70 Ibid. 172.
71 'From: RO Fullbrook, Wellington. Date: 28 February 1923. Subject: For Information Regarding Patent Rights of Enemy Subjects', NANZ File No. R24671907, containing the letter from Mr Fullbrook and the answer from Frances HD Bell, the Ministry of Justice, 5 March 1923.

Act 1903.[72] As in Britain, this statute served to 'extend the powers of the Governor-General during the continuance of present hostilities to make regulations'.[73] It gave the Governor-General the power to make regulations for avoiding or suspending, in whole or in any part, any patent or licence the person entitled to the benefit of which (and any registration for a design or trade mark the proprietor whereof) was the subject of any State at war with the King.[74] In reality, that power was soon delegated to the Attorney-General. It extended to any person resident or carrying on business in the territory of a State at war with the King, and any company managed by a subject of an enemy State or managed wholly or mainly for the benefit of such a subject.[75] The provisions also applied to applications.[76]

The 1914 Act also enabled the Minister to grant a licence over such a patent or design (but not a trade mark) to anyone not a subject of an enemy State. This was on any terms and conditions, and for the whole term of the patent or design registration or for a shorter period, as the Minister saw fit.[77] In 1915, the Commonwealth added to this, by clarifying that it was an offence for anyone else to use a suspended patented invention, registered design or trade mark.[78]

Regulations underpinning the 1914 Act were enacted on 3 December 1914.[79] These were to all intents and purposes mirrored in New Zealand's provisions, set out above. The procedure to be followed for applications to avoid or suspend patents clarified that the applicant had to produce evidence at a hearing, either orally or by statutory declaration, that:

- the patentee/licensee or design proprietor was a subject of a State at war with the King;
- the applicant intended to manufacture the patented/design article or carry out the patented process;
- it was in the general interest of the Commonwealth or a section of the community, or of trade, that the article be manufactured or process carried out; and
- the applicant was not an alien enemy.[80]

---

72 Patents, Trade Marks and Designs Act 1914 (Cth), s. 1.
73 Ibid. preamble.
74 Ibid. s. 3(a)–(b).
75 Ibid. ss 3–4.
76 Ibid. s. 3(c).
77 Ibid. s. 3(d).
78 Ibid. s. 3.
79 Ibid. via Statutory Rules 1914 no. 174.
80 Patents (Temporary) Regulations 1914 (Cth), reg. 3(1). See also Statutory Rules 1914, no 188, which amended the Regulations to state that the Registrar could require an applicant to furnish evidence that he/she was not a subject of an enemy State.

The rightsholder could appear at the hearing in opposition to the application.[81]

As noted above, by 1914 there were 15,811 patents registered pursuant to the Patents Act 1903. In 1915, the Parliament produced a report on the number of enemy-owned patents – defined as those owned by German, Austrian, Hungarian and Turkish citizens or companies – and found that 631 patents came under this definition.[82] Of these, 567 were owned by German residents. Comparatively, there were many more enemy-owned patents in force in Australia than New Zealand (around 4 per cent compared to 0.5 per cent), and, in contrast with New Zealand, there was no lack of applications to make use of enemy-owned patented inventions in Australia.

These patents are tabulated in Tables 15.1 and 15.2. Of the 28 patents for which avoidance/suspension was sought, 20 were successful (though one suspension was subsequently reversed). Four were suspended in favour of the Engineer-in-Chief of the Commonwealth Railways (two of these also to the State of New South Wales), and 10 were suspended in favour of the Minister of State for the Navy. Only three applications were refused. However, two of these were in competition with the Commonwealth. In all four cases where civilians applied for avoidance/suspension in competition with the Commonwealth, the civilians withdrew or were refused, and the Commonwealth was successful.

On 16 December 1914, the Attorney-General gave notice that, during the continuance of the war, 'no patent would be sealed in favour of, and no registration of a trade mark or design will be granted to, subjects of any State at war with the King'.[83] Subjects was defined to include:

- 'a firm which by reason of its constitution may be considered as managed or controlled by such subjects or the business whereof is wholly or mainly carried on on behalf of such subjects';
- 'a company which has received its constitution in an enemy's State'; and
- 'a company registered in the King's Dominions the business whereof is managed or controlled by such subjects, or is carried on wholly or mainly on behalf of such subjects'.[84]

---

[81] 'Procedure under Patents (Temporary) Regulations 1914, Trade Marks (Temporary) Regulations 1914, and Designs (Temporary) Regulations 1914', para II, published in (1914) 20(49) AOJP 2160. See also 'Amended Procedure under Patents (Temporary) Regulations 1914, Trade Marks (Temporary) Regulations 1914, and Designs (Temporary) Regulations 1915', published in (1915) 22(39) AOJP 1088; and (1916) 24(15) AOJP 364.

[82] See Commonwealth, 'Patents: List of Commonwealth Patents Granted in Favour of Residents of Germany, Austria, Hungary and Turkey (16 June 1915) cited in Bond, '"This is not a Bill to legalize looting"' (n. 4) 84.

[83] (1914) 20(49) AOJP 2160, para II.

[84] Ibid. para II.

Table 15.1 Applications to avoid or suspend patents or licences[*]

No.	Title and Patentee	Applicant and Date of Hearing	Result
Cth 9063	'Clamping Apparatus for Pressing Together Railway Rails Girders and the Like'. Hans Goldschmidt and Karl Goldschmidt	Henry Teesdale Smith (VIC), 13 January 1915.[a]	Withdrawn.[b]
		Henry Chinn (VIC), 26 January 1915.[c]	Refused.[d]
		N/A[e]	Suspended in favour of the Engineer-in-Chief for the Commonwealth Railways,[f] the Chief Commissioner for Railways and Tramways for the State of NSW and the Minister for Public Works for the State of NSW.[g]
Cth 12,807	'A New and Improved Process for Joining Metal-Pieces'. Hans Goldschmidt	Henry Teesdale Smith (VIC), 13 January 1915.[a]	Withdrawn.[b]
		Henry Chinn (VIC), 26 January 1915.[c]	Refused.[d]
		N/A	Suspended in favour of the Engineer-in-Chief for the Commonwealth Railways.[f]
Cth 16,313	'New or Improved Apparatus for Use in Butt-Jointing the End of Rails'. Hans Goldschmidt and Karl Goldschmidt	Henry Teesdale Smith (VIC), 13 January 1915.[a]	Withdrawn.[b]
Cth 660	'Improvements in Apparatus for Trimming the Ends of Rails and Other Metal Bars'. Hans Goldschmidt and Karl Goldschmidt	Henry Teesdale Smith (VIC), 13 January 1915.[a]	Withdrawn.[b]
Cth 2534	'New or Improved Apparatus for Use in Butt-Welding of the Ends of Rails'. Hans Goldschmidt and Karl Goldschmidt	Henry Teesdale Smith (VIC), 13 January 1915.[a]	Withdrawn.[b]

No.	Title and Patentee	Applicant and Date of Hearing	Result
Cth 5713	'An Improved Method of Joining the Ends of Rails and Other Metal Pieces'. The Goldschmidt Aktien Gesellschaft	Henry Teesdale Smith (VIC), 13 January 1915.[a]	Withdrawn.[b]
Vic 18,559	'A New and Improved Process for Joining Metal-Pieces'. Hans Goldschmidt	Henry Teesdale Smith (VIC), 13 January 1915.[a]	Withdrawn.[b]
		N/A	Suspended in favour of the Engineer-in-Chief for the Commonwealth Railways.[f]
NSW 11,383	'A New and Improved Process for Joining Metal-Pieces'. Hans Goldschmidt	Henry Teesdale Smith (VIC), 13 January 1915.[a]	Withdrawn.[b]
		N/A	Suspended in favour of the Engineer-in-Chief for the Commonwealth Railways,[f] the Chief Commissioner for Railways and Tramways for the State of NSW and the Minister for Public Works for the State of NSW.[g]
Cth 19,859	'Translucent or Transparent Ferr-Concrete Structure'. Friedrich Ludwig Keppler	John Edgar Tonks (NSW), 27 January 1915.[c]	Suspended.[d]
Cth 5187	'The Manufacture and Production of New Materials Suitable for Use in Tanning'. Badische Anilin & Soda Fabrik	The Calder & Mersey Extract Co Ltd (UK), 1 July 1915.[h]	Suspended.[i]
Cth 5188	'Improvements in Tanning'. Badische Anilin & Soda Fabrik	The Calder & Mersey Extract Co Ltd (UK), 1 July 1915.[h]	Suspended.[i]
Cth 2941	'Adjustable Dredger Head for Suction Dredges'. Otto Fruhling	Arthur Huge Poole, Alfred Henry Hasemer and George William Poole (NSW), 23 March 1916.[k]	Suspended.[j]

No.	Title and Patentee	Applicant and Date of Hearing	Result
Cth 19,209	'Improved Method of and Arrangement for Removing Dredged Material from Ships' Holds, Hopper Barges, and the Like'. Otto Fruhling	Arthur Huge Poole, Alfred Henry Hasemer and George William Poole (NSW), 23 March 1916.[k]	Suspended.[j]
Cth 7720	'Improvements in or Relating to the Manufacture of Reinforced Tubular or Hollow Bodies from Plastic Material'. Louis Hermann Rentzsch	Edward Lucas (SA), 24 March 1916.[j]	Refused.[k]
Cth 19,488	'An Improved Flock and Fibre Teasing Machine'. Aloysius Wilden	Leslie George Goldie (NSW), 27 November 1916.	Abandoned.[l]
Cth 13,543	'Improvements Relating to the Electrolysis of Aqueous Solutions'. William Herbert Waters	Refractory Zinc Ore Treatment Co (USA and UK), 18 January 1918.[m]	Suspended.[n]
Cth 3999	'Improvements in Receiver Connections for Wireless Telegraphy'. Gesellschaft fuer Drahtlose Telegraphie mit Beschrankter Haftung (DE)	N/A	Suspended, in favour of the Minister of State for the Navy, 22 April 1918.[o]
Cth 6051	'A Wave Detector for Wireless Telegraphy'. Gesellschaft fuer Drahtlose Telegraphie mit Beschrankter Haftung (DE)	N/A	Suspended, in favour of the Minister of State for the Navy, 22 April 1918.[o]
Cth 6840	'Improvements in Wireless Electric Signaling System and Apparatus Therefor'. Gesellschaft fuer Drahtlose Telegraphie mit Beschrankter Haftung (DE)	N/A	Suspended, in favour of the Minister of State for the Navy, 22 April 1918.[o]
Cth 7391	'Improvements in Systems of Wireless Telegraphy Applicable to Railway Trains and the Like'. Gesellschaft fuer Drahtlose Telegraphie mit Beschrankter Haftung (DE)	N/A	Suspended, in favour of the Minister of State for the Navy, 22 April 1918.[o]
Cth 7392	'Improvements in Receivers for Wireless Telegraphy'. Gesellschaft fuer Drahtlose Telegraphie mit Beschrankter Haftung (DE)	N/A	Suspended, in favour of the Minister of State for the Navy, 22 April 1918.[o]

No.	Title and Patentee	Applicant and Date of Hearing	Result
Cth 14,377	'Apparatus for Producing Rapid and but very slightly Damped Electrical Oscillations'. Gesellschaft fuer Drahtlose Telegraphie mit Beschrankter Haftung (DE)	N/A	Suspended, in favour of the Minister of State for the Navy, 22 April 1918.[o]
Cth 19,477	'An Arrangement for Producing Electrical Oscillations more Particularly for the Purposes of Wireless Telegraphy'. Gesellschaft fuer Drahtlose Telegraphie mit Beschrankter Haftung (DE)	N/A	Suspended, in favour of the Minister of State for the Navy, 22 April 1918.[o]
Cth 2512	'Improvements Relating to Electric Oscillation Circuits and their Connections'. Gesellschaft fuer Drahtlose Telegraphie mit Beschrankter Haftung (DE)	N/A	Suspended, in favour of the Minister of State for the Navy, 22 April 1918.[o]
Cth 5572	'A Method and Arrangement for Increasing the Duration Uniformity and Economic Working of Discharge Tubes with an Incandescent Cathode.' Robert von Lieben, Eugen Reisz and Siegmund Strauss (AT)	N/A	Suspended, in favour of the Minister of State for the Navy, 22 April 1918.[o]
Cth 9132	'Improvements in Receivers for Use in Wireless Telegraphy and Telephony'. Edwin Philipps (VIC), as communicatee of Gesellschaft fuer Drahtlose Telegraphie mit Beschrankter Haftung (DE)	N/A	Suspended, in favour of the Minister of State for the Navy, 22 April 1918.[o]
Cth 2287	'Diving Dress'. Anton Reznicek	Robert Billington, (NSW), 28 May 1919.[p]	Application lapsed with expiration of patent.[q]
Cth 4266	'Improvements Relating to the Floods of Chilian [sic] Mills and other Analogous Appliances'. Hugo Salomo	Unclear; not listed.	Suspended, 14 October 1918. Suspension cancelled, 25 January 1921.[r]

Notes
* A similar table appears in Bond, '"This is not a Bill to legalize looting"' (n. 4) 87–8. [a] (1914) 20(50) AOJP 2204; [b] (1915) 22(10) AOJP 196; [c] (1915) 22(1) AOJP 3; [d] (1915) 22(10) AOJP 197; [e] We presume that applications for suspensions in favour of the Government (whether Federal or State) were not advertised, as we found no such notifications; [f] (1916) 22(10) AOJP 198; [g] (1915) 22(40) AOJP 1127; [h] (1915) 22(23) AOJP 590; [i] (1916) 24(20) AOJP 496; [j] (1916) 24(26) AOJP 652; [k] (1916) 24(9) AOJP 21; [l] (1917) 26(11) AOJP 262; [m] (1917) 26(26) AOJP 1262; [n] (1918) 28(30) AOJP 734; [o] (1918) 28(15) AOJP 355; [p] (1919) 30(18) AOJP 476; [q] Bond, '"Through the dreadful circumstances of fate, a broken man"' (n. 4) 61; [r] (1921) 34(7) AOJP 168.

Table 15.2 Applications to avoid or suspend applications for patents

No.	Title and Patentee	Applicant for Avoidance or Suspension and Date of Hearing	Result
Cth 11,232	'Method of Trimming Parallel Faces on the Ends of Rails and Other Objects for Butt-Welding'. The Goldschmidt Aktien Gesellschaft	Henry Teesdale Smith (VIC), 13 January 1915.[a]	Withdrawn.[b]
Cth 11,636	'Process of Welding Rails and the Like Laid Already in Paved Roads'. The Goldschmidt Aktien Gesellschaft	Henry Teesdale Smith (VIC), 13 January 1915.[a]	Withdrawn.[b]
Cth 11,637	'Process of Enlarging the Space Between the Ends of Rails Laid Already in Paved Roads'. The Goldschmidt Aktien Gesellschaft	Henry Teesdale Smith (VIC), 13 January 1915.[a]	Withdrawn.[b]

Notes: [a] (1914) 20(50) AOJP 2205; [b] (1915) 22(10) AOJP 197.

Such subjects could still apply and their applications would be treated the same as other applications, until the point of acceptance.[85] Inventions communicated by such subjects would be treated as if made by the same.[86]

Finally, such subjects could not oppose a patent or trade mark of a British citizen or alien friend. Others could oppose the patents and trade marks of such subjects, but the proceedings were suspended until the end of the war.[87]

4. SECRECY, DEFENCE AND INVENTIONS

4.a Provisions Regarding Secrecy: New Zealand

In September 1916 the NZ Government learned of British and Australian precautions regarding secrecy around certain inventions. While recognising that 'such cases in New Zealand would be rare',[88] on 18 December 1916, the Governor made an Order in Council granting the Registrar of Patents, Designs and Trade-Marks the ability to delay the acceptance of a complete specification for a patent or registration of a design, if the Registrar was satisfied that

85 Ibid.
86 Ibid.
87 Ibid.
88 'New Zealand War Histories' (n. 37) 5.

'on account of the war it [was] desirable to withhold publication of the invention or design'.[89] The Registrar could subsequently prohibit:

- the publication or communication of the invention or design;
- application being made for the protection of the invention or design in any enemy or neutral country; or
- application being made for the protection of the invention or design in any allied country or in any of His Majesty's Dominions, without the permission of such person or persons as the Ministry of Defence may appoint in the matter.[90]

The Regulations required that any person wishing to file for a patent or design in a foreign country or anywhere in His Majesty's Dominion had to first give notice to the New Zealand Patent Office, together with a provisional specification. The Registrar then had a month to decide whether it was desirable to withhold publication of the invention or design.[91]

The Regulations, however, had been made without consulting patent attorneys, who were of the opinion that the one-month delay was unnecessary and placed NZ agents under a 'disability'.[92] On that basis, on 2 April 1917 the Regulations were subsequently amended by an additional Order in Council. If the Registrar was 'satisfied that the invention or design was one with respect to which the powers of prohibition conferred … could not be exercised with propriety', the Registrar could give leave for the grant of the patent or registration of the patent or design before the month lapsed.[93]

Enforcement was an issue and it was unclear how the Registrar could police whether an invention was being published or communicated, or a patent was being applied for overseas.[94] Britain and Australia suggested using postal censorship, however this was not feasible as 'inter-Empire censorship was virtually nil'.[95] As a result, the Munitions and Supplies Board of Advice, which

---

[89] 'Withholding Publication of Inventions and Designs on Account of the War Regulations 1916 (NZ)', first published in (1916) 5(26) NZPOJ 570.

[90] Ibid. cl. 1.

[91] Ibid. cl. 2.

[92] See letters from Baldwin and Rayward to the Registrar of Patents (11 January 1917) and Climie, Coates & Co (12 January 1917) in 'Legislation War Emergency Withholding Publication of Inventions and Designs on Account of the War (1914–1918)', NANZ File No. R18323788.

[93] 'Amending Regulations Under the War Regulations Act 1914, Withholding Publication of Inventions and Designs on Account of the War Regulations 1916 (NZ)', first published in (1917) 6(7) NZPOJ 131, 132.

[94] 'New Zealand War Histories' (n. 37) 5.

[95] Ibid.

provided support and direction to the Registrar in this area, ultimately permitted such applications to proceed without issue.[96]

In the administration and application of the Regulations, different approaches were taken for different inventions. While some inventions were withheld from application for the duration of the war, as will be discussed below, in other cases the inventions were ultimately accepted before the cessation of hostilities. For example, on 1 November 1916, Stephen Allwill made an application for an invention relating to an aeroplane, designated patent number 39089. Nearly a year later, during its 17 September 1917 meeting, the Munitions and Supplies Board of Advice advised that a report should be produced providing further information on whether the application should be withheld.[97] The specification was subsequently published on 18 February 1918.

These Regulations were subsequently revoked on 25 March 1919[98] and, as a result, all cases that had been withheld from acceptance were released and publication could proceed.[99] Table 15.3 represents a list of complete specifications, by patent number, subsequently accepted in 1919 that were withheld until the Regulations were revoked. It was compiled through multiple documents, including entries in the New Zealand Patent Office Journal and documents held by the National Archives of New Zealand.[100]

It appears that Nobel's Explosives Co Ltd had to assure Attorney-General Alexander Herdman that its society in Glasgow had severed itself from the German interests in connection with the Nobel Dynamite Trust. 'Negotiations to this end were carried out with the full approval and cognisance of the Imperial Government and with the aid of a neutral Power.'[101]

4.b Provisions Regarding Secrecy: Australia

It is, unfortunately, not possible to create a similar table for Australia. Although similar provisions were introduced, the breadth of the Australian experience makes it impossible to feasibly document.

---

[96] See generally 'The Munitions and Supplies Board of Advice. Minutes of Proceedings' in 'Legislation War Emergency Withholding Publication of Inventions and Designs on Account of the War (1914–1918)', NANZ File No. R18323788.

[97] Ibid. 16 (17 September 1917).

[98] (1919) 8(7) NZPOJ 174.

[99] (1919) 8(10) NZPOJ 252.

[100] See generally 'The Munitions and Supplies Board of Advice. Minutes of Proceedings' (n. 96).

[101] 'Nobel's Explosive Coy', NANZ File No. R21371836, containing a letter from the Chief Agents for Nobel's Explosives Co Ltd (dated 13 August 1915) to Mr Herdman, and a reply from the Attorney-General (dated 16 August 1916).

Table 15.3 Complete specifications accepted after 25 March 1919

No.	Title	Applicant	Date
37856	Shell	John William Rooney (New Zealand)	30 August 1916
38312	Aeroplane Controlling Means	Geoffrey de Havilland (England) and George Holt Thomas (England)	19 December 1916
38313	Explosive	Nobel's Explosives Co Ltd (Scotland)	19 December 1916
38359	Explosive	Nobel's Explosives Co Ltd (Scotland)	10 January 1917
38609	Carburettor	Andrew James Peterson (New Zealand)	13 March 1917
38835	Aerial Conductor	John Hettinger (England)	23 May 1917 (Convention date 2 May 1916)
38989 (in addition to 40424)	Gun-Firing from Aeroplanes	The Sopwith Aviation Co Ltd (England) and Harrys Alexis Kauper (England)	30 June 1917 (Convention date 29 January 1917)
39117	Amorphous Titanium Dioxide Oxygen Compounds, Converting into Crystalline Compounds	Victor Moritz Goldschmidt (Norway)	3 August 1917 (Convention date 14 October 1916)
39118	Pigments Manufacture	Victor Moritz Goldschmidt (Norway)	3 August 1917 (Convention date 14 October 1916)
39119	Four-Valent Titanium Compounds, Producing	Hjalmar Olsen, Christina Förland and Tormod Förland (Norway)	3 August 1917 (Convention date 9 August 1916)
39275	Charcoal Manufacture	Allan Burgess (England), Thomas Sanderson (England) and Frederick Howard Sanderson (England)	18 September 1917
39294	Distillation of Wood, etc. Destructive	Philip Poore (England)	18 September 1917
39316	Artillery Range for Instructional Purposes	Richard Fitz Power (Lieutenant in the Royal Flying Corps of the British Army, England)	27 September 1917
39333	Explosive	Adolphe Segay (England)	26 September 1917
39407	Gun-Trigger Actuating	Gogu Constantinesco (England) and Walter Haddon (England)	19 October 1917

No.	Title	Applicant	Date
39431	Aeroplane	The Sopwith Aviation Co Ltd (England) and Thomas Sopwith (England)	25 October 1917
39445	Liquid – Fuel – Heated Furnace	Dudley Wright (England)	26 October 1917
39489	Aeroplane	Humphrey Francis Parker (New Zealand)	7 November 1917
39641	Wireless Telegraphy	Marconi's Wireless Telegraph Company Limited (England)	20 December 1917
39711	Explosive	Nobel's Explosives Co Ltd (Scotland)	16 January 1918
39712	Feeding Liquid-Wave Transmission-Lines	Gogu Constantiesco, Walter Haddon (England)	16 January 1918
39971	Artificial Limb	Alfred Charles Adams (England)	20 March 1918
40007	Ammonia, Synthetic Production	Harold Cecil Greenwood (England)	3 April 1918
40008	Ammonia, Synthetic Production	Harold Cecil Greenwood (England)	3 April 1918
40009	Ammonia, Synthetic Production	Harold Cecil Greenwood (England)	3 April 1918
40010	Compressed Gases, Mixing in Definite Proportions	Harold Cecil Greenwood (England)	3 April 1918
40023	Cartridge Magazine, Filling Machine	Harry Robert Northover (Canada)	3 April 1918
40161	Breech-Block	Armes Automatiques Lewis Societe Anonyme (Belgium) and Frederick William Hulse (England)	13 May 1918 (Convention date 17 July 1917)
40162	Machine-Gun Magazine	Armes Automatiques Lewis Societe Anonyme (Belgium) and Frederick William Hulse (England)	13 May 1918 (Convention date 17 July 1917)
40160	Wireless Telegraphy Thermoionic Device	Marconi's Wireless Telegraph Co, Ltd (England)	13 May 1918
40424 (addition to 38989)	Gun, Firing from Aeroplane	The Sopwith Aviation Co Ltd (England) and Harrys Alexis Kauper (England)	9 July 1918 (Convention date 14 July 1917)
41025	Can-Cover Lock and Seal	Joel Deeble (New Zealand Medical Corps) and Oswald Bourbeau (Auckland Infantry)	18 December 1918

On 12 July 1916, Australia enacted the War Precautions (Patents) Regulations 1916, supported by the War Precautions Act 1914 (Cth). That statute granted the Executive broad-ranging powers to make regulations with respect to all manner of areas it deemed relevant to the current hostilities. As with all other forms of law created in Australia during this period, the 1916 Regulations were amended multiple times.

In effect, the Regulations created the Patents Inquiry Board, which had the role of investigating the effects of publication of an invention with respect to detriment to public safety or the defence of the Commonwealth, assisting the enemy or endangering the successful prosecution of the war.[102] As enacted, the Board consisted of three persons. This was increased to five persons on 18 October 1916,[103] as it was difficult to find a time for the three members to meet and make a quorum.[104]

The Commissioner of Patents was required to forward the following patent applications to the Board:

- those filed on or after the date of the making of the Regulations, unless the Commissioner of Patents believed that the publication of the invention would obviously not be detrimental as described above;[105] or

---

[102] War Precautions (Patents) Regulations 1916 (Cth), reg. 3(3) (as enacted). This initially had three members, with a military member, a naval member and a secretary from the Patents Office.

[103] As per Statutory Rules 1916, no. 256.

[104] The initial three members consisted of a military member, a naval member and a secretary from the Patents Department. Upon expansion, there were two military and two naval members. See the letters between the Patents Inquiry Board and the Department of Defence (4 October, 15 November and 20 December 1916), National Archives of Australia (NAA) File No. 376570.

When the Draft Regulations were sent around, the Director of Engineers suggested that the member from the Patents Office act as secretary. This is because, since 1 April 1916, 375 applications for patents had been lodged, which equated to around seven applications per day. The Director of Engineers calculated that this meant that each member would have to spend around an hour every day dealing with the applications, and there would be a considerable amount of office work, which would take a secretary an additional hour or two a day. See Department of Defence Minute Paper 'Draft Regulations Regarding the Publication of Inventions', Director of Engineers, 22 May 1916), NAA File No. 356576.

[105] War Precautions (Patents) Regulations 1916 (Cth), s. 3(1) (as enacted). The proviso for 'obviously' non-detrimental inventions was added in a re-draft before the Regulations were enacted, to 'reduce the number of applications to be dealt with by the board': Attorney-General's Department Minute Paper 'Draft Regulations Regarding the Publication of Inventions', 8 June 1916, NAA File No. 356576.

- until 31 October 1917,[106] those applications filed before the date of the making of the Regulations and not yet accepted, if the Commissioner of Patents believed that the publication of the invention might be detrimental as described above.[107]

As enacted, the standard was whether the publication *might* be detrimental, as described above. Upon a positive determination from the Board, the Commissioner of Patents was to notify the applicant and decline to proceed further with the application, unless the Attorney-General directed otherwise.[108] The applicant was then forbidden from publishing or communicating the invention 'in any way', within and outside the Commonwealth, without the permission of the Attorney-General.[109]

In March 1917, the Board raised concerns with the Department of Defence that:[110]

- No provision had been made for the Board to report to the Military or Naval authorities that certain inventions might be of practical utility to the Commonwealth (and also to Britain).
- No provision had been made for coordination between the Board and the Military or Naval authorities.
- No authority had been given for the Board to utilise the services from Government experts, such as the Director of Munitions.

The Department of Defence agreed that these concerns should be ameliorated.[111] However, the Regulations were only amended to reflect the third of these concerns, thereby allowing the Board to obtain additional expert advice from a member of the Public Service 'deemed to be qualified to report upon the nature and utility of the invention'.[112] It appears that there was only one example of this, where the Board sought expert advice from the Central Flying School.[113]

---

106 This was removed by Statutory Rules 1917 No. 283.

107 War Precautions (Patents) Regulations 1916 (Cth), reg. 3(2) (as enacted).

108 Ibid. reg. 3(5) (as enacted).

109 Ibid. reg. 3(6) (as enacted)

110 Patents Inquiry Board, letter to the Secretary for Defence, 16 March 1917, NAA File No. 356576.

111 Department of Defence Minute Paper, 'Patents Inquiry Board', Chief of Ordnance, 31 March 1917, NAA File No. 356576.

112 Statutory Rules 1917 No. 283, adding reg. 4B.

113 Captain CS Barber, Patents Inquiry Board, letter to Major Sheldon, Central Flying School, 31 October 1918, NAA File No. 358451.

From 31 October 1917, applicants for patents were forbidden from publishing or communicating their inventions within or beyond the Commonwealth.[114] The ban would be lifted in individual circumstances if the Commissioner notified the applicant that the invention was 'obviously' not detrimental, as described above.[115] The same amendment changed the role of the Board to investigating whether, having regard to public safety, defence of the Commonwealth and the successful prosecution of the war, the publication of the invention should be absolutely prohibited, or should be permitted 'with limitations and subject to the terms and conditions specified by the Board'.[116] On 5 February 1918, it was clarified that it was also possible for the Board to permit publication without limitations, or terms and conditions.[117] The same Amendment gave the Commissioner of Patents the right to direct that there be no further publication of the invention, if the Commissioner decided that the continued publication was detrimental, as described above.[118]

The 1916 Regulations also required that any person in the Commonwealth who wished to apply for a patent outside the Commonwealth first give notice of this intention to the Patent Office, together with a specification and (from 7 February 1917) drawings, 30 days before posting the application overseas.[119] The Commissioner of Patents was then required to refer this notice to the Patents Inquiry Board.[120] In October 1916, the Chief of Ordnance[121] questioned the necessity that the Board look at all such notices, because, 'even though they can be disposed of quickly by the Patents Enquiry Board, there is considerable time taken at the Patents Office extracting the pith of the subject from detailed descriptions, typing etc.'[122] As a result, from 7 February 1917, the Commissioner did not have to forward a notice to the Board if it was 'obviously' not necessary.[123]

As enacted, the Regulations required the Board to investigate whether the publication of the invention outside of the Commonwealth might be detrimen-

---

[114] Statutory Rules 1917 No. 283, repealing and replacing reg. 3(2).

[115] Ibid.

[116] Ibid. repealing and replacing reg. 3(3).

[117] Statutory Rules 1918 No. 36.

[118] Ibid.

[119] War Precautions (Patents) Regulations 1916 (Cth), reg. 4(1) (as enacted). The application form was published in (1918) 28(42) AOJP 1042.

[120] War Precautions (Patents) Regulations 1916 (Cth), reg. 4(2) (as enacted).

[121] The Chief of Ordnance was a member of the Military Board together with the Chief of the General Staff, Adjutant General and Quartermaster General.

[122] Department of Defence Minute Paper 'Suggested Amendment to War Precautions (Patents) regulations 1916', Chief of Ordnance, HW Dangar, 24 October 1916, NAA File No. 356576.

[123] This was added by Statutory Rules 1917 No. 22.

tal, as described above.[124] This was changed on 31 October 1917, to allow the Board to decide whether publication should be absolutely prohibited or subject to terms and conditions.[125] If the Board determined this in the positive, the Commissioner of Patents had to direct the application not to proceed with the application.[126] The applicant was also restricted from publishing or communicating the invention in any way.

Between March and May 1918, the Department of Defence and Attorney-General's Department questioned the efficacy and necessity of the Board.[127] This arose when there was difficulty in finding a fifth member and secretary for the Board.[128] The prior Secretary had been from the Patent Office, and the Department of Defence felt it had been beneficial to have someone 'conversant with Patent Office procedure'.[129] In February 1918, the Attorney-General's Department wrote to the Commissioner of Patents, seeking a recommendation for this position.[130] The Commissioner responded that due to enlistment, death and resignation, the staff of examiners had been so reduced such as to leave him unable to make any recommendation.[131]

The Chief of Ordnance stated that '[e]xperience has shown that the majority of cases dealt with do not require very great consideration as to whether they are likely to endanger the welfare of the Commonwealth or assist the enemy'.[132] With a view to simplifying the situation, the Attorney-General's Department agreed, finding that, '[h]aving in view the experience gained from the assistance rendered by the Board in the past', the Commissioner was best placed to regulate the secrecy of inventions.[133] Draft Regulations to this effect were drawn up.

Following this, the Chief of Ordnance, Lt Colonel Horace Dangar, suggested that the Board be abolished or at least the number of referred cases

---

[124] War Precautions (Patents) Regulations 1916 (Cth), reg. 4(2)–(3) (as enacted).

[125] Statutory Rules 1917 No. 283.

[126] War Precautions (Patents) Regulations 1916 (Cth), reg. 4(4)–(5) (as enacted).

[127] For a compilation of the Patent Inquiry Board's work, see NAA File No. 358451.

[128] Department of Defence Minute Paper, 'War Precautions (Patents) Regulations – Discontinuance of Patents Inquiry Board', Chief of Ordnance, HW Dangar, 27 March 1918, NAA File No. 356576 (hereinafter Department of Defence Minute Paper, 'War Precautions, HW Dangar').

[129] Department of Defence Minute Paper, 'Appointment of Secretary – Patents Inquiry Board', Chief of Ordnance, 21 February 1918, NAA File No. 356576.

[130] Department of Defence Memorandum for the Commissioner of Patents, 25 February 1918, NAA File No. 356576.

[131] Department of Patents, Memorandum, Commissioner of Patents to the Secretary of the Department of Defence, 28 February 1918, NAA File No. 356576.

[132] Department of Defence Minute Paper, 'War Precautions, HW Dangar' (n. 128).

[133] Attorney-General's Department Minute Paper, Acting Secretary to the Secretary of the Department of Defence, 25 April 1918, NAA File No. 356576.

should be reduced.[134] Lt Colonel Dangar noted the possible ineffective nature of the Board's role:

> The information obtainable regarding the many varied and extensive subjects touched on by Patent Applications is so meagre that it is generally impossible to say definitively that publication will release valuable and novel information.[135]

The Chief of Ordnance also alluded to the futility of action from Australia in an international context:

> Prohibition has been recommended as a precautionary measure rather than on a definite knowledge of harmful results likely to ensure [sic] on publication, as it is extremely difficult, if not impossible, to know the latest developments in any particular subject or the scope of the information already available to the public of other countries.[136]

Put another way, it was difficult for the Board to make decisions about the impact of publication overseas, because it could not definitely know about the state of the art outside of the Commonwealth. More specifically regarding applications originating in Australia, the Chief of Ordnance stated:

> no case has yet been found making a complete departure from known methods. The greater number are modifications of practice, while a few apparently new ideas have, when submitted to the British Authorities found to be already known.[137]

Between the lines is a commentary on the quality of Australian inventions. Upon closer investigation, none were particularly novel in the Commonwealth, and all were known in Britain. Lt Colonel Dangar commented:

> Past experience would indicate that applications originating in Australia are unlikely to effect the War, and it is probable that the Commissioner under the proposed amending Regulations could adequately deal with these, with expert Naval or Military assistance in special cases.[138]

---

[134] Department of Defence Minute Paper, 'Patents Inquiry Board', Chief of Ordnance, HW Dangar to the Attorney General's Department, 21 May 1918, NAA File No. 356576 (hereinafter Department of Defence Minute Paper, 'Patents Inquiry Board, 21 May 1918').

[135] Ibid.

[136] Department of Defence Minute Paper, 'War Precautions, HW Dangar' (n. 128).

[137] Ibid.

[138] Department of Defence Minute Paper, 'Patents Inquiry Board, 21 May 1918' (n. 134).

The Chief of Ordnance further alluded to the potential senselessness of keeping secret applications from outside of the Commonwealth:

> The safeguard of prohibiting publication of a patent originating outside Australia is not always apparent, but this has been done in the majority of cases under instructions to that effect from Great Britain.[139]

He recommended that the Commissioner of Patents should work together with the British and other Allied countries' patent offices, as it made no sense for Australia to make something secret if it had been published elsewhere, and vice versa.[140]

In a similar vein, on 12 September 1918, Captain CS Barber of the Patents Inquiry Board wrote to the Commissioner of Patents regarding an application pertaining to rubber,[141] stating:

> it would be illogical to permit publication in Australia, and prevent it in other countries, but the Board is of [the] opinion that permission could be given to apply for A Patent in Great Britain with the right to obtain permission from the Imperial Authorities to apply for patents, and publish the invention in other countries.

If published in other countries, freedom to publish in Australia would naturally follow.[142]

On 22 January 1919, the Chairman of the Patents Inquiry Board wrote to the Department of Defence, suggesting that the Board be 'dispensed with', as the need to control applications had 'greatly, if not entirely, ceased', and Great Britain had removed their restrictions on patent applications.[143] These Regulations were repealed on 5 February 1919.[144]

5. CONCLUDING THOUGHTS

Although the Armistice came into effect on 11 November 1918, it took many months, and in some cases years, for countries to dismantle the legal regimes

---

139 Department of Defence Minute Paper, 'War Precautions, HW Dangar' (n. 128).

140 Department of Defence Minute Paper, 'Patents Inquiry Board, 21 May 1918' (n. 134).

141 Regarding Application No. 3364/17.

142 Captain CS Barber, Patents Inquiry Board, to the Commissioner of Patents, 12 September 1918, NAA File No. 358451.

143 Department of Defence Minute Paper, 'War Precautions Patent Regulations', Chairman of the Patents Inquiry Board, to the Secretary of the Department of Defence, 22 January 1919, NAA File No. 356576.

144 Statutory Rules 1919 No. 29.

created during wartime. This included Australia and New Zealand, and the treatment of IP rights in both nations.

Overall, the Australasian experience with patents during the First World War highlights that both nations took patent law very seriously (even if they did not fully understand it), as well as their role in the British Empire. Both Australia and New Zealand sought to protect interests that were seemingly important for the war. However, we have shown that reality seldom aligned with the rhetoric.

Ultimately, both jurisdictions introduced many changes to the law and regulations, which mostly created significant unnecessary bureaucracy, using resources that could likely have been more effectively used elsewhere. This is illustrated by the fact that very few patents in New Zealand were 'enemy'-owned, and none were considered useful by New Zealand Government Departments, or industry, as no applications for suspension/avoidance were made. Even in Australia, there were 631 'enemy'-owned patents, but we only found 28 applications for suspension/avoidance – that is only 4.4 per cent of the 'enemy'-owned patents, and 0.1 per cent of all patents.

Regarding secrecy provisions, these were used in New Zealand and in Australia, although the latter experience is more difficult to map. In Australia, it is apparent that the provisions required a lot of work for very little gain. In particular, both jurisdictions hinted at the futility of trying to control information in a semi-globalised world. Neither jurisdiction could realistically track dissemination/publication overseas. Moreover, there was no sense in keeping secrecy in Australasia when a patent might be published in Britain or elsewhere, or when the patents at home were not particularly novel or inventive, as appeared to often be the case.

Even in the twenty-first century, New Zealand and Australia are influenced by foreign governments and international obligations, and both remain relatively unimportant patent destinations in an increasingly globalised world. In Australia in 2018, for example, less than 10 per cent of the 29,957 applications for standard patents were made by Australian applicants.[145] For the same period, only 15 per cent of complete specifications filed in New Zealand were from domestic applicants.[146] Though not in wartime, when adopting patent provisions, the questions both countries should be asking remain the same: How does this affect local innovation? Does the change mostly introduce

---

[145] IP Australia, 'Australian Intellectual Property Report 2019', 'Figure 1: Standard Patent Applications Filed in Australia, 2009–18', 8.

[146] IPONZ, 'Facts and Figures', https://www.iponz.govt.nz/about-iponz/facts-and-figures/, accessed 21 August 2019.

bureaucracy? What is the importance of foreign patents locally? What is the relevance of globalisation?

Index